THE ANGLO-FLORENTINES

THE ANGLO-FLORENTINES

The British in Tuscany, 1814–1860

Diana and Tony Webb

BLOOMSBURY ACADEMIC
LONDON • NEW YORK • OXFORD • NEW DELHI • SYDNEY

BLOOMSBURY ACADEMIC
Bloomsbury Publishing Plc
50 Bedford Square, London, WC1B 3DP, UK
1385 Broadway, New York, NY 10018, USA

BLOOMSBURY, BLOOMSBURY ACADEMIC and the Diana logo are trademarks of
Bloomsbury Publishing Plc

First published in Great Britain 2020

Cover design: Terry Woodley
Cover image © *Florence: Painted by Colonel R C Goff, described by Mrs Goff*, published by
A & C Black, 1905 and All Canada Photos / Alamy Stock Photo (background image)

A catalogue record for this book is available from the British Library.

ISBN: HB: 978-1-3501-2279-6
         PB: 978-1-3501-3361-7
       ePDF: 978-1-3501-3600-7
      eBook: 978-1-35013-602-1

Typeset by Integra Software Services Pvt. Ltd.
Printed and bound in Great Britain

To find out more about our authors and books visit www.bloomsbury.com
and sign up for our newsletters.

For Eleanor and Richard

CONTENTS

COLOUR PLATES

ABBREVIATIONS

ASCF   Archivio Storico Comunale di Firenze

BC   The Brownings' Correspondence, edited by Scott
                Lewis, and others (Waco, Texas, in progress
                1984–)

Church   Miscellaneous letters etc, St Mark's Church,
Letters   Florence, ordered by decade and number

CMB   Church Minute Books, St Mark's Church, Florence

DNB   Dictionary of National Biography

EM   Diaries of Elizabeth Maquay, Harold Acton Library,
                British Institute of Florence

JLM   Diaries of John Leland Maquay, Harold Acton
                Library, British Institute of Florence

FO   Foreign Office, National Archives

LMA   London Metropolitan Archives

LPL   Lambeth Palace Library

RG   Registrar General, National Archives

TNA   The National Archives, Kew, London

INTRODUCTION: BACKGROUND AND SOURCES

The background

With the fall of Napoleon in 1815, the map of Italy was redrawn, but not completely restored to its pre-war appearance. Many of the Italian dynasts returned to the thrones from which French armies had driven them, and with them came an army of a different kind, which was still in occupation when, less than half a century later, the restored order crumbled from Milan to Palermo and the single Italian kingdom, which many observers had thought impossible, came into being. From 1814 on, thousands of Britons who had been starved of a peaceful view of the Mediterranean flocked across the Alps. In his study of Protestant influence on the *Risorgimento*, Giorgio Spini noted this 'swarming over the peninsula of Englishmen of every kind, mentality, profession and social class'. He thought it timely to ask what impact it had on Italian politics and society, remarking that 'The history of English immigration into Italy in the first decades of the nineteenth century is in large part still to be written.'[1]

This book is intended to give a fuller picture than has hitherto been attempted of the variety of Britons who inhabited the Grand Duchy of Tuscany between the end of the Napoleonic Wars and the absorption of Tuscany into the Kingdom of Italy after the flight of the last Grand Duke. Religion plays an exceedingly important part in the story, but it is not our chief focus as it was Spini's. We have tried to depict residents and visitors going about their business, reacting to their Tuscan setting and to the sometimes momentous events that affected it in the last years before Italian unification.

It is difficult to make a clear-cut distinction between residents and visitors. An individual or a family might reside in Tuscany for 6 months, a year or even more, or wander from one continental resort to another, spending substantial periods in each. Long-term residents might go home to die after years in Italy. Everywhere the British went, migratory clergy and half-pay naval and military officers were to be found, and with them the British hoteliers, shopkeepers and physicians who ministered to their fellow-countrymen. More often than not, the sources (including the Italian ones) speak of the English when referring to the British (and often quite clearly to Scots). One of our chief protagonists was a Dublin-born Presbyterian who called himself English even while referring to the Irish as his fellow-countrymen. Here we use the word 'British' when it seems proper to do so.

Our major focus is on Florence. The city harboured one of the largest British colonies on the continent outside Paris, which it resembled in being at once residence, tourist destination and transit camp. There was a seasonal pattern of comings and goings. Many fled from the summer heat to the spa town of Bagni di Lucca, or to the seaside, Germany or Switzerland, while the autumn saw large numbers of arrivals, some of whom went on after a few weeks to overwinter in Rome or Naples. Florentine residents had frequent contacts with the lesser Tuscan centres of British settlement, notably the port of Livorno, always called Leghorn by the British and so called in this book. Winston Churchill thought it quite preposterous that it should ever be called anything else.

Leghorn was above all a commercial city, which owed much of its character to the Grand Duke's decision, late in the sixteenth century, to create a free port and to offer inducements to merchants, including a measure of religious toleration. The British established a consulate and the so-called British 'factory', an association of traders and shippers. Its members suffered badly from the French invasion and occupation of Tuscany, and, although the 'factory' was rapidly re-established after 1814, Leghorn by mid-century was past its best as an international port. In 1849 the consul estimated the British population at a little over 400 (a high proportion Scots). There was a sprinkling of more leisured residents in the vicinity, and the city had a secondary role as a seaside resort, to which some Anglo-Florentines went in the summer.

Pisa and Bagni di Lucca ('the Baths') can in some respects be regarded as a pair. Pisa owed its British popularity to the persistent belief that its mild winter climate was peculiarly healthy for invalids, especially those suffering from pulmonary complaints. In the summer, many Pisan residents migrated to the cooler air of Bagni, as did others from Florence and Leghorn. Bagni lay in the minuscule Duchy of Lucca, which (under the terms of the Vienna settlement) was ruled by a supposedly independent Bourbon prince until, in 1847, it was absorbed into Tuscany. There were only a few permanent British residents, chief among them being Colonel Henry Stisted and his redoubtable wife Clotilda, the 'uncrowned queen of Lucca'. Siena did not flourish as a place of British settlement to the degree that its modern tourist popularity might suggest. Some went there in the summer from both Rome and Florence, and for a time, the British colony was sufficient to justify the existence of a Protestant burial ground, of which only pathetic fragments can now be seen in a corner of the present municipal cemetery. In 1856 one of the few remaining residents, John Fenton Newbery, decided to emigrate to North America with his half-Italian family and handed over what was left of the property of the Anglican congregation to the care of the church in Florence. Other cities, such as Pistoia or Arezzo, are even less commemorated in our sources.

Only a few years after 1814, the number of Britons abroad aroused anxieties about the threat continental travel posed to their conduct, religion and even identity. In 1818 the Reverend J. W. Cunningham sounded an alarm which is worthy of attention because he raised issues which would continue to exercise commentators.[2] He addressed himself not to mere holiday-makers but to those who settled in foreign countries or who undertook so prolonged a tour 'as to allow themselves leisure to catch something of the manners and spirit of the countries which they visit'. The word 'catch' is significant, for he was afraid of infection. The British owed their unquestionably blessed state largely to their isolation, and they were spending too long abroad. Many had no very specific objective, which was dangerous; many were young, which made them impressible; and too many were both young and female, which scarcely bore thinking about. It was hard to keep children who had been educated abroad within the bounds of authentically 'English' ways of thinking and feeling. Worse, it was now not merely 'persons in the highest ranks of life' who travelled. These were to some degree (or so at least Cunningham believed) proofed against foreign influence by their 'lofty and aristocratical' spirit, but 'the subordinate classes of society have also caught the same mania', while lacking the wherewithal 'to sustain them against the tide of foreign habits'.

Cunningham was now approaching his most pressing concern. The traveller all too often acquired 'that species of latitudinarianism which is dignified by the name of liberality … He has no low-minded partiality for one mode of faith, because he has no regard to any.' Cunningham was quick to equate this indifferentism with indifference to vice itself. He saw the Catholic nations of Europe as sharing undesirable characteristics, such as a weak attachment to the domestic hearth, a tendency for women to live in public and the 'prevalence of marital infidelity'. Could Englishmen possibly be justified in exposing their womenfolk to such influences for any prolonged period?

With obvious reference to recent eruptions of social unrest and blasphemy prosecutions, Cunningham lamented that so many of the appointed leaders of society had taken themselves off to the continent just when they were most needed at home. He believed that 'a large and important body of our countrymen' was threatened with demoralization. Some already exhibited 'the plague spot', and 'fresh materials for diffusing this moral pestilence' might be daily expected. The vectors, to clarify the point, were returning travellers, brimming with eagerness to communicate the pestilence to their stay-at-home brethren. Was England, which had for so long, under divine supervision, 'swayed the political destinies of Europe', now to 'truckle to receive her morals at the hands of the vanquished – to receive from them, opinions and practices which have been the very elements of their own degradation and ruin?' If travellers were to persist in travelling, they must not only constantly pray but read the Scriptures and keep the Sabbath, for Cunningham had already identified the failure to do so as among the major defects of Catholic Europe.

The sheer volume of British travel abroad was often remarked on in this early post-war period. On 4 March 1817, the *Times* reported estimates of over 800 English families resident in Florence, Leghorn and Pisa. By 24 December 1822, there were 9,000 Britons at Rome and Naples 'and more than 5,000 at Florence, Pisa, Genoa, and the north of Italy.' These figures compared with an estimated total of about 35,000 at Paris. On 10 February 1825 the *Morning Chronicle* reported that 'Tuscany at present overflows with English residents; they are reported to exceed in number 2000 persons.' Leigh Hunt recollected that 200 English families had been living in Florence when he was there in 1825.[3] Cunningham had made passing reference to material issues, such as the amount of money that was being spent abroad and the effects of so many absent consumers on employment and production at home. In the *Morning Post* of 20 April 1827, a correspondent named 'Philo' relayed a report that over 6,000 British subjects had been in Florence at one moment in 1823. A minimum of £300,000 of British money every week had been spent on the continent since the peace, a loss that no nation could be expected to sustain. 'Philo' denounced this predilection for putting money into the pockets of foreigners and tried to disabuse his fellow-countrymen of what he thought to be their mistaken belief that it was cheaper to live abroad.

He would have had a hard job to do so. An 'Old Traveller', quoted in the *Caledonian Mercury* on 4 January 1834, reckoned Florence to be the cheapest city in Europe, estimating that a single person could live there 'at the first-rate inns, bed and board, annually, faring sumptuously every day and including every expense whatever' for £100 sterling. Rome or Paris would cost him £50 more, Naples £70, Frankfurt twice and Calais three times as much as Florence. For some who were feeling the pinch, Florence could serve as a place of retrenchment, or escape. In the first chapter of *Nicholas Nickleby*, Charles Dickens imagined that 'A mania prevailed, a bubble burst, four stockbrokers took villa residences at Florence.' Walter Savage Landor was a conspicuous example of the long-term resident who was driven out of Britain first by debt and later in life by a lawsuit. There was no extradition treaty between Britain and Tuscany, and a disappointed creditor or victim of actual fraud might have to seek redress through the Tuscan courts, which was unlikely to be easy or fruitful. Some expatriates were merely accused of neglecting responsibilities at home. Absentee landlords (particularly the Irish, who were thought now to be travelling more than they had previously done) came in for special criticism, and a watch was kept on British legislators who spent overlong in the pleasant Tuscan climate.

Giorgio Spini's discussions hint at an irony. British statesmen helped to establish and guarantee a reactionary settlement of post-Napoleonic Italy and Europe; yet both they and the mere visitor to Italy possessed certain characteristics which, from the point of view of a genuine enthusiast for the *ancien regime,* made them somewhat suspect. Not only were most of them Protestants but virtually all espoused a doctrine of monarchy far removed from absolutist orthodoxy. The two defects were inextricably linked in the eyes of nervous Catholic defenders of that orthodoxy – and in Italy they became more nervous as time went by. Already in the 1820s England was a refugee camp for Italian dissidents, such as Antonio Panizzi, the future librarian of the British Museum. Duke Francis of Modena condemned Panizzi to death in his absence in October 1823 and sent him a bill which included the expenses of his own execution. Panizzi replied from Liverpool, sending back 'a facetious rejoinder from his departed soul, presumably now dwelling in the Elysian Fields. There was an Italian gesture which he was unable to enclose'.[4]

John Bull as dangerous revolutionary seems incongruous casting, but it was well known that heresy and political subversion were in the habit of lurking under the same bush. Some of the proverbial British enthusiasm for the Risorgimento was focussed on its religious rather than strictly political possibilities. For many the past and present association of Catholicism with tyranny and oppression was taken for granted; in a liberated Italy, the Gospel would be free to do its beneficent work. In the fourth chapter of *Father and Son*, his rueful memoir of his relationship with his fundamentalist father, Edmund Gosse recalled the atmosphere of his 1850s childhood, when 'We welcomed any social disorder in any part of Italy, as likely to be annoying to the papacy'. What Gosse called 'the faith and sufferings of the dear persecuted Tuscans' undoubtedly interested many British Protestants who were anomalous sympathisers with subversion. In Chapter 7 of his last novel, *Lothair*, published in 1870, Disraeli depicted the social-climbing Mrs Apollonia Putney Giles, who, although 'a violent Protestant and of extreme conservative opinions', allowed 'her Italian predilections' to lead her into dubious company, including Mazzini and Garibaldi.

One result of this spiky Protestant consciousness was anxiety not only for the souls and liberty of enslaved Italians but, as the Reverend Cunningham had already shown, for the moral and spiritual well-being of God-fearing Britons in papist territories. Spini remarks as 'a sign of the times' that the British in Italy were now much more concerned than their eighteenth-century predecessors had been with ensuring their access to Protestant worship, even seeking permission to build churches where this was possible.[5] In Tuscany this resulted, around 1840, in the opening of purpose-built Anglican churches at Leghorn, Florence and Bagni di Lucca, which in itself indicates that for many years after the Congress of Vienna British visitors to Tuscany experienced little to incommode them.

The year 1814 saw the restoration of the former Grand Duke, Ferdinand III, who had acceded to the title in 1790 when his father, Peter Leopold, abdicated in order to succeed his brother Joseph II as Holy Roman Emperor. Ferdinand died on 18 June 1824 and was succeeded by his son Leopold II, who proved to be the last Grand Duke of Tuscany. For Ferdinand and even more for his son, Peter Leopold was an inescapable and somewhat problematic presence. No constitutional monarch, his 'enlightened' government constituted a kind of gold standard that his successors tampered with at their peril. As the apostle of free trade and (still more) the enemy of ecclesiastical privilege, he had British admirers. Some Catholic clergy who hankered after the good old days were less enthusiastic and, both after 1814 and after the failed 1848–49 revolutions, thought they saw an opportunity.

It would be tedious to attempt to list all the occasions on which the government of the Grand Dukes was described by British observers as 'mild'. The negative corollaries of this mildness – feebleness, indecisiveness, vacillation – were also widely recognized, and it was a sad fact that these agreeable Tuscans, including the relatively well-educated and prosperous peasantry, were Catholics. However, there was a lot more to complain about everywhere else in the peninsula, and the new kingdom of Piedmont-Sardinia had yet to assume the mantle of constitutionalism and Italian patriotism. Nevertheless, the close kinship of the Tuscan ruling dynasty with the Austrian emperor remained a fact of crucial importance. In 1821 Austria intervened with armed force to suppress the constitution that had been extorted from the king of Naples, and although neither this episode nor the more considerable continental disturbances of 1830–31 had much effect on Tuscany, the British noted some disturbing signs that the Grand Ducal government was (in their view) unnecessarily nervous.

There followed a prolonged calm period, during which the Anglo-Tuscan colonies flourished. Symptoms of tension multiplied from 1847 on, and amid the revolutionary upheavals of 1848–49, the Grand Duke displayed all the symptoms of a fatal malady: weakness. First he granted a constitution and took on the protective colouring of an Italian patriot; then he remembered that he was a Hapsburg and an autocrat and fled from his capital in February 1849, only to return in the wake of an Austrian army, which remained in occupation of the duchy for 6 years. Superficially, normality seemed to be restored for a few years after it left, but in the face of renewed revolutionary stirrings, Leopold again abandoned Florence on 27 April 1859, and this time, there was to be no return. In less than 2 years the integration of Tuscany into the Italian kingdom was an established fact. Through it all, the British in Tuscany lived on.

The sources

The principal focus of this book is on the British view of the British in Tuscany, especially in Florence. The sources are mostly ones they themselves generated and reflect both their self-image and their opinions of Italy and the Italians. While varied and frequently intelligent, they were also often arrogant and unreasonable. A recently published guide to the sources available in public and private archives in Florence for the history of the British in the city offers a quite daunting range of further, non-English, possibilities.[6] The Tuscan police and the Florentine municipality, for example, were both interested in what British residents and visitors were up to. An online index to the municipal archive (the Archivio Storico del Comune), which incorporates useful summaries of the records, gives some idea of the dealings the British had with the town council.[7]

Our principal sources can be described under the following headings.

The Maquay diaries

The diaries of John Leland Maquay (1791–1868) and his mother Elizabeth (1762–1845) are among a collection of family papers that were donated to the Harold Acton Library of the British Institute in Florence by the heirs of Maquay's grand-daughter Marjorie, who died in Florence in 1982 at the age of 94.[8] We were introduced to these by the former archivist Alyson Price, to whom our indebtedness for this and other benefits is beyond our power to estimate.

John Maquay, born in Dublin and brought up a Presbyterian, spent much of his young manhood in business in Canada and embarked on his Italian travels only in 1822. By this time, he was consciously in search of a wife but probably did not expect that she would be a Sienese Catholic 15 years his junior. He and Elena Gigli were married in Florence early in 1828 but did not finally settle in Florence until 1832. Here their four sons were born and here, in 1840, Maquay entered into partnership with Captain John Pakenham to found a bank, which survived his own departure from Italy in May 1858. For almost every day between 1812 and 1862, he kept a diary.

Written in a small, crabbed and sometimes difficult hand, this is no literary masterpiece, frequently maddeningly terse on interesting subjects and rarely expressive or introspective. Its humdrum character is, however, a large part of its value. It offers a host of mundane trivia, notes of expenditure, a fairly complete record of the Florentine weather and hundreds of names, for John liked to give big parties and listed the people he invited, British, Italian and other, whether or not they came. Apart from his banking business, he was active in the affairs of the English Church (and in clandestine 'Bible-running', which he himself does not mention). He lived through a communications revolution, and not the least valuable feature of the diaries is his description of the routes, speeds and modes of transport he used on his journeys to and from Tuscany.

His mother, Elizabeth, probably never expected or wished to become a permanent Florentine resident, but was marooned there in 1833 and died late in 1845 at the age of 83. Especially in her last years, she was often in Florence when her son was engaged on one of his trips back to Britain, and also during his long absence in the West Indies in 1839–1840. She reveals occasional shafts of humour, which are rare in his diary, and her Italian spelling is a joy. We obtain other glimpses of her from David and Isabella Wilmer, who (travelling to save money) were in Tuscany between late 1834 and early 1837. We are most grateful to their descendant Georgina Maltby for access to extracts from their unpublished journals and permission to quote their impressions of her and of many other people and things.

The Foreign Office records

The correspondence of the Foreign Office with the British Ministers in Tuscany and the consuls at Leghorn is contained in a series of 215 folio volumes in the National Archives, numbered FO79. Of these, a mere twenty cover the period 1781–1813, the rest the years 1814–1860. After the creation of the Foreign Office in 1782, consideration was given to establishing permanent diplomatic representation in the capitals of Europe. The reason for establishing the Tuscan mission was to keep an eye on the papal dominions and the remaining members of the Stuart dynasty and also, more generally, to monitor French and Austrian activity in Italy. It was located in Florence because it was deemed impossible to establish formal diplomatic relations with the papacy. This need for a presence in central Italy was felt even more keenly in the changed situation after 1815, and critics objected in vain that the extinction of the Stuarts and the obvious Austrian hegemony in Italy made the Florentine embassy an unnecessary expense. To his oversight of Rome and the Papal States, the Minister added responsibility for the duchies of Modena and Parma, effectively (like Tuscany) Austrian client-states, and also for the duchy of Lucca for as long as it existed.

The correspondence of a typical year is contained in one or more volumes of despatches from the Foreign Office to the Minister in Florence, one or more of despatches from the Minister and a volume devoted to the affairs of the consulate at Leghorn, which might also contain miscellaneous correspondence from private individuals relating to Tuscany, although that sometimes merited a separate volume. Supplementary material is to be found in other Foreign Office series, which will be noted in their place.

The consul at Leghorn was primarily concerned with the movements of British trade and shipping. He could apply his visa to passports and issue them to British subjects; he might be called upon to protect Britons (including drunken sailors) who got into trouble with the local police. For such purposes, he interacted directly with the Italian authorities, but whenever larger issues of British interests or policy arose, or recourse was necessary to the Grand Ducal government, he was required to proceed by way of the Minister in Florence. It followed that some of his surviving correspondence was with the Minister and some of it with the government at home. The relationship with Florence was unclear, and occasionally the Minister complained that the Consul had been negligent or tardy in communicating with him. During the period under review, only two men (both Scots) held the post, while nine ministers came and went in Florence.

This correspondence is by no means all about high diplomacy and trade statistics. A surprising variety of incidents required attention, and they sometimes involved individuals whose names are unknown to fame or history. When British subjects got into trouble with the gendarmes, the Minister or the consul might have to intervene to secure justice or just to smooth ruffled Tuscan feathers. Explanations might have to be sent home, especially in cases which aroused attention in parliament or the press. The religious crisis of the early 1850s, in which a number of British subjects got involved, made several such interventions necessary. Mixed marriages also caused problems if the parties failed to comply with Tuscan and Catholic law.

Church records

There was only one British church in Tuscany before the Napoleonic wars, at Leghorn. Here the merchants had freedom of worship but not (until 1840) a purpose-built church; they did, however, have a burial ground, for long the only place in Tuscany where a British Protestant could be buried. In 1828 the Swiss Reformed Church, with Grand Ducal permission, opened a new cemetery in Florence, which became henceforth the burial place of choice for most Anglo-Florentine Protestants. By this time, after more than a decade of peace, the burgeoning congregation in Florence was gradually taking on some kind of organization, which was more or less complete by 1833 but was overhauled after a crisis in its affairs erupted at the end of 1839. At Siena, Pisa and Bagni, where much smaller and more seasonal numbers were involved, the development of churches was yet more informal and hard now to reconstruct.

The Leghorn church was and remained distinctive in that, because it served a consulate, its existence was recognized by the British government, which (after 1826) subsidised the chaplain by paying towards his upkeep an amount equivalent to the voluntary subscriptions of the congregation. It also approved the appointment of the chaplain. The consul was *ex officio* the chairman of the church's management committee and annually submitted its accounts, subscription lists and the minutes of meetings to the scrutiny of the Foreign Office. These are therefore to be found in FO79.

The other Anglican churches were unsubsidised and as far as possible ignored by the British government, but it came to be acknowledged that they owed obedience to the bishops of London and after 1842 Gibraltar. Their surviving records have mostly found their way via the Guildhall Library to the London Metropolitan Archive. They include a fragile volume, which records much of what little is known about the church at Siena, and also subscription books and other material from Pisa and Bagni. The Minute Books which were kept from 1839 onwards by the men who managed the affairs of the English Church in Florence remain in the care of the present place of Anglican worship, St Mark's.[9] Our heartfelt thanks are due to Penny Mittler, the former archivist of St Mark's, and to Father Maclean, formerly the priest in charge, for enabling us to have access to these documents. Among other archival material preserved at St Mark's, we have been able to make use of some items among a recently rediscovered cache of letters and other miscellanea.[10] There is a small quantity of sometimes very valuable supplementary material in Lambeth Palace Library.

Unfortunately, almost no documentation of the Florentine Church survives from before 1839. Retrospective references in the extant Church Minute Books give some idea of records that have now apparently vanished. In a report delivered to the Annual General Meeting of the Church on 30 January 1846, the secretary, Christopher Webb Smith, was able to take 'a retrospective view of the Proceedings of the Church Committee from the year 1828 to the present time', and at a subsequent committee meeting, he cited these proceedings more precisely by date. A little later he produced an index of the proceedings from 14 January 1827 (John Maquay refers to a meeting on that day). What happened to these records is unknown. They were not available to Catherine Tassinari when she wrote her valuable history of the English Church early in the twentieth century.[11]

Of all the records generated by these churches, arguably the most important are the registers of baptisms, marriages and burials. These do not, however, constitute a complete record of British life events in Tuscany. British Catholics received the rites of the parish church which they attended. A visitor to the cemetery which lies just below the church of San Miniato al Monte will discover a number of English and Italian tomb inscriptions, mostly of late nineteenth-century date, which record the burial of British nationals, and there are even a few inside the church itself. The *Chiostro dei Morti* at Santa Maria Novella contains a handful of illuminating inscriptions. Vigilance in other churches has occasionally been repaid and there is clearly still much to be discovered.

On the opposite wing of the Christian faith, the Disruption of 1843 resulted in the implantation of one Free Church of Scotland congregation in Leghorn and a smaller one in Florence. Another source of baptisms thus came into being. Although the dissenting dead continued to share the burial grounds with their Episcopalian compatriots, and marriages were celebrated at legation or consulate in order to ensure legal validity, they were no longer registered by the Anglican clergy. British Jews too were of course separately catered for. Occasional help in all these categories comes from notices of births, marriages and deaths in the British newspapers, not, of course, a complete or systematic source.

In theory a comprehensive inventory of British births, marriages and deaths could be compiled by combing the records of all the Tuscan communes in which Britons might have been resident, but this Herculean task has not been undertaken here. Thanks to mixed marriages among other things, British or half-British individuals are not always easy to spot, and English-looking names may equally well be North American or Antipodean. Many Britons lived in Tuscany for a considerable period without getting married, giving birth or dying there. Conversely, it was perfectly possible for individuals to be born, married or buried in Tuscany without being residents in any meaningful sense, for example while in transit to or from Rome and Naples. With all these limitations, the Anglican records name names (sometimes including those of the witnesses at weddings), offer clues to family relationships and help us to chart the life cycles of both long-term and short-term residents.

Thanks to the varied histories of the several churches, their registers have a complicated history of their own and are to be found in two principal London repositories. Broadly speaking, the returns from Leghorn down to 1824 are to be found with the records of the Registrar General in the National Archives, those after 1824 at the London Metropolitan Archive. The Leghorn registers abruptly and inexplicably cease in 1851; no one appears to know what happened to them thereafter, and we become dependent on a miscellany of sources including newspaper notices and the ongoing work that is being carried out by Matteo Giunti on the city's archival material.[12] We are very grateful for some fruitful exchanges with him.

The Reverend Thomas Hall, chaplain at Leghorn until his death in 1824, entered some Florentine life events in his register. Until 1828, Protestant Anglo-Florentines were anyway buried and registered at Leghorn. Otherwise, before 1833, Florentine marriages, which mostly took place at the embassy and might have important implications for property back home, are better recorded than baptisms and have found their way into the National Archives.[13] After 1833, the chaplains returned registers, by now including the burials which took place at the new cemetery, to the bishop of London (later Gibraltar). These are at the London Metropolitan Archive, as is everything produced by the joint chaplaincy of Pisa and Bagni. The embassy in Florence continued to submit notices of marriages to the Foreign Office down to 1852, and many were copied into FO79, with the result that some are recorded in two places or even three, with occasional varying detail.

The records of the Protestant cemeteries of Tuscany should be mentioned here. The Swiss managers of the so-called English Cemetery of Florence kept their own records, which can be cross-checked with the registers made by the Anglican clergy; there are also partial records of funeral expenditures, which can be illuminating. Above all, there are the monumental inscriptions in the cemetery itself. Here we must record another of our special debts, to the cemetery's indefatigable custodian, Sister Julia Bolton Holloway. She introduced us to these resources at our first meeting in 2004, and her welcome since has been never-failing. She has also been responsible for making all the inscriptions available online.[14] At Leghorn, the old English cemetery closed in 1840, but the inscriptions which were still legible were published in 1906.[15] Nothing comparable has yet been done for the newer cemetery (now itself closed) in Via Pera.

The newspapers

Mention has already been made of one useful feature of the British newspapers: the notices of life events. There is a great deal more to be discovered from them, and the appearance of online databases in recent years has made it easier to do so.

The London papers were read in Florence itself. The reading room opened in 1820 by the Swiss bibliophile Jean Pierre Vieusseux kept a wide range of British newspapers and journals. Some Anglo-Florentines read the newspapers at their bank, and it was possible also to have a subscription with the Paris publishing house of Galignani, which published a weekly digest (the *Messenger*) of the news of the continent. Naturally, the English papers took time to arrive, but if the news was a little elderly, that has to be seen in the context of the general speed of communications. The pace quickened as the century went on and speed, anyway, wasn't everything. The content of the English papers – including their coverage of Italian affairs – differed markedly from anything the Tuscan or Italian papers were likely to be able to publish.

Tuscan residents wrote letters to the London papers and also sent reports, anonymously or pseudonymously, on matters of interest. These were sporadic additions to a fairly constant stream of information about happenings in Tuscany and the rest of Italy, which obviously gained volume at times of political emergency, much of it finding its way into the provincial press. This coverage, if not deep, was wide; newspaper-readers anywhere in the British Isles would have had access at least to abbreviated versions of the reports which were appearing in London. They were not interested solely in politics narrowly defined. There was a constant and growing concern with the fate of Protestantism on the continent. In the early 1850s the Grand Duke's renewed Catholic zeal coincided with the irritation of British public opinion by the so-called 'Papal Aggression' and the re-establishment of a Catholic hierarchy in the British Isles. All of this prompted an enormous quantity of press reaction.

In addition, there was a quantity of gossip and occasionally scandal. The *Morning Post* in particular, especially in the 1820s, carried gushing notices of the doings of the great and good in Florence as in other continental centres: even such trivia as the runners and riders at the Florentine races received coverage. For a short period, a prominent Anglo-Florentine, Arthur Vansittart, reported in the sporting press on horse racing in Tuscany, while he himself was among the victims of the *Satirist*, a weekly scandal sheet in which the reputations of some of the leading figures in expatriate society were freely traduced. When major political events were afoot, as in 1848–1849 and 1859–1860, these frivolities were superseded by purposeful and lengthy reporting from regular correspondents such as the anglicized Piedmontese exile Antonio Gallenga, who was sent to Tuscany by the *Times* in the summer of 1859. Contemporaneously, the weekly *Athenaeum* was receiving frequent bulletins from Theodosia Trollope, a long-term resident of Florence with her husband Thomas, elder brother of the more famous novelist.

We should also notice the *Gazzetta di Firenze*, which has been consulted for the period 1814–1846.[16] This publication appeared three times a week and contained a mixture of summaries of the world's news, theatre reviews, official announcements, legal notices and (of most interest for present purposes) advertisements. British householders inserted notices to make it known that they would not be held responsible for debts contracted by their servants, and British nationals gave notice that they were opening shops or offering tuition in English or other services. Similar information was included in a short-lived English newspaper produced in Florence, the *Tuscan Athenaeum*, which had the wider purpose of commenting on current issues and cultural events. Its thirteen issues appeared between 30 October 1847 and 22 January 1848, in distinctly interesting times.[17]

Letters, memoirs and guidebooks

This is naturally a very miscellaneous category. It includes, for example, memoirs written by retired diplomats who had served their time in Florence and innumerable travelogues of varied interest and value. We have made extensive use of this class of material, without presuming to claim that we have exhausted it, still less that we have uncovered more than a very few of the many unpublished examples which could be added to it.

It is understandable that more should hitherto have been written about literary celebrities in Tuscany than about lesser mortals, for they have made it easier to do so by writing about themselves. If (as Giorgio Spini perceived) Byron and Shelley should not dominate our mental picture of the British presence in Italy around 1820, Robert and Elizabeth Barrett Browning should not be allowed to dominate the picture of Florentine expatriate society a generation later. In many respects it was uncongenial to them and they did not participate in it. This is no reason to ignore what they have to say about their Tuscan life and the people they knew, which is often outstanding both in quantity and interest.

It is from these miscellaneous sources that we get many of our glimpses of what might be termed the support staff, the other British on whose services the leisured depended. Although both middle- and upper-class expatriates hired servants, including cooks and coachmen, from the local population, they also contributed to a lower-class British presence in Tuscany by bringing servants with them from home. It was not just the Brownings' maid Elizabeth Wilson who made an Italian marriage as a consequence. Valuable information on what we have called 'the service sector' comes also from the guidebooks, such as those produced by Mrs Mariana Starke and then by the publishing house John Murray. These gave practical information about hotels, shops and other amenities, often noting where English was spoken or where a hotelier or other tradesman was English. When it comes to special subjects such as the straw hat industry or the Tuscan railways, there is a range of secondary literature on which we have had to draw, in addition to what can be found in the Foreign Office correspondence, the newspapers and elsewhere.

Two very different but valuable sources may also be mentioned here. First, the Vieusseux subscription registers (*Libri dei Soci*) have been preserved complete from the very beginning and are available online.[18] Anglo-Saxon names predominate in its pages, and it is noteworthy that a considerable majority of subscriptions were for a week, 15 days or a month, which makes subscriptions for longer periods the more interesting. Some British subscribers attempt to use Italian, some doughtily sign up in English and others use French because this was the common currency.

Second, the National Archives possesses a substantial number of wills made by British residents in Tuscany and proved in England before the Prerogative Court of Canterbury (PCC). The PCC series ends in 1858; wills of a later date can be found in the Probate Registry. Many are brief and convey little information about relationships or property, while others are full of meat.

The structure of the book

This book consists of fifteen chapters, some broadly chronological, others thematic in character. No single approach would suffice.

The first chapter asks who the British in Florence were and how they were identified. The next three describe the peaceful development of expatriate society under the four ambassadors who held office during the years 1814–1846, a period largely though not entirely unaffected by revolutionary alarms in Italy. The fifth and sixth deal, respectively, with the ways the British amused themselves and with the development of the Florentine Anglican Church during this tranquil period. Chapter 7 focusses on the Tuscan life of one 'English' widow who is well known to us through her diary, Elizabeth Maquay.

The eighth chapter deals with the years between 1846 and 1849, in which Tuscany experienced revolutionary stirrings which the Grand Duke proved unable to manage. His reaction to these events, and the consequent Austrian occupation of Tuscany, had their most troublesome consequences for the British, and especially for British Protestant activists, down to 1853, as described in Chapters 9 and 10. Chapter 11 moves into the temporary calm of the mid-fifties, when the Austrians at last departed and an old Florentine resident, the Marquis of Normanby, was British ambassador. Three chapters are then devoted to particular varieties of Anglo-Florentine resident: physicians and seekers after health, men who came to Tuscany to do business, notably straw-hat manufacturers and railwaymen, and finally the very varied 'service sector' – servants, hoteliers, bankers and shopkeepers.

The last chapter sees the end of John Maquay as a Florentine resident and then of the Grand Duke, to be followed by the annexation of Tuscany to a united Kingdom of Italy. A brief Epilogue looks a short way forward into the next few years of the British in Florence.

This book has been a long-drawn-out labour of love, and it is a pleasure to thank those who have helped it to see the light of day. We have already mentioned some of our principal obligations. On top of her other good deeds, Alyson Price read a first draft and ventured immensely helpful and detailed suggestions. We are also grateful to the many people who have been put in touch with us by Alyson and by Julia Bolton Holloway, usually with enquiries about their Anglo-Florentine ancestors. Trying to answer their questions has often proved exceedingly illuminating for ourselves: our apologies if we cannot remember or name them all. We must, however, mention Francis Plowden, whose researches into his ancestor Charles, a prominent banker in Florence, have been a pleasure to share.

Thanks must also go to the staff at the various archives and libraries which we have used, above all the British Institute in Florence, the National Archives at Kew, the British Library, the ever-surprising London Library, the London Metropolitan

Archive and Lambeth Palace Library. A special word should go to the staff at the Wardown Park Museum in Luton, who were exceedingly helpful to us in our early efforts to unravel the mysteries of straw hats. We are exceedingly grateful to Sarah Purdy, a descendant of John Leland Maquay, for permission to reproduce portraits of him and of his wife Elena, which are in her possession. Our grateful thanks must also go to those at I.B. Tauris/Bloomsbury who have been involved in the acceptance and production of the book: first Dr Lester Crook, and latterly Jo Godfrey, Olivia Dellow and the many others who have assisted in the laborious process of making our project into a physical reality.

A note on currency

Comparisons with the present day are notoriously inexact and debatable, but as a rough guideline, £1 sterling in 1830 would be worth approximately £50 today. The problem of calculation is compounded by the fact that many European coins were in circulation in Tuscany, at least in Leghorn, and different people adopted different modes of keeping accounts. The fundamental unit of money was the *lira* or Tuscan pound, divided into 20 *soldi*, each *soldo* divided into 12 *denari*. The pound sterling, as some readers will remember, was before 1971 similarly divided into 20 shillings, with each shilling divided into 12 pennies, but there were around 30 *lira* to £1 sterling. However, the Tuscans rarely used the above terms on the street, preferring the 'paul' or *paolo*, two thirds of a *lira*, itself divided into 8 *crazie* or 40 *quattrini*. A *paolo* at 45 to the £ sterling was worth over 2 pence and more than 5 pennies. In addition to this, we find the *scudo* or *francescone* in use, equalling 10 *paoli* or 23 pence around 4 shillings and 6 pennies. There were 4 florins (*fiorini*) to the *francescone*. Then there was the sequin, a gold coin of 2 *scudi*. Also found in circulation were Spanish or Roman 'dollars', which were worth just under 10 pauls. Many of the English carried Napoleons, which despite the emperor's demise had a widespread exchangeability in Florence at around 36 pauls (roughly 80 pence or 16 shillings). We have generally expressed amounts in the text in pre-1971 currency terms since this is what the contemporary sources used.

Notes

1   Giorgio Spini, *Risorgimento e Protestanti* (third edition, Torino, 1998), p. 101.
2   Reverend John W. Cunningham, *Caution to Continental Travellers* (London, 1818). The author was 'late Fellow of St John's College, Cambridge; Vicar of Harrow, Middlesex; and domestic chaplain to the Right Hon Lord Northwick'.
3   Leigh Hunt, *Lord Byron and Some of His Contemporaries, with Recollections of the Author's Life, and of His Visit to Italy* (Paris, 1828), Vol. 3, p. 254.
4   Harry Rudman, *Italian Nationalism and English Letters* (New York, 1940), p. 199.
5   Spini, *Risorgimento e Protestanti*, p. 101.

6   Alyson Price, *Florence in the Nineteenth Century: A Guide to Original Sources in Florentine Archives and Libraries for Researchers into the English-Speaking Community* (Florence, 2011).

7   www.comune.fi.it/archiviostorico/index.html.

8   We have also made occasional use of the one surviving volume of the travel journals kept by Elizabeth's own daughter, Betsy, who died at Pisa in 1817, and the travel journals of John Leland Maquay senior, who made a 2-year continental tour in 1814–1816 as part of the great post-war wave of British tourism.

9   St Mark's succeeded Holy Trinity, which was opened in 1844 and now, somewhat altered, is used by the Waldensians. Two volumes of the Minute Books concern us, hereafter cited as CMB 1 and CMB 2. The first runs from 27 December 1839 to 26 January 1854; the second, commencing 27 January 1854, covers the rest of the Grand Ducal period and beyond.

10 Cited here as *Church Letters*, with decade, number and date. Some of these letters were written before 1840 and shed light on the 1839 disputes.

11 Catherine Danyell Tassinari, *The History of the English Church in Florence* (Florence, 1905).

12 www.leghornmerchants.wordpress.com.

13 RG33/117 (Hall's register) and FO170/6, as well as in the relevant volumes of FO79.

14 www.florin.ms/cemetery.html.

15 Montgomery Carmichael (ed.), *The Inscriptions in the Old British Cemetery of Leghorn Transcribed by G. Milner-Gibson-Cullum and the Late F. Campbell Macauley* (Leghorn, 1906).

16 Many volumes are available online, and the British Library possesses a complete file on microfilm.

17 The only surviving complete run is in the New York Public Library. The authors have a copy courtesy of the New York Library.

18 www.vieusseux.it.

1 NATIONALITY, IDENTITY AND DOMICILE

In 1851, Augustus Billington, aged 10, was living in the household of his father, the rector of Kenardington in Kent. According to the census, he was a British subject, born in Florence. If faced with a demand for proof of his son's birth and nationality, the Reverend Billington would have been able to refer to the Bishop of London's office, for the baptism, in Florence on 8 September 1840, was recorded in a register which was transmitted to the bishop in his capacity as overseer of Anglican churches abroad. If Augustus had been born in Florence 10 years earlier, there is a very good chance that no record at all would have been made by anyone outside the family.

In 1846, Mrs Mary Losack asked Bishop Blomfield to institute a search for a record of the baptism of her son in Florence in 1829. On 2 September the bishop replied illuminatingly:

> The Chaplain at Florence was not under my jurisdiction in the year 1829. Every English Clergyman who baptised a child on the Continent ought to take some record of preserving the fact, but he is not required to do so by law, nor is there any established mode of proceeding in such cases, the regulations of our common & statute law not being in force out of the British Dominions. In the case of Chaplains who are appointed by the British Government it has been usual for them to send the registers of baptism to the Registry of the Diocese of London.

His Lordship concluded rather despairingly, 'I am sorry to say that I am wholly unable to point out to you any course of proceeding for supplying the omission in the present instance.'[1] Had the young Losack been baptised by the chaplain at Leghorn, a record would probably have reached the bishop, but in 1829 the church in Florence was still undergoing slow informal growth and the systematic keeping and transmission of registers was correspondingly gradual.

At Leghorn, the chaplain Thomas Hall had kept a register throughout the war years. In a letter to Bishop Howley of London, written towards the end of 1820, Hall sketched the course of his early life and subsequent career, speaking of the 'incredible hardships' he had undergone under French occupation, which were slightly mitigated by the fact that the French regarded him as an American national. Born in Philadelphia in 1751, he left America after the Revolution and had been in Leghorn since 1783.[2] In his enforced isolation before 1814, Hall entered in his register the burials that were performed at Leghorn (before 1828, the only burial place in Tuscany for British Protestants) and not only the baptisms and marriages that he himself conducted but some that took place elsewhere in Tuscany which he was requested to record.[3] He continued in this practice until his death in 1824.

His successor, Charles Neat, had different views and refused to register some certificates which were sent to him by the *chargé d'affaires* Fox-Strangways at Florence. Neat took his stand on English practice and his responsibilities to the Tuscan authorities, who required him to take account solely of his own Protestant congregation. He was using printed English register books which 'do not admit of entries of Marriages, Baptism and burials solemnized in any other places than Leghorn'. Primly he declared that 'The old register books were very irregular, and afford no precedent', and he thought it 'right to follow, as closely as possible, the established custom of Parishes in England'.

Faced by Neat's punctilio, Strangways sought guidance from the Foreign Office, 'as it is a subject of considerable importance to the numerous British families settled in Tuscany'. He wanted to know

> First, whether in future, all registers of Baptisms and Burials at Florence are to be sent home as those of Marriages always are, through the Foreign Office, to the London Registry Office; and if so, I beg to know what fee will be required. Secondly, whether the certificates always kept in the Office of this Legation, of such Rites of the Church as may have been performed here, constitute a sufficient and legal Registry of the same, and would be so considered in England?[4]

The Foreign Office confirmed Neat's opinion and told Strangways that His Majesty's law officer had reported 'that there is not at present any provision established by Law for the registration of any Acts of the nature which you describe'. It would be difficult to frame one, as 'British subjects settled abroad, are in strictness liable to be reckoned among the Inhabitants of the Country where they reside'. Therefore 'the legal registration of an Act done in a Foreign country, under the Law of that Country' would (it was assumed) be accepted as evidence in Britain. However, in 1815 the Bishop of London, presumably reacting to the new ease of travel and settlement abroad, had directed that certificates from consuls, chaplains and even individuals should be received by the registrar of his Consistorial Court. Even so, 'the legal effect of such Entries has not been ascertained, by any use that has hitherto been known to have been made of them'.[5]

Hall had made the irregular entries of which Neat complained only if he was requested to do so. Three of the children of Captain Charles Montagu Walker RN illustrate how practice varied. On 19 July 1819 Hall himself baptised

Florence Fletcher Walker, who doubtless took her name from the city, as Florence Nightingale would do the following year. This baptism took place at a villa near Leghorn, but on 27 November in the following year, the Reverend Trevor Trevor certified that he had baptised Florence's brother Arthur de Noë at the Villa di Brock near Florence. No recourse was had to Hall, but the baptism was eventually entered in the register of St Mary, Hampton, the Walkers' Surrey parish. This was also done when Harriet Horatia Fletcher was born in Florence in 1826 (by which time the disobliging Neat was chaplain at Leghorn). On both occasions the certificate also carried an attestation of the births of the children, signed by the attendant Italian physician. It seems that the parents were going to some lengths to obtain evidence of the legal existence of their foreign-born children without either troubling the Leghorn chaplain or using the machinery provided by the bishop of London (if they were aware of it).

The private baptism of Florence Nightingale in July 1820 at the Villa Colombaia at Bellosguardo overlooking Florence was not entered by Hall but, although performed by an Anglican clergyman, was later inserted in the Nonconformist Register at Dr Williams's Library in London.[6] It is anyone's guess how many more such baptisms remain to be discovered in British parish registers. Warren Hastings Anderson and his wife, Mary Dewar, were prominent social luminaries in Florence in the 1830s. The baptism of their daughter Maria Magaretta was entered in the register of Tranent in East Lothian under the date 22 June 1832, with a note that she had been born on 29 April and baptised by 'the Reverend Frederick Apthorp, acting Chaplain to the British Mission at Florence, and rector of Gumley in Leicestershire'. None of the baptisms that Apthorp doubtless performed in Tuscany was ever reported to a bishop or to the Foreign Office. One further example is instructive in that the ceremony in question was performed by Neat. On 16 August 1830 he baptised Carlotta, the daughter of Thomas Andrew Vyse, 'at Lucca Baths', but because the event did not take place at Leghorn, he adhered to his own rule, simply providing the parents with a certificate; the entry is to be found in the registers of the Vyses' home parish, St Mary's Hornsey.

For some years, therefore, we are reliant for our knowledge of Florentine baptisms on such records as were transmitted to the Foreign Office, supplemented by newspaper notices and other anecdotal information. The haphazard nature of this record-keeping is well illustrated by the fact that the births of the sons of an *attaché* at the Legation, Ferdinand St John (the eldest son of the third Viscount Bolingbroke by his second marriage), passed unnoticed. John Henry St John, born on 2 January 1829, achieved only a notice in the *Morning Post* on the 28th of that month. On 2 March 1831 he was joined by twin brothers. The habitually penniless St John had requested Sir Robert Lawley to purchase a Guards commission for a son if he should have one. As a sporting man Lawley agreed to do so if the pregnancy resulted in twins. The first boy, Charles Louis, duly appeared, to be followed hours later by his younger brother. The news of the second birth was brought to Sir Robert on the racecourse, at which he flung up his hands and exclaimed, 'What ill luck is this? Three of my horses beaten, and twins – all in one day'. The younger twin, Frederic (who himself served as *attaché* at the Legation in the 1850s), recalled that Lawley and Lord Rendlesham were his godfathers, but no official record appears to have been made of his birth or baptism.[7]

The system of civil registration introduced in England and Wales in 1837 (1855 in Scotland) did not cover British subjects living on the continent, but as Blomfield implied in his reply to Mrs Losack, there had been some change. From 1833 registers were sent regularly to the Bishop of London and later Gibraltar. Before then, or retrospectively, how did officialdom, at home or abroad, know for certain that a child was indeed 'a British subject born in Florence'?

The answer seems to be that (like a great deal else) the information was taken on trust. One corollary of this bureaucratic imprecision was that British representatives abroad were expected to extend their protection, and sometimes their hospitality, to 'British subjects', a species to which there was no authoritative identification guide. From time to time dubious characters claimed that protection and demanded passports, but proved on examination not to be what they professed to be. Eugenio Latilla, an artist who resided in Florence during the later 1840s, furnished a contrary example.

In 1850 Latilla complained to Lord Palmerston about the Secretary of Legation, Peter Campbell Scarlett, who 'instead of protecting is continually annoying English residents, of which I am by no means a singular instance'. Eight years previously, Latilla had obtained a French passport, but on applying for a new British one, 'to my great astonishment I was told, I was not a British subject and Mr Scarlett would not give me one'. Two letters to Scarlett had produced no change of heart, and Latilla therefore applied to the Foreign Secretary, saying that he was a Protestant, born in London to an Italian father long resident in England and an English mother; he was also a member of the Society of British Artists, which admitted no foreigners. He enclosed a certificate from the Florentine chaplain, George Robbins, to the effect that he had seen a record of Latilla's baptism in London in 1808.

Latilla was not alone in objecting to Scarlett's reluctant discharge of the more humdrum duties of his post, but in this instance, it is possible to have some sympathy for the secretary. He explained that Latilla had signed his application 'Eugenio Latilla', without making any reference to his nationality. Taking him to be Italian, Scarlett had replied that, as he had a French passport, he did not see that he needed another one and that, in the absence of any proofs that he was a British subject, he must refuse his application. Otherwise 'I should not have refused him a Passport which every British Subject is entitled, if necessary, when his nationality is ascertained.'[8] Clearly there was no set procedure to be followed when applying for a passport and no standard form of proof of identity. Lord Normanby as Minister referred only to one rule which he took to be universally observed: that no new passport was issued unless the old one was surrendered: 'With the large floating English population always passing through Tuscany, this precaution is very necessary'. Even so, exceptions could be made.[9]

Latilla could claim to have been born British, but others had more exotic origins. On 25 January 1841 John Maquay attended a large ball given by Madame Coesvelt for her house-warming.[10] William Gordon Coesvelt was born in the West Indies in 1767, the illegitimate son of a Danish merchant. Having moved to London and becoming a banker and a wealthy man, he was naturalized in 1822. In October 1836 he was married in Paris to the Spanish widow of a French soldier, and made ready to leave England by disposing of both his house in Carlton Gardens (later occupied by Palmerston) and his art collection; the Tsar had already bought some of the choicest items. The Vieusseux records attest that he was settled in Via Ghibellina by July 1839.[11] What documentation (if any) did such a man carry about with him to prove not only his own but his wife's claims to the protection of the British crown?

Two of the most prominent members of Anglo-Florentine society for much of the century were only slightly less exotic. In 1786 the American-born Reverend Thomas Hall was married to Maria Kleiber, who belonged to a Swiss merchant family of Leghorn. Their son Horace, born in 1790, entered into what would be a lifelong association with Emmanuele Fenzi, for many years the dominant Florentine banker and businessman. His connections and knowledge of the Florentine scene proved of immense value to Anglo-Florentines, who needed informed help and advice.[12] His much younger brother Alfred established an import-export business in Leghorn but joined with Horace in a number of commercial enterprises, often in association with Fenzi, and, after mid-century, became a stalwart of the Florentine Church. Unlike Horace, Alfred made an English marriage, but he did not have to go to England to find his bride, Mary Eliza, a daughter of the expatriate James Matthews. Their children were born in Florence and Thomas Trollope remembered Alfred as 'the father of a family, one of the most respected and popular of the English colony during the whole of my Florentine life'.[13] On 2 May 1863 a report in *The Lady's Newspaper* complained that the marriage of the Prince of Wales had been ignored by 'the whole body of British subjects' in Florence, with one shining exception: 'The only attempt I have heard of at rejoicing was a party given by Mr Alfred Hall, at his villa, when visitors were liberally regaled; and in the evening a good display of fireworks were exhibited.' This paragon of English patriotism and identity was the son of an American-born father and a Swiss mother, born and married in Tuscany and destined to die there.

Special rules were thought to apply to married women. Henrietta, one of the sisters of George Robbins, the long-serving chaplain of the English Church, was first married to Viscount Weymouth, but after his death, she became the wife of the Marchese Inghirami. In 1850, again widowed, she expressed her wish to be readmitted to the privileges of British citizenship. Sir George Hamilton sought the advice of the Foreign Secretary, who acknowledged that 'questions as to the national character of individuals' under similar circumstances 'have not been very clearly and satisfactorily settled by writers upon international Law'. The Queen's Advocate thought that by her marriage she had become a Tuscan subject, assuming that Florentine law conferred Tuscan nationality on a foreign woman who was married to a Florentine. On this assumption, now that he was dead, she retained Tuscan nationality for as long as she continued to reside in Florence. 'But if Madame Inghirami should think proper to return to, and reside within the dominions of Her Majesty, and to resume her original British character, she would be entitled again to be considered a British Subject.'[14]

This has something of the air of being made up as it went along, but Henrietta may in fact have taken the advice. When John Maquay visited Robbins at his Northamptonshire rectory in June 1853, he found her in residence along with her sister (also the widow of an Italian nobleman) and remarked that the house had been 'beautifully furnished by Madame Inghirami', which implies that she had previously spent some time there.[15] She did not change her permanent residence. John's diary reveals that she was in Florence again in 1854, and like her brother, she died there in 1873. That she regarded herself as a member of Anglo-Florentine society is indicated not only by the fact that she subscribed to the English Church fund and purchased sittings at Bagni in the summer but by the fact that she put her name to the memorial got up by the British inhabitants in 1861 praying for the restoration of British diplomatic representation at Florence.[16]

Among other women who did so was Grace Galeazzi, one of John Maquay's longest-standing British friends in Florence. An Irish-born widow, she had been married in 1826 to Major Michelangelo Galeazzi, late an officer in the Austrian army, who died in 1859 and was buried in the English cemetery. If there was a question mark over the nationality of his wife, before or after his death, there is no evidence that it troubled her. Harriet Guastalla, formerly Burdett and born Willans, was another signatory to the memorial and may have been similarly placed if her husband, the Jewish-born Marco Guastalla, was a Tuscan subject. By signing as 'widow Burdett', she may have sought to establish her right to be interested in the question of British representation in Florence.

If the Tuscans were to accept the British view of the opposite case, that is that an Italian woman married to a British subject acquired his nationality, it was necessary that the marriage itself be regarded as valid. John Maquay obtained the appropriate licences to marry Elena Gigli in 1828, and the wedding ceremonies were performed according to the rules, whereupon Elena became a British subject. Their four sons all received Protestant baptism. John Fenton Newbery married Adela Travaglini in Siena in 1840, and they had at least eight children: five boys and three girls. The girls were brought up as Catholics, the boys as Protestants.[17] These and many other mixed marriages seem to have caused no trouble, but the rules had to be observed.

At some time in the summer of 1850 Thomas Downie, a Scottish engineer, was married at the Leghorn Consulate to Albina Fontana, a native of Massa in the duchy of Modena, where Downie had been working. Albina was born a Roman Catholic, and at 20 was underage. The couple returned to Massa after the wedding and a child was born to them. Trouble started when it was not presented for Catholic baptism. Under British law the marriage was valid, but the Modenese would have none of it, as no licence had been sought from the Catholic authorities. Consul Macbean and the Foreign Office chose to take their stand on the automatic validity of the ceremony at the consulate and the transformation of the bride into a British subject, now forcibly and improperly separated from her husband. The British huffed and puffed, but the Modenese were immoveable. They accused the couple of cohabiting and expelled them from their territory. The Consul was at fault in not insisting that the local rules were obeyed, but there is no evidence that the couple experienced any trouble from the Tuscan authorities.[18]

Thorny issues might arise concerning not only a woman's change of nationality upon marriage and upon the death of her husband but also the nationality of children born in Tuscany to a British father. Both issues arose in the case of Frederick Stibbert.[19] Tourists today can visit his extraordinary house and collection, with its dark wooded garden (unquestionably English in feeling), on a hillside overlooking the centre of Florence. His father, Colonel Thomas Stibbert, was born in 1771, the eldest of three sons of a man who had handsomely enriched himself in India. Thomas served in the Peninsular War, came into full possession of his fortune on the death of his mother in 1815 and embarked on a life of travel. His brother Giles remained in England and lived a life described by Stibbert's biographer as *molto regolare*. From the Vieusseux subscription books, we know that Thomas visited Florence on several occasions between 1822 and 1831, but it was only in 1835 that he settled there and in 1837 that he first made the acquaintance of Horace Hall, who became his banker and would play a vital part in the family's future.

He also got to know Giulia Cafaggi, a woman of lowly social status, who proceeded to bear him five children, of whom Frederick and two sisters survived childhood. It was not until 1842 that the couple were married, going to Malta for the purpose. Giulia later said of her husband that he had few friends and acquaintances in Florence and lived a retired life.

He told me that he had left England at his mother's death, had never gone back there and had no intention of doing so. He had been away for such a long time and had become so accustomed to life abroad and so contented with it and its ways that he had decided never to go back again. He said too that he had no particular friends in England and only one close relative, Giles Stibbert.

Thomas himself, in the year before his death, told his brother that

The motive which has induced me to fix my residence in Florence is the mildness of the climate, the protection afforded to all foreigners, and the liberty of living unfettered by any restraint or odious civil obligations. Hitherto I have not made the purchase of a house but have taken up my quarters in one of the most select streets of Florence, and which I have consequently furnished as becomes my rank in Society and the respect I owe to my lady and the comfort of my little family.

Giles would never acknowledge Thomas's 'lady' and 'little family', and he probably heartily disapproved of his brother's desire to live 'unfettered by any restraint or odious civil obligations', a repudiation of what every English gentleman was supposed to be and do and a shocking reason to wish to live abroad. Absence of restraint did not, for Stibbert, mean a debauched social life, rather the reverse. Horace Hall confirmed both that he had 'lived a life almost exclusively confined within his domestic walls' and that 'from what I could observe of his general behaviour and the tenor of our conversations he seemed to be, and I was convinced of it, definitely settled at Florence'.

Stibbert died on 31 May 1847, when Frederick was not yet 9 years old. His will named his wife and Horace Hall jointly as executors in Tuscany and guardians of the children. Giles was appointed one of three executors for the English property, but he and his two colleagues in England renounced any claims and responsibilities. Thomas also appointed a 'family council', a common Italian expedient. Its members (Giulia's relatives) were empowered to check that the guardians fulfilled their responsibilities and to act for them should either or both default or die. By virtue of Thomas's right under English law to dispose freely of his own inheritance, Frederick became the sole heir to a considerable fortune consisting entirely of investments, since Thomas had never wanted to possess real property either in Italy or in England. It was estimated in October 1847 at £130,000. Arrangements were made for the children's education, and already in the year of Colonel Stibbert's death, it was agreed with the family council that Hall was to be solely responsible for administering the English part of the inheritance.

Not until April 1851 did Hall and Julia have to defend their position. Frederick's academic performance was not brilliant, and it was decided to send him to school in England. Getting wind of this, the family council summoned the guardians and intimated their desire to become more involved with the children's lives. The underlying motive may have been to obtain control of the English property, but ostensibly it was concern for the children's upbringing. The council insisted that they be given a Catholic education, in view of the fact that the mother was born a Catholic and that they were living in a Catholic country. This demand was backed by a decree from the *pretore* of the Santa Croce district.

Hall had no doubts about the real intentions of the family council, and his advice was to send Frederick to England forthwith and make him a ward of court. Giulia set off with her son in August, but the family council was determined to fight. The legal issue was the nationality of the children and the laws to which they were subject, and it was no simple matter. Hall sought the opinion of the distinguished lawyer James Freshfield, who in September 1851 put forward the view that Colonel Stibbert had been domiciled in Tuscany, 'behaved as subject to the law of Tuscany' and made his will accordingly. To Freshfield, it seemed that Giulia was a Tuscan subject 'and because of her husband's death loses the rights she made by means of him as an English subject'. The children, thanks to their British father, 'have a right in virtue of the English law to the privileges of English subjects but they were natural-born Tuscan subjects being born there'. This view would presumably have made Tuscans of John Maquay's four sons. Freshfield concluded that 'Colonel Stibbert, Madame Stibbert and their children are all, though in different degrees, subject to the laws of Tuscany'. This was not perhaps the clearest or most helpful formulation. Henrietta Inghirami had been told that she remained a Tuscan subject even after her husband had died, whereas Giulia Stibbert, in Freshfield's opinion, forfeited her temporary British nationality when Stibbert died.

Rather clearer were the consequences of the Lord Chancellor's wardship. It would remain in force until the subject was 21, and Frederick would be unable to leave Britain without his Lordship's permission. If his mother proposed to return to Florence, it would be necessary to appoint a guardian in England and to make arrangements for his accommodation during school holidays. Since his uncle Giles refused to recognise the existence of his brother's children, the English guardianship fell to the director of the bank which handled the English end of the estate. Giulia and Hall now prepared a memorandum arguing that Colonel Thomas had always retained British citizenship, with the consequence that his children and his wife were British citizens too. The family council declared that Giulia was putting personal gain before her religious duty, that the removal of Frederick to England was illegal and that he must be returned to Florence.

The case was aired before the *pretore* of Santa Croce on 18 December 1851. Perhaps surprisingly, he found in favour of the guardians, expressing the view, as Giulia and Hall explained in a further memorandum addressed to Scarlett early in the following March, 'that the Wards Stibbert, were foreign Subjects and not Tuscans, and that consequently in all relations as to their person, the guardianship falls under the Jurisdiction of the English Authorities'. In the *pretore's* opinion the family council should confine itself to ensuring that the patrimony was divided among the heirs in accordance with 'the laws to which the said children by their birth are subject', in itself a rather ambiguous statement.

The family council appealed against this decision, and the case went before the Tribunal of First Instance. Hall thought it proper to interest the British authorities in the case. Scarlett was requested to confirm that Giulia preserved 'the character of English subject' that she had acquired by marriage. If she stayed in her husband's house, it was because her children 'still continue their residence provisionally in the character of foreigners'. Whenever she had needed a passport, she had obtained it from the British Legation. Madame Inghirami had been told that if she wished to reclaim her British nationality, she must come and live in England; it seems to be hinted here that Giulia had been advised to do the same if she wished to maintain the nationality she had acquired on her marriage.

Scarlett now applied to the Tuscan minister Casigliano, seeking the government's intervention on behalf of the guardians. He treated it as self-evident that the children were British subjects and made no reference to any suspicion that the motives of the family council were mercenary. The air was thick with religious controversy at this moment, and Scarlett made so bold as to declare that Her

Majesty's government could not tolerate an attempt 'to convert Protestant English Children who are minors and wards in chancery, to another form of religion during their infancy and residence'. Were they of age, they would be entitled 'to act according to their consciences' for, as Scarlett complacently pointed out, 'Your Excellency is aware that religious toleration is justly the pride of the Country which I have the honor to represent'. On 14 March he was able to report that his application had been successful.[20] This might seem surprising, in view of the bad blood that had lately been created by British support for Protestant evangelism in Tuscany, but Horace Hall was an influential figure, and perhaps no one wanted to grasp this particular nettle. In reality, also, there was no way the Tuscan courts could enforce Frederick's return against the will of the Lord Chancellor.

A few years previously, Hall had been appointed by another British testator to another family council. Hugh Macdonell led a long and adventurous life and well illustrates the complexity of nationality.[21] Born into a Scottish Jacobite family, probably around 1760, he went to North America with his father, brothers and other relatives only 2 or 3 years before the outbreak of the War of Independence. The Macdonells to a man fought as loyalists and were forced to flee from the American colonies to Canada. Early in the new century Hugh left for England, where he obtained sufficient patronage to be appointed commissary general at Gibraltar in 1804–1806, a military post which subsequently entitled him to half-pay. In 1812 he became consul general at Algiers. According to his second wife, Ida Ulrich, the daughter of the Danish consul there, he arrived a widower, with four daughters. It seems that he and Ida were married in 1815, when she may have been barely 16 and he 55 or more. Understandably he referred in his will to the large discrepancy in their ages, expressing his gratitude for her care and attention to their common children. At Algiers he was twice in danger of his life at the hands of successive Deys, and in 1824 he was compelled to leave. The family eventually arrived in Florence by way of Malta and after some years purchased Casa Annalena, a converted convent in the Via Romana.

By the time Hugh died, aged at least 87, in 1847, four children had been born to Ida in Florence and three of his daughters by his first marriage had been married there. Although he had a Protestant funeral, and all the Macdonell children born in Florence received Protestant baptism, the family had strong Catholic affiliations. One of the daughters in 1840 married the Marquis Aguado de las Marismas, a Spanish grandee, and later became a lady in waiting to the Empress Eugenie. Another became a nun; yet another daughter married a Protestant Austrian soldier and others married British officers, while the two sons entered the British army, the younger, Hugh, later becoming a diplomat.[22] The family knew and entertained a wide range of people, but the cosmopolitan upper reaches of their acquaintance might have looked distinctly foreign to some of the humbler and more determinedly Protestant members of Anglo-Florentine society.

Macdonell made his will on 25 May 1845, 'in a small apartment on the ground floor looking towards the garden' of Casa Annalena.[23] The family council was to consist of the brothers Charles and Joseph Poniatowski, the Marchese Luigi Torrigiani, the Cavaliere Rocco Massaroni and 'Horatio' Hall, all of whom Macdonell thought would be willing to serve, although he did not envisage that they would actually be needed. They were named solely in case it should be discovered that the guardianship of his underage children was in any way dependant on 'the laws or tribunals of Tuscany'. He thought that this was not so, simply because he was a foreigner. He described himself as 'a native of the County of Inverness in Scotland and for many years domiciled and residing at Florence'. When had he last set foot in Scotland?

It was the meaning of the word 'domiciled' that was to bother his executors during the next few years. Hugh, as it turned out, furnished a test case. On 8 February 1853 the *Morning Post* reprinted an article from the *United Service Gazette* in which this case was discussed, in the surely correct belief that large numbers of half-pay officers, both naval and military, were potentially affected by it. Macdonell's executors, setting out to claim £170 of arrears of half-pay on behalf of his estate, had offered to pay British legacy duty on it. They were met by a government claim for duty on his entire estate, in Tuscany as well as in Britain. This was based on a House of Lords ruling in 1845 that if a man died domiciled in Great Britain, all his property, wherever it might be, was liable to legacy duty; if he died domiciled elsewhere, none of it was. The assertion that Macdonell had died domiciled in England rested in its turn on the presumption that the receipt of half-pay prevented a man from abandoning his British domicile in favour of a foreign one. The executors were advised to resist, and the case was about to come before the Court of Exchequer when the Crown's legal officers indicated that the claim was being dropped.

The article spelled out the very positive implications of this decision for the families of deceased officers who had hitherto been deterred from claiming arrears of half-pay because of the presumed liability to legacy duty. As everything depended on having a valid foreign domicile, it also explained what that meant. Serving officers abroad had no choice in the matter and were regarded as retaining their British domicile. To acquire a foreign domicile, it was necessary to be on half-pay or otherwise at liberty to choose one's place of residence. It was not necessary to know for certain that one would live in that place forever; it was even permissible to have the intention of coming home should circumstances change. Provided that the residence in question was not an obviously temporary one (e.g. the long stays sometimes made in one place by avowed tourists), it would constitute legal domicile, even if death should occur while the individual in question was paying a visit to England. It was, however, indispensable to ensure that one's will was made in accordance with the laws and forms of the country of residence.

That many residents of Florence, as of other continental resorts, were potentially affected by this ruling is obvious, but it is scarcely less so that the definition of domicile offered here left room for debate. This was made very clear by a lawsuit which resulted from the death of James Robert Matthews, whose life, although shorter than Macdonell's, similarly combined military and diplomatic phases outside England. Married in London in 1810, he had fathered seven sons and four daughters. In the Napoleonic wars he served in the army of the king of Sweden and in 1816 he was appointed consul at Cadiz, where a daughter was born to him who would later become the wife of Alfred Hall of Leghorn. He was consul at Lisbon from 1822 until 1833, when the British consular service was terminated because of the civil strife in Portugal. He was living in Worthing when his wife died in 1838 and he himself suffered an attack of 'apoplexy'. His physician advised a milder climate and he set off in October 1838 for Italy. In May 1839, he purchased the Villa Lorenzi at Montughi, on the lower slopes of the Apennines just north of Florence, which remained his home until his death. Until 1846 he made annual visits to England, and in 1848 he took the waters in Germany. He died in Florence, aged at least 70, in July 1850.

On 2 August 1843 Matthews made a will, drafted in Italian. In the English will that he made on 28 July 1845 he referred to this as his 'Tuscan codicil', reaffirming its provisions and naming his old friend and solicitor Alfred Turner, together with a Thomas Hoskins, as his executors. The Prerogative Court of Canterbury on 8 November 1850 granted probate on both testaments (the 'codicil' having been translated into English).[24] Difficulties arose and in January 1855 the case of Hoskins v. Matthews was heard in Chancery. The Vice-Chancellor ruled that Matthews had died domiciled in Tuscany, a verdict upheld on appeal, by two votes to one, by the Lords in Chancery in the following November. Judgment was reserved until the following January, when the appeal was finally dismissed. Each of these phases of the litigation was reported in different publications in different amounts of detail, and inevitably much of the same ground was traversed several times.[25]

Some technical issues were discussed which it is neither necessary nor possible to attempt to analyse here. More important are a number of sometimes humorous insights into the attitudes of an Anglo-Florentine exile to both his native and his adopted lands. These were relevant to one of the central issues at stake. It was not in doubt that Matthews had been physically settled at Florence for some years before his death in 1850 and that he had no other abode, which under the definitions offered in the wake of the Macdonell case might have been thought to settle the matter. What was in dispute was whether he remained a would-be British resident at heart or, to use the lawyers' phraseology, whether Florence was his domicile not merely *de facto* but *de animo*.

In support of an English domicile, it was urged that his money was mostly invested in that country, where he had three bankers, and that his letters home showed 'his having used expressions of dislike to many of the habits and institutions of Italy, more especially the religious practices of that country'. In a letter written in 1840 he described his mind as 'on a spring cable, looking towards England'. Although it could be contended that Matthews increasingly saw no practical prospect of a return, the plaintiffs maintained that his ultimate intention to do so remained unchanged. His fixed residence in Tuscany, his liking of the climate and his purchase of property there were not in dispute. He remained in Tuscany solely on account of his health, and this should not be regarded as altering his domicile.

In rejecting the plaintiffs' case at the first hearing Vice-Chancellor Wood had referred to the 'Tuscan codicil', in which

the *indicia* of domicile were very plain. The testator had his family at Florence. There was a lady taking care of them, of whom it might be observed, in passing, that she had treated them with all the care and attention of a mother. Whenever these children went to England, or to other parts of the continent, as they appeared to have done, they always found their father at Florence on their return. It was there that he had what was called by some of the jurists his '*instrumentum domesticum*', by others his '*lares*'. It also fell within another definition of domicile, that when he left that abode he might be said to be travelling, and returned to it as his home.

His Honour then referred to the terms of the codicil, which he observed clearly contemplated a residence in Florence till the time of his death, and that his children would also reside there till their marriage or settlement in life. What stronger *indicia* could be had?

On the details of Matthews's life in Florence, some prominence was accorded to the testimony of Mrs Stephens, the mother-substitute mentioned above, who had remained in the Matthews family to look after the children in accordance with the deathbed wish of Mrs Matthews. Mrs Stephens had clearly run the household and by the 'Tuscan codicil' was left in charge of it; she was entitled to live there for as long as she remained single and had discretion to admit the Matthews sons to the Villa Lorenzi or exclude them from it while the youngest child, William Edgar, to whom it was bequeathed, was still a minor. One of the sons, George Theodore, was excluded altogether, thanks to his 'ungentlemanly and disreputable conduct'. Matthews's daughter, Louisa, who had lived mostly in England, could stay there if she made a downpayment of £80 in advance to Mrs Stephens.

On arrival in Florence in April 1839, Matthews had spent 4 or 5 weeks in a hotel (as was usual) and then purchased the Villa Lorenzi with its furniture and fittings and 7 or 8 acres of land, for a sum equivalent to £2,800. This implied that he had in mind a stay of some duration. Mrs Stephens stated that before he bought it, Matthews had thought of buying a residence in England, but not thereafter: 'I never heard him express any intention of residing again in England. He said frequently that it was a climate which he could not live in.' In 1840 he had bought an additional 5 acres, which was near the villa and evidently used to supply produce for it. In 1844 he tried but failed to make another purchase, and in 1848, he made another in the Tuscan mountains, 'because he enjoyed the air and because it produced oil, which was wanted for the villa'. Matthews jocularly referred to the villa as his 'Winchmore Hill', the place of Mr Turner's residence. That he could not live in England continued to pain him. Mrs Stephens claimed that he had even sometimes regretted buying the villa: 'He often said there was no country like one's own to live in.' He regretted also being separated from many of his family, especially during the school holidays, but much evidence was adduced to show that (like many other expatriates) he was convinced that his health demanded warmth.

On the other side, some stress was laid on his determination that his sons should receive an English education and with it English feelings: two of them were at one time intended for the navy. Only the youngest, to whom the villa was bequeathed, had lived there with his father, and even he was put under a tutor to be prepared for Eton. Of the four daughters, all but Louisa had lived with Matthews at Montughi, the third leaving in 1842 on her marriage to Alfred Hall. More generally, it was possible to show that Matthews remained, positively, an Englishman at heart and negatively a foreigner in Tuscany.

Like Colonel Stibbert, Matthews was a Protestant and a British subject, who did not mix in Florentine society. The same could have been said of many Anglo-Florentines, and he was not unusual in his somewhat contradictory attitudes to his adopted country. In May 1839, at the very moment of concluding the purchase of the villa, he described it to Mr Turner as being near 'this happy town'; the climate was favourable and the government as liberal as need be. Perhaps as the years went by, he became less enthusiastic about some aspects of Tuscan life. Mrs Stephens attested, 'He was not at all attached to the habits and modes of living of the Tuscan people, or to their opinions.' If Matthews was unenthusiastic about Roman Catholicism, there was nothing extraordinary in that. Referring to some processions he had witnessed, he remarked to Mr Turner that to 'make these things palatable to an Englishman and a Protestant; it is no go'. Some amusement may well have been caused in the banks and reading rooms of Florence by his reported reaction to the patent of nobility awarded to him by the Grand Duke in recognition of his contribution to the building of a new road from Florence to Fiesole. He had apparently said to Mrs Stephens, 'Take it, bury it, it is no use to me.' (Lord Justice Bruce commented, 'It is as if a man was made a nobleman of Islington.') Matthews took no part in public affairs, had no business or occupation and never applied to be made a naturalized subject of Tuscany. In accordance with the Tuscan law that foreigners should have governmental permission to reside there renewed every 6 months, he regularly did so and paid the required tax on the renewal.

By the time the Tuscan government showed signs of becoming less liberal, Matthews's health would have so deteriorated as to rule out any departure from Tuscany. The three appeal judges differed as to the implications. In concluding that at the time of his death Matthews possessed a Tuscan domicile, Vice-Chancellor Wood and Lord Justice Turner agreed that not only was his residence there permanent as a matter of fact but it had been a matter of choice and not compulsion. Lord Justice Bruce was disposed to think otherwise, but did not feel confident in differing from his learned brethren.[26]

While this was not the only lawsuit to be generated by disputes about the applicability of Tuscan or British law to property in the one country or the other, the documentation of the Matthews case is unusual in the flesh with which it clothes the legal bones. Reluctant or not, the result of his exile and his large family was to establish an enduring presence in Tuscany, especially if we take into account the descendants of Mary Eliza Matthews and Alfred Hall. No fewer than six of his children were laid to rest there, including all four of his daughters.

Many Anglo-Florentines might have recognized something of themselves in the picture of Matthews that emerged from the lawsuit. Several arrived in Florence having lived and worked abroad and then, perhaps, discovered that either the expense of living in England or the climate, or both, were disagreeable. There were numerous Indian veterans among them. One was John Fombelle, who, as it happened, witnessed Matthews's will in 1845. Born in London in 1763, he had entered the Bengal civil service at about the age of 20.[27] Probably widowed shortly before 1800, in 1809 he took as his second wife Elizabeth, the young daughter of another high-ranking Company servant, Burrish Crisp, Fombelle's close contemporary and a founder member of the Asiatic Society of Calcutta. Mrs Fombelle was the better part of 30 years younger than her husband and extremely musical. If she had Indian blood, she would have been by no means alone among the British inhabitants of nineteenth-century Florence.

Fombelle evidently returned to England in the summer of 1817. At some point he and Elizabeth moved to Cheltenham, where they met the Maquays; in 1833 they joined them in Florence. When Fombelle made his will in 1839, he described himself as 'late of Cheltenham but now residing in the city of Florence in Tuscany'. This hardly told the whole story of his background, let alone his wife's, but he seems to have expected, or hoped, that she would regard England as her home: 'It will be a consolation to me in my last moments to reflect that my beloved wife has wisely determined to pass the remainder of her days in England should I die abroad and she should survive me.'[28] Those last moments were delayed for another 10 years; Fombelle died in November 1849 at the age of 86, predeceasing Matthews by some months. In the meantime he had added a codicil to his will, by which he left all his Florentine property and monies to his wife, making no reference to her future plans. If it had ever been her intention to reside in England, she did not, but died at Florence on 8 January 1865 at the age of 72.

Not long before the Fombelles arrived in Florence, John Maquay had attended the funeral of Joseph Pouget, who died in July 1833 aged 73; it was attended by 'about a dozen carriages'. Pouget had been 30 years in the service of the East India Company. To judge from the fact that he is listed in an 1830 directory as a resident of Exmouth, he had not been long in Tuscany, although the Vieusseux registers bear witness that he had visited Florence earlier in his retirement. During his brief time in Tuscany, he purchased properties at Montughi, where James Matthews would reside a little later. In the will he made on 2 January 1833, he explained that the purchase price had not yet been fully paid and gave directions for doing so.

Aside from jewels and other precious *objets d'art*, which he described in minute detail, Pouget had East India stock to dispose of. His bequests to his second wife, born Maria Perkin, whom he had married in Devon in 1814, were at first hedged with conditions. Although 'perfectly convinced' of his wife's 'uncommon share … of the discretion allotted to her sex', he could not rule out the possibility that she might be lured into marrying again, and therefore provided that her enjoyment of virtually everything she had been bequeathed would cease from the moment of remarriage. In a codicil dated 18 April, Pouget removed these conditions.[29]

Mrs Pouget was left in comfortable circumstances. Early in December 1833 Elizabeth Maquay drove out to see her villa, which exemplified a combination highly prized by the British: 'I never saw comfort and elegance so happily blended.'[30] Mrs Pouget apparently vanishes from the Maquay diaries early in 1834, shortly after John had inspected her 'small villa', presumably with a view to buying or renting it. However, on 15 September 1841 he was negotiating successfully with a Madame Celestini, who turns out to be the erstwhile Mrs Pouget. Having joined the ranks of Anglo-Florentine widows, she had been married at some unknown date to a Francesco Celestini, but she did not change her religion and was buried in the English Cemetery in 1847. Her first husband's late change of mind had assured her of affluence both before and after her remarriage; Maria Perkin's life had been dramatically and totally changed by the move to Tuscany.

Another Indian medical veteran was Sir Thomas Sevestre, who was described as 'late a Surgeon in the service of the Honourable East India Company' when Andrew Buchanan of the Legation and the physician Dr Delisser witnessed his will on 9 December 1842.[31] He was tempted out of retirement at least once, in rather unusual circumstances. Thomas Trollope relates how he pleaded with him to come to the deathbed of a duellist at Bagni in September 1840. Trollope strangely describes Sevestre as 'a very old man', although he was only 57 when he died early in 1843. He consented to come, but only in a custom-made conveyance:

> he allowed me to get an arm-chair rigged with a couple of poles for bearers, and place himself in it – not before he had taken the precaution of slinging a bottle of pale ale to either pole of his equipage. He wore a very wide-brimmed straw hat, a suit of professional black, and carried a large white sun-shade.

Conveyed thus by bearers, with Trollope running alongside, he arrived at the scene and quickly pronounced the case hopeless.[32] Possibly the precautionary bottles of pale ale tell a story: his East India Company years may have left their mark on both Sevestre's ideas of transport and his liver. Sir James Annesley, 'late President of the Medical Board at Madras' and author of a voluminous work on the diseases of India, died at Florence in December 1847, having been there for well over a decade, and received an obituary notice in the *Morning Chronicle* on the following 10 January. There is nothing in his very English will to suggest that he had Tuscan property to dispose of and no evidence that either he or Pouget practised medicine in Tuscany.[33]

Unlike Fombelle, Sir Charles D'Oyly was born in India. It has been said of him that his official duties as a civil servant 'did not keep him too busy' and that he was 'of significance only as an artist'.[34] It was at his house at Bankipore in August 1824 that Christopher Webb Smith, Judge and Magistrate of Ghazupore, was married to Anne Jessie Mackenzie. Born in Blackheath, probably in 1793, Smith had entered the Company's service as a writer in 1808. By all accounts a more zealous official, Smith shared D'Oyly's artistic interests and they collaborated in the production of two large illustrated volumes, *The Feathered Game of Hindoostan*, published by D'Oyly's private press at Patna in 1828, and *Oriental Ornithology* (1829). Smith's only child, Helen Jane, was born at Arrah (Patna) in 1828, by which time he was Judge and Magistrate of Shahabad. In 1831 D'Oyly engraved a view of his residence at Arrah and also sketched his friend's Dickensian person seated inside the bungalow.[35]

On 15 November 1838 D'Oyly is recorded as a guest of John Maquay in Florence, and he was followed by Webb Smith. It is not clear exactly when the latter arrived in Tuscany with his wife and daughter, but he was well enough established there to be elected a member of the church committee on 11 November 1844. Like Fombelle before him, Smith had had hopes of being elected to the directorate of the Company, and offered himself as a candidate for election in 1842.[36] He nurtured these hopes even after arriving in Tuscany, for on 27 November 1844 the *Times* printed an announcement that he had intended to renew his application, but continued ill health in his family made it necessary for him to prolong his stay on the continent. D'Oyly meanwhile had fixed his residence at the Villa Ardenza near Leghorn, and Smith had entered John Maquay's circle. Their common involvement in the affairs of the English Church ensured close contact. On 22 September 1845 the two of them were sharing a 'most interesting religious conversation' with the chaplain George Robbins at the house of the American sculptor Hiram Powers when Smith was called away by the news of D'Oyly's sudden death.[37]

Many years later Smith was remembered humorously and affectionately by another long-term resident, James Montgomery Stuart. The passage merits extensive quotation, not least because it sheds an unexpected light on the ways in which the Indian experience might affect Anglo-Florentine society:

Some thirty years ago English society in Florence was divided into two distinct parties – the Macaulayites and the anti-Macaulayites. The old Guelfs and Ghibellines, the old Bianchi and Neri were not much fiercer in their enmity than these two factions. At the head of the Anti-Macaulayites was a gentleman who had occupied a high place in the Indian Civil Service, and who, I have not the shadow of a doubt, discharged all his duties there, as he played his part in the Anglo-Italian society of Florence, with honour, integrity, and zeal. He filled a large space in that society, literally and physically, as well as morally. For he was a big man with big thews and sinews, with a broad chest, large head and large eyes, big hands, and a big purse from which he dispensed charities.

At Christmas and other holidays he sat at the head of a table groaning with huge sirloins of beef and big plum puddings, which he distributed to all his guests in the hearty spirit of his big honest hospitality. He was large-handed and large-hearted in every good Christian work; if all people employed their means and opportunities of doing good as carefully and conscientiously as he did, our poor shabby old world would be a much pleasanter place than it now is. Columbus himself had not a deeper sense of the responsibilities involved in the name which he received at the baptismal font that was felt by Christopher Webb Smith. But old Christopher had his weak point, an insuperable and quite irrational antipathy to Macaulay.

Smith even objected to Macaulay's personal appearance, saying he resembled 'a dumpy, stumpy tailor'. Stuart speculated that 'old Christopher and Macaulay must have had more than one tiff at the India Council Board'.[38] This quirk apart, what is striking about the description of Smith is its incorrigible Englishness.

While it is impossible to account for visits to England that may have gone unrecorded, it seems a fair conclusion that D'Oyly, Smith and Fombelle, like Hugh Macdonell, all spent most of their lives in foreign parts. Of John Fombelle's 86 years, approximately 36 were spent as a resident of England; for his wife the score may have been as low as 16 out of 72. Attention here has been focussed on some of those whose varied experiences had already accustomed them to expatriate living and possibly disposed them to prefer it or at least to prefer the Tuscan climate. It would be easy to multiply examples of Anglo-Florentine residents who spent much more of their lives abroad than in their putative country of origin.

Francis Joseph Sloane was set apart in a different way. Born to Catholic parents in 1794, possibly in Rome, he received a Catholic education in England, at St Cuthbert's College at Ushaw, County Durham. In 1815 he went to Russia as tutor to the princely Bouturlin family and in 1817 came with them to Florence. In 1824 Prince Bouturlin acquired what is now the Palazzo Niccolini in Via de' Servi, and this remained Sloane's home for many years, even after he married Isabella Edmunds in 1839. He acquired immense wealth as a result of the exploitation of the mineral rights which (together with the Hall brothers) he acquired from the Grand Duke in 1837. He has been criticized for the alterations he made to the Medicean Villa Careggi, which he bought in 1848, but his major legacy to Florence was the funding of the completion of the façade of the Franciscan church of Santa Croce, for which he also commissioned a window depicting the dogma of the Immaculate Conception, proclaimed in 1854.[39] Childless, he left everything to the Bouturlin, and was buried, in 1871, in the cemetery of the *Misericordia*, the most famous and prestigious of Florentine charitable institutions.[40]

Sloane's Englishness was therefore of a very particular type, which took some of its colouring from the current state of relations between the British government and the Catholic Church. On 11 November 1850 the Dublin *Freeman's Journal* published an account of a reception he had given at the Palazzo Bouturlin for

Cardinal Wiseman; he was described as 'an old and cherished college friend' of the cardinal. Among the guests were all the Tuscan government ministers, many Catholic diplomats 'and most of the nobility of the city, with many English … On the following evening most of the English residents, of their own accord, came to pay their respects to the cardinal'. The paper obviously wanted to emphasize the point that non-Catholic Britons were among those invited and indeed eager to pay homage. According to Thomas Trollope (one of the invited), the cardinal was irritated by 'the ultra-demonstrative zeal of the female portion of the mixed Catholic and Protestant assembly, who *would* kneel and kiss his hand'.

Trollope describes Sloane as a fervent Catholic who always remained on intimate terms with the Grand Duke and remarks that he 'used to give great dinners on Friday, the principal object of which seemed to be to show how magnificent a feast could be given without infringing by a hairs breadth the rule of the Church'. Trollope clearly respected the man's abilities, but there is a hint that he was not entirely above exploiting the favour he enjoyed with the Grand Duke, who attributed the success of the mining operation he had undertaken with the Hall brothers entirely to him. The Halls 'subsequently considered themselves to have been shouldered out of the enterprise by a certain unhandsome treatment on the part of the fortunate tutor' (a reference to Sloane's early role in the Bouturlin household).[41]

Inasmuch as he spent very little of his life in Britain, Sloane differed little from many other Anglo-Florentines. He was careful to subscribe to causes of common interest, such as the collections for the relief of distress caused by the Irish famine, the Crimean War and the Indian Mutiny, and the petitions in favour of the restoration of British diplomatic representation at Florence after Tuscany was annexed to the Italian kingdom. As a businessman he had good reason to remain interested in Britain, for a high proportion of the copper produced by the mines at Camporciano which had helped to make him rich was exported in its crude state to the United Kingdom. That he interested himself in the cultivation of the potato in Tuscany should surely also have endeared him to his compatriots.[42]

He was not the only Anglo-Florentine with first-hand knowledge of Russia. Henry Yeames was born in St Petersburg in 1791, the son of the first British consul in that city. His nephew, William Frederick Yeames, the third son of his brother William, British Consul in the Crimea, won fame as the painter of *When Did You Last See Your Father?* Henry was married to Adela Bastogi, sister of Pietro Bastogi, a prominent banker, and had settled in Florence by 1842.[43] In the 1850s he effectively took charge of his orphaned nephew's artistic training, providing an Italian base for him whether he was in Florence or Rome: 'They allotted him a pretty room on the ground floor of the palazza [*sic*], overlooking the garden, and to which he had access by day or night through the good offices of the butler on the ground floor.' He was thus enabled, while studying the Old Masters, not only to entertain but also to go to student parties 'and such-like joyous bachelor entertainments', unattended by his relatives.[44]

Through his wife's family, Yeames had privileged access to Italian society and unsurprisingly, given his background, he was also thoroughly acquainted with the Russian set in Florence. Adela loved to entertain and her husband once surprised Lady Walpole with Madame Donnanberg, the wife of the general who commanded the Russian army at the battle of Inkerman, 'comfortably seated in the smoking-room, each with a big cigar in her mouth'. Although Adela was supposed to have been much attached to her relatives by marriage, we do not hear anything more about her English guests, and neither John Maquay nor the Brownings ever mention Yeames. Like Sloane, he subscribed to the collection in aid of sufferers from the Crimean War. Such collections afforded an opportunity, like the already-mentioned petitions for the maintenance of British diplomatic representation in Florence, for expatriates of very varied backgrounds to affirm their British sympathies and identity.

Notes

1   LPL, Fulham Papers, Blomfield 44, f. 274.
2   LPL, Fulham Papers, Howley 4, ff. 561–4. See also 'Letters of Rev. Thomas Hall', *William & Mary Quarterly*, 22 (1914), pp. 145–58; O. Lohrenz, 'The Life, Career and Political Loyalties of the Reverend Thomas Hall of Revolutionary Virginia and Leghorn, Italy', *Fides et Historia*, 31 (1999), pp. 123–36; M. Sanacore, 'Il Reverendo Thomas Hall, cultura e affari in una città commerciale', *Studi Livornesi* 7 (1992), pp. 41–54. On 27 July 1824, the *Gazzetta di Firenze* advertised the sale of Hall's very extensive collection of antiquities and *objets d'art* at his house in Leghorn.
3   Hall even recorded a baptism that had taken place at Naples in 1797 with Sir William and Lady Hamilton as sponsors.
4   FO79/45, Strangways to FO, 1 November & 22 November 1825 (enclosing Neat's letter). The only British burials that can have taken place at Florence at this date were presumably those of Jews or Catholics, but the query was pertinent in principle.
5   FO79/46, FO to Strangways, 6 January 1826.
6   Mark Bostridge, *Florence Nightingale* (London, 2009), p. 22.
7   Frederic St John, *Reminiscences of a Retired Diplomat* (London, 1905), p. 2; Lord Malmesbury, *Memoirs of an Ex-Minister: An Autobiography* (London, 1885), p. 40. In the 14th edition of Burke's *Peerage* (1852), John Henry was wrongly stated to have been born in 1828 and no date at all was ventured for the twins. These errors were corrected in later editions, presumably from information in the family's possession.
8   FO79/145, Latilla to Palmerston, 12 November 1850, Scarlett to FO, 9 December 1850. Scarlett rejected the charge that he was neglectful of the British in Florence, most of whom, he said, he knew well.
9   FO79/195, Normanby to FO, 9 April 1857.
10 JLM, E10 f. 135.
11 *Times*, 11 May 1837, and the catalogue compiled by Mrs Anna Jameson: *Collection of Pictures of W.G. Coesvelt, Esq., of London* (London, 1836). From the will Coesvelt made on 29 April 1841, it is apparent that he still had numerous works of art to bequeath, mostly now drawings and works of sculpture, TNA, Prob11/1996. The will was witnessed by the banker Charles Plowden and by Edward Erskine and Spencer Cowper of the Legation, but the house was left in trust to Fenzi and Horace Hall, each of whom received a small bequest for their trouble. Coesvelt died in Rome in 1844.

12   See references to Hall in Andrea Giuntini, *Soltanto per denaro: La vita, gli affari, la ricchezza di Emanuele Fenzi negoziante banchiere fiorentino nel Granducato di Toscana (1784–1875)* (Florence, 2002). The connection was probably originally forged by way of Hall's maternal uncle, Sebastian Kleiber, a business associate of Fenzi, and cemented in about 1835 by Horace's marriage to Fenzi's widowed sister-in-law Costanza Lamberti, whose first husband died in 1831. JLM first records the appearance of 'Mr and Mrs Hall' at a party on 28 October 1836, E10 f. 24v.

13   Thomas Trollope, *What I Remember* (2nd ed. London, 1887), Vol. 2, p. 91. Trollope later added a third volume, but his Florentine reminiscences are in the second.

14   FO79/142, FO to Hamilton, 30 March 1850. There are a number of crossings out and amendments in the draft. Unmentioned in these discussions was the interesting detail that, also in 1850, Mme Inghirami was awarded a title of nobility by the commune of Fiesole: Ed. Marcella Aglietti, *Nobildonne, monache, e cavaliere dell'Ordine di Santo Stefano: modelli e strategie femminili nella vita pubblica della Toscana granducale* (Pisa, 2010), pp. 112–13.

15   JLM, E11 f. 112.

16   FO45/4, Memorial to FO, 12 February 1861.

17   At least three of the boys were baptised in Tuscany, the oldest being Fenton Thomas, baptised by George Robbins at Pisa, 1 May 1842. The family later emigrated to Canada, where more than one of the daughters made Catholic marriages.

18   FO79/148 to 151.

19   The following account is derived largely from Simona di Marco, *Frederick Stibbert 1836–1906: Vita di un collezionista* (Turin, 2005), which has been summarized in English by Christina Clearkin and Simona di Marco, 'A Tale of Three Cities: Calcutta, Southampton and Florence: The Stibbert Family and Museum', *British Art Journal* 9 (2009), pp. 43–54.

20   FO79/158, Scarlett to FO, 14 March 1852. Scarlett enclosed his letter to Casigliano and the memorandum composed by the guardians. Frederick Stibbert never settled in the British environment and ended his days in Florence in 1906, leaving his remarkable collection to the city; in 1861 his sister Sophronia made another interdenominational marriage when she became the wife of Alessio Pandolfini.

21   It is not easy to construct a coherent narrative of Macdonell's life. Writers who know about his early years in North America know nothing about his later life. For his Algerian experience, see Robert L. Playfair, *The Scourge of Christendom: Annals of British Relations with Algiers Prior to the French Conquest* (London, 1884); Anne Macdonnell, *Reminiscences of a Diplomatic Life* (London, 1913).

22   For Emily, see Macdonell, *Reminiscences*, pp. 68–9; for Hugh, see DNB. He had a distinguished career as both soldier and diplomat and started on the latter career by serving as unpaid *attaché* in Florence in 1854 before moving to Constantinople in 1858.

23   Hugh's will, translated from Italian, is in TNA, Prob11/2088.

24   TNA, Prob11/2122. There were technical issues about the effectiveness of the 'Tuscan codicil', which it is not important to try to elucidate here.

25   The first hearing was extensively reported in the *Times*, the *Daily News*, the *Morning Chronicle* and elsewhere, all giving slightly different details. The appeal was reported most fully by the *Morning Chronicle*. The proceedings of January 1856 are reported at length in the *Times* and the *Morning Chronicle*.

26   The judgment of January 1856 did not mean the end of the family's litigation. After one of the daughters, Marianna Octavia, died at Montughi in August 1857, notice was given of a suit brought by Charles James Matthews against his brother William Edgar, to whom their father had left all his Tuscan property.

27 There are frequent references to him as an administrator in Upendra N. Singh, *Some Aspects of Rural Life in Bihar: An Economic Study 1793–1833* (Patna, 1980). For his interest in natural history, see Mildred Archer, *Natural History Drawings in the India Office Library* (London, 1964), p. 22. Back in England, he offered himself as a candidate for election as a director of the Company, placing an advertisement in the *Times*, 27 January 1818, in which he summarized his 34 years of service in India.

28 TNA, Prob11/2116.

29 TNA, Prob11/1828.

30 EM, C4 f. 28.

31 TNA, Prob11/1974.

32 Trollope, *What I Remember*, Vol. 2, pp. 146–7.

33 TNA, Prob11/2058.

34 DNB; also M. Archer, *Company Drawings in the India Office Library* (London, 1972), pp. 99, 115, 116, and *British Drawings in the India Office Library, 1, Amateur Artists* (London, 1969), p. 135.

35 Shortly afterwards D'Oyly went to South Africa on leave, and Smith also spent time there in 1837–39. Mildred Archer gives an account of Smith's Indian drawings and natural history interests in 'Birds of India', *Geographical Magazine* 36 (1963–64), pp. 470–81. D'Oyly's drawing of him at Arrah is illustrated p. 480. See also the more recent Jagmohan Mahajan, *Splendid Plumage: India Birds by British Artists* (Hong Kong, 2001), especially pp. 15–17. Many of Smith's drawings and notebooks are now in the possession of Cambridge University.

36 On 3 October 1844 *The Friend of India* included his among 'names of distinction in the administration of our eastern empire' who had unaccountably failed to achieve election. His career down to 1833 was summarised in the *Asiatic Journal*, 1 February 1844.

37 JLM, E10 f. 251v. The *Morning Post* reported on 6 November that D'Oyly had gone to Tuscany for the benefit of his health.

38 James Montgomery Stuart, *Reminiscences and Essays* (London, 1884), pp. 36–7.

39 Sloane's life is outlined by Luigi Zangheri, *La Villa Medicea di Careggi e il suo Giardino* (Florence, 2006), pp. 39–47. See also Nancy Thompson, 'The Immaculate Conception Window in Santa Croce and the Catholic Revival in Nineteenth-Century Florence', *Nineteenth Century Art Worldwide*, 12 January 2013 (www.19thcartworldwide.org/spring13/thompson).

40 In Via degli Artisti, close to the English cemetery.

41 Trollope, *What I Remember*, Vol. 2, pp. 90–2.

42 *Rapporto Generale della Pubblica Esposizione dei Prodotti Naturali e Industriali della Toscana fatta in Firenze nel novembre MDCCL nell' I.E.R. Palazzo della Crocetta* (Florence, 1851), Vol. 2, pp. 123–4. The collections and subscriptions mentioned are dealt with later in this book.

43 His first subscription to Vieusseux was apparently taken out in 1841; he was a regular thereafter. Pietro Bastogi bore a major responsibility for floating the loans of a cash-strapped Grand Duke.

44 M. H. Stephen Smith, *Art and Anecdote: Recollections of William Frederick Yeames RA, His Life and His Friends* (London, 1927), pp. 73, 85. Smith was a nephew of the artist. Yeames died at Baden-Baden in 1865 and was brought back for burial in Florence.

2 THE BURGHERSH YEARS, 1814–1830

John Fane, Lord Burghersh, future Earl of Westmorland, was the first and longest-serving of the nine men to serve as Envoy Extraordinary and Minister Plenipotentiary at the Court of Tuscany between 1814 and 1859. He was accompanied to Florence by his wife Priscilla, a niece of the Duke of Wellington. On their arrival towards the end of November 1814, like many other Britons, they 'stayed some time at an Hotel and then moved into a house which they occupied during the 16 years they remained in Florence'. This was Palazzo Ximenes in Borgo Pinti, where Napoleon had stayed on his sole visit to Florence in 1796. Like other Britons, Priscilla thought that 'The climate was delightful, the house charming and living in Florence was at that time so cheap that they could afford to live far more luxuriously than they could possibly have done at home.' Her husband, having been a soldier, was 'glad to accept employment in another line for which his connections with foreign countries, his knowledge of languages and his general abilities admirably fitted him'.[1] Not everyone shared this positive assessment of Burghersh's talents.

While Burghersh acclimatized, the Foreign Office issued instructions to the newly appointed consul at Leghorn, John Falconar.[2] They covered the need to 'pay the strictest attention to the Orders which you may from time to time receive from His Majesty's Minister at Florence'. Falconar was to submit to him 'such Complaints and Applications of His Majesty's Subjects' as he thought required the attention of the Grand Duke; he was also to keep his Lordship 'constantly and regularly informed of every occurrence of Interest within Your Consulship, respecting either the Trade of His Majesty's Subjects, or that of other Nations at Peace or at War'.

Neither under Falconar nor under his successor Alexander Macbean was the relationship thus outlined always easy, but no relationship involving Falconar was. He seems to have been notably abrasive, which was the more unfortunate as the situation which he inherited at Leghorn was fraught with peculiar difficulties. The British society which developed at Florence was almost entirely new and predominantly leisured, with a strong aristocratic tinge. However bulky the material luggage that its members brought with them from home, they did not carry the psychological baggage which weighed on the reconstituted mercantile community at Leghorn. This included men who had been there in the previous century, most but not all of whom had been forced to leave by the French invasions. The church registers reveal that members of the following families were in Leghorn at some point during the Napoleonic occupation: Jago, Degen, Panton, Grant, Webb, Darby, Pate, Polhill, Routh, Furse, Porter, Pollard. There may have been others. These men had lost property and in some cases been subjected to insult and even imprisonment by the invaders; they nursed profound convictions of what was due to them, but their claims for compensation were doomed to disappointment. The British government would not assume responsibility for the economic casualties of war, and neither the new French nor the Tuscan government could be held to account for damage inflicted by a regime that both regarded as having been an enemy.[3]

These old stagers rubbed shoulders with newcomers, who hoped for peacetime profit, and they made a determined effort to restrict the privileges of membership in the so-called 'factory' to themselves, admitting new members only after a period of probation. Falconar aggravated their discontent by accusing some of them of having collaborated with the French (which was quite probably true). In 1824 he produced a report intended to show that no such corporate body as the 'factory' had ever existed in any legally meaningful sense, and early in 1826, the Foreign Office effectively endorsed this opinion.[4]

The Reverend Thomas Hall and a few others at Leghorn represented genuine continuity from the war years. How many survivors of the Napoleonic epoch did Burghersh and the other newcomers find in Florence? The Reverend Samuel Oliver signalled his presence there on 4 December 1810, when he solemnized the marriage of Anne Amelia Megit and Charles Hoofstetter, and again when he made his will on 10 May 1813.[5] A native of Leicester, he lived in Via Fiesolana, 'exercising the profession of Teacher of the English Language'. He mentioned no English property, made no English bequests and died in 1828 without altering his will. After 1814 he officiated occasionally, notably when he baptised John Arthur Fane, the first child born to Lord Burghersh and Priscilla, on 12 February 1816.

Anne Megit, whose marriage ceremony Oliver performed, was the eldest of at least five children born to a shopkeeper and hotelier called John Megit (his surname occurs in a remarkable number of variants), who is first documented in Florence in 1779 and survived to see the peace, dying in October 1814.[6] Anne and her brother Gabriel seem to have spent their entire lives there, dying in 1833 and 1837 respectively; their sister Catherine had died in Florence in 1804. On an altogether different social level was Anna, the widow of the third Earl Cowper, who for many years in the later eighteenth century had made his Villa Palmieri, on the hills to the north of Florence, a social hub.[7] Very early in 1814 she and her sister Emily raised a monument in the Leghorn cemetery to an elderly servant of their father, who had died in Florence. Lady Cowper died in 1826 'at her Villa del Cipresso near Florence', which Cowper had also owned; Emily died at Pisa in 1832.

The survivors were therefore a varied bunch, as were the new arrivals. After Lady Cowper's death, her late husband's Villa Palmieri continued in English hands, those of a single lady, Mary Farhill, who lived there inconspicuously from 1824 until her death 30 years later. John Maquay reported that she died in her bath one night in April 1854; she had lived at what he called 'Villa Boccaccio' for half of her life and no one knew who her relatives were. The daughter of one of the tutors of Queen Victoria's father, the Duke of Kent, she bequeathed the villa to the Grand Duchess, Maria Antonia, with whom she had formed an intimate friendship, and like many other long-term Tuscan residents never troubled the representatives of the British Crown. Her good works in the locality were praised in 1838 by the commune of Fiesole.[8]

A lady from a rather different background, who seems to have come to Tuscany at about the same time, outlasted Miss Farhill. Grace Barton, the daughter of Thomas Barton of Grove, Tipperary, was first married to Lieutenant-General Kingsmill Pennefather, who died in 1819, leaving her with two daughters. John Maquay, who knew the Bartons and Pennefathers in Ireland, encountered her and some of the Bartons at Siena on his first visit there in May 1825, when he also noticed a 'Maggiore Galeazzi'. In the spring of 1826 Maquay caught up with Mrs Pennefather in Florence, at the Villa Gondi outside the Porta al Prato; on 3 May Major Galeazzi too was there and John observed 'imagine all is sorted'.[9] It presumably was, for, back in Italy in October, he called not on Mrs Pennefather but on Madame Galeazzi. He knew the couple well for the rest of his time in Florence and they were still there when he left 30 years later.

Other new arrivals illustrate the point that an individual's position in Anglo-Florentine society was determined, as at home, largely by blood and wealth, but also to some degree by talent and deliberate choice of associates or way of life. Seymour Kirkup, the son of a diamond merchant, was not poor, but his chosen lifestyle was bohemian. For some time after his arrival in Florence from Rome in 1824, he lived under the same roof with the writer Charles Armitage Brown, 'the friend of Keats', and a succession of mistresses. Brown himself had arrived in Tuscany in 1822, with his illegitimate son, whom he always called 'Carlino', and after a brief sojourn in Pisa moved to Florence, where he lived until 1835. We can see something of one way of Florentine living in the letters he wrote to correspondents, who included the artist Joseph Severn (another friend of Kirkup) in Rome and Leigh Hunt.[10]

The core of Brown's acquaintance was artistic and literary. Leigh Hunt for a time lived near him at Maiano, 'on the slope of one of the Fiesolan hills', and remembered that Brown had occupied a little ex-convent nearby, where he offered jovial hospitality, discoursing 'of love and wine, in the apartments of the Lady Abbess'.[11] When Hazlitt visited Florence in 1825, he sought out his old friend Hunt and enlarged his circle by making an uninvited visit to the famously irascible Walter Savage Landor, who had taken up residence at Fiesole in 1821, and bringing him into communication with the others.[12] The group also included the Irish peer Viscount

Dillon, whose departure for Florence was announced in the *Morning Chronicle* on 15 August 1815. Brown reported in 1826 that Dillon called on him once a week. His Lordship's literary pretensions were evidently somewhat out of proportion to his abilities, but they seem to have aroused no more than affectionate mockery in his friends. Kirkup later recalled that Landor never laughed at Dillon's poetic efforts, but offered 'gentle and inoffensive advice, saying that Dillon's smiling handsome fair face was like a ray of sunshine in Florence'.[13] One day in 1819 Dillon was in the reading room when he observed 'a young man very earnestly bent over the last Quarterly'. It was Shelley, reading a review of *The Revolt of Islam* which likened him, as a doomed blasphemer, to Pharaoh overwhelmed by the Red Sea. At this Shelley burst into hysterical laughter and went off down the stairs, still laughing.[14]

Hunt called Dillon 'a cavalier of the old school' and an incident which took place within a year of his arrival in Florence perhaps demonstrated that character. In July 1816 the duke's chief minister Count Fossombroni complained to Burghersh that Dillon had stopped a policeman beating a blind beggar in one of the public walks by the simple expedient of taking his stick from him (he afterwards returned it). The officer had been carrying out orders and Dillon had prevented the beggar's arrest. Burghersh's enquiries (presumably he simply asked Dillon for his version) suggested that the beggar had been soliciting alms from Dillon himself and that his Lordship was not convinced that the policeman had to use his stick so vigorously in the mere 'fulfilment of his duty'.[15]

Like many other British families, the Dillons established an enduring connection with Florence and experienced birth, marriage and death there. His Lordship's daughter Margaret was born on 3 February 1816, and in 1822 his second son was drowned in the garden of his Florentine home. Just before the family left the city in the autumn of 1826, his daughter Henrietta was married to Edward Stanley, the future Baron Stanley of Alderley and Whig officeholder. In 1842, Dillon's fourth son and eventual heir, Constantine Augustus, was also married in Florence. The names of both this son and another, Gerald Normanby, betray his Lordship's kinship with Constantine Henry Phipps, Viscount Normanby and Baron Mulgrave, a long-term if intermittent Florentine resident, who in 1855 became the British ambassador.[16] Dillon and Normanby were cousins: Dillon's mother was sister to Normanby's father, Earl Mulgrave. Another of her brothers (and therefore Normanby's uncle), Augustus Phipps, had been married to Maria Thellusson, sister to the first Baron Rendlesham, whose nephew John, the second baron, was another long-term Florentine resident during these years. On 6 March 1819 the *Morning Chronicle* reported that Lords Dillon and Rendlesham were among the few British remaining in Florence as the seasonal exodus began. Rendlesham was joined in 1820 by his cousin Charles Thellusson and his bride, and later by his own brother Frederick, who became the fourth baron in 1839. Both Charles and Frederick put down roots in Florence and became prominent among the horse-racing fraternity.

Whatever his literary turn, Dillon's connections dictated some parts of his social life. He was among those who attended the superb entertainment at which, on

13 July 1818, Burghersh invested Admiral Sir Thomas Fremantle with the Order of the Bath; and like others of his rank, he evidently felt obliged to offer a certain style of hospitality. In November 1825, Charles Brown wrote with immense amusement to Leigh Hunt, who had returned to England after the 'very disconsolate time' he had spent in Tuscany:

> The strangest piece of news that I can tell you is that Landor, within the last week, has been to TWO BALLS! – one given by Mr Hare and the other by Lord Dillon – besides which, he lately went to a Musical Conversazione. I hear he is quite gay in his new element, joking and laughing *ad libitum* among the flounced and feathered company.[17]

Francis George Hare was the son and grandson of ecclesiastics, and brother to Julius, the well-known archdeacon of Hurstmonceux, but his own character was far from ecclesiastical. Evidently a man of considerable intellectual gifts, he was also a spendthrift and dandy who lived abroad after losing a great deal of money on horses in 1816–1817. Between 1819 and 1826 he was mostly in Italy, earning a reputation for lavish hospitality at Rome, Florence and Pisa. The Earl and Countess of Blessington and Count Alfred d'Orsay were among his fashionable friends.[18]

Dillon was not alone among Anglo-Florentine aristocrats in cultivating the arts. Burghersh's musical and Normanby's theatrical accomplishments will receive attention in a later chapter. When Charles Greville called on Burghersh early in 1830, he found his Lordship 'at breakfast – the table covered with manuscript music, a pianoforte, two fiddles, a fiddler in the room. He was full of composition and getting up his opera of "Phaedra" for to-morrow night'. Greville attended the opera, 'which was very well performed; pretty theatre, crowded to suffocation'. He breakfasted with Normanby and was struck by his style of living. He occupied

> a house extending 200 feet in front court, garden, and stables for about 200*l* a year, everything else cheap in proportion, and upon 2,000*l* a year a man may live luxuriously. His house was originally fitted up for the Pretender, and C.R.'s are still to be seen all over the place.

On the following day Greville rode out to Normanby's villa at Sesto, 'a large and agreeable house, gardens full of fountains, statues, busts, orange and lemon trees, shrubs and flowers'. Not all of Greville's impressions of Florence were so favourable. He described its society as composed of

> the refuse of Europe, people who come here from want of money or want of character. Everybody is received without reference to their conduct, past or present, with the exception, perhaps, of Englishwomen who have been divorced, whose case is too notorious to allow the English Minister's wife to present them at court.[19]

Lady Burghersh did not dwell on her husband's musical activities in her memoirs, merely mentioning the 'constant dinners and balls and musical parties which they were especially fond of'. They also 'kept open house for all the English in Florence'.[20] How open was this house and how many English did it take to make 'all'? Are we to take literally the statement in the *Morning Post* of 2 January 1823 that 'all the English residents' attended a Grand Ball given by Burghersh in honour of the king of Prussia? The Minister certainly acquired the reputation of encouraging people who were distinguished by talent rather than by birth. According to a correspondent of *Borrow's Worcester Journal* on 28 November 1822, he had established himself at Florence 'as the patron of poets, painters, and philosophers'. On certain days his table was open 'to the whole three classes indiscriminately', but unfortunately many of them were unable to take advantage, 'for the want of almost every article of decent raiment'. Charles Brown implied that it was the lack not of decent raiment, but of an invitation or an inclination on his part to solicit one, that kept him from his Lordship's table: 'I am not, and perhaps never shall be invited to Lord Burghersh's, – unless I'm at the trouble to procure a letter to him.'[21]

Priscilla's memoirs sometimes give the impression that she lived in a world exclusively populated by the highest ranks of the *ton*. She spoke with great warmth, for example, of Marie Louise, previously the wife of Napoleon and now Duchess of Parma, with whom she continued to correspond until the other died in 1847.[22] Such notabilities, however, were not the whole story. In 1830 that raffish and unreliable adventurer Captain Edward Trelawney, friend of Byron and Shelley, told Mary Shelley's half-sister Claire Clairmont that of all his 'intimate friends' in Florence, Lady Burghersh was 'the most interesting and most admired by me'; she was 'all heart and genius'. Early in 1831 he wrote to Mary Shelley about the manuscript of *Adventures of a Younger Son*, on which he had been working in Florence:

> Landor, a man of superior literary acquirements; Kirkup, an artist of superior taste; Baring, a man of the world and very religious; Mrs Baring, moral and squeamish; Lady Burghersh, aristocratic and proud as a queen; and lastly, Charles Brown, a plain, downright Cockney critic, learned in the trade of authorship, and has served his time as a literary scribe; all these male and female critics have read and passed their opinions on my narrative.[23]

That Priscilla was aristocratic and very likely proud as a queen might be inferred from her own reminiscences, but Trelawney saw more in her.

During her time in Florence, although 'she had never imagined herself to possess the smallest talent for drawing', she took up painting. Like other aspirants, she set to work 'copying the best pictures in the Florentine Gallery'. Her rank ensured that she could obtain not only the necessary materials but the best coaching: none other than Sir Thomas Lawrence advised her on 'the mechanical processes of painting'. She began to paint her children during summer holidays at Leghorn, where the family had a villa, and progressed gradually to 'historical and other subjects'. Greville in 1830 found her 'in a brown robe, in the midst of oils, and brushes, and canvas', remarking that she had 'received the gift of painting as if by inspiration'.[24] Allegedly what had set Lady Burghersh painting was her dissatisfaction with portraits of her children by a painter whom she did not name. Lord Burghersh is known to have shown favour in Florence to George Hayter (later portrait painter to Queen Victoria and knighted in 1842), but as Hayter was well-known for his studies of children it might seem surprising if it was he. Hayter's stay in Florence in 1826–1827, which ended in tragedy and scandal, shows us another man with a foot in two worlds.

Even if he was not guilty of everything he was accused of, Hayter was a determined self-publicist who won the good opinion of distinguished patrons more readily than that of his fellow-artists. Charles Brown, now living in Piazza Duomo, entertained him and his friend Charles Hamilton on Christmas Day 1826 and a few days later told Severn, 'I don't like Mr G. Hayter so much as I expected I should'. He went on criticize some of Hayter's artistic productions, including a sketch of 'a rape of Circassian women, [which] is full of murders, daggers, blood, screaming women, and gleaming sabers'. A couple of months later, Brown amplified his criticism. He could pardon Hayter's considerable vanity, but he was 'unpleasant, requiring one's services on every petty or useful occasion, and paying for them with manners just within the boundary of rudeness'.[25] Brown's view of the 'rape of Circassian women' (now lost) was clearly not universally shared: one correspondent thought that 'Nothing can surpass the effect of this production'. It was to be sent to London for exhibition, and 'it will, no doubt, create the same pleasure there that the Connoisseurs have experienced in viewing it here'.[26]

Himself the father of an illegitimate son, and living much in Kirkup's company, Brown was unlikely to be much disturbed by the fact that Hayter had with him in Florence a long-term mistress, Louisa Cauty, who was kept in the shadows as he built up his social connections. By October 1827 reports in the London papers indicated that Hayter had succeeded in establishing his studio in the Palazzo Ginori as a place to visit. Not long afterwards, Louisa Cauty took arsenic and died. Brown reported this tragedy to Severn in two letters.

He focussed first on the likely social outcome. The Florentines were unanimous in their censure, but 'It remains to see how the English will act towards him'. The women, he thought, would all be hostile and Hayter would need powerful and influential support to make headway against this sentiment in the small expatriate society of Florence. In his second letter he reported as fact that Hayter had wanted to turn away a serving maid and replace her by another of his mistresses. Louisa's refusal to accept this humiliation had decided him to send her back to England.[27]

Brown was right that Hayter would be unable to face down the feeling against him. By the end of the year, he was in Rome, whence he wrote a lengthy letter to the duke of Bedford, giving his version of events.[28] According to him, Louisa had been unhappy because she could not be received in Florentine society; after years of cohabitation, she apparently entertained the delusion that this would be possible.

Hayter also admitted that she might have been jealous of his models, but it was entirely against his will that she had insisted on returning to England. Having, to all appearances, made the arrangements for her departure with perfect calmness, she took poison the day before she was due to leave. Mr Baring had come that day to commiserate with him on Louisa's departure and 'Ld Burghersh called to see my pictures'. Among those who had treated him 'with the utmost kindness', he named Baring, Baring's son-in-law Mr Kerrick [*recte* Kerrich], Burghersh and (he needed hardly say) Lord William Russell, the duke of Bedford's second son, a frequent visitor to Florence. Both Hayter's general unpopularity and the continued support he received from the Baring family were substantiated by Henry Fox, the future Lord Holland and British minister at Florence, who visited the city in 1828, at the right moment to be given the generally accepted account of this affair.[29]

It was a curious situation: a woman who could not be introduced in society was nonetheless so open a secret that her lover could be excoriated by that same society for his treatment of her. Hayter maintained his campaign of self-defence with a letter, published in the *Times* on 3 January 1828, which was presumably written at approximately the same time as the one to the duke of Bedford. His friends had all been very kind to him, and Burghersh, having exhibited the *Circassian Women* at his house for 3 days, had assured him how 'universally admired' it had been. His Lordship himself was 'highly complimental' about its pictorial qualities. Hayter's decision to remove himself from Florence, and ultimately from Italy, may have relieved Burghersh of a potential problem.

If Hayter was a determined social climber, Charles Brown was evidently content to live in a different sphere from his country's Minister. John Leland Maquay belonged to yet another category. The descendant of affluent Dublin merchants on the one hand and Waterford gentry on the other, with connections to the Irish clergy and the military, he was introduced to Burghersh at a masked ball on 30 January 1823, where his Lordship affably asked after his uncle, probably meaning Sir Moore Disney, brother to John's mother and a veteran of the Peninsular War, in which Burghersh had also served.[30] John would spend his Florentine years in contact with the courts of the Grand Duke and the British Ministers and with the major luminaries, British, Italian and other, of the city's society. Balls (including those he gave himself) played a part in his life that they did not in the life of a Charles Brown or (usually) a Walter Savage Landor.

Some of the London papers at this period enthusiastically covered the activities of the Florentine upper crust. On 19 January 1825 the *Morning Chronicle* reported that Burghersh had concluded his concerts for the season but continued to give 'splendid balls, to which most of the respectable Foreigners in Tuscany are invited. Lord Burghersh is particularly attentive to the English'. (It is tempting to remark that so one would hope.) In addition,

> The Prince Borghese gave a grand ball and supper, two days ago, at his noble palace at Florence. Twenty-six rooms in this large mansion were open for

the occasion. The English Ambassador, Lord Burghersh, and the Secretary of Legation, Lord Marcus Hill, were present, together with all the other Ambassadors now resident at the court of Tuscany. The *Princess Borghese was not there.*

Camillo Borghese was the (estranged) husband of Napoleon's sister Pauline. In Rome in 1824 Elizabeth Maquay had lamented that he could not remove his fine collection of pictures from the Villa Borghese to Florence, 'which he makes his residence it is 17 yrs since he has been here when he was a very slight figure tho' now such a porpoise'.[31]

The *Morning Chronicle* correspondent also dwelt on the hospitality of Prince Demidoff, who had left Paris for Florence and opened 'his fine mansion twice a week, to all the people of distinction and respectability in Florence, especially the English, to whom this liberal old gentleman is greatly attached'. Nicolai Demidoff was the immensely rich descendant of a weapons-maker who had been ennobled by Peter the Great in 1720. He invested largely in industry and charity as well as in hospitality; awarded the title of Count of San Donato in 1827, he died the following year, but had already begun to build the Villa San Donato (now no longer standing) on marshland north of Florence. Individuals of this stripe exercised a magnetic attraction throughout the reign of the last Grand Duke for those British residents and visitors whose own wealth and social standing, even if more modest, enabled them to hold their heads up in such company. One traveller, J. D. Sinclair, endorsed the social importance of Demidoff and Borghese, and commented on the wisdom of the Grand Duke in welcoming them to Florence, where their hospitality and other benefactions were much appreciated.[32]

When Burghersh left Florence in 1830, the *Gazzetta* carried a highly laudatory report praising his Lordship's hospitality and musical 'genius' and also the 'applause in Painting' which had been earned by her Ladyship and had led to the honour of her election to the Accademia delle Belle Arti.[33] Priscilla's kinship with the Duke of Wellington was another peg on which graceful tributes could be hung. It was recalled in an undated printed poem in Italian, addressed *A Lady Priscilla Burghersh*, which spoke of the 'genius' which at Waterloo had at last met the 'high European challenge'. The poem is signed 'Vitorio Fossombroni', the chief minister of the Grand Duke.[34]

There was a negative side to the coverage which Burghersh received in the English newspapers. This resulted from a mixture of hostility to the man himself, as a Tory placeman, with a belief that the Florentine mission served no useful purpose and might usefully be abolished in order to save money. This rested partly on a realistic assessment of Italian politics. British observers of Tuscany in the first 20 years or so after the restoration of the old order found themselves having to strike a balance between their almost universal approval of the Tuscan mode of government and their awareness of Austria's Italian hegemony, in which Tuscany was embraced. To what extent was Austria to be regarded as free to do anything it deemed necessary to defend the Italian position which had been secured to it by the Vienna settlement?

Reporting to the Foreign Secretary at the end of January 1815, Burghersh thought that this position was insecure and entirely dependent on military force. Two months later, he was lamenting Tuscan passivity in face of the emergency caused by Bonaparte's escape from Elba.[35] According to the *Caledonian Mercury* on 20 May, the Grand Duke 'has displayed great weakness in the late affairs, and shewed himself of a pusillanimous turn of mind'. This crisis passed, but towards the end of 1820, Austria was expected to march troops through the peninsula to suppress the constitution that had been extorted from the king of Naples. Reaffirming his belief in Italian hatred of the Austrians, Burghersh indicated that once again the Tuscans were quaking. Fossombroni had characterized the Austrian government of their Italian provinces as 'ungenerous', observing that they excluded Italians 'from almost all places of trust and emolument', so that even the judiciary was staffed by German-speakers. Burghersh himself had made a very similar diagnosis 5 years previously.[36]

The situation had its impact on British residents in Tuscany, even though the Grand Duchy was not directly affected by the Austrian incursion. On 16 April 1821 the *Times* printed a report from Leghorn, dated a week previously, relating how Mr William Peel, a respectable merchant of the place (and a cousin of the future Prime Minister), had been summarily expelled from Tuscany. Baffled to know what he had done wrong, Peel went more than once to see the normally Anglophile governor of Leghorn, Pompeo Spanocchi, who professed himself helpless to countermand the directives of superior authority. According to the *Times*, the commissary of police told Peel 'in vague and general terms that he was considered a bad subject, and that every thing going on in his house was not right'. This apparent slur on his morals came as a surprise to Peel, but when he again saw Spanocchi, the governor 'asked him if he had not sometimes been incautious in speaking on political topics'. Peel at last realized where he had gone wrong: on the strength of his own commercial correspondence with Naples, he had expressed scepticism about the official bulletins reporting Austrian successes in the south. It was also speculated that a disgruntled former employee of his firm had gone to the authorities with tittle-tattle, which may indeed have been the case, for disgruntled Italian former employees (even when not armed with knives) were the periodic bane of English businessmen.

If Peel was required to leave Tuscany, it was not for long. His presence in Leghorn is attested later in the 1820s and thereafter, but the alarm created by his treatment was not confined to his merchant brethren in Leghorn itself. The Manchester Chamber of Commerce addressed a memorial to Lord Castlereagh on the subject and the question was aired in the Commons. The *Times* hinted that the British would have had better cause for complaint had they themselves not wielded similar arbitrary powers under the Aliens Act; but, from the standpoint of the expatriate colony in Tuscany, the threat was obvious. It was expressed in a memorial from the Leghorn merchants: 'What is Mr Peel's case to day, may tomorrow be that of each or all of your Lordship's memorialists.' They went on to speak of 'the incalculable evil, that must fall upon them if they can be thus attacked, thus dealt with, thus persecuted on the most unfounded suspicions'.[37]

If Peel had made the comment alleged he was not the only one. On 28 March, at about the moment his expulsion was ordered, the *Morning Chronicle* printed a letter written by 'an English gentleman' in Florence, who declared that 'You will scarcely learn the truth of what is passing between the Neapolitan and Austrian armies'; the Austrians had in fact suffered both casualties and desertions. The king of Naples had temporarily taken refuge at Florence. On the day it reported Peel's expulsion, the *Times* sardonically noted that as of 5 April the king was still there; he had had a splendid function performed in the church of Santissima Annunziata 'to offer up thanks to Almighty God for the victories gained by the Austrians over his people, and the temporary destruction of the forms of constitutional freedom in his kingdom'. The note struck by the *Times* tended also to be that of the *Morning Chronicle*, while the *Morning Post* at this period was inclined to the view that all discontent in Italy was the work of Bonapartist malcontents; the Austrians were justified in doing whatever it took to shore up a position that had been awarded to them by international treaty.

The English resident in Tuscany might therefore be perfectly comfortable in his ordinary course of life but never totally able to banish apprehension. On 11 January 1823 Charles Brown, still living at Pisa, wrote to the bookseller Thomas Richards:

> Tuscany's is, to my thinking, the best Government in Europe, if by the best, we are to understand a Government which makes the most happy, – that is, with means to live, & without tyranny. Where so many are miserable, as in England, Ireland & Scotland, you may talk of your *free-borns* as you will, I say that Government is the worst.[38]

Brown was not the only British observer to bring his awareness of extreme poverty and inequality at home to bear on his judgement of the Tuscan scene. Even for those who did not make that comparison, it was a commonplace that the inhabitants of Tuscany were better off than those of other parts of Italy. At almost the same moment that Brown was writing the words just quoted, John Maquay was leaving the states of the church on his way north to Florence, remarking that 'the difference in the appearance of the peasantry after Tuscany is entered is very perceptible. They all appear comfortable and well off whereas in the Roman State misery and squalidity are the reigning features'.[39]

In the course of 1823 Brown moved to Florence, and in another letter to Richards, written on 22 August, he revealed a more negative aspect of Tuscan life. Richards had apparently written incautiously to him on political affairs; the letter had been cut open and reached Brown a week late.

Since some late events every one is cat-watched. Banishment would be a nuisance, as I like the country. The being tongue-tied on certain matters, as we are at present, is no nuisance to me, as my mind seldom wanders on those things which I can neither further nor retard.[40]

Brown was not alone among expatriates in feeling able to live with restrictions which he felt no missionary zeal to challenge, but, as Peel had discovered, one might infringe unawares. On 31 July 1824 the *Morning Chronicle* uttered a warning: 'however comfortably you may be settled for the season at Pisa or Florence, you must shift your quarters at a moment's warning, when Prince METTERNICH gives the word.'

Brown's quiescence in face of the Tuscan way of doing things and the accompanying want of freedom of speech received more vigorous expression from James Cobbett, son of the radical William.[41] The Tuscans might live under a despotism, but they were '*actually* free'. Admittedly dependent on 'a foreign power', their ruler did not imitate Austrian severity, and his absolutism was accepted by his people, who assumed he was bound to deal justly. Consequently, 'there is a sort of understanding between the two, grounded on custom and tradition'. The Grand Dukes had encouraged personal access to themselves in cases of injury to their subjects, which had enhanced their popularity. In all this the Tuscans were the opposites of the British. Cobbett noted the thinness of the Italian press, but in a tirade worthy of his father made it clear that he was not deceived by superficial comparisons with the situation at home: 'Perhaps the people of this country are, as relates to the Press, in the next best state to that of being *completely free*; they have *no freedom at all*.' They knew it, and therefore they were not deluded, as the British were: 'John Bull dotes upon his *Press*, which cheats him into the conviction that nobody is so free as himself.'

Nevertheless, when a correspondent of the *Times* on 6 April 1821 declared that 'The Grand Duke of Tuscany is one of the family and exists only by her [Austria's] permission', he was not using a figure of speech. The death of the Grand Duke Ferdinand on 18 June 1824 gave rise to some reflection on this relationship as well as on the late prince's personal character:

Ferdinand was just the prince for the Tuscans: he was good-natured and affable, and is said to have divided almost all his time between music and books. If he thought himself obliged to subserve to the views of his brother the Emperor Francis and of the Holy Alliance, he did it in as gentle and unscandalous a manner as possible, and shewed a desire to be peaceful and liberal with all parties.

Like James Cobbett a few years later, this writer commented on the popularity and affability of the Grand Dukes, which, admittedly, 'costs little in a despotism and gains much', and on the natural advantages of the country in climate and fertility, which made it easy for the people to put up with so mild a regime. As to Ferdinand's successor, 'Little is known of the new Sovereign, but he is said to be fond of the fine arts.'[42]

Thanks to the sheer abundance of travel narratives, written often on the strength of quite brief sojourns in Tuscany, similar sentiments were oft-repeated. Sinclair, who made his tour at much the same time as the young Cobbetts, was impressed by the availability in Florence of foreign periodicals and editions of authors such as Voltaire and Rousseau, who were banned elsewhere in Italy; the city thereby became a focus for the learned, who were welcomed by the courteous and hospitable Tuscans. To him, too, Tuscany seemed the happiest country in the peninsula. Its people were none too fond of either the French or the Austrians, but they forgot the Grand Duke's Austrian origins and regarded him as Tuscan born and bred. Leopold was 'this liberal young prince, who is the only Italian sovereign possessed of popularity amongst his subjects.'[43]

It was a fact universally acknowledged that the ruler of Tuscany had limited room for manoeuvre, even had he wanted it, and this helped to fuel opposition to the maintenance of the British mission in Florence. Criticism on grounds of cost and uselessness was aggravated by the perception that Burghersh was too much absent from his post while still drawing his salary. There was a small flurry of such complaints in early 1822. The *Times* pointed out that the mission had been created to meet the Jacobite threat, which had passed, and there was now an anomalous situation, in that Tuscany had no embassy in London, where the Austrian mission handled all 'the affairs of the states governed by branches of the Austrian family'. To make matters worse, the ambassadors to Vienna, Frankfurt and Florence, costing more than £20,000 between them, were currently all in England.[44] In April 1822 a gentle caricature of his Lordship was published in London over the title 'A View of Burghersh'.

Early in 1826, Burghersh was again seen on English soil, and on 12 March the *Sunday Times* asked whether this rival to Paisiello and Rossini could not 'cultivate his high musical powers without this country paying the piper'? The Florentine Embassy was 'another profligate job'. In 1829–1830, as his tenure drew to a close, Burghersh's expenses were under scrutiny, in parliament and in the press, and the musical jokes continued. His trip to Rome early in 1829 to observe the papal conclave cost £674. On 13 May the *Times* objected:

Had his Lordship bribed the Conclave, and bought the election of a Pope, there might have been some ground for this charge. Nothing of the kind of course was done; his Lordship was probably content to bribe the Pope's Chapel-master for the score of the last anthem.

A year later, the issue of British diplomatic establishments was again before parliament, and on 8 May 1830 the *Times* recapitulated all its criticisms, concluding that 'Our Consul at Leghorn is capable of doing all our diplomatic business in

Tuscany'.[45] The British government was recurrently subjected to similar attacks, and more was heard of the argument that the Austrian domination of Tuscany, Modena and Parma made a separate diplomatic accreditation to those courts redundant. So far as the Florentine legation was concerned, His and then Her Majesty's government was unmoved. The Tuscan Legation accordingly remained the butt of occasional criticism, which for the most part replayed and elaborated themes stated already before 1830.

Whether or not the existence of the Legation was justified, the despatches sent home by Burghersh and the successive secretaries who served as *chargés d'affaires* in his absence provide us with a quantity of information about British expatriates, whose reasons for being in Tuscany were varied and who experienced a variety of problems. William Peel inadvertently got into trouble with the police for political reasons, but it was also possible to do so because of misbehaviour, which in its turn arose from multiple causes: ignorance or incomprehension of local mores, arrogance and even, we may guess, simple boredom. How often did young Englishmen at a loose end get into trouble, not least during the summer holidays at Bagni di Lucca?

When this occurred and diplomatic intervention proved necessary, British officials had to deal not with the Tuscan government, but with the Marchese Mansi, chief minister of the Bourbon Duchess of Lucca. In early September 1818 Burghersh reported to the Foreign Office on a fracas that had recently taken place at Bagni involving two sons (the elder not yet 21 years old) of William Edwardes, Baron Kensington.[46] The young men had set out to shoot at a target a little way from their lodgings; a gendarme intercepted a servant who was taking a rifle to them and demanded to see a hunting permit or gun licence. When neither was produced, he tried to confiscate the weapon, and in the scuffle that followed, he was slightly hurt. When Lord Kensington (or 'Hisington', as he sometimes appears in the police reports) was told what had happened, he declared his willingness to pay the wounded gendarme some compensation for his 'scratch'. His tone spoke volumes: 'It is a little extraordinary that Gentlemen should be prevented amusing themselves in such a way by the insolent interference of the Gend'armes.'

Just under a year later, Burghersh, who was himself at Bagni at the time, reported to the Foreign Office on a dispute that had occurred between a Mr Wardle and an Italian called Santini. The former was identified as the son of the former MP Colonel Gwyllym Wardle; in fact three of that gentleman's sons had been involved. In origin it was trivial enough, but it is difficult to ascertain the truth, because, as was almost always the case, the account espoused by the local authorities was at variance with the depositions of the British gentlemen. The outcome was usually a stately minuet performed by the Minister or his representative and the Italian officials, each maintaining the veracity of their compatriots and claiming to report the 'facts'. In this instance Mansi blandly rounded off his version of what had happened with the words 'Voilà, Milord, le fait tel qu'il est arrivé' ('Here, my Lord, are the facts as they occurred').

According to the young gentlemen, the quarrel had originated in a cafe where some lemonade was spilt over Santini, not by young Mr Wardle, but by a friend in his company. Apologies were offered, they said, but not accepted, and the affair escalated until the police were called. The Englishmen were alleged to have offered violence to the officers of the law and they were arrested and conveyed to Lucca. It was claimed (and eventually admitted) that they had been marched through the streets in chains, exposed to the insults of the populace. Faced with complaints from the boys and their mother, Burghersh submitted that, while they had reacted with excessive vigour to their arrest (although they themselves denied it), there was no excuse for the humiliation to which they had been subjected, 'like the lowest of malefactors'. The duchess was conciliatory and on 30 August Burghersh was able to report that she had expressed her regrets about the violence committed by the police and had ordered the punishment of those responsible.[47] The young Wardles seem to have had a gift for getting into hot water. Before the year 1819 was out Edward and William Wardle had brought an action for attempted homicide against one L. Noccioli. If Burghersh got to know about this, it seems that he did not find it necessary to report on it to the Foreign Secretary, and there is no knowing whether or not the attempted prosecution was in any way related to the fracas that had taken place at Bagni.[48]

Another incident, more widely noticed because of the celebrity of the protagonists, took place at Pisa on 24 March 1822 and involved Lord Byron, Shelley and Trelawny. Returning from a ride outside the walls, they were rudely disturbed by a dragoon, who rode right through the party. An altercation ensued and the dragoon called upon the guards at the city gate to arrest the Englishmen, who had spurred their horses on towards Casa Lanfranchi, the house (still to be seen) where Byron lived on the Lungarno. The dragoon caught up with them here and a further confrontation took place, during which both Shelley and Trelawny were struck. This was witnessed by a Dr John Crawford, who was also living on the Lungarno and supplied testimony which Byron sent to the Legation together with his own report.[49] Byron had no complaint against the government, 'which has hitherto been apparently impartial, and may continue so', but the offender was a native Pisan and (with apparent reference to the recent trial of Queen Caroline) Byron remarked 'we have seen in England of what Italian witnesses are capable'. In this particular instance, the authorities dealt with the matter by absolving Byron and his distinguished associates of all responsibility but punishing some of their servants (who were not English) instead.

This is perhaps the more noteworthy as Byron was (unsurprisingly) a marked man. In a letter dated 4 October 1821, Aurelio Puccini, president of the Segreteria di Finanza at Pisa, told the Buongoverno in Florence that

We are aware about the political attitude of this Englishman, who combines with a high birth, literary celebrity, and a considerable fortune, a great determination to favour all political novelties … the most careful and secret instructions should be sent for the supervision of the aforesaid foreigner.

Byron's desire to bring all his furniture from Ravenna without paying any duties and his importation of a menagerie of subversives, not to say his mistress Teresa Guiccioli, aroused Puccini's wrath and made the Palazzo Lanfranchi a place to be watched. His departure from Tuscany later in 1822, after Shelley's death, was greeted with relief.[50]

While all these incidents differed, it is possible to see how the assumptions of English gentlemen were challenged by certain aspects of the Italian environment. They were not used to manned gates in town walls, still less to gates manned by armed men, nor to being routinely policed by gendarmes who asked to see their firearms licences. The notion of humble submission to such representatives of the majesty of the state was clearly, in every sense, foreign to them. Another incident, which took place at Pisa in December 1816, turned on a more commonplace problem, which on this occasion led to violence.

Captain (later Admiral) Charles Napier RN had arrived in the city with his family; two porters fastened on to him, of whom he consented to hire one, the other, however, continuing to tag along while the captain found lodgings. The man who had actually carried Napier's bags pronounced himself dissatisfied with his fee and the other, who had done nothing, demanded payment. Finding that they were prepared to offer him violence, so Napier related, he contrived to break the arm of one of his assailants, but when he left the house to make his complaint to the local authorities, he found that a hostile mob had gathered outside, which effectively chased him to the tribunal. When the case was heard, Napier was affronted to discover that the judge wanted him to 'compromise' the matter by making a payment, which Napier would have regarded as an admission of guilt on his part; he insisted on his right of self-defence. The police believed that no threat had been offered to him, but that he 'merely broke a Man's Arm for demanding more Money'. Napier was not the last British litigant to encounter the desire of the courts to achieve closure by means of a monetary settlement rather than to reach a verdict in favour of one party or the other.[51]

Disputes about tips must have been commonplace, but rarely led to such lively consequences. Travelling a decade or so later, James Cobbett commented on the necessity of either bribing or submitting to annoyance at the custom-houses; provided an adequate something was offered, the luggage of English travellers would not be searched. Another of his observations amounts almost to an explanation of what could so easily go wrong. The English were always treated with respect, despite their very different manners, and were always assumed to be rich. However, they were deemed to be *orgogliosi e disprezzatori*, 'proud and contemptuous', which did not surprise Cobbett at all: 'most Englishmen deserve it, judging from their conduct as travellers out of their own country'.[52] The results could be serious: on 16 February 1825 the *Morning Chronicle* reported the fatal stabbing of one Captain Bulkeley near Florence by a disgruntled ostler, remarking that 'our countrymen would certainly do better to carry with them a greater spirit of conciliation, and to leave at home that aristocracy of feeling and severity of manner which renders them ridiculous to foreigners, without gaining them respect'.

If the Englishman, rich or not, really was proud and contemptuous, he would not hesitate to show his resentment of importunities or interference of a kind to which he was unaccustomed. If he was young and somewhat at a loose end as he was dragged around the continent, matters might be made worse. Sometimes the family's excursion was more in the nature of an exile than of a tourist trip, and this was the situation of the young Wardles, who got into trouble at Bagni in 1819. Their father, Colonel Gwillym Lloyd Wardle, had won notoriety as an MP by spearheading a parliamentary campaign against corruption in the award of army contracts, which ended by forcing the resignation of the commander in chief, the Duke of York, in 1809. Thereafter his popularity evaporated and his business affairs went to ruin, forcing him to take refuge abroad in 1815. Charles Brown knew and liked him, telling Hunt in 1829 that he saw him every Sunday.[53]

A curious picture of Wardle appeared in a potpourri of anecdotes published very early in 1833, shortly before his death. It occurs among the supposed oral reminiscences of a loquacious widow, ironically termed a 'Woman of Few Words', who, a year before she wrote down 'her' recollections, had (interestingly) 'heard mass' with Colonel Wardle in Florence. 'She' said that he was 'much courted' by English society, but somewhat 'discountenanced' by Burghersh. His Lordship may well have regarded the old troublemaker with some disdain, but the supposed widow thought that Burghersh required more 'incense' than Wardle was prepared to offer. He was 'a fine, gentlemanly old man – with venerable grey hair – a most agreeable companion' and, albeit cheerful, not happy in his enforced exile.[54] Sorrows had indeed pursued Wardle to Florence: in April 1828 his daughter Charlotte, married a year previously, gave birth to a son there and died 10 days later. Of his sons, William seems to have remained in Tuscany after his father's death and become a 'merchant'. His father's bequests to him included a share, amounting to 42,000 *lire*, in a silk concern in Florence.[55]

Wardle was not the only fugitive ex MP in Tuscany. Henry Grey Bennet presented a more pathetic spectacle. He made a sad brief will at Pisa on 6 April 1826, leaving everything he had to his dearly beloved wife Gertrude, with reversion to their two daughters. Gertrude was the niece of the sixth Duke of Bedford and cousin of the brothers Lord John Russell, the future prime minister, and the endlessly peripatetic Lord William Russell, whose distinctive neat hand makes frequent appearances in the Vieusseux subscription books. Bennet's alleged offence was of the kind that dared not speak its name. He had enjoyed a distinguished parliamentary career as a supporter of liberal measures, but in 1825 it was reported that he had made improper advances to a valet at Spa, which was enough to make him resign his seat and forswear his native land for ever. His wife was periodically seen by her

Russell relatives at Florence or Viareggio and became 'poor Gertrude' in their correspondence. Her husband was not mentioned.[56]

It is unknowable how many other prolonged Italian exiles may have arisen from similar causes or from a desire to pre-empt any such embarrassment. Several lifelong bachelors are identifiable among the Anglo-Florentines, but there is no reason to suppose that all were evading scandal; the absence of family ties or responsibilities may simply have made it easier to settle into a comfortable expatriate existence. Born in 1770, Robert Ladbroke was the grandson of a Lord Mayor of London and son of a banker and MP. He must have settled in Florence shortly after the end of the war, for in 1822 he was described as having been a resident for 'some years'.[57] He lived a very retired life but acquired extensive properties in Tuscany, which included a house in Florence, estates in the vicinity and also lands and houses near Leghorn, where he rented a pew in the English Church from time to time. In his will he remembered his Tuscan domestic servants, his agents and his 'peasant' at Montisoni, an estate just south-east of Florence. Ladbroke had retained extensive properties in England under the terms of his father's and grandfather's wills, and he left the bulk of what he possessed to his brother and other English kin and friends, authorizing the sale of Montisoni as soon as was convenient. He wished to be buried in the family vault at Christ Church Spitalfields, and this indeed happened on 12 May 1845.[58] There is no clue to the reasons for his long residence in Italy, and there may indeed be nothing to discover apart from the desire of a man of means to spend his time both more warmly and more cheaply than he would have done in England.

At some point in the 1820s Ladbroke must have made the acquaintance of another exile, Captain John Gordon, formerly an officer in the service of the East India Company. When Gordon died in 1829, his nephew Alexander, whose mother had given him to understand that he had expectations from his uncle, applied to the Foreign Secretary to know whether Captain Gordon had left a will, telling what he probably found a slightly embarrassing story. In 1803 at Bath 'an unhappy domestic occurrence' had brought about the Captain's separation from his wife and his decision to leave England.[59] How long he had been in Florence is unknown, but he had made a will, naming Ladbroke and Isaac Grant, a prominent Leghorn merchant and Florentine resident, as his executors. He had remembered not only Alexander (who was referred to Ladbroke & Co's bank in London for further information) but also 'Mrs Teresa Mazzaroli who has lived many years with me'. She was to have an annuity of £200 'to be paid to her twice yearly during her life on her drafts on Messrs Coutts & Co'.[60]

Whether this lady had been the cause of Gordon's marital estrangement or a consolation subsequently discovered is unknown, but Englishmen certainly found what might be termed 'emotional companionship' in Tuscany, either to replace or to supplement a marriage. The latter appears to have been the case of Sir Robert Lawley. A baronet by inheritance, like Ladbroke, he was among the early subscribers to the Vieusseux reading room when it opened in 1820. He had already devised a project for bringing political enlightenment to the Italians. A 'private letter' to the *Morning Chronicle* of 26 March 1819 reported that he was planning to publish a periodical journal designed to reawaken in the Italians 'the spirit of their proud and glorious ancestors. It will cost him a great deal of money, but that he regards not.' In 1822 Lord William Russell took the lease of the Serristori Palace from Lawley and found his servants installed there and his cook 'most admirable.'[61] Money was certainly not his problem. In 1831, when he was created Baron Wenlock, he was described as 'possessed of vast estates in the midland counties'. He had, with his lady, 'for some time resided in Italy', and on 15 April 1831 the *Belfast News Letter* declared that he 'sustains, at his splendid palace in Florence, the system of old English hospitality upon a scale quite unknown to modern Tuscany'. He had recently 'purchased a large estate, almost a principality, situated upon the banks of the Arno, between Pisa and Florence', which had cost him between £30,000 and £50,000 sterling.[62]

Lawley did not live long to enjoy his peerage or his Florentine 'principality', dying in Tuscany on 10 April 1834. On the 28th of that month the *Morning Chronicle* remarked that he had 'lived on terms of great cordiality and affection' with his wife but, the marriage being childless, had left his Tuscan property to 'a natural son'. The couple had been married in 1793, and it is therefore likely that when Lawley began spending time in Tuscany, he knew that he would have no legitimate heir. In an Italian codicil he added to his English will in April 1832, he declared his desire to appoint guardians for what he called his 'four adopted children that is to say Roberto Elisa Francesco Enrico Lawley dwelling in Tuscany born of Signora Giacoma Carolina de Val'. He had formally adopted these children in 1830 and appointed as their guardians their mother, the banker Horace Hall and the Abbé Luigi Fioravanti. Roberto, the eldest child, was to be Lawley's principal heir for all his goods and chattels.[63] It seems unlikely that the existence of these children was in any way secret. In 1830 the American sculptor Horatio Greenough, now settled in Florence, told a friend that the English sculptor Wyatt was going to make a portrait of Sir Robert Lawley's children.[64]

In being both able and willing to provide for no fewer than four illegitimate children, Lawley contrasted markedly with a lower-class Briton, whose predicament Burghersh had to deal with shortly before he left Florence. Lady Dorothy Campbell had told him that a servant of hers, named Samuel Heskeath, was to be imprisoned 'for a trifling offence'. The Tuscan authorities did not take the same view. For more than a year, Heskeath had been conducting an affair with an unnamed woman, which had resulted in a child who had to be taken into care. This flagrant affair had been 'accompanied by the most scandalous circumstances', which were deemed damaging to morality (*al costume*). Heskeath was to be imprisoned for 10 days and banished from Tuscany, and the affronted authorities pointed out that they had had the 'delicacy' to warn his employer of the sentence. Burghersh's final word to the Foreign Office is revealing: 'I did not think it my duty to take any further steps in the business, but I find that a few dollars properly applied have entirely overcome all difficulties and the man is allowed to remain.'[65]

Although morally culpable, Heskeath was part of an established household. In the summer of 1825 Fox-Strangways plaintively sought 'any Instructions there may be as to the disposal of the vagabond English who are for ever turning up here and whom I know not what to do with'. The Tuscan government expected him to cope with them according to instructions that they presumed he had but that he could not find. In reply he was sent a copy of the directions issued to British consuls at foreign ports, who had to deal with discharged or unemployed seamen and other flotsam.[66] The consul at Leghorn did indeed from time to time list the hard-luck cases to whom he had been obliged to render assistance. The British subjects concerned were meant to be distressed, not delinquent, but delinquency could of course lead to distress and distress to delinquency.

It is unfortunate, if not surprising, that we get less information about the lower-class misfits or victims of circumstance who came to the notice of HM's ministers than about their upper-class counterparts. One of the odder examples of the latter was George Baring, born in 1781 the fifth son of Sir Francis, founder of the famous bank.[67] Having displeased his family by marrying Harriet D'Oyly (sister of Sir Charles) in Calcutta in 1806, he left a career in the family business to be ordained in 1813 and was briefly vicar of Winterbourne Stoke in Wiltshire. He was very much under the influence of his sister, another Harriet, who on being widowed in 1815 became the lynchpin of 'the Baring party', a group of Anglican dissenters, George among them, who seceded from the Established Church. Harriet similarly influenced her sisters Frances, who married the Brighton MP Thomas Read Kemp, and Lydia, the wife of Philip Laycock Story. Both Kemp and Story participated in the secession and both acquired Florentine connections.[68] George spent a few years promoting the sect in the West Country, but in the spring of 1819, he suddenly left Exeter for a tour of the continent, which lasted until the end of 1824, when he settled at Florence.

Here he made a determined effort to establish himself in the forefront of society. We learn this from the published report of a case heard before the Tuscan Supreme Court in 1834, which turned on the question of the legal definition of a merchant, more specifically on whether or not Baring could be so classified.[69] On this depended which tribunal had jurisdiction over other related litigation. Conflicting verdicts had been given by lower courts, but on appeal it was ruled that Baring was to be regarded as a property-owner (*possidente*), whose money had been spent above all to cut a social figure and not to make commercial profits. In the course of the hearing, his biography was briefly recapitulated.

After he had settled in Florence, 'the magnificence with which he displayed himself to the public was extraordinary'. He commissioned for his pleasure a yacht called the *Goletta Enrichetta* (in homage, presumably, to his wife Harriet), lavishly equipped with furnishings and nautical and astronomical instruments obtained for him in London by Signor Routh of Leghorn. Late in 1825 Strangways mentioned this yacht, which Baring had had built in Leghorn and in which he had taken a cruise to Sardinia, only to be refused permission to land on his return without performing 10 days' quarantine. (Tuscan quarantine regulations were a recurrently vexed subject.)[70] Also in 1825, in order to obtain a desirable country residence, he paid 180,000 *scudi* for a villa and estate at Rusciano just outside Florence. This was 'a trifling expense' compared to what he then spent on furnishings and other works. Meanwhile he took care to obtain entry to society by being presented at court and at the British Embassy. We know from other sources that he was among the fashionables who could be seen driving in the Cascine and at the races.[71]

One observer who was less than impressed by Baring and his family was the acidulated Henry Fox. One evening in September 1828 Lady Dudley took him to Baring's villa: 'He is brother to Alexander Baring, and is of course like the rest of the family extremely rich.' Mrs Baring was

a gigantic, large-boned woman, with grown-up children born in every capital in Europe, and about to give her husband a seventeenth or eighteenth pledge. The girls are tall, rawboned, vulgar misses, very underbred and unladylike in their conversation and manners, without any beauty to commend them beyond the beauté de diable and the usual freshness of all English girls. Mr Baring only appeared on the terrace, with a cigar in his mouth, which he hardly removed to speak to Lady Dudley. Afterwards aware that his appearance could in no way add to the agrémens of the dull evening, he very wisely retired to his private rest on undisturbed potations. We were all dragged into the dining-room to sit round a tea-table, where the young ladies did not preside but filled the offices nature had intended for them cutting bread and butter, opening bottles of soda-water and ginger-beer, and by their dexterity and flippancy strongly reminded me of an English barmaid. By such unladylike occupations they may long continue to stoop, but the part appears too natural to them for conquest to ensue.[72]

Despite this unflattering view of Baring's daughters, three of them were married in Florence over a period of 18 years. The first was Harriet, in 1826. Her husband, Thomas Kerrich, came of a Norfolk gentry family and would later profit by his Baring connections to run a bank in Florence. Mary Baring was married to Sir Grenville Temple in 1829 and Marion to Henry Story, a son of her father's erstwhile co-religionist Philip Laycock Story, in 1842. This younger Baring generation maintained a presence in the city for years after the departure of their parents and were joined by several members of the Story family. The genealogical web woven by these and related families was immensely complex, and illustrates the ways in which relationships forged in England were transplanted to Tuscany, while relationships initiated or continued in Tuscany were spun on through the generations and often transplanted back to England.[73]

Baring's social climbing cost more money than he had. It is not necessary to recount here the complicated dealings into which he entered in the attempt to shore up his finances; one involved a consignment of straw hats, another speculative purchases of grain. A number of both Italian and British businessmen were implicated in these transactions. Baring's 'sad position' was unknown in Tuscany when, at the end of October 1830, he decided to leave for England. His family – including his son-in-law Thomas Kerrich, who was living with him at Rusciano – remained behind. Kerrich, who claimed that his father-in-law owed him 574,630 Tuscan *lire* (over £19,000), was among the numerous creditors who went to court to attempt to obtain something from the wreckage. He had the backing of Thomas Baring in London and was most probably motivated by the desire to keep the whole sorry business (and any remaining assets) as far as possible within the family.[74] Baring's behaviour cannot be regarded as typical even of the richer expatriates in Florence, but his ill-fated doings illustrate the complexity of the possible relationships between different elements of the Anglo-Tuscan population, from the merchant houses of Leghorn to the leisured habitués of the Grand Ducal court and the salons of Florence, who were perhaps not always as rich as they needed to be.

Henry Fox was doubtless delighted, if not surprised, to learn of the Baring debacle. It has to be admitted that he approved of few of his compatriots in Florence, which was 'full of the usual flight of English that renders the place odious'. He had nothing specific to say against the Normanbys, whose house was 'very delightful', and he approved of another English residence, Lady Ashburnham's villa:

> I have seldom seen such a happy combination of Italian splendour and English comfort as she has contrived to render this spacious house. We found them all sitting on delicious English sofas under a handsome portico, before a fine garden full of orange-trees.

It was proverbial among English travellers that Italian houses lacked the comfort they were accustomed to at home, and they remarked on it where they found it. Lady Ashburnham herself did not escape Fox's barbs, because she still hoped 'to inspire youthful desires' despite being surrounded by a bevy of grown-up daughters. Her husband (the third Earl of Ashburnham) was at present in England: 'Poverty makes them reside here, and they contrive to live in this magnificent and luxurious economy with an enormous family upon 2,000 a year!'

Lord and Lady Blessington also felt the rough edge of Fox's pen. Their house was 'prettily situated on the banks of the Arno' next to Schneiderff's celebrated hotel, but her Ladyship 'was as usual very Irish and very censorious, vulgar beyond measure, and speaking the vilest French with her native intrepidity'. When Fox dined with them, Lord Blessington got drunk and abused Holland House. Fox disdained to reply, 'because the correction of a drunkard in his own house seems to me impossible for one of his guests to attempt; and when not drunk he is below contempt'.[75] These opinions did not prevent Fox from dining with them again.

The Blessingtons were naturally accompanied during their stay in Tuscany by the inseparable third member of their strange ménage, Count d'Orsay, and it was in Florence that they decided to give effect to the long-laid plan that the count should be married to one of his Lordship's daughters. The resultant contretemps, accompanied by a great deal of ill-feeling, has been narrated by biographers of Lady Blessington and Count d'Orsay in such a way as to suggest that Lord Burghersh deliberately and malevolently set out to sabotage the match, regarding it as socially unacceptable. It was admittedly a transparent contrivance to secure a handsome settlement to the Count. Burghersh is said to have insulted all concerned by telling the French Minister (a friend of both the Blessingtons and the Count) that the Anglican wedding service must take priority over the Catholic – both being necessary – and then to have been rude to Lady Blessington when she waited upon him with the bride.[76]

Burghersh would have been unlikely to commit to writing an account which reflected badly on himself, but his correspondence with the Foreign Office reveals that an issue of principle was involved which had nothing to do with social propriety and everything to do with rules that as a diplomat he was bound to respect. The issue, of recurrent concern to the British in Italy, was that of mixed marriages. Burghersh pointed out that there were recent precedents to be borne in mind, and indeed there was one that he did not mention.

On 27 April 1826, during one of Burghersh's absences from Florence, Charles Grabau, Hanoverian Consul at Leghorn, was married at the Legation to Henrietta Eliza Inghirami. Two months later Grabau informed Fox-Strangways from Genoa that he was afraid to return to his post at Leghorn as he and his wife had been threatened by the governor of that town with imprisonment. The Tuscan government assured the secretary that there was no such threat, but proceedings had been taken against the Inghirami family, who were deemed answerable for their daughter's involvement in what was regarded as an irregular relationship. It seems that Grabau, having obtained a dispensation from Rome, had appeared in the archbishop's court at Florence to sign the marriage contract, gone through the Anglican marriage service at the Legation and then 'refused, or neglected, to be married in the Roman Catholic church'.

Strangways lucidly spelled out the legal position:

In this country a double duty is to be performed towards the Church in order to render a marriage valid. The first, the above mentioned engagement entered into before the Bishop in the quality of Ecclesiastical Judge; the other, the religious ceremony to be celebrated in the Church itself. No marriage therefore is good in this country even between Tuscan subjects, and Roman Catholics, if the performance of either of these duties has been omitted and the fact of having entered into the engagement contracted at this first ceremony is considered binding on the parties to perform the second, without which the marriage is incomplete.

Grabau himself, not being a Tuscan subject, was not liable to any penalty for contracting an illegal marriage; but were he and his wife to take up residence in Tuscany, they would be regarded as cohabiting and compelled to separate. Strangways continued his exposition for the benefit of the Foreign Secretary:

> Altho' the marriage of a Tuscan subject, being a Catholic, with a Protestant would be valid or at least undisturbed in this country, if, celebrated in England, according to the Law of the Land; yet the forbearance of the Tuscan Law does not go so far as to extend the privilege to such marriages as are performed in the houses of Foreign ministers resident in Tuscany so as to enable a subject of the Grand Duchy to withdraw himself thereby from the operation of the Ecclesiastical Law.

Strangways here hints that a mixed marriage contracted far away from Tuscany (preferably outside Italy altogether) would most probably go unchallenged, and this was a tactic that several Britons later would employ. He further commented that the Grabau episode might have been ignored, had it not been that the priests were currently hopeful of tightening their grip on society.

Grabau was surely being disingenuous; he was right in saying that 'a protestant marrying a Catholic woman in his own Church' was not liable to any penalty under Tuscan law, but an accompanying Catholic ceremony was indispensable. He appears to have believed that marriage was an entirely private matter and that the Tuscan authorities and Roman Catholic church had no right to object if his wife's relatives did not. In a second letter he intimated that he would go through the Catholic ceremony as soon as he could do so on conditions acceptable to himself. Canning's reaction was unequivocal: Strangways was to inform Grabau that unless he complied with the Tuscan law, 'his claim to any further protection of H. My's Mission in this affair will be disallowed'.[77]

The precedent Burghersh actually had in mind had been furnished about 6 months before the Blessingtons applied to him. The Chevalier Incontri had obtained a dispensation from the Pope for his marriage with a Miss Irvine and applied to Burghersh for permission to conduct the wedding at the Legation. Unfortunately, the Protestant ceremony was performed first (on 20 April 1827), whereupon the priest refused to perform the Catholic ceremony, 'declaring that the Papal dispensation was done away by the contumacious conduct of the Chevalier, in having first been married in the English Church'. He was supported by his superiors and it took a long time to sort out the mess, during which it was suggested that the bride might have to become a Catholic. This was extremely distressing to her family; the Chevalier might have ended 'perfectly free from all tie to the Lady, who was on the other hand bound to him by the Law of England, both in a religious & in a civil point of view, as his wife'.

If Burghersh was aware that such difficulties could be created if the Protestant ceremony took place first, it would have been both hypocritical and reprehensible for him to insist on this happening. If he wished to obstruct the Blessington-d'Orsay marriage, the failure of the parties to play by the rules gave him the perfect excuse.

He had asked Lord Blessington whether d'Orsay was a Catholic and if so, 'whether the ceremony according to the Rights [sic] of that Church had been performed, or whether any engagement to ensure its' [sic] taking place had been made'. Learning that d'Orsay was indeed a Catholic and that no such arrangements had been made, he informed Blessington that in the light of previous experience, 'I had determined not to consent to the solemnization of marriages under such circumstances in my house'. There was another still more fundamental difficulty: no dispensation had been sought from Rome. The Blessington-d'Orsay biographers make no mention of this issue; Burghersh was simply being obstructive and insulting.

Burghersh strongly urged that d'Orsay should go to Rome and employ the French ambassador as an intermediary in obtaining the necessary permissions. He would then be able to have the Protestant ceremony performed in the house of the British vice-consul. In December Burghersh heard from Count d'Orsay that the vice-consul at Rome had refused to allow the marriage to be solemnized in his presence, 'upon the ground that a marriage solemnized according to the rites of the Church of England, in Rome would not be legal'. The count had therefore betaken himself to Naples, where the English marriage was solemnized, apparently without any previous arrangements for the Catholic ceremony. When Burghersh sought enlightenment from the vice-consul at Rome, he learned that the objections had come not from him but from the English clergyman, Mr Burgess, who was doubtless extremely conscious of the knife-edge on which he and Protestants in general lived and effectively refused to perform the ceremony in any circumstances, either in his own chapel or at the house of the vice-consul. In answer to the vice-consul's request for future guidance, Burghersh strongly recommended him

> in all cases, where the persons contracting a marriage are of different religions, but particularly where the future husband is not an Englishman, not to allow the English ceremony to take place, till after the one according to the rites of the Catholick Church.

Once again, we observe that this advice flatly contradicted the line he is supposed to have taken in respect of the Blessington-d'Orsay marriage.[78]

There can be no doubt of the reality of the issues involved or of their importance to quite a few Britons in Tuscany, male and female. At this very moment, John Maquay was trying to make the arrangements for his marriage to Elena Gigli of Siena. About a week before Lord Blessington made his request to Burghersh, Maquay had waited upon the Marchesa Zandodari in Florence to talk 'about the Pope's licence'.[79] On 7 November, in Siena, he discussed with Pompeo Spanocchi 'the different ways of managing without this dispensation from the Old Pope'. If he was hoping to be able to do without it, he must soon have thought better of it. The diary sporadically charts the negotiations that followed, which involved a Sienese priest, a cardinal and for some reason the Russian ambassador at Rome; it seems that the archbishop of Siena at one point was dragging his feet.

On 5 January 1828 word had still not come from Rome. On the 8th John had 'a long chat' about the Tuscan law of marriage with a Francescantonio Mori. Back in Florence a few days later he rejoined the busy social round of the early New Year, attending a number of balls, including one given by the Mrs D'Arcy Irvine, whose daughter's marriage 9 months earlier had given Burghersh such trouble. On 7 February 'all the necessary papers came from Siena this morning' and on the 9th he triumphantly announced

> at 10 O'Clock this morning was married to Elena Gigli by the RC Curate of the Parish of Sta Maria Novella (Pacini) at her mother's lodgings, present her Mother, Cav and Mad Pieri, and Stewart Bruce and a friar brought by the Curate as a witness – Marchesa Feroni came in too late the ceremony did not last scarcely five minutes. The Marchesa Feroni then took Elena and called for her bridesmaid Miss Barton in the Marchesa's carriage. Bruce, the Cav. Pieri and myself proceeded in another carriage and met them at Lord Burghersh where we were married by Mr Tayler.

This might almost be termed a textbook demonstration of how to conduct a mixed marriage, including the Protestant bridegroom's apparent flirtation with the possibility of evading the issue, the use of influential personages at Rome and also the reactions of Protestant relatives, which are revealed in a couple of family letters.

On 13 June 1827 John had written to Elena from Aix-les-Bains:

> I arrived here on Saturday Morning and found my Mother & Brother well, but I am sorry to say I found them a good deal out of spirits at the idea of my marrying a Roman Catholic. This you know my dear girl I have already fully warned you of and that you will have to expect a less warm reception from different parts of my family than if it had been otherwise and I will even say that my own feelings on the subject would be much stronger than they are if I thought I was marrying a real Roman Catholic but I do not think so for I feel that whatever you may outwardly call yourself you do in fact believe the same as I do on almost all points for the tenets of the Roman Catholic church claim exclusive salvation for its own members you do not claim it and therefore you are not really a Roman Catholic. We have already conversed on the subject of confessing to your priest instead of confessing to your God and of believing that anyone can absolve you from your sins but God himself and I think upon this subject also you really feel as I do. However you may feel obbligata to say you think otherwise this is what I feel regarding your opinions whether I think right or wrong you know best.[80]

Another family member, John's maternal uncle Sir Moore Disney, reacted in a more urbane fashion, writing a letter of congratulation, in which he observed simply, 'Don't let her convert you.' John described this letter as 'very kind'.[81]

The rules could produce bemusement as well as duplicity, and not just on the part of the Protestant English. In March 1828 Charles Brown told Severn that an Italian called Garofanini had called upon him

with a blundering notion in his head that any priest in Tuscany, Catholic or Protestant, could marry his daughter to the Englishman. I assured him it could not be done in Italy without the Pope's consent.

Garofanini went away to make enquiries, and was surprised to find that Brown was right.[82]

The incident underlines the fact that marriages across the divides of religion and nationality were far from uncommon at several levels of society. Different mixed marriages led to different outcomes for the participants and their descendants. On 18 February 1828, only a few days after his own wedding, John 'saw Miss Lees marriage party (Marchese Guadagni) at Lord B's door'. This was Louisa Lee, the Protestant daughter of Lieutenant Colonel Francis Lee of the Royal Marines. Miss Lee's Catholic bridegroom, Donato Guadagni, belonged to an ancient and illustrious Florentine noble family. Their (Catholic) son, Guadagno, would fight for the British in the Crimea and in his turn take an English Catholic wife. His mother evidently remained a Protestant and was buried in the Allori Cemetery in 1886; her mother, Lady Lee, died and was also buried in Florence, in 1865.[83]

The outcome was probably different for Miss Elizabeth D'Arcy Irvine, who became the Marchesa Incontri in 1827. The Irvine family history was rather curious. It seems that thanks to her marriage settlement, her mother, Mrs Irvine, held the family purse strings. In 1822 she made a will, presumably in Florence as it was witnessed by Dawkins as Secretary of Legation; the subsequent death of one of her sons in India and the marriage of her second daughter to Incontri made alterations necessary, and she added a codicil on 1 August 1827, which was witnessed by none other than Lord Blessington, the British chaplain Mr Tayler and the physician Dr Kissock.[84] Mrs Irvine died in Florence in March 1830 and received Protestant burial in the cemetery which the Swiss had opened 2 years earlier. She was, according to the *Morning Post* on 15 April, a 'universally respected and truly amiable lady'. Her daughter, the Marchesa Incontri, died forty years later. That she had gone over to Rome is suggested by the fact that although the newspapers recorded her death in Florence in 1870, there is no record of an Anglican burial. By contrast, her sister Emily died the same year while visiting her and joined her mother in the Protestant cemetery.

As for the Maquays, Elena continued for some years to attend Catholic services. She did so from time to time during the bridal tour to England and Ireland she and John undertook in 1828–1829. They spent some time in Cheltenham, where his brother George had bought a new-built house.[85] John had first visited him there in the summer of 1826. He met there James Stewart Bruce, a connection by marriage, who in the following year would be attached to the Florentine mission, where he witnessed John's marriage and got married himself at the end of 1828. There was also Denham Cookes, only a boy in 1826, who died in a horse-racing accident on the Cascine in 1847.[86] This does not begin to exhaust the list of those who at some time or another would be discovered in Tuscany. In 1827 Sinclair complained that 'I have often seen the same faces from Bath, Brighton, and Cheltenham, transplanted to the Lung'Arno, lounging about, or staring at pictures and statues in the gallery.' 'Manoeuvring mothers' who had failed at Bath or Cheltenham placed their hopes in the influence of the warm south, hoping that it might

> stimulate and inspire the liberty loving sons of Britain with some of its genial excitement, and induce them to take compassion of their fair countrywomen in a foreign land. It is this perhaps which gives Florence so much the appearance of a fashionable English watering-place, and renders it less interesting to travellers who love novelty.[87]

Not all transplanted Cheltonians would be mere visitors. Next door to George, there lived the retired Indian civil servant John Fombelle and his much younger wife. Elena made their acquaintance in 1828 and she was to see much more of them as permanent residents of Florence. The moment at which she and John could themselves settle in Tuscany was, however, delayed by the death of John's uncle John Leland Maquay senior in Dublin in March 1829, during their bridal tour. As principal heir and executor, John had to spend time in England and Ireland. By the time he next saw Florence in 1830–1831, the Burghersh era was at an end.

Notes

1   Kent Archives & History Centre, Maidstone, CKS U137, 1 Weigall Papers, F18, *Memoirs of Priscilla Countess of Westmoreland*, Vol. 1, pp. 253, 266–7. These were compiled from Priscilla's recollections in 1868, by her daughter, Rose Weigall, for the benefit of the latter's recently born son, Fitzroy.
2   FO79/21, FO to Falconar, 14 December 1814.
3   There is a great deal on this subject in FO79 over a period of years. The detailed claims that were vainly submitted to the Foreign Secretary shed light on the history of the British in Leghorn during the war.
4   FO79/43, Falconar to FO, 2 July 1824; 79/48, FO to Falconar, 3 March 1826.
5   TNA, Prob11/1750. The heading, translated from the Italian for the benefit of the Prerogative Court of Canterbury, read: 'Napoleon by the Grace of God and the Constitution of the Empire Emperor of the French king of Italy and protector of the Confederation of the Rhine &c &c &c'.
6   John Ingamells, *A Dictionary of British and Irish Travellers in Italy 1701–1800* (London, 1997), pp. 652–3.
7   Ibid., pp. 245–7. Born Hannah or Anna Gore, she had been married to Cowper at the age of 16, in Florence in 1774, and both were painted there by Zoffany.
8   Marcella Aglietti (ed.), *Nobildonne, monache, e cavaliere dell'Ordine di Santo Stefano: modelli e strategie femminili nella vita pubblica della Toscana granducale* (Pisa, 2010),

p. 113; JLM, E11 f. 127. Miss Farhill's only surviving sibling, Edward, who spent much of his life in France, erected an inscription in her memory in the English Cemetery.

9   JLM, E8 f. 48.

10 For Kirkup see DNB; for Brown, Eric H. McCormick, *The Friend of Keats: A Life of Charles Armitage Brown* (Wellington NZ, 1989); Jack Stillinger (ed.), *The Letters of Charles Armitage Brown* (Cambridge Mass.,1966); Grant E. Scott and Sue Brown (eds), *New Letters from Charles Brown to Joseph Severn* (www.re.umd.edu/editions/ brownsevern).

11 Leigh Hunt, *Lord Byron and Some of His Contemporaries, with Recollections of the Author's Life, and of His Visit to Italy* (Paris, 1828), Vol. 3, p. 253.

12 This visit and its consequences are described by Robert Super, *Walter Savage Landor* (London, 1957), pp. 177–80. Super acknowledges differing opinions about 'how this group came to know Landor' but gives priority to Hazlitt's account (p. 544, note 3). On Landor's first period of residence at Florence, see Malcolm Elwin, *Landor: A Replevin* (London, 1958), pp. 188–250.

13 Super, *Landor*, p. 179.

14 Thomas Medwin, *The Life of Percy Bysshe Shelley* (London, 1847), Vol. 1, p. 358.

15 FO79/27, Burghersh to FO, 20 July 1816.

16 Normanby succeeded his father as Earl Mulgrave in 1831 and was created Marquis of Normanby in 1838.

17 Stillinger (ed.), *Letters of Brown*, p. 237.

18 Malcolm Barnes (ed.), *Augustus Hare, the Years with Mother* (London, 1952), pp. 3–10. Both Super and Elwin have numerous references to the elder Hare's relationship with Landor. He was married, and his first two children were born, in England, but a son and a daughter were born in Tuscany in 1831–1832, Augustus, the youngest, following in Rome in 1834. The Vieusseux registers attest their father's presence in Florence intermittently between 1834 and 1840. He died at Palermo early in 1842.

19 Henry Reeve (ed.), *Greville Memoirs* (new edition, London, 1904), Vol. 1, pp. 305–6, 308. Normanby occupied the Palazzo San Clemente in Via S. Sebastiano (now Via Gino Capponi).

20 Ibid, Vol. 1, p. 288.

21 Stillinger (ed.), *Letters of Brown*, p. 203.

22 Weigall, *Memoirs of Priscilla Burghersh*, Vol. 1, pp. 259–60, 269–75.

23 Some months previously he had told Mary that the Baring here referred to, 'an excellent person', was acting as courier of the manuscript to London. Ed. Harry Buxton Foreman, *Letters of Edward John Trelawney* (London, 1910), pp. 132, 140, 135.

24 Weigall, *Memoirs of Priscilla Burghersh*, Vol. 1, pp. 309–10; Ed. Reeve, *Greville Memoirs*, Vol. 1, p. 308.

25 Scott and Brown (eds), *New Letters to Severn*, 21, 2 January 1827; 22, 17 March 1827. Brown's view of Hayter was consonant with that expressed by Constable in 1832: 'a very prosperous, disagreeable personage – but a great man in his own opinion, he being a person of consequence' (quoted by Barbara Bryant in her DNB article on Hayter).

26 *Morning Post* 10 October 1827; *Times* 12 October 1827.

27 Scott and Brown (eds), *New Letters to Severn*, 23, 23 October 1827; 24, 12 November 1827.

28 Barbara Bryant, 'Sir George Hayter's Drawings at Duncombe Park', *Apollo* 135 *new series* April 1992, pp. 246–9.

29   The Earl of Ilchester (ed.), *The Journal of the Hon. Henry Edward Fox (Afterwards Fourth and Last Lord Holland) 1818–1830* (London, 1923), pp. 318–19.

30   Apart from his uncle Moore Disney (see DNB), Maquay was connected by the marriage of his mother's sister Sally to the Barnards, who included among their recent members Thomas, bishop of Limerick; Sir Andrew Barnard (also DNB), companion-in-arms of Wellington and a courtier of George IV; and Lady Anne Barnard (a Barnard by marriage), daughter of the Earl of Balcarres and also a friend of George IV. There are occasional references to the Maquays in Anthony Powell (ed), *The Barnard Letters* (London, 1928).

31   EM, C1 f. 75v.

32   J. D. Sinclair, *An Autumn in Italy, Being a Personal Narrative of a Tour in the Austrian, Tuscan, Roman and Sardinian States, in 1827* (Edinburgh, 1829), p. 148.

33   *Gazzetta di Firenze* 11 May 1830, reported in the *Morning Post* 9 June 1830.

34   Preserved among the Weigall Papers in the Kent County Archives, slipped into a pocket with the 'Memoirs', it has no separate reference number.

35   FO79/22, Burghersh to FO, 31 January, 24 March 1815.

36   FO79/35, Burghersh to FO, 2 October 1820; cf. 79/22, 31 January 1815.

37   FO79/36 *passim*, but particularly Burghersh to FO, 5 May 1821; *Times*, especially 16 April & 4 July 1821.

38   Stillinger (ed.), *Letters of Brown*, p. 116.

39   JLM, E8 f. 104.

40   Stillinger (ed.), *Letters of Brown*, p. 129. What 'late events' had caused this suspicious mood, Brown does not explain.

41   James P. Cobbett, *Journal of a Tour in Italy, and Also in Part of France and Switzerland* (London, 1830), pp. 149–50, 324–5.

42   *The Examiner* 11 July 1825, also in the *Morning Chronicle* 12 July. John Maquay had seen Ferdinand one day in January 1823 when he was touring the Pitti Palace: 'The Grand Duke passed through the rooms with his family wrapped up in a huge greatcoat not very ducal in appearance.' JLM, E8 f. 111v.

43   Sinclair, *Autumn in Italy*, pp. 129–31, 144, 287.

44   'Scrutator' in *Morning Chronicle* 15 February 1822; *Morning Post* 22 February; *Times* 1 April.

45   That expedient would in fact be adopted for a period between 1860 and 1863, in vastly different circumstances; see Epilogue.

46   FO79/31, Burghersh to FO, 7 September 1818.

47   FO79/33, Burghersh to FO with enclosures, 10 August 1819.

48   *Gazzetta* 29 January 1820.

49   FO79/38, Byron to Dawkins, 27 March 1822.

50   Iris Origo, *The Last Attachment: The Story of Byron and Teresa Guiccioli* (London, 1949), pp. 301ff.

51   FO79/28, Dawkins to FO with enclosure, 19 December 1816. Dawkins erroneously described Napier as an army officer. On 1 February 1862 the *Manchester Times* published a description of the same incident, extracted from the recently published *Life and Correspondence of Admiral Sir Charles Napier, KCB* by Major Elers Napier, one of the captain's stepchildren, who as a child had accompanied him on the dash to the Tribunal. On 15 January 1862 a Dr McCarthy was murdered at Pisa by a disgruntled porter in very similar circumstances. The reputation of the Pisan *facchini* had if anything worsened with the coming of the railways.

52   Cobbett, *Journal*, pp. 70, 113.

53   *Morning Chronicle* 10 October 1827; Stillinger (ed.), *Letters of Brown*, p. 290. For Wardle see DNB. Hunt had benefited from the colonel's pursuit of the Duke of York,

inasmuch as the institution of the parliamentary enquiry in 1809 put a stop to the prosecution of the Hunt brothers for libel against His Grace, but it seems he did not meet him in Tuscany: 'neither then, nor at any other time, had I the least knowledge of Colonel Wardle.' Jack Morpurgo (ed.), *Leigh Hunt: Autobiography* (London, 1949), p. 204.

54   *Whychcotte of St John's, or, the Court, the Camp, the Quarter-Deck and the Cloister* (London, 1833), Vol. 2, pp. 242–7. This curious publication has been attributed to a Reverend Erskine Neale.

55   TNA, Prob11/1832. Wardle himself had had interests in textiles before his enforced departure from England.

56   See the references in G. Blakiston, *Lord William Russell and His Wife 1815–1846* (London, 1972). The observation (p. 132 note) that Gertrude was living at Viareggio, 'perhaps driven there by poverty', suggests ignorance of the real cause. The DNB article on Bennet states that he and his wife lived at a villa on Lake Como until his death, but Bennet died at Florence on 29 May 1836 and it was there that his widow received a prolonged visit from her father. When Bennet's will (TNA, Prob 11/1881) was proved, Claire Clairmont was one of two witnesses who attested to his handwriting: Bennet was here described as 'formerly of Upper Grosvenor Street in the County of Middlesex afterwards of Pisa but late of the City of Florence'.

57   *House of Lords Journals* 19 March 1822, 2 Geo IV. He had had to signify his assent to a petition that his brothers submitted to the House of Lords in respect of the power to grant building leases on certain lands in west London in which he had an interest under the terms of his father's will. He subscribed to Vieusseux on 6 December 1820.

58   TNA, Prob11/2018. The will was originally made in July 1842, and codicils were added in 1843 and 1844.

59   FO79/54, Burghersh to FO, 17 October 1829.

60   TNA, Prob11/1761.

61   Blakiston, *Lord William Russell*, p. 61. Lawley was brother-in-law to the Marchioness of Conyngham, whose son Lord Albert Conyngham was briefly Secretary of Legation at Florence in 1828–9.

62   *Freeman's Journal* 15 September 1831; *Belfast News Letter* 15 April 1831.

63   TNA, Prob11/1833.

64   Nathalia Wright (ed.), 'Letters of Horatio Greenough to Robert Weir' *New England Quarterly* 49 (1976), p. 510 (letter dated 1 May 1830). Richard James Wyatt (1795–1850) lived and worked mostly in Rome. On 31 July 1834 the *Gazzetta* announced the sale of a *palazzo* at 4177 Lungarno, together with various items of furniture, saddlery and wines, all for the benefit of the young Roberto Lawley and on the instructions of Caroline De Val and Orazio Hall.

65   FO79/55, Burghersh to FO, 16 March 1830.

66   FO79/45, Strangways to Planta, 7 July 1825; 45 Planta to Strangways, 26 July. Strangways was further told 'You will herein perceive that if you administer Relief to distressed British subjects, not Sailors, you are to reimburse yourself the Expence you may incur by Bills upon the Ld Coms of HM's Treasury, giving their Ldps due notice of such Bills, & sending them the Acct of the Sums expended together with the Vouchers.'

67   For Baring, see Grayson Carter, *Anglican Evangelicals: Protestant Secession from the Via Media, c. 1800–1850* (Oxford, 2000), pp. 110–22, and also his article in DNB.

68   Ibid., p. 111 note 18. Carter describes the marriage of Lydia Baring and Philip Laycock Story as childless, but three of their children got married at Florence.

69   *Tesoro del foro toscano o sia Raccolta delle decisioni del Supremo Consiglio e dell Regie Ruote civili delle prime appellazioni della Toscana: supplemento al tomo XLIII* (Firenze, 1841), pp. 3–37.

70   FO79/45, Strangways to FO, 30 November 1825.

71   *Morning Post* 23 August 1826; 7 April 1828.

72   Ilchester (ed.), *Journal of Henry Edward Fox*, pp. 318–19.

73   Lord Dillon's eldest son, Charles Henry, was married to Lydia Story (in England) in 1833, the year after his father's death.

74   Rusciano, at least, remained in their possession, for in 1863–64 Emanuele Fenzi bought the villa and its dependent farms from Kerrich, who was on the point of retiring to Jersey.

75   Ilchester (ed.), *Journal of Henry Edward Fox*, p. 234.

76   Nick Foulkes, *Last of the Dandies: The Scandalous Life and Escapades of Count d'Orsay* (London, 2003), pp. 151–8. On p. 152 he quotes the following from the earlier account given by Michael Sadleir, *Blessington-d'Orsay: a Masquerade* (London, 1933), pp. 114–16: 'That the Blessingtons should seriously have intended to celebrate this indefensible marriage under official auspices in Florence, showed a misapprehension of the atmosphere of the English community which, on the part of the Countess at any rate, is very unexpected.' Foulkes betrays no awareness that the match raised the issue of mixed marriages; Sadleir merely observes that both a Catholic and a Protestant ceremony would have been necessary.

77   FO79/46, FO to Strangways, 28 July 1826.

78   FO79/49, Burghersh to FO, 3 November, 20 December 1827, with enclosures (Smith to Aubin, 14 December, Aubin to Smith, 20 December).

79   JLM, E9 f. 87v. The story unfolds over the following pages of the diary until the marriage takes place (f. 95v).

80   Harold Acton Library, British Institute of Florence, Maquay collection, series Maq. II. 1.

81   JLM, E9 f. 94. The letter from Sir Moore, dated 8 January 1828, is in Maq. II.3.

82   Scott and Brown (eds), *New Letters to Severn*, 25, 29 March 1828.

83   For the history of the Guadagni, see www.guadagnifamily.com. It is recorded that the Marchesa's grandson Bernardo, born in 1869, one of the sons of Guadagno Guadagni, lived with her in Florence while attending the technical school there.

84   TNA, Prob11/2091.

85   John remarked in 1826 that it was 'an extremely nice house and beautifully furnished and fitted up' JLM, E9 f. 78. St Margaret's Terrace, which consists of six houses, still stands.

86   Stewart Bruce and his brothers and sisters were the children of the Reverend Sir Henry Hervey Bruce, nephew and heir to the Irish properties of the 'Mitred Earl', Frederick Hervey, Bishop of Derry and fourth Earl of Bristol. Their mother was Letitia Barnard, the sister of the Reverend William Barnard, to whom John's aunt Sally or Sarah, his mother's sister, was married. Stewart Bruce was married to Helen Alves in Florence on 6 December 1828.

87   Sinclair, *Autumn in Italy*, pp. 129–30.

3 UNTROUBLED GROWTH, 1830–1839

On 16 September 1830 the *Freeman's Journal* reported on a meeting held in Dublin to express the sentiments of the Irish people on the revolution in France. It was addressed by the MP Richard Lalor Sheil, who saw the relevance of late events for Italy and asked, 'Who can imagine that the yoke of Austria will be long endured?' The inhabitants of the ancient city states, 'those celebrated nurseries of modern liberty', Florence among them, 'will walk forth in all the dignity of renovated citizenship'. It is unlikely that at the moment these stirring words were uttered, Sheil (or anyone else) had any idea that over 20 years later, he would die in Florence as Her Majesty's envoy to the Grand Duke.

The events which had prompted his oratory heralded gradual if uneven changes in the environment of the Anglo-Florentines and other expatriates in Tuscany. For one thing, the French re-emerged as active players in the politics of Italy. By changing their monarch, they indicated that they did not deem themselves strait-jacketed by the 1815 settlement, and in 1832 they laid down another marker by garrisoning the port city of Ancona, part of the Pope's ill-controlled territories. Britain itself was scarcely exempt from change during these years. Burghersh arrived back in England towards the end of May 1830 expecting to be appointed ambassador to Naples, but his appointment fell victim to the incoming Whig ministry. He spent some energy petitioning the Foreign Secretary for the pension that he felt was due to him in view of the expenses he had incurred in Florence and that Palmerston was equally determined he was not going to have.[1] Reporting his abortive appointment to Naples, the *Standard* of 22 October 1830 added that 'a son of Lord Seymour goes to Florence as Chargé d'Affaires', saving 'some thousands per annum in the expenditure for Tuscany'.

George Seymour announced his arrival at Florence in a despatch dated 1 January 1831; in July he was back in London to be married to Gertrude Trevor and to be appointed Minister, albeit with a salary much reduced by Palmerston (less than half of Burghersh's £5,000). A jaundiced writer in the *Times* of 7 April 1832 judged him to be a mere 'youth', 'a Tory by birth', unfitted to mediate between Austria and France or to represent the current state of British political opinion. This may not have been an entirely accurate assessment. Seymour achieved some notoriety in 1850, when he informed a parliamentary inquiry that he could not conceive of a successful 'diplomatist' who did not give good dinners, but this was clearly not his only qualification.[2]

During the 4 years of his Florentine incumbency, his bulletins to the Foreign Secretary constitute an intelligent, mildly pessimistic and occasionally prophetic commentary on the state of Tuscany and Italy. His abortive efforts to induce the new Pope, Gregory XVI, to adopt reforming policies in the Papal States, which took him to Rome for a considerable part of 1831–32, contributed to his pessimism and led to a change in the management of relations between the Florentine Mission and the Papacy. Captain Thomas Aubin, who for years had served Burghersh as private secretary, was posted to Rome as the quasi-official representative of British interests, paid as an *attaché* of the Florentine legation. Tuscany remained peaceful despite the stirrings of 1830, and Seymour's term of office, together with those of his two successors, constituted a largely untroubled period for British visitors and residents.

The style in which at least some of the Anglo-Florentines expected to live at this date is indicated by an advertisement which appeared in the *Times* on 19 February 1831.

> FLORENCE. – To be SOLD, a FREEHOLD ESTATE, situate within a mile of that favourite city, Florence, with excellent carriage road to it. It consists of a neat and substantially built villa, containing 3 large sitting-rooms, 6 good size bed rooms, and 4 other small rooms, neatly furnished, with kitchen, cellar, coach-house, and stable for 4 horses, hay loft, corn and coachman's rooms. The whole put into complete repair, and painted within these last 6 months, well supplied with spring and rain water, a small garden, and every convenience a small genteel family can want, with about 16 acres of excellent arable land, laid out in the Tuscan manner, which yields excellent wine, fine corn, oil, and vegetables, well stocked with a variety of the best fruit trees, both on the land and in the garden. It returns 5 per cent, and is capable of returning 6 or 7, clear of all expense. Adjoining is also a capital Farm house, substantially built, like the villa, of stone, with 3 stone built vats for the wine, 3 underground cellars, two farming stables. The whole put into complete repair and painted. This is an unembellished statement, and the only motive the proprietor has for disposing of it, is, that he has another villa close by sufficient for his small family. The price of the whole is fixed at £2,000 sterling. Address, post-paid, to A.B., poste restante, Florence.

The sterling price and the placing of the advertisement make it plain that the purchaser was expected to be British; who the seller was is unfortunately unknown.

John Maquay and Elena made a lengthy stay in Florence, together with John's mother Elizabeth and her sister, Mrs Sarah Barnard, in 1830–31. During their journey in the summer of 1830, John heard news of insurrection in France and Belgium, but once in Florence, it was not until 14 February 1831 that he reported 'rumours of revolution' at Rome and of the establishment of Provisional

Governments at Bologna and Modena. On the 22nd Elizabeth Maquay had 'heard of much commotion at Rome many families coming in from thence'.[3] None of this disrupted the routines of Anglo-Florentine society. There were inevitably continual changes of personnel, but the Maquays were able to re-establish contact with old friends such as Major Galeazzi and his Irish wife, and Elena was reunited with her mother. They made their appearance at court: on 10 November 1830 'Elena was presented a second time ie as a British subject' and Sarah Barnard was presented on the following 9 February, when the rooms were 'intolerably hot'.[4]

Among new faces in Florence one family group was to be of particular importance to the Maquays. John first mentioned Lady Elizabeth, the widow of Admiral Sir Home Popham, when he met her travelling with her son, Captain William, in Switzerland in the summer of 1830. They arrived in Florence in the autumn, shortly after the Maquays, and John commented, 'I think they will be pleasant people.'[5] Lady Popham spent much of her old age in Florence, with an extended family clustered around her. One reason that they clustered may have been that her husband had left her everything when he died in 1820, not perhaps anticipating that she would be 95 when she died at Bath in 1866.[6] In addition she enjoyed a life pension from the British government, as she acknowledged in a letter written from Florence and published in the *Morning Post* on 6 August 1838, laying heavy emphasis on how well deserved it was, considering the services her husband had rendered his country.

The Maquay diaries are full of the Popham sons and daughters and their spouses. Caroline Popham was married to the naval officer John Pakenham, and they and their children became part of the Maquays' most intimate circle. Harriet, the youngest daughter, had taken an Irish Catholic husband, Daniel or Donal MacCarthy.[7] Later in the 1830s MacCarthy entered into a banking partnership with Thomas Kerrich, and in this capacity had the pleasure of showing Thomas Babington Macaulay the sights of Florence in 1838. Macaulay said of him that 'He declared himself a Catholic, but he seems a liberal and sensible one', who proved it by speaking scornfully of lower-class Italian superstition.[8] In 1835 MacCarthy was the moving spirit behind an ephemeral journal, *The Tablet*, which lightheartedly indulged the cultural interests of a group of friends, including the musical impresario Rowland Standish, Mary Boyle, grand-daughter of the Earl of Cork and Orrery, and the Ruxtons, a family from County Louth, who were well known to John Maquay both in Ireland and in Tuscany. MacCarthy also wrote three historical novels on Italian themes, and we know that John Maquay read at least one of them, presumably in manuscript. This would have been *The Siege of Florence*, published in London in 1840. It was dedicated to another Florentine resident, George Irby (the future Lord Boston, who had contributed at least one piece to *The Tablet*), and was nicely puffed in the English press.[9]

Other names with a future appear in the Maquay diaries during these months. Already in 1822 it had been reported in the British press that the soprano Angelica Catalani proposed to settle in Florence and that while on tour in England and

Scotland, she had spent a great deal on 'elegant furnishings and commodities, to fit up her house in the English style and fashion'. A visitor to her villa much later reported that she 'swears by England; she has English grates, English carpets, English chairs, English bedsteads and bed-curtains, and the beds are covered with our counterpanes'.[10] John Maquay may have remembered how as a young man back from Canada, he had heard her sing in London in 1812. On 23 February 1831 he and Elena drove out to visit her and she 'most good humouredly sang us several songs she is the most natural person in manner I have almost ever seen'.[11] From now on they saw her frequently, and her husband, Paul de Valabrègue, and her sons were given to dropping in on them.

On 16 March 1831 the Maquays entertained the Valabrègues at a dinner party which was also attended by the Macdonells. The fact that there were Macdonells of virtually all ages enhanced the family's social value. An anecdote related many years later by the younger Hugh's wife Anne sketches Macdonell's whist-playing set at this period: the Reverend Mr Sanford, the diplomat Ferdinand St John and the wealthy Catholic Francis Sloane were all present one night at Casa Annalena when Hugh saw the ghost of a nun. St John's son, Frederic, affectionately remembered the family and childhood days at what he miscalls Casa Magdalena.[12] John Maquay's references to the Macdonells, more or less continuous whenever he was in Florence, are extremely numerous. Although he never alludes to the fact, it must have been of interest to him, with his own experience of Canada, that old Hugh had spent much of his earlier life there.

Other new names appear in the diaries during 1830–31. A 'Tenison' is mentioned, probably the Thomas who seems to have been a resident since 1829 and who later got into trouble with the authorities for acting as second in a duel. On 8 April 1831 John went to a party at which both the fashionable physician Dr Bankhead and 'the Hon. Col. De Courcy' were fellow-guests. Bankhead he had met years before, but although he had known members of the De Courcy family in his earlier years in Ireland, it is not clear that he had previously made the acquaintance of Colonel Gerald de Courcy (a son of the Earl of Kinsale). The colonel and his family had been in Florence for some years. His eldest daughter, Geraldine, had been one of the young people who participated in Lord Normanby's entertainments in the 1820s, and in 1830, she was married to another member of the same set, Captain William Perry. John would often mention the family in the future.

Of the cosmopolitan notables who had played a conspicuous part in Florentine life, Prince Borghese was to die in 1832, but an important role was still played by Anatole Demidoff, younger son of the late Nicolai. Equally prominent were the Poniatowski, the children of a nephew of the last king of Poland, who had settled in Florence after living in Rome. Prince Joseph possessed a genuine musical talent, both as performer and composer, and displayed it at numerous amateur and semiprofessional appearances in Florence and elsewhere, in which his elder brother, Charles, and Charles's wife, Elisa, also participated. By early 1831 John Maquay was sufficiently well acquainted with 'Poniatowski' to send one of his own horses to him to try; both brothers were enthusiasts for horseflesh.[13] His progress towards establishing a Florentine household and social circle was then interrupted by the need to attend to the settlement of his uncle's estate in Ireland. He and Elena, with his mother and aunt, left Florence in April 1831, not to return until the autumn of 1832. Only then can his permanent residence in Florence be said to begin.

Meanwhile Seymour was learning. At first inclined to believe that Tuscany had little reason to fear a handful of foreign agitators, given that the Tuscans were generally contented with their government, he came to realize that the capacity of the Tuscan government to be alarmed was not necessarily proportionate to the actual dangers it faced, and that it might feel under pressure from on high to be alarmed. In February 1831, during a conversation on the subject of the temporary success of insurrection in Modena, Count Fossombroni acknowledged that the British thought Austrian intervention undesirable, but asked, 'what I should say of that man's prudence, who should decline assisting to extinguish a fire in an adjoining house for fear of giving offence to some person who lived at the end of the Street'.[14] It was anyway the Austrian doctrine that their intervention in Italy was not 'foreign'; they were re-establishing order in their legitimate sphere of influence.

For the time being Tuscan attention was focussed more on French troublemakers than on the British, but in March 1831, Seymour had an expulsion to deal with. A Mr Hubbard was said to have thus described the French attitude to monarchy: 'if the King behaved well he was allowed to reign – if not he was dethroned'. On learning of these words (spoken at a private party), the Austrian ambassador immediately applied to the Tuscan government for Hubbard's expulsion. Seymour was able to do nothing to reverse the sentence, but his attempted intervention offended the Austrians. Fossombroni could only allow Hubbard longer to get out of the country and promise 'to facilitate his return' as soon as tempers and suspicions were somewhat soothed.[15]

A year later Seymour found Fossombroni in a state of high alarm at the news that the French were to garrison Ancona, which he thought would inevitably lead to armed confrontation with Austria. To Seymour 'the further decline of Italian independency' as Austria reacted to unrest was one of the 'evil consequences' of recent agitation. On this view, Tuscany was being driven semi-reluctantly into an increased reliance on Austrian 'support'. The practical consequences were likely to include 'a distrust of Strangers and increased rigour of Police Regulation of which some of Her Majesty's Subjects, or rather Persons under British Protection, have had reason to complain'.[16] The reference was to Ionian students, entitled to British diplomatic support because of the British protectorate over the Ionian Islands, who were regarded as suspect by the Tuscan government. Fossombroni besought Seymour to consider

that there are some thousand English Subjects in Tuscany, that they give the Government no cause of uneasiness and they are in consequence treated as well as ourselves – but that with the Greeks it is quite a different thing, there are among them many persons embued [sic] with the wildest principles of liberty and such we cannot consistently with our own safety tolerate amongst us.

Seymour acknowledged that after this conversation, Fossombroni had been accommodating as far as the Ionians were concerned, but there was a hint of a darkening of the atmosphere.

Within a few weeks Seymour himself was *en route* to Rome, where he remained until September. Back in Florence in early October, he had an interesting conversation with the Grand Duke, lately returned from a royal progress through his dominions and so gratified by the enthusiastic reception he had met with as to be for the moment in love with popular acclaim. This popularity had been earned partly by recent measures he had taken to stem arbitrary arrests and imprisonments, and he was critical of the Pope's 'obstinacy in refusing to adopt a system of Government more suitable to the Age and to the wants of His Subjects'. His Ministers were quite alarmed by all this, but Seymour sardonically observed that there was little reason to think 'that His Imperial Highness entertains any intention of relinquishing any portion of his Authority' and no truth in rumours that Leopold intended to grant a constitution to Tuscany.[17]

So things stood on the public front when John Maquay and Elena returned to Florence in November 1832. There were straws in the wind, but as yet no real reason to fear that life would become difficult for British subjects in Tuscany. John and Elena could once more pick up the threads and hope to establish themselves at the centre of a stable social circle. In these early years Elena's musical talent exerted an important influence on the formation and character of that circle. Friendship with the De Courcys owed much to these shared enthusiasms. On 8 January 1833 'Lady L. Stephenson brought Miss De Courcy to see Elena as they are to sing together in a chorus of Don Giovanni'.[18] Miss De Courcy's visits to the Maquays became frequent, and soon they were calling on Mrs De Courcy; perhaps for reasons of health, she seems to have been more called upon than calling. In March the colonel arrived, presumably from England or Ireland, and it did not take long for him to join in. His only son, Captain John de Courcy, appeared in Florence occasionally.

Lady Lucy Stephenson was the third daughter of the Earl of Limerick, and she and her family also became important members of the Maquay circle. In 1834 her husband Rowland (or as Italian sources called him, Orlando) changed his name (and hers) to Standish.[19] His connection with Florence went back some years. In 1828, he commenced the building of a *palazzo*, designed by himself, in Via S. Leopoldo (now Via Cavour), which was described in 1842 as possessing a fine theatre and a huge and beautiful garden.[20] His musical and theatrical activities involved him with the Poniatowski siblings and other distinguished amateurs. Both Maquays became fond of Lady Lucy and her children, especially their daughter Caroline, who was familiarly known as 'Pussy'. When Standish died suddenly in 1843, Elena was assiduous in her attendance on the distraught Lady Lucy and John visited the family in England long after Lady Lucy died there in 1845.

Another new acquaintance that owed something to shared musical interests was with the Andersons. John first mentions the impressively named Warren Hastings Anderson (Warren Hastings was his godfather) among the guests at a 'man party' he attended on 8 December 1832 (Seymour Kirkup was another). A native of East Lothian, Anderson had been travelling with his wife, born Mary Dewar, for several years before coming to rest in Florence; their presence was noted in Naples in 1829 (where Mrs Anderson gave birth to twins) and in Rome in 1831. A daughter was born to them in Florence in April 1832 and given the names Florence Mary Margaretta. They were far from alone in calling a child Florence (not yet the exclusively feminine name that it has become) in recognition of the city of its birth, but the 'Mary Margaretta' indicates their close relationship to another Florentine resident, who, by marked contrast with themselves, lived a retired life. Mary Margaretta, Lady Don, was the illegitimate daughter of a Scottish peer, Patrick Murray, fifth Baron Elibank, and the widow of Sir George Don, governor of Gibraltar from 1814 until his death in 1831. Lady Don's will, made in Florence in February 1842 and amplified by no fewer than ten codicils, reveals her attachment to Anderson, who was her executor and residuary legatee, and his children. Whether out of disposition, health or simply age (she was 90 when she died in January 1855), she seems to have played no part in Florentine society, although she was sufficiently concerned about the welfare of the expatriate English poor to leave a useful sum of money for their benefit.[21]

As the Maquays reacclimatized, Seymour continued to monitor subtle alterations in the Tuscan atmosphere. In March 1833 he registered a sense that the Grand Duke 'no longer reigns as hitherto in the affections of his subjects'. There was economic distress and it was believed that Leopold wished to restore the Jesuits and to establish a firmer clerical control of education. On several recent occasions, the government had demonstrated its fear of liberal opinions and those who held them. Some indication that this timidity was producing effects inconvenient to British travellers emerged some months later, when Falconar complained to Seymour that he was having difficulty obtaining passports from the Leghorn authorities unless he gave 'a kind of security for the good conduct of the person for whom the passport is required'.[22] Falconar objected that this was unreasonable if the individual in question was totally unknown to him; Fossombroni assured Seymour that it was a mere empty formality, and Seymour advised the consul to comply with it until he could persuade the Tuscan government to drop it.[23] The novelty was not the severity of the present discontent, but the fact that it existed at all, and Seymour feared the consequences of Fossombroni's declining influence. Minor incidents, including arrests, later in the year were calculated to deepen British suspicions of the trend of Tuscan policy.[24]

In June 1833 Seymour reported to Palmerston on the arrest of Francesco Guardabassi, the acknowledged leader of liberal opinion at Perugia and as such *persona non grata* to the papal authorities.[25] Guardabassi had English friends, notably John Craufurd, who had divided his time in the 1820s between Rome,

Florence and Corfu, where he became treasurer-general of the Ionian Islands; he had patronized Joseph Severn and was known to Charles Brown.[26] Two of his children, Robert and Georgiana, had been born in Florence, in 1824 and 1829 respectively; Georgiana would become the wife of Aurelio Saffi, one of Mazzini's chief lieutenants and a Roman triumvir in 1849.[27] During a visit Craufurd paid to Guardabassi while on his way to Corfu in 1833, one of the Craufurd children fell ill and was left in Guardabassi's care. When it was recovered he took it to Ancona; no sooner had he made arrangements with the British consul for its despatch to Corfu than he was arrested by the papal authorities. Guardabassi was eventually released thanks, at least in part, to British intercession.[28]

In the latter half of 1833 the Maquay circle received several additions. The decision John and Elizabeth Fombelle now made to settle permanently in Florence was surely influenced by information received from the Maquays, but we have no details except that on 3 March John wrote 'a long letter to Fombelle' and on 13 August was looking for a house for them. The couple arrived on 15 September and briefly stayed with the Maquays while house-hunting continued; they were driven on the Cascine and introduced to the English Church, the Pophams and Angelica Catalani. On 1 October they went into temporary lodgings in Via della Scala until they could move into their own house, which John called Casa Gherardesca (not to be confused with the Villa Gherardesca at Fiesole, long occupied by Landor). Another new arrival at much the same time was William Moffat, who brought with him his second wife and several daughters. He was the only son of a London banker and MP who died in 1822 and left him a wealthy man; Turner painted two views from his riverside house at Mortlake in 1826–7.[29] The Moffats were invited to a party John gave on 7 January 1834 and featured frequently in the diary until they left the city in 1841; like Fombelle, Moffat became part of the little group which managed the English Church.

A much more fashionable new acquaintance was the Duc de Dino, whom John first mentions among the guests at a party he gave on 22 November 1833. This was Edmond de Talleyrand-Périgord, the nephew of the celebrated Talleyrand. He had effectively been packed off to Florence, where he made himself comfortably at home. His gambling habits, which had contributed to his estrangement from his wife, Dorothea de Courland, would certainly not have made him unduly conspicuous there, and, if Dorothea's biographer is to be believed, even gambling was believed to be cheaper at Florence.[30] He became a reasonably frequent presence in John's diaries, both as Duc de Dino and (after 1838) as Duc de Talleyrand.

In October 1833 Elizabeth Maquay returned to Florence from Rome. She was struck by the style in which her son was living: 'quite a palace every Luxury & elegance to be seen there'.[31] As for the Fombelles, whom she found installed in Florence, there were beautiful grounds attached to their house. On 19 April 1834 Elizabeth recorded that she spent the evening there, 'Concert Ball & Supper every thing in best Style beautiful Supper &c blaze of light every where'.[32] She was told what all this cost them. On a flyleaf of one volume of her diary, she recorded that

'Fombelles expences last year were £700 including every Thing & including both their Dress – House rent & Carriage.' The carriage-horses and coachman cost them 27 *francesconi* a month, and they had given ten dinner parties and a ball; their house rent was £72 for the year and the carriage (in which they often took Elizabeth to church) cost the same. It is not clear exactly to which year these figures refer, but it may have been 1836. John, musing on his finances in the summer of 1837, remarked 'I mean to try for a year on the principle of spending £700 pr Ann exclusive of house rent but am doubtful whether I shall succeed in my plan at Florence.'[33]

On 11 August 1834, the best part of two years after he and Elena settled in Florence, John confided to his diary his plan of building a house of his own.[34] There had been no previous hint that he was not going to be contented with the renting and frequent house moves common among his compatriots. As it happened, the new house was as much of an investment as it was a permanent home, and he frequently rented it out in whole or in part. He soon made a start, and on Elena's 28th birthday (28 September 1834), he was able to inspect the progress that was being made. For some weeks he was going to the building site almost every day, but news of his brother's death in Cheltenham, which reached him on 30 October, compelled him to go to England. When he returned in mid-February, he went promptly to see how the building was progressing.

In early December 1834 Seymour felt able to inform the Duke of Wellington, now for a short time Foreign Secretary, 'that at no period of my residence here has Central Italy enjoyed a state of such complete tranquillity as during the last three or four months'. He immediately entered a *caveat* to the effect that this tranquillity was 'held upon the most insecure tenure'. The weak point was the complete alienation of the subjects of the pope's temporal government.[35] In this diagnosis Seymour was prophetic if by no means unique. Of Tuscany he had at this moment nothing specific to say, but the expulsion of more Ionian students early in 1835 seemed to him another example of the government's tendency to overreact to trivial alarms. He told Wellington that police activity appeared to have increased in inverse proportion to 'the restored tranquillity of the Country'. He himself was probably more concerned by the potential effects of a severe winter drought on the economy of an almost totally agricultural country, thinking it likely to produce unrest.[36]

That the Tuscan government remained amicably disposed to the British was indicated by their handling of a regrettable affair, which Seymour reported to the Foreign Secretary on 1 October 1834. The enduring attachment of gentlemen to their 'honour' periodically caused trouble for their diplomatic representatives in Tuscany, where duelling was regarded as a serious public-order offence. On this occasion, a Mr Rigbye had fallen out with the German Prince de Reuss Köstritz at Bagni di Lucca, ever fertile soil for such disputes. Their initial plans for a meeting were frustrated by the police, and they removed themselves across the Tuscan border to a location near Barga, where the duel took place. Thomas Tenison acted as second to Rigbye, who was slightly wounded. The deliberate relocation of the affair on to Tuscan territory was regarded as aggravating the offence, and Prince Corsini regretfully informed Seymour that the two Britons involved would have to leave the country. In order to communicate this decision 'in the least offensive manner', the Grand Duke wished Seymour himself to notify it to the parties concerned and also to indicate that Rigbye would be able to return after 2 months and Tenison after one.

Tenison was back in Florence by 22 November, when he took out a 3-month subscription to Vieusseux, and Baldwin Rigbye was able to take part in an amateur play performed on New Year's Day 1835.[37] The Prince de Reuss meanwhile, hearing what had happened, delayed his own return to Florence, but not for long. On 5 November Seymour notified the Foreign Secretary that the marriage had that day been celebrated at the Mission of Henry, 69th Prince de Reuss Köstritz, to Matilda Harriet Elizabeth Locke, the daughter of General John Locke. (It is unknown whether she had anything to do with the quarrel between her prospective bridegroom and Mr Rigbye.) Almost no sooner had this marriage taken place than Seymour found himself marginally concerned with the latest episode of an ongoing saga involving the Reverend Thomas Harvey, the minister of the British church at Leghorn, who had been at Bagni during the summer. His enemies, who pursued him unwearyingly, put it about that he had been involved in the recent affair to the extent of actually being present at the duel. The Bishop of London was fed this story and asked Palmerston if he could discover the truth. Seymour, who was sympathetic to Harvey, sent to the Foreign Office copies of testimonials which the clergyman had obtained from the Duke of Lucca, Rigbye, Tenison and Mr John Brock Wood, all exculpating him.[38] The Duke of Lucca himself had caused a mild sensation 2 years earlier, when his (temporary) conversion to Protestantism had been widely reported.[39]

Few incidents during Seymour's term of office can have been more widely noticed than the death of one private individual. The inscription on his monument in the Leghorn cemetery tells the story:

> Sacred to the Memory of Lieutenant Colonel the Honourable James Forbes of HBM Coldstream Regiment of Guards (eldest son of General Lord Forbes of Scotland) who in the prime of life, and at a moment of participation in the splendour and festivities of a ball in the Pitti Palace at Florence on the 25th of February 1835 was suddenly removed from this world by an attack of apoplexy in the 38th year of his age thus affording an awfully striking instance of the instability of human enjoyment and of the uncertainty of human life.

The Reverend Hutton elaborated his register entry: 'dropped down dead whilst waltzing at a Ball at Court on the evening of 25h Feby 1835. Awful proof of the truth "In the midst of life we are in death."' Isabella Wilmer was present at the ball, and confirmed that the dance which saw Colonel Forbes's end was a waltz. Everyone thought he had had a fit: 'Mr Harding came to his assistance, but alas it was of no avail, he died five minutes after he left the room. I never felt so shocked at anything in my life. I was delighted to get home.' John Maquay noted that he himself had left the ball shortly before; his mother baldly recorded 'Mr Forbes dropped down dead dancing at Palace'.[40] The Waterloo veteran was taken to Leghorn to join his mother in the cemetery, and his death was reported in the *Morning Post*, the *Hampshire Advertiser* and the *Aberdeen Journal* among other papers.

It was only a few days later that John Maquay learned of a distressing occurrence in the De Courcy family. On 3 March 1835 De Courcy came to John 'much affected' by a letter from Perry 'about his daughter's run-in with Capt Murray'. This reference to the colonel's eldest daughter, Geraldine, heralded Perry's action against Murray (eventually brought in June 1837) for damages in respect of the latter's seduction of his wife. The case was followed in Tuscany, for John's friend Horne came in on 7 July, presumably just having obtained the newspapers, 'to shew Perry's trial'. The following day De Courcy himself sought John's help in composing a letter to Captain Murray's father.[41] There followed a petition for divorce, which was heard by the House of Lords in March 1838.[42]

The papers reported how Perry had met Miss De Courcy, 'a young lady who had been educated abroad, was highly accomplished, and possessed very great personal attractions'. She had taken part 'in the fashionable amusements going on' in Florence, in which Perry also participated. The resulting intimacy had led to their marriage. As far as Perry's lawyers were concerned, no more apparently needed to be said, but Captain Murray's attorney thought he saw an opportunity to exonerate his client. Perry was to blame for ignoring the obvious implications of his wife's upbringing. He should have made it his duty 'to protect her from temptation, or from the arts of the dissolute', for

> she had been educated in a foreign land, had associated almost entirely with foreigners, acquiring habits which happily as yet were in some degree alien to our country, and was just the sort of person who would require the most watchful conduct of the husband to prevent her falling into the dreadful calamity which had visited her.

Nearly 20 years earlier the Reverend Cunningham had foretold the dire consequences if young Englishwomen were not educated in that respect for domestic values, which was essential to the nation's happiness. For Geraldine de Courcy the consequences were indeed unhappy. On 25 August 1843 John Maquay recorded that 'De Courcy came to me in the evening to consult me about his daughter Mme P who is now reduced to nearly the last stage of degradation & prostitution at Naples'.[43] This was not the last occasion on which a marriage contracted in Tuscany fell apart back home, some at least of the blame being placed on the evil effects of the Italian environment on a young Englishwoman.[44]

In the spring of 1835 Seymour had to deal with the fall-out from another affair of honour. This took place in the Kingdom of Naples and involved one of his own *attachés*, Ferdinand St John, with results that were unfortunately fatal for St John's adversary and inconvenient for himself, inasmuch as he was imprisoned at Rome, with doubtful legal justification. Captain Aubin testified to St John's 'honourable and becoming conduct' throughout, but more significant was Seymour's description of him as 'still nominally an attache to this Mission', although he had been absent from it 'for over eighteen months'. This last phrase was probably underlined in the Foreign Office.[45] The details of St John's employment at Florence, if such it can be called, shed light on contemporary ways of doing the nation's diplomatic business.

St John was unreliable at best. Well-known on the racecourse and on horseback in Florence, he was also known never to have a penny to his name. In July 1837, 2 years after Seymour said he had been absent from the Legation for over 18 months, Abercrombie told the Foreign Office that he had still not been seen. Another 2 years after that, St John himself wrote to the Foreign Office asking to be reattached to the mission: 'having paid my debts in Florence I wish to join Mrs St John there immediately'. A memorandum produced in response to this request on 10 October 1839 stated that he had taken leave from the Legation in October 1833, 'since which time he has not returned to his post.' Two days later, Palmerston added a note 'that after an absence of 6 years he cannot again be attached to Florence, but I will consider him as Candidate for Employment Elsewhere'.[46] It is hard to know which is more surprising from a twenty-first-century perspective: that an absence of 6 years should go virtually unremarked or that the individual concerned should be considered for further employment. Diplomatic business was indeed conducted in a relaxed fashion. In May 1835 Seymour sought permission to spend a couple of months at Leghorn for the sake of his wife's health, remarking that 'the business of the Mission can during the summer be conducted as well at Leghorn as at Florence', which would soon be deserted by both the court and the *corps diplomatique*.[47]

Falconar's problems with passports grumbled on, but, more seriously, as the summer advanced, so did a major outbreak of cholera. Meanwhile John Maquay's new house progressed. On 14 April he had concluded the purchase 'of a house next to my new one in Via Maglio', the first time he betrays its whereabouts. After another trip to England he found the house 'much advanced' in October, but it was another year before it was ready to fulfil one of its most important functions, as a showcase for John's hospitality. He doubtless hoped that its scale and fittings would enable him to hold his own alongside the Macdonells, the Andersons, the Fombelles and others who were capable of making an impressive display. In December 1835, just before he received his recall and appointment to Brussels, Seymour was able to report an item of news which, as he observed, was of some importance to British residents. The Grand Duke proposed to make it possible for any foreigner not only freely to purchase property in Tuscany but to bequeath it by will, a privilege which, Seymour noted, was not available in the duchy of Lucca.[48]

Seymour seems to have made himself popular with the Anglo-Florentines. John Maquay was now a prominent member of that society, and his diary records a succession of meetings at which thanks were voted to the imminently departing Minister. On 3 December Fombelle gave a handsome dinner for Seymour, and on the 4th another meeting took place at Johnston's Bank, where a motion was proposed by Sir Bourchier Palk Wrey, seconded by Frederick Thellusson, to open a subscription to present Seymour with 'a specimen of the Florentine Belle Arti', in the form of a bust of Mrs Seymour. Seymour was praised for

> the manner in which you have promoted our advantage, your own credit, and the honour of your country. Particularly would we record our high appreciation of your punctuality in official duties, and the willing, energetic, and inflexible exertion of your powers in all emergencies.

Not all Florentine ministers would receive (or deserve) such applause.[49] Yet all was not harmony even among Seymour's admirers. On 9 December John Maquay recorded 'meeting about Seymour much difference of opinion adjourned', and 2 days later, there was 'meeting again, near unanimous quarrel Horne & Sanford'.[50] Presumably we are to understand by this shorthand that it was Horne and Sanford who quarrelled. They were two very contrasting characters, one of whom was intimate with John, while the other was no more than an acquaintance. They illustrate different ways of acquiring the wherewithal to lead a comfortable expatriate existence.

Mr Sanford, the second son of John Sanford of Nynehead in Somerset and an aristocratic mother, was, unsurprisingly, the vicar of Nynehead; it is more surprising that his wife had previously been married to the Irish peer Lord Cloncurry, who divorced her by Act of Parliament in 1811. Sanford thus became associated with her daughter by Cloncurry, Mary Margaret Lawless, who in her turn was divorced from her first husband and in 1828 married to Lord Sussex Lennox, son of the Duke of Richmond, to whom she bore three sons and a daughter. This marriage proved to be less than a model of happiness or propriety, and *The Satirist*, a London scandal-sheet which delighted in pursuing the allegedly dissolute British abroad, remarked on 19 December 1841 that Sanford 'ought to be, and no doubt is, ashamed of his connexion with the SUSSEX LENNOX "lot"'.[51] Mary Shelley knew the family, but while visiting Florence in 1842, she wrote wryly to her half-sister Claire Clairmont, who had been governess to the Sanfords' daughter, that she did not see much of them, 'for rich & poor don't get on well together'. In addition, 'Their English set is by no means good'.[52]

Sanford looks like the classic clerical absentee. He was subscribing to Vieusseux already in 1829–30 and early in 1832 sought to compensate for failing to serve the parishioners of Nynehead by offering to serve the English Church in Florence if he should be needed during his residence there.[53] His chief distinction was as a collector of Italian art, some of which went to adorn his Somerset church when he eventually returned home.[54] Edward Horne by contrast was the youngest son of a Quaker coal merchant from Southwark, who had left his sons well provided for.

He subscribed to Vieusseux for substantial periods in 1820, the first year of the reading room's existence, and on 18 October 1831 took out a year's subscription, which suggests that by now, if not before, he was a resident.

John may have first got to know him during that year, if he was the Horne who joined a party to Pratolino in April, but until about the middle of 1833, he continues to refer to him as 'Mr Horne'; thereafter, he was gradually transformed into the more familiar 'Horne'. Their intimacy is suggested by the fact that when the Maquays' third son, Tommy, was baptised on 14 February 1839, Horne spent the evening with them as one of a small select party. Horne collected pictures, but rather more modestly than Sanford; he had three to leave when he died in 1851, including a Pierino del Vaga. His will showed that he still possessed the property at Star Corner, Bermondsey, that his father had left him; certain annuities intended for his Italian servants were charged upon that property.[55] John received a bequest and arranged for Horne's burial close to the tomb of his own mother in the English Cemetery.

In February 1836 Seymour addressed a valedictory assessment of the state of Tuscany to the Foreign Secretary. He hoped that he was justified in supposing that the present tranquillity of the country rested on a surer foundation than it did in the Roman dominions. He believed that the Grand Duke's conduct during the recent cholera outbreak had earned him genuine popularity and even found some grounds for optimism in Tuscany's economic prospects, mentioning in particular the benefits that might be gained from the proposed railroad between Florence and Leghorn. There were shadows over the picture, however. Seymour gave Leopold credit for good intentions, 'very correct and upright feelings' and 'a clear and practical understanding'; but he was surrounded by mediocrities who ranged from the timorous to the outright reactionary, while Fossombroni was approaching the end of his active career.

Seymour's successor, Ralph Abercrombie (or Abercromby), was the only son of Sir James Abercrombie, recently elected speaker of the House of Commons. On 14 April 1836 the Morning Post reported that he had established himself 'at the beautiful Villa Corsi', and also that he would return to London in the summer for a 'matrimonial engagement'. Introduced to him on 6 April, Elizabeth Maquay 'was much [taken] with him none of the offensive affectation of Diplomacy'.[56] However, the new Minister seems to have been a trifle accident-prone, at least in his dealings with women rather younger than Elizabeth Maquay. No sooner had he arrived in Florence than his peace was rudely disturbed by the arrival of a Mrs Mary Wyatt, who, one guesses, was aware of his impending 'matrimonial engagement' and less than pleased about it.

The first inkling the Foreign Secretary had that his newly appointed Minister in Tuscany was being pursued by this avenging fury came from the lady herself, who in July 1836 demanded an interview with him. She had gone to Florence 'to get back Property of considerable Value belonging to me in the possession of Mr R. Abercrombie paid £120 Money lent to him in 1831', but the Tuscan authorities had been set upon her. She did not mince her words, complaining of 'so great a

Violation of the rights of a British Subject as was perhaps ever perpetrated'. She was, she said, dragged forcibly to her carriage at 2 o'clock in the morning, with a broken arm, and removed under escort from the Tuscan states, with no charge against her and no chance to appeal. The governor of Leghorn begged she would not blame his government, for it was all the doing of the British Minister.[57]

Palmerston avoided meeting Mrs Wyatt face-to-face, demanding a full written statement of her grievances, which she never supplied. Two months later, Abercrombie gave his own account of the episode.[58] Mrs Wyatt had arrived in March 'for the purpose as she openly avowed, of insulting me, thereby creating a disturbance which must have violated public decorum'. At his request, a friend had 'induced her to proceed to his house instead of forcing an entry into mine'. The friend told him that 'her sole intention in going to Florence was for the purpose of insulting and trampling upon you' and that she had 'used the most violent expressions of menace & revenge against you for having abandoned her society'. Abercrombie now applied to the Tuscan authorities, who expelled Mrs Wyatt only to be compelled to renew the sentence when she reappeared in July. On this second occasion, according to Abercrombie, she was permitted for a time to remain in her hotel in order to rest, but forbidden to leave it. However, she 'eluded the observation of the Police and proceeded to take possession of my house, from which she declared, that she would only be removed by force'.

The outcome must have been the violation of the rights of a British subject, of which Mrs Wyatt complained to Palmerston. Abercrombie enclosed a letter, dated 20 September, and intended in the first instance for submission to the Tuscan Minister, from the friend whose help he had invoked in March. This was none other than the Reverend John Sanford, no stranger to scandalous women. Sanford said that he had gone to see Mrs Wyatt at Prato in the hope of deterring her, and had received the impression that she had appeared in Tuscany in violation of an agreement made at Milan by which an annuity had been settled on her. He had himself reported her intentions to Count Fossombroni, who promptly ordered her to leave Tuscany. Now, in September, the undaunted Mrs Wyatt was proposing to come to Florence for a third time, and Abercrombie again sought the protection of the Tuscan government, who took the view that by persistent disobedience to their directives, she had anyway forfeited the protection of the British name.

Almost no sooner was Abercrombie relieved of the immediate threat of Mrs Wyatt than he quarrelled with Edgecumbe, his Secretary of Legation, and his wife. On arrival at Florence, he had asked Mrs Edgecumbe to present English ladies at the Tuscan court (by convention the job of the Minister's wife) and she had done so throughout the summer. Unfortunately, an angry exchange between Abercrombie and Edgecumbe, not fully explained in the despatch, caused her to speak so offensively to the Minister that he dispensed with her services and announced that he would for the time being undertake the presentations himself. Mrs Edgecumbe thereupon sought a personal interview with the Grand Duchess and Dowager Grand Duchess in order to inform them that Abercrombie had deprived her of her privilege. The change took effect on the occasion of a court ball on 16 November, and the dispute made sufficient impact to merit an entry in John Maquay's diary: 'great work between Abercrombie and Mrs Edgecumbe about Court presentations'. John himself went to the ball and reported that 'many ladies staid away as Mr Abercrombie was to present'. Abercrombie for his part took grave exception to Mrs Edgecumbe's initiative in seeking an interview with the royal ladies before he himself had been able to notify them of the change. He tried to use Prince Poniatowski as a mediator, but without result.[59]

The acrimonious exchange of notes between Abercrombie and the Edgecumbes is preserved in the Foreign Office correspondence, but the Minister's superiors were not best pleased with his conduct. The Foreign Secretary regretted that he 'should have thought it necessary to make the matter to which that Despatch relates the subject of official correspondence', criticized the tone of his letters and thought it unfortunate that he had not called upon an English resident if there was need of mediation. All parties were urged 'to consign to oblivion a mere quarrel of Society, in which very possibly all may in turn have been to blame' and to remember 'that the credit and character of His Majesty's Mission cannot fail to be affected by a recurrence of such Bickerings'. There is a magisterial 'P' at the bottom of the draft.[60] Clearly the sooner Abercrombie had a wife at his elbow to protect him (and to present ladies at court), the better.

The *Morning Post* continued to report the movements of the *ton* between England and Italy and between the Italian capitals. On 14 April 1836 it carried a typically effusive account of Mrs Hastings Anderson's *tableaux vivants*, mentioning among the many guests present Lady Popham, the Marchese Torrigiani, Colonel de Courcy and Mr Sanford. Many houses had been taken for the winter and a 'brilliant season' was anticipated, reviving the glories of former times. On 12 October, however, it was reported in the same newspaper that there were fewer English than expected, possibly because cholera had intervened during the summer. There were still names for the *Post* to report, including the persistent Sanfords and Henry Fox and his wife Lady Augusta, the daughter of the Earl of Coventry. The duc de Dino, too, was 'giving dinners and parties'.

By now John Maquay was ready to enter the fray, for the new house was ready. His mother noted that it had cost him £2,520 [113,400 *paoli*] to build.[61] On 14 October 1836 he gave his first dinner party and 'opened my drawing-room'; on the 28th he gave a large party, with music and dancing, which lasted until half-past one in the morning. The Poniatowski siblings provided the music together with Elena, Mrs Fombelle and others. The guest list gives a fair idea of the Maquays' social circle in its extended form. It included acquaintance both old and new, although some stalwarts, such as Lady Popham and the MacCarthys, were prevented from attending by the bad weather or some other cause; so too were the Horace Halls and Francis Sloane. Several Macdonells were present, as were the Duc de Dino and Mr Anderson, Tenison, Horne and the banker Plowden. The Fombelles and Kerriches were there and from the Legation Mr and Mrs Edgecumbe. Mr Moffat came with his wife, a daughter and a son, and the physician Dr Harding with his daughters. Regrettably among those present, although John can scarcely be blamed for this, were three of the conspirators who less than 4 years later would plot a massive fraud on the banks of Europe: the Marquis de Bourbel (together with the English wife he would later desert), William Cunninghame Graham and Allen Bogle. Among the Italians were Torrigiani, Lanzoni, Cerretani, Frescobaldi and Spinola. 'All parties seemed well pleased', John remarked complacently, 'and liked the new English house very much'.[62] The billiard-room certainly proved a magnet for males of all nationalities.

Of the ninety-three who attended this party, John calculated that sixty-five were English and twenty-eight 'foreign', while those who failed or were unable to come were almost equally divided, twenty to nineteen. Among these Lady Lee and her daughter, the Marchesa Guadagni, would presumably have been reckoned among the 'English', the Marchese among the Italians. To judge by the number of times John refers to the Lees they were never intimates, but they figure on his guest lists with moderate regularity and Sir Francis would be included if he happened to be in Florence. On John's return from England in July 1839, he brought some papers for Lady Lee and went with her, the Guadagni, De Courcy and the Fombelles to the Legation, 'where they were all legalised'.[63] While we do not have complete guest lists for all the parties John threw, there always seems to have been a strong Italian presence and later numerous Americans as well as other 'foreigners'.

The winter numbers that failed to materialize at Florence in 1836 evidently did so in 1838. On 12 November the *Morning Post* reported, 'This delightful city, the Athens of Italy, appears almost, by general assent, to have become the principal rendezvous of the nobility and gentry travelling this autumn in this country.' Never had there been so many prominent English families gathered there. The major hotels were full, 'yet private lodgings are not much dearer than ordinary. A single gentleman may obtain two very genteel rooms in a good part of the town for ten scudi (about 2l 5s) a month.' The weather was 'unusually fine and genial'. On 17 December the paper reported an estimated '17,000 strangers here on one day. Most of them have resided here a considerable time, and 2,800 have lately taken apartments for the winter'. Towards the end of the year, while the numbers at Florence remained considerable, the usual seasonal migration had taken place south to Rome, Naples and elsewhere. A year later, the picture was similar; on 3 December 1839, according to the *Post*, Florence was crowded with strangers, a hundred and ten new arrivals having been presented at the last court ball.

The majority of strangers came and went, but there was also a constant flow of recruits to the ranks of the residents. Arthur Vansittart was the son of an MP and cousin to a former chancellor of the exchequer, Nicholas Vansittart (ennobled as Lord Bexley). His ancestral lands were at Shottesbrook in Berkshire and he was clearly a rich man. Since his marriage in 1831 to Diana, one of the daughters of General Sir John Crosbie, he had spent most of his time abroad. He first settled in Florence in 1835, to judge by the fact that early in November he took out a 6-month subscription to Vieusseux, but he was not on the guest list for John's gala house-warming just under a year later. John first mentions him in April 1838, when Vansittart showed an interest in renting the house, but they could not agree on terms. A few days later John was trying to price a pair of horses for Vansittart and Poniatowski.[64] Vansittart periodically intervened in church affairs, and he and John socialized from time to time, but their worlds were differently focussed.

William Blundell Spence, artist, guide-book writer and still more art-dealer, settled in Florence at around the same time as Vansittart. Born in 1814 in Drypool, Hull, the son of another William Spence, a prosperous merchant and entomologist, he spent many of his formative years abroad with his parents, including a spell at the Istituto Bellini in Florence in 1829, where he met Austin Layard and Landor's son Arnold. This was followed by a period in Paris under the tutorship of Ingres; there seems to have been no parental opposition to his becoming a painter. As soon as he reached his majority he removed himself to Italy, married a Sienese, Alisia Teresa Renard, on 23 July 1835 and set up shop in Florence. He was to remain there for nearly 65 years, but is one of several well-attested long-term residents whom John Maquay never mentions.[65]

Spence's Italian marriage apparently never caused a problem for the authorities. In 1832 Lord Malmesbury encountered another such couple. The British husband was 'a Scotch banker of the name of Lawrie' who had married 'a most beautiful girl of poor parents in Florence, having taken her as a child and educated her for his wife'.[66] The banker was Walter Kennedy Lawrie, a native of Galloway, who was a much younger man than Malmesbury here makes him sound. His poor and beautiful wife was Clorinda Aretini, 'a very pleasant and ladylike person' according to his Lordship, and they had a single child, a boy who was given his father's names. Lawrie died in 1837, aged only 31. Malmesbury credited him with 'a very good gallery of pictures', and in his will, he authorized the sale of a supposed Raphael, as long as it was for 'more than thirty thousand scudi'. In fact it remained in his son's possession.[67] The younger Lawrie was clearly left a man of property, and he equally clearly grew up and died a Catholic, although his father received Protestant burial. Whatever his social circle was, it does not seem to have included the Maquays.

There were those who on settling in Tuscany left their past life behind them; others kept a sharp eye on their homeland and even expected to exert a continuing influence on its public affairs. On 7 September 1828 the *Morning Chronicle* reported that the Marquis of Normanby intended to reside at Florence for 2 years, returning to England occasionally during the sittings of parliament. On 6 April 1831 the *Morning Post* revealed that he had done just that, returning to lend his support to the Reform Bill. A correspondent of the *Chronicle* complained on 7 August 1833 that not everyone made the effort: it was 'an insult to common sense' that 'while leading a life of dissipation in Florence, Rome, or Naples' a peer should be able to vote by proxy on 'the decisions of the Legislature of this great nation'. The baronet Sir Bourchier Palk Wrey may have been living in Florence for 4 years or more when he learned, late in 1836, that his agent, James Whyte, had been canvassing for Sir Thomas Acland during the electoral campaign for the North Devon constituency. Wrey rebuked him for using his name, opining, from the Palazzo San Clemente, that while he felt the greatest respect for Acland, he deemed the policies of the Tories detrimental to the interests of the country.[68]

Property constituted another tie with the homeland. At this date John Maquay still owned the house in Fitzwilliam Street, Dublin, which he had inherited from his uncle, and was drawing rent from it; Mr Fombelle still owned his house in St Margaret's Terrace Cheltenham, and was presumably doing likewise. On 10 January 1839 John talked to his mother about 'Fombelle's Cheltenham house' and was soon discussing a possible bargain with Fombelle himself. A few days later he received the news of the death of his cousin and close friend John Adair, which had further financial implications for him, thanks to his investment in Adair's struggling Trinidad plantations. On a visit to Cheltenham in March, he looked over Fombelle's house and offered £1,500 for it and the furniture, which he later raised to £1,650; this was accepted and he took possession in early May. This did not, of course, mean that he was going to live there, either now or in the future. Before he departed for Trinidad early in September he had arranged for the sale of Fitzwilliam Street. When he later made up his accounts for the year, he noted that the Dublin house had netted him £150 over the fourteen and a half months that preceded the sale, and also that he had exceeded his intended expenditure for the year (£700) by just over £22.[69] Other British residents who were reliant on income from British properties and investments must have been engaged in similar transactions and calculations.

Abercrombie's dealings with Mrs Wyatt and Mrs Edgecumbe were probably more exciting than most of the public business he had to transact during his time in Tuscany. There were further problems with passports when Austria demanded a personal description of the traveller. Abercrombie's instant reaction was that until he received fresh instructions he could not impose this unprecedented formality on British travellers, and Palmerston predictably supported him.[70] He was in England for some time in 1838 and on 20 September was married to Lady Mary Elliot, the eldest daughter of Lord Minto. As the wedding approached, Mrs Wyatt renewed her importunities to the Foreign Office, where Fox-Strangways, once *attaché* at Florence, was now assisting Palmerston. On 2 August he told his chief, 'I should be sorry to write anything tending to irritate Mrs Wyatt at such an inauspicious moment.' Something (one suspects money) deflected the lady from her quest for vengeance, and after a final rather gnomic communication to Palmerston on 8 September, nothing more is heard of her.[71] Strangways had brought more than diplomatic experience back from Tuscany. On 23 May 1839 the *Morning Chronicle* reported that there were wild tulips from Florence in his gardens at Abbotsbury.

No sooner was Abercrombie married than he was appointed to serve at Frankfurt as Minister to the Germanic Confederation. Captain Aubin was briefly brought back from Rome to preside over the Legation, as Edgecumbe too had departed to become secretary at Hanover. At the very beginning of 1839, Henry

Fox, who had penned malicious sketches of various Anglo-Florentines in the 1820s, was appointed British Minister to the Court of Tuscany.

Notes

1   FO79/69 is totally dedicated to the exchanges between Burghersh and the FO. In fairness to Palmerston, there had been more than one passage of arms between Canning and Burghersh about expenses – for example FO79/41, Canning to Burghersh, 14 May 1824, 'I now tell you, in distinct terms, admitting of no exception, that no expense for couriers will henceforth be allowed to the mission at Florence. Your lordship will be good as to take the warning in this dispatch as peremptory & final.'

2   He was destined for a distinguished diplomatic career, with future postings in Brussels, Lisbon, St Petersburg and lastly Vienna at the end of the Crimean War. A reviewer in the *Morning Post* on 1 May 1857 thought he saw Seymour in the character of the diplomat Sir Horace Upton in Charles Lever's recently published novel *The Fortunes of Glencore* (written in Florence). Lever undoubtedly knew and admired Seymour from his time as physician to the legation at Brussels, but it seems likely that Sir Horace's exquisite hypochondria owes something to Sir Henry Bulwer, whom Lever knew at both Brussels and Florence.

3   JLM, E9 f. 175; EM, C2 f33v. Interestingly Elizabeth reported 'alarming accts [*sic*] from England on 18 November 1830'. There is no clue as to what these were about, but it may have been a reference to reformist agitation or the Swing disturbances.

4   JLM, E9 ff. 168v, 174v.

5   JLM, E9 f. 166.

6   *The Annual Biography and Obituary for the Year 1820*, p. 307: 'The whole property is left, for life, to Lady Popham, and at her death, to be equally divided among their children.' For Sir Home and the Popham family, see Frederick Popham, *A West Country Family: The Pophams from 1150* (Kemsing, 1976); Hugh Popham, *A Damned Cunning Fellow: The Eventful Life of Rear Admiral Sir Home Popham KCB, KCH, KM, FRS, 1762–1820* (Tywardreath, 1991).

7   They were married at His Majesty's mission in Naples in 1832, but we may infer that there was also a Catholic ceremony, for their children appear to have been baptised and brought up as Catholics. MacCarthy's name is very variously rendered, but it appears in this form on the title pages of his novels.

8   William Thomas (ed.), *The Journals of Thomas Babington Macaulay* (London, 2008), Vol. 1, p. 33.

9   John noted on 15 June 1838 that he had 'finished MacCarthy's novel' JLM, E10 f. 67v. Several newspapers, including the *Times* on 25 November 1840, quoted from the *Morning Herald* a notice which read in part 'The author's style is forcible, his dialogue dramatic, his descriptions are marked by great beauty, and the situations into which his actors are thrown are natural and striking. There are passages in his volumes that are not excelled in beauty or power by any romance writer of the day.' MacCarthy later published *Masaniello: An Historical Romance* (1842) and *The Free Lance* (1844), both in the customary three-volume format.

10 *Morning Post* 5 April 1822; *The Standard* 24 March 1837.

11 JLM, E9 f. 175.

12 Anne Macdonnell, *Reminiscences of a Diplomatic Life* (London, 1913), pp. 73–5; Frederic St John, *Reminiscences of a Retired Diplomat* (London, 1905), p. 7.

13 JLM, E9 f. 175.

14 Both these despatches, and several others for 1831, are to be found in FO171/2, a miniature series of volumes which temporarily coexists with FO79.

15 FO79/58, Seymour to FO, 15 March 1831. According to a letter printed in the *Times* on 18 January 1834, which clearly refers to this incident, Hubbard sought out the Duke of Lucca, who was a personal friend, but the latter sent him on his way.

16 FO79/63, Seymour to FO, 23 February 1832.

17 FO79/66, Seymour to FO, 7 October 1832.

18 JLM, E9 f. 221.

19 His father, Edward Stephenson, possessed seats at Farley Hill in Berkshire and Scaleby Castle in Cumberland. His mother was the granddaughter of a Ralph Standish, whose male descendants proved remarkably fragile; in 1807 her brother (and therefore Rowland's uncle), Thomas, took the name and arms of Standish. According to the *Satirist* (21 May 1843), the reason for Rowland's name-change was the desire to avoid confusion with a disgraced banker called Rowland Stephenson, who had fled to America.

20 Federigo Fantozzi, *Nuova Guida ovvero Descrizione Storico-Artistico-Critica della Città & Contorni di Firenze* (Florence, 1842), p. 467.

21 TNA, Prob 11/2211. Lady Don was one of Lord Elibank's children by Mary Mortlock of Guildford, but was given the names of his legitimate wife, who had died before any of these children were born. On Lady Don's fund, see chapter 11.

22 FO79/75, Seymour to FO, 25 May 1834.

23 FO79/76, Seymour to FO, 5 June 1834.

24 FO79/70, Seymour to FO, 7 March 1833; 79/71, 4 June 1833; *Morning Chronicle* 24 September 1833.

25 FO79/71, Seymour to FO, 8 June 1833.

26 Grant F. Scott, *Joseph Severn: Letters and Memoirs* (Aldershot, 2005), pp. 155, 251, 255. Brown too makes several references to Craufurd: Grant E. Scott and Sue Brown (eds), *New Letters from Charles Brown to Joseph Severn* (www.re.umd.edu/ editions/brownsevern) 6, 6–7 June 1823; 8, 5 November 1824; 10, 28 April 1825. On 5 November 1824 he says that Craufurd is 'as discontented with Florence as ever'.

27 For the family's relations with Mazzini, see the references in E. F. Richards (ed.), Mazzini's *Letters to an English Family*, (3 vols, London, 1920–22). The diplomat Henry Drummond Wolff, who was a kinsman, remembered 'seeing at their house in London … at different periods, Mazzini, Orsini, and once a Garibaldian soldier in a red shirt': *Rambling Recollections* (London, 1908), Vol. 1, p. 12,

28 Giovanni Pennacchi, *Cenni biografici di Francesco Guardabassi* (second edition, Perugia, 1876), pp. 15, 20–28. Guardabassi had once met Palmerston in London, and the latter now requested the devoutly Catholic Irish peer Lord Clifford to monitor the proceedings against him and to let him have an early copy of the sentence. In 1830 Clifford's brother-in-law had become Cardinal Weld.

29 'The Seat of William Moffat Esq. at Mortlake Early Summer Morning' (1826) is in the Frick Collection, New York, and 'Mortlake Terrace' (1827) in the National Gallery of Art, Washington. Turner also made several sketches of the property.

30 Philip Ziegler, *The Duchess of Dino* (London, 1962), p. 184.

31 EM, C4 f.23.

32 EM, C4 f.39v. It was evidently some way from the centre of Florence: Isabella Wilmer said in June 1835 that it was 'most delightful … town and country combined.'

33 JLM, E10 f.45.

34 JLM, E9 f.256v.

35 FO79/77, Seymour to FO, 6 December 1834.

36 FO79/78, Seymour to FO, 15 January, 21 February 1835.

37 FO79/77, Seymour to FO, 1 October 1834.

38 FO79/77, Seymour to FO, 15 November 1834. The testimonials form only part of a sizeable dossier.

39 *Christian Remembrancer*, November 1833, p. 658.

40 Carmichael, Montgomery (ed.), *The Inscriptions in the Old British Cemetery of Leghorn, Transcribed by G. Milner-Gibson-Cullum and the Late F. Campbell Macauley* (Leghorn, 1906), p. 69; JLM, E9 f. 267v; EM, C4 f. 69v. For the Wilmer journals, see Introduction. The Florentine register for 1833–9 is in the LMA; it is most unusual for a cleric to make such a comment.

41 JLM, E10 ff. 35, 43.

42 Both sets of proceedings were reported in the *Times*, respectively on 27 June 1837 and 29 March 1838.

43 JLM, E10 f. 203.

44 Captain, later Admiral, Henry Codrington, was married in Florence on 6 April 1849 to Helen Smith, the only child of the long-serving Secretary of the English Church, Christopher Webb Smith, 'a gentleman of great respectability'. The marriage ended in the recently instituted Divorce Court in 1864, as reported at length in the *Times*, 30 July. Mrs Codrington had developed improper attachments, principally to a Colonel Anderson – the eldest son of an old Florentine habitué, Warren Hastings Anderson. It is not impossible that he and Helen Smith first met each other as young things in Florence in the 1840s. The Queen's Advocate remarked, 'Miss Smith had been brought up in Italy, and her manners were not formed in the school of English society; she was more lively, or, perhaps, more what might be called frivolous than most English women.'

45 FO79/78, Seymour to FO, 30 April, 7 May 1835.

46 FO171/3, Abercrombie to FO, 3 January 1837; FO79/95, Palmerston to St John, 18 October 1839 (memo attached to letter).

47 FO79/78, Seymour to FO, 12 May 1835.

48 FO79/79, Seymour to FO, 2 December 1835.

49 JLM, E9 f. 281; *Morning Post* 5 January 1836.

50 JLM, E9 f. 281v.

51 *The Satirist, or Censor of the Times* ran for 924 issues between 1831 and 1849, achieving at its height a circulation of 9000. Its editor, Barnard Gregory, was frequently sued for libel and served several prison terms.

52 Betty Bennett (ed.), *Letters of Mary Wollstonecraft Shelley* (Baltimore, 1989), Vol. 3, p. 49.

53 *Church Letters*, 1830s, 10, 15 January 1832.

54 Julian Orbach & Nicholas Pevsner, *the Buildings of England: Somerset South and West* (second edition, London, 2014), pp. 503–4. A Filippo Lippi portrait which once belonged to Sanford is now in the Metropolitan Museum of Art, and part of his collection went to Corsham Court, the Wiltshire seat of Lord Methuen, to whom Anne Horatia, the Sanfords' only child, was married in 1844: Jim Cheshire, *Stained Glass and the Victorian Gothic Revival* (Manchester, 2004), pp. 66–7. Sanford's sister was married to a Neapolitan aristocrat, Paolo Marulli d'Ascoli, who commissioned works from Canova and Thorvaldsen.

55 TNA, Prob11/2132.

56 EM, C5 f. 22v. Abercrombie did not in fact get married until 1838.

57 FO79/84, Mrs Wyatt to Palmerston, 23 July 1836.

58 FO79/83, Abercrombie to FO, 20 September 1836.

59 FO79/83, Abercrombie to FO, 17 November 1836; JLM, E10 f. 25v.

60 FO79/81, FO to Abercrombie, 6 December 1836.

61 EM, C5 f. 1v.

62 JLM, E10 ff. 23v, 24, 24v.

63 JLM, E10 f. 89.

64 JLM, E10 ff. 65, 65v. It is quite likely that John was being employed as an arbitrator in a deal between the two horse-fanciers.

65 John Fleming, 'Art Dealing in the Risorgimento II', *Burlington Magazine* Vol. 121, 1979, pp. 568–80;

66 Lord Malmesbury, *Memoirs of an Ex-Minister: An Autobiography* (London, 1885), p. 40.

67 TNA, Prob 11/1892.

68 *Trewman's Exeter Flying Post*, 2 February 1837.

69 JLM, E10 ff. 80, 80v, 83v, 85, 105.

70 FO171/3, Abercrombie to Palmerston, 20 April 1837.

71 FO79/92, Strangways to Palmerston, 2 August 1838, Mrs Wyatt to Lord Palmerston, 8 September 1838.

4 PUBLIC CALM AND PRIVATE TROUBLES, 1839–1846

Henry Fox, who became Lord Holland on the death of his father in October 1840, was ambassador in Tuscany for over 7 years. His personal talents scarcely rivalled those of Burghersh or Normanby, but Thomas Trollope believed that he was 'the right man in the right place'. Trollope recorded favourable opinions of his 'great *omnium gatherum* dinners and receptions – his hospitality was of the most catholic and generous sort'. His powers as an amusing conversationalist were even better displayed in frequent, more intimate gatherings, but some who came to the bigger parties resented not being invited to the smaller.[1] A different grievance, justified or not, was reported by the *Morning Post* on 30 October 1841: 'The English complain here that the hospitality of the Embassy is confined principally to foreigners.' Holland and his lively wife, Mary Augusta, who brought a touch of spice to the Legation, were responsible for supporting George Frederick Watts during his sojourn in Florence. They installed him at the Villa Medici at Careggi, which he decorated with frescoes. He also painted and drew Lady Holland (as well as other British members of their circle) several times. When Mary Boyle arrived in Florence with her mother and brother in 1847, they found Watts still at Careggi (which Holland, no longer Minister, had made over to them for the summer) and she recalled with amusement the difficulty they had in winning his confidence.[2]

Occasionally Holland's hospitality recalled the old days, notably the fancy-dress ball he gave in February 1840 to celebrate Queen Victoria's marriage. The Grand Duke and many of his family attended, as well as the Duke of Lucca. Leopold himself proposed the health of the royal couple and desired Holland to convey to Her Majesty not only his good wishes but 'the lively interest and affectionate regard he must ever feel for H.R.H Prince Albert', who had visited Florence the previous year.[3] Among the many British guests, as reported in the *Morning Post* on 28 February, was the 'authoress', more properly scientist and mathematician, Mary Somerville. She had recently arrived in Italy with her husband, the retired naval physician William Somerville. While in Florence she was permitted to borrow books from the Grand Duke's private library in the Pitti Palace, which inspired her to resume work on her *Physical Geography*. She was not particularly complimentary about her benefactor when she met him at an evening reception where she was 'bored to death'. He came up to her, 'said not a word, and after a time asked me some questions in French which I answered, then he looked down exactly like an old buffalo, stood still for a minute, and then walked away'.[4]

The environment enjoyed by the Anglo-Florentines remained calm, and no more than Abercrombie did Holland feel obliged to undertake political analyses of the kind Seymour had composed. It was a sign of the times that more occurred at Rome than in Tuscany to require the Minister's attention, and other Florentine residents had their eyes trained on events in the papal capital, notably the Craufurds, who a few years earlier had been involved with Francesco Guardabassi. They had made the acquaintance of Mazzini in England in 1838, just before they returned to Italy, and among their other liberal friends was the educationalist Enrico Mayer, a Tuscan subject of mixed national origins.[5] On 23 July 1840 John Craufurd wrote to his brother William in London, informing him that Mayer had been arrested at Rome and urging him to bring the matter to Palmerston's attention. His informant had told him that the only hope for Mayer was the 'decided and energetic' use of British influence. In the eyes of Rome, Mayer's dubious friends, together with his Protestantism, substantiated the accusations against him. In applying to the Foreign Secretary, William Craufurd recalled the case of 'that admired Man Mr Guardabassi' and the decisive and successful action Palmerston had then taken. On 7 September he was able to write to the Foreign Office conveying the welcome news of Mayer's release, with many expressions of gratitude for Palmerston's intervention.[6]

Early in 1840 Mayer had been in London, where he suggested to the Piedmontese political exile Antonio Gallenga that he should take employment in the Craufurd household in Florence, where he could live safely under their protection. Gallenga did so, assuming the name of Luigi Mariotti, and served the Craufurd children as a tutor. He thinly disguised the family as the 'Crawleys'. They inhabited 'a large, grim, fortress-like old palace on the Lung'Arno, on the left bank of the river'. Craufurd/ Crawley was 'a man of about sixty, of a very lofty and dignified appearance, and a quiet, unassuming demeanour'. Gallenga noted that in all the adult members of the family

> two distinct natures were blended. As English men and women they were proudly aristocratic, and ultra-Conservatives both in matters of Church and State. To the ignorant Italians who *milorded* and *miladied* them, they were always anxious to explain that they 'had no titles and would be sorry to have any' – that the members of the House of Lords were for the most part mere upstarts, and that the true nobility of England was the old landowners – the county families – before whose names men only placed the plain Mr and Mrs, by which they themselves, the Crawleys, preferred to be designated.

Eventually Gallenga became disillusioned with what he regarded as the dilettante society of aristocratic Italian liberals who frequented the house, and attached himself in preference to the circle of Gino Capponi, the *eminence grise* of the moderate constitutionalists. He was also offended by Mrs Craufurd's condescending attitude to him. He left a rather eccentric portrait of her in his admittedly unreliable memoirs (according to him, she converted to Judaism). It was allegedly a snub from her that determined him, against the advice of Mayer (now back in Tuscany) to leave the menage.[7]

At least as depicted here, the Craufurds represented an extreme among the Anglo-Florentines, inasmuch as they not only identified themselves with Italian patriotic politics but gathered around themselves an Italian rather than English society and spoke Italian for preference, thus making a deliberately nonconformist statement. John Maquay was absent from Florence for a substantial proportion of the time that they were resident there and would certainly have found them uncongenial. Mary Shelley, on the other hand, thought them 'very civil' and hoped that her son, Percy, would 'get on intimate terms there – where he could get singing and dancing quietly to prepare him for the balls'.[8]

It does not seem that the presence of these dubious radicals in Florence resulted in any trouble for Fox/Holland. Much of his time was in fact taken up by scandals of a nonpolitical nature generated by his fellow-countrymen. The case of Miss Julia Rice, which demanded his attention soon after he took office, well illustrates the sort of problem that involved the Minister's time and trouble and ended in the overruling of his judgment.

Miss Rice, born in London in October 1826, had been taken to Florence by an aunt after losing her mother at a very young age. Possibly around 1830, the aunt became the wife of a courier named Pasquale Cipriani and died some years later; she may well have been the 'poor Madame Cipriani' whom Elizabeth Maquay visited on 29 May 1838.[9] In the meantime Julia's father too had died back in England, and her brother George decided to take steps to repatriate her, professing great anxiety about her if she should remain in Florence under the care of his late aunt's husband.[10] Cipriani refused to yield Julia up unless compelled to do so, and early in 1839, Fox was instructed to take steps to obtain the assistance of the Tuscan authorities. In the course of the resulting correspondence, he expressed the opinion that Cipriani seemed to be genuinely fond of the girl and that he had spent sufficient on her upkeep and an excellent education to justify his claim for monetary compensation. George Rice doggedly refused to comply, out of either a genuine conviction that Cipriani deserved nothing or a disinclination or even inability to pay up.

While clearly believing that Rice was being unreasonable, Fox was obliged to seek Julia's repatriation and succeeded in obtaining the backing of the Tuscan government. In November 1839 Julia was consigned to the custody of Colonel and Mrs Alcock, who undertook to take her back to England, although this did not happen for some months.[11] Cipriani, backed by his government, continued to press unsuccessfully for compensation. The Foreign Office had been induced to believe that he had his eye on a bequest that was due to Julia when she came of age. Fox clung to his opinion that Cipriani deserved compensation, but Rice refused to accept his arbitration, hinting darkly that Mr Fox was unaware of the full circumstances. Was he afraid that his sister would convert to Catholicism, as her aunt may well have done? In 1845, while still a minor, Julia was married to a Post Office clerk, and died a childless widow in Sussex 60 years later. Who knows what recollections she preserved of her upbringing in Florence, or whether her lot would have been happier or unhappier had she remained there?

John Maquay had been absent from Florence for much of 1839. When he returned from Trinidad in March 1840, he found the English Church in turmoil, and shortly afterwards, a scandal erupted in which several of his acquaintances were deeply involved. On 12 May his mother was told about 'This diabolical swindling Society headed by Bourbel Graham and his son'.[12] This was a conspiracy, masterminded by the Marquis de Bourbel, which involved the production of forged letters of credit drawn on the London bank of Glyn, Halifax, Mills and Co. On 26 May the *Times* broke the story to English readers, quoting continental newspaper accounts and naming fourteen individuals who were said to be implicated. Bourbel was 'the chief of the gang', which included William Cunningham Graham, 'a resident of Florence, Italy, for some years', his son Alexander, who went under the name of Nicholson, and Allen Bogle, Graham's son-in-law (*recte* stepson). Bogle was 'chief of the firm of Bogle, Kerridge (*recte* Kerrich), and Co., bankers, of Florence'; his stepfather was described as a partner in the bank, an error later corrected. Of the other conspirators, the only one domiciled in Florence was Freppa, 'an Italian, who keeps a curiosity-shop'.

Back in England in the summer, Bogle sued the *Times* for libel, contending that he had been no more than an unwitting bystander or dupe. The case was eventually heard in August 1841 at the Surrey Assizes. Bogle won, but was awarded a derisory one farthing damages and refused his costs. The *Times*, which reported the court proceedings at considerable length, treated the verdict as a victory and published an account justifying its own conduct throughout. This is the principal source for the episode.[13]

Bogle and the elder Graham were active in the English Church. 'Of ancient family and good estate' in Perthshire, William Cunninghame Graham had been driven abroad by debt in 1828. He settled in Florence in 1832 or 1833 with his wife, two daughters and the son who would be involved in the conspiracy. Not long afterwards they were joined by Allen George Bogle, the son of Mrs Graham's first marriage, who after some time in the navy was now on half-pay. By the end of 1837 he had become a partner in the bank of Kerrich and MacCarthy. John Maquay invited both Bogle and Graham to a big party he held on 6 April 1840, shortly after his return from Trinidad, but neither came. On the 18th, 3 days before the intended launch of the conspiracy, Bogle gave a whist party which John attended. On the 27th he came with a number of others to play whist with John, by which time, although no one in Florence knew it, one of the conspirators (Perry *alias* Ireland) had been arrested at Ostend on a steamer bound for London and made a confession.

On 11 May, John learned of 'the extensive forgeries of Graham & Bourbel and their implied accusations against Bogle', although 'no one feels any suspicion against him'. He went to see 'poor Bogle' the following day. There is then a silence on the subject in his diary until on 21 September he was all morning at the bank with 'Mr Dobie Solicitor of the Times, Bogle affair'.[14] The *Times* meanwhile had been far from silent. On 26 May it had published the contents of the statement made by Perry/Ireland and of certain letters that had passed between the conspirators. These proved (certainly as far as the *Times* was concerned) not only Graham's complicity but also Bogle's. Two weeks after John Maquay had said that no one entertained any suspicions of him, he had been publicly named as a principal in the affair, identified as the unnamed 'banker of Florence' of the published correspondence.

Bourbel seems to have been an unpleasant and dangerous character, who had killed at least one man; 'a gambler, a duellist, and a *roué*', he was also by common consent accomplished in the arts and as a sportsman and linguist. Married to a wealthy Englishwoman (Constance Bulkeley), he had moved with her and their children to Florence during the early 1830s. According to the *Times*, 'he entered very generally into the dissipations and intrigues of Florence, and was universally looked on as a specious, agreeable, but thoroughly *mauvais sujet*'. This reputation he reinforced early in 1838 by leaving his pregnant wife for an opera-dancer. The injured Madame de Bourbel died in childbirth in the spring, and the Marquis found it advisable thereafter to live in a retired fashion at his villa near Leghorn. Here he was sometimes visited by Graham, who possessed a remarkable ability to produce copies of engravings and other works of art by mechanical means. Bogle's role was to obtain possession of a genuine letter of credit from the bank so that his stepfather could copy it and the bankers' signatures on it.

When the case came to court, Bogle's erstwhile partner, Thomas Kerrich, and Colonel Thomas Alcock, one of the bank's customers, appeared as witnesses. Their testimony gave local colour to the proceedings and some insight into the way banking business was done at Florence. It was explained that a Mr Robert Nicholson (it is unclear whether he was a party to the conspiracy) deposited his letter of credit at the bank for safe-keeping. Colonel Alcock thought this unusual and never did it himself. One day Bogle came to Kerrich to ask for the letter, as Nicholson wished to make a withdrawal. Kerrich appears to have thought nothing of this and Bogle returned the letter after a couple of hours; no one apparently noticed whether he left the bank with it in the meantime.

On 21 April, Kerrich was puzzled when Bourbel was closeted with Bogle for 2 hours in a locked room at the bank, but (here as elsewhere) he does not seem to have asked too many questions. When Bourbel left, another conspirator, called the Comte de Pindray, appeared and, producing a letter of credit for £2,000, demanded £200, which he received in gold. Thus emboldened, he made the mistake of trying to obtain more money from a shopkeeper called Philipson, who like many others 'discounted' bills, that is, paid an amount reduced by what we would term commission. Alerted by some sixth sense, Philipson refused to pay. On his way to return the letter of credit to De Pindray, he met Daniel MacCarthy in the street, and coincidentally Colonel Alcock too ran into them. What Philipson actually said is unknown, but MacCarthy scented something amiss and tried to make contact with Bogle. Failing to find him he left him a note, which Bogle said the following morning had quite spoiled his appetite.

As an accomplished conman, de Pindray evidently now calculated that his only course of action was to play the wounded man of honour and insist on repaying the money to the bank, where Kerrich found him the following morning in earnest confabulation with Bogle and MacCarthy. He asked the bankers to make enquiries of their 'correspondents' (i.e. Glyn & Co) and thus 're-assure yourselves on the matter', knowing that such enquiries would take weeks to complete. All was now quiet at Florence until 9 May, when Kerrich received a letter from Cologne, warning him that forged letters of Glyn & Co were in circulation. That same evening Henry Fox sent Kerrich a parcel of papers which had already been shown to the Tuscan government. They included the depositions of the conspirator Perry/Ireland, which named not only Graham and Bourbel but Bogle.

Kerrich was asked at the trial what Bogle's reaction had been to these incriminating passages. He replied, 'I do not recollect his precise words. He appeared greatly distressed; so much so that it was painful to witness.' Bogle seems not to have been made of the stuff that any right-thinking conspirator would desire in his colleagues, but simply collapsed, declaring that he was 'ruined'. By the following day he had taken to his bed, insisting that he must withdraw from the firm at once. Still, as John Maquay testified, no one suspected him of wrongdoing. Presumably it was thought, as he himself tried to maintain, that he was an innocent catspaw.

From now on he remained in a state of seclusion, only going out in a closed carriage to have dinner with his mother. Efforts to get him to show himself and assert his innocence were met with the reply, 'I cannot; I have no spirits.' On 22 May he received an order to leave Tuscany forthwith. Greatly distressed, he asked Kerrich to accompany him to see Fox and beg his intercession with the Tuscan government, but Fox refused. Sarcastically the *Times* asked whether it was to be believed that 'the mild Tuscan government' had suddenly become 'Tatarish, Turkish and despotical' or that Fox too had abandoned his inherited kindliness – or was there simply convincing evidence of Bogle's guilt?

On the very day that Bogle received his marching orders, Captain John Pakenham came to John Maquay with a pressing invitation to join him in founding a bank. John immediately informed MacCarthy. Both Pakenham and MacCarthy were sons-in-law to Lady Popham, and for reasons that he does not spell out, Maquay was anxious to consult her before he made a decision. Pakenham, however, demanded an answer, and on the 23rd John announced with characteristic portentousness that he

was therefore obliged unwillingly to say yes, as I could not let the opportunity slip, though I much wished a communication with Lady P., therefore the new house of Mackay and Pakenham commences from Thursday and I pray the assistance of the Almighty in enabling us to carry it on our principles consistent with his service and glory.[15]

On 28 May Bogle left Florence, and on the 29th or 30th Mrs Graham and her daughters received a government order to do likewise. Before leaving, they asked Kerrich to take custody of 'a great number of things' which had belonged to Graham, which were duly stowed away in a store room at the bank. It was not until some weeks later that Kerrich examined them more closely. They included the lathe which Graham had devised to enable him to execute the forgeries. By this time Bourbel, who had retired to his villa, had thought it best to leave Tuscany. According to Kerrich's own account, it was as a result of some curious conversations which he had with a Mr Roster that he belatedly remembered how Bogle months before had asked him for Mr Nicholson's circular letter. Roster (who subsequently took refuge in his status as a Tuscan subject and refused to answer questions) had seen it in Graham's possession and even helped him to copy the signatures on it.[16]

As the *Times* remarked on 19 August 1841: 'It is not to be supposed that in the neighbourhood of a gay and brilliant city, such as the capital of Tuscany, there are not at all times many persons resident of more than equivocal character.' This was a favourite theme of the muck-raking London weekly the *Satirist*, whose Florentine correspondent gave Holland some trouble during this very period. Although often crudely abusive, the *Satirist* professed a kind of moralistic agenda and regularly congratulated itself on exposing the unrighteous. One imagines a readership of middling folk who regarded themselves as patriotic and hard-working, and were both titillated and incensed by tilts at those who were richer, socially more eminent, politically more influential or all three. At best the latter revealed feet of clay, at worst betrayed their trust and harmed the innocent, while enjoying asylum in pleasant continental climes. On 1 December 1839, the paper informed 'A Creditor (Brighton)' that

> The last we heard of the ex-M.P. for Lewes, THOMAS READ KEMP, was, that he was doing the penance of economy at Florence. It is almost impossible for a man to have run himself so completely out at elbows as he has done. Whether he plays now or not, we are unable to say. It is well known he has played, and the fool, too, to 'pretty considerable' disadvantage.

Kemp, after whom part of Brighton is named, had in his time been an adherent and promoter of the rebel Anglican sect to which George Baring belonged, and was married to one of Baring's sisters, which in itself seems to have been enough to arouse the *Satirist*'s hostility. Its Florence correspondent made the Bourbel–Bogle affair the vehicle for slurs and innuendoes against several people. In the issue of 21 June 1840, an individual named Baring (not apparently mentioned anywhere else) was said to have been among those arrested at The Hague (*recte* Ostend). Later in the same piece, with seeming inconsequence, 'Kerrich is married to a Miss Baring'. A week later, the correspondent introduced a new theme which became a favourite. 'The firm of Bogle undoubtedly arranged the plot, but their opposite neighbours, Count (!) Plowden and Co, had, it is rumoured, a hand in the business.' The guilt is now not merely Bogle's but his firm's, and Plowden & French are implicated, with the addition of personal insults: 'Plowden being son of an old Catholic gentleman by his cookmaid, and inheriting all the slippery qualities of the latter'.

The *Satirist* returned to the attack in a piece published on 27 September, quite clearly intended to discredit Kerrich, who was now allegedly showing around the letter in which Bogle announced his intention of suing the *Times*. He is accused of some dubious conduct in connection with another credit letter, which had been stolen from Mr Thellusson and offered to him for payment. While he did not pay out on it, he did nothing to deliver the thief to justice and only belatedly informed Thellusson. Kerrich was 'a high Conservative, nay, an Orangeman'. This, by implication, qualified him to be the banker of the English Church, which at the time occupied a room in the ambassador's house, but Kerrich had lately refused to produce his accounts. Here at least there was an authentic echo of the troubles that had been convulsing the English Church. On 1 November it was reported that Kerrich was telling everyone that the solicitor of the *Times* was with him for several hours every day. Dobie allegedly could speak not a word of Italian and was therefore 'driven to seek information from such men as Kerrich, French, and Plowden, all of whom were more or less implicated in the *circular* affair'.

Kerrich's involvement, even if only 'more or less', is here more explicit than before. It is certainly possible to seize on some oddities in his version of events, things that he apparently did not notice or let pass at the time, and his willingness, even after having read the documents Fox sent to him, to believe in Bogle's innocence. That he did what the *Times* and Mr Dobie wanted of him, including going to Paris to identify the handwriting of the conspirators on documents in the hands of the French authorities, might be uncharitably interpreted as turning queen's evidence. The *Satirist* put it more crudely on 11 July 1841. He had gone to England, 'some say to get some more blunt out of the proprietors of the Times for his information against his former friend and partner, Boyle [sic]'. As for his bank, 'What money or pretensions this firm can have to be bankers, I know not, nor do the *Florentines*.'

Even if there are observable oddities in Kerrich's conduct, it is hard to see on what evidence Plowden and French were implicated. On 17 January 1841 the *Satirist* gave its own version of the origins of the firm. French was Irish and had arrived in Florence 'with very little, save a fine brogue and a full carpet bag, but a full share of impudence and assurance'. Plowden, having been a clerk at a bank in Paris, now closed, had already arrived, 'determined to astonish the Florentines with his Parisian manners'. He opened a broker's office and French joined him, promising to bring him the business of Galway and all Ireland. We are now told how they had earned their titles of nobility from the Grand Duke, and how they had recently played a trick on the other bankers, who took their working rate of exchange ('generally one or two points less than the legal exchange at Leghorn') from them. Finding he was losing clients, Plowden on a sudden 'offered the *full amount* for English bills', to the fury of his fellow-bankers.

John Maquay's diary for 27 November 1840 includes the two words 'Plowden exchange', presumably a reference to this episode; so it was clearly not totally imaginary. The *Satirist* could explain why Plowden was (allegedly) losing customers: it was his 'downright pride and insolence … I know Captain Lynch left him on that account, though this lying *Count* says it was because the Captain was jealous of his wife and Plowden'. That Plowden should be guilty of sexual irregularities merely completed the set. Monotonously and repeatedly, he was designated 'that son of a fat cook'. It becomes difficult to explain how he and French managed to run their bank with apparent success for so many years.

The *Satirist* carried numerous notices of Florentine and other Italian incidents in earlier and later years, but its Florentine assaults were concentrated in 1840–1841, more precisely between 21 June 1840 and 21 February 1841. This was probably not because the antics of the British there were uniquely scandalous during that period, but because the paper had a 'correspondent' in place. On 13 February 1841 John Maquay went to a men's party at Lord Vernon's, where it was said that the articles had been 'traced to Mr Anthony Mahon who is ordered away by the government'.[17] In June Lord Holland was asked by the Foreign Office to supply information about Mahon. The governor of Genoa had raised objections to his continued residence in that city on the grounds that while in Florence, he had 'libelled some English ladies in the Florence newspapers'.[18] The libels had not in fact been directed solely against the ladies.

Holland replied on 28 June, observing that Mahon had been expelled from Tuscany some time before. All he knew was that during the previous summer and autumn, while he himself was in England, 'a series of scandalous articles' had appeared in the paper. On his return he had been asked by several of the gentlemen whose womenfolk had been slandered to request the Tuscan government to set the police on the trail of the culprit; 'a large sum of Money was offered to procure this desired piece of information'. He did not comply. Both he and his wife had been among those slandered, and he therefore refrained 'from acting as if I was taking advantage of my official situation for the purpose of redressing any private wrongs'. Then, just before he had left Florence in the previous November, a new article appeared,

> full of Libels and Calumnies not only against British Subjects, but virulently attacking persons of other Countries, and some near Connexions of Florentine families of High Rank and great Influence, besides some Contemptuous phrases respecting the Grand Duke and His Government.

As a result a ban was put on the *Satirist* at the Tuscan Post Office and during the winter, Mr Mahon was sent away by the police, 'since which time, I am told, no more libellous articles from Florence have appeared'. Even as Holland wrote, more were imminent.

When Cowper, as *chargé d'affaires*, had asked why Mahon had been expelled, the Tuscan Minister avoided any explicit reference to his main offence, saying that he had been accused of cruelty to a Tuscan servant. Holland suspected that this oblique approach revealed a desire to avoid any 'Breach of the Peace either by assault or Challenge'. This, he thought, would almost inevitably have occurred if Mahon had been publicly identified, 'so great was the Irritation, and so numerous were the Parties aggrieved'. Holland claimed that he had not even known of Mahon's existence before he heard him named as the suspected author of these libels, but he was now able to return the compliments he and his wife had received. Mahon had been a resident at Florence for some time, living with a married lady who had so far failed to obtain a divorce from her husband. It was also said that he had been forced 'to leave Ireland, in consequence of some disgraceful story about play'; in short, he was precisely the sort of person he pursued and denounced in his writings.[19]

The *Satirist*'s favoured targets were adultery and gambling, of which malpractice at the racecourse was a subset. Arthur Vansittart and his brother-in-law, the baronet Sir Joseph Hawley, received an intensive barrage on both counts. Hawley, who would become a highly successful racehorse-owner in England, had married Mrs Vansittart's sister Sarah in June 1839, and their daughter, Mabel, was baptised in Florence in the spring of 1840. Recent childbirth, if Mahon was to be believed, did not prevent Lady Hawley from cuckolding her lord (or hoping to do so). As for Vansittart, he had had an affair with Mrs Fox, who was 'very gay'. Vansittart was 'declining somewhat into the vale of years', a strange way to describe a man who in 1840 was 34 years old. He 'was a party to all the petty doings at the last races, and is the author of the trash written under the title of "A Turfite in Italy"'. This alluded to Vansittart's current contributions to the English sporting press.[20] Vansittart had rented part of Casa Standish (which he had), 'very much to the annoyance of *Lady Lucy*', who apparently did not want her daughter to witness Mrs Vansittart's goings-on. Standish himself was a 'regular little old goat, laying siege to every petticoat in Florence', a claim which may not have been wholly without foundation.[21]

'Mahon' challenged Mrs Vansittart to deny an assignation at 4 o'clock in the morning in the gardens of Casa Standish, and in a later piece (8 November) described an imaginary performance of *Love Laughs at Locksmiths* at Standish's theatre, in which she would appear in the garden at that very hour, 'in her lace-trimmed nightcap', in order to admit her lover, the Comte de Ballou. There now 'appears an old goat, with the smoke of a cigar issuing from its mouth. Upon near approach, this is recognised to be Standish, who has posted himself there by appointment to meet the lady's-*maid*'. Meanwhile Vansittart is peacefully asleep in his own room, 'his nightcap being raised off his head by the luxuriant growth of his antlers'. Much merriment is aroused by the fact that Vansittart ran a horse called *Antler* (which he did).

Further racing bulletins appeared on 1 November, with accusations of chicanery, of which 'silly Sir Joseph' was a victim and the hotelier Gasperini a perpetrator. On the 28th, Gasperini again figured prominently as 'president' of a 'gambling, smoking, betting, begging society'. Its chief members were Vansittart, 'that seven-foot piece of squint-eyed humanity' (it is attested elsewhere that he was very tall), and the cuckold Hawley, 'about the most empty-headed, greasy-looking specimen in the whole Baronetage, trying to knock everyone down with his purse'. Hawley was oddly called Vansittart's son-in-law, but as we have seen, the *Satirist* had curious ideas about Vansittart's age.

On 10 January 1841 'Mahon' depicted the 'wailing and gnashing of teeth' that had accompanied Lady Holland's recent temporary departure from Florence. The afflicted included her supposed paramour, 'Beauty' White, Mrs Walker (the widow of Captain Charles Montagu RN, commonly called 'the Duenna' by Mahon) and her 'romping' daughter, Frederica. These two lamented the loss of Lady Holland for slightly different reasons: the mother because she would no longer have the loan of her ladyship's carriage and the daughter because her ladyship's hospitality had afforded cover for her assignations with Charles Poniatowski. 'Mahon' now mentioned that Poniatowski, Vansittart, Hawley and 'honest Kerrick' [*sic*] had applied to the Government to have the *Satirist* excluded from Tuscany.

It is not entirely easy to match the sequence of the extant articles with the chronology Holland supplied to the Foreign Secretary. The offensive article of November 1840 can presumably be identified as the one that appeared on the 28th of that month, in which Charles Poniatowksi was named not only as one of Arthur Vansittart's horse-racing set but as 'cavalier' to the wives of both Vansittart and Hawley. It is, however, hard to see where the 'contemptuous phrases' about the Grand Duke and his government occur. Nearer to this particular mark was the piece which appeared on the following 17 January, where the writer made mock of the titles of nobility which had lately been awarded to Plowden and French:

The Grand Duke gave orders that a road from Florence to Fiesole should be made; but as this would cost money, which the Grand Duke does not much like throwing away upon pounding stones, he issued an order that the title of Baron could be purchased for 100*l*, and that of Count for 50*l*, all of the money to go to the making of this road; so this accounts for our highway nobility in the persons of Messrs French and Plowden, together with a few others whose names you shall have anon.

This, we may note, was the occasion on which James Matthews also was awarded noble status. On 24 January there followed an uncomplimentary account of the background of the Poniatowskis.

If John Maquay saw this piece, he could have added himself to the list of those personally affected by Mahon's scribblings. He had 'become banker, and pretends to great religion', but Elena was the chief victim. It was alleged that Charles Poniatowski had misbehaved with Frederica Walker at a Maquay musical party at which the writer claimed to have been present. It was not to be wondered that Mrs Maquay permitted this conduct, considering that she 'is an Italian, and that her conduct with the singing master "Juliani," is quite notorious'. John was a credulous cuckold, who, when his wife was away from home, 'innocently' said that she was practising music with Giuliani. Whatever the truth of these allegations, there is no trace of the name Mahon in any of John's party lists down to this date.[22]

John heard on 13 February that Mahon had been expelled, but that was not inconsistent with the appearance of further articles in the issues of 7 and 21 February, which would have had to be sent from Florence several weeks before publication. There was then a gap of some months, but on 4 and 11 July, two fresh articles appeared, which must have been written and transmitted to England even as Holland pondered his reply to the Foreign Office. The article of 4 July certainly bears the usual hallmarks. Much of it was devoted to the recent races, where Joseph Poniatowski and Gasperini had conspired to nobble one of Sir Joseph's horses; the jockey whom Hawley held responsible for the loss of the race was threatening to sue him for defamation, with the support of 'Prince Poloney'. Mahon thought Vansittart was not in on this particular plot, and certainly in his guise as the 'Turfite' the latter gave a very different account.[23] It is also recorded that over the winter, Vansittart and his 'chaste Diana' had had a terrible row, which had resulted in her taking refuge at Pisa at the invitation of Sir Joseph, with whom she had had an affair before his marriage. Vansittart meanwhile 'remained at Florence, and had a little affair with a Madame Garland, with whom he got acquainted at Leghorn'. She was an Irishwoman, whose husband, driven mad by jealousy, cut his throat.[24]

There is a year-long gap in the Satirist's Florentine coverage after 11 July 1841, but there is also incontrovertible evidence that a Mr A. C. Mahon was in Florence late in that year. An 'English gentleman' of that name took space in the Gazzetta of 21 November to disclaim any responsibility for debts incurred by his servants. If this was the scandal-monger he had no qualms about advertising his presence and his address. Then in July and August 1842 a series of pieces appeared concerning an affair which was noticed in the regular press, for example in the Morning Post of 20 July 1842, and the Times on the following day. It can be briefly summarized.

Mr Delamore was an Englishman who was given to a game of cards but rarely played for high stakes. Mr Baldwin was a young American who goaded him into wagering larger and larger sums. Delamore persistently won, which only prompted Baldwin to goad him further, but still he won. At this point, unable to pay his losses, Baldwin accused Delamore of cheating. John Maquay became marginally involved, probably because he was Delamore's banker. He reported on 17 May that Delamore had made a statement about the episode and on 26 June seems to say that Baldwin had sent his victim a challenge, although Delamore's own account suggests that he himself had previously challenged Baldwin.[25] Delamore was on the point of leaving Florence. On 17 July John received a letter addressed to him from Baldwin, which he opened and answered.[26] Nothing more seems to be said, in the newspapers or elsewhere.

The *Satirist*'s treatment of this episode has a very familiar ring. It was notably lengthy, continuing well into October, with much detail, abuse and repetition. The issue of 31 July, which reported the facts as they appeared elsewhere, set the scene. The 'gay cities of the continent' provided an income for 'a large class of the expatriated adventurers, who, having worn out their vocation in their own country, go abroad for the double purpose of profit and pleasure'. On 14 August the paper printed a letter from a correspondent at Paris who praised its efforts to suppress gambling. Delamore was to be condemned for 'imprudence and impropriety' in having allowed himself to be inveigled to continue to play, but otherwise his conduct had been entirely honourable, in contrast with the 'disgraceful and unprincipled … conduct of the Yankee'. This anti-American tone was later strengthened: Baldwin was typical of his nation and could not be expected to pay his gambling debts promptly or honourably.

Then, to no one's surprise, Plowden and French were implicated. Plowden, as Baldwin's 'friend', declared on his behalf that he 'would neither *fight, pay or apologise*'. Asked why they were taking Baldwin's part French 'very coolly' explained that it was in their interest to do so, since if Baldwin were obliged to pay Delamore, he would be unable to meet his very considerable debts to them. 'Not a soul in all Florence but these two men, and a person of the name of Wood (whose wife is a Frenchwoman) could Mr B find to side with him.' Putting everything together, we find that to be American (Baldwin), French (Mr Wood's wife, by whom he was probably corrupted), Italian (Elena Maquay), Irish (Anthony French) or Catholic (Plowden and French) was to be morally suspect. We might perhaps add 'Scottish', on the strength of the issue of 24 October 1841. A 'Correspondent' had supposedly asked, 'What has become of Mrs Hastings Anderson – the once celebrated Scotch beauty?' Various cryptic insinuations are made against the lady, but only 'our correspondent at Florence' could supply the answers, which were apparently wanted by someone who wished to give 'a lecture on Scotch morality'.

Was the coverage of the Baldwin affair by the same hand as the *Satirist*'s bulletins in 1840–1841? They share an agenda and an animus and they quite clearly pander to an all-too-familiar popular xenophobia on the part of the paper's readership; however, not all the content can have been invented behind a desk in London. How much independent knowledge did readers have of the Anglo-Florentines who were libelled – if libelled they were? And why should the man in the English street have been at all interested in Arthur Vansittart, Elena Maquay or Thomas Kerrich, if not simply as specimens of the idle rich and their hangers-on?

Sometimes the *Satirist* is silent when one might expect it to be noisy. In the summer of 1841, almost a year before the Baldwin–Delamore affair, its *bête noire* Plowden had been involved in a fatal encounter at Bagni di Lucca. The episode, which received some coverage in the London newspapers, seems ultimately to have owed much to the rather erratic favouritism of the Duke of Lucca, as well as to dubious elements in the society that clustered at Bagni during the summer months.

On 22 June 1840 the *Morning Chronicle* reported that three British physicians, Crook, Gifford and Dowling, had been tried by the Tuscan supreme court for being concerned in a duel. Although it had taken place on Lucchese territory, a recent law had provided for such offences to be prosecuted in Tuscany, doubtless because those who remained obstinately attached to affairs of honour had been known to slide back and forth over the border between what were still two states in order to avoid criminal proceedings. Despite or perhaps even because of this misdemeanour, Crook attracted the attention of the duke, who made a favourite of him as he was somewhat prone to do, appointing him court chamberlain.[27] According to one version of events, this aroused the jealousy of Henry Cottrell, lately himself a favourite, but now no longer. Crook was said to be 'gentlemanly, well educated, respectful, accomplished and endowed with all the qualities' that Cottrell totally lacked. Plowden became the means by which the latter could obtain his revenge.

Plowden passed the summer of 1841 at Bagni, where he opened a seasonal branch of his bank. In passing, we may notice that the contemporary author of a guidebook to Bagni remarked that the firm was well-known and had been 'for some years established, conducting business in the most satisfactory manner.'[28] Plowden encountered Crook and it seems made insulting remarks to him, evading his demand for 'explanations' and alerting the police chief Bedini to the possibility of a duel. (It would have been known that Crook had already been involved in such an affair.) A few days later Crook publicly accosted Plowden and called him a slanderer, a liar and a coward. A mutual friend somehow managed to prevent a violent outcome and to hush the matter up. Thomas Trollope's account of the affair, which differs in several respects, makes Plowden the victim of a bullying campaign by Dr Crook.[29]

On the evening of 4 September a ball took place at 'the Club', a recently founded institution set up by the British in answer to the French-run Casino. During the evening, Crook and Plowden had words, seemingly because Plowden had spoken insultingly to a Mrs Newton, a widow of whom both were apparently enamoured but who preferred Crook. Now that it seemed that a duel was genuinely imminent, Cottrell set about ensuring that it took place. When the police chief was again invoked, Cottrell put him off with assurances that the affair had been settled peaceably, while in fact the principals and their seconds were getting organized and setting off for a place on the border between Lucca and the Duchy of Modena.

When the signal was given, Plowden aimed low, but succeeded in hitting Crook in the groin. Crook fired as he fell, but missed. It immediately appeared that his wound was mortal, and a doctor who was called to attend him felt unable to attempt to extract the bullet. Already the news of the duel was out and, according to Bedini, the holiday makers of Bagni flowed to and fro visiting the dying man.

Plowden was arrested, but released when it was established that the duel had not taken place on Lucchese territory, and he departed for Pisa and apparently then for Paris. Crook died after 36 hours; the duke was reported to be thunderstruck and inconsolable and still grief-stricken in October. Cottrell busied himself organizing the funeral at Leghorn, which was also attended by Colonel Stisted and by the Reverend George Robbins, who currently served the congregations at Pisa and Bagni. Crook apparently died heavily in debt, with 30 *paoli* in his purse, and his entire movable property amounted to no more than 500 *lire*.

On 23 September, the *Morning Post* published an account, derived from Galignani's *Messenger*, that differed in a number of respects from the foregoing. Galignani's correspondent thought that Crook had insulted Plowden at the ball and that the latter had sent a friend to demand an apology, which was peremptorily refused. It was also stated that Crook and Plowden had shaken hands after the fatal wound had been inflicted, and that Crook had said, 'I forgive you, you have acted rightly.' Furthermore the duke, even though attached to Crook, was said to have believed that Plowden had been forced into the affair. Trollope's contrasting version was that the duke, 'in unblushing defiance of all equity and reason', blamed Plowden entirely and strained every nerve to get him banished from Tuscany; the Grand Duke was 'more just and reasonable' and refused to do so. Plowden was permitted to return to Florence. In the short run he may have anticipated trouble, if we can trust the recollections of a son of the clergyman at Leghorn, Mr Gambier, who claimed to remember his father hiding Plowden in their attic until he could smuggle him out of the country.[30]

It is curious that a year after this widely reported incident took place, the *Satirist*, while denouncing Plowden and French for their part in the Baldwin-Delamore affair, said no more about Plowden's activities at Bagni than that 'It was only last year that Dis-"count" Plowden, as he is universally called, was publicly posted at the baths of Lucca.'

Some years later the paper revisited Bagni, prompted by the duke's decision, taken not long before he ceased to rule his pocket principality, to ban gambling there. The author of a piece published on 18 October 1846 remarked on the important role that English visitors had played in supporting this, 'one of the smallest, if not the smallest Italian dukedoms', and asked what effect the new ban would have on their numbers, given that (so he believed) only a few came to enjoy the climate, 'the majority the excitement afforded at the gaming tables'. He hoped that Bagni's attractions would be increased for 'those really respectable families who resort to the Continent for the education of their children' and who had hitherto been 'deterred from visiting this delightful spot by the fear of the much dreaded Casino'.

As to what had prompted the duke to take this step, given that he was not averse to a little flutter himself, the *Satirist*'s correspondent was inclined to give the credit to 'those highly respectable Protestants, Colonel and Mrs Stisted, of the Baths of Lucca'.[31] The mere existence of such a couple, who had only lately built the Anglican Church at Bagni, alongside the gamblers and roués, might have reminded this writer of the essential duality of 'English' society at Bagni, as in Florence and indeed the rest of Italy. The diarist Provenzali declared in 1846 that 'Bagni society is rascally (*scelerata*) and composed for the most part of nameless English, vulgar and thieving', but a modern historian of Bagni has commented that alongside such people, 'there was another society, of people who had no love either for play or for the evening dances at the Casino or the Club'; they came simply to relax.[32] There are sufficient descriptions of the British at Bagni and their humdrum occupations – their walks and rides, picnics and water-colour sketching – to suggest that the scandalous may in fact have been in a minority.

A series of anonymous articles on Bagni in the year 1840 might be read in support of either view. The writer had arrived there in early May to enjoy both relatively cool weather for scrambling about the mountains and relative peace before the hordes of visitors arrived. When May was over, the pace quickened, and not for the better:

> English carriages laden with luggage and children now arrive daily. Next month the duke arrives; the Casino Reale, that plague-spot of the place, opens, and balls, soirees, and all the dissipation of a watering-place, take place of our moonlight rambles and quiet country life.

The *contadini* too detested the casino, regarding it as the ruin of 'many respectable families' and the probable cause of bad weather and bad harvests.[33]

It would be rash to suppose that Anglo-Tuscan society, including some of the people the *Satirist* chose to attack, was not guilty of immorality, cheating and excess or that some guilty parties escaped unpunished. Mrs Mary Light was as scandalous as 'Mahon' could have desired. Born Mary Bennet, an illegitimate daughter of the second Duke of Richmond and Lennox, she was married in 1824 to Colonel William Light, artist, surveyor and founder of Adelaide, and later accompanied him to Egypt. He separated from her in 1832; Isabella Wilmer noted her arrival in Bagni in August 1836 under the name of Mrs Bowen. It was evidently known that she had 'gone off with Captain Bowen leaving her husband in Egypt'. On 7 October 1841 (now a widow) she was married at the Florentine Legation to Alfred Lambert (interestingly described as 'late secretary to the Grand Duke of Tuscany') and Lady Holland gave a breakfast on the occasion, as the *Morning Post* noted on the 30th. It was presumably to Bowen that she had borne the three children who (aged 12, 11 and 10) were baptised at Florence by the Reverend Robbins on 13 January 1846 under the name of Light.[34]

The *Satirist* was not alone or innovatory in detecting the presence in Tuscany of British undesirables. According to the *Morning Post* of 18 January 1843, 'British vulgarians and swindlers have desecrated Florence and other of the most *recherché* abodes of travelling *virtuosi*'. Among their likely victims were young men of the propertied classes who led an idle, wandering existence. On 26 July 1841 the *Freeman's Journal* covered a case that had been lately heard in the Insolvent Debtors' Court in Dublin. The Honourable Henry Alexander Savile, a younger son of the Earl of Mexborough, had been arrested as he attempted to cross from Ireland to England. He had several creditors, mostly foreign, and the debts laid to his charge amounted to over £9,000. Savile was called 'reckless', but the word 'feckless' might have been coined to describe him. The paper related that, having sold out his commission in the Hussars in 1834 and spent the proceeds, he had lived mostly on the continent and had married a Miss Pennefather, an Irish lady, in the previous August at Florence. The marriage settlement had been drawn up by Captain Pakenham, who also, it appears, advanced him £500. His wife had a few jewels, but no money, although she did have property in Tipperary worth about £200 a year. Perhaps that was why he had come to Ireland.

John Maquay must have known this unfortunate young woman, one of Madame Galeazzi's two daughters, since she was a child. He notices the imminent marriage with a touch of disapproval and foreboding: on 7 August 1840 Pakenham was much engaged with Madame Galeazzi on the subject, 'great hurry I think too much so no settlements prepared'. John was invited to the wedding on the 17th but did not go.[35] How much he knew about Savile's history we can only wonder, but as revealed in the newspaper report, it was pathetic, discreditable and faintly ridiculous all at once. He had wandered over the continent, giving one valuable gold watch to a lady of pleasure, whose name he could not remember, and parting with another when he was 'in difficulties' at Munich, where he had also purchased a large quantity of gold plate, which was seized by his creditors. A gold box had been stolen from him in Paris when he was at the races on the Champs de Mars. With part of the money he had received from Pakenham he had bought a carriage, which he had pawned at Brussels to a man to whom he owed £50, and he had left a valuable dressing-case in pawn at Florence. Other debts were mentioned, one of which he had assumed his father would pay as he approved of his marriage. He estimated his annual expenditure at £1,000; his father made him an allowance of £400. He had (it was said) 'great expectations'.

It seems to have been accepted that Savile had never tried to deceive anyone and had been the gullible victim of moneylenders who led him into further debt on the expectation that he would somehow be bailed out. A letter from the representatives of one of his Florentine creditors was read out in court, stating their willingness to see him released from custody and their faith in his 'honourable character'. Kate gave birth to their son, William, in London on 8 October 1841 and the couple must subsequently have returned to Florence, for on 18 May 1842 Major Galeazzi came to tell John Maquay that Savile had been arrested at the behest of the shopkeeper Sam Lowe. John discovered that the arrest was 'good', although he had received a legal opinion that it was not; he was angry, but to no avail.[36] This and Pakenham's involvement in Savile's affairs suggest that Maquay and Pakenham were the young man's bankers, and one good reason for John's annoyance may have been that Lowe's action would give him priority over the bank as a claimant to any money

Savile might be able to muster (rather as Plowden and French had laid a prior claim to any money from Baldwin).

Savile was released from gaol on 1 June, but there was to be no happy ending. On the following New Year's Eve, John heard that Kate was very ill; labour had come on and it was not thought that she would survive. She died the following day. The *Standard* on 20 January gave the cause of death not as childbirth but as consumption. John went to her funeral and reported that Savile was so distraught that he could scarcely stand, although supported by his elder brother, Lord Pollington, and Colonel Lindsay.[37] We may well feel a pang of compassion for Kate Pennefather: a young woman in poor health, married to a wastrel and not spared the rigours of pregnancy despite her frailty.

How many other Henry Saviles were there in Tuscany or elsewhere on the European continent at any one moment? As a banker, John Maquay ran the occupational risk of coming up against them. It seems likely that some obscure entries in his diary for April 1846 reveal – or conceal – such an experience with a titled debtor. On the 19th he heard that Lord Drumlanrig was leaving Florence, which moved him sufficiently to insert two exclamation marks. The following day 'Lord D's affair much talked of, and my conduct canvassed, people however see that I could do nothing else'. On Tuesday he was writing notes about the affair, on Thursday it was still causing 'much remark', and on Saturday he had a conversation with Lord and Lady Vernon on the subject.[38] Nothing further is said, and whatever it was, this episode did not merit – or receive – newspaper coverage. Quite probably John had felt compelled to identify Drumlanrig publicly as a bad debt, perhaps even seeking his arrest, as Sam Lowe had sought Henry Savile's.

The Savile story was at bottom pathetic; a grimmer one unfolded in the summer of 1841, a few weeks after Henry Savile was released by the Dublin court, and was reported in the English papers, which took it from the *Court Journal*. A full version appeared in the *Manchester Guardian* on 11 August, which merits quotation for the picture it gives of the setting:

Two sons of Lord Aldborough (who has a villa near Florence) went into the town a few days since to look at some horses at a livery stable, when a quarrel ensued, and words ran high between them; nevertheless, they returned home apparently reconciled to each other, and dined and slept as usual under their father's roof. The next day they again went out, ostensibly to shoot; but the younger brother, a lad of 18, still nourished a deadly resentment against his elder brother, a young man of 23, on account of the dispute of the preceding day, and upon a bird getting up, he deliberately levelled his gun and aimed at his brother; but only succeeding in slightly wounding him in the side, he drew a pistol and took a surer aim by shooting him in the back of the neck, and raising up part of the skin of the head. As soon as his brother had fallen, this modern Cain fled into a neighbouring vineyard, where several *contadini* seized him, and remonstrating with him upon his horrible conduct, told him that he would come to the galleys at last. To which he replied, with great defiance, 'No, no, thank you, I shall never come to the galleys!', drew another pistol from his pocket, and, opening his mouth, shot himself dead on the spot. The corpse of this unfortunate suicide and fratricide was left to blacken for many hours unheeded beneath the scorching rays of an Italian sun, while the wounded body of the elder brother was conveyed home to his father, who is said to have exclaimed on seeing it – not knowing the fate of his other son – 'If that most unnatural wretch escapes the gallows it will not be my fault'. His Lordship was heard the next day giving, with self-collectedness, a detailed account of this horrible affair at Fenzi's, the bankers, previously to his departure for Leghorn. A council of some hours' duration was held at Lord Holland's as to whether the suicide should be buried in consecrated ground or not; it was at length decided that he should; so, accordingly by torchlight, with no other attendants but the clergymen and the sexton, the body was consigned to the grave; and thus closed this fearful domestic tragedy, worthy of the Borgias and their times. The life of the wounded brother is still precarious.

The *Times* had already printed the story on 10 August, but cut it slightly and suppressed the name of the family.

The Florentine Church records confirm that on 21 July 1841 Gustave Stratford was buried, having died by his own hand on the 18th. The Reverend George Robbins officiated on behalf of the Reverend Tennant, who made and signed the entry. The deceased was one of several sons of Mason Gerald Stratford, fifth Earl of Aldborough, and, unknown to the clergy, he may have died unbaptised. Over 10 years later, on 7 July 1851, the *Freeman's Journal* carried a curious report that the late Lord Aldborough had never permitted any of his children to be either baptised or buried. This was prompted by the discovery of a child's bones in an attic of his villa at Leghorn, which was raided by the police in 1849, not because of any suspicion of such unconventional behaviour, but because three of the Stratford sons had been active in revolutionary politics.[39] The report seems to be in part substantiated by the fact that no fewer than nine Stratford children of all ages were baptised after his lordship's death in 1849, one of them on 18 November in that year and eight on a single day, 15 March 1850.

It can well be believed that his late lordship was somewhat eccentric; certainly his marital affairs were highly irregular. He was married to Mary Arundell at the Embassy in Paris in 1826, some time before his first wife, born Cornelia Tandy (to whom he was married at Gretna Green in 1804), was granted a divorce by the Court of Arches on 7 December that year. Despite his denials that Cornelia had ever truly been his wife, her claim to be the countess and her eldest son's right to succeed his father in 1849 were upheld. This meant that the Stratfords of Florence and Leghorn, the earl's numerous children by Mary Arundell, were excluded from any inheritance.[40] When the sons got into serious trouble during the disturbances of 1849, they were said to be exceedingly poor, and we may well believe that the earl was in need of cash when we find him advertising Holloway's Liver Pills. A letter supposedly written by him from the Villa Messina [*recte* Messori], Leghorn, on 9 October 1845, testifying to their miraculous properties, appeared endlessly in the papers both before and after his death.

The Savile and Aldborough affairs got into the British press; others did not. In 1843–1844 Holland had to grapple with a minor convulsion, known only from the Foreign Office correspondence, in the otherwise little publicized British society of Siena.[41] On 13 September 1843 the Recorder of London, Mr Charles Law, wrote to Viscount Canning at the Foreign Office, enclosing two letters about the recent experiences of his son Charles. He demanded that Lord Holland should be required to send home 'copies & minutes of all Applications by whom & when made to him against my Son in reference to the distressing affair of Lady Eleanor C. Law'.

The son had expectations from his father's childless elder brother, Lord Ellenborough, formerly governor-general of India. He and Lady Eleanor Howard, the eldest daughter of the Earl of Wicklow, had been married in November 1840, when he was only 20 years old and she some 3 years older. They arrived in Siena in April 1843, but one night in August, so a Mr Hills wrote to the elder Law, Lady Eleanor fled from their house to a lodging nearby. Miss Emily Souper appears in the story henceforth as her constant companion and virtual bodyguard. No one could prevail upon Lady Eleanor even to see her husband, whose violence she claimed to fear. She was taken under the protection of Colonel James Knox, a son of the first Earl Ranfurly, an acquaintance of her father and well-known, like the rest of his family, to John Maquay. Mr Law for his part took refuge with Mr Hills, who reported to the elder Law that the laws of Tuscany were of no help to him. It was for precisely that reason that Lady Eleanor had for some time been meditating flight: 'it was to seek protection from the Laws of Tuscany, the Laws of England in her case affording no redress, that she had recourse to so desperate a measure.' That the Italian laws would not simply award a husband custody of his wife's person owed more to the notion that a woman always remained part of her father's family than to any belief in female self-determination.

Mr Hills was indignant that Colonel Knox had so one-sidedly taken the woman's part. When Knox was told of Mr Law's distress at his wife's refusal to see him, he allegedly remarked that he would not care if the young man blew his brains out or cut his throat the next moment. An English physician called Flewker and the resident clergyman, Mr Roberts, were employed fruitlessly as intermediaries. Flewker was also called upon to examine Law and subsequently gave evidence in court about his sanity. Apparently he thought the young man perfectly sane but in an extremely 'irritable' state. He gave him medicine to assuage the 'irritation' and thought it as well to order the removal of pistols or sharp objects from him, for fear not that he intended harm to his wife (as she and her party maintained) but that he might harm himself. He stated firmly that he had attended Law solely as a medical man and did not want to know about his private relations with his wife.

It was Colonel Knox who on Lady Eleanor's behalf requested Holland to obtain the protection of the Tuscan authorities against her supposedly violent husband. Holland probably had no alternative but to ask the Tuscan government to send the necessary instructions to the Sienese authorities. This was represented to the elder Mr Law as a request for his son's arrest, which not unnaturally annoyed him. In a second letter, Mr Hills complained of 'the ruthless manner, in which Lady Eleanor's cause is espoused and defended by her friends, or rather her new formed acquaintances, at Siena'. He further asked, 'How far an Ambassador or Minister is within the sphere of his duties in taking the violent course which it appears Lord Holland has taken, on statements necessarily ex parte?'

Meanwhile, Randall Plunkett, another old acquaintance of John Maquay, who in 1848 became the fifteenth Lord Dunsany, had arrived in Siena for a couple of weeks for a change of air, only to find himself embroiled in this 'painful event'. On 23 August he wrote to Andrew Buchanan at the Florentine legation explaining that all that was wanted was some police surveillance over Mr Law, as Lady Eleanor believed herself to be in mortal danger from him. Her father was expected to arrive shortly to take charge of her. To Mr Hills the younger Law seemed innocent and distraught; Plunkett, however, stated that he had made himself 'sufficiently notorious' at Siena. 'He has beaten his own servants, insulted the townspeople & in short conducted himself in a manner perfectly ruinous to the character of our own Countrymen in the eyes of foreigners.'

John Maquay was in Siena between 13 and 16 August and records among the people he saw the Hills and Knox, who we know were ranged on opposite sides in the Law dispute, but he says not a word about it.[42] In the event, young Law consented to leave Siena for England, apparently travelling under some kind of friendly supervision. On 21 September Holland rejected the Tuscan government's request that he should take steps to prevent Law from returning to Tuscany. The visa on Mr Law's passport which would enable him to do so was not under his control but theirs. As if to answer his critics, he pointed out that while he had recommended Lady Eleanor to the government's protection, he had not felt justified in asking for Law to be expelled or exiled from Tuscany, where he had hitherto not been guilty 'of more than most threatening & extraordinary language.' He transmitted to the Foreign Office both the correspondence in which he had been personally involved and transcripts (untranslated) of the depositions that had been taken at Siena from Lady Eleanor, Miss Souper and a host of Italian witnesses, including servants of both husband and wife. No attempt will be made here to pass judgement on this somewhat one-sided testimony. No London newspaper published any account of the affair and the sequel remained wrapped in discretion.[43]

Becoming a banker did not totally alter John Maquay's social life, but arguably added a dimension to it. We can discern that he assisted old friends such as Horne and De Courcy with their business affairs, and he is to be found witnessing wills, as other bankers such as Plowden regularly did. When the widowed Lady Lucy Standish was forced to leave Florence by the news of the serious illness of her son, he effectively became the agent for Casa Standish, arranging lettings; he would help new arrivals in Florence to find lodgings. One such newcomer was Dr Frederic Septimus Leighton. Mrs Leighton's health provided the pretext for the family's continental travels from the late 1830s onwards, but wherever they went, the doctor's son, another Frederic, had drawing lessons.[44] In Florence Dr Leighton was lodging in Borg'Ognissanti when he subscribed to Vieusseux for 9 months on 29 July 1845. A few days later, the Leightons were guests at a Maquay tea party and on two occasions a little later in the year John drove Dr Leighton to inspect villas for sale. In October Leighton required four sittings at the English Church.[45] It is possible that the children's fancy ball that young Fred attended in Florence dressed as Punch (thus acquiring an enduring nickname in the family) was one of those that John gave during this same winter. At all events, the relationship thus formed was sufficiently cordial for young Leighton to call on the Maquays in the 1850s when as a rising artist he travelled to and from Rome.[46]

John's involvement with the English Church brought him into close contact with several new Florentine residents, in one case rather to his regret. Morgan Thomas was a non-practising barrister, who between 1832 and 1863 made no fewer than five attempts to be elected Tory MP for Coventry, succeeding at the fifth. Like so many Florentine refugees, he was less wealthy than he would have liked, although his pretext for residing there was his wife Louisa's health. During a stay which lasted, off and on, from about 1841 to 1852, he evinced a determination both to make himself felt in Anglo-Florentine society and to demonstrate his disapproval of it. His daughter left a revealing picture of this truculent and aggressive Welshman:

> My father disliked Society – he loved his home; my mother on the contrary liked Society. My father did not like women to wear low necked dresses; my mother on the contrary wished to be like other people. My father's opinion was that eleven o'clock at night was a respectable hour for leaving parties, this was the hour at which parties began. He obliged my mother to come home just at the time when she was beginning to amuse herself. My father would not call on this lady or that lady, or visit Madame A because she had a lover, or Madame B because she received Madame A. He would not even set foot at the English Embassy while Lord Holland was Ambassador, because gossip was afloat concerning Lady Holland. He seemed possessed with a passion for virtue, and he had been nicknamed at Florence 'the policeman of Society'.

As a member of the Church Committee he would frequently clash with John Maquay.[47]

Other less contentious characters became John's friends. The names Dennistoun and Vere appear in his party lists from 1842 onwards. Archibald Campbell Dennistoun of Edinburgh was married to Mary Vere in Florence on 16 December 1841 and two daughters were born to them there. They drank tea and played whist, and Dennistoun came for billiards. He already had family links to the city, for his younger brother, Richard, with his wife and her mother, Mrs Hannah Meiklam, had been great friends of Elizabeth Maquay there in the previous decade. It was in the 1850s that Dennistoun became part of the ruling coterie of the English Church, and he did not leave the city until after the death of his wife in 1877. Another arrival in the early 1840s, the ex-Indian civil servant Christopher Webb Smith, was sufficiently intimate with the Maquays to be a guest at the party John gave on the evening of their fourth son's christening on 3 April 1845; like Dennistoun, he would witness and survive two Tuscan revolutions.[48]

A slower start was made by William Reynolds. A Liverpool broker, he was still living in England when the census was taken in June 1841.[49] His wife had died in 1839 and he may have felt the time was ripe to retreat to a warm climate and leave the sometimes contentious business of share-dealing to his sons, who were occasional visitors to Tuscany. It was probably he who subscribed for a month to Vieusseux on 28 May 1844 and for 6 months on 12 September. In the autumn of 1845 he applied for five sittings in the church, which suggests that he had been accompanied to Tuscany by his four daughters. A few years later he was elected to the church committee, and it was later still, it seems, that he got to know John Maquay well. Also slow to take an active role in the church was Maurice Baruch. The combined witness of the Maquay diaries and the Vieusseux subscription books suggest that he was in Florence by 1846; one of John's party-lists identifies him as 'German', but in the fullness of time, he clearly became not only accepted as a member of British society but of central importance as manager of the church library.

In the summer of 1842, Maquay spent some time in Siena and met the Reverend George Crossman, his wife and daughters, remarking that he liked Crossman's preaching style.[50] By the end of that year, the family had moved to Florence and rapidly became part of the Maquay inner circle. In June 1845 John mentions for the first time Major Charles Gregorie, an intimate friend of the Crossmans, who had just bought the Villa Colombaia at Bellosguardo. Here he lived with the Crossmans until his death in 1858, and the Maquays were ceaseless visitors.[51] Another arrival at much the same time was Dr Peter Luard, who first subscribed to Vieusseux in June 1845 and was listed among new subscribers to the English Church in the autumn of the same year. His movements from one Florentine address to another can be followed, with some chronological gaps, for the next 11 years and he makes quite frequent appearances in the Maquay diaries.

The arrival of a more celebrated new resident was registered when in October 1843 John met 'Mrs Trollope who has come to settle in Florence & her son, most undistinguished looking person possible'.[52] Surely this meant the mother rather than the son. Thomas Trollope would become a valuable commentator on Florence and the English in Florence. In Paris before his arrival in Italy he had met both Sir Henry Bulwer, who became Minister in Florence in 1852, and his sister-in-law Rosina, Lady Bulwer, the estranged wife of the novelist Edward Lytton. She had 'an apartment far larger than she needed' in the Palazzo Passerini in Florence, and it was with her that the Trollopes first stayed while they were looking for lodgings after their arrival in September 1843.

Trollope gives a sympathetic picture of Lady Bulwer: she 'was brilliant, witty, generous, kind, joyous, good nature, and very handsome', but also 'wholly governed by impulse and unreasoning prejudice' and totally devoid of prudence and judgement. Rather like the spoiled child, she could be furiously angry the moment she was inconvenienced. Trollope recalls an incident when she burst into tears, while climbing up through the Boboli Gardens towards the Belvedere, simply because it was too hot. The Trollopes never fell out with her, but they were often sorely vexed by her behaviour, not least when she complained of her poverty, which meant that she was reluctant, not to give to her friends, but to pay her bills. Trollope gave no countenance to the rumours circulating in Florence about the propriety of her conduct, regarding it 'almost a matter of course that such a woman as Lady Bulwer, living unprotected in the midst of such a society as that of Florence in those days, should be so slandered'. He argued, probably rightly given his range of acquaintance, that if there had been any scandal, he would have known about it.[53] John Maquay never mentions her.

Arthur Vansittart remained in Florence, occupying a prominent position in English society but a marginal one in John's circle. He was cultivated and musical, but also a sportsman and a gambler; John was not, despite a keen interest in horses as befitted his Irish origins. One evening in April 1843 he recorded how he had played whist with Vansittart, 'the others bearing my stakes, as they play high'.[54] In 1844 Vansittart paid 300,000 *lire* for the Villa Salviati north of the city, which had been much neglected. He lavished money on it, in the words of William Blundell Spence sparing 'neither care nor expence in having it completely restored and refurnished in a most princely style of magnificence suited to the character and period of the building'.[55] As this investment might suggest, Vansittart had no plans at this moment to return to England, but another of the racing fraternity did so, after many years in Florence. Early in 1840, Frederick Thellusson, who had become Lord Rendlesham the previous year, marked the birth of a son and heir by sending £50 back to England to be distributed among the grateful tenantry of Rendlesham and the surrounding district. When 3 years later he stood as if by divine right for election to the East Suffolk constituency, his opponent referred to 'his long Italian sojourn' and suggested, to laughter, that he might have studied the works of Machiavelli 'near the fair city of Florence'.[56] His Lordship won comfortably.

Some members of parliament, while mindful of the need to be seen to do their duty, saw no reason to deprive themselves and their families of the delights of the winter season at Florence. On 23 January 1843 the *Morning Post* let it be known that Viscount Pollington, MP for Pontefract (and elder brother of the hapless Henry Savile), would be returning to England to attend parliament, leaving his wife to return in the spring. On the following 13 September the same paper carried a sententious announcement from Captain Hamilton, MP for Aylesbury and now at Bagni di Lucca, that he intended 'to return as soon as the severity of the ensuing winter is passed' and to take up those duties to his constituents, 'which having undertaken, it is imperative on every Member of Parliament, according to the best of his ability, to perform'.[57] In December 1845 Lord Normanby had scarcely settled into the enjoyment of the Florentine season, with every intention of remaining for 6 months, when he was urgently summoned home by the news that Lord John Russell was forming a new administration.[58]

On 3 November 1844 Florence experienced a humanitarian disaster, a devastating flood. John Maquay wrote on the 4th, 'The tales of misery and devastation of property are heart rending every shopkeeper along the Arno ruined £80,000 of goods in the Custom House destroyed, 14 lives lost that are known of in short almost every one more or less suffers.' His mother spoke of 'the numberless distressing Scenes which I hear of every hour people not being able to get out of their houses animals of all kinds floating down the River all dead furniture of all sorts passing down at same time the Duke is indefatigable in relieving the distresses of the poor'.[59] As John himself commented, the 5th was 'a curious day' to have a dinner party (which Elizabeth attended), but it had already been arranged, and on the following evening, he went to play whist with Mrs Trollope. The British may have maintained their social arrangements undisturbed and the opening of their newly built church proceeded as planned on the 17th, but they were not unresponsive. In 5 consecutive weeks, beginning on 12 November, the *Gazzetta* published the names of contributors to a relief fund. Over 200 British individuals were represented, and on 19 December the paper noted in addition the collection that had been made at the opening of the *Chiesa Anglicana*, which raised the equivalent of £82 sterling.

Lord Holland's time at the Florentine embassy may have been more disturbed by the disputes and peccadilloes of his fellow-countrymen than by political crises, but underlying Tuscan realities did not change. On 18 March 1841 the *Freeman's Journal* reported that Austria had obtained the Grand Duke's consent to the establishment of a stricter system of surveillance and espionage at Florence, which it said had been 'a long time the peaceable abode, where foreigners from all countries come and seek repose or alleviation to their corporeal sufferings'. Now more than ever, they could reckon that their letters would be 'opened and read by the Austrian police, they are also irrevocably kept back if they contain any equivocal sentences, no matter how important may be the contents of letters for the private interests of the persons to whom they are addressed'.

There was, then, the continuing possibility of annoyance to foreigners, innocent and otherwise, and there were signs of mounting internal tensions, on which Holland commented in a long despatch written on 9 March 1846, almost at the end of his term of office. The Grand Duke's desire to introduce into Tuscany a new order of nuns, closely allied to the Jesuits, who planned to open an educational establishment for girls at Pisa, had elicited a protest from the professors of the University of Pisa. They were rebuked for their presumption, but were gathering support around Tuscany. Unconsciously recalling sentiments earlier expressed by

Seymour, Holland remarked that these demonstrations, mild in themselves, had made a deep impression because in Tuscany 'popular feeling is rarely excited and never expressed'. This was the more so as the discontent emanated from the upper classes.[60]

This was not the only sign that a long period of stability, if not somnolence, in Tuscan politics was over. In September 1845 Gregory XVI's misgovernment of the Papal States had at last provoked rebellion, notably in the Romagna. The revolt had been suppressed with Austrian assistance during the winter, and political refugees had poured over the frontiers to lie low in Florence. The Grand Duke incurred considerable odium by surrendering one of them, Renzi, to the papal authorities, and the government's unpopularity was aggravated when it expelled the popular Piedmontese nobleman Massimo D'Azeglio for a pamphlet criticizing the Tuscan government's policy.[61] However, some refugees were permitted and even aided to escape. The Tuscan Foreign Minister Humbourg, Holland and the French ambassador de la Rochefoucauld cooperated (using D'Azeglio and Trollope as intermediaries) to remove as many as quickly as possible to cooler climes. The granting of British and French passports to non-nationals was effectively winked at by the Tuscan government. The Foreign Office approved Holland's conduct 'on this occasion', implicitly discouraging any repetition.[62]

By the time Holland was recalled in May 1846, he had been assisted for 2 years by Peter Campbell Scarlett, second son of the first Lord Abinger, who was appointed Secretary of Legation early in 1844 and would remain in post for over 10 years. Thanks to the ill health of successive Ministers and the deaths of two of them, he served for considerable periods as *chargé d'affaires* and (perhaps unfortunately) had the management of situations trickier than any that had bothered Seymour, Abercrombie or Holland. If we add that he returned to Florence in 1859 to become (as things turned out) the last British Minister Plenipotentiary to the Court of Tuscany, it becomes apparent that Scarlett's Florentine career embraced the most interesting of times, although it began quietly.

Notes

1   Thomas Trollope, *What I Remember* (second edition, London, 1887), pp. 93–4.
2   Sir Charles Boyle (ed.), *Mary Boyle Her Book* (London, 1901), p. 201. Four of Watts's portraits and a drawing of Lady Holland are illustrated in Barbara Bryant, *G.F. Watts Portraits: Fame & Beauty in Victorian Society* (London, 2004), pp. 40–9, as are a number of portraits of members of their Florentine circle, including a drawing of the *attaché* Edward Erskine (p. 64) and a caricature of Count Henry Cottrell, one-time favourite of the Duke of Lucca and later a friend of the Brownings (p. 65).
3   FO79/97, Fox to FO, 18 February 1840.
4   Dorothy McMillan (ed.), *Queen of Science: Personal Recollections of Mary Somerville* (Edinburgh, 2001), pp. 189–90. Compiled by Martha Somerville, the *Recollections* were first published by John Murray in 1873.
5   Numerous references to the Craufurds are to be found in Arturo Linaker, *La Vita e i Tempi di Enrico Mayer con documenti inediti della storia della educazione e del*

Risorgimento Italiano (1802–1877) (Firenze, 1898) and *Lettere di Giuseppe Mazzini ad Enrico Mayer e di Enrico Mayer a Giuseppe Mazzini* (Florence, 1907). It was reported that when he was in Florence, Mayer sought the company of Craufurd (*La Vita*, p. 302).

6   FO79/99, Craufurd to Palmerston, 4 August 1840. William Craufurd was introduced to Lord Leveson at the Foreign Office by Fox-Strangways, who stated that he had been 'for many years intimately acquainted' with John Craufurd in Florence. There is no trace of Palmerston's intervention on behalf of Mayer in the Tuscan correspondence.

7   Antonio Gallenga, *Episodes of My Second Life* (London, 1884), Vol. 2, pp. 52–3, 61–77.

8   Betty Bennett (ed.), *Letters of Mary Wollstonecraft Shelley* (Baltimore, 1989), Vol. 3, p. 49, to Claire Clairmont, 29 November 1842. Drummond Wolff confirmed Gallenga's recollection of the Craufurds: 'All spoke Italian in preference to English': *Rambling Recollections* (London, 1908), Vol. 1, p. 12.

9   EM, C6 f. 22v.

10   The long-drawn-out documentation of this affair begins with a letter from Rice to the Foreign Office (FO79/95, 10 January 1839) and is spread over several volumes of the Foreign Office correspondence until Fox's final somewhat resentful despatch (FO79/97, 25 June 1840). Some of the ancillary correspondence is to be found in the miscellaneous FO79/99.

11   The Hon. Mrs Alcock, sister of Viscount Doneraile, died in Florence on 1 February 1840. On 30 April Fox told the Foreign Office that Alcock had made the arrangements for Julia's return to England.

12   EM, C7 f. 20v.

13   The court proceedings were reported on 17th and 18th August, with an overview of the entire case on 19th August.

14   JLM, E10, particularly ff. 113v, 115, 115v, 116, 124v.

15   JLM, E10 f. 117v.

16   William Blundell Spence a few years later mentions a Roster, who made 'copies in water colours in a very forcible style': *Lions of Florence* (Florence, 1847), p. 62. He also mentions Freppa as a dealer in curiosities (p. 67). In 1823–4 JLM had taken Italian lessons in Florence from a Mr Roster, who, he said, was English. The Roster of the Bogle affair, whatever his origins, was clearly a Tuscan subject.

17   JLM, E10 f. 136v. A Mr A. Mahon subscribed to Vieusseux on 29 April and 16 August 1840, for a month on each occasion, and a Mr Mahon for 2 months on 1 November 1840.

18   FO79/100, FO to Holland, 15 June 1841; 79/101, Holland to FO, 28 June 1841.

19   In 1841 a person of this name published in London a volume of verse entitled *London as It Was and Is*, complaining in the 'advertisement' that he had been defrauded by the executors of a will. On 19 December 1842 reference was made in the *Freeman's Journal* to an Anthony Mahon, who owed money for his defence on a charge of 'criminal conversation'. In 1848 an insolvent Captain Mahon, who said that he was once a lieutenant and paymaster in the Marines, was imprisoned for perjury at Taunton, and on being asked whether he had run away with the wife of a Mr Tuke, he said that he was not bound to answer (*Daily News* 21 April 1848). An Anthony Mahon is involved in other litigation subsequently. Any or all of these individuals might be identified with the *Satirist*'s supposed correspondent.

20   *Satirist* 28 June 1840.

21   *Satirist* 27 September 1840.

22   A Mr and Mrs Mahon were invited to a party in October 1845, but they did not come. On the face of it, it is hard to imagine that this can have been the author of the

libels. There is a Giuliani musical score in the Biblioteca Nazionale Centrale Firenze, 783.2 (13) 'Le romanze/composte e dedicate alla nobil donna la signora Elena Maquay nata Gigli da Michele Giuliani', which would no doubt provide straw from which some might build bricks.

23 For Vansittart's contrasting account of this race, see Chapter 5.

24 *Satirist* 4 July 1840. Augustus Lester Garland died at Leghorn on 14 February 1839. The burial register gives no hint of suicide.

25 An exchange between Baldwin and Delamore appeared in the *Gazzetta* on 21 and 24 May.

26 JLM, E10 ff. 169v, 172v, 173v.

27 The story is told by Bruno Cherubini, *Bagni di Lucca* (Lucca, 1977), pp. 177–82; see also p. 174. Cherubini draws on the diarist Pietro Provenzali, and it may be due to him that Cherubini constantly refers to Plowden as 'Plander', in which he is followed by G. Lucarelli in his brief summary of the affair in *Lo Sconcertante Duca di Lucca: Carlo Ludovico di Borbone Parma* (Lucca, 1988), p. 130. Cherubini refers to Crook as the duke's 'beniamino'.

28 William Snow, *Hand Book for the Baths of Lucca* (Pisa, 1846), p. 56.

29 Trollope, *What I Remember*, Vol. 2, pp. 142–8.

30 James W. Gambier, *Links in My Life on Land and Sea* (London, 1906), p. 14.

31 On 25 November the *Morning Post* attributed the duke's decision to 'the ruin which gambling tables have entailed on many visitors to the baths of Lucca'. The Casino at Bagni, as also that at Viareggio, was to be converted into a reading-room.

32 Cherubini, *Bagni di Lucca*, p. 175.

33 'The Baths of Lucca in the Summer of 1840', *Metropolitan Magazine* 30 (1841), pp. 402, 406.

34 They had been born, respectively, at Aix-en-Provence, Genoa and Florence. Mary had had a Tuscan connection in the person of her sister Caroline, the wife of Captain Henry Napier, who died at Florence in 1836. She herself died at the Villa Capponi in 1879. For Colonel Light, who died in Adelaide in 1839, see the *Australian Dictionary of Biography*. Alfred Lambert was living at the Villa Corsi when he subscribed for 3 months to Vieusseux in December 1851. He was later interested in the Carrara marble business; see Chapter 13.

35 JLM, E10 ff. 122, 122v.

36 JLM, E10 f. 169v.

37 JLM, E10 f. 187. Savile's one surviving child lived until 1903, but he himself died in 1850, aged only 38, at Pau, another continental resort much frequented by the British.

38 JLM, E10 f. 264v.

39 See Chapter 9.

40 In reporting the story of the fratricide, the *Manchester Guardian* had pointed out that according to *Burke's Peerage*, his lordship had only two legitimate sons, neither of whom could have been involved. This was echoed, perhaps in a mischievous spirit, by a number of papers.

41 FO 79/109, Law to Viscount Canning, 13 September 1843.

42 JLM, E10 f. 202. Two Laws had been guests at a party he gave in Florence on 9 January (f. 188) and he dined at Mr Law's on 7 February (f. 190).

43 There was no divorce. Lady Eleanor can be glimpsed in her father's household after her return from Italy and seems to have devoted some of her time to translations of French devotional writings. She died in 1852, aged probably no more than 35. Charles remarried no fewer than three times, and by his second marriage obtained an heir to the Ellenborough barony, which he at length inherited in 1871; see *Burke's Peerage*.

44 Mrs Russell Barrington, *The Life, Letters and Works of Frederic Leighton* (London, 1906), Vol. 1, pp. 37–8.

45 JLM, E10 ff. 248v, 252, 252v; CMB 1, Committee 6 October 1845.

46 JLM, E11 ff. 119, 120v, 135, 181 passim. In May 1853 Leighton's mother quoted to him a letter written by Mrs Maquay to Miss Pakenham in which he was approvingly mentioned: Barrington, *Frederic Leighton*, p. 134. The Leightons' stay in Florence may have had another later consequence, the marriage of Frederic's sister Augusta to Arthur, the son of James Robert Matthews. It is also possible that the two families had become acquainted earlier, in Frankfurt.

47 Brian Thompson, *A Monkey among Crocodiles: The Disastrous Life of Mrs Georgina Weldon* (London, 2000), p. 21. In 1856 Thomas adopted the surname Treherne. He became deputy lord lieutenant for Surrey, in which county he died (in a mental hospital in Long Ditton) in 1867.

48 JLM, E10 f. 241.

49 He had started life as a clerk and throve sufficiently to be elected honorary secretary of the Liverpool Sharebrokers' Association: William A. Thomas, *Provincial Stock Exchanges* (London, 1973), p. 17. In 1840–1 Reynolds's firm was involved in a somewhat acrimonious lawsuit concerning a deal in shares in the Grand Union Railway.

50 JLM, E10 f. 145.

51 JLM, E10 f. 244v. It has sometimes been supposed that Mrs Crossman (born Anne Oakes) was Major Gregorie's sister, but the kinship link was in fact between Gregorie and her husband. Crossman's mother was born Elizabeth Brickdale and her brother John was married to Catherine Gregorie, the major's sister. In his will (Principal Probate Registry, 8 December 1858), Major Gregorie left Mrs Crossman and her daughters, whom he described as 'in easy circumstances', a legacy of £350 and permission to remain in the villa for 6 months after his death. He nowhere refers to her as his sister, naming the children of his late brother as his universal heirs.

52 JLM, E10 f. 205v.

53 Trollope, *What I Remember*, Vol. 2, pp. 82–9. This is not the place to evaluate the depths of bitterness and the accusations which informed the exchanges between Lytton and his wife, which even by Victorian standards were fairly extreme.

54 JLM, E10 f. 194v.

55 Ovidio Guaita, *Le Ville di Firenze* (Rome, 2005), p. 53; Spence, *Lions of Florence*, pp. 143–4. The villa, which Guaita calls by its more recent name of Villa del Ponte alla Badia, was bought from Vansittart in 1852 by the tenor Mario and his wife, the soprano Giulia Grisi.

56 *Morning Post* 5 January 1836; *Times* 12 March 1836; *Morning Chronicle* 3 March 1840; *Ipswich Journal* 20 April 1843.

57 *Morning Post* 13 September 1843. Captain Hamilton's brother became British Minister in Florence in 1846, which encouraged his continued absences in Tuscany.

58 *Freeman's Journal, Morning Post* 10 November 1845; *Morning Chronicle* 18 December 1845.

59 JLM, E10 f. 231; EM, C7 f. 133v.

60 FO 79/118, Holland to FO, 9 March 1846.

61 FO 79/118, Scarlett to FO, 11 February 1846, Holland to FO, 1 April.

62 FO 79/118, Holland to FO, 17 March 1846; 117, FO to Holland, 7 April. Thomas Trollope describes his own role in *What I Remember*, Vol. 2, pp. 95–6. There is no reason to doubt what he says, which matches the detail in FO79.

5 JOHN BULL AT PLAY

On 18 September 1820 the *Bristol Mercury* described how the British were making themselves at home in Italy. There had been 'a regular double-wicket cricket match – Eton against the World' near Naples; fox hounds had been imported to Rome; and 'At Florence, they establish races on the Cascine, after the English manner, and ride their own horses, with the caps and jackets of English jockeys'. A writer in *Borrow's Worcester Journal* on 10 April 1828 reiterated that wherever John Bull went, he 'carries his own sports with him', finding the amusements of foreigners 'too insipid'. Two days of horse racing at Florence had recently demonstrated the point, but the horses 'were not of first-rate character'.

The Florentine races were sometimes reported in the British press as part of a coverage of expatriate social activities which began to appear soon after the post-war resettlement of Florence. It petered out in the course of the 1830s, either because of changes in Anglo-Florentine social life itself or because the subject lost its appeal. Many amusements were not in the least newsworthy. It was routine to drive, ride or walk on the Cascine, to give and attend dinner parties, balls and musical evenings, to play whist or other card games and (partly as a consequence) to gamble. To go to the theatre or opera or to participate, if only as a spectator, in the diversions of Carnival, was similarly unremarkable. The quantity of newspaper coverage in the 1820s owed much to the presence of Burghersh and Normanby. The genuine musical gifts of the one and the theatrical abilities of the other produced performances of exceptional calibre and their rank ensured an eager, sometimes sycophantic, press.

Together their Lordships provided opportunities for their compatriots to exhibit their talents, or lack of them. Lord Dillon may have entertained delusions about his histrionic as well as his literary abilities, for in 1825 Charles Brown suffered an 'internal pain' when seeing him perform in one of Normanby's private theatricals: 'decency forbad me the relief of a hearty laugh – it was really very comic'.[1] Five years later John Maquay delivered a crisper verdict on George Irby, the future Lord Boston, who performed in an amateur play at Lady Normanby's and 'made a failure'.[2] The occasional professional lent a hand. On 5 December 1826 the *Morning Post* reported that 'Mrs BRADSHAW, late Miss TREE', visiting Florence with her husband, 'occasionally delights the audience of Lord NORMANBY's private theatre'. Miss Tree, more of a singer than an actress, had compulsorily retired from the stage on her marriage a year before.

Accounts of Burghersh's lavish entertainments and opera productions appeared not only in England but sometimes in the *Gazzetta di Firenze*, which doubtless helped to reinforce his belief that he was enhancing British prestige at his own considerable expense. Already at New Year 1815 he gave a glittering ball at his residence, and a few weeks later another which celebrated the birthday of Queen Charlotte and was fully reported in the *Gazzetta* on 24 January. The British newspaper reports were gleaned from anonymous 'private letters', which read very much like press releases. The *Morning Post* on 23 May 1816 recounted that Burghersh had given a 'grand fete to celebrate his Sovereign's Birth-day'. It was 'attended by most of the Nobility and Foreigners of distinction' and began at about 10 o'clock in the evening, 'in a great hall magnificently lighted up, and lined with orange trees'. About midnight 'a sumptuous supper' was served for 300, after which the dancing resumed and lasted till after 4 am. The *Gazzetta* covered the event at some length on 11 June, adding that Consul Falconar at Leghorn had given a dinner on the same occasion, to which the governor of the town and all the members of the Factory were invited: repeated toasts were drunk to the King, the Prince Regent, the Queen, Princess Charlotte of Wales, Lord Burghersh and the Duke of Wellington among others. This kind of celebration was evidently part of the job: on 24 July 1821 the *Gazzetta* noted that the consul had given a dinner to mark the day fixed for the coronation of George IV.

On 13 July 1818 Burghersh, on behalf of his King, invested Admiral Sir Thomas Fremantle with the insignia of the Order of the Bath. The Grand Duke was present, as were other members of the royal family and also Marie Louise. The hall was decorated with busts of the Prince Regent, Wellington, Pitt and Mr Percival; the royal family and court party were placed at a separate table of forty covers, and the company altogether numbered more than 300. A ball followed the ceremonial.[3] On 14 March 1820 the *Morning Chronicle* reported on a flurry of cultural activity. Burghersh with other English residents had staged a play called *The Honey Moon*, 'well got up, and performed with spirit', and there were 'symphonies' of his Lordship's own composition between the acts. News of the death of George III had brought these entertainments to an end, but the paper also mentioned that Burghersh had hosted a private exhibition 'of Sir Thomas Laurence's portraits of the Pope, Cardinal Consalvi, the Emperor of Austria, &c'.

Large-scale entertainments were customarily given during Carnival, which preceded Lent. On 19 March 1827 the *Morning Chronicle* related that Burghersh's 'last Carnival and Fancy Ball … was the most splendid of the season'. Nearly 700 were present, attired in the costumes of all nations and apparently periods. George Hayter, whose private affairs were soon to set Florentine society by the ears, had designed the dress of a beauty of the period of Louis XIV, while 'Lady Burghersh was splendidly attired as a Lady of the Westmorland Family'. The *Chronicle* of 10 October recorded that 'the first assembly of the season' at Florence took place at Count Demidoff's French play (he had already produced French plays during the summer at Bagni). The British notables mentioned included the Burghershes, Normanby, Lord and Lady Blessington, the Wardles, Mr and Mrs St John, Mr Perry, and Mr and Mrs Medwin.[4]

If the British had taken the initiative in establishing racing on the Cascine, they did not remain alone in their enthusiasm. John Maquay attended a race meeting on 14 December 1826 which he said was well-attended despite bad weather; Demidoff and the Austrian ambassador were involved alongside Normanby and Captain Medwin.[5] On 7 April 1828 the *Morning Post* carried a lengthy account of the spring meeting. Among non-English names familiar elsewhere in the annals of Florentine society was that of Demidoff's natural son Mr Romanowitz, the news of whose death in a duel in 1830 put an end to a reception at the British Embassy.[6] On the British side, Normanby and Burghersh headed the field, accompanied by the baronet Sir Hedworth Williamson (Normanby's brother-in-law and later a Whig MP), Mr Thellusson, Thomas Kerrich, George Baring, Mr Lee (probably the Royal Marine officer whose daughter had very recently become the Marchesa Guadagni), Stewart Bruce from the Legation and Mr Perry.

The Arno Stakes were in their second year and the system of handicapping was significant: 'Horses not thorough-bred to carry 9st. 10lb; thorough-bred horses that have not run in England, 10st. 8lb; and thorough-bred horses that have run in England, 11st.' The Chianti Stakes were for all horses that had never run in Italy. Mr Baring offered a gold cup and Thellusson a silver cup which was won by Mr Lee's *True Blue*. In a two-horse match (a typical feature of meetings at this date), Baring's *Rob Roy* was conclusively beaten by Baron Smirnoff's *Malvina*. At the autumn meeting later that year, Burghersh, Normanby, Williamson, Thellusson and Mr Perry all had runners, but Baring's name was apparently absent; although he had not yet been forced to leave Florence, he may have been beginning to feel the pinch (*Morning Post* 13 November).

The coverage of Anglo-Florentine entertainments reached a crescendo in the closing years of the decade. On 27 December 1827 the *Times* reported that Normanby's Shylock and her Ladyship's Portia had been 'the subject of general panegyric. Lord Normanby has also performed the part of *Richard the Third* to the admiration of the *cognoscenti* of Florence'. In January 1828 the Burghershes hosted a masked ball, which was attended by some 800 'Persons of high rank, of both sexes, native and foreign'. (John Maquay, who was present, said that 850 were invited and about 700 attended.) The following week, Lady Burghersh gave a ball for 'about 200 of the children of our own Nobility, and of the foreigners of distinction in this place – all in elegant characteristic dresses'. In April there were 'concerts of vocal and instrumental music' for which 'The music was taken from two of his Excellency's works, the one entitled *L'Eroe di Lancastro*, already well-known, and the other *Il Torneo*'. The music was entrusted to professionals, reinforced by 'a number of eminent Dilettanti, both Florentine and English'; there were fourteen harpists, and a chorus of forty or more ladies, elegantly dressed alike with white flowers in their hair. 'Both Concerts were attended by the most eminent personages of both sexes in this City, and elegant refreshments were served up.'[7]

On the last day of 1828, under the heading 'English Fashionables in Italy', the *Morning Post* printed a bulletin from a 'Florentine friend and constant reader', who announced that 'Florence has been more than usually gay during the present season' and provided a list of recent aristocratic visitors to add to 'the regularly-established English Residents, amongst whom we can boast many distinguished names'. This was reproduced in the *Morning Chronicle* on the following day. Normanby's private theatricals, which had included *The Merchant of Venice* and *Much Ado about Nothing*, were highlighted:

> the admirable stage arrangements, studied attention to costume, and scenic effect, have been the admiration of all, as displaying a correct and highly-cultivated theatrical taste. Of the acting at these delightful performances, so unlike ordinary amateur attempts, it is unnecessary to speak in praise, since, owing to the affability and kindness of the Noble Lord and his interesting Lady, there are few of our travelled countrymen who have not had an opportunity of judging for themselves of their merits.

Meanwhile, Burghersh had produced 'an Italian Opera of his own composition' in 'a pretty temporary Theatre in his Palazzo'. 'The chorusses, which were very effective, were brilliantly executed by no less than forty amateurs, English and Italian.' This correspondent was also looking forward to the Spring Races.[8]

The opera referred to was undoubtedly *Il Torneo*.[9] According to a report (very probably from the same correspondent) in the *Morning Post* on the following 15 January, the piece had received five performances 'with scenic apparatus and perfect dramatic effect' at Burghersh's Palace. It was greeted with rapturous applause by an audience of 'Noble Personages', who marvelled that 'in the few moments of leisure he has to spare from the important duties of his Office', Burghersh had achieved such excellence. On one evening he added 'a Scene and Aria' to be sung by the wife of the Austrian minister, Bombelles, whose fine musicianship was well-known. The opera was followed by *The School for Scandal*, in which Lady Burghersh played Lady Teazle. The *Morning Post*'s correspondent showed little restraint, adding that 'the dignified and polite manners of Lord and Lady BURGHERSH shed on these, as on every similar occasion, a fascinating charm over all the entertainments'.

If another account of this production is to be credited, not everything behind the scenes was as it should have been. Among the members of the chorus on these occasions was young Charles James Mathews, whose stage fame would in time surpass that of his father, the comic actor Charles Mathews. At this moment a student of architecture, he had been touring the continent with a companion, Matthew d'Egville. Arriving in Florence in September 1828, he promptly contracted smallpox, but once recovered, he was recruited by Normanby to take part in his private theatricals.[10] His involvement rapidly amounted to a great deal more than merely performing.

On 16 January 1829 he told his mother that he and D'Egville had effectively been rebuilding his Lordship's theatre, a 'delightful' task, carried out at high speed because of the shortness of what Normanby 'most managerially' called his season and his need to return to England. Lady Normanby, Matthews told his mother, was 'a pet that you would love most sincerely'. He and d'Egville had spent Christmas with the Normanbys and on average dined with them three times a week, 'in that quiet snug way that is so pleasant and so English. Quiet cosy evenings, sketching and talking, with no boring [sic] to show off in any way, without even being once asked to sing'.

The new theatre accommodated about 200, and 'the stage is exactly the same depth and width as the Haymarket'. Matthews was seriously complimentary about the quality of production and performance:

Lord Normanby is himself an actor that might at any time supply Charles Kemble's place with credit, considerably resembling him too on the stage, and moreover understands thoroughly all the management of the theatre, superintending the scene-painters, machinists, lighting everything, with an experience of twelve years, having had an annual season regularly during that period.

To Mathews one of the charms of these theatricals was that the female parts were undertaken not by professionals but by women of status and refinement, notably Lady Normanby herself and her sister Lady Williamson: 'The Masquerade Scene in "Romeo and Juliet" was quite enchanting; all the lovely English girls here of high fashion, dressed in most beautiful fancy costumes, performed the dance in a manner that captivated everybody'.

The performances did not pass off entirely without incident. During *Romeo and Juliet* a lady in the audience had hysterics; when the prompter left his post to attend to her, he was forcibly prevented by a Mr Cornewall, who announced 'you are prompter here, and, by G—, prompt you shall.' This Cornewall, called by Mathews 'a Plantagenet' and a person 'of gigantic stature and powerful feelings', was the only person ever to criticize Lord Normanby's acting and imply his own superiority.[11] Normanby caused a sensation by offering him his choice of Hotspur or Prince Hal when *Henry the Fourth* was given after the enlargement of the theatre. Cornewall chose the prince, but an unexpected complication arose. Sir Robert Lawley begged to be allowed to play Worcester,

than which nothing could be more ridiculous, as his whole appearance, manner, and utterance are so eminently ludicrous that it appeared to be a fit of madness that induced him to request it. However, he would not be refused, and ordered two most splendid dresses, one of gilt chain armour, to be made for this occasion.

Cornewall was driven nearly frantic by the prospect of acting with Lawley and concocted a scheme by which Sir Hedworth Williamson would understudy the part while someone else invited Lawley out to dinner on the day and got him drunk, which it was apparently easy to do. He was unable to secure the necessary cooperation, and at 8 o'clock the performance was due to begin. There was no sign of Lawley, nor had he appeared by 9 o'clock. Cornewall was restrained with great difficulty from making a public announcement that 'old Lawley isn't come, and I only hope he has broken his neck!' At last Lawley did arrive. Matthews (who was playing Falstaff) believed the explanation for his tardiness to be that he had been so taken with his appearance in his gold chain armour that he could not resist showing his 'martial mien' off to 'a certain chère amie of his' (perhaps the mother of his four half-Italian children). Cornewall meanwhile proved that he was not the actor he claimed to be, but Matthews thought the play 'by far the most perfect of any yet done'; even Sir Robert was better than anyone expected.

According to Matthews, Burghersh's decision to erect his own theatre and stage his operas properly was motivated by the justified suspicion that his guests were tired of mere concerts. In *Il Torneo*, an entirely amateur performance, the choruses consisted of about thirty female and thirty male singers, including 'all the pretty English girls in Florence, splendidly dressed, and forming a brilliant *coup d'oeil*'. When the opera had received its five or six performances, the egregious Cornewall prompted Lady Burghersh to ask the Normanbys whether they would mind her putting on just one play in her temporary theatre. Fully understanding that Cornewall was seeking to showcase himself once again, Normanby lent every assistance in his power.

The play chosen was *The School for Scandal*. Cornewall was to be Sir Peter, Lady Burghersh Lady Teazle, Lord Douro (son and heir to the Duke of Wellington) Joseph Surface and Burghersh's secretary, Captain Aubin, Charles. Between these personages

> before the first rehearsal was over, a civil war broke out. Each wished to be manager, all had different ideas upon the subject, and none of them knew anything about the matter. The difference of the rival houses was well described, the one as a 'mild despotism', the other, a 'turbulent republic'.

Mathews himself was involved as Sir Benjamin Backbite. All this British activity inspired the French ambassador to put on plays at his house, but he encountered the same problem, finding that his players 'would all be kings or queens or nothing', and abandoned the enterprise.

In February 1829 the Burghershes hosted their customary Carnival masked ball, which was attended by Marie Louise and celebrated with breathless praise by the correspondent of the *Morning Post* on 27 March. Marie Louise, together with the Grand Duke and Duchess and the Prince of Saxe-Coburg, also attended a performance of *L'Eroe di Lancastro* on 19 March, which took place on the eve of Burghersh's departure for Rome and the conclave which elected Pope Pius VIII. Perhaps it was Burghersh himself who sent to the Foreign Office a cutting from the

Gazzetta which praised the music and the august company which had attended.[12] On 11 July the *Morning Post* reported two further airings of the opera, given in response to 'the solicitation of a numerous and select auditory who crowded to hear it'. Burghersh next branched out with two performances of a Mass of his own composition, earning predictable praises from the *Gazzetta* on 24 July and the *Morning Post* on 5 August.

It was an inevitable consequence of the ebb and flow of Anglo-Florentine society that their Lordships had to cope with an ever-changing cast list. The visiting Lord Malmesbury acted in Burghersh's theatre in 1828.[13] As the 1829 season approached, it was reported that Normanby had lost Lord Blessington, but in compensation, 'several of the minor branches of the English nobility' were arriving for the winter season and would provide reinforcements.[14] On 5 December several English papers carried reports of the Florence autumn race-meeting, which the *Times* thought 'may not be unacceptable to our sporting readers, who will recognize several well-known English racers'. Normanby put up no fewer than six runners, while Count Poniatowski and Count Lowenberg were new non-English names.

Perhaps appropriately in view of Normanby's Yorkshire connections, the *York Herald* on the same day carried the most interesting account:

Florence Autumn Races seems to present a sort of Italian Newmarket, except that the parties who contribute to these sports being principally English noblemen and gentlemen, consider pleasure rather than gain the object of their contention. Lord Burghersh, Lord Normanby, Mr Perry, Mr Thellusson, Mr Kerrich, Mr St John, Colonel Gascoigne, Mr Holt, and two or three foreign noblemen, managed this year to get up three days' admirable sport. Horses, the pride of Tuscany, regularly bred, and riders of experience, some of them from Newmarket. powerfully contended for the various stakes and deposits. Lord Normanby and Mr Perry however seem to have been the owners of the best blood, for their horses were generally the winners. We understand many parties came from Naples, Rome, and Milan, to be present at this meeting. Lord Burghersh and Sir H. Williamson were the stewards.

If Normanby and Perry owned the best blood, it must have been partly due to their purchasing policy. The *Morning Post* reported on 21 December that Normanby had paid 500 guineas for a 'famous horse' called *Kildare*, who was on his way to Florence, 'where he is matched against Mr PERRY's horse *Starch*, who, during the last Races in the Tuscan capital, won everything'. This is only one of several notices of a traffic in horses between England and Tuscany.

His Lordship meanwhile had opened his theatrical season on 8 December with two old favourites: *Henry IV* (Part Two), followed by *Simpson & Co*. Mathews was again Falstaff and his colleague d'Egville played Poins, but there were new names elsewhere. Several of the Legation participated, Aubin as the Earl of Worcester, the recently appointed Edward Bligh as the Earl of Westmorland, and Mr St John doubling as the Earl of Douglas and Gadshill. Mr Thellusson took the small part of Peto. Normanby himself was Hotspur, while King Henry was played by a Colonel Lane and Prince Hal by Mr Craven, who was said, along with Normanby and Mathews, to have displayed the greatest talent.[15] Along with many familiar faces, the talented Mr Craven and the equestrian Mr Perry were also in the cast of a very new play, *The Follies of Fashion* by Lord Glengall, which Normanby was preparing as the year 1829 drew to a close. The *Morning Chronicle*'s report of this production, which appeared on 6 January 1830, suggested that Burghersh and Normanby were about to join forces to produce drama and opera alternately, but the careers of both were shortly to take a different direction.

Burghersh ended his long Florentine sojourn on a high note. The *Gazzetta* of 9 February reported that his Lordship's comic opera *Lo Scompiglio Teatrale* had received five performances in his own theatre as part of the celebrations of carnival; individual pieces received special praise, and several had been printed by the publisher Ricordi. Three of Burghersh's own children, together with other high-born young people, had taken part in a 'un graziosissimo ballo' during the intermission. The spring of 1830 saw three performances of *Fedra*, which was received with the usual enthusiasm, and a selection of Italian plays, which included works by Alfieri and Goldoni, and English comedies, including Vanbrugh's *Provok'd Husband.*

The year 1830 witnessed a substantial dismantling of the society that had produced this flurry of cultural activity. It was later gilded with nostalgia. Writing in the 1860s in his fictional persona of Cornelius O'Dowd, Charles Lever (who only became a Florentine resident in 1847) cobbled together what must have been other people's reminiscences to paint a picture of a golden age.[16] Early in 1836 Normanby wrote to Matthews, recalling 'what we cherished at Florence – the legitimate drama'.[17] Neither his Lordship nor his critics could ever throw off these memories, and there were repeated suggestions that he would have been both happier and more gainfully employed had he devoted himself to the theatre. A writer in 1841 described a meeting in Hyde Park between Normanby and Matthews and his wife, the famous actress Madame Vestris: 'Ah, my good lord, you were a happier man when living in Florence and cultivating the Arts.' Normanby was grey and lined now, as a result not of age, but of 'place'.[18] This writer was by no means the only one to remark on how rapidly his Lordship aged, and others were more directly critical of his fitness for political office. His performance as governor of Jamaica attracted some poor notices. The *Morning Post* on 2 February 1833 judged that it would be good for his own reputation and the well-being of the people he had misruled if he returned 'to his theatricals and his novel-writing in this country, or in Florence'.

A melancholy footnote was added in 1839, when it was reported that Normanby's 'elegant little theatre' at Florence had been recently pulled down.[19] Twenty years later, when his opposition to the Tuscan revolution was making Normanby unpopular with British enthusiasts for Italian independence, a writer in the *Morning Post* (29 August 1859) declared, 'If the plain truth must be told, Lord Normanby mistook his vocation, or, rather, his social position did not allow him to embrace it.' Even now, he glowed when remembering 'the time that he first played "Romeo", forty years ago, in the Palazzo San Clemente' and took pride in reflecting that 'The chief actors, with scarcely one exception, have all risen to Cabinet Ministers, and the very Sampsons and Gregorys have become Under-Secretaries of State!'

Clearly the usual routines of entertainment and hospitality continued under Seymour and his successors, but there is no suggestion that any of them emulated the style, still less the accomplishments, of Burghersh and Normanby. It was probably partly for that reason that press reportage of the kind they had attracted died away. Musical leadership passed into other hands, notably those of the Poniatowski siblings and for some years the Englishman Rowland Standish, while a few enthusiasts kept up a tradition of amateur dramatics, but for our knowledge of what was going on, we become almost entirely dependent on the recollections of individuals. John Maquay and his mother offer glimpses of races, balls, musical evenings and theatricals at Florence and elsewhere. John's involvement as a spectator was stimulated by Elena's as a participant, and he was well acquainted with many of the English (and others) who were most actively engaged, from the Poniatowskis and Standish to Arthur Vansittart.

There were continued productions of amateur plays, in which Irish expatriates were prominent. On 5 December 1833 John recorded a performance of *Bombastes Furioso* at 'Mr Ruxton's', noting that about fifty people were there. Ruxton on this occasion performed together with Colonel De Courcy and the banker Charles Plowden.[20] This production was followed early in the New Year by *Raising the Wind* and in February by *The Rivals*. Both Mr and Mrs Ruxton appeared in *The Rivals*, as did a Miss Jackson, Miss Moffat (daughter of John's associate on the Church Committee) and the recurrent Colonel De Courcy. Most of the performances just mentioned clearly took place at the Ruxtons' residence, but *The Rivals* in February 1834 was performed at Casa Standish, and on New Year's Day 1835 the amateurs gave there the comedy *A Cure for the Heartache*, with *The Liar* as an after-piece. By a happy chance two accounts of it survive, by Daniel MacCarthy and Mary Boyle.[21]

MacCarthy praised above all the hospitality Lady Lucy offered to a large party, not all of whom she knew. She had chosen the play and appointed the date, with triumphant success on both counts. Both MacCarthy and Mary Boyle regarded the production as 'ambitious'. A careful correlation of his review (which does not name the female performers) with Miss Boyle's reminiscences and the text of the play reveals that it was she who scored a triumphant success as 'Miss Vortex'. Probably Miss De Courcy was also among the cast. Jessy, MacCarthy said, was played by one who 'has on many former and eminently on a recent occasion gratified admiring audiences'. The men involved included Ruxton, James Annesley (veteran of the Indian Medical Service), a Mr Gooch, Mr Popham (it is not clear which of the clan this was), Edward Standish, son of Lady Lucy, Mr Rigbye (who had recently been involved in a duel at Bagni), Mary's brother, Captain Charles Boyle, and Sir Thomas Gage. Oddly, MacCarthy did not mention George Edgecumbe, Secretary of Legation, whom Mary Boyle remembered as a star performer. Mary composed the *Prologue*, which was spoken by Mr Annesley, hailing Lady Lucy as the 'Guardian spirit' who had produced 'A Panacea for our social woes', a reference to the depressed state of society in the depths of winter. It was presumably during this visit to Florence that Mary and her friends put on 'a magnificent *ballet d'action*' in which she and Miss De Courcy performed alongside the young Marquis Talleyrand de Perigord, the eldest son of the Duc de Dino, while 'Standishes of all ages and both sexes took part in this brilliant spectacle.'[22]

The focus here is on the musical and theatrical activity of the British themselves, but there was of course professional performance, notably at the Pergola theatre, where Lady Popham and others hired boxes. The *abbuonamento* (season-ticket) to the Pergola worked out at 2 ½ crazie per performance in 1847. In theory, this gave admission only to the pit but one was perfectly free to enter the box of any acquaintance. At less than the equivalent of one penny, this was seriously cheap. The audience waited for carriages afterwards in 'an exceedingly comfortable but very parsimoniously-lighted large room, which was a grand flirting place.'[23]

On 4 January 1836 John Maquay went to the Pergola to see the soprano Felicia Forconi make her debut in *La Cenerentola*. Some 18 months earlier, on 26 July 1834, Rowland Standish had made an Italian will in which he left a monthly sum of 130 Tuscan *livres* to be paid to Forconi, from the moment of his death for the term of her natural life. She was residing in the Via Larga, and anything that belonged to him in the house in which she lived was also to be hers. There can be little doubt that he had established her there, nor that his family knew about her. The Via Larga was continuous with the Via S. Leopoldo, where Casa Standish stood (the two together later became Via Cavour). When Standish died suddenly in April 1843, the Italian codicil was opened, read at the request of his eldest son Edward and pronounced to be valid. John Maquay mentions Forconi, uninformatively, while dealing with his late friend's affairs.[24]

While Standish lived, his theatre witnessed innumerable theatrical and musical performances both amateur and highly professional. Among the latter John Maquay noted and attended the appearances of the Norwegian violinist Øle Bull (a 'second Paganini') on 3 June 1834, of Liszt on 8 November 1838 and of another piano virtuoso, Theodor Döhler, who enjoyed the patronage of the Duke of Lucca, on 1 December 1840.[25] Standish also made his theatre available to gifted amateurs, and his association with the Poniatowski family (who later acquired his *palazzo*) was particularly fruitful.[26]

A pleasant picture of the social and cultural scene in the year 1837 was drawn by Charles Hervey, looking back at his first visit to Florence from the much-changed standpoint of the 1880s.[27] He recalled a cosmopolitan environment in which the British participated, rather than one that they dominated, noting the Italian noble residences and families that were most frequented by society and also the house of Angelica Catalani and her husband Paul Valabrègue, where she would respond to the insistence of her guests and seat herself at the piano, singing in 'a voice tremulous with age, but still full of expression'. In a piece on 'Vocal Music', which Rowland Standish contributed to Daniel MacCarthy's *Tablet*, he paid lengthy tribute to an anonymous 'Lady, with whom many of our readers are acquainted', surely to be identified as Catalani. According to Standish, her triumphs were to be attributed to assiduous practice.[28]

Catalani's well-attested willingness to sing the National Anthem, which naturally endeared her to the British, fitted with her well-documented Anglophilia. On 3 April 1845 the *Times* reported that she had organized a benefit concert for the support of a poor artist; Poniatowski conducted the orchestra and at the end asked her to sing 'the English national air', which of course she did, with little voice but the 'deepest feeling'. This was thought likely to be her last public appearance. She was more than Anglophile, however, for a letter published in the *Caledonian Mercury* on 14 December 1840 recorded that she had asked the writer to convey greetings to mutual friends in Scotland and 'as a *souvenir* of Scotland', she sang *Of a' the airts the wind can blaw*, and *Scots wha hae wi' Wallace bled*. We can name one of her Scottish visitors, the phrenologist George Combe, who was charmed with her in 1843, not least because of the warmth with which she greeted his wife Cecily, a daughter of Mrs Siddons, whom Catalani remembered well. Combe did not fail to note Catalani's physical and phrenological characteristics and appended his verdict on her husband: 'a good-natured, rounded-headed, shallow-looking little man'.[29] Hervey remembered him as an enthusiast for billiards and a great socialite who knew nothing about music.

Surely the Combes also visited the Fombelles, as one of Mr Fombelle's daughters was married to a son of Mrs Siddons. Hervey remembered theirs as 'A very agreeable and thoroughly English house ... where the *elite* of the British colony was always to be found.' Here he heard the 'delightful improvisations' of 'that admirable pianist, John Baptist Cramer'. He also had a good deal to say about the operatic productions of the Poniatowskis, which took place in Rowland Standish's theatre. It was so small, and space so limited, that 'it was considered rather a feather in one's cap to obtain a card of invitation'. Another participant was 'The fashionable music-master Antonio [*recte* Michele] Giuliani'. Hervey was also aware of Joseph Poniatowski's other consuming passion, for the races on the Cascine took place largely as a result of his exertions and those of 'one of the best-known members of the English colony, Mr Vansittart'.

Elena began to take singing lessons from Giuliani soon after she and John returned to Florence in 1832. By the summer of the following year, she had got to know another of his pupils, the youthful Emilia Goggi (1817–1857), a native of Prato who 20 years later would create the role of Azucena in *Il Trovatore*, but died young.[30] Giuliani was a frequent visitor to the Maquay house. Elizabeth Maquay described him already in April 1834 as 'quite domesticated there', a circumstance which later gave rise to libellous allegations about his relationship with Elena.[31]

He took English lessons from John, played whist and billiards and shared the common interest in horseflesh. Hervey noted the enthusiasm of Florence's male society for billiards, and both Valabrègue and the Marchese Torrigiani, who was reputedly the best player in Italy, were among those who made use of the table in John Maquay's opulent new house. Another was Colonel De Courcy, while Warren Hastings Anderson played both whist and billiards.

Not all music-making was formal or public, and some houses were more suitable than others for concerts or plays, as indeed for balls. On a warm day in May 1833, John gave a small dinner party, which was attended by Catalani and Valabrègue, the Andersons, Giuliani, De Courcy and also the Marquis and Marquise de Bourbel. In the evening more guests arrived and there was 'piano on the terrace, singing and dancing'.[32] Madame de Bourbel was among those who gave 'French plays' at her residence, and in the summer of 1836, she took part in an 'amateur play' performed for charity at a theatre next door to the Andersons' summer residence at Bagni.[33]

Catalani marked the New Year of 1836 by giving an entertainment at her villa. The Seymours and Lady Popham were among the many English residents present, 'too numerous to mention' as the *Morning Post* said on 26 January. Prince Poniatowski sang on this occasion. The *Post* added that both Countess Orloff and Lady Popham proceeded to give splendid parties, which were attended by much the same people: 'the fact is, at each house almost the same persons generally meet.' Now that Burghersh and Normanby were gone, much of the high-society performing that attracted press attention seems to have been the result of female initiative. The *Post* singled out among the entertainments which enlivened the Lent of 1836 a 'most brilliant exhibition of *tableaux vivants*' given by Mrs Hastings Anderson on 15 March, describing at great length her impersonation of Judith with the head of Holofernes, of Walter Scott's Rebecca and of a Madonna of Murillo, the part of the infant Christ being taken by one of her own children. These *tableaux vivants* required a great deal of rehearsal, as John Maquay well knew, for Elena was among the performers. So too was her friend Miss De Courcy, whose contribution won praise from the *Post*; her father, the colonel, was watching.[34]

In general, cultural life was thought to be in good health in the late 1830s. On 21 December 1838 the *Morning Post* reported in glowing terms on the 'musical parties' at Standish's theatre, which attracted all the best vocal and instrumental talents and 'the *élite* of our fashionables'. Arthur Vansittart was also an enthusiast for amateur dramatics, but it was with the revival of racing in Florence that Charles Hervey retrospectively associated him. His articles for English sporting journals described not only meetings at Florence and Leghorn but allied topics, such as the races held in honour of St John the Baptist on 24 June.[35] It must be confessed that they were written in a tiresomely overblown style, which did not spare the reader the proofs that Vansittart had received a gentleman's classical education, but they shed their own light on a chapter of the social history of the British in Tuscany.

Although they name numerous owners, the Turfite's bulletins reveal that a relatively small group was dominant among them, with the Poniatowskis at their head. Another noteworthy personality of a different stamp was the hotelier and coach-maker Silvestro Gasperini, who was deeply involved as Secretary of the Jockey Club, at this time an impermanent, almost *ad hoc* organization. In one of his articles Vansittart describes a visit to Gasperini's hotel, the *Pelicano* in Piazza Santa Trinità, to observe him at work. In his company he found the Poniatowski brothers, Baron Lowenberg, some other members of the fancy and some rather more plebeian English figures, including Joseph Gamgee and James Huband. Both of these were proprietors of livery stables and also ran horses on their own account.[36] Patrons ran their horses in their own livery with coloured caps and jackets *à l'anglais*.

The Turfite's first report described the autumn meeting of 1838. It began:

> The races at Florence, which, since the retirement of Lord Normanby, Sir Hedworth Williamson, and Messrs Thelluson, St John, and Perry, had sunk into insignificance, bid fair, this autumn, to surpass, in excellence of sport, the most brilliant meetings of that truly sporting era.[37]

Vansittart recurred on later occasions to nostalgia for the bygone days of Burghersh and Normanby. If the Maquay diaries are any guide, there does seem to have been a lull in Florentine racing during the 1830s. John records going to the meeting on 2 fine days in early March 1831, but silence then falls until the spring of 1837, the year remembered by Charles Hervey, when several days of racing took place despite unfriendly weather.[38] According to John, Lord Burghersh, visiting Florence, attended the autumn meeting in 1838, which was 'fairly good'. A report published in the *Times* on 16 October also listed Burghersh, Vansittart himself and Prince Metternich among the spectators. In this writer's opinion the races had been a great improvement on the previous year's.

The Arno stakes aroused great interest, focussed on the respective prospects of Prince Charles Poniatowski and Gasperini. The former engaged 'a first-rate jockey' for the occasion, but 'Gas' was not caught napping and wrote to his friend Mr Perry, who had adorned Florentine society in the 1820s and subsequently became master of the horse to the Lord Lieutenant of Ireland, none other than Lord Normanby. Perry sent out a jockey called George Maxted, who had been winning prizes at country meetings in England. His arrival was cloaked in secrecy until a few days before the meeting and the Turfite gave him the credit of the victory.[39] *Galignani* named the victorious horse as *Selim*, 'a colt out of the Duke of Richmond's stable'. Both accounts agreed that a good deal of money changed hands.

Many horses came from England. Gamgee went frequently to England to buy stallions for Italian patrons and played a major role in the recruitment of jockeys and trainers from reputable stables, such as Scott and Prince in Yorkshire and Newmarket. In his piece on the Carnival of 1839 Vansittart mentioned that Charles

Poniatowski had imported a grey from Yorkshire, 'whose name, pedigree & performance are kept profoundly secret'.[40] There is a good deal of evidence of the trading of horses both between England (especially Yorkshire) and Florence, and also between owners in Florence. Towards the end of 1840, a Colonel Anson sold his 2-year-old Derby colt, *Traffic*, who was taken from stables at Malton by railway, *en route* to Florence. The purchaser was the Honourable Richard Bingham, brother to Lord Lucan. According to Vansittart, *Traffic* ran for him in the Arno Stakes in the spring of 1841 and came second to Joseph Poniatowski's *Antrim* (a suggestive name in itself), narrowly beaten only because badly ridden. Shortly afterwards we are told that *Traffic* was jointly owned by Bingham and Charles Poniatowski, who bought out Bingham's share immediately after this defeat for 200 *Louis d'or* and the very next day won with him.[41] The *Hull Packet* on 7 May reported erroneously that Poniatowski, having won the Arno and two other races with *Traffic*, 'means to give us another ball on the strength of his winnings', while 'Sir Joseph Hawley leaves Florence on account of his losses!'[42]

Chateau Lafitte was another horse which changed hands several times. The famous Tattersall had bought him as a 2-year-old for Gasperini, paying the Duke of Richmond £30; in Florence, Gasperini sold him to Baron Lowenberg before Sir Joseph Hawley bought him for 300 *louis d'or* (about £240) in 1840.[43] Vansittart (Hawley's brother-in-law) thought that the horse was only defeated in the 1841 Arno because the jockey disobeyed orders as to how to run the race, but a less kindly observer thought that he had been nobbled by arrangement between Poniatowski and Gasperini.[44] Another aristocratic owner was the erratic Ferdinand St John, *attaché* at the Legation, who achieved several victories. The Anglo-Florentine market in horseflesh continued beyond the period of the Turfite's coverage and was not confined to racehorses. In 1849 it was reported that Gamgee had purchased four superior coach horses, three of which had won prizes at various Yorkshire shows and were on their way to Florence from Howden railway station, together with two others which had been entrained at York.[45]

It was far from unknown for owners to ride their own horses and for gentlemen to show off their equestrianism. On the third day of the autumn meeting in 1838, Henry Cottrell rode the Turfite's own horse *San Leopoldo* in a match against Mr Onslow on his *Grey Momus*, 'made merely to amuse the ladies' and to display the two gentlemen's skills. In another match, between Mr Lousada's *Lucca* and Mr Singleton's *Sultan*, the former won 'entirely by the superior riding of Mr Lousada'. Lousada belonged to a ramified family of Portuguese Jewish origin and was ennobled by the Grand Duke in 1845, while his wife became a *dame d'honneur* to the Grand Duchess.[46]

In his account of this meeting Vansittart kept alive the spirit of the earlier 'golden age' by discussing opera alongside the racing. Charles Poniatowski had announced *L'Elisir d'Amore* at the Standish theatre for the evening of the first day of the meeting, to do honour to no less a person than Prince Metternich. Unfortunately, Giuliani, who was to sing Nemorino, was ill and Metternich was thus deprived of 'the richest treat that can be imagined'. Vansittart lavished praises on Charles Poniatowksi, who was to have sung the charlatan Dulcamara, and his wife Elisa, who would have been the heroine Adina. Thanks to Giuliani's illness, the opera became a ball, which on its own terms was clearly a glittering success. *L'Elisir d'Amore* saw the light of day on the following 27 January, during Carnival, with the recovered Giuliani as Nemorino, and a few days earlier *Il Barbiere di Siviglia* had been performed with a similar cast. These performances were noticed by the *Gazzetta*, for they were given in Standish's theatre in aid of the Florentine orphanages.[47]

The Turfite anticipated criticism from his readers: What was he doing writing about opera in a sporting magazine? His answer was, effectively, that 'in so effeminate a city as that our fair one of Florence', there was so little sport as a red-blooded Englishman would understand it that he had to write about something. The Carnival of 1839 Vansittart regarded as an altogether limp affair, thanks largely to the fact that many major social luminaries had migrated southwards, and he did not expect much of the forthcoming spring meeting other than a certain entertainment value: 'As to the racing, it is below mediocrity'. Sardonically he predicted that the occasion would be 'brilliant' because of 'the extreme badness of all the horses, and the utter impossibility of deciding which is the worst of an abominable string of cripples'. Nevertheless, he supplied the readers of the *Sporting Review* with an account of the meeting, which saw the first and (he expected) only hurdles in Florence. A proposed repeat performance was banned because of safety concerns on the part of the Tuscan authorities.

Vansittart spent the summer of 1839 at Leghorn and endeavoured to set up an autumn meeting there, which did not prevent him from returning to Florence to see the October races. When describing the autumn meeting of 1840, he remarked on a considerable recent increase in gambling. This meeting was enlivened by an accident when *Chateau Lafitte* slipped and sent his jockey, Carter, on an 'aerial flight': 'Prompt assistance was given, and he was transported to the *cafe* on the Piazzone, where Drs Kissock, Bankhead, and Harding lavished every attention on him that medical skill could suggest'. The fortunate Carter was unhurt and even survived this welter of medical intervention.[48]

The Turfite's account of the spring meeting of 1841 seems to have been his swansong, and it was perhaps in the awareness that he was writing a valedictory bulletin that he expressed his views on the present state and future prospects of racing in Tuscany. He began with some typically British reflections. There was no kind of 'rural sport' in Tuscany except horse racing, which accounted for the enthusiasm with which it was embraced by all classes. Hence it was that

> not only all the English idlers, but so many of the Florentine nobles, have embarked heart and soul in the only manly pursuit to which the enervating effects of a sultry climate, the luxurious manners and mode of living of the inhabitants, and their constitutional indolence of temperament have not denied them access.[49]

Vansittart urged the Tuscan government to lend its aid to the promotion of horse racing, for it would then cease to be dependent on 'the exertions of any English turfites, whom chance, choice or necessity may detain in Tuscany'. The present Jockey Club had been founded to last only for 5 years and would cease to exist with the forthcoming autumn races, unless the Florentine nobility bestirred themselves.

Despite these forebodings, the spring meeting 'in sport and interest was unusually rich, and attracted company from every part of Italy'. It was enlivened by some more accidents which proved not to be serious and by the appearance of St John's 12-year-old son (John Henry), riding his own horse 'in the gala dress which he sported at Poniatowsky's Fancy Ball last winter'. The Turfite seems not to have covered the autumn meeting, which was to be the last held under the auspices of the evanescent Jockey Club, but an account appeared in the *Morning Post* of 30 October, which reported that the Tuscan nobility were absent because of the death of the young Archduchess. 'Our fair countrywomen' had nonetheless filled the grandstands and there were some distinguished Russians in attendance.

Thereafter English press coverage was scanty. *Bell's Life* gave a brief account of runners at the meetings of autumn 1845 and spring 1846, revealing that Lords Vernon and Drumlanrig (heir to the Marquis of Queensberry) were now among the owners involved. John Maquay's diary during these years contains few mentions of the races, which could be explained in a number of ways, on some occasions by his absence from Florence. Elena went to the spring meeting of 1841, but he did not, simply hearing that there was great betting on the Arno Stakes. There is then compete silence until April 1845, when he attended on a couple of days, recording on the 21st that 'Poniatowski as usual lost everything almost'.[50] Races took place in October, but he went neither then nor in the following March; in the spring of 1846 Elena took a friend one day, but he did not accompany them.

He next attended on 19 April 1847 and had cause to regret it. His motive for going may well have been that his young friend Denham Cookes was riding. Clearly the concerns of the Tuscan authorities had been overborne, for the last race of the day was over hurdles. Cookes was riding a horse of Lord Ashtown, but a collision over the first hurdle resulted in his falling on his head, the horse then falling on him. He never regained consciousness; the combined efforts of Drs Trotman, Harding and Wilson proved unavailing. John and two of the physicians watched over him through the night, but he died on the 21st.

The accident seems to have shaken Florentine society beyond the ranks of the British. On the 24th John was one of the chief mourners at Cookes's funeral, as *Borrow's Worcester Journal* reported in its extensive coverage on both 6 and 13 May:

His pall was born by Prince Demidoff, Lord Ashtown, Mr J. P. Knox, Mr Wild, Mr Tyser, and Captain Bennett; and John Maquay and Wm. Cave, Esqrs. were his chief mourners. Among numerous other instances of the respect and regard in which the late Mr Cookes was generally and deservedly held, we may mention that Prince Poniatowsky, from the time of the accident until its fatal termination, sent messengers every half hour to enquire how he was; while another distinguished nobleman, Prince Demidoff, evinced his sincerity and good feeling, by directing – what he is taught by his church to consider efficacious – a solemn service to be celebrated in the Greek Church for the repose of his soul.

John's shaken and sententious reaction reflects his increasing religiosity as he felt old age coming on (he was now 55): 'thus ends poor Denham cut off in the midst of health and gaiety without a moments preparation. Let us hope he was prepared, and let it be a warning to us all to prepare for a like exit.'[51] From now on, he had little appetite for the turf.

Women of course were merely decorative spectators at the races, but elsewhere English ladies rode in a manner which surprised the natives and occasionally endangered themselves. In 1845 Lady Drumlanrig underwent 'a sad accident', as the *Times* reported on 9 December. She was riding one of Vansittart's race-horses in the Cascine when she was thrown

with great violence against a tree. For awhile it was thought her ladyship was killed, as she lay senseless, her nose perfectly flattened, with several gaping wounds on the forehead.

She proved to be made of stern stuff. 'No bones were broken, and to-day the faculty pronounce her out of danger.' On 14 December the *Satirist* remarked that

had the same accident happened to Drummy, considering the thickness of his skull, the tree would have had the worst of it. His lordship's refined taste is backing boxers, rejoicing in the office of stakeholder, and writing (see last Bell's Life) slang letters to sporting papers. Verily our aristocracy are improving.

'Drummy' evidently had *Bell's Life* sent out to him, for he wrote from Florence to express his opinion on the refereeing of the Caunt-Bendigo bout, which had taken place on 9 September 1845 near Oxford and became a subject of impassioned debate among followers of bare-knuckle fighting. This gave rise to a lively correspondence, in which his Lordship received almost as much abuse as the fighters.[52]

The Turfite's last article in fact concerned not English racing, but a major annual event in the Florentine calendar which attracted a great deal of attention from both visitors and residents: the celebrations on 23 and 24 June of the feast of the city's patron St John the Baptist. The chaotic bareback racing through the streets, which was one of its major features, tended to be regarded by the British with a mixture of incredulity and contempt. Published in 1842, Vansittart's account probably described the events of the previous year. He recorded fatalities among the spectators, including women and children: 'Who cares for the spilling of blood?' Gasperini's *Tipsy* won, as she had done several times before. She sounds like an English horse, which the Turfite probably meant to imply when he credited her with 'all the indomitable resolution and pertinacity of a through bred English mastiff!'[53]

The fireworks and other festivities were generally more congenial to the British. The diaries of the Maquays, mother and son, bear ample witness to these annual jollifications, although as the years go by, John sounds a little jaded by repetition. In June 1841 Elena took the children to see the horse races, but both John and Elizabeth stayed at home, John noting that two people were killed by a horse running away.[54] Earlier that same month he had taken Elena and their son George to Pisa to see the illuminations that celebrated the feast of the local patron San Raniero, another tourist attraction. Their friends the Crossmans were there at the Palazzo Roncioni on the Lungarno. The event was put in doubt when a storm came on and lightning struck the cross on top of the cathedral, but it cleared up and they 'certainly witnessed a magnificent spectacle.'[55]

The Jockey Club could be regarded as one of a number of forms of distinctively masculine sociability. From time to time John Maquay gave all-male dinner parties and recorded that he had attended similar parties elsewhere. For a few years Irish patriotism produced an annual celebration, which was also an all-male affair.[56] On 17 March 1833 John observed: 'Patrick's Day and a very wet one, and I dare say my countrymen will make it wet inside as well as out.' There is no mention here of any special celebration, but a year later there was to be a dinner for St Patrick, which was highly organized. On 10 March a preliminary meeting was held to discuss the arrangements and on the 13th there was 'a rehearsal dinner of the Stewards'. The dinner itself was held at the York Hotel; Colonel De Courcy was president, John one of the stewards, thirty-five sat down to dinner and proceedings continued until 2.30. Seymour was a guest and 'all past over very well & harmoniously'.

The following year, on 10 March 1835, a preliminary meeting was again held, and the 17th was a doubly special day. The Maquays' first child, George, was born on the 15th and baptised on St Patrick's Day, which did not stop John from attending the dinner at the York Hotel. Again he was a steward; of the thirty-four diners, twenty were Irish, and De Courcy was again in the chair and Seymour, with Edgecumbe, again a guest. Seymour 'in a pretty little speech proposed the health of Master George Maquay and I had to return my due thanks some good singing particularly Mr French'. Charles Hervey remembered the banker French's musical talents: 'he had a sweet tenor voice, and sang Moore's melodies, notably "Love's Young Dream," with exquisite taste and feeling', which doubtless went down well on St Patrick's Day.

For a moment it may have looked as if the dinner would become an institution, but in 1836 no one attended the preliminary meeting, and on the day itself, John remarks simply that he dined at the Roast Beef Club, without specifying whether this was in connection with St Patrick or not. In neither 1837 nor 1838 is there any sign of a dinner; in 1839 John was in England; just back in Florence in March 1840, he betrays no awareness of any celebration. In 1841 he states explicitly that there was no dinner, and in 1842 he was again absent from Florence. Things were different on 17 March 1843, when thirty-six guests sat down at a dinner at the Hotel d'Italie, Pakenham made a couple of good speeches and John got home by 11 o'clock. Elizabeth Maquay went to see the tables laid out for this dinner, which she states explicitly was for St Patrick.[57]

In 1844 the saint's day fell on a Sunday and the dinner was postponed on to the following day. Rather oddly, John was hosting his own party that evening and he remarked that not many people came because of the large St Patrick's dinner, held at Palazzo Ximenes, to which, for some unexplained reason, 'I would not go'. In 1845 the day fell in Holy Week and no dinner took place; some of the other lacunae may be similarly explained. The next dinner, in 1846, again took place at the Italia hotel, attended by thirty persons, with the Marquis of Normanby as the guest of honour. The news of the Irish famine portended a permanent dampener on the celebration, followed as it soon was by political upheavals in Italy.

As early as August 1825, John was introduced at the Casino de' Nobili, with 'great form about qualifications'.[58] This institution, which stood at the corner of Via Tornabuoni and the Lungarno, over the years hosted a variety of social events, but there were recurrent attempts to establish imitations of the English club. The Roast Beef Club, where John noted that he dined for the first time on 13 January 1836, met at Madame Hombert's hotel in Via Porta Rossa.[59] How long this club lasted he does not tell us, but in January 1842 he was discussing with Talleyrand the formation of a 'Union Club' and was named one of a committee of seven who were to draw up its rules, which were approved on 31 January 1842.[60] No sooner had it been founded than John ceases to mention it, but it may be identifiable as the 'Cercle de la Réunion', which was thus advertised in the *Tuscan Athenaeum* of 15 January 1848:

New Reading Rooms and Circulating Library. This Establishment, conducted upon the principals [sic] of the London Club-Houses, is open to all travellers, by the Week, Month, or an [sic] Year; it is well provided with the Newspapers of most countries and a House dinner is provided for subscribers, daily at ½ past Five oClock. The entrance is at 3348 Borg'Ognissanti.

On 27 February 1844 John records having become a member of 'the new Casino'.[61] This was housed in the former Borghese Palace in Via Ghibellina, sold by the prince's heirs in 1843. A distinct sense of *dejà vu* is induced when we read that on 21 December 1846 John attended a dinner at what he called the 'Cerchi de l' Union', when there were 'proposals as to forming a club'.[62]

If it becomes more difficult to observe the British at play in any great detail after about 1845, it may be because the available sources change. Vansittart ceased to write his 'trash', although he lived in Florence for another 5 years, and the

Florentine races were now scarcely mentioned in the British press. The *Satirist* dries up and the London newspapers were less interested in the kind of trivial social reportage they had published in the 1820s. For as long as he remained in Florence, however, and even as he became less energetic with advancing age, John Maquay continued to chronicle the various diversions enjoyed by his social group.

Mrs Fombelle, much younger than her husband (in fact much of an age with John himself), continued to preside over entertainments such as the otherwise undescribed 'tableaux arranged by Mussini', which took place at her house on 25 June 1847.[63] 'Tableaux' were clearly grander and more public affairs than the 'charades', which were a popular feature of Anglo-Florentine parties. Other entertainments sound rather more cerebral. On 21 January 1843 the Maquays were invited to 'a recitation of Dante at Lady Vernon's', but could not go. Only a week later John attended a similar event at Colonel Lindsay's (but only for half an hour).[64] It is hard to imagine that there was a regular competition among British householders to stage events of so rarefied a character, but that Lady Vernon should have done so was hardly surprising. Her husband, since 1835 the fifth Baron Vernon, 'devoted his whole life to Dante' and this became a family occupation.[65]

Thomas Trollope is a valuable supplementary witness to the amusements available to the Anglo-Florentines. He makes much of Florence's cheapness, one of the original reasons that he and his mother settled there. A flask of excellent Chianti, equivalent in size to three bottles, might cost a paul (just over 2 pence) and the same sum purchased a good fowl in the market.[66] There were all the entertainments on offer that could be desired, without the need to offer anything in return, but they had not been long in Florence before the gregarious Mrs Trollope established a weekly Friday reception, at which whist became an ever-more frequent and regular activity. John visited her frequently for whist, and not only on Fridays. Some of her entertainments were more lavish. In January 1846 'Mrs Trollope's Ball was held at the Casino' and in February 1847 she produced 'a representation of the witches in *Macbeth* with Locke's music, extremely well got up'.[67]

The Tuscan Court remained an important social centre. Holland presented anyone to the Grand Duke who asked for it, thus avoiding some of the petty jealousies which had dogged earlier Ministers, but his successor, Sir George Hamilton, adopted a stricter policy, adhering to the recognized rule that only those who had been presented at home could be presented at the Florentine court. As a result 'the Grand Duke's receptions at the Pitti became notably weeded' and Hamilton soon received a hint that the Grand Duke would be pleased if he was a little less prescriptive. The Ambassador replied 'He shall have them all, rag, tag and bobtail.' As a result, Leopold supposedly declared that he 'kept the worst drawing-room in Europe'. His motive, Trollope was sure, was to enrich his subjects by doing everything to encourage 'the gold-bringing foreigners from that distant and barbarous western isle'.[68] Leopold himself always seemed ill at ease; his clothes never fitted him and he shifted from foot to foot, with nothing to say.

In the 1850s John Maquay presented visiting Americans, who had no diplomatic representation at Florence at this date. Trollope relates that on one occasion, John helpfully whispered in the Grand Duke's ear that 'the gentleman was connected by descent with the great Washington, upon which the Duke, changing his foot, said "Ah! Le grand Vash"'.

Trollope gives a graphic description of balls at the Pitti. No court dress was required except at the New Year, when the Grand Duke held a formal reception. No invitations were issued to those who had been before, only to newcomers (usually through their embassies); having once attended, one was welcome ever after. There was always an abundant supper and people used to line their pockets unashamedly with food. The English made a beeline for the bonbons, but Trollope records seeing Italians seizing a

> large portion of fish, sauce and all, packed up in a newspaper, and deposited in a pocket. I have seen fowls and ham share the same fate, without any newspaper at all. I have seen jelly carefully wrapped in an Italian countess's laced mouchoir!

Apparently a full bottle of wine was the only commodity off limits.[69]

Amateur theatricals clearly continued, but it becomes increasingly rare for John Maquay to give any particulars of the performers or even the titles of the plays. On 15 April 1842 he attended 'an English Amateur Play in Piazza Vecchia Lady of Lyons, Lady Louise Tenison, Mr Kay & de Courcy acted well, can't say much for the others'. His mother thought it 'admirably got up Lady Louise Tennison De Valebregue & De Courcy admirable Sir Francis Vincent so so Mr Thompson quite a Stick'.[70] (Mr Thompson was presumably one of John's 'others'.) Amateur plays, English and French, and charitable performances, were sometimes given at the Cocomero Theatre; John went there with Elena to see The Road to Ruin and The Mayor of Garratt in April 1845.[71]

We learn more from Thomas Trollope, who became involved in theatricals in his early Florentine years. Arthur Vansittart was a leading light:

> He engaged the Cocomero Theatre for our performances, and to the best of my remembrance defrayed the whole of the expense out of his own pocket. Vansittart was an exceptionally tall man, a thread-paper of a man, and a very bad actor. He was exceedingly noisy, and pushed vivacity to its extreme limits.

It seems appropriate that he should have come on in The Road to Ruin 'with a four in hand whip in hand'. He was also 'inexhaustibly good-natured and good-humoured, and gave us excellent suppers after the performance'. Others involved were Edward Hobhouse, 'far and away the cleverest and best-educated man of the little set', his wife and her sister Miss Graves. Sir Francis Vincent, 'a heavy actor with a good elocution and delivery', played Falkland in a production of The Rivals, in which Trollope himself was Bob Acres; Mrs Trollope was Mrs Malaprop and 'brought the house down' nightly. Later, Trollope made the role of Sir Anthony Absolute his own.[72]

Mary Boyle, who had adorned the theatricals of 1835, returned to Florence a decade or so later. On this visit she became friendly with the Vansittarts at Villa Salviati. Here she remembers her brother and herself amusing their hosts with 'a ballet d'action on a small scale' and being smothered with flowers from their magnificent garden at the conclusion. The Irish novelist Charles Lever arrived in Florence in 1847 and after a while rented Casa Standish with its private theatre. He loved either to act in a small group or deliver humorous monologues and promptly invited Mary to become his '*prima donna*', as he had heard she had previously done 'with so much honour'. To Mary, Lever was the complete type and model of an Irishman – 'warm-hearted, witty, rollicking' and 'often blind to his own interests'. He assembled an 'excellent' company. She remembered particularly a Captain Elliott, who was lodging with his charming wife in Piazza Pitti and was peculiarly suited, with his graceful and courteous demeanour, to play first lover. Elliott appeared as Joseph Surface in some 'detached scenes from the School for Scandal', in which 'our host and lessee gave a decided and Irish colouring to the reckless humour of his namesake "Charles"'.[73]

The plays are named at least sometimes, but the music which formed so important a part of Anglo-Florentine entertaining is rarely identified. For John Maquay, small dinner parties were punctuated by big set-piece affairs, with music and dancing. The music, seriously rehearsed and performed, played an important part, but we have no idea what it was. Emilia Goggi sang for them on 18 March 1841, her 'last time of singing before she comes out on the stage'. A year later the Poniatowski siblings were among the musical talent who helped to provide the '7 pieces of music' that preceded the dancing at one of their large parties, as they had done at John's housewarming in 1836 and did on other occasions.[74] On 29 January 1847 John held a ball with 'some supper, tho' not a regular one', which ended before 4 am; 367 were asked and some 225 turned up, but 'a few more not remembered' enlarged the number. Thirty or thirty-five were children, most of them in costume, who were asked to come at 8, the adults at 10. Such numbers appear large, but Poniatowski 5 days previously had opened his new *palazzo* with a ball for 600.[75]

We obtain the occasional glimpse of entertainments offered by the ambassador. In July 1848 Maquay heard his compatriot, the 'Hibernian prima donna', Catherine Hayes, sing at a party given by Sir George Hamilton, but, he says, 'I don't much like her voice.' He heard her sing again at Mrs French's in early November but made no further comment, perhaps because the lady had agreed to do him a good turn: she was going to take charge of his second son, John Popham, on his way to England to embark on his military training.[76]

Unlike Lever, Trollope or Vansittart, John Maquay was never a performer. His diaries continue to chronicle the usual social activities, but a good deal may have gone on that he did not know about, or at least participate in, as his age, infirmities and religiosity increased. During his later years he more than once records attending dinner parties, where the other guests were principally clergymen and the subjects of discussion were 'serious'. It was in harmony with this sober frame of mind that in the autumn of 1847 he sought to slake his thirst for clubs by promoting a Book Society. On 6 September he went to Christopher Webb Smith's Villa Lamporecchi to draw up the rules.[77] The usual difficulties experienced in sustaining any kind of club were probably aggravated in the difficult political times that were imminent, and John was anyway absent in Rome for a lengthy period in 1847–1848. Smith, conscientious as usual, maintained his interest, proposing in 1849 that an arrangement be made for exchanging books with the Pisan book club, but the Pisan side rejected the idea as it was attended with 'many inconveniences'.[78] In March 1850 Maquay and Smith decided that they should call a meeting of the Book Society 'this year', and it seems thereafter to have maintained a reasonably regular existence, until in 1857 it was decided to bring it to an end.

During the winter of 1847–1848, the *Tuscan Athenaeum* carried serious notices of cultural events, but it sheds little light on the activities of British amateurs in Florence. Arthur Vansittart contributed occasional reviews of opera at the Pergola, in one of which (27 November) he complained that all social gatherings seemed to be 'devoutly forsworn and avoided as if plague stricken by the Haute Société'. The *Athenaeum* at least afforded him the opportunity on 11 December to mention the races which were intended for the following spring. Whatever enterprises were afoot, there was now no single British impresario of the stature of Burghersh, Normanby or Rowland Standish; and, as far as the English newspapers were concerned, there would henceforth be more important Tuscan affairs to write about than the amusements of the Anglo-Florentines.

Notes

1   Jack Stillinger (ed.), *The Letters of Charles Armitage Brown* (Cambridge Mass., 1966), p. 255.
2   JLM, E9 f. 170v.
3   *Morning Post* & *Morning Chronicle* 1 August 1818; *Gazzetta* 16 July 1818.
4   The Medwin referred to was presumably the biographer of Shelley.
5   JLM, E9 f. 53v.
6   As reported in the *Morning Chronicle* 22 February 1830.
7   JLM, E9 f. 94v.; *Morning Post* 10 March & 10 May.
8   *Morning Post* 31 December 1828.
9   The British Library possesses a copy of the libretto of *Il Torneo, Dramma posto in Musica da Milord Burghersh, & rappresentato nel Palazzo di sua residenza in Firenze l'anno 1828*. It contains some pencil markings as if made in the course of rehearsal.
10   Mathews's account of his Florentine theatrical experiences is in Charles Dickens (ed.), *The Life of Charles James Mathews, Chiefly Autobiographical, with Selections from His Correspondence and Speeches* (London, 1879), Vol. 2, pp. 7–25. The editor was the son of the famous novelist.

11 Cornewall was probably one of the two sons of Folliot Herbert Cornewall, Bishop of Worcester, who died in 1832. These Cornewalls belonged to one branch of a family which claimed descent from an illegitimate son of Richard of Cornwall, son of King John and brother of Henry III; hence the 'Plantagenet' sobriquet.

12 FO79/53, 19 March 1829. It is bound into the volume with no cover.

13 Lord Malmesbury, *Memoirs of an Ex-Minister* (London, 1885), p. 18.

14 *Hampshire Telegraph* 3 August 1829; *Morning Chronicle* 31 August. Lord Blessington's departure had been noted in the same paper on 27 October 1828.

15 This may have been Fulwar Craven, born 1810, whose mother was Laura, daughter of George Vansittart of Bisham Abbey, Berkshire, and therefore related to the Vansittarts of Shottesbrook in the same county. One of his brothers was given Vansittart as a second name. He would have been young in 1829, but not perhaps too young to play Hal.

16 Charles Lever, *Cornelius O'Dowd upon Men and Women, and Other Things in General* (Edinburgh, 1864–5), Vol. 2, pp. 93–101.

17 Dickens (ed.), *Life of Mathews*, p. 79.

18 *The Odd Fellow* 24 April 1841. Henry Fox records going to see Vestris perform in Florence in 1828 (*Journal*, p. 316).

19 *Freeman's Journal* 12 December 1839.

20 JLM, E9 f. 241.

21 Sir Charles Boyle (ed.), *Mary Boyle Her Book* (London, 1901), pp. 147–8. MacCarthy's review was in the first issue of *The Tablet*, pp. 4–6.

22 *Mary Boyle*, p. 150.

23 Thomas A. Trollope, *What I Remember* (second edition, London, 1887), Vol. 2, pp. 100–1.

24 JLM, E10 ff. 8, 198, 198v. British newspaper notices reveal that during 1841 and 1842, she was singing with success in Berlin and Copenhagen, her star roles being in Donizetti's *Gemma di Vergy* and *Lucrezia Borgia*.

25 JLM, E9 f. 252, E10 ff. 75v, 130v.

26 He was also the owner of some noteworthy Italian pictures, one of which (by the Venetian Vincenzo Catena) is now in the National Gallery in London. The painting, *A Warrior Adoring the Infant Christ and the Virgin*, is illustrated in D. Robertson, *Sir Charles Eastlake and the Victorian Art World* (New Jersey, 1978), p. 133.

27 Charles Hervey, 'Florence Forty-Five Years Ago', *The Graphic*, 31 March 1885.

28 *The Tablet*, 5, pp. 69–71. For an outline of Catalani's career, see the article by Elizabeth Forbes in *The New Grove Dictionary of Music and Musicians* (2nd edition, London, 2001).

29 Charles Gibbon, *The Life of George Combe* (London, 1878), Vol. 2, p. 69.

30 Several Verdi biographers give some account of Goggi, including M. J. Phillips-Matz, *Verdi, a Biography* (Oxford, 1993), pp. 308, 311, 313, and David Kimbell, *Verdi in the Age of Romanticism* (Cambridge, 1991), p. 289, who quotes a letter from Verdi to Joseph Poniatowski about her qualities.

31 EM, C4 f. 39.

32 JLM, E9 f. 228.

33 JLM, E10 f.18.

34 *Morning Post* 14 April 1836. John records rehearsals on 4, 11 and 12 March, with a dress rehearsal on the 14th. JLM, E9 ff. 10v, 11.

35 In order of appearance these articles were: in *The Sporting Review* 'Florence Races', Vol. 1 (1839), pp. 33–9; ibid. 'Florence and Florentine Sporting: The Carnival of 1839', pp. 260–4; ibid. 'Florence Races, April 1839', pp. 448–53; ibid. 'Autumn on the Arno', Vol. 2 (1840), pp. 354–66; ibid. 'Leghorn and her Sports', Vol. 3 (1840), pp. 178–90;

ibid. 'Florence Races', pp. 450–2; ibid. 'Florence Autumn Meeting 1840', Vol. 4 (1841), pp. 348–53; ibid. 'Sketches of Horse Racing in Italy', pp. 423–9. In the *New Sporting Magazine* 'The Forest of Pisa and the Grand Duke's Stud Farm', Vol. 1 (1841), pp. 33–4; ibid. 'Florentine Races, 1841', Vol. 2 (1841), pp. 18–24; ibid. 'The Festival of St John the Baptist at Florence', Vol. 3 (1842), pp. 67–72.

36 'Autumn on the Arno' (1840), pp. 354–6.
37 'Florence Races' (1839), p. 33.
38 JLM, E9 f. 175v, E10 ff. 37, 73.
39 'Florence Races' (1839), p. 34.
40 'Florence and Florentine Sporting' (1839), p. 263.
41 *York Herald* 5 December 1840; 'Florentine Races' (1841), pp. 20, 21.
42 Joseph Hawley (on whom see DNB) was to be a Derby winner five times between 1851 and 1869 and recorded several other classic victories. Supposedly his interest was kindled in Florence, and he first went into partnership as a trainer with John Stanley, who was also to be seen at the Florentine races, but is never mentioned by the Turfite. In compensation he is mentioned frequently, and in no friendly spirit, by *The Satirist*.
43 'Florence Autumn Meeting' (1840), pp. 350, 352.
44 *The Satirist* 4 July 1841.
45 *Hull Packet* 26 January 1849, *York Herald* 27 January.
46 'Florence Races' (1839), p. 38. Lousada was married in London in November 1834, but not before he had threatened to horsewhip his future father-in-law Sir Charles Wolseley. He later entered the British diplomatic service and died in 1870 as HBM's consul at Boston. John Maquay never mentions him, although he knew other members of the family.
47 'Florence and Florentine Sporting' (1839), pp. 251–2; *Gazzetta*, 10, 19 & 29 January 1839. Besides supporting the orphanage as indicated, Standish also hired orphans from the *Istituto degli Innocenti* to help out in the theatre.
48 'Florence Autumn Meeting' (1840), pp. 348, 351.
49 'Florentine Races' (1841), p. 18.
50 JLM, E10 f. 242v.
51 JLM, E10 ff. 286v-287. The Greek Church referred to was probably the one in the Russian Embassy.
52 See the reports in *The Era* 9 & 16 November 1845.
53 'The Festival of St John the Baptist at Florence' (1842), p. 72.
54 JLM, E10 f. 172; EM, C7 f. 73v.
55 JLM, E10 f. 171v.
56 JLM references to the celebrations; E9 ff. 225(1833), 247v(1834), 268v(1835); E10 ff. 11(1836), 192v(1843), 218(1844), 243(1846).
57 EM, C7 f. 93v.
58 JLM, E9 f. 25.
59 JLM, E10 f. 8v.
60 JLM, E10 f. 159v.
61 JLM, E10 f. 216v.
62 JLM, E10 f. 278. A *Circolo dell'Unione* is said to have begun meeting at Demidoff's villa in 1852 and to have moved its meetings in 1853 to a sixteenth-century *palazzo* in via Tornabuoni (which still bears its name). The raison d'être of this society was the promotion of horse racing, but the word 'Union' in its title supposedly disturbed the Grand Duke because of its liberal connotations and it was rechristened the 'Jockey Club': Antonio Fredianelli, *I Palazzi storici* (Florence, 2007), p. 325.

63 JLM, E11 f. 6. Mussini was a notable painter who had opened a school in Florence in 1844.
64 JLM, E10 f. 189.
65 See the article in DNB. While continuing to be called Lord Vernon, the fifth baron in 1837 assumed the surname of Warren, in accordance with the will of a relative, Lady Bulkeley. The *Tuscan Athenaeum* in its tenth issue (31 December 1847) reported with pleasure his election as a corresponding member of the Accademia della Crusca, Italy's nearest equivalent to the Academie Française. Like Vansittart, Vernon returned to England in 1851 but was back in 1857. John Maquay had seen quite a lot of him and it looks very much as if he acted as his man of business, house-hunting for him and disposing of his furniture after his departure from Florence.
66 Trollope, *What I Remember*, Vol. 2, pp. 99–101. Trollope also gives an exceedingly useful guide to Tuscan currency. The lira, for instance, no longer existed as a coin (though it made a comeback after unification). The scudo was used, for example, for buying and selling land rather like the English guinea. The gold zecchini or 'sequins', Trollope says, were used for paying prizes in the lottery.
67 JLM, E10 ff. 260v, 284. Between January and May 1846, when Maquay left for England, there are eighteen references either to his going to the Trollopes or the Trollopes coming to him for whist and other entertainments.
68 Trollope, *What I Remember*, Vol. 2, pp. 93–5.
69 Trollope, *What I Remember*, Vol. 2, pp. 101–6.
70 JLM, E10 f. 167; EM, C7 f. 67v.
71 JLM, E10 f. 242, f. 260.
72 Trollope, *What I Remember*, Vol. 2, pp. 208–10. Trollope refers to the continuance of these amateur performances into the period of Italian unification, but the personnel (himself apart) must by then have been very different.
73 Boyle (ed.), *Mary Boyle*, pp. 205, 210–11.
74 JLM, E10 f. 138, f. 164.
75 JLM, E10 ff. 274v–275v, 276–276v, 281–3 all contain complete party lists and give some idea of the scale of John's acquaintances as well as the frequency of his entertaining at this date.
76 JLM, E11 ff. 24v, 29v, 30. An account of Hayes is given by Basil Walsh, *Catherine Hayes 1818–1861: The Hibernian Prima Donna* (Dublin, 2000).
77 JLM, E11 f. 9.
78 LMA, CLC/387/Ms22926, f. 25.

6 JOHN BULL AT PRAYER

The British paid particular attention to Protestantism in Italy at two moments in the history of the restored Grand Duchy. The first coincided with the move towards the removal of Catholic disabilities in Britain in the late 1820s; the second with the so-called Papal Aggression in the early 1850s, which aggravated British sensitivity to the perceived persecution of Protestants in Italy. At the earlier date, Tuscany enjoyed a British reputation as a haven of moderation and even toleration on the very doorstep of the Pope. Peter Leopold's legacy included a substantial measure of resistance to papal dictation and ecclesiastical privilege, but by 1850 that legacy seemed to be under threat and Tuscany's liberal reputation was fraying.

In October 1816, acting on instructions from the Foreign Office, Burghersh obtained from Count Fossombroni answers to certain questions about ecclesiastical affairs in Tuscany. Many indicated the determination of the Tuscan government to uphold the Leopoldine controls over episcopal appointments and the possession of church property. The final question, with its answer, read as follows[1]:

> What is the relative establishment or toleration of the Sects of Religion different from the Dominant Religion – and what are the Civil and Military Privileges which the Subjects belonging to such Sects are capable of enjoying?
>
> No Individual of any Religion whatsoever wishing to establish himself in Tuscany would be excluded from any Civil Rights, but excepting the Jews (who have public Synagogues in several towns of the Grand Duchy) there is no public worship excepting according to Roman Catholic rites. In the town of Leghorn however, the schismatic Greeks & other Heterodox professions are allowed to pursue in public their particular modes of worship. These, as well as the Jews, enjoy all Municipal privileges & honors annexed to their professions, but they are never employed either in civil or Military Service.

At Leghorn the old-established British church had maintained a ghostly existence throughout the war years under the direction of Thomas Hall, who told the Bishop of London that he had 'never neglected a single Sunday performing divine service, either in French or English.'[2] With the coming of peace, the situation rapidly returned to what passed for normality, although many of the incomers were anything but loyal Anglicans. There were Presbyterians, Methodists, Anabaptists, Unitarians and others, while even some of the Anglican clergy Hall encountered were 'methodists in their hearts'. At Leghorn these intrusive Methodists attracted police attention by their hymn-singing, and Hall was constrained to point out to them 'the impropriety of presuming to exercise the same liberty, in a foreign Country, where the Roman Catholic religion was established, as they had hitherto done in England'. Only 'the English episcopal Church' was officially sanctioned and to the police Hall was its licensed minister. He was pleased to be able to report that the dissenters and Presbyterians (mostly Scots) had in the course of time become pillars of his church, and at the most recent major festivals, he had had nearly a hundred communicants. Despite this optimism, dissenting undercurrents continued to afflict the Leghorn church.

Hall revealed also that since 1783 he had had no contact with any ecclesiastical superior, although he believed he was technically subject to the Bishop of London. His own desire to get this clarified had been thwarted by a party among the merchants who feared for their control over the appointment of the chaplain, but their successors were more amenable. It was as a result of contact with another émigré Anglican that Hall was finally convinced that the Bishop of London was his diocesan. The Rev. Trevor Trevor, prebendary of Chester, had spent some time in 1818–1819 trying to re-establish Anglican worship at Genoa and in the course of so doing discovered that he was theoretically responsible to Bishop Howley.

In 1816 the Leghorn mercantile community applied to the Tuscan government for permission to build themselves a church, which was granted on terms spelled out by the governor, Pompeo Spanocchi. The church was to be unobtrusive and to have no external sacred emblems, inscriptions or bells. It was to be built, and the chaplain maintained, entirely at the expense of the congregation; the chaplain must register the name of everyone who considered himself to belong to it and must provide the municipality with registers of baptisms, marriages and burials, which would have the same force of record as the registers of other (Catholic) parishes. It was made very clear that the chaplain's remit extended only to born Protestants; the Tuscan authorities were and would remain sensitive on the issues of proselytism and conversion. In broad terms the same conditions were imposed years later when Anglican churches were built not only at Leghorn but at Florence and Bagni.[3]

Unfortunately the congregation proved unable at this date to raise the necessary money, but by the time Hall wrote to Howley in 1820, the Grand Duke had ceded to the congregation the chapel of the suppressed Jesuits, for which they paid a moderate annual rent. This had been fitted up 'very neatly & commodiously after the manner of an English Church', which had a salutary effect on local opinion. Now that the Anglicans were no longer worshipping 'in a private room', they looked more like Christians. It had been entirely normal for migrant Protestants in Catholic Europe to conduct their services in a 'room' and so it remained, at Florence and elsewhere, for years to come.[4]

With an occupying force, a shrunken congregation and no contact with a bishop, Hall had not unnaturally become something of a law unto himself. He told Howley that he had catechized and instructed the young, admitting them to communion when they were sufficiently prepared. In this as in other respects, his pragmatism seemed after a decade of peace to be no longer in order. His successor, Charles Neat, asked in 1825 whether it would be possible to organize confirmation for his young people. Wishing as he did to conform as far as possible to standard Anglican usages, he was also perplexed to discover that marriages were contracted without banns or licence, and asked whether some means could be contrived whereby he could grant licences. The problems this situation could create were vividly illustrated when on 2 August 1827 he solemnized the bigamous marriage of the opera impresario Joseph Glossop with his mistress, failing (so Falconar maintained) to make adequate enquiries into Glossop's marital status.[5]

In the latter half of 1819 the Reverend Trevor moved from Genoa to Florence, where the ambassador's private chapel became the nucleus of the British church. Trevor was typical of the migratory clergy who were always to be found in Italy, and held several Cheshire livings during the years he was abroad.[6] John Maquay had often been in Chester, where his maternal grandmother and other relatives lived, and when he attended service in Florence early in 1823, he made himself known to Trevor and subsequently visited him at his 'very prettily situated' Villa Gondi outside the Porta Prato. It was Trevor who introduced him to Lord Burghersh.[7]

At this date the provision of Protestant worship in Catholic Europe seems to have been seen by men on the spot as a practical and pastoral problem rather than as matter of controversy. On 19 November 1822 Trevor wrote an informative letter to Burghersh, which was evidently intended for circulation as far as the Foreign Office.[8]

To whatever place our Countrymen resort in such numbers as they do to Florence, the necessity of having some one at hand to administer the spiritual relief and the Rites of our Church must, I think be apparent. I have now performed the duties of a Parochial Clergyman here for upwards of three Years and can assure Your Lordship that I never was more frequently called upon to exercise them in England, than I have been here. Our Congregation in your House on Sundays, from the beginning of October to the end of April or middle of May, has amounted to 150 & from that to 200 Persons, in the other months, the number has been less, but always respectable; the number of communicants at the Lord's Supper has been peculiarly large, & I am happy to say has been uniformly so, seldom less than 50 and at Christmas & Easter never less than 100, and often considerably more.

This was not a matter simply of numbers and performing the service. The Anglican clergyman offered pastoral support 'in almost every instance of distress, whether it arises from mental suffering or pecuniary want'. It was to this that Trevor had bent much of his energy, and he was grateful to his Florentine congregation for their liberal support. The purpose of the letter was to obtain authorization for a formal appointment as British Chaplain at Florence, if possible with remuneration but more likely without. The Foreign Secretary, Canning, had no objection to Trevor's holding the title, as long as it was understood that it implied no claim, pecuniary or otherwise, on His Majesty's government.

The last recorded marriage that Trevor performed at Florence took place on 12 March 1823, the last baptism on the 18th. It must have been around this time that Burghersh made him an *ex gratia* payment of £50 (which the Foreign Office refused to reimburse). For more than 4 years of his Florentine ministry, the clergyman had been 'in affluent Circumstances' and needed no remuneration, but 'some failures in England' had so reduced his income that he was scarcely able to afford the journey home.[9] For some months he may have had no regular replacement, but by the autumn of 1824 the Reverend Archdale Tayler, who had previously been in the service of the East India Company, was officiating, sometimes calling himself 'acting chaplain'.

The provision of facilities for Protestant worship (and burial) formed part of the larger issue of toleration. The journals kept by the Maquays on their continental travels shed an unselfconscious light on this subject. Presbyterians by nurture, they had no objection to attending Anglican services either in England or in Europe. In Leghorn with her parents in 1815 John Maquay's sister Betsy remarked that 'the English chapel' was 'not so well attended as it ought to be, considering the numbers of English here'; at Bagni there was no public Protestant worship to be had and 30 July was 'the first Sunday we have been without church since leaving Nice'. On the 5 Sundays her uncle, the elder John Maquay, spent in Bagni, he read the service to the servants (an expedient his nephew later often adopted, in Florence and elsewhere). At Florence he records reading the service on 17 September and subsequently merely remarks 'service as usual'. One may suppose that he attended the Ambassador's chapel; certainly he met Lord Burghersh.[10]

As John Maquay roamed around Italy during the 1820s he described varied provision, where it existed at all. In Florence on 2 November 1823 he noted that 'church' (presumably the ambassador's chapel) was 'very much crowded', which would not have surprised the now departed Dr Trevor.[11] At Rome a year later he attended services given in the *palazzo* occupied by the guidebook writer Mrs Starke, but on 26 December 1824 he 'walked to the new church … a room outside the Porta del Popolo'.[12] At Siena in the summer of 1825 he made no reference to Sunday worship until on 12 June, when he went to 'family prayer' with Mrs Colquitt, one of his many Irish expatriate acquaintances. This engagement was repeated on several Sundays, until on 17 July he rather oddly recorded how a Church of England service had taken place 'at Mr Bowyer in very old lodgings he an Anabaptist Clergyman'.[13] In the following weeks this became 'church'. Everywhere, the private reading of the service and sermons were possible expedients.

Although clearly sincere in his faith, John was not so zealous that he could not quite often be deterred from going to church not only by bad health but by bad weather and other distractions, and it was in no way unusual that he chronicled a great deal of attendance at Catholic spectacle. This included not merely services at the great churches with their accompanying music but such oddities as the baptism of Jews or the profession of nuns. The latter seems to have had a peculiar, almost morbid, fascination for the British. The rigorous Protestant might scent danger in the allurements of colour, sound and ritual, and might well also be alarmed by slack Sabbath-keeping. John, like others, would commonly go from service on a Sunday morning to tourist activities in afternoon and evening. Nowhere does he betray any frustration or annoyance about the facilities for Protestant worship. There was, and always would be, a difference between those who were content to work with what they found and those who demanded the unconditional recognition and concession of 'rights'.

Charles Brown believed that guests in a foreign land were obliged to respect the laws of the host country, including those which governed religion. On 13 December 1828 he wrote to Joseph Severn expressing unfavourable views of the evangelizing efforts of militant Protestants he had heard of in Rome.[14] He must have approved of the pamphlet that his friend Colonel Wardle published in the same year as his contribution to the British debate on Catholic emancipation.[15] Wardle refused to accept that Protestantism was inseparable from liberty, civilization and the 'social compact'. He had lived for 12 years among continental Catholics and had found them 'liberal in their sentiments upon all subjects, and upon that of religion, infinitely more so than very many of my Protestant countrymen'. Others with similar experience, he thought, would agree, and he was prepared to confront another treasured British Protestant belief. Like all Catholics, the Italians

> hold it to be wiser and better, that the reading of the minister be the reading of the flock, rather than that the flock should read each after his own manner. It is not that they cannot read the word, but that it is interpreted to them according to the reading of those who are supposed better to understand it.

Wardle did not pretend to decide which was better, but believed that Tuscany proved 'that the reading the Bible is not necessary to the establishment of good government, of which morality is an integral part'. It is hard to imagine a statement that would have been more comprehensively rejected by many British Protestants, both at this moment and 20 or 30 years later.

On 5 October 1827 the *Standard* reported the consecration of the Swiss chapel and the imminent opening of the Protestant burial ground that had been built at Florence with the aid of a contribution from the King of Prussia, praising the inhabitants for their readiness to support it and observing that 'in general strangers live quite at their ease among the polished inhabitants of Tuscany, and under its mild government, and have no kind of intolerance to complain of'. This was fighting talk. As the domestic debate on Catholic Emancipation gathered momentum, its British opponents drew attention to Protestant disabilities in Catholic countries.

A bald statement of the supposed position in Italy appeared in the *Cambridge Chronicle* on 26 December 1828: 'In Italy no Protestant can hold a place under

Government, and a Protestant is even prohibited worshipping his Maker according to the dictates of his conscience.'[16] The Earl of Hardwicke replied, contending that the employment of Protestants depended entirely on the ruler in question and, by way of answer to the second point, describing the chapel that had been established at Rome, where service was performed twice weekly from November until May. He also pointed out that 'at Genoa, Turin, Florence and Naples, there are places of worship for Protestants of the Church of England'.[17]

This mild rejoinder went a great deal too far for some. A certain 'Philocles' wrote an immediate response, which appeared in the *Chronicle* on 9 January, focussing on the difficulties and restrictions which had attended the English Church at Rome, and this was echoed by a correspondent, ominously code-named 'Luther', who declared in the *Morning Post* of 31 January that 'the Papists will not suffer a single English Protestant Church or Chapel to be built throughout all Italy or Piedmont'. The Leghorn merchants, if asked, might have corrected this assertion. 'Luther' now embraced Florence in his attack:

> Even at Florence, where so many English constantly reside, and spend so many hundreds of thousands of pounds, no Protestant English chapel is allowed to be built, and the only accommodation for us Protestants is to ask the favour of our Ambassador to be allowed, under his protection as ambassador, to attend in his parlour when his chaplain reads prayers, or delivers a sermon, and this parlour cannot contain the tenth part of the English who would wish to get a chair there, and it is the same at Turin and Naples. So much for Roman Catholic liberality and Christian charity!! and I defy any one to contradict these facts who has lately been in Italy.

The challenge was taken up by 'Veritas' in the *Morning Post* of 4 February, 'at Florence there is a Chapel for the Lutherans, to which the King of PRUSSIA has been a contributor; at Leghorn the same. You will observe, Sir, that these are Chapels, not attached to Embassies, not in Ambassadors' houses'.

'Luther' was strictly correct in stating that there was no 'English Protestant church' at Florence, but there is no evidence that the English had so far sought to build one, or that they would have been refused permission if they had. They would have had to pay for it themselves, and, as 'Veritas' indicated, an alternative was available. The 'Lutheran' chapel he referred to had been authorized by the Grand Duke on 24 July 1826 and opened on 5 September in a *palazzo* at 1921 Via Maggio. Albeit under the patronage and protection of the Protestant King of Prussia, it was the work of the Swiss colony in Florence. The English took an interest in it from the beginning. The fifty-six subscribers to the fund raised for its maintenance included the half-Swiss Horace Hall, son of Thomas, and the shopkeeper Samuel Lowe.[18]

On 14 January 1827 in Florence, John Maquay noted in his diary that there was a 'meeting of English after service'. He does not tell us what it was about, but it marked the beginnings of a church organization.[19] In October, through Horace Hall, the 'English' sought permission to hold services in the Swiss chapel at times that would not inconvenience its proprietors. The negotiations were not brought to a successful conclusion until June 1828, when it was agreed that the English would hold their Sunday service at half past twelve, paying an annual rent of 120 *francesconi*. The first service took place on the first Sunday in November 1828, by which time John Maquay and Elena were in Ireland. It is unfortunate that they spent so much time away from Florence during the next few years, for John's diary might have shed light on the growth of the English Church during a period for which very few records survive.

With the Reverend Archdale Tayler, we begin to see the transformation of the clergyman who served the ambassadorial chapel into the minister of the English Church. In 1830, having spent much of his life abroad, he returned to England and the rather different environment of Stoke Newington, and was replaced by Frederick Apthorp. Like so many others, Apthorp was a pluralist, chief among his benefices being the rectory of Gumley in Leicestershire, where he died in 1853 at the age of 74.[20] The Maquays encountered the Apthorps during their stay in Florence in 1830–1831 and briefly again when John and Elena returned in the autumn of 1832, but neither John nor his mother says anything about him in his professional capacity, mentioning only balls and concerts given by Mrs Apthorp. When the Apthorps left Florence late in 1832, John took over their furniture and the lease of their lodgings in Palazzo Quaratesi in Borg'Ognissanti. This apartment enjoyed a special asset in the form of a private box in the adjacent Teatro Solleciti.[21]

With Apthorp's successor Charles Henry Hutton, graduate of Balliol and fellow of Magdalen, we enter the period in which the English Church was taking on a more defined organization and John was in Florence to observe it. Hutton announced in a letter written on 8 December 1832 that he would commence his duties on the first Sunday of the New Year, making it clear from the outset that he would be absent during the summer. He was among the guests at a dinner party John gave on 25 January 1833, and 2 days later, on Sunday, he came again to dine 'and read us a sermon in the evening.'[22] It was only now that baptisms, marriages and burials began to be registered with some regularity and (in time) submitted to the Bishop of London's office. Hutton recorded his first marriage on 18 January, his first funeral on the 28th and his first baptism on 11 March. John attended church reasonably regularly at this time, but often also 'read to the servants' on a Sunday evening. There were two services on a Sunday and 'Mr Hutton catechized the children' after the evening service, sometimes apparently with John's assistance.

Meanwhile, cooperation with the Swiss had its problems, caused by the timing of the services and the growing size of the English congregation. On 3 March, a fine day, John 'walked with Kissock looking for a place for a new church.'[23] If the English were thinking of setting up by themselves, the idea for the moment came to nothing, perhaps because the Swiss had no wish to lose the annual rent the English were paying. They may also have thought it prudent for Protestants in Florence to present a united front. At all events, it was decided that the two congregations should move to a more commodious site. By the autumn of 1833 it had been agreed that the English were to pay two-thirds of the rent of 'the large hall on the first floor of Palazzo Magnani-Ferroni, 6 Via dei Seragli', which served as the joint church for the rest of the decade.[24] The palace also accommodated the British legation.

The management of the burial ground and the building of a mortuary chapel there were also under consideration. At some time in the spring or early summer of 1833, Maquay and Kissock, together with Hutton and Horace Hall, were appointed a sub-committee to consider whether the British could or should lay claim to a bigger say in the direction of the cemetery. John makes more than one reference in his diary for June to a 'report' on which he was working.[25] It was concluded that the English had no grounds for asking 'for any extension of privilege or share in the management', and that everything they could wish for was being provided by the Swiss, who were owed a considerable debt of gratitude.

The meeting to which this report was presented took a momentous decision, which we know about only because it was recalled over 6 years later at a time of crisis in the church's affairs. At a meeting held on 27 December 1839 it was stated that before 1833 'the management of the Affairs of the Church was in the hands of the Annual Subscribers'. Presumably they met *ad hoc* with little or nothing in the way of a constitution, although they were clearly capable of appointing committees and receiving reports. On 21 June 1833, the five gentlemen who had been appointed to oversee the congregation's move to bigger premises recommended the appointment of a managing committee of eleven subscribers, five to form a quorum, who were supposed to hold an Annual General Meeting. This suggestion was adopted. Neither the five gentlemen nor the eleven original committee members are named, but John was surely among them.[26]

Almost no sooner had these decisions been taken than church services ceased for the rest of the summer of 1833, to resume in September. Hutton went off on a 'tour', notifying both Seymour and the church committee that he intended to return on 7 September. Mr Yelverton (a well-connected Irish clergyman) proposed to spend the summer in Florence and 'kindly engaged to undertake any occasional duty which may occur'.[27] In the interim John sometimes recorded his private reading of morning or evening service; Elena was still attending Mass from time to time. Services resumed on 8 September, but Hutton himself was temporarily incapacitated by an operation for piles on the 21st. This affliction seems to have bothered him off and on, but he was presumably fit to attend the opening of the winter session in the new rooms on 17 November.

Isabella and David Wilmer arrived in Florence late in 1834 and stayed for a time with the Reverend Edward Peacock, who for some months assisted at the church, and his wife, Selina, David's half-sister. Church on several Sundays was so full that they were unable to get sittings, 'for which they charge three pauls each'. On 23 November, however, Mr Peacock took the clergyman's seat and Isabella was able to get in. She had a treat: 'Mr Yelverton reads prayers and Mr Hutton preaches. He gave us a very good sermon upon Death.' A Mr Burrard added to this little consortium of available clergy. Peacock looks a particularly good example of the affluent wandering clergyman, whose social routine was in no wise narrowly clerical. The Peacocks both gave parties and attended them, including fancy balls and masquerades. In the summer of 1835 they were off to Bagni and then to Viareggio and Rome. In April 1836 Peacock wrote to David Wilmer from Naples: he was 'thinking of being in Florence next winter if he can get the church here'. If not, they would return to Rome after a summer in Sorrento.

For some years the English Church was run, well or badly, by a clique of which John was one. Part of the problem which erupted late in 1839 was that the original volunteers had become a self-perpetuating body, which took decisions without involving the congregation, even to the limited extent of holding an Annual Meeting. Inferences about its membership can be made from a miscellany of sources, including John's diary. It was not a totally unchanging group, if only because people came and went from Florence: for example, Dr Kissock moved to Rome, probably in 1834. Horace Hall and Thomas Kerrich were clearly prominent members; John Fombelle and William Moffat rapidly joined both this group and John's social circle. By this date William Cunninghame Graham and his stepson Allen Bogle, whom John certainly knew well, were also members. The banker William Gracie Johnston was secretary and treasurer until John took those functions over from him in 1837.

Despite the attitude taken by the British government, and in contrast to the policy adopted by later ambassadors, both Seymour and Abercrombie were involved with the church to the extent of acting as chairmen of the committee.[28] On 12 May 1834 Seymour called on John to discuss 'Yelverton's appointment', which presumably means that the latter had indicated a desire to succeed Hutton, but 2 days later, he failed 'to come forward' at a committee meeting. Hutton did not leave Florence until the end of the year and Yelverton went to Genoa, as an indirect result of events which had unfolded at Leghorn.

It is impossible here to narrate all the troubles of the Reverend Thomas Harvey, who succeeded Neat as Leghorn chaplain in 1831, but they cannot have gone unnoticed at Florence. They were certainly noticed by Seymour, who saw the official correspondence on the subject and indeed wrote some of it. Harvey received some warm support and testimonials to his piety and integrity, but it seems clear that throughout his life, he had a gift for making enemies, notably among 'presbyterian' elements in his various flocks.[29] At Leghorn this resulted in a secession of certain members of the congregation, who preferred the ministry of the Reverend William Hare.[30] One of the most vociferous was Captain James Pattison Stewart RN, who had already quarrelled with the Reverend Neat and criticized the consul for not doing enough to encourage visiting seamen to attend church. Stewart's personality may be judged from a remark in a letter to Palmerston against Harvey: 'I presume that the testimony of an old officer in H. M. Service will have at least as much weight and influence with your Lordship as that [of] Merchants Clerks and Shopkeepers.'[31] In April 1833 there was an unseemly dispute between Harvey and Stewart at the graveside of a Mr Turner, a Pisan resident who had opposed Harvey and whose family tried to prevent him from conducting the funeral service. Stewart now denounced Harvey's chief supporters as either contaminated by Catholicism through family ties or never to be seen at church, or both. Palmerston directed Falconar to investigate.[32] This was a symptom of troubles to come on the subject of the burial ground.

Ironically in view of the struggles of the Florentine congregation to obtain government funding for their church, Stewart and his party favoured the withdrawal of that funding at Leghorn in order to secure its total independence. Many of them, a decade or so later, would form the congregation of the newly minted Free Church of Scotland. In the summer of 1834 Harvey's opponents accused him of helping to foment a duel at Bagni di Lucca and even being present at it, which as he himself remarked would have been the act of a madman. He had been offered the Genoa chaplaincy, but decided not to retreat before his accusers and Yelverton took the Genoese post. It was not long, however, before Harvey did leave Leghorn, only to experience repeated difficulties elsewhere. There may be one distant echo of these upheavals in the Maquay diaries. On 11 October 1835 John heard the new Florentine chaplain, the Reverend James Hutchinson, preach for the first time and was not entirely pleased, fearing that his style would 'prove what is erroneously called Evangelical hope not as it will create a party spirit we have hitherto been free from'. His mother some months later was, however, delighted with 'a very beautiful & impressive sermon' from Hutchinson.[33]

Hutchinson had scarcely taken up the reins when an incident took place which suggests some local hostility to the Protestant burial ground. On 5 November Horace Hall indignantly told Seymour that the cemetery had been vandalized during the previous night. Twenty-two monuments were 'flattened and dispersed, and offer such a dismal sight, that is really heart-rending'. The Swiss were going to seek redress through the Prussian Minister, but Seymour was requested to add his voice and said he would do so.[34] The outcome is unknown and nothing suggests that the incident was repeated.

Like most of the chaplains so far, Hutchinson was not destined to stay long; after about 9 months, he received the offer of a post at Rome. This rapid turnover of personnel doubtless helped to foster the belief among the leaders of the Florentine congregation that the clergyman was an employee who could be hired and fired at will, an attitude which drew strength from the fact that, as they were more than once told by their government, their church was an entirely private matter which they had to finance themselves.

Hutchinson's successor, the Reverend Hartop Knapp, proved a little more enduring. Knapp had been Gladstone's tutor at Eton in the 1820s, and the great man remembered him with a touch of affection.[35] Hutchinson favoured the congregation with 'a very good farewell sermon' on 26 June 1836 and the church then closed for the summer recess, but Knapp was in Florence already in July, subscribing to Vieusseux and meeting the church committee.[36] Services resumed in September, and on the 4th, John reported that Knapp's delivery was 'very drawling and monotonous, but his language appeared good'. His mother concurred: 'a most humdrum sermon language not amiss but deliver'd in a most monotonous Tone of Voice'.[37]

John's diary intermittently reveals small details of the incidents of church life, and in 1838 he began to chronicle new developments. On New Year's Day there was a church committee meeting at Abercrombie's residence, where a proposal was put forward 'of building a chapel &c'. In accordance with instructions he received at this meeting, Abercrombie wrote to the Tuscan government to ascertain whether any objection would be raised, and on the 3rd he was able to tell the committee that he had been assured 'that no impediments will be offered provided the proposed Building does not bear any external mark of being constructed for the express purpose of serving as a Protestant place of worship'. This was entirely consistent with the guidance the Leghorn congregation had received over 20 years earlier and again in 1837, when they revived their plans to build a church. Abercrombie advised the Florence committee that if they were able to collect sufficient funds to begin building, they should follow the example of the Leghorn Building Committee and submit 'the plan of the elevation' to the Tuscan government as soon as they had agreed on it.[38]

Another meeting took place on 12 January, when Knapp submitted his resignation. On the 18th Abercrombie despatched the following notice to the Vice Chancellor of the University of Cambridge:[39]

A vacancy being about to occur in the Chaplaincy to the British residents in Florence, the committee give notice, that all qualified clergymen of the Church of England who may be desirous of proposing themselves for the same, are requested to forward their applications (free of postage) accompanied with the proper testimonials, addressed to John Maquay Esq., Treasurer and Secretary to the Church Committee, Florence, before the 13th of April next; and that the election will take place on the 1st May next, 1838. N.B. The stipend is £100 sterling per annum, exclusive of surplice fees; and it is desirable that the candidates should state whether they are willing to take pupils, should such offer, and whether their views are directed to a lengthened residence in Florence.

It was a Cambridge man who was appointed, and during his incumbency, the English Church would experience unprecedented convulsions and receive a reformed constitution.

Robert John Tennant had performed a kind of spiritual odyssey before he became Florentine chaplain. His biography can be broadly reconstructed from the memories and correspondence of his Cambridge contemporaries, with assistance from a letter of recommendation (unconnected with the Florentine vacancy) that the Irish novelist Maria Edgeworth wrote on his behalf to the Archbishop of Canterbury on 23 July 1837.[40] He was born in 1809, the younger of two sons who both became clergymen. According to Maria Edgeworth, his father was 'a great manufacturer of broad-cloth at Leeds', who got rich and then over-reached himself and became poor. Tennant's Cambridge friends would see poverty as one of his major problems. While still a schoolboy at Christ's Hospital, he attracted the notice of Samuel Taylor Coleridge, and at the end of the century, Hallam Tennyson recalled that as a follower of Coleridge, he 'had been shaken in his belief, & had hesitated, like many others then, to take orders'.[41]

At Cambridge, Tennant became one of the 'Apostles', which accounts for his appearance in the letters and recollections of Arthur Hallam, Alfred Tennyson and their circle. Their various testimonies evoke a personality that had its difficult side. In July 1831 Hallam was worried that Tennant might have taken offence at something he had said or done and commented:

> It is Tennant's misfortune that with a soul yearning for sympathy, and capable of feeling and glorifying the tenderest, and the most exalted passions of which our nature is capable, he should be perpetually defeating his own end by the *pugnacity* of his intellect, and the capriciousness of his wilful humanity. The essential parts of him are worthy of all honour, admiration, and affectionate regard; yet the causes I have mentioned often make his conversation unpleasant, and give one a sensation like that of sitting near a hedgehog.[42]

This sounds like the man who later became chaplain at Florence. In 1834 Tennant was teaching at a school in Blackheath and urging Frederick and Alfred Tennyson to send their younger brother Horatio ('Rash') there. At about this time he decided to take orders and became Julius Hare's curate at Hurstmonceux.

When Maria Edgeworth wrote her letter of recommendation to Archbishop Howley, Tennant was in love and, she said, too poor to get married. His intended bride was born Mariquita Eroles, one of the daughters of a Catalan exile, Don Antonio Jesus Eroles. Her first husband, David Reid, had died at Florence in November 1833, and her sister Rosa was married to Maria Edgeworth's stepbrother Francis. She and Tennant were married at Clewer near Windsor on 2 January 1838, a few days before Knapp submitted his resignation to the Florentine committee. On 25 April John decided with Fombelle and Horne to support Tennant's candidacy and went to consult Moffat on the subject. When the committee met on 2 May, the names of no fewer than twenty-six candidates were put before them, but only two received any votes at all, seven in favour of Tennant and five, prophetically, for George Robbins, who at this moment was serving at Pisa and Bagni di Lucca and would be the Florentine chaplain in time to come.[43]

After a momentary hesitation on Tennant's part, he arrived in Florence on 29 August and immediately called on John, who on the following day drove him around to meet members of the committee. When church opened on the 2nd,

'Mr Tennant officiated for the first time, a most impressive discourse, and which made quite a sensation among the congregation'. John again drove the new minister around on the 4th to meet members of the congregation and completed the Tennants' induction into Anglo-Florentine society when a few days later he gave what his mother called 'a very handsome supper' for them, to which the members of the committee, their families and a few others were invited to the number of 'near 30'.[44]

As it happens, we know the content of that impressive first discourse, for it was included among the Florentine sermons which Mariquita published after her husband's early death.[45] What might the audience have found sensational about it? Presumably they were not unaccustomed to being reminded that they were sinful, but were they surprised by the slightly melodramatic picture Tennant drew of the hazards of their position?

> I feel a fearful responsibility rests with me, far removed as we are from our own land, and from the advice of the spiritual overseers of the Church; I feel as if leading a little flock here in the wilderness; and if the lion and the bear should come and take a lamb from the fold, it may require the courage and the faith of David to smite them and deliver the lamb.

This may have been taken as a coded reference to the perils of Catholic conversion, but in the light of later developments, it is tempting to wonder whether both the glancing allusion to episcopal authority, which the church had done without for so long, and Tennant's implied vision of his own role raised a few eyebrows. Preaching, he said, although foremost among his duties, was not the whole: 'in preaching, we are God's ministers towards you; in praying we are your ministers towards God'. Was there a hint here of the priest as intermediary, which may not have gone down well with the independent-minded elements in the congregation? It was certainly not the only example in Tennant's sermons.

There was mundane business to attend to, such as 'revising the poor list', and on 19 September John drove Tennant and his wife to see 'Casa Tough which is bought for the Church'. With this casual reference he introduces what proved to be an exceedingly contentious issue.[46] A little over a week previously Captain Aubin, *chargé d'affaires* at Florence, had written to Count Fossombroni, referring to the church's previously announced plan to buy or build new premises. An opportunity had arisen to purchase Mr Tough's house, on the left bank of the Arno between the Santa Trinità and Carraia bridges. The only necessary alteration might be the insertion of new windows. Fossombroni replied approvingly and a contract was drawn up by which the committee undertook to pay Tough 10,300 *francesconi* (around £2,300) over 6 years. The committee members named were Mr Bogle, Thomas Kerrich (the Treasurer), Horace Hall, John Maquay as secretary and Messrs Fombelle, Graham and Moffat. No one seemed concerned that they had not consulted the body of the subscribers before entering into this agreement or that they were not assured in advance of obtaining the money.[47]

On the First Sunday in Advent, which in 1838 fell on 2 December, Tennant issued an invitation:

> to join with me on every future Sunday, not only in the morning, but in the evening service of public worship. Beginning with next Sunday, I shall, with God's blessing, be ready to do the office of a priest, and to lead your evening prayers at the footstool of God's throne. The service will be read next Sunday evening, at seven o' clock, at my own house. Let me account all my congregation as my friends, and invite you to join with me at that hour in the holy offices of devotion.[48]

There had been an evening service in the days of Hartop Knapp, but it seems that it had ceased, either for want of demand or because it did not fit with the Swiss demands on the church premises. In reintroducing an evening service at his own house, Tennant was obviously seeking to encourage piety, but was also running the risk (as he may have realised) of promoting a holier-than-thou party spirit.[49]

Henry Fox was now ambassador at Florence. Services continued to be held in the *palazzo* which also housed his Legation, but in response to the offer of the 'Presidentship' of the committee, he wrote on 26 January 1839

> that it does not appear to me adviseable [sic] that the Minister representing Her Majesty's Government who may be called upon to protect & assist the interests of the Church Committee should himself form a component part of it.[50]

This attitude differed from that taken by his predecessors, but it was soon to be put to the test.

On 5 July 1839 John records for the first time serious symptoms of the troubles that were about to be visited on the clergyman and the church: 'Church meeting at Bank strong resolutions as to committee powers in opposition to chaplain think that Tennant puts forward pretensions beyond what he ought'. Possibly John was recording what was 'thought' by some rather than what he thought himself. On the following day he went to see Tennant, 'conversations about yesterdays business'.[51]

There is one stray clue to what was amiss, which is fortunately consonant with such other evidence as we possess. In May 1839 Bishop Blomfield of London wrote what was clearly a reply to a letter from Tennant, cautiously affirming his willingness to offer help and advice. As things stood he had no jurisdiction over the Florentine Church, but if the chaplain's stipend were to be paid by the government, 'the Secretary of State would require the chaplain to be licensed by me'. Were the residents to express a desire for the chaplain to be licensed, 'which is not infrequently the case under circumstances of a like description', that might be a different matter. As to the management of church affairs, he agreed 'that the money which had accumulated was best expended upon the important object of securing a permanent place of worship for the English Residents at Florence'.

Demands on the finances of the Church in England meant that he could offer no assistance towards liquidating the debt.[52]

For what happened next we are largely reliant on the minutes of the extraordinary General Meeting of subscribers which was held on 27 December 1839.[53] The meeting was chaired by Fox, who read a statement which must have been prepared for him and included a summary history of recent events. Quite deliberately it made limited reference to individuals and leaves a great deal unclear. Clearly two issues had come together and demanded resolution: the status of the clergyman in relation both to his congregation and to his putative ecclesiastical superior in London; and the recent management, or mismanagement, of the church's affairs by its committee. The scrappy evidence suggests that the proximate cause of the conflict was Tennant's support for a party within the congregation which was challenging the committee's control of the church.

In terms of the supposed church constitution as established in 1833, the committee had been proceeding irregularly for some years. Now that matters had come to a head, it was put on record that this had been recognized even before Tennant's arrival in Florence. At a meeting held on 18 April 1838 it was acknowledged that 'some irregularity has unintentionally taken place in the formation of the Committee'. A General Meeting was therefore to be called (none had been held since 1833), at which subscribers would be recommended to confirm the present committee and all their actions, and to empower them to fill up future vacancies as they occurred: that is, to sanction for the future the manner in which the committee had been conducting itself. The proposed meeting was duly held, attended by the committee and only two other subscribers, with John Fombelle in the chair, and everything that the committee desired was done. Ironically, perhaps, this was but 2 days before the governing clique decided to back Tennant as the new chaplain.[54]

For 18 months things went on as before. This apparent indifference on the part of the subscribers, and their willingness to let a virtually self-appointed body of activists get on with it, seems entirely typical of clubs and societies at all times and places. Something had to happen to galvanize the rank-and-file. On 24 May 1839 Horace Hall, Fombelle and Bogle wrote to Thomas Kerrich referring to Tough's 'non fulfilment of his duty' and the need for repairs which he should be required to make to the house.[55] This merely added to the gathering disquiet about the committee's handling of the negotiations for the purchase of the house. By autumn, there were signs that a party among the congregation was beginning to organize itself in opposition to the ruling junta. It emerges from a terse note from Colonel James Lindsay to Kerrich on 4 October that a General Meeting had been requested but not granted by the committee. Kerrich's note to this effect 'was by this Meeting deemed unsatisfactory'. How and by whom this 'Meeting' was constituted we are left to speculate. Colonel Lindsay, formerly a Tory MP, had not been long in Florence, but furnishes a good example of a relatively short-term resident, a man of some rank and distinction, who thoroughly involved himself in the activities of Anglo-Florentine society for as long as he was there.[56]

A few days later, Tennant wrote to Kerrich about a sermon that he proposed to preach in support of a collection for the new church.[57] He had been in contact with Horace Hall and had suggested to him 'that it might be as well to have the annual general meeting next week, before the Sermon, as it will probably increase the Collection by giving satisfaction to the seatholders'. Perhaps disingenuously, Tennant continued

> I presume there would of course be a meeting this year and only suggest that it should be now. Mr Hall seemed to think the annual meeting unnecessary, but on looking over my notes of the Proceedings I cannot agree with him in supposing that we as a Committee are wholly severed from the Congregation. However Mr Hall has promised that he will see you to speak on the subject. If there is no objection to my calling the meeting I should give notice of it on Sunday at the same time with the notice of the Sermon. I think it would give satisfaction to the seatholders because several have spoken to me about it, and because it might tend to remove various mistakes and prejudices respecting the new Chapel, which is the object of the Collection.

The committee's response to these stirrings seems extraordinarily ill-conceived. On 6 November the rain was pouring down in Trinidad and John Maquay could not leave the house; back in Florence, the committee held a meeting at which it was declared that the failure to hold an annual meeting during the present year was due to his absence. Taking the offensive, they pronounced 'the total inefficacy of the annual Meetings hitherto advertised to be held' and resolved to discontinue them forthwith unless or until one was thought necessary by a majority of themselves.

It must have been obvious that this course of action would arouse accusations that they were afraid to have their actions submitted to scrutiny. They emphasized that they had always 'given their time and trouble gratuitously' and declared that any annual subscriber who was interested could always consult their minute and account books at Bogle and Kerrich's Bank. It was further resolved that the committee should be enlarged to twenty, if so many could be found who were willing to serve. Their dissatisfaction with Tennant was not forgotten, and he was reminded that his position was dependent on their approval. At a subsequent meeting it was resolved that he should be dismissed, but this was apparently modified into a vote of censure on him.

We have no record of these contentious resolutions other than the summary given in Fox's statement. We do, however, have an undated scrap of paper on which Tennant wrote and signed the following:

> That according to the original constitution of the Committee they are responsible to the general Body of Annual Subscribers called together in an Annual Meeting and the Committee is not competent of themselves to abolish the Annual Meeting.[58]

Did he produce this note at the meeting of 6 November, which he would have attended *ex officio*, or write it afterwards?

The subscriber worms now collectively turned. Their demand for a General Meeting was countered with the offer of a meeting no earlier than the following June, when many subscribers, it was pointed out, would be absent from Florence. The committee's next move was to offer to prepare a copy of the accounts and make it available by the end of January, after which a meeting might be called if the demand still existed. Unsurprisingly, this was not thought satisfactory and a substantial number of subscribers applied to Fox to convene a meeting.

One result was a note addressed by Kerrich to Tennant on 22 December. He obviously thought it sufficiently momentous to keep a copy.

Sir, In consequence of a letter from Mr Fox informing me in my Official capacity as Secretary to the Church Committee that he had taken upon himself to request you to call a General Meeting of the congregation from the Pulpit for the 27th Inst & seeing that it was utterly impossible owing to the lateness of Mr Fox's communication to call a full Meeting of the Committee to take into consideration his request I have to inform you that a Quorum consisting of the following Gentlemen Mr Fombelle Mr Moffat Mr Hall Mr Graham & Mr Bogle & myself acquaint you that if you take such a step without the sanction of the Body who elected you the consequences must be upon yourself.

This speaks volumes about the committee's conception of their relationship with the Minister who represented the Queen, with the congregation and with their chaplain (as they evidently considered him).[59]

The contested General Meeting took place in the chapel at the Palazzo Magnani-Feroni on 27 December 1839 and with it the extant Minute Books begin. Among the indications that the committee itself was divided was a flurry of resignations in the days immediately beforehand. The *attaché* Edward Erskine (perhaps leant on by his chief) suddenly discovered that he was finding it difficult to attend committee meetings because of his duties in the legation chancery. It may have been genuinely coincidental that George Crawford had been summoned home to take command of the Royal Artillery at Devonport, but the letter written late on Christmas Eve by the physician James Playfair provides more evidence of the disquiet aroused by the committee's conduct. He had learned that a quorum had voted to lay a copy of a letter they had addressed to Mr Fox on the table of the public reading room. We have no idea what this letter said, but Playfair had signed it, not thinking that it was going to be thus made public; he had hoped only 'that some portion of it might lead to an amicable termination of the existing differences'. He therefore withdrew his signature and declared that if it was not expunged from the exhibited letter he would feel compelled to lay a copy of his present letter alongside it. At the same time he submitted his resignation. It may be significant that he was the favoured physician of the Legation.[60]

The resolutions taken at the meeting on 27 December may be briefly summarized. They were, first, that every person subscribing for a specific purpose had a right to see that his money was properly employed: therefore all who subscribed for 3 months or contributed 4 dollars in the year were entitled to attend and vote at General Meetings. Second,

> That the Assembly of British subjects for Worship in Florence, commonly called the British Church, is an Assembly according to the Doctrines, Discipline and Rites of the Church of England, and that the officiating Clergyman is responsible for his Ecclesiastical Duties solely to his Ecclesiastical Superior the Bishop of London in whose Diocese the Certificates of Baptisms and Marriages in Florence have always been registered.

There followed two resolutions concerning the future holding of General Meetings and the constitution of the committee, which was to include the clergyman, a member of the British mission, and thirteen members chosen from the subscribers, five to constitute a quorum. Their powers would terminate with every annual meeting. Like the first two resolutions, these were carried unanimously. The fifth disbanded the existing committee – in response, it was said, to their earnest desire to be relieved of the responsibility – and elected a new one, which included not only those who had headed the requisition to Fox but also John Maquay. It is hard to know whether it was felt that he could not be held responsible for actions taken by the committee in his absence or whether he was simply thought to guarantee a measure of continuity.

After these practical measures had been taken, Fox addressed the meeting and moved that the vote of censure lately passed on the Reverend Tennant should be expunged from the Minute Books

> as contrary and repugnant to the feelings of this Meeting, which takes this occasion of expressing their sense of deep obligation and sincere respect for the conduct of Mr Tennant since the commencement of his ministry at Florence up to the present day.

This motion, seconded by Captain Pakenham, was carried by acclamation. It all amounted to a pretty complete repudiation of the late committee, and it is not surprising that some of its members, such as Thomas Kerrich, never served again.

The day after the meeting Fox wrote both to the Foreign Secretary and privately to Fox-Strangways.[61] Among the contested issues, he gave priority to the position of Tennant. Tennant had asserted that the committee's claim to be able to dismiss him at pleasure 'was the doctrine of an Independent Chapel, but not of one, as he esteemed this to be, of the Church of England'. Faced with their continued intransigence, he had appealed to a General Meeting. It was this, as Fox presents it, which had provoked the committee, 'which had long been dreading any interference with their assumed powers', to resolve to abolish the

General Meeting. On top of this came 'a great feeling of dissatisfaction' about the committee's proceedings in respect of the house purchase. Fox himself had been a signatory, with over forty other respectable householders, to a petition addressed to the committee requesting a meeting before the end of 1839. This had met first a refusal and next 'a very evasive and unsatisfactory reply'. Fox had then received a requisition from well over fifty subscribers and had no hesitation in convening the meeting which had taken place the previous day. He names those who had headed the list as Lords Rendlesham and Farnham, Sir Henry Bethune, Colonel Lindsay, Mr Vansittart, Mr Millingen and Colonel Alcock.

Fox explained that his principal reason for troubling his Lordship with the matter was the possibility that violent attacks on himself would appear in the London papers. To Strangways he said, 'I am told Messrs Kerrich Fombelle Graham Moffat, Hall and Bogle intend to write flowing articles in the London papers against Mr Tennant the clergyman and myself.' It does not seem that these articles ever appeared, but what is one to make of this lineup of forces? Are we seeing loyal churchmen (including those sporting gentlemen Rendlesham and Vansittart) belatedly stirred into action against a gang of crypto-dissenters? We know that the absent John Maquay had been baptised and brought up a Presbyterian; that Hall, half-Swiss by birth, was closely associated with the Swiss Evangelical Church; that Bogle and Graham (currently plotting to defraud the banks of Europe) were Scots and probably Presbyterians; and that Thomas Kerrich was married to a daughter of George Baring, once an ordained clergyman of the Church of England who had seceded from it.

The British government's desire to ignore the existence of the Florentine Church as completely as possible stemmed primarily from its determination not to pay a penny towards its upkeep. It was and remained its firm contention that the Anglo-Florentines were there for their own amusement and not to forward the national interest through trade; the institutions they created had no claims on official support and as individuals they could seek the protection of the embassy only if they were denied the legal protection of the Tuscan government under international custom. Predictably, therefore, Fox was informed that Her Majesty's government had nothing whatever to do with the church and it was not proper for him in his capacity as HM's Minister to take any part in its disputes. To this Fox replied briefly but to the point.[62]

He was rightly able to claim that he had so far abstained from involvement as to decline becoming president of the committee as his predecessors had been,

but at the same time I must remark to Your Lordship that the Tuscan Govt have hitherto sanctioned and protected with guards, the British Place of Worship at the intercession and under the protection of the Mission – that the Committee have been recognized as a Body and permitted to acquire property in consequence of an application of Mr Aubin's; and should that official intercession and Protection which has hitherto existed, be withdrawn, it would doubtless be productive of serious evil to the British Community in Florence, and I conclude such is far from being Your Lordship's wish and intention, tho' Your Lordship justly observes that Her Majesty's Minister should in no way officially interfere with the differences among Subscribers.

Fox might have further argued that a Tuscan government which was utterly familiar with the concept of a state religion, not merely countenanced but enforced by the secular authorities, would have some difficulty in comprehending the British government's disavowal of any concern for Anglicans in Florence. As he had already made clear, he not unreasonably took the view that if divisions between British subjects in a foreign land were going to arouse publicity or even scandal, he was within his rights to act, certainly when requested to do so.

The Foreign Office may never have been aware of an exchange between Fox and the Tuscans, which demonstrated the truth of what he had told them. On 20 January 1840 he informed Fossombroni about the December meeting. In consequence Neri Corsini, the Secretary of State, issued an instruction to the Florentine municipality, stating it to be a maxim of the Tuscan government that neither the place of worship of a heterodox nation which possessed a Legation nor the individuals who administered it were officially recognized, unless the Legation itself gave its approval to both. The Florentine commune was to take note of the information now supplied by Mr Fox, notably that the previous committee was dissolved.[63]

By this time the new committee had run into difficulties with the old. Its attempts to get control of the church funds currently held by Messrs Bogle and Kerrich encountered legal difficulties because of claims arising out of the purchase of Tough's house.[64] The late committee delayed handing over documents and accounts. They also intimated that they had no intention of resigning and would justify their conduct at the postponed meeting to be held on 5 February. Horace Hall read a statement at this meeting 'explanatory of the conduct and proceedings of the late Committee' and proposed that no changes should be introduced until John Maquay returned, which was rejected. On 10 February the new treasurer was instructed to get hold of the funds that were still in the hands of Bogle and Kerrich and to transfer them temporarily to Messrs Guerber Gonin & Co. The new committee moved to discover the discrepancy between what was owed to Tough for the purchase of the house and what funds were actually available, and to achieve a total review of the project, including a valuation of the house.[65] It was also decided to investigate the possibility of making alterations to the accommodation currently being used for worship,

On 12 March John Maquay arrived back in Florence, horrified to discover the dissensions that had erupted in his absence. The next day, an adjourned General Meeting (which he attended) received a detailed report on the condition and potential of Tough's house, which recommended, reluctantly but unanimously, that it should be sold as soon as the price set on it by the congregation could be obtained. The wounded John moved that it should be retained as an investment, but was defeated. The meeting then voted a salary of £130 per annum to Tennant, with £20 for house rent. John confided to his diary that 'if I see my remaining on the committee is likely to be of any good I shall not flinch from the charge'.

For some weeks, unsurprisingly, he made numerous references to church affairs. He saw Tennant and others on church business, while the late committee maintained a phantom existence in which he participated. It was probably in part as their representative that on 6 April he proposed that a respectful letter should be written to the Bishop of London, explaining the difference of opinion that had arisen about the degree of control the congregation should exercise over their clergyman and asking his Lordship to state what authority he deemed himself to have over the Florentine Church. Would those who nominated the clergyman exceed their powers if they dismissed him, or if they sought to dictate the dates and purposes of charity sermons? The latter question reveals what had been one burning issue between Tennant and his would-be masters.

The resolution was slapped down by another, proposed by Lord Rendlesham and Colonel Alcock, to the effect that the church had already decided it was

an Assembly according to the Doctrine, Discipline & Rites of the Church of England, and that the officiating Clergyman is responsible for his Ecclesiastical duties solely to his Ecclesiastical superior the Bishop of London.

The meeting then proceeded to approve an application to the bishop for a licence for Tennant. On the following day, Lindsay as secretary wrote the desired letter; on the 13th, the late committee met and resolved to send its own memorial to the bishop.

On 25 April Maquay 'sent Col Lindsay all the Church papers'; perhaps he had at last extracted them from Kerrich. The difficulties he experienced as the sole survivor of the old committee and a would-be intermediary are strongly hinted at on 27 April, when he noted that he was 'as usual in minority' and that Colonel Alcock had declared 'his intention of moving a vote of censure on me' (which he evidently did not fulfil).[66] Also at this meeting Lindsay read his letter to Blomfield. We have the bishop's reply, written on 20 May, and also one that he wrote 3 days later to John Maquay.

The two cover much of the same ground. Blomfield acknowledged that as things stood, he had no authority over the Florentine chaplain, but he was of the firm opinion that every Anglican clergyman ought to acknowledge an ecclesiastical superior, and he could hardly suppose that any congregation would desire to withdraw from all episcopal superintendence. If a clergyman were licensed by a diocesan at the request of the congregation, they had no power to suspend or dismiss him. Blomfield also stated 'that the Chaplain ought not to admit any authoritative disturbance on the part of his congregation as to whether any, or what Collections should be made, in the Chapel, or at what time'.[67]

Lindsay had told Blomfield that Fox had chaired the great meeting of 27 December, and he wanted a copy of the minutes, signed by the Minister. Rather significantly, he said he had written to Palmerston desiring to be informed whether the Foreign Secretary had received any report from Fox, but at the time of writing, he had received no answer. The bishop's letter to Palmerston was written on 28 April, but it was not until 25 May that Palmerston deigned to draft a reply, saying only 'that HM's Govt have nothing to do with the appointment of a British Chaplain at that Place'.[68]

Lindsay read Blomfield's letter at a meeting held on 1 June, and 2 days later another meeting considered the reply that was to be made to it. John described this meeting as 'very strong and unconciliatory altho I went determined to do all in my power to put all right'. Nothing in the minutes really explains what prompted this remark.[69] A great deal of ill feeling had been created, but there was now no doubt that this was an Anglican congregation and that the chaplain would be licensed by the Bishop of London (it was not until the following year that the licence was actually issued). The subscribers had foregone all power to dismiss him, although for a few more years they retained the power to choose him.

The meeting of 1 June saw another demonstration of the new committee's enthusiasm for their clergyman. Colonel Alcock proposed that Tennant should be thanked for his recent excellent sermon in aid of the *Misericordia*, the most illustrious of Florentine charitable institutions, which extended 'its relief in the pure spirit of Christian charity to persons in distress of whatever Religion or country'. Tennant was to be invited to make a fair copy available for perusal in the Public Reading Room, and fifty copies of an Italian translation were to be printed for circulation 'among the native inhabitants most zealous in the cause of humanity'. Fox was to be requested to present one copy to the Grand Duke

as a testimonial of our readiness at all times to co-operate with his own subjects in general acts of Beneficence – and of our humble gratitude for the ease and security which the English uniformly experience under his enlightened and protecting government.[70]

Tennant's published sermons include one delivered in aid of the *Misericordia*, quite likely the one which aroused such admiration.[71] Like many of his sermons, it laid stress on the peculiar position of his auditors as Protestant strangers in a Catholic land. He set out to counter what he took to be a general view among his compatriots that they need not feel obliged to relieve the wants of the poor of the country in which they happened to be living. He could find no scriptural warrant for a refusal to recognise these unfortunates as fellow-Christians. His hearers should be grateful that as foreigners they enjoyed all the benefits enjoyed by the natives and that 'we are permitted to assemble ourselves together, though against the customs of the country, to worship God in our own manner, and the manner of our forefathers'. 'Shall we not willingly repay to the needy that which we have received from the condescension of the prince?' Tennant added a practical consideration: when at home, the English knew their neighbours and who the deserving poor were, but in Florence, they were vulnerable to imposture. By working through the *Misericordia*, they ensured that their benefactions were handled by people with local knowledge.

Reviewing Tennant's published discourses, we may think back 25 years or more to the alarm with which the Reverend Cunningham viewed the dangers of British travel in Catholic countries or, a decade later, 'Luther's' evident belief that freedom of worship was a right that the Protestant abroad should be able to demand. In other sermons Tennant came closer to the Reverend Cunningham's tone and cautioned the British against forsaking their native values, for example in the matter of Sabbath observance, but he explicitly rejected any intention to 'proselyte' those to whom he had no commission.[72] There were those among his congregation who in years to come would feel no such inhibition.

The English Church was thus described in an 1840 guidebook[73]:

English Divine Service

Divine worship according to the Service of the Church of England is performed every Sunday morning at 12 o'clock in the *palazzo Feroni, via di Serragli*. Seats may be taken by the year, month, or day, and although tickets are disposed of at the door before service, it is recommended that they should be procured from the *custode* at the Chapel the day previous, as many persons object to the paying money at the door of a Chapel, which the committee would have gladly avoided had it been possible; but after long experience, they found that until that method was adopted, the receipts fell so far short of the expenses that the Chapel would otherwise have had to be closed. There is a spacious gallery left open for free admission to servants and such persons as are not disposed to contribute to the expenses of the Church. The present Chapel (1839) is only a hired room; but a subscription has lately been set on foot to procure a permanent establishment, and sufficient money having been subscribed to pay the first instalment (about one third of the price) a commodious house on the Lung'Arno has been purchased which will shortly be fitted up for the purpose and for the Chaplain's residence; and the committee trusts to the liberality of their fellow-countrymen to enable them to meet the other instalments.

The notice continued by listing those empowered to receive subscriptions, beginning with John Maquay, treasurer and secretary, and concluded 'The Rev. R.J. Tennant, MA of Trinity College, Cambridge, chaplain, has an Evening service at 7 o'clock on Sunday evenings, to which all those who attend the chapel are invited.' In addition it appears that Tennant was keeping a school, or at least offering to do so, for the guidebook specified the terms on which he would prepare pupils aged 8 or more for the universities, either as day scholars or as boarders.

In October 1840 John resigned from the church committee. He still attended church regularly, taking young George (now 5 years old) with him, but when a General Meeting took place on 17 November, he did not attend. It was possibly just as well, for the secretary and acting chairman, his friend and business partner Captain Pakenham, delivered an address that might have irritated him. The report which Pakenham read to the subscribers displayed all the fervour and pomposity which marked his later history. His emphasis on the disinterested manner in which the present committee had conducted their business over the past year implied a contrast with their predecessors, and this, with his effusive praises of the chaplain, was scarcely calculated to soothe still-wounded feelings. It was not enough that Tennant should be thanked for continuing the service during the summer months and adding an evening service at other times, or that his inadequate salary, though not complained of by himself, should be increased. Pakenham's view of the chaplain's vocation could scarcely be more loftily conceived: the Minister was to be 'emphatically described as an Ambassador from God and as praying us in Christ's stead', a distant echo of Tennant's own inaugural sermon. Both his personal respectability and his total independence in the exercise of his office were therefore matters of the deepest concern to his flock. Pakenham went on to express the hope, forever doomed to disappointment, that it might be possible to obtain financial support from the British government now that the status of the church as an Anglican establishment had been confirmed.

After all this he announced the committee's decision to try to bury the hatchet with their predecessors, and a vote of thanks to the gentlemen of the late committee was therefore proposed. This met with a chilly response from Thomas Kerrich, reported at the meeting of 7 December: the members of the late committee declined to accept the thanks, not understanding why they were voted now and not last year. On 9 June 1841 a letter was drafted in pursuance of the quest for government financial support. Holland (as he now was) transmitted it to London, supporting the petition on the grounds that this would be the best means of obviating disputes of the kind 'which at one time ran so high as to endanger the whole Establishment & to create much excitement among the English Residents in Florence'. The answer was predictably negative. Palmerston's marginal comment on this despatch might well have been inspired by the recent example of Leghorn: 'They would quarrel a great deal more, look at all the Cases under the Consular Act.'[74]

Rumblings, if not quarrels, continued. At a committee meeting on 14 October 1842, Godfrey Byng Webster reported that there were still 'painful feelings' aroused by the second resolution that had been passed at the meeting of 27 December 1839, that is, the declaration that the congregation belonged to the Church of England and the clergyman owed obedience only to his ecclesiastical superior. Pakenham, as the only person present who had attended that meeting, tried to explain the real intention behind the resolution. The committee decided that it had been intended simply to establish for the future that the church was under the jurisdiction of the Bishop of London. John, presumably informed of these proceedings by a friend, perhaps Webster or Pakenham himself, noted in his diary 'resolutions carried exculpating the last committee and thus I hope restoring harmony by a tardy acknowledgement'.[75] Shortly after this, he left Florence for a visit to England and Ireland, but in his absence, it was proposed, on 6 November, that he should be invited to rejoin the committee as secretary. The timing seems significant, and his reinstatement ensured that he was in place during the momentous period of the building of the new church.

Tough's house had remained a millstone round the necks of the congregation, and in the autumn of 1841, the committee applied through Holland to the Tuscan government for renewed permission to sell it. He and they were reminded that the option of using the house as a place of worship would not be available to a purchaser, and that if in future another private chapel should be erected for the Protestant rite, 'that could only take place under the special influence of the English Mission and on the same conditions which had been established for the one which has ceased to exist'.[76] The inference was clear: the church in Florence was assumed to be a branch of the Established Church of England.

In other respects the moment was propitious. The Leghorn community had at last built its splendid neoclassical church (opened on 28 June 1840).[77] The Anglican congregation at Bagni had obtained permission to build a church for themselves, granted by the Duke of Lucca despite the vigorous opposition of the Archbishop of Lucca to the erection of a heretic temple, and were seeking a loan from their co-religionists at Florence.[78] Among his other eccentricities, the duke was given to fits of Anglicanism as well as Anglophilia, while the Grand Duke Leopold was at this moment far from the state of pious paranoia that would possess him after 1849. Not only did the much larger Florentine congregation not wish to be left behind but there was additional urgency, explained in a report delivered to the Annual Meeting of 2 November 1841.

The lease of the present chapel was due to expire in November 1842. When it had previously come up for renewal, an increased rent had been demanded and paid, but now it was understood that the *palazzo* might be put up for sale and there was a real prospect of 'being deprived even of our present Establishment'. Everything pointed to the desirability of building 'within the walls of this Ancient and renowned City'. Thanks particularly to the efforts of Mr Irving and Captain Lynch, there was already a substantial building fund. The new enthusiasm ensured that the report was carried unanimously, with the recommendation of an expanded committee to give effect to the proposals. Messrs Tenison, Whyte, Millingen, Vansittart, Knox, and Captains Bridges, Lynch and Pakenham were joined by Lord Mandeville and Messrs Delamore, Rowland, Spencer Perceval, Morgan Thomas and Webster. All possible avenues were to be explored, from raising funds locally to seeking support in England by personal approach and public advertisement, as well, of course, as a renewed approach to the British Government for help and assistance.

In fact there were to be a number of frustrating delays, and it was 3 years before the new church was opened. The committee perhaps distracted itself by first trying to find suitable buildings for conversion and it became clear that a timetable for completion in November 1842 could not be met. The first floor of the Palazzo Magnani-Feroni was now completely occupied by the British Embassy, and it was necessary in the summer to take temporary accommodation for the church on the ground floor of a *palazzo* in the Via Maggio. Further delays were imposed by the absence of most of the committee during the summer months and by the untimely death of Tennant on 24 July, which meant that as soon as committee meetings again became quorate the process of finding, a new chaplain had to be initiated. In the autumn the church again shifted premises to the Via Palagetto (now Via Guelfa). The one long-term gain from these moves was disengagement from the Swiss, with whom relations had become increasingly fraught because of an inability to agree on service timings.

The year 1842 had been disappointing for the church. The Annual Meeting in November had been informed not only of Tennant's death but of another *non possumus* from the British Government on the subject of financial support. When approached by aspirants to the vacant chaplaincy, the Foreign Office resolutely disclaimed any responsibility for the appointment.[79] It might therefore have seemed logical for it to leave the church to write its own letters requiring obedience from overseas churches to the new Bishop of Gibraltar; yet on 22 December 1842, Buchanan at the Legation acknowledged receipt of Lord Aberdeen's Circular 'intimating to me the desire of Her Majesty's Government that the Congregation of the English Church established at Florence should be placed under the Spiritual Superintendence of His Lordship'.[80]

On 17 February 1843, the appointment of the Reverend George Robbins as chaplain was confirmed, and the pace began to quicken. Robbins was thoroughly familiar with the Tuscan scene, but it was July before he could take up his responsibilities. At the same meeting the committee resolved to seek land on which to erect a purpose-built church. They alighted on a suitable piece of ground to the north of San Marco in the Via del Maglio (now the Via La Marmora), near the house which John Maquay had erected in 1838 and not all that far from the burial ground by the Porta Pinti. In April, Holland wrote to Corsini on behalf of the church, asking first whether the Grand Duke would waive his rights over what had been part of the royal demesne and allow the purchase from the present owner, and second whether the government would approve of the use to which the land was to be put. Corsini replied that the proposal would encounter no opposition, provided only that the 'edifice in question is constructed in such a manner as to give no exterior indication of the existence of the private chapel it is intended to establish there'.[81]

A new building subcommittee (consisting of Buchanan, Morgan Thomas, Webster, Hall and once again John Maquay) had been appointed in February and they now set vigorously to work. The purchase price was 1,725 *francesconi* (£386) payable immediately, and estimates and plans were drawn up. The original rather optimistic estimate for the building was for £1,743, payable according to contract in three instalments, the third and last being held against remedy of defects and settled within 3 years of completion. The final cost was some £2,680, but this included initial fittings and furnishings. Once the contract was concluded in September 1843, it took little more than a year to build the church, against a background of intense fund-raising.

In April 1844 Dr Tomlinson, the new Bishop of Gibraltar, visited Florence, an event recorded with unusual fullness in John Maquay's diary.[82] On 23 April he went

> after breakfast with Plunkett and Robbins to call on the Bishop with whom I was much pleased, and at 9 o'clock I took him up to see the new church where he remained a couple of hours and seemed to like it much.

The following day there was 'a handsome dinner for 20 persons' at Plunkett's for the bishop, his wife and chaplain, Robbins and his wife, such Anglican ecclesiastics as were in Florence and their spouses, Sir Charles Webster, and 'Pakenham & self'. This followed a confirmation of fifty-three young persons (an interesting pointer to the size of the British population). Lord Holland gave another dinner on the 25th with a slightly different guest list: the Bishop and Robbins (but no other clergymen), Lord and Lady Drumlanrig, the Plunketts, Messrs. Macdonnell, Bannerman and Cottrell and again 'Pakenham and self' together with Holland's artist in residence, George Watts.

On the 26th John loaned his carriage to the bishop for the whole day and gave his own dinner in the evening, an all-male affair of twelve, including his young Irish cousin John Adair. 'Mrs Tomlinson came in the evening', together with a number of other women who had no doubt been busy at the bazaar held during the day at Plunkett's, which had raised £140 for church funds. On Saturday John 'brought the bishop to my house to meet the committee where we talked over various matters and every one seemed much pleased with him'. On Sunday the 28th 'Bishop preached today and administered the Sacrament and collected for the church and he preached again in the evening when I attended and I rec'd the sacrament in the morning.' Finally, on Monday night, John held a Grand Ball, to which 191 were invited. The bishop must have departed exhausted on the 30th; he certainly did not lack for social life while in Florence, and there was no doubt who had been the chief moving spirit behind it all.

The new church opened on Sunday 17 November 1844, a fortnight after the disastrous overflowing of the Arno. John had been busy over the previous couple of days, among other things arranging the seating: 372 seats were taken. There had had to be some modifications to the exterior to meet the government's requirement that the building should be in no wise recognizable as a church. In June, Robbins had broken his leg when he was thrown from his carriage and was therefore out of action during the crucial discussions of furniture and fittings. The 17th was a very fine day, and service was attended by over 500 people, who made a collection for the flood victims.[83] Although the church was not formally consecrated till 2 June

1845, when the bishop made a return visit, the English community now had what they had long desired: a centre which they could call their own and which was forever England.

The immediate need to fill the church and attract custom was reflected in the circular notices organized by the committee and sent to all the hotels.

English Church at Florence

The new Church in the Via del Maglio is now open and Divine Service is performed there according to the Rites of the Established Church of England every Sunday Morning at 11 O Clock and every Sunday afternoon at 3 O Clock. The seats in the body of the Church are subject to a Tariff for Morning service, a box is provided for voluntary contributions at afternoon service and a spacious gallery is appropriated to free seats.

As it is found necessary to collect money from Non subscribers by means of tickets for the support of the Church funds, and as the Committee wish to avoid as much as possible the disposing of these tickets at the Church door on Sundays they earnestly request all Non subscribers to provide themselves with such tickets as they may require previously for which purpose the Custode has orders to attend at the Church on Saturdays from 2 till 5 o Clock at which time seats also can be subscribed for. All non Subscribers must [enter] in the church either by the door in the Maglio or by the garden.

There followed the arrangements for carriages and the notice concluded

As a considerable sum is still required for the completion of the Church the Committee confidently trust in the liberality of their fellow countrymen to enable them to carry out their purpose. Subscriptions will be received by all the English Bankers, by the Revd Geo Robbins chaplain and by the undersigned.

J L Maquay Tres & Secy[84]

It was perhaps inevitable that, with the main objective achieved, warfare would break out at the Annual Meeting on 20 November over the internal fittings of the church. Alternative plans were circulated and entrenched positions taken up. Robbins's moderating influence had unfortunately been largely absent since June, and there was clearly some resentment of decisions that had been made by the committee. The report for the year was finally adopted subject to Vansittart's olive-branch motion that furniture and fittings remain temporarily where they were, indicating that further consideration by the whole congregation was necessary. This was no sooner passed that Morgan Thomas, Captain Lynch and Randall Plunkett all resigned from the committee. Mr Webster then moved that, subject to the approval of the Bishop of Gibraltar, two churchwardens should be elected in place of the committee to assist the clergyman in managing the affairs of the church. This was a proposal with a future, but for the present, it was not accepted. John Maquay's comment on this meeting adds colour:

Annual Meeting at the Church very stormy and unsatisfactory Thomas attacked me and I replied and he ultimately resigned his seat on the Committee. He had taken seats for 20 servants to inable (sic) them to vote and they followed in Mr Thomas's tail from one side of the Church to the other as the voting went!!![85]

Three exclamation marks signal the height of drama in John's diary.

On 2 December there were calls for a General Meeting as soon as possible, and both Pakenham and Samuel Lowe submitted their resignations. The meeting demanded was held on the 16th, where it was agreed to hold the Annual Meeting in future on the last Friday in January and to elect the new committee then. Meanwhile what was left of the existing committee would stay in office and give effect to the necessary revision of the rules. This allowed tempers to cool while providing the congregation with the instant action the situation required.

On Friday 31 January 1845 the first Annual Meeting under the revised rules was held and a new committee was elected by ballot. This took place while the proposed new rules were being discussed, which set a precedent. John Maquay was mildly triumphalist: 'Morgan Thomas and his tail signally defeated much more decidedly so than I had anticipated and myself and all my friends were elected by ballot by large majorities.'[86] The new committee consisted of Plunkett (once again), Maquay, Webb Smith, Horace Hall, March, the Reverend John Prior and J. D. Thomson. It was a heavyweight committee, which contained elements of both continuity and new blood: Webb Smith was to prove a priceless stabilizing asset during the last years of the Grand Duke.

Of the new rules drawn up by the committee for the approval of the meeting, the eleventh was the only one to be substantially amended. As proposed, it provided that in the event of a vacancy in the chaplaincy, the committee (consisting of a minimum of six members) was to elect a clergyman to fill it, immediately notifying the Bishop of Gibraltar 'for his Lordship's approval and licence'. A temporary appointment for a period not exceeding 3 months could be made by a quorum in case of necessity. The amendment was epoch-making. The proposed arrangement for a temporary appointment remained unchanged, but: 'In the event of a vacancy in the Chaplaincy the Bishop of Gibraltar shall elect a clergyman to fill it.' At a stroke, the English Church in Florence ceded the patronage to the bishop. Rule 16 provided for the rules to be forwarded to the bishop and to remain in force until altered or repealed at a General Meeting. The question of furniture and fittings was to be dealt with by the committee as part of its governance.

This did not in fact suffice to bring instant and total peace. A special meeting was demanded for 17 February, at which there was evidently renewed discussion of Rule 11. As the proceedings were subsequently expunged from the record by order of a special General Meeting on the 25th, we do not know exactly what transpired, but from Maquay's perspective, the meeting was 'a complete scene of disorder and factious opposition God knows where it can end it quite upset me and I could eat no dinner'. He and his 'friends' adopted the strange tactic of addressing a memorial to the special General Meeting but resolving not to attend the meeting itself. As a result their memorial was read but not 'received' or recorded, and the opposition 'then had all their own way they erased everything that was resolved in last meeting and now I hope they will be contented with their triumph'.[87] It sounds very much as if John and his party had hoped to reinstate the original form of Rule 11, that is, to retain the committee's right to appoint the clergyman. This impression is strengthened when we learn that Morgan Thomas, on the 25th, proposed that the Bishop of Gibraltar be immediately informed that the right of presentation was now vested in him.

Morgan Thomas might no longer be on the committee, but he made himself felt. In September 1845 he and John, as secretary, were at odds over the manner in which a new distribution of seats was to be carried out. This resulted not only in a remarkably lengthy exchange of letters, which at least on Morgan Thomas's part were fairly vituperative, but in John's resignation from the committee, which he notified to a special meeting on 22 September. In his diary John referred to the renewal of his old adversary's 'captious ungentlemanly behaviour'.[88] He refused to reconsider his resignation, and this provided the opportunity for Christopher Webb Smith to inaugurate his career as secretary and treasurer.

When Smith read his annual report to the Annual General Meeting on 30 January 1846, he expressed the committee's 'great pleasure in being enabled to congratulate the Congregation upon the flourishing state of its Institutions and in ascribing that prosperity to the Great Head of the Church, the Author and Giver of every Blessing'. This happy state did not prevent Morgan Thomas from proposing no fewer than five amendments, two of them attempts to get the meeting adjourned. The flavour of one of the others will suffice:

> the Committee of the English Church at Florence is nominated by the Congregation and derives its power and authority from it. That the Committee is bound on all occasions to give effect to the Resolutions passed at any General Meeting of the Congregation duly convened – that the Committee was therefore bound to confine the new Benches within the lines laid down at the last Annual General Meeting as a rule for their guidance in the fitting up of the Interior of the Church.

Practical problems of all kinds nonetheless continued to preoccupy the men who governed the church. Experiments with the mode of collecting subscriptions led to some loss of income in 1846, particularly from the short-term visitors who were in Florence for less than 3 months. This was among several issues discussed at length at the Annual Meeting of 29 January 1847. Another was the ongoing problem of the burial ground.

The English now had a church building but no burial ground; the Swiss had a burial ground but no church building (they still leased premises in Palazzo Magnani Feroni). In the 18 years to the end of 1845, there had been 210 burials in the Swiss-owned cemetery, an average of about 1 per month, and English burials accounted for two-thirds of the income.[89] In 1834 there had been a proposal to erect a chapel for the reception of coffins, the accommodation of the minister and the conduct of the burial service in bad weather. The English had offered to pay for it, but Swiss sensitivity on the subject of ownership, combined with the subsequent full engagement of English finances, ensured that nothing happened. In 1846 it was proposed to renew the offer, but from the outset, the negotiations seem to have been bedevilled by misunderstanding.

The Swiss apparently suspected that no offer could be that generous; either it would be used to lever a shared proprietorship out of them or the majority users of the cemetery would attempt to manipulate burial fees to their advantage. The most they were prepared to concede was a mortuary chapel erected at the expense of both churches. They reiterated, with reference to burial rates, that the English would always be subject to the same charges as Protestants of every other denomination. Somewhat offended by what they regarded as a rebuff, the committee resolved that, while they would consider a plan and estimate for a chapel, they would also ascertain, before submitting new proposals, whether any pledges had ever been given as to burial fees. It was discovered fairly quickly that there had been no guarantee that fees would not be raised. There was no regulation of the fees charged by officiating ministers or for that matter by the *custode*, and those billed could not always distinguish between authorized and unauthorized charges.[90]

On 29 January 1847 the Annual General Meeting received a report to the effect that the *Consistoire* had refused any proposal which would give the English 'a part interest in the Cemetery, based on their paying half the expenses incurred in forming and enclosing the Cemetery'. Nor would they offer a guarantee that the burial fees would not be increased – an unreasonable demand, anyway, given that the *Consistoire* could not bind its successors or allow for inflation. The committee abandoned the idea of building a mortuary chapel and threatened to open negotiations for an independent cemetery. Faced with naked economic power, the Swiss caved in. Although they still refused to yield a *half* proprietary right in the cemetery, they promised to construct the Mortuary Chapel, to permit the consecration of the cemetery (by the Bishop of Gibraltar), to convert their leasehold into a freehold tenure, and to give a solemn pledge never to raise the present Tariff of the Burial Fees. Whether or not the threat to pursue an independent cemetery was bluff, it is clear that the English had no real appetite for the heavy outlay (at least 9,000 *francesconi*, over £2,000) that would have been required. The committee advised the subscribers, at a special meeting held on 21 April, 'to rest satisfied with your present position'. All things considered, there was good reason not to seek a separation. British Protestants would continue to be buried in the cemetery until 1877.[91]

The Annual Meeting of January 1847 was further enlivened by another clash between Morgan Thomas and John Maquay. John proposed the appointment of an assistant curate, who should run a school. Morgan Thomas (always seconded by Captain Lynch) moved repeated amendments, the third of them to the effect that as the patronage had been vested in the Bishop of Gibraltar, no such appointment could be made either by the committee or by the chaplain for the time being. John tersely reported the outcome: 'Morgan Thomas attended as usual but was able to do nothing and what we wanted was carried.'[92] This was not quite true, for a further amendment (not from Morgan Thomas, but carried) proposed that application be made to the bishop for the appointment of a curate. The idea foundered on the passive resistance of George Robbins, who informed a special meeting on 21 April that he regarded himself as perfectly equal to the discharge of his duties and did not want an assistant, but he evidently had no disposition to keep a school.

Morgan Thomas may have persisted in his flank attacks on the committee, but he is not again mentioned either by John Maquay or in the church minutes. As a partner in the banking firm of Maquay and Pakenham, John necessarily remained close to church affairs and he was again elected to the committee in June 1848. By this time the Florence in which the English Church lived was facing changes of a magnitude which was for a time hard to estimate.

Notes

1   FO79/27, Burghersh to FO, 28 October 1816. Much of this information the government had already in its possession in the form of 'A memorial on Tuscan Legislation in Ecclesiastical Matters, delivered to Lord Burghersh by order of the Secretary State for Foreign Affairs in Tuscany and ordered by the House of Commons to be printed 11 July 1815'.
2   LPL, Fulham Papers, Howley 4, pp. 561–4.
3   FO79/31, Burghersh to FO, 12 September 1818, enclosing a petition for government support; FO79/52, Falconar to FO, 10 October 1828, enclosing a copy of the conditions. Falconar claimed that by drawing a salary from the London Society for the Conversion of the Jews, the chaplain, Charles Neat, was at least potentially violating the clause that restricted the church's ministry to born Protestants. Leghorn had the largest Jewish population in Italy (estimated at the time at around 18,000 or nearly one-fourth of the population).
4   LPL, Fulham Papers, Howley 4, pp. 561–4.
5   There is an extensive correspondence in FO79/49 & 50 in particular.
6   Richard V. H. Burne, *Chester Cathedral* (London, 1958), pp. 226–7, 235. Trevor participated from time to time in disputes within the chapter. The double 'Trevor' is not a mistake.
7   JLM, E8 ff. 110, 111v, 112.
8   FO 79/38, Trevor to Burghersh, 19 November 1822.
9   FO 79/39a, FO to Burghersh, 5 June 1823.
10   Elizabeth Maquay junior, D ff. 5v, 32, 32v, 34, 39; John Maquay senior, A4 f. 105.
11   JLM, E8 ff. 73v, 107v, 153v.
12   JLM, E8 ff. 190v, 191, 193.
13   JLM, E9 ff. 20v, 23.
14   Grant E. Scott and Sue Brown (eds), *New Letters from Charles Brown to Joseph Severn* (www.re.umd.edu/editions/brownsevern) 28.

15   Gwillym Wardle, *Colonel Wardle to His Countrymen* (London, 1828).

16   This seems first to have appeared in a rather jumbled account of Catholic oppression of Protestants in the *Durham County Advertiser* 6 December 1828.

17   Hardwicke's riposte was reproduced in the *Bury & Norwich Post* 7 January 1829, *Morning Chronicle* 10, *Leicester Chronicle* 17 and the *Sheffield Independent* 24; it was paraphrased in the *Liverpool Mercury* 23 January 1829.

18   For a summary of these events, see Catherine Danyell Tassinari, *The History of the English Church in Florence* (Florence 1905), pp. 14–17.

19   JLM, E9 f. 66v.

20   His obituary in the *Gentleman's Magazine*, 1854, p. 651, referred to the various preferments which (implicitly) resulted from his marriage to a niece of the Bishop of Lincoln. Nothing is said about his spiritual qualities, but he was an assiduous magistrate.

21   JLM, E9 f. 217v, 27 November 1832. The theatre was many years later transformed into a Baptist church, still to be seen today.

22   *Church Letters*, 1830s, 16, 27 January 1833; JLM, E9 f. 222.

23   JLM, E9 f. 224.

24   Tassinari, *English Church*, pp. 19–21.

25   Years later, when the burial ground was again under discussion, what was probably this report (said to be dated 20 June 1833) was quoted in the church minute books CMB 1, 21 April 1847.

26   Christopher Webb Smith's researches in 1846 (CMB 1, p. 209) revealed that John had been 'a Member of the Church Comtee in 1832 – received a vote of thanks 27 Dec 1835 for his indefatigable exertions in conducting the affairs of the Church – was a Member of all SubComtees on every important occasion'.

27   *Church Letters*, 1830s, 21.

28   Seymour formally accepted this position in a letter dated 16 January 1832: *Church Letters* 1830s, 11.

29   The British Library possesses a large number of pamphlets generated by his travails wherever he went and documenting his complaints against a wide variety of people, including Lord Aberdeen and (especially) Bishop Blomfield of London (various shelf-marks, e.g. 1414.e.66). There is little here about Leghorn, but voluminous documentation of events is there in the Tuscan correspondence, beginning in FO79/59, 28 May 1831, when Seymour writes privately to Palmerston: 'It appears that the intimation of Mr Harvey's appointment to the Chaplaincy of that place has been received with considerable dismay.'

30   On 5 January 1833 Seymour sent the Foreign Secretary a massive dossier including the pamphlet warfare generated by the schism at Leghorn (FO79/80).

31   FO79/73, Stewart to Palmerston, 11 January 1833.

32   FO79/73, Stewart to Palmerston, 19 April 1833; Palmerston to Falconar, 22 May.

33   JLM, E9 f. 279 (the underlining is John's); EM, C5, f. 30v.

34   *Church Letters* 1830s, 28.

35   JLM, E10 f. 13v. Gladstone recalled that 'My tutor was the Rev. H.H. Knapp (practically all tutors were clergymen in those days). He was a reputed whig, an easy and kind-tempered man with a sense of scholarship, but no power of discipline, and no energy of desire to impress himself upon his pupils. I recollect but one piece of advice received later from him. It was that I should form my poetical taste upon Darwin, whose poems (the "Botanic Garden" and "Loves of the Plants") I obediently read through in consequence.' Quoted by John Morley, *The Life of William Ewart Gladstone* (2nd ed., London, 1905), Vol. 1, p. 29.

36   JLM, E10 f.1 6.

37 JLM, E10 ff. 16, 20v; EM C5, f. 37v.

38 JLM, E10 f. 57; *Church Letters*, 1830s, 37. Progress at Leghorn was sufficiently fast for the congregation to take possession of their new church in the summer of 1840, and this provided a natural stimulus to activity at Florence. FO79/91 contains initial correspondence and plans.

39 *Lancaster Gazette* 17 February 1838; *Blackburn Standard*, 21 February 1838.

40 LPL, Ms.2185, f. 132. See also the references in Peter Allen, *The Cambridge Apostles: The Early Years* (Cambridge, 1978) and Jack Kolb (ed.), *The Letters of Arthur Henry Hallam* (Columbus, Ohio, 1981), esp. pp. 346–7.

41 Hallam Tennyson, *Alfred Lord Tennyson: A Memoir by His Son* (London, 1897), Vol. 1, p. 177.

42 Kolb (ed.), *Letters of Hallam*, p. 453.

43 JLM, E10 ff. 65–65v.

44 JLM, E10 ff. 71v-72; EM, C6 ff.33v-34.

45 Robert J. Tennant, *Sermons Preached to the British Congregation at Florence* (London, 1846), pp. 12–13. William Gladstone subscribed for six copies of this edition and his brother John for one, which is now in the possession of the present authors. William met Tennant once when he was visiting Hallam at Cambridge.

46 JLM, E10 f. 72v.

47 Tassinari, *English Church*, pp. 23–5.

48 Tennant, *Sermons*, pp. 96–7.

49 In another, presumably later, sermon (ibid, pp. 368–9), he cautioned: 'Let not these our Sunday evenings be a mark or badge or party; let not those which are present judge those who are absent, as if they were not brethren; nor let it rather be a bond of Christian joy and charity; the voice of each one stirring up the spirit of the others to a watchful, earnest, and consistent life.'

50 *Church Letters*, 1830s, 52.

51 JLM, E10 f. 89.

52 LPL, Fulham Papers, Blomfield 20, ff. 65–6.

53 Transcribed by Tassinari, *English Church*, pp. 26–33. CMB 1 begins with these minutes.

54 John records both meetings in his diary without any additional comment whatsoever. On 21 May he records what he calls the 'annual church meeting', again without further elaboration: JLM, E10 ff. 64v, 66. It is a pity that only 3 weeks after he thus gave notice of the gathering storm, he himself left Florence, to go to Trinidad to look into the affairs of his late cousin John Adair, not to return until March 1840.

55 *Church Letters*, 1830s, 54.

56 *Church Letters*, 1830s, 45. Colonel James Lindsay (1791–1855) was a grandson of the fifth Earl of Balcarres. Once MP for Wigan, he was defeated standing for Fifeshire in 1837. A decided Tory, he had entertained changing views of Catholic Emancipation but had opposed electoral reform. He subscribed for 6 months to Vieusseux on 2 November 1839 and from time to time appears on John Maquay's guest-lists. John was house-hunting for him in July 1842. Father of a Crimean war hero, he died at Genoa in 1855 on his way to Florence.

57 *Church Letters*, 1830s, 53.

58 *Church Letters*, 1820s, 2. This note has been assigned to the wrong decade.

59 *Church Letters*, 1830s, 2.

60 *Church Letters*, 1830s, 51 (Erskine), 57 (Crawford), 58 (Playfair). Curiously, John never mentions him, and it is only because of his resignation from the committee that we know he was a member of it.

61 FO79/97, Fox to FO and to Fox-Strangways, 28 December.

62 FO79/96, FO to Fox, 17 January 1840; 79/97, Fox to FO, 30 January.
63 Tassinari, *English Church*, pp. 33–4. Fox distanced himself from further discussions of the rules and procedures of the new committee. Colonel Lindsay chaired the adjourned General Meeting on 5 February, but Fox did chair a subsequent adjourned General Meeting on 13 March, which was concerned largely with the premises issue.
64 CMB 1, meeting of 22 January; also *Church Letters*, 1840s, 21 & 22, to Bogle & Kerrich from Tough and Hall respectively, both dated 16 January 1840. Accounts of subsequent meetings all from CMB 1 unless otherwise stated.
65 An undated rent roll shows that Tennant was occupying a first-floor apartment in the house rent-free and was also renting a second-floor apartment, perhaps in connection with his school: *Church Letters*, 1840s, 23.
66 JLM, E10 ff. 111–16 cover the period between his return to Florence and the meeting of 4 May, when he noted that 'Col. Alcock did not attend to bring his motion of censure forward.'
67 LPL, Fulham Papers, Blomfield 25, ff. 43, 45.
68 FO79/99, Blomfield to Palmerston, 28 April 1840; FO to Bishop of London, 25 May.
69 JLM, E10 f. 118. Blomfield's letter (dated 23 May) is printed by Tassinari, pp. 41–2.
70 The first two proposals were carried unanimously, the third and fourth deferred for consideration at the next meeting.
71 Tennant, *Sermons*, pp. 540–58.
72 Tennant, *Sermons*, p. 483.
73 Capt. M.J. Jousiffe, *A Road Book for Travellers in Italy* (2nd ed., Brussels, Paris and London, 1840), pp. 51–3.
74 FO79/101, Holland to FO, 11 June 1841.
75 JLM, E10 f. 179.
76 CMB 1, pp. 46–7.
77 *Morning Post* 16 July 1840.
78 Bruno Cherubini, 'Dissensi fra Governo a Curia per un Tempio Protestante' in *Bagni di Lucca fra Cronaca e Storia* (Lucca, 1977), pp. 203–17. In the late summer of 1842 the Lucchese government also granted permission for a Protestant burial ground at Bagni, 'provided it be in a lonely and sequestered situation, where it cannot be complained of on account of the Public Health'. On 25 August Buchanan acknowledged the permission with thanks for 'the gracious consideration with which the Duke of Lucca has always met the wishes of my Countrymen residing in his dominions' (FO79/105).
79 CMB 1, 10 November 1842; FO79/106 Rev King to FO, 11 August 1842.
80 FO79/105 Buchanan to FO, 22 December 1842. Buchanan chaired the meeting on 7 December, in which the church declared its compliance.
81 Tassinari, *English Church*, pp. 45–58, contains an account in some detail of the site and building of the new church. Nothing of this correspondence between Holland and Corsini appears in FO79.
82 JLM, E10 ff. 220–221v.
83 JLM, E10 f. 232.
84 CMB 1, 11 November 1844.
85 JLM, E10 f. 232.
86 JLM, E10 f. 237.
87 JLM, E10 ff. 238–238v.
88 JLM, E10 f. 251.
89 These calculations are based on the registers of burials in the LMA and the English cemetery records. The cemetery in Piazzale Donatello is owned by the Swiss Church to this day. It was originally just outside the walls, but now echoes to the sound of

traffic as the ring road parts and swings either side of it. At what point the name 'English cemetery' became attached to the site is not certain.

90 For these transactions, see CMB 1, 30 January, 2 March, 6 April, 7 December 1846.

91 There continued to be a few burials in the cemetery and some scatterings of ashes after this date, particularly where there were existing familial links, but to all intents and purposes, the Allori, 3 miles south of the city centre, became and remains to this day the main non-Catholic burial ground for Florence.

92 JLM, E10 f. 281.

7 A WIDOW IN EXILE: ELIZABETH MAQUAY

At the end of 1845 a great change overtook John Maquay. His mother, Elizabeth, died on 10 December at the age of 83: 'such an emaciated form I would not have believed could live.'[1] He recorded her funeral on the 12th, and immediately succumbed to a heavy cold and a week later to an attack of neuralgia, which confined him to his bed until he struggled to the dinner table on Christmas day. Unprecedentedly, he made no diary entries between the 21st and 25th and did not begin to mend until the very end of the year. Whatever his relations with his mother had been, and despite the fact that he had had ample warning of her death, there seems little doubt that he was deeply affected by it.

Elizabeth's Florentine residence seems to have begun almost by chance and perpetuated itself from year to year until it became apparent that there was in every sense no going back. Probably restless by disposition, in earlier life she had been an indefatigable continental tourist, but by 1827, when she was 65 and her elder and favourite son, George, was installed in his fine new house at Cheltenham, she may have been ready to embrace a more settled mode of life. George's unexpected and unwelcome decision to get married precipitated fresh upheavals. The wedding took place in May 1830, while she and her sister, Sally Barnard, were on their way with John and Elena to Florence. Elizabeth did not return to Cheltenham until the summer of 1831, and the following year, she was off again with Sally, just ahead of John and Elena. It was not until the autumn of 1833 that they returned from Rome to Florence and what proved, for Elizabeth, to be a permanent domicile.

A summer trip to Switzerland in 1834 was her last excursion outside Italy. On her way there she said goodbye to her sister; they would never see each other again. She returned to Florence in November to hear of George's death in Cheltenham, which had more than merely emotional consequences for her. George had been left by his father with the responsibility of paying what was due to her under her marriage settlement, but he had no idea of the value of money and left a will with which his brother as executor struggled for years.[2] The value of George's bequests to his wife alone exceeded the value of his assets, and her father was quite determined that she was going to receive as much as possible, with some justification inasmuch as it was discovered that she was pregnant. Worse was to come when in the autumn of 1835 she unexpectedly entered into a second marriage, to the Reverend Henry Creed, which Elizabeth denounced as 'unkind and disgraceful'.[3] It was in every sense a disaster. The couple soon separated, and in the then state of the law, the Reverend Creed was left in possession of all his wife's assets.

These troubles were not of Elizabeth's making, but for others, she arguably bore some responsibility. She and John were probably not as close as she and George had been. At no time during her Florentine years was there any suggestion that she should live with him and Elena, and quite possibly nobody desired that she should. Her determination to maintain her own establishment led her to make one decision, which may have bred at least temporary resentment. On 6 November 1834 John recorded that 'she will not part with her servants during my absence'; she therefore would not move in with Elena, who was well advanced in pregnancy, during his absence in England.[4] Henrietta de Courcy stepped into the breach, but on New Year's Day 1835, Elizabeth 'din[e]d alone the first time in my life on this day'. In fact she had not been abandoned, for she had seen Elena only a couple of days previously.[5] Some ill feeling may have persisted, and there were minor squalls in the weeks and months that followed the baby's birth in March 1835.

The incident cannot have sweetened John's disposition towards the servants, whom (as he must have thought) his mother put before her daughter-in-law. It is not clear whether Elizabeth's maid Nanette, first mentioned by John in Cheltenham in 1827, was French or Italian, but her manservant, Tommasi, first certainly mentioned in the summer of 1832, was a native of the Lucca area.[6] It would be interesting to know more about his background; clearly he had business interests outside Elizabeth's household. He and Nanette were married in Florence in February 1834. It was not unusual to be served by a married couple, and Elizabeth's diary is full of the praise of her servants, who were so attentive to her wants, making sure that wherever she went everything was beautifully arranged for her arrival. There were troubles ahead, but in 1834 they lay some time in the future.

Elizabeth's social circle was inevitably much less Italian than her son's. One day in February 1837, she recorded as if surprised that she had 'gone to Johns in the evg unasked when I found them surrounded by Italians'.[7] Her education and early travels had habituated her to the use of French as a common currency, and this left its mark on her ideas of Italian and its spelling. Elena's music master was always 'Juliane' to her. She went several times to court but more than once refers very inappropriately to the 'Petit' Palace. She enjoyed an excursion, but we sometimes see her destinations through a glass darkly, as for example when on a disagreeable day in March 1834 the coachman, instructed to take them for a drive, 'chose the Bela Sguardia'. Among other victims of her orthographic creativity were the Boblie or Bobbly Gardens and the villa of 'Pioggio imperially', and one morning in July 1835, she walked in the 'Stroutzie' gardens. By becoming Madame Galeazzi, the former Grace Pennefather imposed an almost impossible strain on Elizabeth's spelling, as Miss Lee had done by becoming Madame Guadagni; 'Guardania' was one common rendering.

Elizabeth may have seen more of Lady Lee and her daughter than her son did. Sir Francis was unwell at the end of December 1840, and in late January 1841, Elizabeth was lamenting that having been a great deal better he had been 'thrown back'. He returned to active service, but on 12 November 1841, Elizabeth drove to see Lady Lee, only to be informed by her servant 'that she had just the acct of her husbands sudden death which sorely grievd me, I had been askd that evening to meet her at Mrs Mackenzies'.[8] Lady Lee clearly formed part of a feminine social network whose visits, tea-drinking and little supper parties are naturally little reflected in John's diary.

It was natural that Elizabeth should seek the acquaintance of other widows in Florence, of whom there were several, some merely visiting, some living with son or daughter, some presiding over their own households. Mrs Mackenzie was living with her desperately ailing daughter, who died in the autumn of 1838. She would come to Elizabeth's aid at a moment of crisis in her life. Then there was Mrs Hannah Meiklam, who paid an extended visit to Tuscany with her daughter, also Hannah, and son-in-law Richard Dennistoun. Elizabeth first mentions the family and Mrs Meiklam (sometimes 'Micklam') shortly after their arrival in Florence in November 1833, and they were fixtures in her diary for as long as they remained there.[9]

Her circle inevitably overlapped with her son's. Elizabeth found the Fombelles established as a ready-made addition to her acquaintance when she returned from Rome in October 1833. The Pophams and the Pakenhams were friends in common, and Elizabeth lived long enough to become acquainted with Mrs Trollope. However metamorphosed, Grace Galeazzi was Irish by birth, and the Irish in Florence, whether residents or visitors, formed an important part of Elizabeth's circle, belonging as they did to an intricate web of friends and relations familiar to her from youth. A typically breathless entry on 7 October 1842 shows her welcoming envoys from the world of the Irish gentry:

> spent a very pleasant evg at Websters who sent a very friendly invitation at Dinner time to go to meet the Gledstanes her Sister & the Plunkets & two or 3 Men I had never seen Plunket for thirteen years when he was a boy at Pisa with Ld Dunsany his Father I had never known Gledstanes but we met as old acquaintances as being connected wth Pallisers.[10]

Similarly qualified were Colonel De Courcy and his family, Lady Lucy Standish, the Ffolliotts and the Ruxtons, whose amateur theatricals Elizabeth patronized and appraised. Early in January 1834 she attended *Raising the Wind* at the Ruxtons' and in February *The Rivals* at Casa Standish, in which she thought Miss Moffat 'a great Stick', which was not a compliment, while the Colonel and Mr Ruxton were 'very good'. It was customary to pay calls on 'the Amateurs', as Elizabeth did the next day, to congratulate them on their achievement.[11] On New Year's Day 1835, she missed out on the theatricals at Casa Standish, but the Fombelles attended, for Elizabeth complained that they put her off for 'Lady Lucy's play'. On 15 March 1836 she went to see Mrs Anderson's much publicized *tableaux vivants*, opining that they were 'very well got up, but there was too much of a good thing 20 in Number, every one tir'd heat intense room very small & crouded [*sic*], half the company never saw any thing'. At nearly 74, Elizabeth liked her comfort, which was not always to be had on these occasions. On the following night there was a 'fine musick party at Lady Popham's very good singing', but 'very formal Circle all stuck against the Wall'.[12]

Her enthusiasm for music was undoubted and she had her opinions as she did about acting. On 2 June 1836 she went with the Wilmers to hear the distinguished Austrian mezzo Carolina Ungher in Donizetti's *Marino Faliero*. David Wilmer noted that she did not much like Ungher. Elizabeth herself was more exact: 'the Prima Donna a very fine scientifick singer but screamed too much'. In the following October, at a music party given by the Fombelles, she heard an unnamed gentleman who 'playd & sung Handels musick most delightfully much Taste & feeling he has a charming sweet Voice'. This was probably a Mr Noakes, whom she heard on other occasions; in the following May, she lamented that she had heard his 'sweet pipe' for the last time. She also judged the daughter of the Reverend Mr Apthorp to be one of the most accomplished 'private' singers she had ever heard.[13] Like her son, she knew and visited Angelica Catalani. On 3 January 1844 she went 'to congratulate Madame Catalani on her resurrection her death having appeared in the Papers'.[14]

Elizabeth had got to know David and Isabella Wilmer during the summer of 1835 and she introduced them to a number of people, including the Fombelles. On 9 July Isabella confided to her journal her view that Mrs Maquay was 'such a nice kind old lady'. On the 21st she took tea with her: 'The conversation is all in French, a French girl being of the company.' Elizabeth was not totally uninfluenced by her surroundings. On 27 January 1836 she gave a dinner party, which Mrs Wilmer described:

We sit down 12 in number to a beautiful and excellent dinner quite in the Italian style, the dessert being on the table all the time and every thing handed. The gentlemen left the dining room with the ladies.

The last-mentioned departure from English custom is particularly interesting. The hostess herself thought, 'Dinner very handsome and all went off very well.'[15]

On 17 June 1836 Elizabeth met Mrs Landor, probably in the Cascine, and there was a polite exchange of visits; but although she was invited to name a day when she would go early up to Fiesole and spend the day, there is no clear indication that she did so, and she last mentions Mrs Landor in May 1837.[16] Julia was somewhat shunned by Anglo-Florentine society; as for her husband, who in 1835 had left her and returned to England, he was distinctly uncongenial to Elizabeth. During her stay in Florence in 1830, she had made several efforts to call upon the Landors, without success. Then one day in December 'Mr Landor called whose face I hope I shall never again see from the appalling principles he sported'.[17] Elizabeth's principles were indeed quite different. Like many of her fellow-countrywomen, she was a connoisseur of clergymen, and dearly liked a good sermon and a little theological reading.

Like other Florentine residents, Elizabeth usually abandoned Florence during at least part of the summer: she went at different times to Bagni, Leghorn, Montecatini and Viareggio. In 1835 she found the Dennistouns at Bagni before herself proceeding to Brandeglio in the Lucchese hills, where Tommasi had relatives. On this first visit to Brandeglio she was conveyed up the 'mountain' by a 'Chaise a porteur':

> & a most frightful undertaking it was for an hour & half I was most dreadfully frightened not from any real danger for the men did not make a false step but carried me perfectly safe I do not think I should have been more frightened carrying me up Vesuvius

However, all was delightful at the top. One day Mrs Meiklam came to visit her and Elizabeth gave her a remarkable meal at the height of an Italian summer:

> a very nice dinner the best Irish Stew she said she had ever eaten a very large fine Trout loin of Veal Bacon salted in house & such Peas as I have not seen since I left England True Marrowfat.[18]

When Elizabeth returned to Brandeglio in the summer of 1836, she was visited by the Wilmers, who on 18 August found her 'looking very much older and changed poor woman', but nonetheless spent a delightful day with her, talking and walking. This rather pessimistic view of her condition was corrected in October when David, visiting Florence from Pisa, reported that she 'was looking better than I expected, or indeed ever saw her look, she was as kind as ever'.

Elizabeth went again for a week to Brandeglio in 1837, but she had had enough: 'formerly when all was new to me it did very well for tho I no longer desire to partake of much gaiety yet absolute seclusion is more than I could desire.' Bagni provided more variety, and her chronicles of her several stays there shed light on the Anglo-Florentine summer holiday. At the end of August 1837 her harmless diversions were rudely interrupted by storms and flooding. At Ponte Serraglio 'the desolation was appalling houses Mills and roads all carried away'. On 1 September 'there is a collection making for the poor Sufferers whose houses & bit of ground all carried with every thing which they possessed'. For a short time there was no getting out of the place, but she was able to leave on the 4th.[19] When she made a brief visit the following year, she took note of the repairs that had been done to the roads and prolonged her stay 'in the hope of doing something about the poor people for whom the money was collected last year in order to rebuild their house but I found nothing had been done for them'. She was disillusioned: 'I have staid to little Purpose the money has got into bad hands.'[20]

Wherever she went, she attended divine service, if it was to be had. At Bagni in the summer of 1837 she was much taken with the well-connected Reverend Frederick Ricketts, who was there with his wife, a niece of the celebrated fifth Earl of Shaftesbury. On 13 August Mr Ricketts conducted the service 'in my great Room, where there were above 70 people'. At the end of the relevant volume of her diary, Elizabeth noted Ricketts's address in Merionethshire and also, alongside recipes for a toothache remedy and for a cement which would mend glass and crystal, the title of his *Considerations on the Condition of the Soul in the Intermediate State*, published in 1831. At Bagni in 1841 she no longer had to have the service held in her hotel room, but was able to attend the recently built church, 'on which there has been a ridiculous Sum laid out'. She had modestly contributed to this outlay by subscribing (as her son also did) for a copy of the book that Mrs Stisted wrote to raise funds for the building.[21] Unsurprisingly, Elizabeth at least once rendered Mrs Stisted phonetically as 'Mrs Tisted'.

Of the Florentine clergy, Elizabeth has most to say about the Reverend Tennant. On his arrival she was 'very much pleasd' with him and she was among those who took up his invitation on 9 December 1838 to attend evening service at his own lodgings. On several occasions subsequently she took her son there in her carriage. On 14 February 1839 Tennant came to John's house to baptise his third son, Thomas, and stayed on for the evening. Elizabeth describes

a very nice dinner but a very stupid day John Mr Horne & the Fombelles (who never play indeed not playing better than you and I) sat all the evening at whist so that Mr Tenant Mrs John and I sat over the Fire he a most excellent person but not given to small Talk.[22]

She was not an uncritical admirer of Tennant, whom she pronounced guilty of 'a woefully prosing Sermon' on 31 May 1840.[23] A year later she recorded that she did not go to church because she disapproved of the cause for which the collection was to be made, but she does not say what it was. John also chose that day to stay at home and read the service to the boys, but does not say why.[24] It was not unknown for charity sermons to provoke contention.

One day in November 1839 Elizabeth had 'much conversation' with Tennant, on what we are not informed, although it might well have been about the troubles in which he was currently embroiled with the church committee. It would not have been surprising had they at some time talked about Archdeacon Hare, Tennant's late employer at Hurstmonceux. In January 1833 in Rome, Elizabeth had heard Hare preach to great effect on the text 'What went ye far to see?' Using 'most beautiful' language

he offended many very much by probing too deeply the causes or rather the objects for which people quitted their homes their connections & everything which should be most dear to them and what for?

The question is echoed in one of Tennant's published sermons, which may have given similar offence:

My brethren, you are most of you come lately from your native land, and are travelling now among strangers, in new scenes. What are you searching for? It may be that some of you are thirsting after happiness, which hitherto you have not found, and so you wander from place to place, as if by change you sought to satisfy the craving of your souls.[25]

Elizabeth herself had done a fair amount of 'wandering' in earlier years, but by now she could scarcely have been said to have abandoned responsibilities at home, even if she still hankered to return.

It is difficult to be sure when she finally realized that she would never be able to return to England or exactly why that was so. After George's death she still had brothers and sisters there, but it seems that there was no feasible home for her with any of them. On 18 March 1839 she received a letter from her sister Sally, in consequence of which she wrote, 'I have finally decided upon not going to England which has been a woeful blow to me.'[26] To judge from this, it was not merely the state of her finances that precluded her return, although there is the occasional hint in her diary that she had to watch her expenditure. At the age of 77, she was apparently still prepared to contemplate going back and perhaps continued to hope, but those hopes may have been dampened when in November 1841 she received a letter from her brother Sir Moore Disney 'giving the lamentable acct of my poor Sister's situation'.[27] As so often, what exactly this meant is unexplained.

It was more important, therefore, that she should be secure in her Florentine residence. In late February 1836 an incident had occurred which, ominous in the light of later developments, remains unexplained in the diaries of either mother or son. It involved Tommasi and a Captain Cuppage, whom it is hard to identify with certainty among several possibilities. On 25 February Elizabeth announced dramatically 'the grand blow was struck John came here directly when I told him every thing'. Had Elizabeth rashly invested some money in a business venture in which Cuppage was also somehow involved? On the following day she said that John 'did not come', but John himself says that he did, having in the meantime had an 'extraordinary interview' with Tommasi.[28] Certainly relations between mother and son were strained for a month or more.

On 13 May, Elizabeth recorded that John 'forced me much against my Inclination to go & sign some papers at Mr Abercrombies'. From John's own diary, it is clear that he was setting up an annuity for her and he sometimes later refers to taking her money to her on the due dates.[29] It is quite likely that he himself had provided the capital, which may be why Elizabeth was reluctant, but whether the immediate stimulus for it was the fall-out from George's will and his widow's remarriage, the recent disaster with Tommasi and Captain Cuppage, or both, is unknowable. We can imagine what John's opinion would have been if he knew, or believed, that his mother was confiding any of her own money to Tommasi's enterprises. This is speculation, but we do know from Elizabeth's diaries that from time to time she offered hospitality to Tommasi's father and other relatives in her house at Florence. John believed in keeping servants in their place.

Meanwhile she pursued her usual activities and took her usual summer excursions. In August 1838 she was quite rhapsodic about her stay in Leghorn, where she took a course of baths. Tommasi and Nanette obtained the most desirable lodgings for her on the sea front (Dr Kissock had insisted on this). The sunsets were beautiful, and Elizabeth was surprised by the concourse of walkers, 'so handsomely & well dressd', who made a show greater, she thought, than on the Cascine in Florence. There was constant

amusement looking out of the window at the passengers & that lovely sea always alive with Vessels sailing up & down the Sea breeze always refreshing of which I have the full benefit 3 Windows open alway[s];

One minor flaw was promptly remedied. On her first day, her dinner, which was supplied by a *traiteur*, was 'very indifferent and not enough', but on the next, it was 'very good & ample'. Church too was up to scratch although not all that well attended: 'large Church a very small congregation not above 70 People Service very creditably performd a place good Sermon on the necessity & advantage of prayer by Dr Perry.'[30]

Meanwhile Tommasi continued to do business on his own account. We hear early in 1839 of his desire to buy the house where 'Mrs Clark had kept her boarding house when I formerly came here', and in August of the same year, he had let 'his apartments' for a month and a half. On 14 November she unexpectedly remarks 'a word has not passd between T & me for upwards of a Week'.[31] This surely means Tommasi, but the entry seems to be completely without sequel or explanation. More than once it is noted that he was absent from the household in pursuit of his own affairs, and when Elizabeth was staying at Leghorn in the summer of 1841 he took himself off to Florence because he 'could not content himself here'. She returned to Florence only a few days later and received an unwelcome visit from John, back from Siena. He 'made great complaint of Tommasi impertinence which agitated me much fearing what might be the consequence'. Tommasi was prevailed upon to apologize for unintentionally causing offence, but in the meantime, Elizabeth spent a sleepless night, 'fearing I might be oblig'd either to break with John or part with Tommasi'.[32] It is striking that she should have seen this as the choice before her.

Then, early in April 1842, Elizabeth noted, 'Such a row with Nanette as has made [me] quite ill', to the extent that when the Pakenhams called, she could not receive them. The following day she returned home after paying calls and refused to have any dinner, 'which I believe annoyd them much'.[33] Elizabeth was now approaching her 80th birthday and may well have been guilty of capriciousness, which she was hardly likely to describe or even perhaps to be aware of. On 2 May Caroline Pakenham and Kate came to tea 'much to the annoyance of –'. Apparently they invited themselves and came despite heavy rain; Elizabeth 'was very unequal to receiving them having fallen off my long chair when turning round & lay on the floar [sic] for three hours unable to get up'.[34] Where were her servants then? As on other occasions, calm and normality appear to have supervened; John came to dinner, others to tea, without any apparent difficulty. The departure later in May of some old friends whose company she had enjoyed induced a sobering reflection: 'no one now remains (except my dear John) who I should see depart without a sigh'. The expression is confused, but the sentiment clear enough.[35]

During the summer, which for once Elizabeth spent in Florence, she recorded outings with Nanette and expressed great concern when the latter was seized with stomach cramps, which seem to have continued intermittently for months. Her only mention of Tommasi is to note that on 10 July he 'went to his Manufacture', the nature of which is unclear.[36] Then on 10 January 1843, without warning or preamble, she recorded that she had given him warning.[37] What happened next remains obscure. On 1 February she dined with her son, who said that her 'affairs [were] still going on with Tommasi a proper blackguard he is' and 'how ungratefully has she been served both by him & Nannette, principally however by the former, and now her eyes are partially opened.'[38] (The 'partially' is noteworthy.) A long silence then falls in both diaries, until on 1 April John casually observes that he was late home, 'having been taken up a good deal with Mother's lawyer'. From the 19th to the 21st of the month there were further discussions, which involved Pakenham, about 'Mother's lawsuit'. It was decided 'against the lawyers advice to concession or abandon it'.[39]

On the following day 'new insults from the servants' resulted in Elizabeth's decision to leave her own house. These events are related rather differently by mother and son.[40] According to John, he

> prepared a bed for her with us but Mrs Mackenzie to whom she was to go for a month next week got her room ready in time and after a bustley day I got her things out of the house and deposited her safely with Mrs M. at 8 o'clock.

That it had apparently already been arranged that Elizabeth should go for a month to Mrs Mackenzie suggests that perhaps an anticipated crisis had arrived a little early. Had she decided to leave her present house and dismiss the servants who had now become adversaries?

From Elizabeth's own account one would not know that John had had any part in her rescue. She was forced

> by the insolence of Tommasi and his wife … to go over to Pakenhams where I was advised to pack up every thing & leave the house as soon as possible, Kate P came home with me when it was a day's labour what with packing and

writing over my Will having it witnessed and other business with Lawyers &c so that I was not able to get off until almost dark I was receivd in the most friendly kind Manner by my most excellent friend Mrs Mackenzie and I hope to feel a little tranquility.

The reference to her will is ominous. It seems clear that Tommasi and Nanette were being written out of it; to what extent they had been in it is unknown. Elizabeth had made more than one will during her time in Florence, but this was to be the last and would be proved by John in London in the June after her death. It was witnessed by Pakenham and Walter Johnston, who was helping at the bank. Elizabeth made bequests to her sister Sarah, to her niece Hester (Sarah's daughter) and to Elena; her dear son John Leland Maquay was her residuary legatee and sole executor.[41]

Elizabeth was so disturbed by these events that she started to narrate them all over again in her diary as if they had occurred a week later than they actually did. For John they were rapidly overtaken by the sudden death of Rowland Standish, and also by plans for the building of the new English Church. For Elizabeth there were continuing annoyances. On 10 May she was particularly offended to learn that Nanette had told her lawyer that she had not been paid any wages for 20 years. It is easy to believe that Elizabeth had not kept any kind of record of payments to a person in whom she had invested not merely reliance but confidence and even affection. It is easy also to believe that her servants had had virtually a free run of her household and had received a great deal in kind rather than in money. On 17 May, however, she was able to write 'got this day out of the hands of my Tormentor', although exactly what is meant by that remains once again unexplained. It appears that her servants remained in possession of her house for some time; perhaps at last they had been ejected.[42]

On 1 May Nanette's place had been taken by 'Williams', who was probably the English maid of that name whom Elena had engaged for her own service a year previously.[43] One can readily imagine John and Elena holding a rapid consultation about what was to be done with the old lady and deciding that Williams was part of the answer. At all events, she remained with Elizabeth for the rest of her life and went with her to Bagni in the summer of 1843, where Mrs Maquay had the company, among many others, of the Pakenhams and her old friend Dr Kissock. On her return, she resumed her usual activities with only minor interruptions caused by bouts of ill health.

Can Elizabeth Maquay in any sense be regarded as a typical Anglo-Florentine resident, if there was such a being? Her age and limited command of the language helped to ensure that she lived, as many others did, on the surface of Italy, and she was certainly not alone in being confined to communication in English or French. That she lived (and insisted on living) alone in her own household made her overdependent on servants who were more at home in the local environment and this too may not have been an unparalleled situation. On the other hand, she differed from most elderly British widows in having a son with an Italian wife; John spoke the language and could deal with Tommasi and the lawyers if his mother permitted him to do so.

Typical or not, Elizabeth's diaries shed light on some of the trivial occupations and annual routines of a British householder. We might take as an example the matter of carpets. Putting down the carpets for the winter was an important part of ensuring that minimal degree of comfort which expatriates were so conscious of needing in an Italian environment which, as it seemed to them, often conspicuously lacked it. Chilled to the bone one October day in 1835 Elizabeth toasted herself in her dressing room where the carpet had been put down and the stove was lit. Taking the carpets up in the spring correspondingly indicated a faith that summer was on its way. In 1836 Elizabeth had this done at the end of April, although the temperature did not yet really warrant it; the following year she was wiser and it was the end of May before this 'great job' was undertaken. Late in October 1837 she agreed to go with her brother Sir Moore Disney to Rome and they were in a great bustle laying all the carpets down, in the hope of being able to let the house. One may guess that the hoped-for tenant was British. The drawing-room carpet was put down early in October in 1838, with the comfort of visitors presumably in mind, the rest on 10 November. In the following July, Elizabeth visited a Mrs Armstrong at her delightful villa and learned that her monthly rent would increase if she stayed long enough 'to require carpet'.[44]

Like most British residents, Elizabeth lived in rented accommodation and her diary chronicles her moves from one house to another. It is hard to know whether these moves were more or less frequent than the average. On their arrival in Florence in October 1833, she and her sister stayed at an unnamed hotel and after a little house-hunting and mind-changing decided on an address on the Lungarno, where they must have stayed until they set out northwards in the following May. Probably knowing that she did not propose to return for 6 months, Elizabeth relinquished the rental of the house, and on arriving back in Florence in early November, she had once again to take up her quarters in a hotel. This was the height of the season for new arrivals and she was unable to obtain a room at the Hotel de l'Europe, returning instead to her 'old quarters' at 'the little Hotel de l'Arno'. It was here that John came to tell her that George had died. Within a few days she had agreed on the rental of the Casa Maldura, which one Vieusseux subscriber locates in Borgo Santi Apostoli, just north of the Arno, and reported how her servants

> went to arrange house which they have made comfortable they buying all necessaries in the most liberal way I paying them 15 Sequins the sum I was to have paid the owner had he furnished bare necessaries.[45]

Comfortable it may have been, but this house did not detain her long. It was the first of four addresses that she occupied between the autumn of 1834 and her death just over 11 years later, all of them in a quarter of the city which was convenient for the Cascine, where she drove or walked frequently. In the spring of 1835 she was house-hunting again and in May moved into 4355 Via della Scala, which ends at its south-eastern extremity in Piazza Santa Maria Novella. Clearly her summer holidays within Tuscany did not require her to give up her house, and she remained in Via della Scala for 4 years. When her visiting brother Sir Moore Disney prevailed upon her to accompany his party to Rome in the autumn of 1837, she hoped to be able to let the house during her absence, which lasted until the beginning of the following March. Given that this was a peak period for short-term residence in Florence, it may have been a reasonable expectation. It was this that prompted the carpet-laying.

In May 1839 she moved to the Via delle Belle Donne on the other side of Piazza Santa Maria Novella. If her account of this move is to be believed, houses, or apartments, could be left in a state which required a great deal of reclamation. Her servants first made the drawing room ready for habitation, 'all the rest of the house in confusion', but on the following day, there was still a lot of cleaning to be done, '2 men still to be employed for several days'.[46] This stay lasted 2 years. Elizabeth was house-hunting again in the early summer of 1840 but without result, and it was not until 3 April 1841 that she moved, not very far, to the Palazzo 'Ambron' at 4207 Via dei Banchi.[47]

Elizabeth sometimes went to the trouble of hiring a hotel room to get a better view of the illuminations at carnival and the festive seasons. In 1835 she paid three *francesconi* for a window at the Hotel dell 'Arno and was most gratified:

the fire works far exceeded my expectations & far surpassed any thing I had ever seen the Boats moving up & down was a most animated Scene some of them most gaily decorated & lighted Mr Standish had a very magnificent one filled up like an Indian Pagoda he had I heard a very handsome Supper in it.[48]

In 1841, when she had moved to Via de' Banchi, she discovered that the terrace afforded her a grandstand view of the illuminations of the Duomo and Piazza. In the following year, the weather was unfavourable. John recorded that on the eve of the feast, 23 June, 'dreadful gust of wind this evening carried away all the preparations on the bridge for fireworks and none could take place, my hat & papers carried away!' He went with Mr Webster to call on his mother, who wrote that they arrived just as she was sitting down 'in my Cabinet where Tea was laid that I might admire the lighting of the Duomo' and joined her in there instead of in the drawing room: 'it was a compleat squeeze but they enjoy'd it much.' With the exception of her summer holidays and the untoward imbroglio with Tommasi and Nanette early in 1843, here she remained for the rest of her life.

She went again to Bagni in the summer of 1844 and pointedly remarked on her return to Florence early in September how 'gratifying' it was to find the house in such nice order and to be so kindly received '& that by people whose good will had not been purchas'd by ever having given money to any one the gardener excepted'.[49] That November she was a witness to both the Florentine floods (she contributed to the relief fund) and the opening of the new English Church. The diary gradually peters out during the early months of 1845 and ends with the entry for 7 March; but John is our witness that despite some more prolonged bouts of illness, Elizabeth spent at least part of the summer of 1845 away from Florence. In October she received news from her brother of Sally Barnard's death, and in November, her son began to chronicle her final decline.

Notes

1   JLM, E10 f. 257v.
2   TNA, Prob11/1841.
3   EM, C5 f. 12v.
4   JLM, E9 f. 260v.
5   EM, C4 ff. 66–66v.
6   JLM, E9 f. 79; EM, C3 f. 10v. At the time of this first mention, Elizabeth was in Paris on her way to Italy. In 1823 in Rome he remarks that his mother has engaged a new maid, an Italian, JLM, E8 f. 154v; this may have been Nanette.
7   EM, C5 f. 51.
8   EM, C7 ff. 37, 58v.
9   The Vieusseux subscription books reveal Mr Dennistoun subscribing from a variety of addresses between January 1835 and April 1836, and on one occasion, Mrs Meiklam's name is bracketed with his. Richard was an Edinburgh 'Writer to the Signet' (solicitor). He and his brother Archibald shared a common but distant ancestor with the celebrated James Dennistoun, historian of the dukes of Urbino. Richard died in Glasgow in 1848, but his widow returned to Florence, dying there in 1867.
10   EM, C7 f. 83.
11   EM, C4 ff. 30v, 34v.
12   EM, C5 f. 19v.
13   EM, C5 ff. 28, 38v, 58. Unger (1803–77), a favourite of Donizetti, sang in the first performance of Beethoven's 9th Symphony.
14   EM, C7 f. 113. Catalani's alleged death was widely reported in the British press.
15   EM, C5 f. 16v.
16   EM, C5 ff. 30–30v. Elizabeth says that she had not seen Mrs Landor for 20 years; it is possible that they had met at Como in 1816.
17   EM, C2 f. 31v.
18   EM, C5 f. 4.
19   EM, C5 ff. 65–70v.
20   EM, C6 ff. 30–30v.
21   EM, C7 f. 51v; Mrs Henry Stisted, *Letters from the Bye-Ways of Italy* (London, 1845), p. viii.
22   EM, C6 f. 47.
23   EM, C7 f. 22v.
24   EM, C7 f. 42; JLM E10, f. 143.
25   EM, C3 ff. 38v–39; Robert J. Tennant, *Sermons Preached to the British Congregation at Florence* (London, 1846), p. 417.

26 EM, C6 f. 50.
27 EM, C7 f. 59.
28 EM, C5 f. 19; JLM, E10 f. 10.
29 EM, C5 f. 25v; JLM, E10 f. 13v. On the following 2 November, he again took his mother to the Minister to sign a power of attorney (JLM, E10 f. 24v).
30 EM, C6 ff. 31v–33.
31 EM, C6 ff. 44v; 62v; C7 f. 9.
32 EM, C7 f. 52v–53v.
33 EM, C7 f. 57.
34 EM, C7 ff. 69 r–v.
35 EM, C7 f. 71.
36 EM, C7 f. 74v.
37 EM, C7 f. 90v.
38 JLM, E10 f. 189v.
39 JLM, E10 ff. 193, 194v.
40 JLM, E10 f. 194v; EM C7, f. 96.
41 TNA, Prob11/2037.
42 EM, C7 f. 97v. Nanette's claim that she had been unpaid for 20 years may substantiate the suggestion above that she was hired in 1823.
43 JLM, E10 f. 169v.
44 EM, C5 ff. 10, 24v, 59v, 77; C6 ff. 36v, 39, 58v.
45 EM, C4 f. 64.
46 EM, C6 ff. 53v–54.
47 Recte the Palazzo Amron, the name of the then owner, now Palazzo Mondragone.
48 EM, C4 ff. 78v–79.
49 EM, C7 f. 130.

8 THE LONG REVOLUTION, 1846–1849

That Holland should be recalled in May 1846, after 7 years in Florence, was in itself reasonable, but the appointment of Sir George Baillie Hamilton to replace him meant that a new man was in post at a moment when experience was needed. The problem was aggravated by Hamilton's bouts of ill health. For a couple of weeks in November 1846, as John Maquay reported, his life was despaired of, and there was another emergency in December.[1] The oversight of affairs on these and subsequent occasions was left in the relatively untried hands of Peter Campbell Scarlett.

Much has been written about the impact of the election of Pius IX on 16 June 1846. Against all expectations, given his apparent frailty, Giovanni Mastai Feretti was to be pope for longer than any other. He died in 1878, having succeeded both in turning the church upside down and in contributing, albeit unintentionally, to the unification of Italy. Observers were initially misled by the contrast with his predecessor Gregory XVI, who had seen much change and opposed all of it. Pius's amnesty on 17 July 1846 'took the world by storm'.[2] The effect on his next-door neighbour, Tuscany, was immediate and obvious. If the Pope was not prosecuting his rebels, there was no reason for the Tuscan government to do so; there was not even much reason for refugees from the Romagna to move on. Worse, as the Pope embarked on the reform of government in the Papal States, the Tuscan government, hitherto regarded as something of a model of enlightened autocracy, could not be seen to be lagging behind, and it rapidly lost control of timing and process.

It is impossible here to rehearse the multiple causes of the European crisis of 1848. Tuscany had its particular problems. The government had arguably spent money unwisely, for example in absorbing Lucca in 1847.[3] It had compounded the problem of bread supply by failing to prevent the unlimited exportation of wheat from Tuscany; whereas there had been 400,000 sacks in store at Leghorn in January 1846, there were only 34,000 by January 1847. In addition to having to find funds to stabilize bread prices, the government had to sacrifice revenue by allowing the free import of all grain and vegetables from 16 January.[4] Nonetheless, Scarlett believed there was no serious fear of scarcity, despite one of the hardest winters ever known in Italy. John Maquay records wet and cold throughout the autumn, culminating on 13 December 1846 in 'a regular Canadian fall of snow', which lasted 10 days before being dissolved by rain over Christmas. Further snow in mid-February was followed by prolonged cold and more heavy rain which continued into April 1847.[5] This was on top of an earthquake in August 1846, which did considerable damage from Volterra westward to the coast.[6]

That much of the Foreign Office correspondence with Tuscany concerned the doings of the new pope merely reflected where the Italian spotlight fell (as well as the absence of formal diplomatic representation at Rome). Any energy left over for Tuscan affairs was used to recommend free trade to the Tuscans with religious enthusiasm. Much of the early part of 1847 was taken up with negotiations for a free trade treaty, and in April, Richard Cobden visited Tuscany with his wife, Kate, and spoke eloquently on the virtues of free trade at a public dinner held in his honour. A total of 110 people assembled in the magnificent gallery of the Borghese palace. The chair was taken by Vincenzo Peruzzi, Gonfaloniere of Florence, and the *Times* printed the toast to the guest of honour, delivered by Emanuele Fenzi, and Cobden's reply in which, to the delight of his hosts, he waxed eloquent on the great Tuscans of the past who had led the way in freeing trade (including Peter Leopold).

Cobden was elected an honorary member of the Georgofili, a society of Tuscans interested in 'improvement', and was royally entertained during his 16-day stay by the Italians Fenzi, Ridolfi, Torrigiani and Peruzzi as well as by the resident English Lord Vernon and Sir Frederick Adam. John Maquay met him at Lady Vernon's on 30 April. There was time for the Cobdens to visit the art galleries and an industrial school supported by Prince Demidoff to the tune of £4,000 per annum. The only person of consequence Cobden did not meet was the Grand Duke himself, who was not in Florence at the time, but there is no indication that his visit was uncongenial to the government. In his diary Cobden claimed that because of Tuscany's free trade in exports 'there have been fewer riots about the high price of provisions here than in other countries'.[7]

To the British, free trade meant just that: public money was not to be spent on oiling the wheels of capitalism. In March 1846 the merchants of Leghorn petitioned the British government for the establishment of a regular direct postal service home via Gibraltar, instead of the uncertain land post via France and Spain. The request was supported by a memorial of British bankers and merchants, signed by Plowden & French, Horace Hall, Maquay & Pakenham, James Tough and others. It also had Scarlett's support, since 'The present means of conveyance through Tuscan, Roman, Austrian and Sardinian Post Offices renders it almost impossible for Her Majesty's Minister to write with any freedom'. The Treasury's response was negative.[8] British traders must stand on their own feet and residents tolerate communications with the mother country which could take 18 days or even longer, with the prospect that their post might be opened by inquisitive Tuscan clerks or the much more sinister Austrian spy network. As for the embassy, it could use code or employ a courier, provided the matter was important enough to justify the expense.

If such an issue could not persuade the British government to loosen the purse strings, there was no prospect of its reconsidering financial support for the English Church in Florence or any other institution established by British residents. Its obligations to distressed British subjects who wished to return to the mother country were met reluctantly and within strict criteria. British settlers in Tuscany were kept at a distance. They chose to live there; they could not expect support against the legitimate demands of Tuscan authority, and the British government certainly had no means to protect them against revolutionary unrest. Nonetheless, between 1848 and 1859, it was forced to give much more consideration to British subjects who fell foul of the Tuscan system of arbitrary government than it had had to do in the generation after 1815, when more relaxed attitudes and informal contacts usually provided solutions.

In January 1847 Scarlett reported that the Austrian ambassador, Neumann, had severely criticized the Tuscan government for its failure to control anti-Austrian demonstrations and placards. There followed some attempts at repression; by March there had been no fewer than 200 arrests since the beginning of the year, which both disconcerted and puzzled the Florentines. Among possible explanations for these unaccustomed disturbances were communist *agitators* (a new term in the vocabulary) and Austrian *agents provocateurs*, whose activities were intended 'to bring about at last a military occupation of Tuscany'.[9] The Austrian military movements which led to the occupation of Ferrara in July 1847 were clearly designed to intimidate the Pope, who had just created a civic guard, but also represented a not very coded warning to the Tuscans not to do likewise. The Tuscan government was, however, being driven down that road. Hamilton had remarked in June that the 'tranquillity of this country entirely depends on what occurs at Rome'.[10] In May the freeing and decentralizing of the processes of press censorship followed on the heels of the Roman law of 23 March. Perhaps more significant for its immediate impact on the Anglo-Florentines was the establishment of a civic guard in Tuscany by a decree of 5 September.

The British residents displayed a marvellous capacity to get on with their own lives and to pursue their own quarrels while mayhem erupted around them. A mixed bunch, they represented a wide variety of degrees of integration not only into the host society but into 'English' society itself. Among the best adapted to their surroundings, in their different ways, were John Maquay and Thomas Trollope. Of the two, Trollope is the more useful commentator on the age of revolution, inasmuch as he addresses political issues directly. Maquay is valuable as much for what he does not say, or does not find it necessary to say, as for what he does. He not only moved freely in society both English and Tuscan but (unlike Trollope) was deeply involved with the English Church.[11] After 22 months in Florence (one of his longest continuous sojourns), he was in Ireland when Pius IX was elected and in England when Peel's government collapsed, not returning to Florence until 20 July 1846. For the most part his diary chronicles a continued peaceful existence, remaining what it had always been, laconic and often uninformative where one most wishes it would be expansive. Only with a reference to the civic guard in September 1847 does Maquay betray any awareness that there was something unusual going on in the country.

Two famous residents were largely absent from the conventional social round: Robert and Elizabeth Browning. Much has been written of their time in Florence and much implies or mistakenly ascribes to them a centrality in Anglo-Florentine society. Elizabeth was on her own admission a semi-invalid and, although Robert was out and about somewhat more, entertaining was not really on their agenda, not least because of their modest resources. They lived an unobtrusive, peaceful life, but with the generality of the Anglo-Florentines they had little sympathy and little involvement. They had no interest in the English Church (except, on Elizabeth's part, to criticise it). When they are writing from first-hand knowledge and with the acute observation of poets their letters are of the highest value, but Elizabeth was particularly liable to deliver sweeping judgements and generalisations about things she could not know, reliant as she was on visitors and hearsay. The Brownings spent less time in Florence between 1848 and 1858 than John Maquay did.

They arrived in Leghorn on 14 October 1846, a month after their marriage, accompanied by Elizabeth's maid Wilson. Their early residence was at Pisa, and it was not until April 1847 that they moved to Florence, taking a 2- and later 3-month lease on rooms at 4222 Via delle Belle Donne for £4 a month. On 20 July 1847 they moved to what was to become their permanent residence – seven furnished rooms on the *piano nobile* of Casa Guidi, including free entry to the Boboli Gardens, all for a guinea a week plus 9 shillings a month for concierge. Only in May 1848 did they become permanently settled there at a much cheaper rent, 25 guineas a year for the apartment unfurnished. It was there on 9 March 1849 that their only child, Robert Weidemann, known as Pen, was born.[12]

The letter Elizabeth wrote to her sister Henrietta from Via delle Belle Donne between 24 and 30 April 1847 provides us with a flavour of her style, with its tendency to hyperbole.[13] Mrs Anna Jameson and her niece were staying with them, which was possible because 'the *houses* in Italy would be palaces in England'. In virtuous obedience to doctor's orders, Elizabeth stayed on the sofa and did not go out with them. The Garrows, whom she had known at Torquay in the 1830s, were living very close by, but 'they are to leave Italy we hear, in May, altogether and I hope to escape them in as complete a totality'. This reluctance, at least initially, to associate even with the only people she knew in Florence is typical. Theodosia Garrow became Mrs Thomas Trollope in 1848.

There are priceless nuggets of information, for instance on prices. How does one eat? Why, by arrangement with a *trattoria*:

we have an agreement for dinner at three at the rate of 2s-8d a day, – covering the whole, observe! And they send us soup and three dishes, besides vegetables & pudding or tart. Everything hot – & well cooked – & there are three of us. Wine we have separately – and Robert pays three pence or four pence a bottle for what he drinks.

Robert had his piano, a grand hired at 10 shillings a month, including music. Their payment for the apartment included everything, linen, plate, china: 'we have real cups instead of the famous mugs of Pisa, & a complement of spoons & knives & forks, nay we have decanters & champagne glasses'. A week later, the Jamesons had gone, apparently to Elizabeth's regret, but she was still enraptured by their catering arrangements:

We don't order dinner here, which is delightful. They send us what they like, and everything cooked excellently & well served & hot – as superior as possible to Pisa. Wilson dines after us, & something is always left for supper.

It is doubtful whether Elizabeth was right to conclude that by contrast with England there was here 'no need of management or money'. Poor Robert, constantly thinking of the pennies, was clearly unaware that everything happened by mirrors!

Robert hired a carriage for a month (2 hours a day, 2 shillings and 8 pence, dearer than at Pisa but 'a very easy and most comfortable German barouche') and they made their first visit to the Cascine, which Elizabeth describes delightfully in a letter to Henrietta, ending 'its an improvement on the London Parks', which, if true then, certainly is not now.[14] She was clearly in a mood to be delighted by what she saw, for she let herself go again on the celebrations for the feast of San Giovanni on 24 June. She enjoyed the races in Santa Maria Novella, which were 'childishly innocent', 'no betting, no gambling, no drinking – the most peac[e]able good humour on every side'.

After the races, there were fireworks which started at 9 and lasted for about half an hour. They had a splendid vantage point in a bedroom in a hotel on the Arno which would have been perfect 'if we had remembered to bring a bottle of Champagne'. As Elizabeth admitted, it was her turn to be a child, the experience topped off on the way home by threepence-worth of San Giovanni cakes from a stall on the Ponte Vecchio.[15] She and Robert attended the service in the Duomo, where they were struck by the grandness of the music and the spectacle of the crucified Christ in the dim cathedral lit by a hundred burning candles. It all adds up to yet another piece of evidence of the general good temper of the Florentines on the eve of revolution. When that came, Elizabeth's observations reveal the impressions of the moment rather than the results of mature reflection and have their own value.

Of prime importance to British residents who wished to be informed on the changing situation in Tuscany were, perhaps paradoxically, the English newspapers, even if the intelligence in them was always out of date. Late in 1849 John Maquay records the post arriving from London for the first time in 7 days.[16] The reality during this period was more like 10 days to a fortnight, and that was to presume no interruption because of the political situation. Those who could read Italian had access to the *Gazzetta*, while the French newspapers usually arrived with no more than three days' delay. A chief motive for the foundation in 1847 of the weekly *Tuscan Athenaeum* was to cater for the needs of English residents for up to date information.

John Maquay is suitably laconic about its gestation early in 1847: 'took a 1/8 share in a new English paper Tuscan Athenaeum'; 'formed a society for publishing the Athenaeum Vincent Vansittart Trollope Garrow & myself'.[17] All five participants in the enterprise were long-term residents who had committed themselves to Florence to a greater or lesser degree. Sir Francis Vincent is mentioned in John Maquay's journals as early as 1842; Trollope described him as 'to a great degree a reading man' with 'a considerable knowledge of the byeways of Florentine history'.[18] Joseph Garrow (Trollope's future father-in-law) was the son of 'an Indian officer by a high caste Brahmin woman, to whom he was married'. Educated for the bar by his great uncle, a judge, he was married to Theodosia Fisher, the well-off widow of an English naval officer.[19]

Probably Maquay, Garrow, Vincent and Vansittart put up the money for the paper, with Trollope as editor, able to call on Theodosia and his mother Fanny, as well as Vansittart and possibly also Vincent for articles. During its short life it gives a tantalizing insight into day-to-day life in mid-nineteenth-century Florence. Besides carrying articles on the political situation and subjects of general interest (e.g. the *Misericordia*), it published the hours of the performances in the theatres, the opening times of museums and other sights and reviews of current plays and operas. Every week it recorded new British arrivals, with a note of where they were staying, and carried advertisements for goods and services. There are glimpses of the property market which greeted newcomers, at just the moment of the annual autumn influx, for example in the first issue (30 October):

> To be Let. For 6, 8 or 12 months furnished the well known Palazzo Standish, Via San Leopoldo, with extensive Stabling and gardens. It consists of two floors, which will be let together or separate, each floor making up 10 or 11 beds. Apply to Messrs Maquay and Pakenham, Bankers.

This property was clearly not for short-term tourists and the price was probably negotiable. On 6 November Gamgee, the vet and horse dealer, was trying to let the first floor of the Palazzo Venturi, not far from his home at 4638 Via dei Banchi. A fortnight later, one could have, for £20 per annum, 'A small Villa, in perfect repair, a mile and a half from Florence, with magnificent views of Fiesole and Florence', by applying to Angelo the gardener at the adjacent Villa Salviati (which belonged to Vansittart) to see it. A slightly ominous note was struck when in the fifth issue (27 November) James Tough advertised, at 47½ scudi a month, an 'excellent First Floor apartment on the Lung'Arno with wash house and stabling'. The family now occupying it had 'relinquished their intention of passing the winter at Florence'.

There could have been several reasons why they had done so, but 2 weeks previously the paper had addressed, 'A word to those elderly ladies of both sexes who are afraid of coming into Tuscany because it is in a state of revolution.' In its ironic tone, this article bears Thomas Trollope's imprint. It begins by admitting that Tuscany is in a revolutionary state:

And it is devoutly to be hoped by every friend of humanity that she may continue to be so for some time to come for change is needed, and it is happening at an appropriate pace under an enlightened prince and with a united people, with less upheaval than had attended the repeal of the Corn Laws in England.

Indeed, 'Tuscany was never so secure an abode, so safe from all probabilities of social disturbance as it is at present.' There was only danger from a revolution repressed, not from a revolution 'in which Prince and people advance hand in hand'. It is doubtful whether Trollope would have written the same thing a year later. Clearly he was overconfident of the continuing cooperation between prince and people, as perhaps he was about the prospects of the *Tuscan Athenaeum*.

The fact that the paper lasted only for thirteen issues may well reflect market forces. By and large the British residents were content with what they could already get. In its sixth issue, on 6 December 1847, the *Athenaeum* carried a large advertisement which gave the hours of opening of Vieusseux and the names and range of journals it carried – some 26 in the English language. It was open from 8 in the morning to 10 at night and closed only on Christmas Day, Easter Sunday and the feast of St John, with subscription rates from 2 pauls for the day to 120 per annum in 1847–1848. Besides the main dailies (the *Times, Daily News, Morning Chronicle, Morning Post, Examiner*), there were the reviews (*Quarterly, Blackwood, Athenaeum, Edinburgh*) as well as newcomers and potential subversives like *Punch*. The visiting American could count on news from home from, for example, the *New York Enquirer* and *New York Weekly*, as could the Indian veteran (the *Bombay Times*).

Vieusseux was open throughout the revolutionary period, and the subscription book told one who was in town and where they were staying. While the vast majority of subscribers were male, the registers include a number of women, a high proportion of them English. Elizabeth Browning seems originally to have been under the misapprehension that she was barred from Vieusseux, writing plaintively to Anna Jameson in April 1850: 'I can read the newspapers only through Robert's eyes, who only can read them at Vieusseux's, in a room sacred from the foot of woman.' By 1853, the misapprehension had been corrected: 'I insisted on going out yesterday morning with my husband to Vieusseux's before anybody else had arrived to read the newspapers on our play.'[20]

British newspaper references to events in Tuscany were quite frequent during this period, and with the advent of the telegraph, could be surprisingly quick to appear. Personal news or advertisements which were paid for could be inserted even more quickly, although the usual interval in 1848 for births, marriages and deaths was about 3 weeks. Whereas the small advertisements in the *Tuscan Athenaeum* were addressed to persons already in Florence, these spoke to a wider public at home. Who inserted and who read them at the time?

Apart from the desire to impart or receive information, status and position in the social pecking order were indicated by what and where one advertised. William Wolley could feel well satisfied to get the birth of his daughter Florence simultaneously into the *Times* and the *Morning Post* on 25 March 1848; the 'Esq' proclaimed him to be a gentleman, who was occupying the lovely Palazzo Strozzi Ridolfi near San Niccolo. The birth of the Brownings' son on 9 March 1849 was noticed in the *Daily News* on the 19th, the *Examiner* and *Morning Post* on the 23rd and elsewhere. Marriages might be quiet or spectacular, unnoticed or reported. Thomas Trollope seems not to have advertised when he was married to Theodosia Garrow – the wedding was quiet, and on his own admission, he had very little money. The wedding, a 10-minute ceremony conducted in the embassy chapel by Robbins, 'kind and good a little man as could be', was followed by a wedding breakfast for 'half a score' at Garrow's house in Piazza Santa Maria Novella. The honeymoon was a ramble round the Tuscan cities.[21]

By contrast, on 1 February 1849 the *Morning Post* announced:

> On the 6th ult, at Palazzo Bouturlin, Florence, Il Cavaliere Commendatore Giuseppe Pistoj, Postmaster-General of Tuscany, to Ellen Forster Walford, only surviving daughter of the late Richard Walford, Esq., of Ryde, Isle of Wight, and niece of the late Sir Edward Berry, Bart, KCB.

This was a Catholic wedding at the vast Palazzo Bouturlin, home to Francis Sloane; it was worth mentioning that the bride was the niece of a baronet.[22] Sir George Hamilton's niece had a quiet wedding to the Count de Geneys. Because of Hamilton's continued illness, the invitations were restricted, but the quality was good, according to the *Morning Post* on 22 March 1847. Guests included the Austrian Minister and his English wife, the Prussian and Sardinian Ministers, several other foreign notabilities and, among the English, Mr and Lady Janet Walrond, the Honourable Mrs Vivian, Mr and Mrs Plunkett, Mr and Mrs Thomas, Dr Harding, and the Honourable Campbell Scarlett. The Honourable Miss Vernon and Miss Walrond were the bridesmaids.

Death notices sometimes recorded premature and tragic ends. The *Morning Post* on 16 November 1846 reported that Lieutenant William Douglas had died aged 37: 'for years he had been an inmate of three different lunatic asylums in Florence.' It was not uncommon for notices to appear in one or more of the London papers and also in the local press of the area with which the individual's family was connected. When Scarlett lost his son at the age of only 21 months on 15 October 1847, it was reported in both the *Times* on 1 November and in the *Hampshire Telegraph* on the 6th. The great and good might expect an expanded entry and even a small obituary, for example John Maquay's old friend De Courcy, whose passing on 20 October 1848 was noticed in several newspapers.[23]

As for news, the English resident almost certainly received a more detailed account of natural disasters than he would have received from an absolutist government. The *Times* of 5 September 1846 reported the earthquake at Leghorn on 14 August, reproducing what it called 'an extract of a Private Letter', dated from Florence on the 26 August. The unnamed author, an artist, gave a detailed and vivid description of the sensations created by the quake, his reactions (he was at his easel at the time) and the effects on his house and on the neighbourhood. Revealing here is the assumption, clearly indicated by the fact that the letter was published a mere 9 days after it was sent, that readers at home as well as in Tuscany would appreciate information on this event. The Foreign Office would hardly have obtained it more quickly, even though Macbean had written to Scarlett the day after the quake and Scarlett had posted his despatch 10 days earlier on 16 August.[24]

The resident might also expect to receive from the British newspapers a commentary on political events in Tuscany independent of Tuscan government censorship, even if it was slightly in arrears and reflected the bias of a particular newspaper. The papers also supplied a social commentary, which might gratify both the stay-at-home who read about his compatriots abroad and the Florentine resident who might even see himself mentioned. With or without personal experience of Italy, readers could take pleasure in the notion that the British presence was indispensable to the Tuscans. The year 1847, it was feared in Florence, was going to be a 'bad year' for the numbers of migratory English were expected to be low: 'John Bull is the staff of life to all. It is the annual tide of English that fattens the land.' This gratifying sentiment was reprinted from the *Westminster Review* by (for example) the *Blackburn Standard* on 17 February 1847 and the *Glasgow Herald* on 6 March, a good example of the dissemination of metropolitan journalism.

On 6 May 1847 the *Times* carried a lengthy report of the charity ball that had been given at Florence in aid of the Irish and Scottish famine victims. This was very far from being an Irish or even an 'English' occasion, for the topmost echelon of Florence's cosmopolitan elite became involved. John Maquay had a role in both this event and a more narrowly British initiative. On 26 January he remarked on 'lamentable accounts from Ireland' and thereafter makes several references to a 'Relief Committee'. This body (of which he was treasurer) called upon British subjects in Tuscany to subscribe to a relief fund. The names of those who did were published in the *Gazzetta* on 4 and 15 February. On 13 March John waited upon the Grand Duke himself in connection with the ball, together with Prince Poniatowski, the Duc de Talleyrand and Prince Demidoff, who offered the use of his villa for the occasion.

The ball was completely distinct from St Patrick's Day, on which, John explains, there was 'no festivity from the sense of the state of the country'.[25] On 24 March the General Fast that had been ordered in England was observed by the British in Florence. John's account of the long-awaited ball, which took place on 15 April, is unusually lengthy:

> This was the day for the Great Ball at Demidoffs for the Irish & Scotch. I as one of the Stewards went at 8 ½ o'clock and took George with me to show him the rooms, sending him back when Elena came at 11 o'clock it was magnificent and went off extremely well 982 persons attended ... 4000 francesconi had been guaranteed as the proviso Demidoff required for giving the Ball & paying up all the expenses himself. Refreshments in abundance Scotch & Irish music express from Paris. Supper was prepared at 5 ½ o'clock for the Lady Patronesses, Patrons & Stewards and their respective consorts and we got home at 7 o'clock it had been a hard night.[26]

The *Times* report, which appeared a mere 3 weeks after the event, confirmed John's account in several respects, but added a lot of descriptive detail. It is full of assumptions, not least that its readers would know something about Demidoff: 'There is no need to tell those who know San Donato, either by happy experience of its hospitalities, or by report, that the music, the refreshments, the lighting up &c, were the best, the most abundant, and the most elegant that taste could suggest or wealth and liberality supply.' The Grand Duke arrived early, and 'it was high tide in the ball-room about 1 o'clock.'

Great events were now stirring. In his diary, for 12 September 1847 John records the joy with which the Tuscans celebrated the granting of the Civic Guard.[27] There was 'a great demonstration of the whole country', and. 24,000 marched to the Pitti,

> clergy and laity, Tuscans, Italians, French, English American etc etc etc. The sight there was said to be most imposing and I was very sorry they had it on the Sunday and that I could not see any of it. The whole city was illuminated at night and everyone seemed wild with joy and wonderful to say not the least outrage of the person or insult occurred the whole 24 hours.

A similar note (without the sabbatarian touch) was struck by Elizabeth Browning. Writing to her sisters on 13 September from her grandstand view in Casa Guidi, she captured the carnival atmosphere: 'A vast procession which included everyone even foreign groups all with their national flags.' (One would love to know the names of the English involved.) She commented on 'the mixing of elegantly dressed women in all that crowd and turbulence with the sort of smile which proved how little cause there was for fear ... and without a single discord to mar the harmony'.[28]

This was the culmination of a fortnight or more of demonstrations. Hamilton noted on 27 August that 'An entire paralysis seems to have seized the Authorities.' Perhaps, 'in the present helpless condition of the Government', the best course was indeed 'to establish a civic guard and place arms in the hands of those who have property to defend, and enable them to guard their houses from Pillage'. A regular guard had by this time been put on the Austrian embassy. Baron Neumann was absent at the time, which Hamilton thought just as well, 'as his position, at Florence would be very disagreeable'. Hamilton had additional reason to be sensitive about any embarrassment for Neumann, whose wife was Lady Augusta Somerset, eldest daughter of the seventh Duke of Beaufort.[29] A writer in the *Daily News* on 11 November credited the new civic guard with some adverse consequences, including the appearance of beggars on the streets of Florence, which had always 'in my recollection' been free of them. By implication, the 'right to beg' was seen as one of the new freedoms which were dawning.

Another who observed the fevered state of Tuscany in 1847 and compared it with the past was the archaeologist and diplomat Austen Layard. Although born in Paris (in 1817), Layard spent most of the first 12 years of his life in Florence. He had been given sick leave from the embassy at Constantinople and was on his way home via Florence, where he met many old friends of his mother and father, both Italian and English. He mentions in particular Francis Sloane, whom he had known as a boy. As a Catholic and intimate of the Grand Duke, Sloane no doubt gave Layard his own slant on the current situation. Layard wrote to his aunt Mrs Austen on 10 December 1847, 'At this moment the Italians are little removed from downright craziness.' Every popular demand, in Tuscany and the papal dominions, was being met. This aroused inflated expectations, particularly among educated professionals, who seemed to aim at 'Nothing short of a general confederation of the Italian States'. These views were spreading to the lower classes, and coffee houses were being rechristened 'the "Fratellanza Italiana," or the "Italiani Uniti," or something of the kind. Every one is mad for the Civic Guard and endless uniforms strut up and down the street.'[30]

It was probably Trollope who endorsed these impressions in the *Tuscan Athenaeum* on 18 December. Epithets which had hitherto applied to the Florentines such as 'bella, artistica, gaia, docile, pacifica' had been absorbed by the single word 'bellicosa' and 'four words were better than a government passport – 'Italia, Independenza, Unione, Lega'. He suggested a new name for the Cafe Doney, 'the Cafe dell'Alleanza dei popoli'.[31] Layard thought that 'few really know what they want', but that in consequence of the formation of a national guard, and the arming of the people, at both Rome and Florence, 'people will shortly be able to dictate what terms they like', if they were determined to follow the lead of the handful of would-be opinion-formers. As a sincere lover of Italy, he hoped for the best but feared the worst: 'as yet one hears of no serious, sober man competent to form and control public opinion'.

The devil of the civic guard lay in the detail as far as some English residents were concerned. The only persons exempted from full service were clergy, military, government officials, day labourers, shopmen and servants in employ, and these were to form a reserve which might be called out in extraordinary circumstances. Foreigners of ten years' consecutive residence, or those who in addition to five years' residence owned land or property or were members of a commercial establishment, were liable to serve and were required to take the oath of allegiance. On 17 September George Gower, long established at Leghorn, wrote to Consul Macbean asking for guidance as to how he stood as an Englishman if bound to serve. He was unhappy to be involved 'between Governing and the Governed, especially when political changes are going forward, in which foreigners have no right to interfere'.

In forwarding this to Palmerston, Hamilton observed that according to his understanding of British law, any person taking the oath would be disqualified from owning British ships: 'There are individuals at Leghorn who have interests in British shipping and want to know how they stand.' Meetings took place at Leghorn on 2 and 15 November. 'Her Majesty's subjects were fearful that they might be compelled in a manner which may compromise their conscientious scruples or their position towards their own Government' and therefore declared that 'by serving in the Tuscan Civic Guard they do not intend in any way to prejudice their nationality or to forfeit their right to the protection and countenance of the British Government'. The Foreign Office reply on 5 November was the reverse of helpful, stating firmly that British residents 'cannot claim exemption from assisting in the defence of the State in which they may have established themselves'. Since to change British law would be inconvenient, however, the Tuscans should be asked to change theirs and release British subjects from taking an oath of allegiance. Fortunately the Tuscan government, beset by other problems and not wishing to provoke a quarrel, proved amenable and dispensed with the oath for foreigners.[32]

Very few traces have been left of English service in the civic guard before it was disbanded in 1849. The *Tuscan Athenaeum* recorded that Protestants would be exempted from attendance at Catholic religious festivals on personal application to their commandants. The Civic Guard appeared at the New Year's Day Reception of the Grand Duke for the first time when English would have been present, the Grand Duke wearing the dress of General of the Guard.[33] A number of English residents remained unhappy about the requirement to do military service at all.

As 1847 shaded into 1848, the newspaper reports, together with the revolution itself, acquired a more serious political edge. The *Times* on 14 January hoped that the carnival would not get out of control and that there would be no 'Italian puppet-show of freedom, followed by a revel of anarchy, and terminated by the strong hand of Austrian power'. The conservative *Morning Post* on 24 January nailed its colours to the Austrian mast, looking to their presence 'as a providential preserver against the horrors of revolution, and as a sort of strait-waistcoat against its mad fits'. Salvation from that quarter seemed unlikely in the short term, however, as the *Times* lamented on 30 March: 'Austria is dissolving like a giant in snow.'

In February 1848 Hamilton informed the Foreign Secretary that (after much dithering and even denial) the Grand Duke intended 'to grant such a constitution to His People, as the desires of His Subjects and the necessity of the times required in Italy'.[34] Elizabeth Browning reacted predictably to the news:

Good Grand Duke! I clapped my hands with all my heart at him. Such an excellent constitution he has given to Tuscany, with every religious distinction abolished at one sweep, & this, by his free will & after long reflection – Nights after nights he has spent, they say without sleep in painful thought- & his face expresses it – I like him and I like his face.

She went on to report how he had been recognized a few nights later at the Opera, with the result that the music had to stop and the crowd 'carried him home to the Pitti in a triumph', at which he 'wept like a child'. No one could have doubted Leopold's temporary popularity. Nevertheless, with some percipience, Elizabeth remarks, 'the north of Italy is under the cloud, & God knows how all may end, as the thunder ripens'.[35]

One of the many consequences of Leopold's grant of the constitution was to put negotiations for a commercial league with Great Britain on indefinite hold. As Hamilton remarked on 1 March, 'No favourable disposition exists towards the admission of English, or indeed any foreign, manufacture', and 'at one time there was a cry in Florence against the English merchants established here, which very much alarmed them, that feeling seems now to have subsided'.[36] The new electoral law published on 9 March was inclusive, allowing male foreign residents eligible for the civic guard and over the age of 25 to vote or even become deputies. However, with the arrival of the news of the fall of Metternich and of events in Lombardy, it became clear that the Tuscan government had lost control. It was announced that 'the hour of the complete regeneration of Italy having unexpectedly arisen', all regular troops were ordered to the frontier; Florence itself was left in the hands of the Civic Guard. Two days later the Austrian arms over the embassy were pulled down and burnt, although no insult was offered to those of any other nation; a crowd stood outside the British embassy and cheered. On 10 April the Tuscan representative was recalled from Vienna and the Austrian representative in Tuscany was given his passports. Elizabeth Browning told Henrietta that she was not at all frightened by the burning of the arms on the Austrian embassy, but asserted, 'Many of the English are flying from Florence, tranquil as Florence is, and absurd as all fear is.' She had also heard that 'all the packets for the next three months are engaged by fugitives from Italy'.

To describe as 'cowardly' what she believed to be the common British reaction seems a typical overstatement. If many British treated Florence as if it were Cheltenham, with a better climate, they could hardly be blamed for leaving if it suddenly became less cosy. Even if she herself made light of it, one person in her own household was worried. Tuscany was quiet, all soldiers having departed to do battle, but Wilson, who was, after all, the person who had to go out to get the shopping and transact other necessary errands, was not convinced of the power of the civic guard to protect her. Putting arms in the hands of irregulars with little training was ever a hazardous business. Elizabeth speculated as to the worst that might happen if the Austrians did come ('Our knapsack is soon made up'), and asked Arabella rhetorically, 'What's to happen to the English, I wonder, who keep in-doors & shut their windows?' Such people had obviously not flown; and Elizabeth herself kept indoors, whether or not she shut her windows. Her favourite physician, Dr Harding, who deplored the unnecessary alarm, was in himself proof that the settled for the most part remained so. In June Elizabeth nevertheless stated with even more emphasis: 'nearly everybody English has run away'.[37]

John Maquay's diaries tell a rather different story. For 6 months from the end of October 1847, he was in Rome on banking business. He returned to Florence on 2 May 1848, disturbed on the way only by a row at an inn in Spoleto, where another family (nationality unspecified) had engaged all the best rooms. He found 'business languishing', but otherwise says little to indicate any alarm among the many English that he knew. During May he saw Knox, Trollope, Fombelle, Crossman and Burdett among others, and discussed church affairs with George Robbins and Christopher Smith. Lady Popham left Florence on the 8th; it is not explained why, but she was an old lady who may not have relished the prospect of disturbance.

Discussions on banking business occupied much of John's time, principally because, to his surprise and regret, his partner, Captain Pakenham, had decided to retire from active involvement. This resulted in a number of discussions over the ensuing weeks, a couple of trips to Leghorn and the preparation of new circulars and forms consequent upon these changes. The complex settlement finally achieved is described in a somewhat tumultuous entry for 3 July:

> My partnership with Pakenham dissolved but his young son Montague comes in in his place and the firm remains the same Maquay and Pakenham. The Roman house is merged with an Anonimi!! British and American banking ho. JP[akenham], CBS[myth] and self leave in our capital and JG Hooker from New York is the director, CBS, Montague Pakenham and myself open a separate house at Leghorn.[38]

Highly relevant, and a cause of rejoicing, was the opening of the completed railway line from Leghorn to Florence on 10 June – for the first time, it was possible to get there and back in a day.[39] It is also interesting to note that on 18 June, in the midst of the negotiations, Pakenham left Florence as usual to set up the bank's seasonal branch at Bagni; clearly the customary summer hordes of English were expected there. The church minute books show an actual rise in receipts from April to May, from 1116 to 1998 pauls. There was a diminution between June and October before receipts (significantly) rose again, but this can be explained by nothing more than the usual seasonal exodus from Florence during the hot season. It is worth noting also that there continued to be a service throughout the summer.

If one looks at the list of subscribers to Vieusseux, there was in 1848 a drop in the number of people taking out short-term subscriptions, that is of a fortnight or less, but some fifteen individuals took out subscriptions of 2 months or more, indicating a stay of some length if not necessarily residence. Conspicuous among the residents were those with subscriptions of 6 months or a year: the retired physicians Luard and Bankhead, the businessman Thomas Andrew Vyse, John's friends Horne and the retired William Reynolds and Barron from the embassy. These match up well with the numbers in this category in 1847.

Vieusseux is an imperfect guide, for some who we know were in Tuscany at the time did not subscribe. More pertinently, recorded births amongst those residents who gave their children Anglican baptism were only one fewer in 1848 than in 1847. Although marriages were down by 25 per cent from 1847, they were more than in 1845, and deaths show a resumption of the steady numbers of the early 1840s. For some reason 1847 has the highest number of deaths amongst the Anglican residents of any year between 1815 and 1862. Fewer visitors there may have been, but it is by no means clear to what extent the insouciant and intrepid British traveller was deterred by a small war on the frontier of what he regarded as a civilized country. As for those creatures of habit, the latter-day grand tourists, the customary period of rotating settlement between November and May, from Florence to Rome and Naples and back, was only marginally affected in 1848, since by the time the fighting started, most were safely settled well to the south of the serious business.

In September 1847 John Maquay mentions an individual who may in fact just have arrived in Florence and certainly remained there until his death in March 1852. Edward Lombe, a Norfolk landowner, should have been the last person to fear revolution, for, in his own words, he was 'ultra-liberal in all matters of Politics, Philosophy, & Religion'. Like many others, he sought to exercise a controlling influence in England from afar, for he supported the *Westminster Review* as long as it published articles agreeable to his beliefs. On 7 September John records that he had let his house to him for 8 months. When Lombe actually took possession on the 16th, his landlord said that he was 'very off hand but appears fidgetty and I shall have something to do for some days in contenting him'. Sure enough, after a month he had to settle some differences with Lombe about the house.[40]

Another more conspicuous new arrival in October 1847 was Charles Lever, with his wife and three children. He made a strong impression on everybody. The diplomat Horace Rumbold later remembered him:

I see him now, riding into the Piazzone at the Cascine with his wife and daughters, all mounted on horses of variegated hues and graduated sizes – piebald, dappled, cream-coloured and chestnut, from the raw-boned old hunter down to the shaggy little Sardinian, the strange collection giving the whole cavalcade a decided look of the circus.[41]

It was perhaps not to be expected that such a man would completely avoid trouble in Tuscany, and there was indeed a brush with the courts in 1849 when he refused to pay what he regarded as a monstrous tailor's bill. The exchange became so heated that the tailor fell backwards down the steps of Lever's house and naturally swore, in court, that he felt intimidated and feared violence. Lever was asked to account for his panic and replied flippantly, 'On two grounds, he is a tailor and a Tuscan.' Needless to say, he had to pay 'ample damages'.

The city was raw material for Lever the novelist and journalist. 'Florence', he declared,

> is to the world of society what the Bourse is to the world of trade. Scandal here holds its festival, and the misdeeds of every capital of Europe are discussed. The higher themes of politics occupy but few; the interests of literature attract still less; it is essentially the world of talk.

In this world he revelled, but he preferred some company to others. 'Literary ladies' rather alarmed him, especially Mrs Trollope; his biographer suspected that he was afraid of becoming a character in one of her books. Despite their shared passion for whist, he went to great lengths to avoid having her as a partner, while she was equally keen to secure him.[42]

Perhaps it followed, although Mrs Trollope and Mrs Browning were very different, that he and Elizabeth would not agree. The Levers first called on the Brownings late in 1848, when (to Elizabeth's surprise) they were on the point of going unseasonably to Bagni. She told Arabella, 'He is said to be "better than his books" – which is some comfort, for I never admired them much, you know.' Nearly 2 years later, she reflected on the relationship: 'We never see him, it is curious.' She thought he had called on them in order 'to see that we had the right number of eyes and no odd fingers', and having done so was satisfied: 'In fact he lives a different life from ours; he is in the ballroom and we in the cave, – nothing could be more different; and perhaps there are not many subjects of common interest between us.' The diagnosis was accurate enough.[43] Elizabeth and Lever were unlikely to be at ease with each other; both were accustomed to be the centre of attention. Lever was certainly not stupid and was capable of great charm and sensitivity, but he was not a man for intellectual dialogue, nor (as Elizabeth indeed implies) was he happy unless in society.

While the English probably had little to fear for their personal safety in Florence, things were different in Leghorn. Here the presence of radical elements, led by the lawyer Guerazzi, combined with the port's free status and its volatile politics to make the British residents extremely uneasy. Miss Ann Ward, on her way from Naples to England, had her baggage stolen from Thomson's hotel on 31 March 1848, and the looting of the *Ariel*, a British steamer which went aground on the Vada Reef 10 miles off the coast at Leghorn on 2 June, gave legitimate cause for concern, although the personal safety of the passengers was not threatened. The looting seems to have been due more to criminal opportunism which the local authorities did not prevent than to political unrest. As for the robbery of

Miss Ward, Macbean reported on 16 August that the failure of his enquiries was largely due to the breakdown of policing and authority in general; officials were afraid to do their duty, witnesses to give evidence.[44] In June Robert Stuart, writing from Glasgow on behalf of his family at Leghorn, asked for a British warship to protect interests there.[45] While the government was not prepared to accede to the request of a private citizen at this stage, the situation further deteriorated with the establishment of a Provisional Government at Leghorn in August, which compelled the British government to reconsider its position.

At Florence there was a general calm during late spring and early summer, as everyone awaited with bated breath the outcome of the war in the north of Italy against Austria. Much attention was focussed on the Assembly, which met for the first time in the last week in June. On the 15th John noted: 'attended to give my vote for the Deputy for the first parliament voted for Avv. Landrini'. It is interesting that he should disclose the way he voted; Landrini was a moderate constitutionalist. On the 21st Elena went after dinner to see reinforcements depart for the Tuscan camp. Both husband and wife went into Florence on the 26th for the opening of the chambers 'for the first time' and John heard Gioberti speak at the Casino di Firenze on the 29th.[46] On 4 July Mrs Browning told Miss Mitford, 'The elections have returned moderate men & many land proprietors, and Robert who went out to see the procession of members, was struck by the grave thoughtful faces and dignity of expression.' Elizabeth had not yet ventured to any of the debates; the hour of 12 fixed for meeting was 'sufficiently conclusive against dangerous enthusiasm', given the hot sun.[47]

Meanwhile, John continued to entertain, although there were no grand parties. He mentions among many others De Courcy, Plunkett and 'Lord Ashtown's children', who came to play with his. His young cousin, John Adair, was sufficiently confident to call on them on his way back from Cyprus. On 7 July the Levers are mentioned for the first time. After a remarkably quiet period, there was a little disturbance in Florence on 30 July and bad news from the camp, with the people 'unquiet'. On 4 August, 'The Austrians are said to be in Bologna seems that we may look for them here.' John carefully avoids registering either approval or disapproval. He was under some domestic pressure at this time: there was a great deal of sickness among his servants and John Adair also fell ill. The death of Mrs Goddard, a customer of the bank, on 7 August (leaving a daughter who spent some days with the Maquays during that month), involved him in probate matters; he had been a regular caller on the lady in her last illness. His diary entry for the day before she died is splendidly typical: 'Mrs Goddard in same state, Austrians advancing.' This was followed by rumours of the fall of Milan on the 9th and bad news from the Arona on the 10th, although on the following day, the army was said to have rallied and there were rumours of French intervention. Meanwhile Lever responded with relief to the news from Lombardy, anticipating peace and declaring that 'I like the place better than any I have ever known'.[48]

As August drifted into September the Tuscan government's inability to control the situation began to weaken its hold on power. Tuscan defeat at the battle of Mantua in May had not only led to soldiers streaming back over the frontier, retaining their weapons and often disappearing with them back to their homes, but had raised the spectre of an Austrian invasion of Tuscany. General Welden, commanding Austrian troops in the Legations, accepted British and French mediation in August and was conscious of the need to restore order. He agreed not to invade Tuscany provided it remained quiescent and called off its aggression. According to Hamilton, writing on 7 August, the volatility of the public mood in Florence caused the greatest joy, with hopes of a cessation of war as well as a universal feeling of gratitude towards England for bringing it about.[49] On 17 August the *Times* praised Hamilton for preventing an Austrian invasion of Tuscany; the *Daily News* and the *Morning Chronicle* on the 16th took a more balanced line, noting the joint British and French intervention.

With the imminence of the Austrians, renewed disorder was threatened at Leghorn. Macbean wrote to Hamilton on 25 August that he was being besieged by British merchants who were anxious to know what arrangements existed for their protection and when the Tuscan government would bestir itself: 'We fear much that the rabble may resort to pillage if not also to personal violence.' Writing privately to Bidwell at the Foreign Office a few days later, he said that the state of alarm was extreme, given the reverses sustained by Italian troops and the rapid advance of the Austrians. Few were prepared to volunteer to continue the fight and many hoped for French intervention. There was much Republican activity and hopes were being expressed that the Grand Duke's government would fall and he himself take flight. On the previous Sunday there had been an attempt in Florence to publish a decree 'declaring that the Royal Family of Tuscany had lost its right to reign in this country'.[50] Although Macbean had HMS *Thetis* under Captain Codrington on hand, he doubted whether this would be sufficient.

Codrington too urged action, for the rebels would seize money not only to line their own pockets but also to pay the armed men they hired: Were British merchants to suffer this? As Palmerston had authorized English service in the civic guard, this was all well and good for as long as it was under the command of the recognised government. 'I am not disposed to allow the detention of English vessels. If they play this game, I can play it too.'[51] The proclamation of a Provisional Government at Leghorn might be regarded as the last desperate throw of the dice by Italian nationalists to keep the failing revolution going, but it certainly threatened the fragile peace, as well as the property of British subjects.

This situation was brought into focus on 29 August, when, to his astonishment, Hamilton received a demand, rather than a request, from the Gonfaloniere of Leghorn that he negotiate a full amnesty for the city with the Grand Duke. If Leghorn were to be 'exposed to a hostile assault from the Grand Ducal troops', he could not answer for the lives and safety of British subjects. Blackmail it was, bluff it may have been, but Hamilton simply could not afford to take the chance.

Once again he found himself acting without instructions and interfering in the internal affairs of the state to which he was accredited, urging the Grand Duke to demand unconditional surrender from the Leghorn rebels, with a conditional promise of 'the utmost possible leniency'.[52] Although the Grand Duke's emissary Colonel Cipriani was admitted to Leghorn with 1,600 troops, he failed to arrest the ringleaders or to wrest the initiative from the republicans. His request for English marines to land from HMS *Thetis* to assist him provoked Hamilton's anger as well as his frustration, considering 'the dangers that might beset the English Inhabitants at Leghorn, if an English force interfered at a moment of popular fury'. Hamilton was nonetheless aware of the unpleasant possibility that the Grand Duke's possession of Leghorn might turn out to depend on English assistance and for the first time felt that the throne was in some danger.[53]

The *Times* had much to say on the revolt in Leghorn, notably on 16 September; the report from its own correspondent was dated a mere 9 days previously. On the 27th it described the present state of Tuscany and lamented the lack of strong government. The fundamental message of these accounts is similar. The fault was not in the people but in their leaders: 'the Grand Duke has promised much and done nothing'; the government 'are apparently incapable of any strong exertion'. Even though 'the Tuscans are a most amiable people, and not disposed to commit excess, even in the midst of political license', there were fears for property; at Leghorn prayers were being offered up for foreign intervention. Most of the papers at this stage adopted a more or less conservative line, though not all went as far as the *Standard*, which on 19 August positively rejoiced in the Austrian defeat of Charles Albert. On 18 September the *Daily News* supported the landing of British marines at Leghorn to protect property. There were clearly those among the residents who saw an Austrian victory as the beginnings of the resumption of normal service.

Some stability was achieved at Leghorn under the rule of Guerazzi, who was treated by the population as if he were the official governor. The Tuscan government formally declared its inability to protect English residents there, although (according to the *attaché* Barron, who was sent to Leghorn by Hamilton) they did not consider themselves to be in imminent danger of life and property. Nevertheless Admiral Parker, on station at Naples, acceded to a request for an additional warship as a precaution, given the presence of twenty-nine merchant ships in the harbour. Guerazzi and the Livornese then accepted the appointment of another advanced liberal, Professor Montanelli, as governor of the city, which restored the government's theoretical authority, if not its power to control events.[54] However, the resignation in early October of the Tuscan ministry under Gino Capponi created a government crisis.

Repeatedly and reluctantly, Hamilton found himself compelled to offer advice. He approved of the Grand Duke's attempt to form a ministry under Ricasoli, but deprecated any idea that Leopold should withdraw from Florence, unless a republican ministry were forced upon him. He would not countenance a protest by the diplomatic body against a republican administration, and by the end of October, he was conceding that a Montanelli-Guerazzi ministry should be accepted if it was unavoidable. If it failed, the Grand Duke would be free to choose a ministry to his liking; if it succeeded, 'nothing more could be wished'.[55] The issue was decided when Ricasoli declined to serve.

The turbulence at Leghorn claimed a temporary British victim. On 16 November Captain Codrington complained from HMS *Thetis* that David Polhill, belonging to 'an English Mercantile house of long standing in the Town of Leghorn', had spent

> 24 hours in prison, without food, or any accommodation whatever for passing the night, and that he is sentenced to pay a fine of 30 lire, the sole Complaint against him being, that he declined to do duty in the Civic Guard.

Codrington somewhat intemperately wrote directly to the new governor, Carlo Pigli (appointed by the Montanelli government in November 1848), thus bypassing both Macbean and Hamilton, and pointed out not only that Polhill had voluntarily joined a commercial patrol at the desire of the government during the late disturbances but that 'it was a breach of agreement to subject Commercial business to vexatious stoppages'. Italians who had refused to serve had not been imprisoned.[56] Neither Hamilton nor Macbean was prepared to permit the implication that Codrington acted while they talked. He rightly got his knuckles wrapped for not communicating immediately with one or preferably both of them. Fortunately good sense prevailed; the Montanelli government considered it wiser to exempt all foreign residents in Leghorn from active service in the Civic guard.[57]

Elizabeth Browning's 'dangerous enthusiasm' of July by now appeared to have been replaced by healthy realism. It was

> painful to feel oneself growing gradually cooler and cooler on the subject of Italian patriotism, valour and good sense but the process is inevitable. The child's play between the Livornese & our Grand Duke, provokes a thousand pleasantries. Every now & then a day is fixed for a revolution in Tuscany, but up to the present time, a shower has come & put it off. Brave men, good men, even sensible men, there are of course in the land, but they are not strong enough for the times or for masterdom.[58]

Hamilton was making the same point to the Foreign Office at the same time, less elegantly and at rather greater length.

John Maquay's leisure activities meanwhile continued undisturbed. On 10 September, his 57th birthday, he as usual expressed a pious wish: 'may I the more make preparations for my departure.' He did not mean departure from Florence. One old friend, Colonel De Courcy, did depart in the direction indicated on 20 October; John had made out his will for him on the previous day. For some time he is uninformative about political happenings until, out of the blue, his entries for 21 and 22 November provide a good illustration of his style:

Tuesday very fine day Bank & home same as yesterday. Elena remained with Mad D'Hoggner all day. I gave my vote for Landrini as deputato.

Wednesday very fine day bank & home. The mob forced all the voting places destroying the papers, registers etc dinner & evening at home.[59]

His use of the term 'mob' with its derogatory connotations indicates an opinion which would have been held by the majority of his fellow residents: abhorrence of those who interfered with the processes of orderly government. Otherwise, he reverts to silence on the revolution, despite the advent of the Montanelli ministry.

By this time the Grand Duke and family, not entirely to Hamilton's liking, had departed for Siena. At least this was better than Elba, as the Foreign Secretary ironically observed.[60] In a letter written on 3 December, Elizabeth Browning revealed more of her anxieties. The rumours from Leghorn had caused the Grand Duke 'to send away his family to Siena, and we had "morte ai Fiorentini" chalked up on the walls'. Still, 'I look forward to an unbroken tranquillity just as I used to do', even though the windows of the nearby Ridolfi palace had recently been smashed, in the absence of its proprietor as an envoy to London. Elizabeth was stuck in Florence, heavily pregnant, events were not evolving as she had wished and hoped and life had for a time ceased to be quite so pleasant. She clung to her optimism and wished the Florentines still to be 'amiable, refined, graceful' but a little less of the 'fancy easily stirred into impulse' and more of a 'determinate strength'. Here she was echoing a frequent British grouse about their hosts, and her sentiments, in face of strengthening symptoms of radicalism, were complicated by the fact that she was no radical and no egalitarian.[61]

'Impulse' was well illustrated by the events recorded in a December letter to Arabella. They had heard the 'Generale' (call to arms) beaten below their windows. Wilson, of course, was in a dreadful fright, but Elizabeth and Robert sat in a state of perfect indifference until Robert proposed to venture out to see what was going on. Reality struck and Elizabeth thought she had better be frightened. It turned out to be only a case of 'Down with the Ministry', until Guerazzi went out and harangued the mob, which turned the cry to 'Up with the Ministry and Down with the ringleaders'; 'Such children to be sure!' She told Arabella not to believe that the Grand Duke had fled.[62]

None of Elizabeth's letters is an exclusively political bulletin; most if not all begin with a wealth of family and personal gossip. There are innumerable references at this period to the Cottrells. Sophie Cottrell was born Sophie Tulk and was distantly related to Elizabeth. In September 1847 she was married in London to Henry Cottrell, Chamberlain to Charles, Duke of Lucca, and ennobled by him with the title of Count. He was now footloose in Florence, out of a job with the reversion of Lucca to Tuscany.[63] Sophie had the benefit during 1848 of the company of her father, Charles, and also her elder sister, Louisa, who was expecting her third child in May 1848. The Tulks and Cottrells were frequent visitors to the Brownings. Sophie's first child, Alice, was born prematurely on 14 July 1848 and always struggled to survive, dying at 16 months in November 1849.[64] Sophie seems to have been an unfortunate mother, losing at least two more children in early infancy. Friendship notwithstanding, Elizabeth was somewhat barbed about the Cottrells' apartment and conspicuous expenditure, such as the blue satin curtains on Sophie's bed, and she did not like the situation of the house, 'quite at the other end of Florence in a new piazza … the houses looking like Cheltenham houses … nothing characteristic or Florentine'.[65] At one time Henry dreamed of restoring his fortunes by joining the Californian gold rush.

At Florence as previously at Pisa, Elizabeth was often reluctant to make the acquaintance of people whom she subsequently learned to like. She emphasized that she was not inclined to see strangers; her isolation was very much self-imposed. There was nonetheless a steady trickle of visitors during these months who, according to Elizabeth, were mostly American. There was also Father Prout, who spent evening after evening with them in October and November of 1848. They hadn't the heart or the courage to tell him to go, although his 3-hour smoking sessions could hardly have been good for Elizabeth's lungs, leaving aside the test to Robert's patience of providing an endless supply of wine and a spittoon.[66]

Mary Boyle was at the time living at the Villa Medici at Careggi, which was still owned by Lord Holland. On being introduced to the Brownings, Mary invited them to Careggi; the invitation was refused but Mary was invited to visit them at any hour except between 3 and 5 pm. Soon she was a regular fixture at Casa Guidi, coming, as she herself reported, almost every evening after her mother had retired to rest. 'A little lively aristocrat', Robert opined, and Elizabeth took to her: 'Clever [and] original she certainly seemed in her talk.' Their favourable impression of her was reciprocated to the point of effusiveness. Elizabeth seemed to Mary 'half bird, half spirit': 'I have never in the course of my life seen a more spiritual face, or one in which the soul looked more clearly from the windows.'[67] To Elizabeth's regret, Mary (who was after all but a visitor) joined the 'panic people' and left in the summer of 1848, on her infirm mother's account.

Some residents were away, or went away, in 1848–1849 for reasons of their own. Frederick Tennyson, elder brother of the more famous Alfred, had lived in Florence since 1839, the year of his marriage to Maria Giuliotti, the daughter of the chief magistrate of Siena. Tennyson was deeply musical, though mistaken in thinking that he was a better poet than his brother. He described himself as a 'person of gloomy insignificance and unsocial monomania', to whom society was 'Snookdom', and he particularly disliked those 'who go about with well cut trousers and ill-arranged ideas'.[68] His Florentine circle may have remained restricted as a result, and for some years, he led a wandering existence, which often took him away from Tuscany and his wife. That he was absent in the autumn of 1848 seems in no way strange and not to be attributed to nervousness. On 2 September Maria wrote to him plaintively apologizing for bothering him but pointing out that there had been 'a small revolution at Leghorn'. Her particular reason for concern was that their son, Giulio, was at school there and no letters were arriving. 'At least write to me that I may be happier.'[69]

There were a great many Florentine residents who did not flee, whether or not they were frightened. Seymour Kirkup, now halfway through his long years of residence, had no intention of moving. Although deaf since 1835, he remained a willing talker and was glad to receive people, especially if they put him in the way of accumulating ever more dusty manuscripts which, along with his two spaniels, he described as his family. He had conversed with Landor in the mid 1820s and early 1830s and would do so again in the late 1850s and early 1860s; he came to know the Brownings well through the link of spiritualism. He rarely went out, but as recently as the spring of 1847 had broken with his normal habits and breakfasted at Doney's with G. F. Watts and the American sculptor Hiram Powers. He was also to become a close friend of Jarves, the American artist, with whom he joined in an enthusiastic reappraisal of the Italian primitives. At this stage in his life, he was still basking in the glory of his role in the discovery of the portrait of Dante in the Bargello in July 1840.[70]

Those with commercial interests or investments in business were scarcely disposed to move at a moment's notice, particularly if, like the Hall brothers, their residence had been long-standing, indeed lifelong. Alfred had a flourishing importing business in Leghorn, most of his trade being with England; he had a young family which had been augmented by the birth of a daughter in March 1847. Horace is scarcely absent from the church minute books in Florence at this period, together with the emerging Christopher Webb Smith. Thomas Kerrich had sold out his banking interests to John Maquay in 1843, but remains a social presence in the latter's diary down to 1848; he added a daughter to his family in April of that year. He among other Britons (including the Halls) had interests in the building of the first Tuscan railways, which was proceeding at this moment. Robert Stephenson, consulting engineer for the line between Leghorn and Florence, left England on 16 November 1848 for what one biographer regards as a winter break in Tuscany, inspected the completed line and the girder bridges over the Arno, and returned home in the following February.[71] If there were Irish navvies among the workforce which laid the tracks, they doubtless added their own peculiar colour to the revolutionary mix. Throughout this period of upheaval, English residents were being born, dying or getting married in Florence; like John at the Bank, they were going about their business. At the height of the unrest they may have kept indoors a little more and given fewer large balls and parties, but there was life beneath the surface.

Late in 1848 there was relative tranquillity in Florence and Leghorn and some governmental stability, but news from Rome threw all into confusion. After the murder of the Pope's short-lived Prime Minister Pellegrino Rossi on 15 November and the flight of the Pope himself, the revolutionary junta announced on 29 December the summoning of a Roman constituent assembly. This immediately provoked popular calls for a similar proclamation in Florence, a demand for which Montanelli presented to the Grand Duke on 21 January 1849. Leopold asked everybody's opinion as to what he should do, including Hamilton's, which was, like that of most of the Grand Duke's supporters, negative. Leopold then proceeded to sign the proposal that had been laid before him. Hamilton contrasted the rapturous applause of the Montanelli faction in the Assembly with the more general reaction, which was 'of the most painful description', with people crying in the streets for their Sovereign's weakness: it was now the opinion of all the most influential people 'that the sooner the Grand Duke goes away the better'.[72]

These events sent rumours flying around amongst the English residents, some of which reached home. Letters from an unnamed 'gentleman of Florence' which appeared in *Trewman's Exeter Flying Post* on 18 January 1849 gave a bleak picture of brigandage and rampant criminality:

> It is now little more than a year since the Grand Duke, in the impulse of a most generous confidence, began his career of constitutionalism; and in that brief space he has seen his fair city, the resort of strangers from every land of Europe, actually deserted by all foreigners of distinction; its trading population reduced to absolute beggary; taxation more than doubled; Leghorn wrested from his rule, and given up to the sway of a set of unprincipled demagogues.

The picture seems exaggerated if we compare it with what John Maquay has to say. The statement that Florence had been deserted by foreigners of distinction depends on what is meant by 'distinction', as well as on the unmentioned difference between residents and tourists. It has already been suggested that the evidence for a decline in numbers amongst the Florentine residents, as opposed to short-term visitors who might have been leaving anyway, is far from clear. While it is indisputable that for a period, the land route was interrupted by war, which deterred some birds of passage, sea communication was not interrupted, and in 1849 (apart from Rome, which was admittedly a real problem), the season was not affected at all. Indeed, thanks to the Roman situation, many made their way to the comparative safety of Florence before the French landed at Civitavecchia on 27th April 1849, to be followed later in the year by active participants in the Roman Republic like the American Margaret Ossoli (Fuller). The number of short-term subscriptions to Vieusseux picked up in the spring and again in the autumn, and the English Church remained a going concern throughout the period, despite recurrent anxieties that the uncertain times might have an impact on receipts.

A corrective to the *Trewman's* correspondent appeared in the *Examiner* on 3 February 1849, in the shape of a letter addressed to Walter Savage Landor by 'a well-informed English resident in Florence'. The Pope, in this writer's view, had been 'unmasked at last' and was an object of malediction in Tuscany, now that his opposition to the revolution was patent. Landor was warned 'against all the falsehoods which fill the English newspapers', even (or especially) if 'written with mock preference of liberalism'. According to this correspondent, 'the writers of

Florence are calling for the bible in Italian, and wives for the priests, and the paper and press in general have become nearly Protestant'. There had been an explosion of newspaper titles at Florence, to the number of about twenty, 'two or three of which are called moderate, but all against Austria'. The ministry was 'liberal', the country quiet, but a reaction was to be expected from the assembly, both chambers of which consisted mostly of 'old courtiers'. If the ministry was driven out, an uprising could be expected 'for one chamber and extended suffrage'. The writer was very possibly Arthur de Noë Walker, who was later involved with the Protestant 'martyrs', the Madiai. He certainly expresses the wishful thinking about Italian Protestantism, which was awakened in a number of British enthusiasts by the events of 1848–1849.[73]

By this time, the Grand Duke's nerve had failed. Despite offers of Sardinian forces to restore his power, and against the most earnest advice of the British, he resolved to leave Tuscan territory and join the Pope at Gaeta. On 6 February Hamilton reported that Leopold had gone to visit his family, whom he had left at Siena before Christmas and on the 9th that he had gone aboard a British vessel (HMS *Porcupine*) at San Stefano, placing himself and his family under the protection of the British. A Provisional Government was immediately proclaimed at Florence under Guerazzi and Montanelli, and a plot discovered at Leghorn to set fire to HMS *Bellerophon* and *Porcupine*. On 8 February Mazzini landed at Leghorn and, before going on to Florence, urged the crowd to make common cause with the Roman people. It was just as well he moved as fast as he did, for Hamilton recorded on the 13th the destruction of 3 miles of the only recently completed Florence Leghorn railway and the burning of the station at Empoli.[74] The Republic was duly proclaimed on 19 February.[75] Tuscany faced an uncertain future.

A Mr Loftus, writing towards the end of February from the safety of Cavendish Square, seems to have anticipated a veritable bloodbath of English merchants in Leghorn as a consequence of the British protection given to the Grand Duke, and wanted a substantial portion of the British navy, if not all of it, to be sent for their protection. How he proposed to protect British residents at Florence, where, he alleged, the embassy arms had been torn down, is not quite clear. As it happened, scarcely any of the rumours were true. The Royal Arms remained firmly above the British Embassy in Florence, and, although there was natural alarm, Hamilton reported that his applications to the Provisional Government on behalf of British subjects 'have met with the most marked attention'.[76] How long this moderation would continue, however, was anybody's guess.

Mrs Browning was bound to react to all this. She wrote breathlessly to Henrietta to report the advent of a republic and the rumours that were currently flying around: English ships were at Leghorn to protect English interests; the English ambassador was writing threatening letters in the journals about what he should do if insults were offered to the English. The Grand Duke was tender hearted; Guerazzi was as 'false as falsehood', while Mazzini was virtuous and heroic. As Elizabeth told her sister, she '*could not* move from Florence at the present moment', so there was no point in being fearful, and the republic 'has no more chance of standing than a straw in a storm has'. In this last judgement she was absolutely right. It was doubtless good doctoring on the part of Dr Harding to reassure her by 'laughing it all to scorn – "not the least cause for fear in the world", says he'. Nevertheless, according to Elizabeth, 'The English are all dreadfully frightened such of them as are still resident, Mrs Trollope has everything packed up ready to flee.'[77]

The last assertion is worthy of comment, for we have an account derived from Thomas Trollope's papers by his second wife.[78] In July 1848 the family had gone on tour to Switzerland to escape the heat. Whilst there, Fanny, disquieted about the state of Italy, urged her son to return to Florence, sell up and rejoin them at Vevey for the winter. No sooner had Thomas arrived back in Florence than in September, he received a note from his mother telling him she had changed her mind and was returning to Florence with Theodosia. Her presence by the end of that month is confirmed by John Maquay, who went to a 'little party' she gave on the 28th.[79] On 1 February 1849 John entertained her to dinner, but noted on the 22nd that she was leaving Florence a couple of days later, for what reason he does not say. In fact she had received the alarming news of the illness of her daughter, Cecilia. and was at her bedside in London when she died on 10 April. Whether she had really been sitting with her bags packed for the past few months because of imminent revolution is unknowable.

Theodosia and Thomas in the meantime went on a tour to southwestern France and Thomas commented ironically that we 'quit Florence when it is becoming almost too hot to hold Englishmen'. That he did feel some misgivings at this moment is confirmed by an article written in April 1850 when he was back in Florence. Here he reflected humorously on a much changed city. When in February 1849 he had made 'a rather precipitate retreat' from the 'city of flowers', it had rather more resembled 'a city of bayonets', where

> every Florentine *gamin* was preparing to devour at least a dozen Austrians for his breakfast and hurrah-ing songs about 'giovini ardenti' and 'la libertà'. I return to find the 'giovini ardenti' sadly tamed by paying taxes to the tune of 50 per cent or so, and the *gamins* loud in their complaints that their Austrian foemen devour – if not themselves – at least all their victuals.[80]

This irony at the expense of the Florentine gilded youth strikes an already familiar note. In a book written 10 years later, Trollope made rather more of the troubles that erupted in Florence in 1849, going so far as to say that 'Great numbers of those who could do so now left the city. The rich went to their villas; foreigners hastened out of the country; and a reign of terror began in Florence'.[81] However, he immediately qualifies the severity of this 'reign of terror' and elsewhere does not seem to take it entirely seriously, indeed emphasizes its childish character. The point of the book was in large part to contrast the constitutional moderation of the 1859 uprising, which succeeded, with the more disorderly radicalism which briefly held sway in 1849 and failed; possibly also he was *ex post facto* justifying the anxieties to which he himself had yielded.

John Maquay reacted to events in his own way. He records the institution of the Provisional Government and remarks that there were 'Great crowds about the streets but no excesses came out immediately'. This introduces some of the most explicit references he ever makes to political events.[82] There was still no news of the Grand Duke on 10 February but 'a little row last night calling Viva Leopoldo II many arrests made. I fear we shall see bad work'. John's uneasiness was not assuaged when on 12 February Mrs Knox was frightened by a man abusing her for not giving him money – the first and clearest mention he makes to an actual threat to an English resident in the Florentine streets. On the 15th he did not see the Provisional Government as lasting very long:

No proclamation or protest has yet appeared from the GD who is at San Stefano and Guerazzi and his colleagues are plastering the walls with all kinds of new laws tending towards a Republic but I think a month will tell another story.

On Sunday 18 February he attended church and lunched with Christopher Webb Smith, but in the evening heard the bells ringing, 'we learn not what for, but we heard in town that 20000 Piedmontese had entered Tuscany to reinstate the Grand Duke'. On the following day (when there was a church meeting), 'Tree of Liberty was planted in the Piazza Gran Duca last night and the bells rang. Very contradictory reports today Governo Provvisorio getting frightened and they say running away'. On the 21st, 'A reactionary movement took place among the contadini near Florence and the town was in an uproar all night ringing firing illuminating etc but by 3 o'clock it was all put down'. It was clearly going to be some time before there was any certainty about what was going to happen, especially when the news reached Florence that 'The GD has run away for Gaeta and they say we are to have a republic immediately'.

Other English residents may well have faced the problem which John faced on 12 March: 'a Festa on account of the voting for Costituente, which begins today, the band of Settignano came to bother us in the evening, had to give them money'. It was better to pay up than to risk violence. Certainly there could be no question of any St Patrick's Day celebration: 'not even a Shamrock do I see in any one's hat to mark it or have I heard it mentioned'. Presumably it had been normal to see shamrocks on 17 March in former years in Florence.[83] The social life of the Anglo-Florentines could not and did not take its usual shape during these months.

In the newspapers February was largely occupied by bulletins about the flight of the Grand Duke. Around the 24th there were a number of mentions of disturbances at Empoli, including the destruction of the railroad. The prevailing tone was hostile to the revolution. *Freeman's Journal* on 8 March quoted the *Times*, both unhappy with what they took to be the pro-insurgency drift of British policy. It appears that this supposedly friendly disposition was being exaggerated by reports within Italy, but there were obviously people in Britain either uncertain what to believe or anxious to believe the worst of their own government. Reports were being circulated that Hamilton had left Florence and was in a variety of ways aiding and abetting the Provisional Government, which elicited a widely reported refutation from Brown, the British Consul at Genoa. Hamilton remained at his post as a visible symbol of British presence, leaving the Royal Arms in place in order to give confidence to the 'English population' who were 'in great alarm'.[84]

On 25 February he obtained the release from prison of the 17-year-old Norbone Smith, fresh out of Eton, who had been living near Florence with his parents. He was arrested on the 21st on the grounds that he had been involved in leading a reactionary peasant movement against the Provisional Government. Allegedly, he had had the misfortune to approach the gates of Florence at the same time as a mob of peasants and aroused the suspicions of the Civic Guard. Even when released from prison (where he contracted smallpox), he was expelled from Tuscany, and it took time for the sentence to be reversed.[85] Hamilton could have done with the assistance of Scarlett, on leave in London, who on 16 March was told by Palmerston to return with all due haste. With that inappropriate timing which sometimes distinguished the British Government, the Foreign Office wrote to Macbean on the same day proposing, as part of its general review of consulships, to reduce his salary from £400 to £350 with effect from 1 July.[86]

The brief renewal of war between Austria and Piedmont brought further rumour and counter-rumour, but with the news of the abdication of Charles Albert on 23 March, there could be no doubt of the Austrian victory. As early as 30 March, John Maquay was hearing rumours of a deputation to the Grand Duke, and disturbances in Florence elicited from him on 12 April one of his longest and most explicit entries:

A row broke out yesterday evening between the Livornese Volunteers who had been behaving themselves very badly in Florence and the Florentines. About 15 to 20 of their men were killed, and two or three Florentines among them a Frate, order was restored but the people took a run against Guerazzi, called him every name they could. Viva Leopoldo was the order of the day this morning. The Municipio took the Government on themselves in name of Leopold. Guerazzi hid himself. Shops shut all day and in the evening a spontaneous illumination in town and country so I hope there is some chance of getting peace again.[87]

The Livornese were expelled and the Provisional Government was reconstructed in the name of the Grand Duke to include moderates. Leopold was to be requested to return. The breach between Florence and Leghorn, which still held out against the Grand Duke, as Pisa also did for a time, would ultimately provide the excuse for direct Austrian intervention. In the short term it threatened worse anarchy in Tuscany outside Florence, where some sort of calm prevailed. Leghorn declared its independence and closed its gates. On 2 April Macbean wrote: 'Hitherto I have suffered no annoyance of any sort – but I am told that last night a Municipal patrol was particularly charged with preventing any insult being offered to the Shield of this Consulate.' There was a certain amount of British naval firepower in the Leghorn roads, which no doubt acted as some deterrent to hotheads.[88]

One immediate consequence of these events was that the railway stopped running – indeed Christopher Webb Smith and his wife, coming up to Florence on 12 April, 'were in such danger the train was fired on and a ball struck their carriage the train stopped and they walked 3 miles to a Villa where they passed the night and came on by the road this morning.'[89] The Smiths had probably escorted their daughter Helen and her new husband back to Leghorn, for on the 9th she had been married to the contentious Captain Codrington at the Florentine legation.

The *Daily News* was one of several papers to foresee that current events would serve only to cement the Austrian grip on Italy, observing on 19 April that 'It was vain to hope that Austria would not take full advantage of the victory gained over the only independent Italian power on the field of Novara.' The expected French intervention, undesirable in itself, was desirable inasmuch as the involvement of two powers was better than that of just one: 'The original aim of Austria could be no other than to restore the absolutist regime of the Pope.' Some sort of prize for optimism should go to the writer who proclaimed from Florence on the 18th, 'We assist here at a reaction from subversive and anarchical notions to moderate principles of Constitutional Monarchy.' Such beliefs prepared a welcome home for Leopold.[90] Meanwhile Pisa adhered to the Grand Duke on the 20th, leaving Leghorn 'in a terribly lawless state'.

On 5 May the deputation sent to Leopold at Gaeta returned. Serristori was invested with extraordinary powers to govern until the Grand Duke's return.[91] John noted on the 6th that Austrian troops had occupied Lucca. A few nights previously 'our house in town where the Knoxs are now staying was broken into … and about £50 of things stolen all belonging to Knox except my plated tea urn.' Old Irish friends, Thomas Knox and his wife were leaving Florence for good on the following Saturday, and John felt 'as if he had not a single friend left in Florence, we played a farewell rubber of whist in the evening'.[92] His long-standing friend from Cheltenham days, John Fombelle, after some 16 years in Florence, was clearly failing, although he was to linger on until November. John might well have been feeling a little despondent at this moment, even without the benefit of political events, which had taken such an uncertain turn.

Notes

1   JLM, E10 ff. 276v–277, 278v.
2   Edward E. Y. Hales, *Pio Nono* (London, 1954), p. 57.
3   FO79/125, Hamilton to FO, 5 October 1847.
4   FO79/123, Scarlett to FO, 11 January, 20 January 1847.
5   FO79/123, Scarlett to FO, 20 January 1847; JLM, E10 ff. 277v–283v.

6   FO79/119, Scarlett to FO, 16 August 1846.
7   FO79/123, Hamilton to FO, 3 May 1847; *The Times* 14 May; JLM, E10 f. 287. Miles Taylor (ed.), *The European Diaries of Richard Cobden 1846–1849* (Aldershot, 1994), 22 April 1847.
8   FO79/119, Macbean to FO, 24 March 1846; 118, Scarlett to FO, 28 March, Scarlett to FO, 15 April; 121, Treasury to FO, 15 May.
9   FO79/123, Scarlett to FO, 11 January 1847, Scarlett to FO, 9 March, also 17 April.
10   FO79/124, Hamilton to FO, 23 June 1847.
11   Although he was not a member of the church committee between October 1845 and July 1848, Maquay communicated frequently with members by letter and otherwise. On 3 January 1846 he records having a working dinner with Webb Smith to go through the accounts, since the latter had just become secretary and treasurer. JLM, E10 f. 260.
12   Martin Garrett. *A Browning Chronology* (Basingstoke, 2000), pp. 73–80. In October, unable to renew the lease at the old price on Casa Guidi, they had moved to 1881 Via Maggio at £5.7s a month. Finding it too cold, they had broken the lease and paid 'heaps of guineas' for another apartment in Piazza Pitti opposite the palace.
13   BC14, 2670 EBB to Henrietta, 24/30 April 1847.
14   BC14, 2678 EBB to Henrietta, 16/21 May 1847.
15   BC14, 2681 EBB to Arabella, 22/25 June 1847.
16   JLM, E11 f. 49v.
17   JLM, E10 ff. 280–280v.
18   Thomas A. Trollope, *What I Remember* (2nd ed., London, 1887), Vol. 2, pp. 208–10.
19   Ibid. Vol. 2, pp. 150–51. Garrow's stepdaughter, Harriet Fisher, was to die in Florence of smallpox at the age of 37 in December 1848. Garrow himself died in November 1857 and was also buried in the English cemetery.
20   BC16, 2840 EBB to Anna Jameson, 2 April 1850; BC19, 3199, to Jane Wills Sandford, 3 May 1853.
21   Trollope, *What I Remember* Vol. 2, pp. 153, 167–8.
22   The groom remained Tuscan postmaster-general until the end of the Grand Duchy, and his wife died in Florence, as announced in the *Times* 18 March 1867.
23   For example in the *Standard* on 11 November and the *Morning Post* on 16 November.
24   FO79/119, Scarlett to FO, enclosing Macbean's report.
25   JLM, E10 ff. 281; 284v.
26   JLM, E10 f. 286. The Dublin *Freeman's Journal* carried an account on 28 April.
27   JLM, E11 f. 9v.
28   BC14, 2701 EBB to Henrietta and Arabella, 13 September 1847.
29   FO79/124, Hamilton to FO, 25 & 27 August 1847. Neumann and Lady Augusta were married in both Protestant and Catholic ceremonies in London in December 1844.
30   Austin Layard, *Autobiography* (London, 1903), Vol. 2, pp. 182–4. Layard describes Kirkup, Landor, Burghersh and Normanby amongst others, and never lost his love of Florence, returning whenever he could in later years.
31   *Tuscan Athenaeum* 18 December 1847.
32   FO79/125, Hamilton to FO, 24 September 1847; 79/122, FO to Hamilton, 5 November; 79/127, Macbean to FO, 15 November; 79/126, Hamilton to FO, 16 November.
33   *Tuscan Athenaeum* 11 December 1847; 11 & 18, January 1848.
34   FO79/130, Hamilton to FO, 12 February. On the same day Palmerston drafted a despatch to Hamilton containing his reflections on the subject (FO79/129). He had probably not yet received Hamilton's of 8 February, in which he described how the Grand Duke had warned the leaders of the Civic Guard against demonstrations

in favour of a constitution 'which he should be obliged to refuse, in order not to compromise his old friends, (the Austrians) and his new (the Pope)'. In the meantime an offensive and defensive alliance had been concluded between Austria and the Duchies of Parma and Modena.

35 BC15, 2719 EBB to Henrietta, 22/24 February 1848; 2720 to Miss Mitford, 24 February.
36 FO79/130, Hamilton to FO, 1 March 1848.
37 BC14, 2724 EBB to Henrietta, 7/15 March 1848 to 1 April 1848; 2728 to Arabella, 15/17 April 1848; 2736 to Julia Martin, 20 June 1848.
38 JLM, E11 f.24. A *Società Anonima* was one in which the responsibility of the partners was limited to the amount of capital subscribed. CBS designates Currell Burston Smyth, who belonged to an Irish family well-known to the Maquays.
39 JLM, E11 ff. 22v, 23, 25. Railway business took him to a meeting in Florence 14 July and the AGM of the Leopolda on 17 July, which he attended with John Adair and which detained him till 3 pm. Clearly, with the railway just opened, there was much business to transact: JLM, E11 ff. 24v, 25.
40 JLM, E11 ff. 9v, 11. See the references in Rosemary Ashton, *142 Strand* (London, 2007).
41 Horace Rumbold, *Recollections of a Diplomatist* (London, 1902), Vol. 1, p. 152.
42 For Lever's arrival and early years in Florence, see Edward Downey, *Charles Lever, His Life in Letters* (Edinburgh and London, 1906), Vol. 1, pp. 270–97.
43 BC16, 2887 EBB to Miss Mitford, 7 November 1850.
44 FO79/134, Miss Ann Ward to FO, 22 May 1848, Macbean to FO, 3 & 19 June, 16 August; also FO79/135, P&O Steam Navigation Company to FO, 25 July 1848.
45 FO79/135, Stuart to FO, 3 June 1848, FO to Stuart, 8 June.
46 JLM, E11 ff. 21v–22v, 23v.
47 BC15, 2761 EBB to Arabella, 16/18 December 1848; BC14, 2738 EBB to Miss Mitford, 4 July 1848.
48 JLM, E11 ff. 23v–26; Downey, *Lever*, Vol. 1, p. 284.
49 FO79/132, Hamilton to FO, 7 August 1848.
50 FO79/134, Macbean to Bidwell, 30 August 1848.
51 FO79/132, Macbean to Hamilton, 25 August 1848, Codrington to Hamilton, 27 August. An account of the revolution in Leghorn from a hostile perspective is given by Michael Burke Honan, a loquacious Irishman, Catholic and correspondent for the *Times*; *Personal Adventures of Our Own Correspondent in Italy* (London, 1852).
52 FO79/132, Hamilton to FO, 31 August 1848.
53 FO79/133, Hamilton to FO, 4, 5 & 7 September 1848.
54 FO79/133, Hamilton to FO, 5 & 9 October 1848, Barron to Parker, 2 October.
55 FO79/133, Hamilton to FO, 14, 21, 22 & 27 October 1848; for Hamilton's first positive impressions of the ministry, 6 November.
56 FO79/135, enclosure by Codrington in a despatch to Admiral Parker, 18 November 1848.
57 FO79/135, Codrington to Carlo Pigli. On 26 November, Parker intimated that Codrington should have communicated with Hamilton but forwarded his letter to the Admiralty, which sent it to the Foreign Office on 8 December. The first indication that Hamilton had been apprised is a stiff letter from him to Codrington (23 November), pointing out that he had just received a visit from the Tuscan Minister of foreign affairs and was put at a disadvantage! See FO 79/133, Hamilton to FO, 30 November, for the resolution of the matter as far as English residents were concerned and FO to Admiralty, 19 December, reiterating that British subjects could not claim exemption but that the Tuscan government had itself resolved the issue.

58 BC 15, 2749 EBB to Miss Mitford, 10 October 1848.

59 JLM, E11 f. 30v.

60 FO79/129, FO to Hamilton, 7 & 9 November 1848: 'I have to say that the Grand Duke and His Advisers must be left to judge for themselves as to the expediency of such a step; but it is not every abdicated Sovereign who can return from a temporary retirement to Elba, as Napoleon Bonaparte did in 1815, and there is much virtue in continued possession.' Nevertheless, Hamilton's action in offering advice to the Grand Duke was approved 'in a moment of difficulty, though much to be regretted that the GD should be driven to this necessity'.

61 BC14, 2749 EBB to Miss Mitford, 10 October 1848; 2757 to Julia Martin, 3 December 1848.

62 BC15, 2761 EBB to Arabella, 16–18 December 1848.

63 Sophie's elder sister Caroline married John Gordon, whose sister Anne married Elizabeth Barrett's uncle Samuel in 1833. For the Cottrells, see Simona Berbeglia, 'Count Cottrell at the Court of Lucca', *Browning Society Notes* 33, April 2008, and Scott Lewis, 'Sophie Cottrell's Recollections', ibid, 24, 1997.

64 Her tombstone bore an inscription composed by EBB, which read: 'And here, among the English tombs,/In Tuscan ground we lay her,/While the blue Tuscan sky endomes/Our English words of prayer.' The tomb no longer exists, but the Armstrong Browning Library, Baylor University, has replaced the epitaph with a plaque on the English Cemetery Gatehouse wall. It is perhaps appropriate to emphasize here that the child is a remote cousin of EBB at three removes. Subsequent English Cemetery research has revealed that she was in fact buried with Georgiana Sloper, who died on 2 April 1854. Georgina was a sister of Count Henry Cottrell and married the Rev John Sloper in August 1839. Alice is thus buried with her aunt and with her infant brother, Charles.

65 BL14, 2731 EBB to Arabella, 10/11 May 1848.

66 BL15, 2761 EBB to Arabella, 16/18 December 1848; 2751 to Henrietta, 18/20 November 1848.

67 BL14, 2698 EBB to Fanny Dowglass, 6 September 1847; 2699 to Mary Boyle, 7 September 1847; 2701 to Arabella & Henrietta, 13 September 1847; Sir Charles Boyle (ed.), *Mary Boyle Her Book* (London, 1901), p. 219.

68 Charles Tennyson, 'Tennyson and His Brothers Frederick and Charles', in Hallam Tennyson (ed.), *Tennyson and His Friends* (London, 1911). See also Hugh Schonfield (ed.), *Letters to Frederick Tennyson* (London, 1930), and the article by Michael Thorn in DNB.

69 *Letters to Frederick Tennyson*, pp. 72–3, 87–8.

70 David Robertson, 'Weave a Circle; Baron Kirkup and His Greatest Friends', S. I. Mintz & others (eds), *From Smollett to James* (Charlottesville, Virginia, 1981). Landor reported the discovery of the Dante portrait in the *Examiner* on 16 August 1840, without mentioning Kirkup's name; there were to be wrangles over the credit for the discovery. See Richard T. Holbrook, *Portraits of Dante from Giotto to Raffaele: A Critical Study* (London, 1911); also the report in the *Daily News* 6 January 1857.

71 David Ross, *George & Robert Stephenson: A Passion for Success* (Stroud, 2010), p. 229.

72 FO79/137, Hamilton to FO, 23 January 1849.

73 Walker and Landor were friends; Landor left his writing desk to Walker in his will.

74 FO79/137, Hamilton to FO, 6, 9 & 13 February 1849.

75 FO79/140, Macbean to Bidwell, 19 February 1849 private; 137 Hamilton to FO, 23 February.

76 FO79/141, Loftus to FO, 24 February 1849; 137, Hamilton to FO, 27 February.

77 BC15, 2773 EBB to Henrietta, 10/20 February 1849.

78 Frances E. Trollope, *Frances Trollope, Her Life and Literary Work from George III to Victoria* (London, 1895), Vol. 2, pp. 130–4, 140. The second Mrs Thomas Trollope was born Frances Ternan.
79 JLM, E11 f. 28.
80 *Athenaeum* 1 June 1850.
81 Thomas A. Trollope, *Tuscany in 1849 and in 1859* (London, 1859), p. 173.
82 JLM, E10 ff. 35–36v.
83 JLM, E10 f. 37v.
84 FO79/137, Hamilton to FO, 27 February 1849.
85 On 6 April the FO asked Hamilton to explain the circumstances (FO79/136) enclosing an enquiry from Smith's uncle R. T. Gilpin (FO79/141). On 3 May the FO transmitted Hamilton's report to Gilpin's MP, Sir Henry Meux, and on 7 June told Gilpin that the exile had been rescinded (FO79/141). Trollope believed that Smith had indeed put himself at the head of the royalist peasantry, but he says nothing about his arrest: Trollope, *Tuscany*, p. 189.
86 FO79/140, FO to Macbean, 16 March 1849.
87 JLM, E10 ff. 38, 39.
88 FO79/140, Macbean to Bidwell.
89 JLM, E10 f. 39.
90 *Morning Chronicle* 26 April 1849. Most of the main papers in England and a good number of the provincials have near-daily bulletins from Italy during this period.
91 FO79/137, Hamilton to FO 12, 14, 17 April, 5 May 1849.
92 JLM, E10 f. 40.

9 THE AUSTRIAN OCCUPATION TO 1853

Life's night begins: let him never come back to us!
There would be doubt, hesitation and pain,
Forced praise on our part- the glimmer of twilight,
Never glad confident morning again!

ROBERT BROWNING: THE LOST LEADER[1]

The Austrian invasion of Tuscany was a turning point in the reign of the last Grand
Duke. On 5 May 1849 the Austrians occupied Lucca, on the 7th Pisa, and on the
12th, they entered Leghorn after a cannonade of 3 hours, with 15,000 troops.
Macbean reported that they 'generally acted with discipline and moderation.
Houses of two British residents were entered however, before their officers could
prevent them – much damage done to property of inmates'. The consul reckoned
that at this moment there were 478 British residents, 163 in the town, 202 embarked
on boats in the harbour and 113 temporarily absent.[2]

Leghorn was immediately placed under martial law ('state of siege' in the
current terminology), with draconian instructions from General Wimpffen, which
were retailed by the *Times* on 22 May. Upwards of 200 were shot, many without
trial, for simply wearing the national colours, although there was otherwise perfect
quiet. For the English residents of Leghorn, the reality now on their doorstep must
have been more alarming than the powder-puff Livornese attempts at revolution.

Had the Grand Duke invited the Austrians in? To this simple question
contradictory and evasive answers were given. A proclamation issued on 18 May at
Austrian request merely declared that their presence was necessary to restore order.
On the 25th Florence was occupied by 20,000 troops under Aspre as commander
in chief, who issued another proclamation claiming that they were acting at the
request of the Grand Duke to restore order 'and those days of happiness for which
you were formerly envied by Europe'. This appeared in the *Times* on 4 June.

Hamilton was called upon in rapid succession by Serristori (who had headed
the delegation to Leopold at Gaeta) and by Aspre. The one complained that the
Grand Duke's reputation was being blackened, for he had specifically declared

that he had not called the Austrians in; the other assured the British Minister that the Grand Duke had twice written to the Emperor requesting his intervention. By 10 June Hamilton thought he had unravelled the mystery. Leopold had sent Serristori back to Florence with a proclamation which acknowledged that 'the legitimate authority of the Grand Duke had been restored by the spontaneous acclamations of the people', but explained that order could not necessarily be secured by the same means. Therefore 'the Grand Duke had accepted the friendly offer of Austria' to supply his want of troops. 'The good sense of the Tuscan people' would recognize the usefulness of their assistance. Apparently Serristori's nerve had failed him and he had not issued the proclamation. On the 29th his commission was terminated and a new ministry appointed under Baldasseroni (President of the Council), Landucci (Minister of the Interior) and Casigliano (Foreign Affairs).[3]

There was widespread agreement in the British Press that Leopold's delayed return to Tuscany was to be deplored. The *Times* suspected that his flight had been a put-up job to bring Austria in, given that he was in no imminent danger. A letter from Florence, published on 14 May, suggested that (at the time of writing 8 days earlier) the Florentines still thought the city would not be occupied; it was precisely to avert that fate that the 'demagogic faction' had been expelled. Unfortunately Tuscan troops were insufficient to subdue Leghorn and the need to accept some slight offence to the national honour was reluctantly accepted.

Meanwhile Radetzky came and went from Florence, having held a grand review of Austrian troops, with bands playing and fireworks – bread and circuses for the Florentine population. The Archduke Charles visited and, as Hamilton reported on 8 June, 'Florence has resumed her former appearance of brilliancy and gaiety'. The streets were again crowded with pedestrians and carriages, and all classes seemed to be rejoicing in 'the calm and security which has succeeded to a long state of uncertainty and dismay'.[4] Hamilton's eagerness to make himself agreeable to the Austrians, however diplomatic in every sense, would not be universally admired back home. On 21 June the *Post* reported that Hamilton had given a 'grand dinner' for the Austrian archdukes, Radetsky and Aspre, the foreign Ministers, Demidoff, Orloff 'and several English ladies and gentlemen of distinction'. The *Daily News* on 3 July struck a sour note:

> We are here in the midst of an Austrian carnival. There are found folks not only among the foreign resident families, but even some Florentines of historic lineage, to rejoice in the forcible occupation of this quiet town by an uncalled for garrison of 16,000 Austro-croats. The Israelite banker Bonfils, the Russian slaveholder Demidoff, and the British minister Hamilton, lead the van in this humiliating display.

Bonfils (a converted British Jew) was doubtless principally concerned with the security of the new railway, with which he was deeply involved. 'Ladies of a certain age' meanwhile had had their hopes revived 'on the coming of such a millennium of military gallance'.

Still Leopold delayed, apparently fearing to face the Tuscan people until he felt completely secure. On 2 July the *Morning Post* quoted a letter written from Florence on 21 June which summed up the position: 'in two words: presence of the Austrians – absence of the Grand Duke'. It was not until 24 July that he landed at Viareggio and the 28th that he returned to Florence. Hamilton reported his return almost as an afterthought.[5] On 7 August the *Times* gave its readers to understand that he was enthusiastically received, but the truth was that Leopold was known to be tied to the fortunes of Austria both at home and abroad and so he would remain.

It is admittedly difficult to see how he could have forestalled an invasion, even if he had not abandoned his post in February. Austria's perceived need to secure Italy and to contain French intervention was paramount, and reports in the *Times* on 14 and 20 September indicated a dawning realization that Florence was going to be not merely occupied but occupied for a long time. Leopold's loyal subjects were going to pay the price for this occupation with a massive increase in taxation. John Maquay's reaction displayed his usual mixture of the laconic, betraying very little, and the invitation to read between the lines. On 14 May he received a long account from Currell Smyth 'of last weeks proceedings at Leghorn which has been far worse than any of the newspapers have led us to think'. Two days later, however, he went down to Leghorn in the afternoon with his sons George and Tommy,

> got to the San Marco hotel at 7 ½. Town full of Austrian troops, many persons have been shot by court martial since they occupied it, took tea at Smyths, then went to hotel & spent some time with Mr & Mrs Stewart, great quarrel between Stewart & Smyth!!!'

This quarrel between Stewart (presumably the Scots Free Church Minister) and Smyth clearly interested John as much as the political situation did. He visited the *Bellerophon*, spent time aboard with the officers, got Tommy fixed up with a week's work experience aboard, took tea at Smyth's (where two Englishmen in the Austrian service spent the evening) and returned on Friday to Florence with Tommy, leaving George in Leghorn for a couple of days, apparently without any anxiety about his safety. He arrived to hear the news that Pakenham's house had been searched for Bibles and a number seized. This in the long run would concern him rather more than what the Austrians were doing.

On 24 May he sent Tommy by train to Leghorn for his week with the Navy and on the following day went down to the Cascine with Elena to see the Austrians arrive and bivouack, 'very well behaved'. On 1 June he collected Tommy from the railway, safe and sound and 'much pleased' with his experience. The Austrian band played every evening in the Cascine. Elena went to hear it on the 3rd, and both she and John did so on the 5th, 'a great many people there'. On 8 June,

'Radetzsky arrived in Florence last night and this evening there was a review or parade in the Cascine which I went to see and got the axle tree of my carriage broken in the crowd'. On the 15th John attended 'a remarkably nice ball at Mrs Macdonnell', with Austrians present, before going to Leghorn again to spend another couple of days with Tommy on the *Bellerophon*. St John's day came and went with, significantly, 'no fetes'. There is then no mention of political developments until the Grand Duke's arrival at Viareggio was noted on 24 July: 'the Belvedere fort fired a salute in the evening and all the neighbourhood of Florence was lighted up but not the town itself.' Finally, on the 28th, John recorded Leopold's arrival with his family, but neither he nor his children went to see the illuminations: 'the boys were not well enough and I did not care enough about it to leave them at home.'[6]

Mrs Browning was making the best of a bad job. On 14 May she declared that she was now 'altogether blasée about revolutions and invasions' – particularly a 'revolution made by boys and vivas & unmade by boys and vivas – no, there was blood shed in the unmaking, some horror and terror'. As for the Grand Duke, whose part she had taken hitherto, she gave him up henceforth, for he had resumed his Austrian titles. Just over a week later, she told Henrietta, 'Robert and I agree that it is melancholy work to live on here.' Poor, distracted Italy 'never will lie down quietly for a continuance under the heel of Austria … and she has not wisdom nor energy enough to stand erect for an hour, neither'. By contrast, Austria 'is prepared to do it & will do it'. Elizabeth told Arabella on 6 June that 'the aspect of the city is at once brilliant and melancholy'. Austrians, and the German language, were everywhere. There was in her opinion no 'intercourse' between Austrians and Tuscans, and again she alleges that the English had all gone.[7]

Not only had the English not all gone but, as a letter to the *Times* on 17 May pointed out, English families had not unreasonably fled from Rome when the French bombardment started, taking the road to Florence, one of the few left open to them. There was already plenty of intercourse going on between English and Austrians and between Tuscans and Austrians too. Escape to Bagni on 30 June was perhaps the only way for Elizabeth to avoid confronting the truth that the Florentines had always been adept at getting on with their lives.

There is no doubt that the Austrian occupation induced some fundamental changes to life in Florence. The alteration in the Grand Duke was manifest. Others may have ascribed his restoration to the power of Austrian bayonets or thought that he might have chosen to come back by invitation of his people. Leopold knew that he owed it to the intervention of the Virgin Mary and reacted accordingly; this may subliminally have seemed less humiliating to him than to credit any human agency. To his infirmity of purpose and inability to make up his mind, he now added stubbornness in the one area where he had certainty: religion. Old laws against proselytism and heresy were dusted down, new ones added and a Concordat sought with the Pope. There were some high-profile political trials, most notably Guerazzi's, and Tuscans were tried on religious charges. The death penalty was reintroduced in November 1852 for offences against religion and for acts of public violence against the government.

Among Protestants abroad there was a furious reaction to what was seen as Tuscany's return to medieval barbarism. The new-model Tuscan government impacted also on the Protestant English residents, in ways to be more fully explored in the following chapter. The fact that the British & Foreign Bible Society had little in common with Mazzini was neither here nor there. The Tuscan government took its lead from the Grand Duke and began to see reds under the bed everywhere, sometimes among the English residents, but also among visitors to Tuscany, whose only crime might be that they showed their resentment of customs officers or that they happened to have been in company with a supposed revolutionary. Whereas in the old days such issues might have been settled quickly and semi-informally by the Embassy and the Tuscan Foreign Minister, they now often became locked in tedious claim and counter-claim.

The occupation was punctuated by incidents which occasionally erupted into major diplomatic confrontation involving Austria. The Tuscans, emboldened by the Austrian presence, took refuge in the tactic of admitting nothing and standing on their dignity, while the British, even when in the right, appeared as the bullying Great Power which was continually complaining. When British nationals misbehaved, the Tuscans could claim vindication, which did not help tempers on either side. An incident in the summer of 1849 involving a young artist called Whitburn illustrates some of these difficulties.

Whitburn left Florence on 27 July by public diligence to study paintings at Arezzo. One may question whether it was wise for a young foreigner to choose this moment to enter a zone of active military operations, without a passport and with an out-of-date *carta di soggiorno* (residence permit).[8] Also in the diligence were a Captain Carbonel and his wife, but the key figure was a Mrs Forbes, whom Whitburn said he had never seen before. Mrs Forbes, born Conti, was a native of Siena and the second wife of Colonel Forbes, a *garibaldino* who was now a fugitive (together with Hugh, his son by his first wife) as Garibaldi retreated across Italy from Rome. Given that Garibaldi had been in the vicinity of Arezzo on 23 July and was eluding capture by the Austrian forces in the area, it was not unreasonable that the Tuscan government should keep an eye on Mrs Forbes.

At Arezzo on 28 July Whitburn was arrested, accused of being Mrs Forbes's son, and his effects examined. Carbonel and his wife were also arrested, but fairly soon released. Despite the strenuous denials of all parties that Whitburn was Mrs Forbes's son, he was arrested and released twice, then arrested a third time and, with Mrs Forbes, bundled off back to Florence under escort on 2 August. The next day Landucci released him, accepted that his arrest was a mistake and renewed his out-of-date *carta*.

Whitburn then decided to seek compensation of £100 for the time and expense he had spent under arrest, mostly in the Hotel La Posta in Arezzo with a *carabiniere* outside the door. He wrote both to Hamilton and directly to Palmerston, to whom

Hamilton in his turn submitted the case, having already received a negative answer from the Tuscan government. The Tuscans contended, first, that by being with Mrs Forbes, Whitburn was suspect. Secondly, his 'card of security' was a few days past the time of renewal, and thirdly his second arrest was purely imaginary. (Nothing was said about the third.) Whitburn rightly pointed out that the only grounds for his arrest had been the allegation that he was Mrs Forbes's son, in itself hardly a crime; but in an age of anti-terrorist legislation, it is possible to understand the government's position. Whitburn may have been innocent if naïve, but was Mrs Forbes? Certainly, to the Austrians and Tuscans Colonel Forbes was the equivalent of a terrorist.

Whitburn revealed his naiveté by saying that he had made 'numerous enquiries' and had never heard of anyone being arrested because their *carta* had expired. Sometimes months elapsed before renewal, as it was regarded largely as a matter of form. He thought that the *carta* was only mentioned when Hamilton was pressing the case with the government, by which time it was known that he was not Mrs Forbes's son: 'this excuse was discovered for want of a better.' It was true, as many another disgruntled Briton discovered, that the Tuscans were adept at finding a new justification for proceeding when the original one seemed to be wearing thin, but now, security considerations apart, the charge for renewing the *carta* was a source of revenue, and given the Austrian occupation, the Tuscan government would be much more assiduous in insisting on it.

Technically Whitburn was in the wrong and had added to his problems by having no valid proof of identity on his person. He claimed that he had not only suffered financial loss but had been 'greatly injured'; his reputation had suffered in both English and Italian society at Florence. He was young (about 20) and clearly took a view of his own importance which the Foreign Office did not share. On 29 November Hamilton reported failure to obtain any compensation, and Palmerston noted, 'HM Government do not feel that they can with propriety press the matter further.'[9]

Whitburn had wandered out of his depth. Carbonel was no innocent, having served with Garibaldi in 1848. Early in October 1849 he wrote to Palmerston on behalf of Forbes, in prison at Genoa.[10] Perhaps surprisingly, Forbes had earned the good opinion of the Austrian General Aspre, who, as Hamilton related in a private letter to the Foreign Office, had previously released him from a Florentine gaol at Mrs Forbes's entreaties. Hamilton commented, 'It is sufficient to be an Englishman to insure Gl. D'Aspre's support, even if he is as worthless a character as Col. Forbes.' So much for automatic hostility between Austrians and Englishmen.[11]

Albeit indirectly, the Whitburn case had raised the issue of the precise relationship of the Tuscan State with the Austrian occupying forces, which was to surface again and again during the 6 years of occupation. Was Tuscany independent and fully responsible for the protection of British citizens, her courts open to them and the presence of a British diplomatic mission entirely justified? Or had she become a province of Austria, in which case diplomacy should be pursued at Vienna, the embassy downgraded or abolished and all business transferred to the consul at Leghorn? That proposal had received some support in earlier years.

From the Tuscan point of view, there was an obvious temptation to hide behind the Austrians. The occupation was irritating, but it had yet to be seen that it was not to Tuscany's ultimate benefit. In the short term it did the British no favours, particularly those at Leghorn who lived in a 'state of siege' until 1855. Florentine residents and others who had to pass through Leghorn on their way to and from the steamers had to submit to rigorous Austrian checks. Consul Macbean's presence was helpful, but even he experienced difficulty from time to time as to whether he was supposed to be dealing with the Austrians or the Tuscans.

The question of who ruled in Tuscany was brought to the fore by the claims of British Leghorn residents, who had suffered as a result of the Austrian occupation.[12] There were two principal losers: Alfred Hall, who had had his unoccupied villa plundered to the tune of £3,000 worth of damage, and a widow, a Mrs Bisset, who lost the entire contents of her house. To do Hamilton credit, he conceded that her losses were effectively greater than Hall's because she was poorer. The initial response of the Tuscan government implied an acceptance of responsibility, for they sent a Tuscan general down to the Austrian headquarters to verify the amount of damage on the spot. However, they rapidly had second thoughts, disputing the British entitlement to compensation and claiming *force majeure* for which they were in no way responsible. They also maintained that, as Tuscan subjects who had suffered were unable to sue for compensation, it would be unjust to allow that right to foreigners.

The Confidential Print devoted to this issue ends on 25 September 1850 with no resolution in sight. Advised by the Crown's law officers, Palmerston rejected the Tuscan arguments and would admit no dispute about the justice of the British claim, although he was prepared to entertain arbitration as to the amount of compensation. First the Sardinians offered arbitration (rejected by the Tuscans, probably under Austrian pressure), then Russian and finally Belgian arbitration was proposed. A trifle belatedly, Hamilton was instructed to prepare a detailed dossier on the losses suffered by individual Leghorn residents. A few more claimants appeared and the total sum claimed totalled £1,539 6s (*lire* 46,175 16 8), of which by far the biggest single amount was Alfred Hall's (£1,365 16s 8d), although he had more than halved his original claim.[13]

The depositions shed a vivid light on the Austrian entry into Leghorn. At 10.30 on 11 May 1849, about 100 Austrian soldiers, ignoring the card on the front door which said *Domicilio Inglese* and the protests of the *custode*, broke into Hall's Villa Bacciochi. During a stay of 3 hours, they forced open furniture, got themselves thoroughly drunk on the contents of the cellar (some 150 bottles) and departed with as much booty as they had not smashed up in the meantime. One has sympathy with the view that this could not possibly have been part of any military operation, and the Austrian authorities seem initially to have recognized some responsibility. When apprised by the consulate, D'Aspre had sent a patrol of soldiers with orders to shoot the looters, but they had already gone. Schnitzer indicated that he would do all in his power to secure indemnity, and Wimpffen allowed Hall to put up a notice offering a reward for things returned, particularly items of sentimental value like his wife's wedding trousseau, but to no avail.

Widow Bisset, who was guardian for her underage son Adam, had had a similar experience. Austrian soldiers ignored the notice with the consular seal on the door of her second-floor apartment at 1 Borgo Reale, breaking in and causing damage while she was with her son in Florence. In this instance not only did they compound the felony by assaulting the person who had been left in charge but they were accompanied by women, who left items of clothing behind. The widow's claim for £89 7s 8d (2,682 *lire*) represented a considerable portion of her substance. Again the Austrian authorities seemed helpful at the outset, posting a sentry at the broken door to prevent further looting.

Among the four additional claimants was Elizabeth Kerr, who had retired on the 10th to an English vessel in the harbour, having locked her apartment. When her son, William, returned at 8 am on the 12th, he found the door smashed and her effects scattered; she put her losses at over 181 *lire*. Her neighbour, Humphrey Murray, a poor Scottish artisan, had likewise retreated with his wife, Agnes, to a British ship, and put in a claim for 228 *lire*. The merchant Joseph Pate claimed 1,939 *lire* (over £60 sterling) for his losses from his substantial third-floor apartment at the Stabile Malenchini. His three servants and a shopkeeper who was with them, all Italians, had been molested. The last claimant was John Udny, whose opportunistic claim for repairs to his property of £172 16 8 as a result of damage from an Austrian howitzer shell Hamilton rightly disallowed.[14]

Another insight into the experiences of British residents during the Austrian invasion comes from a voluminous report that Macbean prepared in August 1849. This was a riposte to a letter from David Thomson, professor of natural philosophy at Kings College Aberdeen, published in the *Times* on 8 June, which reproduced one written on 23 May (with publication in mind) by his father, David Thomson, an hotelier in Leghorn. Thomson asserted that Her Majesty's Ships of War 'might just as well have been dismantled in Portsmouth harbour for any good done by them to the British residents during this month of May'. They had not taken British subjects under their protection, or on board, during the assault on Leghorn; residents instead were exposed to great inconvenience and misery on board merchant vessels. This performance was contrasted both with that of the Royal Navy during the Napoleonic wars in defending British lives and property at Leghorn, which some could still remember, and with that of the Americans and the French in respect of their own subjects in May 1849.

Hamilton had been alerted by Captain Baynes of the *Bellerophon* (the same who had received John Maquay's Tommy on board) to the rumours that were circulating Europe in the wake of this letter, which had been published in the widely read Paris-based *Galignani*. Instructed to report, Macbean did so in a despatch nearly fifty pages long, which retold the story of rebel activity from 25 August 1848 onwards, and recounted interviews with Thomson (who stuck to his guns, although he admitted some slight inaccuracies) and others.[15]

The gist of the defence was that Baynes had thought it better to stow civilian refugees on board merchant vessels while the warships stood by in case they were called into action. Interestingly, Thomson's co-religionist, the Reverend Stewart, who with his family had been taken on board the schooner *Lancashire Lass*, supported this position. He had been on a man of war in his time and said that 'even had he had the option he would have preferred being on board of a Merchant Vessel'. If Macbean is to be believed, he had offered to inform Thomson of the arrangements for the embarkation of civilians, to which Thomson replied 'that he was an old man and had seen things quite as bad, and that it was his determination and that of his wife and daughter to remain on shore and to take care of their House'. Macbean insinuated that Thomson might have had a personal grievance. His hotel had once been 'much frequented by British Naval Officers', but for some reason had not been used by those of *Bellerophon, Thetis* and *Porcupine,* 'and I imagine that he has felt much hurt at not having had their support'.

Whatever the rights and wrongs of these allegations, the British navy did not seem able to afford any greater protection on land than the British Consul offered. On 11 January 1850, a fight occurred in Leghorn between three British mariners (Baines, Johnstone and Macmillan), all from the merchant vessel *Euphemia*, and some Greek seamen. Macmillan had allegedly aggravated his offence by resisting arrest by the Tuscan police and stabbing a gendarme in the hand. The police delivered the ritual beating-up, it was claimed, and in accordance with the state of siege turned the sailors over to the Austrians, who did not regard the crime as serious and handed them over to Macbean. Macmillan was promptly rearrested by the Tuscans and carried off to Lucca, his trial fixed for 7 March. Macbean urged an immediate trial so that the evidence of other seamen could be taken and the complaint that all three had been beaten up investigated, but he got nowhere. The Tuscans thumbed their noses at the occupying Austrians, the British Consul and, for that matter, the Royal Navy ships on station at Leghorn.

On 13 February, after a meeting in the Consul's office, a memorial signed by sixty-three Leghorn residents was sent to both Hamilton and the Foreign Office, forcibly making the point that the Tuscan authorities 'had acted unwarrantably' by arresting and detaining Macmillan after the Austrians had taken cognisance of the incident. In the event, the trial did not conclude until the summer, when Macmillan had spent the best part of 6 months in gaol. Remarkably, he was acquitted by the Lucchese judges despite (Macbean claimed) the attempts of local officials to secure a conviction. His defence was paid for by Leghorn residents to the tune of 820 pauls.[16]

In February 1850 the Austrians acknowledged the reality that Florence was no threat by shifting their headquarters to Leghorn. The military convention with Tuscany which was signed on 27 May, and reported by the *Times* on the

29th, limited the number of occupying troops to 14,000, but the duration of the occupation was left entirely to the emperor, who could empower his commander in chief to subject any place and its population to martial law. As the *Times* remarked, this supposedly private agreement would make the Grand Duke very unpopular when it became known.

British governmental uncertainty about the position of Tuscany was reflected in the successive appointments after Hamilton's sudden death in September 1850. First, there was the Irish Catholic Sheil, in the hope this would please both the Tuscans and Rome. His appointment was greeted with surprise, cynicism and misgiving. The Protestant Irishman Maquay was moved to insert two exclamation marks on hearing of it, but he planned a welcome dinner party for the new Minister, which the latter was prevented from attending by a summons to the Pitti Palace.[17] Sheil was scarcely 3 months in Tuscany, from mid-February 1851 until he died on 25 May, but during that time, he showed some notable and perhaps unexpected energy in a number of causes, and his death was to be much regretted.[18] His biographer reported that

> It was utterly disgusting to the dowagers of Tuscan society to see how little he valued ceremony and punctilio; and his straightforward mode of speaking and acting indicated, in the opinion of certain politicals, both Italian and foreign, tendencies in the direction of liberalism deeply to be lamented, if not feared.

Sheil mistrusted the Austrians and was convinced that they planned to exclude British exports from Tuscany.[19] Some years later a pleasant exchange with the Austrian Envoy Baron von Hügel was remembered. As proof that the Italians were unfitted for self-government, Hügel told Sheil 'that for five crowns, you may take away a man's life in the Roman States; for five crowns, Sir!' Sheil replied, 'Well, it's a very handsome price, I can recollect some years in Tipperary when it would only have cost five shillings.'[20]

In May 1851 Sheil had to get Frederick Tennyson released from prison, to which he had been condemned 'for resisting the Police and for having publickly employed exceedingly strong language in denouncing the Tuscan Government'. Sheil had managed to have the sentence commuted to house arrest. The Minister for Grace and Justice was doubtless only too pleased to pardon 'the brother of the distinguished poet' and thereby, as Sheil remarked, to give 'evidence of the wish of the Tuscan Government to do what may be agreeable to the British Government and its representative'.[21] We are unfortunately not told the details of Tennyson's outburst.

This turned out to be a trivial matter; other incidents during the summer of 1851 were more serious or at least more annoying, and they occurred at a moment when Sheil's unexpected death had once more pitchforked Scarlett into responsibility for the British mission. One had to be dealt with somewhat in arrears. Dr William Aiton, an elderly Leghorn resident, had been in transit overland to England in April 1851 when he was held for a day in prison at Pietrasanta and subjected to some rough treatment by the police, as well as being surrounded by a hostile crowd. A retired naval surgeon, he was in poor health: he had come to live in Italy because of a severe bronchial infection and he also had poor eyesight.[22] Macbean found it difficult to account for his treatment, except on the assumption that minor Tuscan officials had got the idea that their superiors were unfriendly to Great Britain and would look kindly on any annoyances they inflicted on British subjects.

The response of the Tuscan government was revealing. The conduct of the police at Pietrasanta was justified on the grounds that Aiton had 'taken up his abode in one of the lowest Inns outside the walls of Pietra Santa' and that he was rather oddly dressed, which attracted a crowd of 'the curious and rude country people'. The gendarmes were within their rights to arrest him when he refused to produce his passport in the presence of this crowd. He was released the following day when he had shown his papers and was left 'in perfect liberty, altho his alledged [sic] inattention to the orders of the public force deserved some reproof'. Here one might suspect the effects of cultural difference; both Aiton's brusque behaviour and his eccentric appearance were held against him. The Foreign Office may have found Casigliano's reply unsatisfactory, but Aiton's complaint produced no further action.[23]

The arrest of the son of the physician Dr Harding at Leghorn in June 1851 illustrated a familiar combination of adverse circumstances. James Harding, an artist, had been returning from Elba to Florence when he was arrested at the Leghorn terminus of the Leopolda Railway after having an altercation with the *Guardia di Finanza*. He had with him a piece of canvas which he said he had originally brought with him from Florence and which he had wrapped round an umbrella. No notice had been taken of it when his luggage was examined and sealed at the San Marco gate, but a few minutes after he had left the Customs House, it was seized by another official. Thereupon 'By Mr Harding's own statement he appears to have lost his temper and to have made use of violent language', under provocation as Macbean thought. This led to his arrest.

Demanding the right to contact the Consul, Harding immediately wrote a letter to Macbean, which he gave to the station master for prompt delivery but was immediately appropriated by a gendarme; two hours later he was allowed to write again. Macbean received the two letters at about the same time and went to the Police Office, where he secured Harding's release by undertaking responsibility for any fine that might be imposed. The canvas, he believed, had been returned, but only after Harding had paid its full estimated value. The consul particularly complained about the interception of the first letter.[24] Harding had reacted irritably, perhaps intemperately, to the contradictory conduct of two officials who seemed to have overlapping jurisdictions, while Macbean was justified, on the available facts, in complaining of an infraction of the victim's recognized right to communicate with his diplomatic representative when in trouble.

In presenting the case to the Tuscans on 21 June, Scarlett chose to treat the incident as an illustration of a general truth. He had 'frequently' been told that British subjects had experienced 'harshness and injustice' and also 'wanton and unnecessary' severity at the Leghorn station, but he had 'often' refrained from bringing these incidents to the government's notice, for want of witnesses and evidence to prove facts of which he had no doubt. The tone was calculated to irritate, but Scarlett explained why he adopted it in a private letter to Palmerston a few days later. He admitted that he thought Harding had largely brought his arrest upon himself, but it would be useful 'to give the Tuscan subordinate authorities a Lecture on their want of courtesy and civility, in which qualities they are too often wanting'.

It was entirely and tiresomely predictable that the Foreign Office, instructing Scarlett to communicate its displeasure, did not mention Harding's bad temper, insisting instead that such a system of administration would have a deterrent effect on foreigners visiting Tuscany. The 'free and perfect right on the part of every British Subject to communicate, either in writing or personally with the Agents of his Government' was magisterially asserted, and an undertaking demanded that this interference would not occur again. It was no less predictable that the Tuscan government should hide behind a legal investigation which made much of Harding's violent and abusive language and very little of administrative incompetence. As Scarlett observed, it failed to deal at all with the issue of consular access, on which a further reminder was necessary. It was eventually explained that Harding's letter had been taken by the police precisely in order to expedite its delivery to the consul (who had gone home by the time it arrived), while the fact that it was unsealed had led them to believe they might read it!

Acceptance of the principle of the right of communication amounted to an apology of sorts and perhaps manifested a desire on both sides to cool matters off.[25] Far from cooling, however, tempers later in 1851 became more heated as incidents multiplied. The summer at Bagni di Lucca managed once again to produce an example of disorderly behaviour on the part of bored young British gentlemen, which showed the breed at its worst and appears also to have brought out the worst in the Tuscan authorities.

On 3 July 1851 in Bagni, Francis Hare got into a quarrel with a Neapolitan prince, which rapidly assumed the status of an affair of honour. When the authorities tried to intervene in order to prevent a duel, Hare allegedly struck a gendarme with a whip. Then he and the Honourable Alfred Stourton rode their horses along a public highway at a furious gallop 'in violation of Article 173 of the existing regulations of the Police respecting fast racing'. When the Italian owner of one of the horses took exception to the animal's treatment, he was belaboured around the head. The gendarmes again intervened, but the young men on their own admission at first refused to obey orders to dismount, because they had been addressed discourteously. Francis's brother William became caught up in the business and was arrested too. He claimed that he was only trying to find out what had happened, but the Tuscans maintained that he was abusive and had also struck a gendarme with his stick.

What happened in custody thereafter was disputed, but there seems little doubt that the gendarmerie indulged in a little roughing-up. Guarantors were then found – an Englishman, William Newton, who was residing at the house of the apothecary Betti, Mr William Anguilleri, Adrian Bell and the hotelier Gustavus Pagnini. The accused were released pending trial, but their case was not helped either by the prejudices of Scarlett, who seems to have assumed that because they were gentleman of 'high respectability' they could not possibly have been guilty of conduct unbecoming, or by the extraordinary letter which their mother sent to the Police Chief. This he returned, claiming to believe that it was not in fact intended for him. Mrs Hare's response revealed the English matriarch in full flow. He was to have the goodness to come to her house immediately (she had already summoned him once), and if he refused, she would notify the Minister of the Interior. She wanted (immediately) the names of the guilty gendarmes 'who have beaten, ill-treated and almost maimed my son', and if these were refused, the Minister would be told of that too.

Mrs Hare was unduly confident that the Minister would see things in the same light as she did. A copy of her letter was submitted for Scarlett's perusal with the rhetorical question whether she could have more openly refused 'the considerations of propriety and respect due to the public authority of the Country in which she lives'. Even Scarlett could only suggest 'that as a mother not in possession of the full information, she might be excused a little unreasonable heat, given the circumstances and her sex'. The Tuscans did not accept that they should apologize to him 'for so gross and voluntary an Insult to the British Nation' and dismiss and punish the offending officers. Throughout the proceedings and the subsequent correspondence, two things became clear, both of which might have stemmed from cultural and linguistic differences. The English refused to obey orders from properly constituted authority unless they were asked nicely, revealing a derogatory attitude to those they regarded as inferiors, while the Tuscan gendarmerie tended to resort to strong-arm tactics when their instructions were not obeyed.

The authorities then proposed to prosecute the unfortunate Mr Newton, who had gone surety for his worthless compatriots, as he plaintively told Scarlett around the beginning of December. Allegedly he had so intimidated the Bagni police by threatening to appeal to Her Majesty's government and 'foreign powers' that he had virtually forced them to release their prisoners. This might anyway have seemed simply ludicrous, but Newton claimed that he could not speak a word of Italian. Scarlett replied that he had laid the case before the Tuscan government and advised Newton to employ an advocate; we hear no more about it.[26]

As far as the principals were concerned, the Tuscans were in no hurry. The Hares had to return to their regiments and Stourton to return to England, which forced them to permit judgement to go by default. It was not until June 1852 that Bulwer reported sentences of 12 days' imprisonment for Francis, 8 days for William and 1 year's expulsion from the Grand Duchy for both. Stourton was entirely acquitted. His minor misdemeanour of riding his horse (at least it was his own) at a furious gallop was overlooked. The gendarmes were not punished for their misbehaviour, but they had been given great provocation by the ill manners of these so-called English gentlemen. The Tuscan judgement was a masterpiece of moderation, in which considerable effort was made to ascertain the facts; the Foreign Office was wise to regard the matter as closed. The Hare brothers were scarcely worth the trouble, as their later careers revealed.[27]

The courts also worked well in another incident which involved Harry Robert Newton, an architect (not apparently related to the Mr Newton at Bagni). Around the end of August 1851, he visited Volterra and took the precaution of presenting himself to the police before embarking on his sightseeing, only to be assaulted by a gendarme, who among other things hit him with his own camp-stool. When he asked how he had offended, he was informed that he had spoken discourteously. When this was reported to them, the Tuscan authorities opted for the pre-emptive strike. Scarlett was told 'that if the Accounts which had reached him were proved to be correct, the Police Officer would undoubtedly be punished', but since Mr Newton had 'taken the course of placing the Affair before a Tuscan legal Tribunal to be tried in the usual way, the Tuscan Government can not interfere now with the regular Course of Justice'.

Placing reliance on 'the regular course of justice' might have been risky, but it worked. The policeman was condemned before the legal tribunal at Volterra to 20 days' solitary confinement in the prison of the Fortress on short rations and a month's suspension afterwards from service and pay. Newton was able to produce several local tradesmen and residents as witnesses; this gendarme may have been a known local quantity. Newton also got his costs, for in an unwonted fit of generosity, the British government agreed to make up any shortfall not awarded to him by the Tuscan courts. Scarlett's complacent assertion on 22 October that 'the Interest taken by Her Majesty's Legation in this Affair has had considerable Influence in hastening and bringing it to a favorable Conclusion' may not have been justified.[28]

While the Tuscan ministers tended to support the behaviour of the gendarmes, the Austrians may have been less happy about the effect of gratuitous violence on international relations. According to a private letter written in October by Lord Methuen in Florence, and partly prompted by the Hare-Stourton affair, Prince Lichtenstein (commander in chief of the Austrian forces at Florence) had told the Tuscan government that 'it would get itself into a serious scrape by its allowing such misconduct on the part of the Gendarmes'.[29] By this time a far more serious case, which did involve the Austrians, had unfolded.

On 7 June 1851 Henry, Edward and Charles Stratford, sons of the late Earl of Aldborough, together with an Italian, were arrested after a raid on their Leghorn villa. They were accused of revolutionary activity and conveyed to the fortress to await trial by the Austrians. Their position was peculiar from the outset. Their late father, Mason Gerard Stratford, Earl of Aldborough, died on 4 October

1849 and was buried in the Leghorn cemetery. The sons now living in Leghorn were illegitimate, although they claimed otherwise and the eldest, Henry, called himself Earl of Aldborough. Charles Stratford had been given unpaid employment in the consulate, but on the day before the raid on the villa, he had resigned on the grounds 'that if he was not worth a salary which should suffice to buy him clothes he could not continue with me'. Macbean had been lending him money throughout this whole period. Charles had clearly been engaged in revolutionary activity while being employed by the consulate.

Macbean's letter to Scarlett, written on 8 June, starts with a masterly understatement. Yesterday there had been 'a very disagreeable piece of work in the neighbourhood of my house'. He had been summoned to the Villa Messori at about 4 o'clock to discover it surrounded by gendarmes, its front door smashed in. On making himself known, he was admitted to the house and told that the Austrian general had ordered a 'perquisition':

> types and printing materials had been found with some copies of inflammatory placards that a quantity of damped paper had been found in a state ready for use, but that advantage had been taken, of the time required by them to effect their entrance, to burn a considerable number of papers.

Macbean refused to come up to the second floor and see for himself. He 'could not defend in any way the conduct of my countrymen', but did not wish to seem either to interfere with the local authorities or to approve their actions. He had no influence over the quick-tempered Stratfords, and his presence 'might have induced them to persist in the offensive language which I heard they had addressed to the Officers & men of the Gendarmerie'. He confined himself to expressing surprised regret that the officers had 'shewn so little consideration to the feelings of the other inmates of the house by effecting their entrance in so violent a manner'. He would remain on the first floor with Lady Aldborough and her younger children, who, he was confident, had no part in any illegal acts.

In a despatch to the Foreign Office dated 10 June, Scarlett not only got the date of the Stratfords' arrest wrong and mistakenly identified Henry as the son who had been employed in Macbean's office but also alleged that prohibited arms had been found. There had been 'great sensation' about this in Florence, the episode said to be one of many proofs of a conspiracy going on under the direction of a Central Committee in London aided by Mazzini. Macbean had not mentioned the discovery of arms, a much more serious offence. Given the brief interval since his letter, what fresh information had reached Scarlett about the further finds that had been made at the villa?

A further letter from Macbean on 13 June added more detail but scarcely justified Scarlett's hyperbole. The consul accepted the justification of the conduct of the police, who only smashed down the door when they were refused admission with violent and abusive language, and subsequently (at Macbean's request) left gendarmes to guard the premises until it could be repaired. He had had a perfectly civil exchange with the local commander de Crenneville, who wished not unreasonably that communications between them should not be considered as official.

Everything seemed to suggest that an early solution might be found. After court martial 'the most guilty might be imprisoned for a Year at Volterra or in some other Prison of that class'. It was true that a dagger and a couple of bayonets had been found, but as Crenneville had only ordered the raid because of the rumoured clandestine publications, he had no wish to make matters worse by mentioning arms. Macbean was able to assure him the family's firearms 'had been deposited in this Office so far back as May 1849'. He had also assured Crenneville that the culprits' mother was English and not Spanish, as Crenneville had believed and had shown him the certificate of her marriage to her late lord at the British embassy in Paris in 1826. Crenneville had not previously regarded the Stratfords as British subjects and would 'in consequence of what I told him have to correct one or two points in his official report'. The nationality of the young men was of some importance, and it emerged later that their illegitimacy and birth outside Britain did put their status in question.

In a brief despatch to the Foreign Office on 15 June, Scarlett sketched a dramatic prospect. There would be trial by court martial, and a fortnight would elapse before sentences were delivered. If the death sentence were passed, the Grand Duke out of deference to Great Britain would recommend exile, provided Scarlett guaranteed that the three removed themselves far from Tuscany. He would advise Admiral Parker in the meantime to be prepared for their removal. He had received the report of the Tuscan government on the 14th, which significantly added nothing to what Macbean had already reported. The Foreign Office reply was sombre: deep concern that Her Majesty's subjects should engage in conspiracy, 'nothing to say in extenuation of an offence which is so repugnant to the feelings', and a plea for mercy from the Tuscans.[30] It is a pity Scarlett was not more specific about the 'great sensation' that these events were supposed to have created in Florence. The Brownings were not in Florence at the time, Trollope says nothing in his memoirs and John Maquay nothing in his journals.

It is hardly surprising that when the story broke on 18 June, with brief reports in both the *Times* and the *Daily News*, the newspapers took the exaggerated line and embellished it. The *Times* hit its stride on the 28th. The young men were discovered *in flagrante delicto*

> with concealed firearms in their possession, a printing press, the third number of a Republican journal, and the new-fashioned infernal machine of walking canes, containing a reservoir from which vitriolic acids may be ejected on the dresses of ladies seen with Austrian officers, or wearing Austrian colours.

Further, 'they were members of that conspiracy, which, under the pretext of regenerating the peninsula, seeks to plant the Red Republic in the centre of Italy'.

After a reference to the disputed succession to the Aldborough earldom, the report continues with the discovery of arms, 'concealed ammunition' and other prohibited items, 'treasonable by virtue of the state of siege'. Had the so-called Lord Aldborough and his brothers been Tuscan or Austrian subjects, 'they would have been tried at the drumhead and shot within an hour', but the Austrians were disposed to be merciful. The report ends by praising the efforts of Macbean and Scarlett and hoping that the facts were not as bad as they appeared, a remarkable sentiment given that the paper had made every effort to make them seem worse. By 7 July the *Freeman's Journal* was reporting the arrest of twenty-two persons in Florence, and numbers in Lucca and Pisa, connected with discoveries at the Villa. The *Nottinghamshire Guardian* on the 10th got things spectacularly wrong, referring to 'Lord Aldborough and his brothers, the Messrs Scarlett'.

Elsewhere reality was beginning to strike home. Throughout the autumn, disquieting rumours began to circulate that the Austrian court martial had indeed passed sentence of death on the Stratfords – a sentence unknown in Tuscan law in 1851. Macbean, who had visited the brothers in the Leghorn fortress where they were being held in passable conditions, could offer no enlightenment. The sentences were secret until confirmed by Radetzsky at Milan, who was presumably in correspondence with Vienna. The Tuscan government was unable to comment because it had no information on the matter from the Austrians; so much for Tuscan independence. It was not until 20 December that the sentences were published. Henry and Edward Stratford had indeed been sentenced to death, but their sentences were commuted by Radetsky to 10 and 6 years' solitary confinement 'for the express purpose of conforming the punishments to Tuscan Law'. Charles, though not acquitted, was considered much less culpable and released on consideration of his previous imprisonment.

While Radetsky seemed to have sufficient political sense to recognise the existence of a Tuscan government, the sentences were harsh, given that no act of rebellion had actually been proved. Scarlett regretted that 'the Austrian Authorities do not appear to act in accordance with the Assurances I have so frequently received', that is, that once the trial had taken place, the passing of sentence would be remitted to the Grand Duke. Further exchanges with the Tuscan government resulted in a statement, on 30 December, that further mitigation of the sentences might be considered. This promised continued hard diplomacy rather than any instant action.[31] The issue was about to become entangled in a major diplomatic row between Britain and Austria over the treatment of a young Briton at the hands of an Austrian officer in Florence on 29 December 1851 – the day before the Tuscans' response about the Stratfords. Scarlett, who except during Sheil's brief tenure of office had been holding the fort ever since Hamilton's final illness in September 1850, was now confronted with a fresh crisis.

Its small beginnings appear in a letter from Mr Twizell Wawn, MP for Gateshead, which reached the Foreign Office on 8 January 1852. On 29 December Mr Erskine Mather, aged 19, and his 16-year-old brother were listening to a regimental band, when the elder was struck from behind by an Austrian officer, with the flat side of his sword, and on his turning round sharply to see by whom and for what he was thus assaulted, he was immediately cut down. In consequence he was conveyed to the hospital, where he now remains in a precarious state. The young man had sufficient self-possession to request his brother to mark well the features of the officer who committed the assault, and has also got the names of other respectable individuals who witnessed the outrage. I have therefore to ask your lordship to write to the Consul [sic] at Florence, and command him to inquire into this outrage upon a British subject, and to demand such reparation as the case requires, otherwise the property, the liberties, and the lives of British subjects will be endangered, and that liberty here accorded to foreigners will be denied to British subjects in other countries where they are aliens.

Wawn enclosed a letter sent by Mr Mather senior, with enclosures from his two sons. John Maquay, it may be noted, heard about the incident on the day that it occurred.[32]

Two important points must be made. Firstly, the British government was in its last throes. Lord Palmerston, the Foreign Secretary, had been sacked in December 1851 for altering despatches after the Queen had signed them, and Lord Granville, who replaced him 26 December, had hardly got to grips with business. He was himself to lose office in February, to be replaced by the less than competent Lord Malmesbury. Secondly, nothing came from Scarlett until a despatch (dated 2 January) and a private letter to Granville (dated the 6th), obviously sent together, arrived on the 12th. It was to be a conspicuous feature of subsequent developments that the elder Mather always seemed to get information from Florence faster than the Foreign Office received it from Scarlett.

So did the newspapers. The first reports appeared in the *Morning Post* on 8 January and the *Times* on the 9th, to be followed by others between the 10th and 12th, often feeding off one another but including three distinct eyewitness accounts, which thus became available to the public in the first fortnight. By the 12th the *Daily News* was in full cry. Florence was peaceful; there was no justification for the substitution of 'the brutal force of an insolent soldiery' for the ordinary processes of law and government. By what right were 'the Austrian allies of the Grand Duke above the laws of the land they are called in to support and maintain'? And were the British who might fall victim to their casual violence obliged to submit? An anti-Austrian tone was already apparent in English newspaper coverage of Italian affairs and was going to get stronger during the 1850s.

Meanwhile the Foreign Office continued to suffer from lack of accurate information. On 9 January Granville received a letter written by Lord Methuen in Florence on the 2nd, forwarded to him by its Baring recipient. It was profoundly misinformed and contributed to the Foreign Office's initially slow reaction. Methuen averred that strong demonstrations of feeling on the part of Scarlett and the English residents had resulted in the Austrians' consent to the trial of the suspected officer and 'justice done to the wounded man'. Granville was told that 'you will not have any trouble about the affair', which could not have been wider of the mark.[33] A request to Scarlett to investigate the truth of Wawn's report, sent off before anything had arrived from Scarlett himself, seemed a mere formality. The lack of news from Scarlett contrasts with what was already in the public domain.

By the time Scarlett's despatch of 2 January arrived Mather had probably received letters from his sons, written on 29 December, assuring him that the wound was superficial and not dangerous. Erskine cheerfully added, 'The English Consul has been applied to and M. Charles Lever & a friend who called upon [me] offering their services.' He expected a rapid settlement of the affair; but the younger brother (who himself went to see Prince Lichtenstein) was beginning to have significant doubts about Scarlett: 'I do not think the Consul did right in treating this case in such a cold manner as if an Englishman his Compatriot was nothing to either him or his Country.' He was nonetheless confident: they had witnesses, including an Italian priest.

A first class row was now brewing, which Scarlett's despatch was unlikely to assuage. Unknowingly contradicting the brothers, he asserted that Mather's life was still in danger from the sabre cut. He had not been recognised as an Englishman; because of the shape of his hat he was probably taken for an Italian (and a liberal at that) which, by implication, explained the attack. Persuaded that it was useless to seek an official enquiry, Scarlett had taken informal soundings. He received the impression that, if Mather would declare he had had no intention of offending the officer, the latter would be ready to declare he regretted his mistake. Even Scarlett admitted that this offer was hardly sufficient, and the Mathers rejected it, demanding an enquiry. Convinced that this would not be granted without Austrian consent, Scarlett went to Prince Lichtenstein, who was very civil, and in effect gave him permission to approach the Tuscan government! Scarlett was 'quite prepared to suspend official intercourse with the Government if all redress were refused', and, in a gesture calculated to strike terror into the Tuscans, privately informed Casigliano that 'if no reparation were granted, I should feel it to be my duty to abstain from appearing at the State ball, and from presenting the English on New Year's Day'. The English population were also prepared to absent themselves.

By paying court to the Austrians instead of putting his demand directly to the Tuscan government and throwing on them the odium of refusal, Scarlett had instantly compromised the vital principle of Tuscan independence. Somewhat ominously, he revealed that Lichtenstein had planted a seed in his mind by suggesting that it would be timely for Lord Westmorland (formerly Lord Burghersh and now envoy at Vienna) to speak to Schwarzenburg about the release of the Stratfords. 'Florence', Scarlett sighed, was 'no longer the post of idleness and tranquillity in these days, that it used to be'. He was grateful for the continued assistance of the *attaché* Barron, seconded from Turin.

Granville seems to have acted with commendable speed and decision. On 13 January a despatch was sent to Lord Westmorland acquainting him with what had happened and warning that if an enquiry was not fairly conducted in Florence Her Majesty would be obliged to ask for reparation from Austria and would expect prompt redress. On the 14th Scarlett was authorized to remunerate the lawyer, Salvagnoli. Clearly, whatever reservations Granville may have had, forwarding an enquiry was the only option for the present, but predictable concerns rapidly became apparent.

On 4 February Mather senior, now in Florence with his two sons (Erskine had left hospital on 17 January), complained to Granville that the proceedings were conducted in secret 'without an opportunity of eliciting truth or rebutting evidence against it'. Salvagnoli 'has not yet been present at the examination of a single witness on either side' and had not himself 'obtained one witness for examination'. Whether there could be a fair outcome given these circumstances his Lordship might decide. As to whether he himself should initiate legal proceedings before the courts of Tuscany, Mather asked how a just decision could be obtained in the circumstances of the country. Even if it were, how was it to be executed against a man supported by the Austrian army? 'I dare not take the responsibility of placing this important question involving the safety of our countrymen abroad in such a fatal position.' Mather thus lobbed an unwelcome ball firmly into the British government's court; they alone could obtain redress.

Mather here raised in stark terms the issue which should have been central from the beginning: Tuscan independence and the willingness and ability of the Tuscan government to fulfil its international obligations. The British government's failure over the next 3 months to bring the necessary pressure to bear, and the increasing evidence that Scarlett was simply not up to the job, raised Mather's frustrations to fever pitch. The backing of his MP ensured that the issue was kept alive in the Commons, the newspapers were in full cry and he had contacts in Florence like Lever, who, whatever they lacked in political clout, certainly had the energy to advise and publicist skills to reach a wider audience. On 19 February the *Times* published a letter from an anonymous American in Florence, who reported widespread doubts about Scarlett's energy and competence. The projected boycott of the New Year's Ball had been averted (only too easily, one imagines) by assurances of 'examination and redress'.

Under pressure in Parliament and the press, Granville on 13 February asked Scarlett when they could expect to hear about the enquiry and urged him to chivvy the Tuscan government. The government's proceedings might have been more focussed if Granville had survived a little longer. One of his last actions was to decide, in January, that a political heavyweight was needed at Florence in the person of Sir Henry Bulwer, but unfortunately Bulwer did not arrive until mid May. Partly this was due to his private concerns – he never moved anywhere without due consideration of his health – but, much more significantly, the Tuscan government took the unusual step of raising a formal objection to his appointment, which inevitably caused delay. Granville would have none of it, and the veiled threat to close the embassy, which his successor Malmesbury had no honourable option but to support, induced the Tuscans to yield, if with gritted teeth. For the time being, Scarlett was left in charge.

The outcome of the Tuscan investigation, transmitted by Scarlett on 19 February, was unpredictable only in the sense that it completely vindicated James Mather's view of events. No Austrian soldiers had been questioned; all further proceedings now awaited a decision from Vienna. The Tuscans could hide behind the Austrian occupation and absolve themselves of any responsibility. On 4 March, James Mather saw Malmesbury in London. What actually passed between them will forever be unknown. Mather was induced to abandon, with extreme reluctance, his initial position that the government was obliged to secure punishment of the offender and proper reparation for the damage done to his son and British prestige abroad. Although there is no evidence that he had previously suggested any appropriate compensation, he consented to name a figure of £5,000 damages, enormous by any standards of the day. In a further exchange with the Foreign Office a few days later he remarked that, if it was Malmesbury's pleasure that personal reparation be entertained, it ought to be proportional to the deed. Otherwise some other term should be employed: 'It would then have been far better for this point to be omitted.' There was no response to this.

Malmesbury's instruction to Scarlett on 12 March, containing a note to be communicated to the Tuscan Government, starts promisingly enough. While Her Majesty's government regretted the way the legal investigation was conducted, it conceded that it manifested a sincere desire to get at the truth; but the Tuscan government could not be permitted

> to repudiate the responsibility of an independent State to protect the subjects of foreign Powers residing peaceably in the territory of that State, on the plea there is no tribunal in Tuscany competent to take cognizance of complaints preferred by such a person.

Tuscany's independence was mutually recognized by the presence of diplomatic representatives at both courts; Tuscany could not claim the rights and privileges of independence and at the same time refuse the obligations.[34]

What followed was surely unforgivable, not only as an abdication of responsibility but because it represented Mather as a money-grubber. Mather senior considered 'that the injury done to his son may be atoned for by a pecuniary payment on the part of the Tuscan Government'. Her Majesty's Secretary of State had received a statement from him 'that he would be satisfied if a sum of £5,000 was paid to his son'. 'Her Majesty's government, however, considers that sum to be greater than they ought to demand of the Tuscan government to pay'. The Tuscan Government was in effect asked to name its own price.

Malmesbury seems to have been satisfied with an exchange of notes with the Austrians during March in which the latter expressed regret for the injury done to Mr Mather, indicating there was no desire to offer insult to a British subject and that they wished to improve relations. Equally they had shown no disposition whatsoever to discipline the soldier concerned. They expressed no opposition to the British quest for compensation from the Tuscan government – that was a matter for them. So the tattered remnants of British prestige amounted to what could be screwed out of the Tuscan government, which was disinclined to cooperate. Scarlett recorded in a despatch of 28 March that the first reaction of the Tuscan government was one of 'infinite surprise'. They had no jurisdiction over the Austrians and, even when Scarlett on his own initiative suggested that an offer of £1,000 might do, their answer was still negative.

Scarlett was probably not helped by his friendship with von Hügel, the Austrian minister, who thought that Mather ought to receive something, but from his own government rather than the Tuscans! He ended his despatch by recording that since it had become known that Mather had made a large pecuniary claim on the Tuscan Government 'the sympathy which was previously evinced in his favour has much abated'. If by this he meant (as other testimony seems to suggest) the sympathy of the English residents, one might ask whose fault that was. All Malmesbury could do in answer was to instruct Scarlett to continue to press the case, ending somewhat lamely that, if the Tuscans refused, he should await the arrival of Bulwer with a view to perhaps withdrawing the mission. This despatch, dated 9 April, was accompanied by a private letter of the same day which reads even more pathetically. Scarlett was to get £500 if he could, as a last resource ask for arbitration, and 'Of course you must not talk of an apology from the officer, as it would be bathos after Prince Schwarzenberg's note.' Two days before his death, Schwarzenberg had apparently told Lord Westmorland that Tuscany ought to have allowed Mather to plead in a civil court. The Austrians also seemed disposed to settle the business by an *ex gratia* payment through the emperor if the Tuscans did not deliver.

At this point Malmesbury contrived to get himself in an even more complete mess, on the one hand hoping Scarlett could get the matter settled before Bulwer arrived, on the other unable to close with the Austrian offer, which would have involved the recognition that Tuscany was no longer an independent state, with all the attendant complications for the mission. Bulwer's instructions, issued on 26 April, were clear if weak. He was to maintain the principle upon which the government's last demands had been made. The Tuscan government 'is bound in honour and equity to compensate Mr Mather for his danger and suffering by a pecuniary payment'. If the Tuscans refused all payment and even arbitration, 'you will close Her Majesty's Mission at that Court. You will also state to the Tuscan Government that ulterior measures will be adopted by Her Majesty's Government to obtain redress.' This presumably meant going cap in hand to the Austrians. Scarlett's instructions meanwhile were anything but clear. There was also the question of what James Mather was going to say about all of this when it came to light.

It was in this rather heated atmosphere that Scarlett conceived the less-than-brilliant idea of linking the Stratfords with Mather, in order to get things settled before Bulwer arrived. Henry and Edward Stratford, it will be remembered, had been sentenced to imprisonment by the Austrians and it was understood that they would be turned over to the Tuscan government to exercise its mercy. In the event, that did not take place till March 1852. Scarlett had reported on 28 March that there would be some further delay because the Tuscans did not 'wish to be seen to act too abruptly following their release by the Austrians'.[35] In other words (in Scarlett's defence) there was further diplomacy to be done here. He had already complained of being overworked and this had to some extent been recognized by an instruction to Horace Rumbold at Turin, sent on 26 April, to get to Florence as soon as possible, permitting Barron to return to Turin.

Meanwhile yet another incident had taken place at Leghorn. On 15 February 1852 Corporal Baggs, a non-commissioned Officer of the Royal Marine Artillery belonging to Her Majesty's Steam Frigate *Firebrand*, who had been given shore leave, was arrested, in uniform but unarmed, put in chains and beaten up. He was then marched through the streets in chains to a guard house where 'Money was extorted from him on pretence that he broke the Chains in resisting the Police and must pay for the Damage he had caused.' Macbean was not informed of the arrest at the time, and Captain Codd of the *Firebrand*, who had gone to Florence, was not told till he returned several days afterwards. Codd went back to Florence and deposited a statement with Scarlett, who went to see Landucci. The latter, he told the Foreign Office, 'coolly justifies the whole Conduct of the Police Force'; the blame was solely that of the drunken corporal, who had 'committed excesses in the Streets' with his friends. Casigliano was scarcely any better. Given the 'notable difference' between the facts as presented by the two sides, only a judicial process could decide, and he severely deprecated 'the Tone of Captain Codd's Letter to the Delegato of Leghorn'.

For once, the worm in Scarlett turned. On 3 March he complained of the too-numerous recent instances of police violence towards British subjects and expressed little confidence in the Tuscan courts, demanding immediate reparation for the insult to the British uniform and making a none too veiled allusion to the Tuscan government's professed inability to deal with the Austrian officer who had struck Mather. As 'a non-commissioned Officer of the British Marine Force', Baggs was 'no more amenable to Tuscan Law Courts than any other Officer of a Foreign Military Force'. In a further exchange of notes on the 8th Casigliano rejected this contention, but Scarlett stuck to his guns, and his vehemence seems to have had its effect. Casigliano's note offered a small concession, if not an apology or a reparation. In reproof of any 'excess of zeal' there may have been, the Superior of the Guard House at Leghorn was recalled to Florence and put under arrest for 8 days. This gesture did nothing for Baggs, but it was enough to prevent the closure of the embassy, which Scarlett had privately indicated to Malmesbury he was prepared to order if the Tuscans yielded nothing.[36]

Back home, Disraeli, Chancellor of the Exchequer but also Commons spokesman on foreign affairs, got a rough ride when he was forced to deny that the government regarded the 8 days' imprisonment as reparation. He also revealed that the Tuscan government had applied to have Captain Codd reprimanded, adding that 'it was scarcely necessary to say that the Government could not listen to it for a moment'. On 8 April the *Daily News* carried a letter from 'Civis' in Florence, who not only defended Baggs's innocence but put the episode into its general context:

> during the last three years there has been a series of insults offered to Englishmen resident in Tuscany, unequalled, indeed unknown, during the period of between 30 and 40 years, during which Tuscany has been frequented by the migratory masses of our idle or dyspeptic countrymen.

This was surely connected with 'the change in administration, and even mastership, of this misguided duchy'. The thirteen cases the writer had before him included Aiton, Newton at Volterra and of course Mather. He now asked the inescapable question: 'Is Tuscany still an independent province?' The presence of 'foreign bayonets' and 'the sound of a harsh, guttural and for her sons and daughters an unknown tongue, justify us in doubting the fact'. 'Civis' returned to the charge on 13 May, describing Disraeli's statement in the commons as 'shuffling, evasive, and quite unworthy one of her Majesty's ministers'. Nothing could better illustrate the interchange between Florentine residents and London newspapers on the subject of Tuscan affairs.

The arrival in Florence of both Fenton and Rumbold proved precious little relief to Scarlett, who became seriously ill early in May. Rumbold too fell ill and then proceeded to engage in a row with Barron over precedence, which must have irritated the Foreign Office no end. He claimed not to like Florence much, because he was 'ill most of the time and in a condition of nervous depression that precluded all enjoyment'. However, he also shared a spacious furnished apartment on the ground floor in the Piazza Maria Antonia with two other gentlemen, 'where we clubbed together and lived in princely style at fabulously low cost'; nor did he fail to pay court to the social celebrities of the day.[37]

Barron told Malmesbury of Scarlett's illness on 9 May, and in a private letter written on the same day also declared, 'The Stratford and Mather cases may be considered as settled.' On the 5th Casigliano had informed Scarlett that 'an indemnity of one thousand francesconi (about £222 4s) would be offered to Mr Mather'. Scarlett pointed out that this was much less than he had been instructed to seek and that he could only accept it if the Messieurs Stratford were instantly released. Casigliano replied that the Grand Duke had every intention of honouring his pledges on this point, but not yet. Two days later, however, he wrote confidentially to Scarlett to the effect that the Grand Duke had yielded 'to his noble impulses' and commuted the Stratfords' punishment into perpetual banishment from his states. Scarlett wished Barron 'to express to the Tuscan Minister his satisfaction at this arrangement and to report the same to Your Lordship'. This letter contained the even more momentous news that (after what might seem a remarkably long delay) the Grand Duke had at last abolished the constitution.[38]

Barron now compounded Scarlett's felony. The date of Bulwer's arrival was uncertain, the Tuscans were pressing for prompt fulfilment and a British ship was ready to take the Stratfords off. On 13 May Barron told Malmesbury that Casigliano had offered 'an explicit declaration of principles on Tuscan responsibility'. It may be that the Grand Duke, or his ministers, had sensed here an opportunity to assert Tuscan independence at low cost, but Barron (who should have jumped at it) decided that this would require 'a fresh discussion of principles'. An 'implicit' declaration would suffice and the passage in question should be expunged. Casigliano had put this to the Grand Duke, who 'had shewn the greatest reluctance to allow this erasure, but had finally consented'. Barron continued, 'I beg to enclose a copy of this passage, which I think your Lordship will allow to have been unnecessary and objectionable.'[39] His Lordship should have allowed no such thing. Never was Bulwer more badly needed. The Stratfords were duly delivered up and whisked out of the country on 16 May.[40]

As far as the Tuscan government was concerned, the Mather and Stratford affairs were settled. What respect can they have had for an embassy which accepted so little? The Grand Duke was going to release the Stratfords at some time anyway; the compensation to Mather was a snip compared with the original £5,000 demanded. On top of that, the embassy chose to wash its dirty linen in public, for on 18 May Rumbold had appealed to Casigliano to recognize him alone, and not Barron, as authorized to treat on behalf of the British Government.[41]

Malmesbury's first instinct was to try to brazen it out. Bulwer was to rap Scarlett's knuckles for making such an agreement, but only when the secretary had recovered from his illness. Although HMG could not approve of the arrangement, they would not refuse to recognize it. It was Addington, under-secretary at the FO, who had the unenviable job of acquainting James Mather with the award of just over £200 and the regret of the Austrian government. The Foreign Secretary was induced by the 'patriotic manner' in which Mather had expressed himself throughout to believe that he would now 'consider our international laws as sufficiently vindicated'. Mather's reply suggested otherwise. The Foreign Office appeared to have retreated all the way along the line and his main contentions were unanswerable. The offer made to him was 'even submitted to me in terms as if it were felt to be most humiliating', and no redress had been obtained at Florence. The Austrian officer was still at large and remained unpunished. He concluded, 'I will not pretend to be a judge of what is due to the honour of England, but I know what is due to my own.'[42] Worse from the government's point of view was the appearance of Mather's letter in the *Times* on 28 May, which gave the lie to Malmesbury's assertion in the Lords that the affair was all but concluded.

The *Times* commented editorially that Malmesbury was perversely both admitting to the Tuscan Government 'that the amount claimed by Mr Mather is excessive' and admitting to Mather 'that the amount obtained for him is inadequate'. On 4 June, it printed a further, longer letter from Mather to Malmesbury in which, among much else, he stressed his own willingness, all along the line, to subordinate private compensation to the national honour. While still in Florence, he had for that reason refused to entertain an offer, communicated to him semi-privately, of £2,000 to £3,000 as a 'compromise'. 'A gentleman now in England of high respectability and literary position' had been privy to this conversation and would bear witness to it.

During the first fortnight of June most of the English newspapers took up the running, the overwhelming majority hostile to Malmesbury, although with different emphases. The *Morning Chronicle* on 31 May wanted to know what had been obtained for the honour of England. 'A personal slight to Lord Malmesbury' would be of less concern than 'indignities which become insults to this country', brought about by his incompetence. Addington's letter was 'really a wonderful production'. The *Examiner* on 5 June gave full weight to Mather's answer to Addington and his follow-up letter to Malmesbury. On the 8th the *Daily News* took aim at Scarlett, quoting Lord Dudley Stuart in the Commons and raising yet more issues:

> there was very considerable dissatisfaction felt by the English residents of Florence with regard to the manner in which the business of the mission was conducted. There was no place of business attached to the mission in Florence, and when any English resident there had business to transact, he was obliged at considerable inconvenience, expense, and loss of time to go to Mr Scarlett's country house. In his opinion it was most objectionable that cause should be given to British subjects to complain, that the money voted by that house was not applied as it ought to be.

This was a well-founded criticism. Stuart had received a letter from W. E. Hickson, which the *News* now published. It described how Scarlett conducted the Legation's business and also accused him of having failed to take the proper measures to obtain sworn depositions from witnesses of the Mather incident. By his own account Hickson had seen Mather's blood on the pavement and had instantly visited him in hospital. He may have been the unnamed 'friend' whom the young Mathers had mentioned to their father.[43] Before leaving Tuscany, he had discerned among both Austrians and English that 'the comparative tameness of our remonstrances' proceeded from a sense of weakness and he foresaw evil consequences for British residents on the continent.

Only the *Standard* and the *Morning Herald* on the 11th took Malmesbury's part:

> It certainly is not for our credit, nor our comfort as Englishmen, that here and there some conceited young man should insult the authorities of the place

which he is visiting, solely on the force of his privilege as an Englishman; or make his countrymen an object of dislike, jealousy, and suspicion in all civilised countries. The English residents at Florence have no great reason to be grateful to Mr Mather [the father or the son?] for his absurd pugnacity, still less will they have to thank him should the Grand Duke remain obstinate, and this nation, with the wisdom, of the man who cuts off his nose to be revenged on his face, suspend its diplomatic relations with Tuscany.

That this writer was in fact expressing Malmesbury's own opinion is indicated by a statement made years later by his Lordship and reported in the *Times* of 13 June 1865. He recalled how in 1852 'an ill-mannered boy interfered with the band of an Austrian regiment at Florence and received a wound'; also (with remarkable inaccuracy) that 'the sum of 350*l* which I demanded in compensation for that offence was, by many persons in this country, thought to be an insufficient sum'. That many Anglo-Florentines had mixed feelings about Mather, preferring to be left undisturbed in the enjoyment of the company of Austrian officers, we may well believe.

The Foreign Office had not waited until the full weight of public wrath hit it. On 29 May no fewer than four despatches were winging their way to Bulwer, who had at last arrived in Florence on the 19th. The first expressed annoyance at Scarlett for waiving the principle of responsibility; Bulwer was to press for its reinstatement, for HMG could not accept money with conditions. If the Tuscan Government would not accede, HMG could no longer regard Tuscany as an independent state and he was to withdraw the mission. The second clarified the Government's justification for reopening the issue, should the Tuscans regard it as settled, and the third was a formal disavowal of Scarlett. The fourth instructed Bulwer that the 'Tuscan Govt must admit that Tuscany is bound to protect the English in Tuscany or the mission is withdrawn.' If the Tuscans admitted the principle, HMG had no interest in 'pecuniary compensation' to Mr Mather, on which point he was indifferent, as his letter of 27 May showed. This was tendentious, to say the least.

We do not have to imagine what Bulwer thought when all this landed on his desk, for he told his brother-in-law, Lord Cowley, at Paris. After describing his state of health – always a first consideration – he continued in his inimitable personal style:

I have had almost an impossible task delivered to my hands. Scarlett asking for liberality & taking it; Ld M apparently approving even as late as 28th – Then disavowing & leaving me to get a principle positively recognized which had always been refused hitherto.

He had succeeded, trying to do so

without too much bullying these poor little people. I suppose the Govt will be contented but I don't know & God is Great. To have broken up the Mission wd have suited my private books – but what shd we then have done? Nothing & thus been as ridiculous throughout Italy as we became in Spain. I don't like playing the Bravo with a woodden [sic] knife. I got last night a little out of town & hope to pick up having had such work as you can hardly conceive 1st to get the principles admitted on which a note was to be written & then to get a note written that stated at all intelligibly such principles: even now some of the phrases are half a mile long & like one of the passages in an Elizabethan house leading when you get to the end of them to nothing at all. But I say again God is Great & has not made every body understand the rules of the Grand Temple.[44]

Bulwer struck up an immediate friendship with von Hügel, who was included in many of the discussions with Casigliano in subsequent days; this obviated the need for three-way communication and secured Austrian goodwill. On 18 June he was able to report that Scarlett's notes, and all subsequent correspondence dependent on them were withdrawn and cancelled, with the singular exception of the Grand Duke's note of clemency for the Stratfords. Scarlett's humiliation was complete, but there was no helping that. After both the Tuscans and the Austrians expressed more regrets about the incident and its effect on relations, Bulwer obtained the declaration sought by the British government: that the Tuscan government recognized its duty to protect foreign nationals and that in any future case, subject to practical considerations, its courts would be open to foreigners to take action.[45]

Thanks to the time-lag, the papers were still excoriating the government for its acceptance of a minimal pecuniary compensation. The last word might be left with *Punch*, which published a full-page cartoon showing Malmesbury accepting the paltry cheque while a wounded British lion sits disconsolate in the background. Early in July it quoted 'A New Handbook for Italy', written by the 'Earl of Marmalade', which advised the traveller always to conform to the customs of the country and particularly 'to take anything that an Austrian officer may provide them, whether it be the flat of the sword or the edge, with the most perfect stoicism'. Like the London dailies, *Punch* could be read in Florence.[46]

Something more must now be said about Scarlett at this low point in his career, particularly about criticisms of his running of the Florentine embassy. He had experienced much personal tragedy: the death of his infant son in October 1847 was followed in September 1849 by that of his wife Frances, aged 23, leaving him two small children to look after. He witnessed the death, in post, of two Ministers in little over 8 months and himself had periodic bouts of ill health; the latest may well have impaired his judgement in May 1852. None of this justifies, but it may explain, his conduct of business, particularly his dealings with English residents. The criticisms voiced by Mr Hickson and Lord Dudley Stuart were neither isolated nor new; Eugenio Latilla's, in 1850, was quoted in an earlier chapter.[47]

In March 1852 Scarlett had somewhat unwisely written to the Foreign Office, complaining that the business of the Legation was 'much prejudiced by the constant presentation of Papers for Signature or Attestation of Signature, such as Half Pay Certificates, Powers of Attorney and Legal Documents, which would more correctly be submitted to a Consular Agent'. He asked whether 'I may direct all those Persons to whom I may not be anxious to grant a Personal Favor to have recourse to Her Majesty's Consul at Leghorn'. The term 'personal favour', then as now, could have unfortunate connotations when used by a supposedly impartial public servant, and the Foreign Office, to do it credit, returned a dusty answer. Attestations had always formed part of the business of an embassy and there was no reason why Scarlett should be exempt.[48] It was doubly unfortunate that this application was fresh in mind when an anonymous letter from one 'Britannicus' was received in the Foreign Office through the prime minister Lord Derby.

'Britannicus' was unusually explicit about the problems faced by ordinary residents in dealing with Scarlett, as opposed to those to whom he was inclined to grant 'personal favours'.

> On the death of the late Sir Geo Hamilton, Minister here, whose official office was in the Palazzo Ximenes although he lived in the Country 2 miles off- Mr Scarlet [sic] Secretary of legation & Charge d'Affairs immediately sent to all official persons a printed letter that he had removed his Chancellerie, to his Villa, Villa Galli 2 miles out of Florence, and that a Letter Box would be placed in the Hotel Pelecani under the care of the Innkeeper to receive and distribute the letters and official papers signed by Mr Scarlett. For instance, it is necessary at the end of the last day in each quarter that all officers of the army and navy on half-pay or receiving pensions to get their declarations signed to be forwarded to London, they are obliged to send them to Mr Scarlett from his Letter Box or to take carriage to his Villa which costs 5 francesconi or 2/3d to have his signature in person

'Britannicus' claimed that many of these officers had 'very little besides their half pay' and could not afford to hire a carriage out to the villa. Scarlett would return the papers

> into his Box, perfectly open so that his factotum Gasperini (an Italian) who speaks and writes English, can make himself aquainted [sic] with any officers ½ pay or pensions, surely my Lord, such things ought not to be tolerated and it is said that his income as Chrge d'Affairs is £1000 a year.

The 'late lamented Mr Shiels' had done things differently, immediately establishing an office in his house. On discovering how Scarlett had conducted himself, Sheil 'declared that all such Declarations signed by Mr Scarlett were illegal and unjust', but as soon as he was dead, Scarlett reverted to his previous practice. In addition,

> Mr Scarlett is very capricious in who he introduces to the Court – this winter a Mr Fosberry applied to be presented on 1st January by letter, as he had not

been presented at the Court of St James he declined (in which he was perfectly correct) to present him. Mr Fosberry a few days after was obliged to call on him, to get some official paper signed at his Villa, Mr Fosberry told him that he was intimate with his sister Lady Stratheden and lived within a Mile of each other – Mr Scarlett then said he would have great pleasure in presenting him to the Grand Duke, which he did. There has not been for the last 25 years any Minister or Secretary, so universally disliked as Mr Scarlett he is barely civil to his Compatriots, except they have Titles, these he worships – poor John Bull without any such aids, can receive hardly any attention or common civility from him, he ought to recollect from what Family he has sprung from, namely Jamaica sugar planters.

'Britannicus' then reverted to his main theme:

The Ministers of Austria, Sardinia, France, Naples and Rome have offices in their houses for the Diplomatic transaction of business and visas of Passports, from 11 to 2 o'clock. If an unfortunate English traveller requires the visa of Mr Scarlett, and arrives at 5 or 6 o'clock in the afternoon, he cannot proceed on his Journey & is the next day most probably detained, because he has to send to Villa Galli, and may be detained 24 hours or more, most likely Mr Scarlett might be out, or gone down to Pisa with his children for a few days. My Lord the whole of this statement is true, not an Englishmen in Florence but would be glad of his removal.

Attached to the letter is an unusually forthright memorandum from Malmesbury, who disputes none of this, indeed says that he knows it to be true. Scarlett's unfortunate application 'to be relieved from these usual duties proves how inconvenient he thinks them'. As a traveller, Malmesbury himself had suffered from the absence 'in different Chancelleries' of appropriate people to visa passports, which was the more important now that the railways imposed their timetable. Avoiding any specific mention of Florence, he wished general instructions to be drafted to obviate the grievances 'Britannicus' had adumbrated.[49]

When Bulwer left Florence early in 1855, he delivered some thumbnail verdicts on the embassy personnel:

Of Mr Scarlett, Her Majesty's Secretary of Legation, it is scarcely necessary for me to speak. Indeed he has hardly been at his Post when I have been residing in Tuscany, and as an old public servant his merits are known to your lordship.[50]

The last phrase might well be deemed two-edged.

During the 3-year period between the Austrian occupation in 1849 and the arrival of Bulwer in May 1852 English residents may have been wondering whether their interests were going to be adequately protected by the embassy. These misgivings were perhaps reinforced by an increase in the taxation of foreigners. On 29 October 1851 a long article in the *Daily News* informed readers what these exactions amounted to. On arrival at Leghorn a foreigner must pay 3s 8d for the visa on his passport and at Florence 5s 6d for a *carta di soggiorno*, usually granted for 2 months. This sum was payable on every renewal. Were he to travel around the Grand Duchy and spend 10 or 12 days in each 'department', he must purchase more *carte* at 5s 6d each. (Tuscan natives were not subjected to these charges.) If the foreigner wished to settle more permanently, he became liable to a personal tax (the *tassa di famiglia*). The amount was supposed to be based on his income, which the commissioners appointed by the government had no way of knowing. The result was that

> an Englishman possessing no property in Tuscany, exercising no profession, and having permission to reside there is called upon to pay a sum varying from 2s 6d to 30*l*, and bearing no kind of proportion to his means, whether he possess a few tables and chairs of his own, or occupy furnished apartments; if the commissioners choose to think him rich he will be mulcted annually to the above amount.

The writer claimed to know three persons 'of equal income, of whom the first has been taxed 2*s*, the second 2*l*, and the third 4*l* 10*s*.' Appeals were in effect more trouble than they were worth, and the excuse was the need to raise money to pay for the Austrian occupation. Many residents, it was alleged, had left Tuscany because of these imposts and the article concluded, while conceding the Tuscan government's right to do what it liked with its own subjects, by averring that it was 'the incontestible [*sic*] right, nay, the duty of the British government, to protect its subjects from unjust, capricious, and arbitrary extortion'.

Duty was one thing and capacity another. As Scarlett pointed out to the Foreign Office, he had on frequent occasions represented to the Tuscan government the arbitrary contributions to which British subjects domiciled in Tuscany were subjected by the operation of the *tassa di famiglia*. Before 1850 (or so Scarlett wrongly said) this tax had only been applied to native Tuscans, 'of whose incomes the Authorities might form a tolerable estimate'. Its application to foreigners was a complete lottery, thanks to the mode of assessment and collection. The government determined the sum to be paid by each *comune*, and the *comune* then appointed 'parochial Commissioners' who made the assessment according to their often unfounded notions of the wealth of each householder.

One British sufferer had been Charles Otley, who also illustrated the difficulties which residents had with Tuscan bureaucracy. He had been threatened 'with pains and penalties' unless he immediately paid 135 pauls in personal tax for 1850. He had no profession, he possessed no property in Tuscany and 'although I have resided here for some years it has always been with a "Carta di Soggiorno" for six months only, so that my residence cannot, I conceive, be legally considered a permanent one'. He had put these arguments forward the previous year, 'when I applied to the Gonfaloniere, who referred me to the Municipal Council, which referred me to the Prefect, who referred me to the "Consiglio di Prefettura", which Council finally resolved that it was incompetent to decide the question, because the Municipal Council had not made a previous decision'. He then let the matter rest, but had since been asked for 162 pauls for 1851 and served with a *precetto* (summons) in respect of 1850, which he had placed in the hands of a lawyer.

Otley went on to complain that other foreigners (whom he names) who were in precisely the same circumstances had obtained exemption, including one who had actually made an appeal to the *Consiglio della Prefettura* on the same day and in the same terms as himself. This he attributed, rightly or wrongly, to the intervention of their ministers. Scarlett did manage to get a stay of execution on the *precetto* from Landucci on 19 December 1851. On 2 January the Foreign Office urged him to exercise caution. He should not contest the right of the Tuscan Government to tax non-Tuscans (income tax in England applied to foreigners), but rather make the case that foreigners were not all being treated equally.

Scarlett's representations appear to have borne some fruit. He obtained an exemption from proceedings for Otley, but more importantly Landucci had told him that the tax would in future be levied on a reformed principle. To become liable a foreigner must have resided in Tuscany for 3 years.

> Those who reside longer than this will be taxed in proportion to their visible expenditure on horses, carriages etc., but if without these luxuries, they will be taxed only according to a fixed scale in proportion to the rent of the houses they occupy.

The tax would thus be put on a somewhat clearer footing, although an assessment of 'visible expenditure' sounds rather approximate. It still meant that English residents of more than three years' standing were going to have to reconcile themselves to a substantial rise in taxation. As for those resident for a shorter time, the need for revenue meant that the rules governing the *Carta di Soggiorno* were going to be much more strenuously enforced, with renewals every 3 months rather than every six. As Scarlett pointed out in January 1852, the Tuscans were running a budgetary deficit averaging well over £200,000 a year on an income of not much more than a million, supporting two armies which cost nearly half the budget between them. Something had to give.[51]

Hopes of immediate improvement were disappointed. Landucci, albeit in charge of the responsible ministry, was simply giving an opinion, and the Tuscan government delayed taking action. Bulwer was obliged more than once to draw Casigliano's attention to the issue. Although he believed that the tribunals would normally respond positively to a reasonable appeal, the fact remained that a municipality could demand the tax and leave the resident to appeal and get his money back. That could only be changed by the passage of a new law, which

Casigliano told him would soon appear.[52] In the face of governmental dither, the Florentine town council took the initiative. On 15 March 1853 Erskine reported (in Bulwer's absence) that this body had considered 'the very objectionable mode in which the "Tassa di Famiglia" is now levied on Foreigners' and would shortly institute a new and probably more satisfactory system. He enclosed copies and translations of two 'forms of declaration' which residents would have to complete: 'mere residents' would not be liable until they had spent 10 years in Tuscany, 'whilst officers on half-pay and other public Servants, who may at any moment be recalled home, will be considered as altogether exempt'.

The proposed system amounted to self-assessment by the householder, on which basis his tax would be levied 'at a rate varying with the requirements of the Public Exchequer'. The French *chargé d'affaires* had suggested alternatively that the amount of house rent should be used as the basis of assessment. This was being looked into, and Erskine trusted that the one course or the other would be eventually adopted. It had also been cause of complaint that Her Majesty's subjects found themselves taxed twice over: as householders, like Tuscans, by the *Tassa di famiglia*, and as foreigners by the *Carta di Soggiorno*. Erskine had been assured that 'this admitted injustice' would be removed, so that those liable to the household tax would pay only a nominal sum for their residence permit. On 19 March he reported that this charge had been reduced to 1 paul (5d.)

On 2 April Scarlett announced the final outcome. For those with fewer than 10 years' residence and no trade or profession, the *Carta di Soggiorno* was renewable every 3 months at the rate of 13 pauls (5s. 6d). Those with under 10 years residence, but exercising a trade or profession, paid *tassa di famiglia* on declared profit or income plus *carta di soggiorno* at 1 paul. Those with over 10 years residence were to be treated as Tuscan subjects in regard to property, paying *tassa di famiglia* on their own declared profit and expenditure and *carta di soggiorno* of 1 paul. While this seems to have settled the issue, inasmuch it does not surface again in the official correspondence, the Tuscan government was in fact introducing a fresh anomaly for those with 10 years' residence. It treated property as permanent while still regarding the people who inhabited it as temporary residents, who could be told to pack up and leave at a moment's notice.[53]

While the many incidents involving the Tuscan government and the embassy may have given cause for concern to informed English residents, most accommodated themselves to the changed situation in Tuscany after 1849. This was demonstrated by a number of marriages between the English and the Austrians and their allies during this period. Among these, on 18 October 1849, was that of Bernard Ernest Jules de Koetteritz to Lady Emma Stuart Bruce, the widow of an Irish baronet; the Reverend George Robbins performed the ceremony at Sir George Hamilton's villa. A native of Leipzig, Koetteritz, although at the time a colonel in the Guards of Nicholas I, was a liaison officer loosely attached to the Austrian army. The *Standard* on 26 September described the wedding in glowing terms: 'Nothing could exceed the gaiety and happiness of the party on the occasion.' Others followed. On 28 May 1850 Ida Macdonnell, daughter of the late Hugh, married Adolf Kleinkauf, a captain in the Austrian army, with the approval of some distinguished Austrian witnesses, including von Hügel, the ambassador. The marriage was a tragically short one. The groom died in April 1851 and their one child, whom they had called Ida, survived a mere 6 hours.[54] The Macdonnells remained closely connected with the Austrians.

Pride of society place, however, went to Elizabeth Farquharson, only child of Major-General Farquharson of the Bombay Army, who on 29 June 1851 captured the Austrian Minister himself, Charles von Hügel. This involved a double wedding ceremony, first a Catholic one in the Austrian Embassy and afterwards an Anglican service at Scarlett's villa performed by Reverend Henry O'Neill, with an extraordinary array of witnesses, from Prince Lichtenstein to the egregious Morgan Thomas.[55] Other weddings of note included that of Henrietta De Courcy, the youngest daughter of John Maquay's late friend Colonel De Courcy, to Chevalier Albert de Knebel, a major in the Austrian army, on 5 August 1851. Newspapers (including the *Times* on the 26th) noted that the bride had the inestimable social advantage of being given away by Prince Frederick de Lichtenstein. Florence Lowe could claim no such privilege, being the child of the mere merchant Samuel Lowe, when on 28 October 1851 she was married to Anton Meissler, described as first lieutenant in the Austrian service. Her sister Charlotte also married an Austrian, 1st Lieutenant Johann Garlik, on 29 June 1854. All of these weddings involved Anglican services but none took place in the English Church, although in every case it was the chaplain or his substitute that performed the ceremony.

There were other marriages across national boundaries. On 15 August 1853 the Marchese Ricci Parraciani and Rosalie Eustace were married by the Archbishop of Florence in his palace. The bride was the daughter of Lieutenant General Henry Eustace and the wedding was widely reported in the English press.[56] Another English family made a habit of contracting Italian marriages. On 7 May 1850 the Marchese Guido Manelli Riccardi was married to Christine Reader in the Duomo, the service again conducted by the archbishop. Rosalie's sister Frances had married Francesco Salviati in October 1843, and another sister, Mary, was to marry Attilio Incontri in November 1850 (an aunt had also married an Incontri in 1827). Influential Italians aplenty were there, with Sebastiano Fenzi (son of Emanuele) a witness. It is interesting here to note that Robbins had performed the Anglican ceremony at the Embassy the day previously; no doubt the pair behaved with due discretion over the next 24 hours. The Readers had a huge extended family in Florence, with almost innumerable links both British and Italian.[57] With the exception of Elizabeth Farquharson, all of the English just mentioned had families which had struck deep roots into Tuscan soil, and they surely regarded Florence as home.

There were English soldiers in the Austrian service. John Maquay had met two of them at the Smyths in Leghorn in May 1849 and Dedham, the purser of the *Bellerophon*, regularly on station at Leghorn during 1850, tried to get a cadetship in the Austrian service.[58] The Austrians would certainly not have lacked for a social life. What the Grand Duke did not provide by way of frequent balls and receptions, the diplomatic community supplemented. John Maquay records balls at the Casino at which Austrian officers were present; he himself was frequently with the families of those who married Austrians and attended events which Austrians would have attended, for example at Demidoff's or Normanby's. Although he himself continued to hold big parties he no longer always provides detailed guest lists. For example on 28 January 1851 he invited upwards of 250 on the birthday of his fourth son, William Henry, with 'dancing till 3 o'clock', but we have no idea who the guests were.[59] As for Italians in the higher social ranks, many, like Ricasoli, had largely retreated to their estates; after the abolition of the constitution in 1852, there was little to occupy them in Florence. There is no obvious evidence at this level of any boycott for national reasons, which appears to be a myth established after unification.

There may have been growing hostility to the Austrian army as a whole because of what it represented, particularly given the behaviour of some of the rank and file, who seemed to the cultivated Florentines like barbarian hordes from the nether reaches of the Empire. One interesting reaction came from an Englishman who settled with his family at Florence during the early years of the occupation. Captain Fleetwood Wilson was married to the Florence-born Harriet Walker in 1850 and shortly afterwards discovered that, thanks to mismanagement by his elder brother, they were virtually penniless. Florence was then 'perhaps the cheapest place to live on the continent' and so there they stayed, clearly without a qualm:

> Florence offered many advantages to impecunious English people. Good education was available, and cheap, and it was constantly visited by what used to be called in those days 'the best English', and this enabled the exiles to keep in touch with English life and English Society. Our home became a sort of rendezvous for many of my father's army and hunting friends travelling, as well as for relatives and connexions of my mother who visited Italy.

With her sisters Gertrude and Florence (the latter also born in the city whose name she bore), Harriet made up what Horace Rumbold called 'the charming English sisterhood composed of Madame Baldelli, Mrs White and Mrs Fleetwood Wilson'.[60] Her husband had known Vienna well earlier in life and was acquainted with many Austrian officers, so that 'at first his sympathies were distinctly Austrian', but gradually he became disgusted with the army's behaviour, commenting in his diary on instances of their brutality (including the attack on Mather).[61] In all these respects he may well have been representative of the English resident under the occupation.

Thomas Trollope and Elizabeth Barrett Browning present contrasting views. Trollope had little to say beyond generalities, asserting that the Austrians behaved well and were favourably contrasted with the French army of occupation in Rome.

As a result they 'were never hated in Florence with the bitter intensity of hate which the French earned in the eternal city'. He qualified this by saying that the Florentines occasionally gratified their Italian patriotism by turning out in the streets and making a row.[62] Mrs Browning, on the other hand, declared that the Austrians were hated: if an Italian dances with an Austrian, she 'is a marked woman and injured in reputation'. She cites one incident, alleged to have taken place at a Grand Ducal Ball, when a woman rejected an Austrian's forcible attempts to dance with her, her husband looking on 'frightened out of his wits & by no means inclined to accept the situation patriotically'.[63]

Trollope's view that the French (or for that matter the Sardinians) were no more popular than the Austrians in the early 1850s may have been true, but in Tuscany, the Austrians happened to be on the spot. English residents probably for the most part kept quiet, for even the most innocent of actions could sometimes incur the wrath of the authorities, particularly with the abolition of the constitution and the granting of extraordinary powers to the police to search premises on suspicion, even without a warrant. There were ways of making a protest. In 1853 Windischgratz, the commander of two units of Austrian troops in Florence and nephew of the hero of the suppression of the revolt in Prague in 1848, was blackballed at the Jockey Club. This created a minor sensation. Although the club had an international clientele under its then president Prince Demidoff, this method of rejection was very English. After governmental displeasure had been made known, the practice of referring membership to a ballot was abolished and election was entrusted to the Committee. Windischgratz was admitted, but the point had been made.[64]

The disposition of the occupying forces to see a Mazzinian round every corner created an understandable nervousness, although it did not justify the thuggery sometimes directed against innocents who had beards or were wearing the wrong type of hat or cloak. In this respect the soldiery differed little from the Grand Ducal government, which, having made its bed in 1849, became increasingly neurotic as the 1850s went on about revolutionary conspiracy real or imagined, and showed a disposition to defend its gendarmerie right or wrong, for fear of the consequences if it did otherwise.

This nervousness could sometimes have its comic side, as the *Times* recorded on 26 January 1853. The police had carried out a search of the houses of a Mr Lawley (whose father Sir Robert had adorned the Florentine social scene in the 1820s) and one Bertolacci, a Corsican native who had served in the British army and was drawing a British government pension. Both lived in the countryside near the railway station at Pontedera, where Lawley had a farm, and Bertolacci was devoted to horticulture. The only suspicious article the police could find in either house was a letter from a friend of Bertolacci in Leghorn,

> thanking him for his present of a magnificent red cabbage, which, as the writer
> declared, had caused quite a *furore* at Leghorn, and was eagerly partaken of

'even by the Austrians'. This mysterious allusion naturally excited suspicion in the minds of the astute police, who could detect the seeds of revolution even in a head of cabbage, and M. Bertolacci narrowly escaped incarceration as a cure for his love of vegetables.

Growing red cabbages was clearly little removed from encouraging red revolution.

Petty vexations continued. In February and April 1853 two British subjects were ordered out of Tuscan territory. The first was George Craufurd, the younger brother of the MP for Ayr, who held an official appointment in the government of Corfu and was on his way thence to England via Tuscany where he had stopped for a few days. The other was Evelyn Waddington, brother of the Home Office junior minister Horace Waddington, who was in Florence for a family wedding.[65] Both were on the surface respectable men, but their pedigrees were sufficiently irregular to arouse the suspicions of the Tuscan government. Waddington, who resided near Perugia, had entered Tuscany on a Roman passport which supposedly had mysterious marks on it, put there by the Roman authorities to indicate that he was not respectable. He had indeed been involved in 1849 in ordering arms for the National Guard at Perugia, which had been seized at Leghorn. He was allowed to stay for the family rejoicings when Scarlett issued him with a British passport.[66]

Craufurd belonged to a family with genuinely Mazzinian affiliations, of which there may well have been memories in Florence. It was admitted that in his indiscreet youth he had 'accompanied a foolish expedition which set out from this place in 1845 to join the insurrectionary movement in the Papal States', on the failure of which he had returned unmolested to Florence. Not only did he know Mazzini; according to Landucci, he was said to be his 'Secretary'. On his way through Italy to Florence, he had stopped for a few days in Perugia to visit that old family friend Guardabassi, and here he had been arrested, largely, he was told, because of the shape of his hat, 'a common wideawake', which he learned was strictly forbidden in the Papal States. The Tuscan government with some difficulty allowed itself to be persuaded that Craufurd, whatever his past, was now respectable, and he was permitted to return to Corfu via Tuscany if necessary.[67]

An indication that it was not merely crypto-revolutionaries or English Protestants who got themselves into trouble is provided by a Mr Shinkwin. It is not clear which member he was of this very Catholic family, which originated from Cork, but the battery of their tombs surrounding the altar in the crypt of the hilltop church of San Miniato bears witness to their faith and the remarkably good standing they must have enjoyed with the monks. One day in the autumn of 1853, Mr Shinkwin was walking out of the Porta Pinti when his *Carta di soggiorno* was demanded; he did not have it with him and was refused permission to pass. When the policeman touched him, 'he very improperly struck him a blow with his stick, and was taken instantly to prison in the Bargello'. Scarlett's private plea for mercy seems to have met with an instant response; Shinkwin was released on the same day.[68]

The gates were a perennial problem, and there was a further incident the following month when Captain Smith and Mr Marshall were refused exit at the Prato gate to go for a drive in the Cascine because they were carrying neither their passports nor their *Carte di Soggiorno*. When they returned with the necessary papers, they were again refused exit because it was believed they were leaving the city for good without proper formality. The temper of the two Englishmen at this apparently irrational behaviour was not improved by seeing others pass through; a Frenchman was allowed to proceed, apparently without presenting any papers. A complaint to Scarlett was inevitable, but whether the two were justified in believing that they were inconvenienced because they were English, rather than because of simple police stupidity, is open to doubt. Baldasseroni was in a responsive mood. He refused to be riled by the accusation of partiality and recognized that the Prato gate, now both the route to the Cascine and from the city to the railway, was a problem. It was solved by dropping all demand for papers at the gate for Florentines or foreigners; in future they would only be demanded at the station.[69]

For the majority of English residents (and Italians for that matter) who did not attract the attention of either the occupying forces or the gendarmerie, it was business as usual, with additional entertainment provided by the Austrians themselves. By June 1849 the band was playing in the Cascine every evening and there were usually band concerts once or twice a week down to the end of 1854. There were also troop reviews, public affairs to which prominent members of the community were invited, and others could watch, as long as they kept out of the way. Added to these were celebrations of special events like the Emperor's Birthday, which fell on 18 August. John Maquay implies that in 1851 the 'continued discharge from the Cannon & Batteries all yesterday from 4 AM to 8 PM' was rather too much of a good thing.[70]

Who were the English residents during these years? Were they any fewer because of the situation? Did people leave or were they deterred from taking up residence? We have a number of helpful pieces of evidence, notably the Vieusseux subscription books and the church registers of births and marriages. If we look at Vieusseux in 1850, we find that there appear to be fewer than in 1849 taking out subscriptions for 6 months or more, although there are a larger number of renewals of shorter terms which may add up to more than 6 months. This might suggest that there was greater uncertainty in 1850 than 1849, but it is a risky speculation. In 1851 Robert Browning appears for the first time, heading the list on 1 January with a 1-year subscription. Others subscribing for 6 months or more included Arthur Vansittart and Captains McCleverty, Bennett and Hammill. Major General Farquaharson took a 6-month subscription to tide him over his daughter's wedding to the Austrian ambassador, and the Free Church Minister, James Hanna, had an unusual 8-month subscription. The years 1852–1855 show the same mixed results, with roughly comparable numbers.

If the Vieusseux records obviously name only those who took out subscriptions, the registers of baptisms, marriages and burials compiled by the Anglican clergy in Florence equally obviously have their limitations in that they record only a proportion of the British population. Not only are Catholics (and Jews) excluded but a few (like the Brownings) preferred to avoid Anglican baptism, although they might be captured by the Protestant cemetery. However, it seems reasonable to suppose that rises and falls in the recorded numbers of Anglican life events bore some proportion to those of the British as a whole. The following figures are based on the registers returned to the Bishop of Gibraltar and the records of the 'English' Cemetery.

Year	Baptisms	Marriages	Burials
1846	14	8	14
1847	19	10	19
1848	17	6	6
1849	9	10	18
1850	14	6	11
1851	19	9	15
1852	14	4	17
1853	10	10	11
1854	15	9	18
1855	13	5	18
1856	9	7	9

It is difficult to extract from these figures a pattern that clearly mirrors that of political events. The number of baptisms in 1849 obviously represents a sharp decline from 1846 to 1848, but there seems no good reason why there should have been three times as many Anglican burials in that year as in 1848, when the number of baptisms was high. The 1848 figure for marriages is low, but higher than in 1852 or 1855, when Tuscany was peaceful. That burials should dip somewhat in 1850 and 1853 suggests happenstance, especially when we observe that the figures for 1852, 1854 and 1855 are surpassed only in 1847. Of all the years recorded here, 1856 seems to mark the lowest ebb in British activity, and by now, the Austrians were long gone. If by any chance Tuscany was becoming a less attractive place to live, it might have been for a combination of reasons: higher prices and taxation, or perhaps insecurity induced by the Tuscan government's religious policy and the behaviour of its police. Reaction may have been a more potent force than revolution in discouraging residence. Yet this too is somewhat speculative, for by 1855 (as we shall see in a later chapter), reaction was a blunter instrument than it had been, certainly as far as foreign residents were concerned.

The evidence seems to warrant the tentative conclusion that the number of English residents between 1847 and 1855 remained reasonably consistent. Naturally there were those who left. Joseph Gamgee was one who returned home because several of his children had done so. Arthur Vansittart had invested in property (the Villa Salviati) and showed every sign of putting down roots, but in February 1851, the childless Lord Bexley died and left 'my cousin Arthur Vansittart' immense properties, on condition that Vansittart spent at least 6 months of every calendar year living somewhere in England. The moment he failed to do so, all the properties would go to the next heir in line.[71] Vansittart took the bait and returned home; he did not return to Italy, dying in London in 1859.

Vansittart shows that not everyone who left Florence in the years of Austrian occupation did so out of fear or distaste. Another very different illustration is furnished by Robert Henderson, a member of the well-known shipping firm. He had been in Leghorn since 1840 but returned to Glasgow in the winter of 1852–1853 to take charge of that end of the business on the death of his brother George. By a happy chance, we know something about the arrangements he made to transport his entire household back to Scotland, a daunting task that must have confronted numerous British expatriate householders.

On 5 February 1853 he wrote to his wife, Jeannie, to suggest plans for her return with their children; he thought a sea passage would do the children good.[72] Of course he knew the vessels and their masters; the Hendersons had doubtless assisted fellow-countrymen to make similar moves, to or from Italy, and the despatch of goods, including works of art, to shipping agents in the British Isles was among the services commonly offered by bankers and other merchants. For Jeannie there was a choice between the *Genoa*, which would sail from Leghorn in April, or, if she thought that too late, the *Livorno*, which was about to sail from Liverpool and would be returning from Leghorn for Marseille, Gibraltar and Liverpool towards the end of February. Robert advised his wife 'to send by the steamer one of the milk goats, which will be a great thing for the children to have sembolino [a kind of milk pudding] and milk every day'. She should also consult Robert's brother Thomas ('signor Thom') about sending home 'some pasta by the "Jane" as the children will be fond of, also some pomidoro etc., a quarter cask of Marsala and my two cases of Superfino port; the other wines may be packed by themselves or sold as Sig. Tom. may see fit'.

Robert was house-hunting in Glasgow, and when he had obtained something comfortable, he would make suggestions as to what furniture she should send home, although this would not prevent her from making her own decisions in the meantime.

> I would say all your bed and table linens, English books and pictures etc., all decided on – some of the best tables and stands, and sofas, chairs, etc., your earthen ware, cutlery, and electro-plate, a great part of which, being English won't pay duty, and a number of other things.

As if this was not sufficient, he added, 'I doubt not but you will be wishing to bring home the piano, two or three good iron bed stands, and if you can barter for something better even than what we have it will be as well.'

There were departures of another kind. For both visitors to Tuscany and residents who had no intention of spending their entire lives abroad, expectations of a return to a British life and death were sometimes rudely disappointed. Many came home without one or more family members. It was relatively uncommon for the deceased to be repatriated for burial; the dead established a permanent British presence in Tuscany. We do not often obtain any insight into the process, which many relatives must have gone through before they left Italy, of erecting the monument which would mark out, as they hoped forever, that precious corner of a foreign field. A rare instance is to be found in the correspondence of the Phillips family of Mold in Flintshire, who in the summer of 1852 were staying at Bagni di Lucca.

On 13 July, Frederick, the father of the family, died there. His son, another Frederick, promptly left for home to take care of the business created by his father's death, leaving his mother and sisters to follow him. On 1 September, the widowed Margaret Phillips wrote to tell him that they would be able to leave earlier than they had thought

> in consequence of the Monument having been finished and put up which I had scarcely hoped would have been the case before the end of this month. It has been completed to my perfect satisfaction, & is really singularly chaste & beautiful, so white, & the lettering, (wh. I have had such anxiety about) clear & as well executed apparently as that of Gibson. It is 5 ½ feet from the ground to the top of the Cross. Gardello says that he is better pleased with the piece with any he has yet done, & all our friends are as thoroughly satisfied as ourselves.

A few days later her daughter Grace endorsed Mrs Phillips' judgement on the monument: 'I like it better than any other in the country & have been making a sketch for Mama, so you can judge how it looks & stands.'[73] The widow did not have long to nurture the sorrowful feelings with which she had left her husband in Tuscany. She died early in the New Year, and was buried at Mold on 25 January 1853. A window in the parish church commemorates the couple.

Given that within any community there is the usual quantum of the disreputable, eccentric, criminal or quarrelsome, it is perhaps surprising that there were not more problems between the British, whether travellers or residents, and the Tuscan government. Among the disreputable was James Dennis, barrister at law, judge on the Western circuit and great-great nephew of the Right Honourable James Dennis, Lord Chief Baron of the Exchequer in Ireland, who became Baron Tracton in 1780. He had all the appearance of a gentleman; the reality was murkier.

Dennis had been cohabiting with his servant, Mary Steele, in London since at least 1834. After the birth of two daughters, Mary and Ann, he was temporarily finished with her and she was married, in 1837, to a Richard Mitton. Then Dennis offered Mitton an annuity in return for a separation and annulment; Mrs Mitton was to return to live under Dennis's roof as his servant. Mitton accepted the offer and two more children, James and Emily, followed.[74] In 1842 Dennis compounded the annuity for £1,600 in return for the abrogation of all Mitton's claims on Mary. He was buying her back totally, and, apparently in this same year, he set mother and children up in Florence, employing Tuscany as a discreet dumping ground for a gentleman's less than respectable appendages. Alas, some years later Richard Mitton turned up again, laying claim to Mary and threatening violence, surely as a means of extortion.

Writing from Cheltenham on 17 June 1852, Dennis wanted the Foreign Office to instruct Bulwer to cooperate with the Tuscan police in having Mitton thrown out of Tuscany, professing the concern of a father for the safety of his children, which depended 'in a great degree, on the conduct which your Lordship may be pleased to adopt'. The Foreign Office consulted the Queen's advocate, and as a result Dennis was told that there seemed insufficient justification at present for instructing Bulwer to take any official action, since 'Mrs Mitton is under the protection of the Tuscan Govt.'[75] That should have been the end of the matter; but it was not.

In February 1853 Dennis wrote to Lord Russell, this time from Casa Morrecchi, Via dei Pilastri, Florence, with a fresh lament. Mitton had instituted a plea of restitution of conjugal rights in the Tuscan courts, and in order to avoid a scandal, the Tuscan government had ordered him out of the country. Bulwer had interfered on the ground that Mitton was a British subject who had done nothing wrong. The Tuscan government countermanded its order, but when Mitton pursued his writ, it decided to expel Mary instead. One might have sympathized if it had expelled them both. As it was, Dennis had a point in arguing that if the embassy intervened in the case of the one it ought also to intervene in the case of the other. He went on to expatiate movingly on the hardships which the expulsion of Mrs Mitton would entail. After 10 years' residence, she 'has made every preparation to render Florence her permanent home'. There was 16 months left on the lease of her house. Her health was delicate and she had 'selected Tuscany by the Recommendation of her medical Adviser'. She had 'a large and young family' and was 'very slenderly provided with pecuniary means having seriously injured her fortune in paying her husband for the Act of Separation'. He omits to mention that the children (not all that young) were his and that he himself was a major contributor to the scandal.[76]

The response from the Foreign Office was blunt and direct. They can barely have received Erskine's of 8 February before declining to direct him to intervene. When Dennis protested that if Mrs Mitton was expelled she could not defend herself against the legal action, the despatch to Scarlett (now back in Florence) was even more emphatic. The most Clarendon would do was to send a copy of Dennis's second protest to use at Scarlett's discretion; he refused to instruct him to interfere.[77] The Tuscan authorities meanwhile achieved admirable clarity. The court noted that Mrs Mitton lived alone in Tuscany with no scandal to anyone and could remain. It also declared that by the British deed of separation and

1 John Leland Maquay, portrayed probably in his early thirties (private collection).

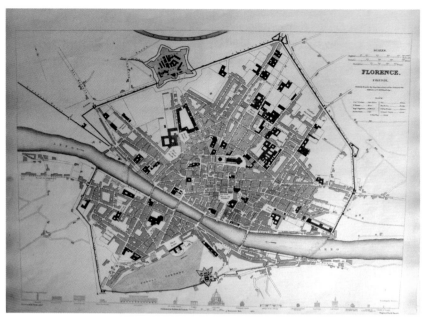

2 Map of Florence in 1835, published by the Society for the Diffusion of Useful Knowledge (authors' collection).

3 Florence from Bellosguardo, the birthplace of Florence Nightingale in 1820 and a favoured place of English resort (authors' photograph).

4 'A View of Burghersh'. Caricature by Robert Dighton, dated 13 April 1822, during one of his Lordship's much-criticised absences from Florence (authors' collection).

5 The Marquis of Normanby. Engraving by H. Robinson after H. P. Briggs, 1833 (authors' collection).

6 The Palazzo Spini-Feroni in Piazza S. Trinità. Madame Hombert's Hotel de l'Europe and the shops run by Thomas Townley and Samuel Lowe were at different times located here (authors' photograph).

7 The Leghorn terminus of the Leopolda railway (authors' photograph).

8 A view of the old Leghorn cemetery (authors' photograph).

9 The neo-classical facade of the Anglican Church in Leghorn, opened in 1840 (authors'
photograph).

10 All that remains of the former British burial ground at Siena (authors' photograph).

11 A view of Bagni di Lucca (authors' photograph).

12 The 'Venetian Gothic' doorway of the English Church at Bagni di Lucca, opened in 1842 and now the communal library (authors' photograph).

13 The tomb of Colonel Henry Stisted in the English cemetery at Bagni di Lucca. He and his wife Clotilda were driving forces behind the building of the church at Bagni (authors' photograph).

14   The former English Pharmacy in Via Tornabuoni, founded in 1843 (authors' photograph).

15 Elena Maquay with her youngest son William, c. 1847 (private collection).

16 The monument to the hat manufacturer Thomas Waller in St Mary's, Luton, 1847. The only known work in England of the Florentine sculptor Pietro Costa (authors' photograph).

AUSTRIA'S COMPENSATION FOR ALMOST MURDERING A BRITISH LION.

Lord M-lm-sb-ry. "OH, DON'T MENTION IT. IT'S OF NO CONSEQUENCE; AND IF AT ANY OTHER TIME YOU SHOULD—I'M SURE—VERY HAPPY,"—&c., &
John Bull Bottle-Holder. "AH! I'D HAVE HAD MORE THAN THAT."

17 Lord Malmesbury accepts a paltry cheque from a youthful Emperor Francis Joseph in compensation for injuries to Erskine Mather: Punch, June 1852 (authors' photograph).

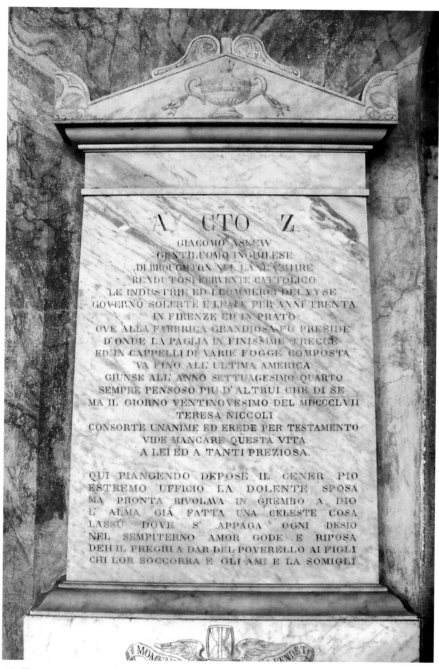

A CTO Z.

GIACOMO ASKEW
GENTILUOMO INGHILESE
DI BROUGHTON NEL LANCASHIRE
RENDUTOSI FERVENTE CATTOLICO
LE INDUSTRIE ED I COMMERCI DEL PASSE
GOVERNÒ SOLERTE E LEALE PER ANNI TRENTA
IN FIRENZE ED IN PRATO
OVE ALLA FABBRICA GRANDIOSA FU PRESIDE
D'ONDE LA PAGLIA IN FINISSIME TRECCE
ED IN CAPPELLI DI VARIE FOGGE COMPOSTA
VA FINO ALL' ULTIMA AMERICA
GIUNSE ALL' ANNO SETTUAGESIMO QUARTO
SEMPRE PENSOSO PIU D'ALTRUI CHE DI SE
MA IL GIORNO VENTINOVESIMO DEL MDCCCLVII
TERESA NICCOLI
CONSORTE UNANIME ED EREDE PER TESTAMENTO
VIDE MANCARE QUESTA VITA
A LEI ED A TANTI PREZIOSA.

QUI PIANGENDO DEPOSE IL GENER PIO
ESTREMO UFFICIO LA DOLENTE SPOSA
MA PRONTA RIVOLAVA IN GREMBO A DIO
L' ALMA GIÀ FATTA UNA CELESTE COSA
LASSÙ DOVE S' APPAGA OGNI DESIO
NEL SEMPITERNO AMOR GODE E RIPOSA
DEH IL PREGHI A DAR DEL POVERELLO AI FIGLI
CHI LOR SOCCORRA E GLI AMI E LA SOMIGLI

18 The monument to the straw-hat merchant James Askew (d. 1857) in the cloister of San Francesco at Prato (authors' photograph).

19 A view of the so-called 'English Cemetery' at Florence (authors' photograph).

20 The tomb of Christopher Webb Smith (d. 1871), long-serving member of the English Church (authors' photograph).

renunciation of rights executed in 1842, Mitton had forever debarred himself from making any claim either upon his wife or children.

Dennis was as dubious a character as Mitton, but neither was a confidence trickster, a species well known to haunt places of resort on the continent. On 2 November 1849 John Maquay recorded, 'Henry Cavendish's affair at the bank!!! great scandal, we lose £22 stg.'[78] The subsequent arrest of 'Cavendish' at Rome must have occurred at about the same time as newspaper reports of his dealings in Florence appeared in England. The Foreign Office sought information from Sir George Hamilton, who reported that 'this person represented himself to be the legitimate Son of the Earl of Burlington, and then to be the natural Son of the late Lord George Cavendish'. 'Cavendish' had married what Hamilton called an English governess, a Miss Ellen Lamb, on 23 October at Leghorn, where he had abandoned her. Only one bank – obviously this was Maquay and Pakenham – had suffered to some small degree.[79]

Perhaps we should not waste too much sympathy on the deserted wife. On the following 13 December, the *Times* published a report from a Florentine correspondent which amounted to an enjoyable textbook account of the conman abroad.

An Englishman, of genteel exterior, plausible manners, and speaking French fluently, lately made his appearance in Florence, under the assumed aristocratic name of Cavendish. He took up his residence at the Grande Bretagne *Hotel*, appeared abroad in a handsome carriage, attended by a servant, and made a few purchases at some of the shops, for which he paid. His first act was to hire an expensive suite of apartments in town, of which he immediately took possession. An establishment of servants was soon found, and liberal orders given for wines, viands, and other necessaries for housekeeping.

After his marriage at Leghorn, 'Cavendish' requested the consul to be prepared to receive his sister, Lady Georgina Cavendish, who would arrive in his yacht with his baggage; he had hired an opulent villa near Florence for her. In his temporary absence from Leghorn, it became known that the Roman banker Torlonia had refused payment on a bill for £300 which he had presented. Of course there was a mistake, as he had had an account at Coutts for years, but he nonetheless thought it prudent to vanish, taking his wife's small amount of money and apparently leaving her to her fate. The hotelier allowed her to remain until she received fresh funds, but when she did, she in turn made off, leaving her bill unpaid.

On 12 August 1852 Maquay heard that 'the swindler Cavendish' had been arrested in Paris, and in 1854 it was reported that he had been tried for forgery there.[80] His career was distinguished for a quite remarkable amount of bigamy; Miss Lamb seems to have been the second wife he took in 1849. This propensity delivered him, in his old age, to Woking Gaol, where he died in March 1877. An inquest was held, as *Reynold's News* reported on 1 April, at which 'an elderly lady in deep mourning, and holding a chaplet of white camellias in her hand' rose and demanded the right to speak. This was none other than the former Ellen Lamb, who claimed to be the lawful wife of the deceased, married to him at Leghorn in 1849. The coroner was understandably disconcerted.[81] How old was Miss Lamb when she encountered the charming 'Henry Cavendish' in Florence? In accepting his advances, was she taking her chance to exchange a dreary servitude, which as many governesses learned was not always a secure one, for something more exciting and more profitable?

A growing element in the Florentine Anglophone population at this time was represented by the Americans. Some, such as the sculptor Hiram Powers, were there long before the revolution and stayed put. Here were the supplies of the Carrara marble that he required, and from 1844 to 1852, he was always seeking to expand his premises. John Maquay seems to have come to know him in the course of 1844, when he recorded visiting him in his workshop and admiring the celebrated *Grecian Slave*. The relationship had blossomed and Powers became a regular on the Maquay party lists.[82] Powers's refusal to serve as an unpaid American consul probably brought them closer, as John came to perform something of that service with the cooperation of his American friend. Another American sculptor, Horatio Greenough, died in Florence in 1851 and Maquay later sorted out his possessions at Casa Standish together with Powers. For Powers the task may have been wholly personal; for John as a banker it was partly business, which involved destroying several of 'Greenough's Busts & Gessi'.[83]

Powers (who numbered spiritualism among his interests) was also well known to the Brownings, but they and the Maquays lived in largely different worlds. John's range of acquaintance in Florence, English, American, Italian and other, was at the most conservative estimate far more extensive than theirs, but there is only one mention of them in his journals. The Brownings do not mention the Maquays at all, and the closest Elizabeth came to John's partner Captain Pakenham was when Wilson and the nurse encountered him at Bagni one day in September 1849 and he admired the infant Pen.[84] An analysis of the Browning letters in fact tends to support the view that long-term English residents were in a minority among their frequent callers and close friends. The Anglo-Florentine bankers, traders, shopkeepers, merchants and retired East Indiamen, some of them active in the English Church, many interested in whist, amateur dramatics, music and dancing in their leisure hours, inhabited areas where the Brownings had nothing to offer. John Maquay in this respect was more representative of the English population. Guy Fleetwood Wilson, born in Florence in 1851, remembered that

The Brownings were a distinct feature of Florence life in my childhood. Mrs Browning used to hold a species of literary state reception once a week when she, her husband and her small son used to receive the worship and the adulation of their admirers, largely composed of American and English birds of passage.

Wilson remembered also the kindness of Lady Normanby and her humorous opinions on the Brownings' unintelligible verse.[85]

The Trollopes might have formed a bridge to the Brownings, but the latter in their early years in Italy saw them as uncongenial. Mrs Trollope especially was an outgoing socialite, whose grasp needed to be avoided as long as possible. In John Maquay's diary for 1852 alone there are forty-one mentions of social meetings with the Trollopes – and that is to leave aside other occasions when they may have met for business or as guests at other people's houses. Mrs Browning sometimes expended her waspishness on Fanny's receptions and whist parties where she would not be seen dead, telling Miss Mitford in January 1849 that 'your friend Mrs Trollope holds royal "drawing rooms" some once a week'. This involved an interesting admission: 'for, remain in Florence quite enough English, in spite of our Italian patriots, to do the English work of routs & whist & double gossip'.[86] This social distance was not indefinitely maintained: Thomas's wife was the Theodosia Garrow, who had known Elizabeth when living with her parents in Torquay, and Thomas himself was acquainted with John Kenyon (Elizabeth's distant kinsman).

Like Maquay but unlike the Brownings, Thomas Trollope became a property owner. In 1850 he purchased a plot of land for a house in what is now Piazza dell' Indipendenza, and then acquired more for a large south-facing garden with orange and lemon trees: 'In a word I made the place a very comfortable residence'.[87] Some of the internal arrangements of the house were elaborate, to judge from an American newspaper report in 1854 which spoke of Mrs Trollope's large and choice private library: 'The library room is an expansive Gothic hall, the furniture being all after the antique, and decorated with statuary and paintings.' Here she held her 'Saturday morning receptions'.[88]

A British settler who did become well-known to the Brownings was a native of Edinburgh, James Montgomery Stuart. In 1845, in London, he was married to Maria Gherardini of Volterra, and in 10 years she bore him at least four children, including twins, in Florence, where his residence can be amply documented (for example, he took out a year's subscription to Vieusseux in September 1849). An indefatigable lecturer on literary subjects, he was a constant presence providing intellectual chat: too constant, according to Charles Eliot Norton, who found his first visit to the Brownings spoilt by having to compete with the Scot for attention. Elizabeth described Stuart as 'one of our few friends in Italy' in a letter introducing him to Anna Jameson, whom he had been hailing, in lectures in Florence and Bagni, as 'the best English critic of Shakespeare'.[89]

Among other sources of much-needed income Stuart did translation work for the Legation. He was first engaged by Scarlett at the end of 1851; a year later Bulwer asked the Foreign Office to authorize a monthly salary for him. The reply was predictable: Bulwer had three secretaries attached to his mission – Why could not one of them do the work? It was a fair question if they were merely idle, less so if they had been appointed without regard for linguistic competence. As Stuart himself told Lord John Russell, as both Sir Henry, his secretary Mr Fenton, and the two Attaches Messrs Wolff and Lytton were all equally unacquainted with the Italian language on their arrival in Florence, it is clear they could not perform this duty he had no choice left but to employ me or some other person equally or better qualified for its performance.

The underlining was done in the Foreign Office; were they really surprised? Stuart declared that between 1 January and 30 June 1852, he had been paid a total of about £15 for his labours and in July and August about £15 for tasks which he describes in some detail. Subsequently, Bulwer had undertaken to pay him 150 *francesconi* a month on his own initiative, trusting (wrongly) that the arrangement would be sanctioned. Among other things Sir Henry had asked him to prepare a daily digest of the relevant news contained in the Italian press, and he also had to make copies of documents 'without receiving a sixpence. Such, I was informed, was the liberal arrangement of the Foreign Office' (more faint Foreign Office underlining). Stuart had felt the impact of recent events:

> Whatever the conditions of one thus employed in the Florence Legation may formerly have been, I can assure Your Lordship from personal experience that it is incompatible with any other regular employment. At least during the past year what with Mather's case, Bagg's case, the Stratford case, Stibbert's case, the Madiai case, Murray's case, the Tuscan Elections, the Customs League, the Education laws, besides the regular finance reports, there has been frequently so much and that required in such haste, that having to act as Translator to the Embassy it has been impossible for me to take, or having taken to keep, any other engagement.

This was not regular employment, but on any given day, he might be landed with a large packet of documents in urgent need of translation. That the times were not normal was, apparently, part of the Foreign Office argument for not paying him a salary.[90] Here then was a Briton who not merely lived in Florence throughout the occupation but obtained employment, if not much of a living, partly as a result of it.

During the Austrian occupation, the Brownings were absent from Tuscany for lengthy periods. They were in Venice, France and England from May 1851 to November 1852, during part of which time the free-thinker Edward Lombe, who was known to Robert, occupied Casa Guidi.[91] From November 1853 to June 1854 they were in Rome. Back in Florence in early 1853, Elizabeth Browning gave an account of their housekeeping. They had one servant fewer than they had previously had, but scarcely lived more cheaply. 'Penini' now ate as much as she did, yet given 'the cheapness of everything, article by article', a saving might be expected. £2 6s covered all weekly supplies, including wine, lamp oil and washing; yet Mrs Tennyson, with four children and several servants, spent no more. Elizabeth was conscious of failing somewhere, but she had no notion where.[92]

As John Maquay chronicles his regular whist parties and snippets of bank business, life under the Austrians appears fairly normal. He opened 1853 with what he described as one of his best dinner parties. It was attended by a cross section of Anglo-Florentine society, including Messrs Erskine, Webb Smith, O'Neill, Harding, McClaverty, John's son George and himself; Mesdames Burdett, Fombelle, Thompson and Lever; Miss Lever and Miss Maclean; and of course Elena. Others invited who could not make it included Wolff and Robert Lytton from the embassy, Captain Smith RN and his Italian wife, Frescobaldi, Madame Galeazzi and Miss Pennefather, Mr and Mrs Dennistoun, Mrs Webb Smith and Major Gregorie. This was followed on 28 January by a birthday party for the 8-year-old William, at which numerous children had conjuring tricks performed for them, 'after which they danced & amused themselves much till 12 O'clock'. Ash Wednesday (9 February) saw John recording his silver wedding, and then on 14 February, he had a big party with music and dancing. Two hundred were invited, including 32 Americans, and 138 turned up.[93]

On 15 March George celebrated his eighteenth birthday and began attendance at the Bank. In the same month there was bad news, the failure of Lampronti's bank; Maquay and Pakenham held some £1,100 of their paper, 'but hope not to lose'.[94] Later in the year there was another chill on the banking front, as Currell Smyth at Leghorn made it clear that he wanted a bigger share of the business, a dispute that would on and off haunt John's remaining days in Tuscany. Florence was no longer as cheap as it once was: he records his expenses for 1853 as £1,232, approximately one and a half times what he was budgeting 20 years earlier.[95] The fact that he now had a pleasure-loving eldest son may well have sharpened his cost-consciousness. George was only too willing to join in Elena's musical activities and to accompany her if she wanted to go to the opera, a concert or a ball. John's own outings, though still quite numerous, were fewer than theirs. Elena and George attended the races in 1853, but in April of the following year, when George went, his father 'did not go near them'.[96] Emilia Goggi visited them occasionally, although it is not clear whether she sang at the musical parties they still regularly gave. In the autumn of 1853 she was performing professionally at the Pergola, where John and Elena heard her on 12 October in *Trovatore*, John remarking sadly, 'she acted very well but voice much gone'.[97]

There were clouds on the international horizon, as Britain's entry into war with Russia became an imminent reality, and John might complain about the uncertainties which afflicted business, but he remained unshaken. By marked contrast with the Brownings, he scarcely left Florence, let alone Tuscany, from the time he returned from Rome in May 1849 until he went to England in the middle of 1853. In 1850 he spent 347 days in Florence, in 1851, 358 days and in 1852, 360. Trips to Leghorn, mostly for a day or two on business, largely account for the rest. In each of 1853 and 1854, he spent a few weeks away in England and Ireland; he was then in Florence throughout the first 5 months of 1855. The fifth month saw the departure of the Austrians from Tuscany.

Notes

1 Written in 1845 in condemnation of William Wordsworth, these lines are almost uncannily prophetic of the Brownings' feelings about the Grand Duke in and after 1849.

2 FO79/138, Hamilton to FO, 14 May 1849. The Confidential Print entitled 'Occupation of Leghorn British Claims' begins with this despatch (FO881/237). Macbean's estimates are in 79/140, 11 May.

3 FO79/138, Hamilton to FO, 7, 20 & 29 May, 10 June.

4 FO79/138, Hamilton to FO, 8 & 10 June.

5 FO79/138, Hamilton to FO, 26 & 30 July.

6 JLM, E11 ff. 40v–44 passim.

7 BC15, 2791 EBB to Julia Martin, 14 May 1849; 2793 to Henrietta, 23/25 May 1849; 2794 to Arabella, 6/7 June 1849.

8 All foreigners arriving in Tuscany required a *carta di soggiorno*, originally renewable every 6 months, soon to become 3 and 2 months as the Austrian occupation bit. Since there was no mechanism for chasing those whose *carte* had expired, it was common for renewal to be dilatory and equally common, before 1848, for the police to renew out of date *carte* without question.

9 FO 79/139, Hamilton to FO, 6 September 1849 (with enclosure from Whitburn) & 29 November (note on back by Palmerston); 79/140 Whitburn to Palmerston, 3 September; 79/136, FO to Hamilton, 27 September. Whitburn, born in 1827, was an art teacher who wrote on the decorative arts and ended up as Honorary Curator of the museum in Guildford, where he spent most of his life and died in 1914. He was in Italy from early in 1849 to 1851.

10 FO79/140, Carbonel to Palmerston, 8 October 1849. Carbonel translated the *Memoirs of Orsini* in 1857. In 1861 he applied to the English Church for money to go to Leghorn and got 2 dollars and 'not a penny more' (CMB 2, 3 April 1861). He died in 1862 aged 42, and is buried in the English Cemetery at Florence.

11 FO79/141, Hamilton to FO private, 6 October 1849. See also George M. Trevelyan, *Garibaldi and the Defence of the Roman Republic* (London, 1928), especially pp. 349–51. Forbes later emigrated to the United States, where he took up the anti-slavery cause, but he reappeared on the Italian scene in 1859 and served with Garibaldi in Sicily in 1860. He died at Pisa 22 July 1892 aged 84. His son Hugh was baptised (at the age of 20) in the English Church at Florence in July 1852 and 6 months later was married there to Laura Passerini. His two children were baptised in 1856 and 1858.

12 The correspondence on this issue down to September 1850 was gathered together in a Confidential Print (FO881/237), from which it is cited here. See for what follows Hamilton to Palmerston, 16 July 1849; Palmerston to Hamilton, 3 August; Hamilton to Palmerston, 13 September; Palmerston to Hamilton, 15 October; Hamilton to Palmerston, 6 November; Palmerston to Hamilton, 27 December.

13 The resulting dossier was included in the Confidential Print.

14 FO881/237, Hamilton to FO, 22 May 1850.

15 FO79/138, Hamilton to FO, 20 June 1849; 79/140 Macbean to FO, 31 August, with enclosures. FO79/141 contains much correspondence vindicating Baynes's conduct.

16 FO79/145, Macbean to FO, 25 February 1850, Macbean to FO, 6 August.

17 JLM, E11 ff. 64v, 70. On 5 June, after Sheil's death, the *Daily News* discussed at some length the adverse reactions which had greeted his appointment.

18 After a Catholic funeral at San Michelino, which was attended by the Tuscan Ministers and the entire diplomatic corps, his body was eventually transported back

to Ireland and interred at his home in Co Tipperary. On 3 June 1851 the *Morning Post* carried an extensive obituary, and other notices appeared on the same day in the *Morning Chronicle* and *Daily News*. Mrs Sheil outlived her husband by a mere 14 months, dying at Leghorn on 4 August 1852. Sheil's brief official career may be followed in FO79/149; for his early career the article in DNB.

19 William Torrens McCullagh, *Memoirs of the Right Honourable Richard Lalor Sheil* (London, 1855), Vol. 2, pp. 428–9.

20 *Morning Post,* 3 February 1859.

21 FO79/149, Sheil to FO, 17 May 1851.

22 A graduate of Edinburgh (1820), Aiton had seen service in the Mediterranean, and published *Dissertations on Malaria, Contagion, and Cholera* in 1832. In 1846 he was asking for new church sittings in Florence, and between 1849 and 1851, he subscribed to the Leghorn church. He died in Glasgow in 1863 at the age of 77. Two of his daughters were married in Italy: Margaret Jemima to the future royal academician, Edwin Long, in Rome in 1853, and Agnes to another painter, John Henshaw, in Leghorn some time between 1855 and 1857. We do not know whether Aiton was present in Italy for either of these marriages.

23 FO79/151, Macbean to Scarlett, 28 August 1851, Casigliano to Scarlett, 13 September; 79/148 FO to Scarlett, 13 October.

24 FO79/153, Macbean to FO, 20 June 1851, containing enclosures to Scarlett 19 June, to the Delegato of Leghorn, 13 June & two letters from Harding to Macbean, 11 June.

25 FO79/148, FO to Scarlett, 11 July 1851; 150 Scarlett to FO, 24 July with enclosures, Scarlett to Palmerston, private, 27 July, Scarlett to FO, 25 August with enclosure.

26 FO79/151, Scarlett to FO, 2 December, with enclosures.

27 FO79/151, Scarlett to FO, 15 September 1851, with enclosures; 79/159, Bulwer to FO, 2 June 1852. The brothers were Francis George (1830–1868) and William Robert (1831–1868), sons of Landor's great friend Francis, nephews of Archdeacon Julius and therefore elder brothers of the celebrated guidebook-writer Augustus. Augustus scarcely knew either of them; both were army men and spendthrifts who lived unruly lives at arm's length from the family. Francis, who converted to Catholicism, was bankrupted shortly before he went to fight for Garibaldi in 1860. He died penniless at La Spezia in November 1868 and was buried in the Campo Santo at Pisa; William died the same year at Brighton. See Augustus Hare, *The Years with Mother* (London, 1952).

28 FO79/151, Scarlett to FO, 5 September & 22 October 1851; 79/148, FO to Scarlett, 3 November. Newton (1828–1889) was the son of the miniature-painter Sir William John Newton, who intervened when a year later Newton was arrested for supposedly sketching the fortifications at Verona, which he denied (*Morning Chronicle* 2 September 1852).

29 FO79/154, Methuen to J. Baring, 10 October 1851. Baring (presumably one of the banking family) sent this letter on to Ponsonby at the FO on 18 October.

30 FO79/147, FO to Scarlett, 24 June 1851; 79/150, Scarlett to FO, 10, 14 & 15 June; 79/153, Macbean to Scarlett, 8 June & 13 June.

31 FO79/152, Scarlett to FO, 20, 21, 24 & 30 December 1851. This volume contains most of the correspondence, much of it a tedious dialogue of the deaf.

32 FO881/255; FO79/162, Wawn to Granville, 7 January 1852; JLM, E11 f.84. All references to the Mather affair hereafter are taken from the Confidential Print FO881/255, unless otherwise stated. While FO79 contains most of the relevant correspondence, it does not contain the exchanges between the British government and the Austrian government in Vienna.

33   FO79/162, Baring to Granville, private, 9 February 1852.
34   Prince Joseph Poniatowski had for some years exercised a kind of roving commission as Tuscan representative, based in Paris but with responsibility also for Great Britain and Belgium.
35   FO79/158, Scarlett to FO, 28 March 1852.
36   FO79/158, Scarlett to FO, 9 March 1852, with numerous enclosures including Scarlett's notes to the Tuscan government.
37   Horace Rumbold, *Recollections of a Diplomatist* (London, 1902), Vol. 1, p. 152.
38   FO79/163. Scarlett's children had been at Pisa for their health; he was summoned there by concern about one of them and himself went down with inflammation of the lungs. Barron had been to see him and taken his instructions, believing it would be a long time before he was fit to return to work, and signed the despatch of 11 May, which notified the presumed agreement with the Tuscan government. The same volume documents the tea-cup storm between Barron and Rumbold.
39   FO79/159, Barron to Malmesbury, private, 13 May 1852; also 881/255 pp. 76–8.
40   They arrived in Liverpool, destitute, at the end of May. The mayor, predictably, received no help from the Foreign Office when he asked what he was to do with them (FO79/162, FO to Thomas Littledale, 4 June 1852), and eventually opened a subscription on their behalf.
41   FO79/163, Rumbold to FO, 18 May 1852. On 26 May Rumbold rightly gets his knuckles rapped for the way he has been behaving, although by that date, one might argue that the damage had been done.
42   FO79/156, FO to Bulwer, 21 May 1852; 79/162, Addington to James Mather, 24 May, James Mather to Malmesbury, 27 May, 14 June.
43   Hickson had been proprietor and editor of the *Westminster Review* until he sold it to John Chapman in October 1851. As such he had been closely associated with Edward Lombe, whose Norfolk rents he is said to have collected, and he must surely have visited him on this trip to Florence. He subscribed to Vieusseux for a month on 28 January 1852, giving Casa Fenzi as his address. See the references in Rosemary Ashton, *142 Strand* (London, 2007).
44   FO519/167, Bulwer to Cowley, 18 June 1852. Bulwer married in 1848 Georgiana, half-sister of Cowley, who was a Wellesley and nephew of the Duke of Wellington. His first view of Florence, delivered to Lord Cowley on 29 May, reveals a certain whimsical character: 'The place very pretty but quite small bad climate and life though cheap not so very cheap as to startle one.'
45   FO79/159, Bulwer to FO, 18 June 1852. Also in State Papers 1852, pp. 536–45.
46   *Punch* Vol. 22, pp. 245–7; 23, p. 19.
47   See Chapter 1.
48   FO79/158, Scarlett to FO, 12 March 1852 with attached FO memorandum.
49   FO79/163, 'Britannicus' to Lord Derby 14 March 1852 with attached memorandum by Malmesbury.
50   FO79/183, Bulwer to FO, 5 January 1855.
51   FO79/152, Scarlett to FO, 16 & 19 December 1851; 79/155, FO to Scarlett, 2 January 1852; 79/157, Scarlett to FO, 31 January & 6 February 1852.
52   FO 79/161 Bulwer to FO, 24 December 1852, enclosing his to Casigliano of 28 June and Baldasseroni's reply, 1 July; FO79/165, Bulwer to FO, 14 January 1853.
53   FO79/165 Erskine to FO, 15 & 19 March 1853; 79/166 Scarlett to FO, 2 April. The Heads of the Diplomatic Body met at Baron von Hügel's House on 1 April by appointment 'to discuss and arrange this question'. When they all agreed, the Tuscan government bowed to the inevitable pressure.

54 JLM, E11 f. 72 says that Kleinkauf died suddenly on Wednesday 16 April, and he was buried with a large military funeral on the Saturday.

55 This union produced the famous theologian Friedrich von Hügel, and another son, Anatole, who became the first director of the Cambridge Museum of Anthropology and Ethnography.

56 For example *Morning Chronicle* 27 August and *Times* 28 August 1853. The bride's brother married into the Foschi family in Florence in 1861.

57 Christine Reader died in 1891 and was buried a Catholic in San Miniato. Her father William died in 1846 and is buried in the English Cemetery. On the English side the Readers were linked to the Walkers (involved with the Madiai), Fleetwood Wilson, Macdouall, Whyte, Moyser, Chichester, D'Arcy Irvine, Hill Trevor; on the Italian Riccardi, Incontri, Bossi Pucci, Salviati, Ulivieri, Lippi. We have identified no fewer than eleven Anglo-Italian marriages within this group of families (often between cousins) and there may well be others.

58 JLM, E11 ff. 40v, 60, 66v. Dedham must have been serious to head for Vienna in pursuit of his ambitions on Boxing Day. His son, Edward, became a great friend of Tommy Maquay during Tommy's visits to the ship and John employed Edward temporarily in the bank.

59 JLM, E11 f. 69.

60 Rumbold, *Recollections*, p. 153.

61 Guy Fleetwood Wilson, *Letters to Somebody – A Retrospect* (London 1922), pp. 33–6. EBB mentions a visit from the Wilsons in a letter to Isa Blagden (BC20, 3427 8 June 1854).

62 Thomas A. Trollope, *What I Remember* (2nd edition, London, 1887), Vol. 2, pp. 194–5

63 BC16, 2848 EBB to Arabella, 3? May 1850.

64 FO79/166, Scarlett to FO, 28 April 1853.

65 We have found no trace of this wedding – it was possibly one of his in-laws. In May 1836 Evelyn Waddington had married at the legation in Florence Marianna Bacinetti, who was clearly Italian although described as from London. The bridegroom was described as from Naples (G23773/4no21).

66 FO79/166, Scarlett to FO, 12 April 1853.

67 FO79/164, Craufurd to Lord Clarendon, 11 March 1853. The affair is first noticed in a despatch from Erskine (FO79/165, 23 February 1853) and in effect ends with a Tuscan apology: FO79/166, Scarlett to FO, 30 April. There are continued indignant denials from the family that they have any intention of fomenting revolution in Italy and mutterings from the Grand Duke that Mazzini had been seen in an English uniform in Naples.

68 FO79/169, Scarlett to FO, 11 October 1853. The same despatch records the case of Mr Butler, placed under arrest at the hotel where he was staying and accused, Scarlett thinks justly, of being a second in a duel, but released the same day on Scarlett's private plea – which again reveals the good sense both of the Tuscan authorities and Scarlett, though not of the British miscreants involved.

69 FO79/169, Scarlett to FO, 1 November 1853.

70 JLM, E11 f. 77v.

71 TNA, Prob11/2126. On 11 June 1851 Vansittart took out a 6-month subscription to Vieusseux, but by October a Colonel Winthrop was residing at Villa Salviati. On 15 May 1852 the *Times* carried an advertisement of the sale of the villa. On 1 November 1852 the *Caledonian Mercury* reported that it had been bought by the tenor Mario, but Colonel Winthrop was still residing there at the end of the year.

72 This letter is transcribed in a typescript history of the Hendersons, which survives among private papers in the possession of a descendant of the family, to whom we are most grateful for permission to quote from it.

73 Flintshire Record Office, Hawarden, Ms D/HE, nos. 606, 607. The reference to 'Gibson' is to Benjamin Gibson, brother of the famous sculptor John Gibson, who lived and worked in Rome. A native of Conwy, Benjamin died in Bagni on 13 August 1851.

74 Dennis's will, made in 1852 (TNA, Prob11/2266), names these children. Mary (born 1835 in London) married an Austrian officer, Carlo Czappele, in Florence in February 1854, with Dennis as a witness.

75 FO79/162, Dennis to FO, 17 June 1852, FO to Dennis, 1 July.

76 FO79/171, Dennis to Lord John Russell, 5 February 1853. 79/165, Erskine to FO, 8 February, the first communication on the subject from the embassy, provides more detail and encloses a statement from Mrs Mitton. Erskine seeks instructions, having been informed by Casigliano 'in a friendly way' that the government was proposing to banish Mrs Mitton. He has managed to get the period of grace for her extended to a month.

77 FO 79/164, FO to Erskine, 16 February 1853 (this could in fact be interpreted as a positive instruction not to interfere); FO to Scarlett, 15 March.

78 JLM, E10 f. 48.

79 FO79/143, Hamilton to FO, 26 January 1850.

80 JLM, E11 f. 94. *Daily News* 16 February 1854 gives a complete account of the Paris trial.

81 *Reynold's News* 1 April 1877.

82 JLM, E10 f. 251v, 22 September 1845. For Powers's life and career see Richard P. Wunder, *Hiram Powers, Vermont Sculptor* (Cranbury, NJ, 2 Vols, 1989–91). His daughter Louisa was baptised in Florence in September 1838 and several other children followed, down to Ellen Elizabeth in 1853. Powers died in 1873 and was buried in the English cemetery; his wife Elizabeth Gibson died in 1894 and was buried in Allori.

83 JLM, E11 f. 116. On the 29 August 1853 'Powers met me before breakfast at Casa Standish to look over Greenough's things.'

84 BC16, 2813 EBB to Henrietta, 20 September. Earlier that year she had mentioned Pakenham only to say that they were not acquainted with him, 'we live like hermits and know nobody in fact' (BC15, 2792 EBB to Fanny Dowglass, 16 May). Later she reacted to the news of his expulsion from Bagni and then from Tuscany.

85 Fleetwood Wilson, *Letters to Somebody* p. 6.

86 BC15, 2771 EBB to Miss Mitford, 30 January 1849.

87 Trollope, *What I Remember* Vol. 2, pp. 190–1.

88 This report, from the *Newark Advertiser*, was reprinted in the *Manchester Times* on 17 May 1854. Mr Trollope had won notoriety in 1832 with her uncomplimentary *Domestic Manners of the Americans*.

89 S. Berbeglia, 'James Montgomery Stuart: A Scotsman in Florence', in Barbara Schaff (ed.), *Exiles, Emigrés and Intermediaries: Anglo Italian Cultural Transactions* (Amsterdam & New York, 2010), pp. 117–30; BC16, 2850 EBB to Anna Jameson, 4 May 1850.

90 FO79/161, Bulwer to FO, 22 December 1852; 79/151, Stuart to Russell, 15 January 1853. The Murray case referred to here involved a British subject put on trial at Rome. Stuart outlasted the Austrian occupation before returning to Britain in 1858 with a loan from Robert Browning and a letter of recommendation to the publisher Chapman. The loan had not been repaid years later. In England he made a name for

himself as a lecturer on literary and political subjects. In the 1860s he became an Italian correspondent of the *Morning Post* and also served as secretary of a company called Florentine Land and Public Works Ltd, established in London in 1866, under his old friend Sebastiano Fenzi. His children continued to live in Italy, and in 1874 in Rome, his daughter Mary Victoria was married to Romeo, son of Antonio Gallenga, erstwhile Piedmontese political exile, *Times* correspondent and deputy in the Italian Parliament. Stuart died at Perugia early in 1889 (obituary in the *Morning Post*, 23 January 1889).

91 BC17, 2906 Lombe to RB, 19 March 1851; 2974 RB to Carlyle, about 22 October 1851. Lombe made his will (TNA, Prob 11/2149), witnessed by Bligh of the legation, on 30 October, and died on the following 1 March. He left everything to his French wife and, after her, to University College Hospital. In 1855 the Council of University College expressed its thanks to Horace Hall for his assistance to the hospital in his capacity as agent for Lombe's executors (*Daily News* 6 November).

92 BC18, 3159 EBB to Arabella, 15–17 January 1853.

93 JLM, E11 ff. 103–4.

94 JLM, E11 f. 126.

95 JLM, E11 f. 122v.

96 JLM, E11 f. 128.

97 JLM, E11 f. 118.

10 PROTESTANTS IN STORMY WATERS, 1849–1853

In 1848 the Anglican Church in Florence was established at the centre of the life of the British residents. The ruling committee had a stable core which included Christopher Webb Smith and John Maquay; the amiable chaplain George Robbins, who had been in Tuscany since 1836, had officiated since the death of Tennant in 1842. The congregation's fervent desire was above all for a quiet life, and this was precisely what it was not going to get as 1848 turned into 1849.

The church might in some respects resemble an English parish, but it was operating in a very different environment. It was a tolerated anomaly within a state which professed a different religion, and there were limitations on the freedom of action and expression not only of its management committee but of individual members of the flock. Protestants of all stripes were only too conscious of being in a minority in a Catholic land, but their reactions to the majority faith varied, from pragmatic acceptance to a missionary fervour which could, and occasionally did, endanger the precarious security of their co-religionists. Contacts between Tuscan Protestant exiles and the agencies of Evangelical opinion back home were nourished by correspondence, travellers' tales and the newspapers. British Protestants could easily be whipped up into indignation about the beleaguered status of Protestants in Catholic countries. The re-establishment of a Roman Catholic hierarchy in England in 1850 provoked a furious reaction in England which echoed in Tuscany, suggesting to the Tuscan authorities that British demands for toleration were hypocritical.

The Florentine Church was not immune to the ecclesiastical controversies which excited mid-Victorian England; the residents occupied the same spectrum of opinion. In July 1845 the artist Eugenio Latilla (who later contributed articles on fresco-painting to the *Tuscan Athenaeum*) volunteered to paint 'the recess of the Communion table' in the English Church. The Committee thanked him for his 'liberal offer', but refused it for the present as they were 'not certain of reaction of congregation to paintings in church'.[1] If anything, the effects of different opinions were sharpened because, in a country which accorded them only conditional toleration, foreign Protestants had little choice of where to go for public worship, baptism, marriage or the burial of the dead. Dissenters and Presbyterians were keenly, and sometimes resentfully, aware of their enforced proximity to Episcopalians.

At Leghorn, Anglicans and the numerous Presbyterian Scots were compelled to share church and burial ground, but the formal establishment of the Free Church of Scotland altered the situation. The key event was the arrival of Dr Robert Walter Stewart in 1845. The first Free Church services were held in Thomson's Hotel and the fortunate passage of three other ministers through Leghorn enabled a Presbytery to be established for the single purpose of ordaining office-bearers for the newly formed congregation. The first office-bearers were Henderson, Thomson, Rae and Robertson, all prominent figures in Leghorn life and commerce. Premises were rapidly acquired, and by 1849 what were described as a church and manse were in being.[2] Peace between the Frees and the Anglicans had already broken down before the revolutionary storm broke over Italy. The brief account that follows hardly reflects the voluminous correspondence and the passions aroused over a period of months.

On 2 June 1847 Thomas Henderson's wife died, and his brother Robert informed Macbean of the family's desire to have her buried by Stewart according to the rites of the Scots Presbyterian church. Macbean, hostile from the outset to the demands of his fellow Scots, demurred: although all British Protestants could be buried in the cemetery, their funerals must be conducted according to the Anglican rite. In order to expedite the burial, Henderson consented to pay the chaplain's fee, accept his participation under protest and hold a Presbyterian service separately. A correspondence ensued on the issue of principle, and the Scots' determination to appeal directly to Lord Palmerston forced Macbean to lay it before his lordship officially.[3] Having received no answer from Macbean, Stewart himself wrote to Palmerston on 30 October.

Palmerston was sympathetic to the Scots, thinking that, whatever the legal position, 'the Free Church Minister ought to be allowed to perform Funeral Service for deceased Members of his Communion'. Meanwhile the trustees of the Leghorn Anglican Church had sought a ruling from the Bishop of Gibraltar, who was prepared to concede that while the Anglican rite might be omitted if it was objectionable, no other could be permitted in the cemetery. Apparently he thought (like Macbean) that the Presbyterians had no funeral ritual and would not be inconvenienced by this prohibition. Apart from the fact that this was hardly an adequate response, the Scots would not accept any ruling from the Bishop. By late February 1848, Stewart had heard unofficially through the Moderator of the Free Church that Palmerston had decided in their favour, but Macbean had not, so the funeral of an infant Rae still aroused dispute. Macbean wrote again to Lord Palmerston on the 26th and Stewart and the Elders followed on the 29th, indicating that it was from him alone that they would accept a decision. Not until the end of March did Palmerston formally communicate with Macbean and Stewart. It seems that the papers had been inadvertently put on one side; the Foreign Secretary may have been temporarily distracted by other less important issues such as revolution in Paris and the downfall of Metternich. With some asperity his Lordship ruled in favour of the Scots, stipulating only that 'order and decency' should be observed at all times and (of course) that 'the proper Fees, sanctioned by HM's Govt be paid on each Interment'.[4]

The existence of an assertive Presbyterian congregation at Leghorn had a ripple effect at Florence, where the Scots established a smaller-scale congregation under the Reverend James Maxwell Hanna. It met for the first time, necessarily on private premises, on 26 September 1849. Among its early members were the Brownings, Frederick Tennyson and the American Harriet Beecher Stowe.[5] At Bagni the Brownings, like others, subscribed to the Anglican Church as the only available place of Protestant worship. Even in Florence, Elizabeth confessed that 'Two hours of dear Mr Hanna are considerably too much for Robert and me'. Hanna was 'really clever & most excellent, but, with all that, the very dullest & slowest preacher I ever listened to ... Three words every five minutes ... in a high Scotch accent'.[6]

The Scots church had never received permission for its presence in Tuscany. In 1848 Stewart somewhat presumed on the continuance of religious toleration when he urged the establishment of the Frees at Florence. When the new Leghorn church was opened in 1849 the sermon of dedication was translated into Italian, printed and circulated. This did not pass unnoticed by the Tuscan Government as reaction set in, and Stewart's own account reveals that he had to answer some awkward questions and tell some half-truths, for example about sermons that had been preached in Italian. He was also accused of distributing heretical books, in particular one called L'Amico dei Peccatori (The Sinners' Friend) which he apparently felt able to say that he had never possessed; he averred also that he had made a point of never giving books to Italians. Perhaps he had not done so with his own hands; he had been absent in Scotland during the autumn and winter of 1848, raising money to buy Bibles among other things. He had eluded immediate danger, but knew now that Italian could not be used in his church – an irritant rather than a fatal impediment. He had been warned and was careful to eschew any direct participation in the Florentine project, beyond encouraging Hanna to establish himself there.

With the failure of the Tuscan revolution both Hanna and Stewart challenged the Tuscan authorities by Bible running, and some members of the Anglican Church were also involved in it. 'Bible running' does not mean the importation of the one Bible which was part of the luggage of most English tourists, intended for their own use (although occasionally that might be confiscated by over-zealous Tuscan officials). It was, rather, the illegal importation of Bibles and religious tracts, smuggled into the country for the deliberate purpose of selling or giving (more often, in the case of tracts) to the native Tuscan population. To carry a Bible or give a tract to someone in England excited little comment and broke no law. It was very different for a merely tolerated church in a foreign state. And what was to be done about Tuscan Protestants, those who did in fact convert? These were live issues, and a potential danger to foreign Protestants, given that the Tuscan government's tendency after 1849 was to equate heterodoxy with political revolution.

The English Church in Florence was not entirely secure financially. Its repeated efforts to obtain a subsidy from the British government were consistently rebuffed. The residents found it hard to accept the government's firm distinction between a consulate (as at Leghorn) and an embassy. Surely both existed to serve British interests. As Scarlett had discovered, he had to offer at Florence the services rendered by Macbean at Leghorn. It might well seem both unfair and anomalous that the Leghorn church had privileges that the Florence church did not. In fact governmental logic tended to break down, for a number of reasons.

The embassy had provided religious facilities for residents and visitors from the earliest days of the post-war British colonization and it remained a favoured location for weddings. The first wedding at Holy Trinity – of an American couple – did not take place until 1853. From Holland onwards, the ambassadors paid pew rents; a slightly undignified correspondence after Hamilton's death reveals the committee in pursuit of his unpaid rent. After 1839 the church proclaimed itself a branch of the Anglican establishment, of which the monarch was Supreme Head. By 1849 it was ministering to significant numbers of Americans; hence serious discussion in the Select Vestry as to whether the Book of Common Prayer would allow prayers for the American President alongside the standard prayer for the Queen. The issue had to be referred to the Bishop of Gibraltar, who consulted Sir George Hamilton, which led to a tedious exchange involving Lord Palmerston and the Archbishop of Canterbury. After 18 months it was ruled that the church could only pray for the English royal family and the sovereign in whose dominions the chapel was situated.[7] As Holland had perceived, the Tuscan government would not understand any disavowal of responsibility for a church which was tolerated only on the understanding that it had the sanction of the British authorities. If the Tuscans discovered reasons to put the English Church in the dock, the British Government was in no position to play Pontius Pilate.

The Church remained dependent totally on subscriptions and pew rents from residents and visitors and such other casual income as it could raise from donations and events such as bazaars, which could meet but a small proportion of its expenses. Collecting subscriptions from residents had always been less of a problem than collecting from visitors, given that there was increasing resistance to the only obviously foolproof method of doing so, at the door. Even passing the plate round during the service – regarded as both unspiritual and undignified – was not without its hazards. Collecting at hotels was beyond the resources and organization of the church, although it was tried from time to time, as was the sale of tickets in various locations around the town. Whether out of negligence or malfeasance, many visitors left Florence without paying. Consideration had to be given to future sources of funding.

This was not the only issue which exercised the congregation during the years of revolution. The Committee came to the Annual General Meeting in January

1849 prepared to lay before the subscribers both a proposal for a revised seat tariff and the idea of establishing an endowment fund to meet the church's financial needs.[8] In his report on 'a year which will long be remembered as one of doubt and perplexity', Christopher Smith was sure that the subscribers would join in devout thanks to God who, 'in these troublous times', had watched over the congregation 'and continued to it the privileges and consolations of His Holy Worship and Service, amid uninterrupted peace and tranquillity'. As past experience had shown, the congregation had an unexampled capacity to disturb its own peace and tranquillity, and a bombshell was dropped on the meeting before Smith could read his report.

He opened the meeting by handing in the lists of 6- and 12-month subscribers and, as usual, proposing a ballot for a new committee. This was at once met with an amendment, proposed by the Reverend Thomas Sleeman[9] and seconded by the Reverend T. Wolley. No prior notice of this had been given, but the Chairman, Lord Dunsany, had no option but to put it to the vote. It read

> That the Meeting being desirous of bringing the management of the Church of Florence into complete uniformity with Ecclesiastical usages and the customs of other Churches, do determine that the duties of the Committee of Management shall now cease, and that two Churchwardens shall be immediately chosen, – the said Churchwardens to be annually elected in open Vestry – One by the Minister and the other by the assembled Congregation.

It was carried by a simple majority. Robbins named Webb Smith as his churchwarden and John Maquay was nominated to act on behalf of the congregation but promptly refused, at which the Reverend Wolley was unanimously elected. Now Arthur Vansittart moved that Robbins and the two churchwardens should be appointed a committee 'to draw up Rules for the guidance of the Churchwardens, as nearly assimilating to those previously in force, as the change of management will admit'. These were to be submitted to an adjourned General Meeting on 23 February. The motion was carried *nem. con.*

Maquay's diary merely hints at his reactions: 'most unexpectedly a party carried a resolution to substitute churchwardens for Committee'. On 5 February he 'as usual dined at Robbins and then to Pakenham for a meeting to consult about Church affairs not at all satisfied with Robbins line of conduct in the late affair'. He was obviously unhappy, but it is not clear precisely why. That Vansittart's motion was unanimously carried suggests a general recognition that there must be some continuity in management. To proceed to the appointment of churchwardens without providing any framework for their operation or any job description seemed at the very least precipitate.

What lay behind the proposal, beyond the stated intention to make the Florentine Church more like an English parish, is unclear. That desire was evidently very strongly felt by some, just as it had been strongly felt that the church must declare its obedience to a bishop and relinquish the right of appointment of its own chaplain. Personal animosities may have had something to do with the proposal sprung upon the meeting, but a lot of people appear to have had misgivings by the time of the adjourned General Meeting on 23 February. Among them was the significant figure of the Secretary of the late committee, and now the clergyman's churchwarden, Christopher Webb Smith. Albeit one of those appointed to draw up the new rules he, with thirteen others, signed a requisition that the meeting should reconsider the decision that had been taken: 'the proposed new system is not suited to the British Church at Florence.'

Differences and hard feelings were immediately apparent. Already the Reverend Sleeman had proposed an informal meeting between the two sides in order to achieve 'an amicable arrangement' and to restore 'peace and unanimity to the Congregation'. Several such meetings had taken place and produced draft rules which proposed a hybrid authority (Select Vestry plus churchwardens), on the dubious supposition that this was what the decision of the January General Meeting intended. The rules were adopted without a dissenting voice and the meeting proceeded to the election of a Select Vestry (or reincarnated management committee). Meanwhile the Chairman requested Robbins to nominate his churchwarden, for Webb Smith had resigned after a remarkably short term of office. Mr Bonnin, a 12-month subscriber, was appointed in his place to serve along with Wolley.

It is not necessary here to follow the tortuous course of the wranglings over the new system which took place over the next few years. Fifty years later, Tassinari summarized the shortcomings of the arrangements as they now stood. The division of responsibilities between churchwardens and Vestry was in practice unworkable. The Vestry retained control of the funds and were to make all expenditures over a certain amount, while the churchwardens did all the day-to-day work of running the church and paid 'all items of ordinary expenditure'. It was quite unclear how the Vestry's general oversight and its relations with the churchwardens were to be managed. As Tassinari comments, 'it is not surprising to find that before three months were out, Select Vestry and Churchwardens were hopelessly at variance, and the latter had resigned their office, declaring it to be impossible to act under existing regulations.'[10]

Even as the Anglo-Florentines argued about the management of their church, the Grand Duke was a fugitive and the Austrians were on their way. A meeting was scheduled for 12 April 1849 to consider 'important questions' raised by the churchwardens, principally anxieties about the church's income. Smith failed to attend because his train from Leghorn was fired on, but he had had the foresight to leave a lengthy memorandum expressing his views. He believed that the finances were in a healthier state than the churchwardens supposed. It had been feared that 'unanticipated political events' might lead to a further diminution of income, but he thought (perhaps ironically) that since late January, there had been 'some improvement [...] in those circumstances which may be deemed to affect the resort of our Countrymen to this City'.

Tiresome disputes continued, in the course of which new names appear. William Reynolds was elected to the Select Vestry in May 1849 and the retired physician Dr Peter Luard became the chaplain's churchwarden in January 1850, when it was agreed that the churchwardens could attend Vestry meetings as of right. Both men figure in John Maquay's diaries as members of his social circle. Luard proceeded to quarrel with his fellow churchwarden, the Reverend Gilbert, who showed a disposition to act without consulting him and eventually resigned (thanks to Smith's diplomacy he was reinstated). Simultaneously Luard complained about the conduct of the *custode,* who was called in for examination and declared that 'He had told Luard he was not a slave'. Luard had 'annoyed him' and he had taken refuge in dumb insolence. He was sacked as from 1 May. With the submission of the churchwardens to the final authority of the Select Vestry and the recognition in 1853 that a sitting member of the Select Vestry might be a Churchwarden, the church organization was at last established on a footing which survived the establishment of the Kingdom of Italy.[11] In the meantime ongoing consideration was given to the vexed question of the church's finances.

The endowment fund was intended to secure an income which would pay the chaplain's salary and make it possible to stop charging for seats. At the fateful Annual Meeting on 26 January 1849 a committee was appointed to examine the issue and draw up a set of rules. It was then discovered that the joint churches of Pisa and Bagni had already issued a prospectus entitled 'Rules for the Guidance of Trustees of the Endowment Fund of British Protestant Churches in Foreign Lands', which the Florentine committee considered at its meeting on 23 February. While there was some resentment that the Pisans had proceeded without consultation, the Florentines decided to seek co-operation with them, but all manner of problems then surfaced.

If the deed of trust, as recommended, were to be drawn up under English and not Tuscan law, two of the three trustees would have to be based in England. Finding persons in England willing to serve with no profit to themselves and arranging for their meetings with the Tuscan trustee presented thorny difficulties. The indissoluble connection between the church and Her Majesty's Minister, if not Her Majesty's Government, was indicated by the suggestion that the Minister should *ex officio* be the Tuscany-based trustee.[12] There were numerous other problems. All monies collected were to be invested in British or Indian funds, yet there were to be two bank accounts, one in London for funds collected in Great Britain and elsewhere (there were hopes of subventions from the United States), another in Florence. There was no clarity about what was to happen in the event of conflict between trustees and church, nor was it at all clear what real incentive there would be for well-wishers from abroad to subscribe.

Although the Pisa-Bagni congregation proved amenable to negotiations, which produced a first draft document for consideration at the Annual Meeting of 25 January 1850, the energy was evaporating from the proposal. Producing a final agreed set of rules took another year, and it was not until January 1852 that a prospectus could be printed. Thereafter practical difficulties came to the fore. Although the Bishop of Gibraltar produced enthusiasm (and £50), there was precious little financial support from elsewhere. George Robbins (now back in England) was prepared to act as a trustee, but the high-profile figures that the committee approached, for example the Earls of Shaftesbury and Wicklow, declined to act. After further negotiations and amendments, the Endowment Fund finally became active with George Robbins as home trustee, John Maquay as local trustee for Florence and Colonel Stisted for the Churches of Pisa and Bagni.[13] By this time expectations had diminished, and the endowment fund ceases to feature regularly in the minutes. Donations continued to be received over a number of years and were put to profitable use, but there was no attempt to replace the existing system for the support of the chaplain.

Even while the effort to establish an endowment fund continued, other means of securing income were discussed. At the beginning of 1850 Robbins expressed his repugnance to the system of collection at the church door and asked for a sub-committee to reconsider the matter, while acknowledging that other expedients had been tried without success. He was prepared to take a salary cut of £50 if that would help. The sub-committee's report, submitted in February 1850, included a useful description of the present situation. They would have been only too happy for the funds to be in such a state that the church could be freely 'thrown open to the Public', and they hoped that endowment might be the answer, but meanwhile pointed out parallels with familiar English practice:

> they cannot see with what good reason any parties can complain of the system now adopted in a Church situated as ours is, in a foreign Country and totally dependent upon our own resources, when they reflect than [sic] in our own native land, it is found necessary to adopt the same system in numerous instances and more particularly in those towns where as in Florence, a great proportion of the Congregation is composed of transitory visitors, such as Buxton, Cheltenham, Hastings and likewise in many private chapels in London Dublin and elsewhere.

Free accommodation was provided; the gallery, which contained almost 150 seats, was never full, but this was intended for servants and the poor. Anyone who 'conscientiously' objected to paying out on a Sunday had only to come on a Saturday afternoon when the *custode* would be available to take their names as weekly subscribers. This arrangement should be publicized and other places in the town named where weekly subscriptions could be obtained.[14] The accounts for the past year revealed that the seat subscriptions (when fully collected) would just about pay the chaplain's salary. Only two sermons in aid of church funds, plus sundry donations, put the account into profit.

The chaplain's basic salary was fixed at £250 in 1846 and it was the same in 1861. In addition he kept the fees from baptisms, marriages and funerals, which averaged about another £50 sterling. As the income of the church was derived solely from the pewage and periodical collections, the state of the funds at the close of the year depended upon the number of English visitors and the balance accruing from the previous year. The figures for the years 1849 to 1854 reveal fluctuations which seem to reflect the impact of public events only rather approximately. In 1850 income fell to 2,190 pauls from the 1,849 figure of 2,570, which might seem predictable, but it climbed back to 2,308 pauls in 1851. There was for some reason a sharp decline to 695 pauls in 1852, but 1853 and 1854 produced end-of-year balances of 3,933 and 5,558 pauls respectively. Neither ordinary nor extraordinary expenses varied greatly from year to year. In 1852 there was passing concern, but never any panic that funds would run dry.

In the absence of any alternative, it was simply not possible to dispense with revenue taken either at the door or by means of tickets sold in advance. Tariffs were here to stay. A printed copy of the revised tariff as at New Year 1854 was inserted at the beginning of a new volume of the Church Minute Books. Subscriptions were available for periods ranging from 12 months down to 1 week, or for a single festival, and the following explanatory rules were appended:

1. The Custode attends at the Church every Saturday from 2 to 5 pm to receive applications for Seats.
2. The Tariff is intended to apply strictly to the Members of one family living in the same house.
3. One Subscription admits to both Morning and Evening Service. The System of giving Tickets is discontinued.
4. For all Seats beyond 8 Seats whether 3, 6 or 12 months Subscription the increase for each additional Seat shall be 1 paul.

Already in 1845 the *custode* had complained that despite his best endeavours 'many persons force their way into the church without paying, and that without an unseemly altercation he cannot succeed in getting them to take tickets'.[15] Robbins's hostility to charging at the door had led indirectly to the purchase of tickets in advance at various agencies around the town; now the task returned to the *custode*. In March 1850 the churchwardens reported that despite their attendance 'on the 10th and 17th of this Month persons entered the Church refusing to pay the Sunday Subscription'.[16] It was not clear what action could be taken against those who turned up on Sunday morning without having bought from the *custode* on Saturday. The Select Vestry had no answer beyond exhorting the churchwardens to explain things to the people concerned, but the system surprisingly lasted out the Grand Ducal years.

The Minute Books reflect an almost ostrich-like concern with matters such as heating and hymnbooks, or whether the church could afford to have the organ reconditioned by Signor Ducci, and might give a misleading impression of the perils that faced the church both from within and without. The latter were obvious and may be briefly stated.

The restored Grand Duke was determined to secure his soul by a stricter interpretation of his religious obligations and a closer relationship with the Papacy. This manifested itself in the Concordat concluded by Cardinal Antonelli and Baldasseroni in April 1851 and ratified by the Grand Duke on 19 June.[17] The spirit was conveyed in the first article, which laid it down as the duty of the lay authority to protect 'morality, worship, and religion' and to be ready 'to give to the Church any aid required for the exercise of the Episcopal authority'. The bishops were accorded extensive powers of censorship and were to be free in their relations with the papacy; the church had the free administration of its property (which must have made Peter Leopold stir in his grave even if he had not already done so). Nowhere in the document was it suggested that the State had any duty other than to support the Catholic church.

If the Concordat for the most part passed the English Church by, determined as it was to remain a closed corporation serving the British only, there were issues which did impinge on the residents. Alarm bells rang over a decree on education issued in August 1852. This ignored the existence of Protestant schools but thoroughly perturbed those running such schools, which not only ministered to children of British Protestant residents but for reasons of economic survival also took in British Catholics and others. The decree was long and involved, but in broad terms both primary and secondary schools were subjected to ecclesiastical oversight. The 9th clause conceded that non-Catholics should not be required to attend religious lessons, but the 68th provided that all teachers who were not Tuscan and Catholic and wished to open a school must deposit documents regarding their religious, moral and political behaviour and prove three years' residence. In his despatch to the Foreign Office outlining this decree, Bulwer proposed, perfectly properly, to confine his remarks 'to British subjects, whether Protestant or Catholic, attending British Protestant schools', as he had already ascertained that schools would certainly not be allowed to remain open to Tuscans unless the law was complied with.[18] As was so often the case with Tuscan decrees in which religion was involved, it took a long time to achieve clarification.

Towards the end of 1853 there was some correspondence about a proposed Protestant school at Leghorn, which had been mooted for at least 2 years and for which land and a house had been purchased. One of the causes of delay was all too familiar in England at the time: the inability of dissenters and Anglicans to agree on the religious content of the education to be given. Macbean had explained to Scarlett that the purpose was to educate the children of British residents and also those of the numerous British subjects currently employed on the Tuscan railways. The latter presented special problems:

It is difficult to induce some of these people to attend churches or to send their children on Sunday to the Chaplain's class; during the week the fathers are entirely taken up with their work, and unless the mothers are orderly and sober (which I am sorry to say is not always the case) the children are neglected and allowed to play about the streets.

Macbean ignored the additional problem that a number of these children were the children of Irish Catholic navvies. Acquiescence was obtained from Landucci. As Scarlett understood it, the minister ruled that all recognized Protestants might attend such a school, but no Roman Catholic subject of the Grand Duke could send their children to Protestant schools: 'the permission to open, and give instruction at, such Schools was conditional on their being strictly confined to Protestant families.'[19] It was not clear whether British Catholics might attend British schools run by Protestants, but there is no record of any English school being closed for failure to adhere to the law, even if the decree put difficulties in the way of the foundation of such schools.

More serious for the members of the English Church who wished to lead a quiet life was the fact that there were some among them for whom the Church existed to provide more than weekly religious solace. One was Captain John Pakenham. In the spring of 1840 Pakenham had become Secretary and Treasurer to the reconstituted church committee and he and his partner John Maquay were later bankers to the church. Having relinquished the secretaryship to Maquay in November 1843, Pakenham resigned from the committee a year later and disappears completely from the Minute Books, except inasmuch as his name occurs in references to the bank. He is next mentioned as an individual when the committee proposed to invite him to discuss endowments with them in January 1849.[20] By this date a lot of water had passed under a lot of bridges and Pakenham's life had been transformed.

The last of his children, Montague, was born in Florence in August 1840, not long after the bank opened, but from then on he experienced more family loss than gain. In the winter of 1840–1841 his daughter Kate was desperately ill, but against all expectation recovered, only for her sister Elizabeth to die in February 1841. His wife of 26 years, Caroline, followed on 2 August 1844. He was left with the young Montague, 4 years old, as well as Kate and Louisa, who was 22 and 6 years later would marry Gerald Lake Brooks in Florence. John Maquay recorded how depressed Pakenham had been during his wife's final illness, although her death found him 'quite calm and resigned'. He spent the rest of the summer at Bagni, where he usually ran the summer branch of the bank, and in October went off with the family to Rome.[21] Here he met the widow Frances Julia Tollemache, born Julia Peters, at a service held in a private house.

Julia later recounted that when she learned that Pakenham had lost his wife 6 months previously her 'romantic self' had exclaimed, 'Oh, poor man!', only to be told (rather remarkably) by a Lady O., 'My dear, spare your sympathy, his heart is not broken.'[22] Soon afterwards the pair became engaged and on 8 May 1845 were married in Lord Holland's house at Florence, Robbins and Maquay being the only witnesses. John had been introduced to Julia two days before and described her pointedly (and percipiently) as 'a ladylike person ma fredda'.[23] The coldness of the second Mrs Pakenham is amply attested by her extraordinary spiritual autobiography. The unfortunate little Montague exclaimed, 'Mamma is kind to me, but mamma does not love me' (which she admitted), and 4 years into their marriage Pakenham himself told her, 'it is not possible for you to be a good stepmother.'[24]

There can be little doubt that Julia was a decisive influence in the transformation of Pakenham's rather pompous piety into a missionary zeal which let nothing stand in its way. In May 1848 he suddenly announced his intention to make over his interest in the bank to Montague. John, who seems to have had no previous inkling of this, was 'very sorry for it'. Social life largely ceased: John records that the Pakenhams dined out for the first time since their marriage on 14 May 1849. That the motive for Pakenham's withdrawal was to devote himself to missionary work is confirmed by his wife.[25] He regarded the 1848 revolution as a golden opportunity to print what he called instructive books in the Italian language. His greatest hope for the inculcation of truth was placed in the dissemination of the Bible in two translations – one by Martini, formerly Archbishop of Florence (which was countenanced by the Roman Church), and the other by Diodati, a sixteenth-century Lucchese version (which was not). Initially he hoped to appease the authorities by printing Catholic versions. This, along with much else, was explained in a long apologia which he addressed to Lord Palmerston from Bagni when the storm had broken.[26]

Pakenham claimed that the 'dissemination' had met little opposition even before 'facilities increased with the recent development of Constitutional liberty' in 1848. Restrictions on imports ceased, advertisements appeared in the papers for Bibles at reduced prices and 'no Bookseller's shop could be visited wh[ich] had not some on sale'. Political upheaval led to distress among the working classes at the end of the year and it occurred to certain members of a society established for poor relief that printing and binding the New Testament might be 'a means of extending relief perfectly in accordance wh [sic] the very spirit of the Book'. With the aid of the British & Foreign Bible Society in London, Pakenham had produced large impressions of both the Martini and the Diodati translations, 'without note or comment' (the necessary hallmark of an acceptable Protestant version). Governments came and went, and when 'the Reaction came around', with its apparent promise of stability, Pakenham approached Gino Capponi, head of the Provisional Government, and (he claimed) was given approval for his actions.

If he had some justification for believing that he had been licensed to continue, he failed to take account of changing times. On 11 May 1849 his premises were raided and Bibles, typefaces, even blank sheets of paper for printing seized and confiscated. His sense of injured innocence and outrage knew no bounds. He told Palmerston that he had resided in Tuscany for 12 years and had never had any dispute with the government; he had 'carefully abstained' from meddling in its political changes, but with the real interests of 'an interesting Country' at heart had 'endeavored by every proper means, to spread amongst them the sound principles of Truth'.[27] He admitted that at the present moment the inhabitants of the Grand Duchy scarcely knew 'by what Regime we are governed'. According to the Constitution there was ecclesiastical censorship of 'all works ex professo of a Religious description'; but – and here he slips into the first person plural, as speaking for a constituency – 'we insist' that the New Testament was not subject to ecclesiastical censorship, but was itself the standard by which all other religious works must be judged. This was a claim repeatedly made and repeatedly, if implicitly, rejected by the Catholic authorities.

Pakenham appealed for redress, and took the precaution of writing not only to Palmerston but to the Bible Society, so that Palmerston found Lord Ashley in his ear on 31 May. In Tuscany, all Pakenham could do was to put the matter in Hamilton's hands; but it was at this moment that his troubles began with the authorities in Lucca. Here he seems to have enjoyed an extraordinary latitude to evangelize, or perhaps in troubled times the authorities were slow to react. In June 1849 the Vicar of the Chapter of Lucca denounced him as the agent of Protestant proselytism, distributing books and pamphlets on religious subjects and keeping an elementary school without leave from the local authorities and even in spite of their repeated prohibitions in 1848 and before. The resultant enquiry produced a substantial dossier incorporating the evidence of a number of local witnesses, which was eventually transmitted to the Foreign Office in 1851.[28]

Not its least interesting feature was the conclusion that Mrs Pakenham was 'a more engaged propagandist than her husband'. Don Bartolommeo Lacchesi, rector of Ponte a Serraglio, perceptively noted that

> As long as the said Pakenham had his first wife he kept to himself as a prudent and honest man should. From the moment he returned here with his second wife about four years ago he gave himself up to circulate and disseminate books containing heterodox opinions and doctrines erroneous and in opposition to our Most Holy Religion.

Pakenham did not deny the charges. It would have been difficult to do so, given the number of individuals, including parish priests, who now had in their possession catechisms, copies of Diodati's Bible, and other Protestant tracts. He apparently promised to discontinue his activities, but did not do so; the school he had opened at Fornoli continued, as did the distribution of books. He even invited the dubious former Dominican Giacinto Achilli to Bagni, 'under pretext of getting him to preach in favour of Italian independence', but in fact he preached Protestantism.

Lacchesi had told his parishioners that they could not keep books given to them by Protestants, and had a number handed in to him. This did not necessarily implicate Pakenham, for there had been an Englishwoman from the Bible Society, who may or may not have been connected with him, also distributing tracts in the area. Lacchesi averred that Pakenham had openly declared his intention 'to make proselytes to his religion; and he repeated that this was a good vineyard, and that in two or three years all would be Protestants'. Faced with further complaints that Pakenham had continued to distribute tracts in defiance of prohibition, the Prefect of Lucca expelled him and his wife from the province in September 1849. On 25 September they left for Florence. Pakenham had ensured that he was a high-profile figure, identified as little disposed to heed Tuscan law.[29]

It was not until 17 October that Hamilton was able to report to Palmerston. He could as yet say little, since the affair was *sub judice*. A large quantity of translated Bibles, illegal by the laws of Tuscany, had been seized and would remain confiscated until the trial of the printers was over. Despite repeated warnings, Pakenham had continued to distribute tracts in Lucca, 'some of which are said to be of a political, as well as religious tendency'. The Tuscan government deemed his conduct 'too outrageous' for them to grant Hamilton's request for a fortnight's delay in his expulsion from Lucca. When Pakenham asked him whether he intended to take any further steps, Hamilton replied by affirming the right of any state 'to eject any Foreigner of whatever rank' (a point on which the Captain had somewhat dwelt), whom they deemed dangerous to good order. He did not think it his duty to do more.[30] The passing reference to Pakenham's status-consciousness is revealing.

Hamilton had overlooked one question which became central to the voluminous correspondence of the next year or so, and the Foreign Office duly asked it. What law was it that Pakenham had broken? The reply might well have closed the case officially. A 1743 law was still applicable and the more recent press law of 1848 had also been infringed. Hamilton was told that if Pakenham had been an Italian he would have been imprisoned; as an Englishman, he was ordered out of Lucca 'by way of admonition' and was not prevented from residing at Florence. This did not prevent him from composing another lengthy apologia for his philanthropy at Lucca and a rebuttal of the charge of 'incorrigible and opinionated proselytism'.[31]

The trial of the printers began on 19 January 1850. John Maquay noted that Pakenham attended as a witness in full British naval uniform. Whatever he hoped to achieve by this piece of bravado, the response from the Tuscan Government was immediate. On the 20th he was ordered to quit Tuscany within 10 days. On the 21st, John reported that the printers had been fined. In fact one of the printers had been acquitted and the other condemned to a fine of 50 dollars, the minimum the law allowed. Pakenham had met Landucci in Scarlett's presence, with the result that his expulsion from Tuscany was suspended 'for the present'.[32] This suspension proved short-lived.

Hamilton said that he had tried to persuade the authorities not to act so precipitately, but they were adamant that they had no option because of Pakenham's 'continued violation of the Laws in endeavouring to make proselytes to the Protestant Faith and his continued distribution of forbidden Tracts'. Had Pakenham really been so insensitive to his future prospects of residence as to continue to break the law? According to Hamilton, he positively declared the allegations to be false. Since returning from Lucca he had remained passive, 'with the exception of having given two tracts to a dying man in hospital'. Perhaps selective memory concealed more such offerings. Hamilton probably felt that he was doing what he could. He even forwarded a medical certificate from Pakenham's physician, which referred to the serious effects that 'mental agitation' from the events at both Lucca and Florence had had on him; if he were to be banished from Tuscany 'at this Season of the Year', it might prove fatal. At the interview with Landucci in Scarlett's presence, it had been agreed that a further investigation should take place. Meanwhile, according to Hamilton, 'every English gentleman, without exception, who has spoken to me on the Subject, blames Captain Pakenham's conduct'. Pakenham had for some time past given considerable offence to native Catholics, at a very sensitive moment.

Even if Hamilton was right, it did not prevent the British residents from launching petitions on Pakenham's behalf, signed in both Florence and Leghorn, which the Minister enclosed to the Foreign Office. Another was produced a few weeks later when Pakenham's expulsion was confirmed, and this too Hamilton sent on.[33] It was rare for the residents – or a substantial number of them – to emerge thus into the open as a body. The first petition read:

We the Undersigned residents in Florence, being subjects of Her Britannic Majesty, beg to represent to you that, having ascertained that the authorities have menaced our Countryman Captain Pakenham with expulsion from the Grand Duchy, on the allegation that he has committed a certain act in contravention of some regulations of the Country, the commission of which act Captain Pakenham directly and positively denies, and we from our knowledge of his character and of his rank in the service of Great Britain, firmly believe that denial to be sincere. Feeling this and perceiving that the Government can and ought to substantiate their accusation if true, we feel called upon, in the interest of all foreigners in Tuscany, but especially of such as are British Subjects, to say, that should the authorities carry into effect their threat, in the arbitrary manner proposed, our residence in Tuscany in future must necessarily be one of insecurity, and the faith we have hitherto reposed in the justice and hospitality of the Country be destroyed.

The signatures make interesting reading. At Florence we find Charles Lever, William Reynolds and Christopher Webb Smith. There were the Anglican clergymen Wolley and George Crossman, the Free Church minister Hanna, and the physicians Trotman and Allnatt. There was also Robert Browning, his one venture into the pages of the Foreign Office volumes. (Elizabeth did not sign, although one woman, Mrs Eddy, did.) At Leghorn, the clerical signatories included the chaplain Thomas Sleeman and the Free Churchmen Stewart and William Wingate. There was also a substantial cross-section of the business community: Henderson, Pate, the Elders, Dunn, Rae, all long-established merchants, and John Maquay's banking colleague Currell Smyth. There were the physicians John Gason and Henry Green, and Arthur de Noë Walker, who had a part to play in a future religious controversy. Not all those who signed the first petition signed the second, in which some new names appeared, including those of the artist Eugenio Latilla, the physicians Luard and Wilson, Edward Lombe and George Crossman's friend Major Gregorie. Browning was among those who signed for a second time.

While there were individuals here whom the Tuscan Government might not have been sorry to see depart, there were also some solid and unexceptionable citizens, whom not even the most fevered imagination could cast as subversives. Still more interesting, perhaps, are the missing names. Trollope, as it happened, was away from Florence, but there was no Maquay, no Plowden and no Sloane. It is hardly credible that this was out of ignorance of what was going on. Plowden and Sloane were both Catholic, both had powerful business interests and both enjoyed Grand Ducal favour. The same, without the Catholicism, could be said to apply to John Maquay. He was close to Pakenham, but had good reason at this stage to wish to keep his distance, nor would he have wanted to have his name associated with a process likely to fail.

Pakenham now decided that the time was ripe to pen another massive epistle to Lord Palmerston.[34] In it he assailed everybody and everything, although he admitted his entire responsibility for the printing of the bibles. He sounded quite disappointed that one of the printers had been acquitted on a technicality. An appeal against the 'impious' verdict was being made to the Court of Cassation and he was keen to impress on Palmerston that the legal issue had not been decided. Meanwhile it was necessary to proceed 'as quietly as possible, in order to avoid the intrigues of the Priests'. He asserted that the trial had caused 'throughout a great part of Italy a considerable sensation'. Now, albeit 'without any angry feelings', he attacked Hamilton.

Had Hamilton displayed energy 'at all commensurate with the necessities of the case', the problems at both Lucca and Florence would have come to nothing. His failure to take vigorous action in respect of Pakenham's expulsion from Lucca 'has led to all that has since transpired and that will yet take place, if some firm ground be not stood upon, and some simple, plain natural principles of justice be not insisted upon'. Since his return from Lucca, he had been subjected to all manner of annoyances. These included being summoned before the police to be interrogated by an 'unwashed dignitary' who was 'in personal appearance and in manner, of the standing of a hackney coachman' (a comment perhaps more revealing about Pakenham than it is about the interrogator). Pakenham denied having done anything detrimental to Roman Catholicism during his 13-year residence; all he had done was to print editions of the New Testament in the vulgar tongue. This was 'an offence which at Rome is unpardonable and the Government of Tuscany are now avowing that they are determined to uphold Roman Power'.

That was true enough, but Pakenham did not seem to think that they were within their rights to do so, asking, 'is it, my Lord, a thing to be permitted, that her Majesty's subjects are to be expelled from Tuscany on orders sent from

Rome?' If it were, it would be neither to the honour of Britain, 'nor for the benefit of the Country, now being driven back either to the darkness and servitude of the middle ages'. At the end of the letter he echoed the sentiment of the petition in his support: 'if some decisive step be not taken for the protection of British subjects in Tuscany, their security will be very small.' He clearly knew all about the petition, describing it as a 'public document'. Collective expressions of grievance are never welcome in an absolutist state, least of all a weak one prone to stand on its dignity.

Certainly the Tuscan Government felt justified in believing that he was a disturber of the peace. It concluded its 'further investigation' in record time, for on 2 February Pakenham was expelled from Tuscany at 12 hours' notice. The most that the embassy could win for him was an extension to 8 days. The second petition from the residents was entirely unavailing. It stressed the main point that Pakenham, whatever his provocations, was being expelled without due process or the production of evidence to which he could reply. It repeated that 'we can no longer feel any personal security, nor any confidence that in a similar manner, unsubstantiated grounds may not be made use of against any of us'. Hamilton told Webb Smith that he had been told that the 'fresh investigation' had given the government no reason to change its decision. He regretted the failure of his efforts, but reaffirmed what he had already told Pakenham, that any Government was at liberty to expel a foreigner without infringing international law and to withhold 'its hospitality from Foreigners, under the impression that their residence is prejudicial to internal tranquillity'.[35]

The British residents started from a valid concern for their own positions under an arbitrary and absolutist government. Pakenham himself had never been put on trial. In sticking to the wording he had received from the Tuscan Government, Hamilton may simply have been covering himself, but he was also clearly reminding the residents that if they wished for a quiet life they should keep their noses out of Tuscan affairs. All Pakenham could do, as John Maquay reported, was to set off for London with his wife 'to see what Palmerston will do'. Before departing, he fired off another broadside, in which he complained of bad faith on the part of the Tuscan Government. Scarlett, he said, had been promised that proceedings would be suspended indefinitely and if renewed would be 'in the form of accusation, enquiry and proof adduced'. Scarlett understood only that 'further investigation' had been promised.[36]

As to what Palmerston would do, or could do for that matter, the answer was, very little. Pakenham was not able to resettle permanently in Tuscany, and the full dossier of evidence was not dug out of the Tuscan Government until mid-1851. Palmerston admitted he had not had time to read it before he left office in the December of that year. This may have been a coded way of saying that he and the rest of the world had lost interest in a tedious self-publicist, prone to use the royal 'we', who wrote numerous long letters (on an unpleasant pale blue paper) which conveyed an inflated idea of his own importance and an incorrigible missionary zeal. Whatever may have been thought in the Foreign Office about the Tuscan laws on religion, Pakenham's capacity to get himself into hot water elsewhere in Italy confirmed that, whether or not he had broken any laws, he was an infernal nuisance. Despite the fears of the English residents there was no threat to those who simply wished to live in Tuscany, and there were no other expulsions of prominent long-term residents on religious grounds.

The Foreign Office therefore continued to keep its distance from Pakenham, who on arriving in England at the end of March submitted a full statement of his case to date and requested an interview with Lord Palmerston. What he got was a reference to the Law Officers of the Crown, who duly reported on 29 April that the Government 'is not called upon to take any further steps in this matter'.[37] Nor is it apparent what the Pakenhams achieved by seeing Gladstone, who recorded in his diary that he saw Mrs Pakenham on 10 July and the Captain on the 20th.[38] The government decided to confine itself to obtaining leave for him to return to Tuscany for long enough to settle his affairs, and would also pursue his (belated) demand to see a transcript of the evidence against him.[39] This last request was likely to prove the more troublesome to fulfil. Hamilton had seen the papers, shown no great interest in them and sent them back.

It was reasonable to request the Tuscan Government, via John Maquay and Hamilton, for 1 month's leave for Pakenham to return to Tuscany to settle his affairs, but this was undermined by a crass and ill-conceived piece of direct action. Pakenham exploited the limitations of nineteenth-century bureaucracy by equipping himself with a passport in Paris, countersigned by the Tuscan Consuls there and at Genoa, and turning up at Pisa, informing only Maquay. Here he was provided with a *carta di soggiorno* before the authorities realized what was happening. If he hoped thereby to stampede all and sundry into bowing to his demands, he was sadly mistaken. John acted immediately:

> found letter from Pakenham at Pisa and went to Scarlett & Minister of Foreign Affairs and then off to Pisa to advise him to leave Tuscany till Landucci sends an answer to his request for permission to come to Florence to settle his affairs … Pakenham had got a carta di soggiorno at Pisa and seemed inclined to brave it out, sent him a letter from Sir G H with the refusal of the government to allow him to come even for (a month) on account of his 'religious fanaticism!!' Poor Pakenham how small a degree of anxiety to teach ignorant people to read the Bible is sufficient to earn people nowadays the title of fanatic![40]

John combines a fundamental sympathy for Pakenham's position with a much greater realism. By contrast Pakenham complained vociferously about everything. There was the Tuscan Government's expulsion of him when he thought he had permission to stay, its continued persecution of him, the unjust confiscation of his property. Then there was Sir George Hamilton's failure to get him permission to return and to secure him justice. Hamilton had quoted the Tuscan Government's accusation of 'religious fanaticism' when he should have protested against it.

Pakenham insinuated that the Tuscan Government was more willing to grant his request for time than Hamilton was to support it.

All these complaints winged their way to Palmerston at the end of August, prompting Hamilton, sick and clearly at the end of his tether, to ask the Foreign Secretary rhetorically on 3 September, 'whether I have not reason to be offended at Captain Pakenham's language'. Complaining of Hamilton's alleged indifference and procrastination, Pakenham had uttered the vague threat that 'such a state of things must be submitted to the British Government and to the Examination of the British public'. Hamilton added that 'The Tuscan Government have opposed no obstacle to the settlement of Captain Pakenham's affairs by his Agents here'. He had that very day sent a passport to Mrs Pakenham at Massa.[41]

It was the last action that Sir George was ever to take. At 2 am on the following day he died; it is debatable how much Pakenham had contributed to that outcome. Scarlett immediately communicated with the Foreign Office and later gave an account of Hamilton's funeral on the 6th, which was attended by the diplomatic body, the Tuscan Foreign Minister and Prince Lichtenstein. Consul Macbean came up from Leghorn, and the Grand Duke expressed his condolences. On the 11th Pakenham was writing from Massa to Scarlett (presumably therefore he had heard the news), unable to believe 'that Lord Palmerston will permit a British Subject to be treated as we have been'.

The instructions that were sent to Scarlett as *chargé d'affaires* on 20 September indicated some change of emphasis. It was thought right that Pakenham should be allowed to return to settle his affairs, given his long residence. Scarlett was directed to ask, perhaps somewhat redundantly, what Pakenham had 'lately done which is so different from his conduct during the long period of his residence in Tuscany, as to require and justify his expulsion from the Grand Duchy'. He was also to ask whether he was such a danger to 'the tranquillity of Tuscany as to make it unsafe for the Government to allow him sufficient time for making those various arrangements in regard to his property which his removal from Tuscany must require'. That Pakenham was 'wrong-headed and pertinacious' was acknowledged, but that was no reason why he should not be treated with fairness and justice. It was to be suspected that he had fallen victim to 'the impulse of a spirit of reactionary Bigotry connected with the turn which political events have lately taken in Italy'.[42]

Scarlett's first attempt, which won 15 days with a possible further extension of 1 month, foundered on the rock of that intractable personality. Pakenham refused to receive anything as an act of grace and insisted on what he saw to be his right to justice. He did not seem to comprehend what irritation he had caused by taking the law into his own hands in returning to Pisa. Scarlett also fell foul of the Foreign Office's demand for plain answers to the questions which had been raised in the despatch of 20 September. His attempts to see officially the documents by which Pakenham was condemned were again rebuffed. Unsurprisingly, the Tuscan Government continued to assert that they had done Pakenham a kindness by not putting him on trial and that they were still willing to allow him back to settle his affairs. Landucci could not resist landing a low blow:

> as Her Majesty's Government have recently shown some susceptibility on the subject of Papal intervention in England he hoped the objection entertained by the Tuscan Government to Protestant interference in a Roman Catholic state would now be thought more pardonable than before.[43]

A more serious blow was landed, or at least threatened, early in 1851, when the Tuscans accused the English Church itself of proselytism. Not only did this compound the difficulties the embattled Scarlett had to cope with, but it compelled an unwilling British Government to take official notice. On 9 January Casigliano wrote to Scarlett with specific allegations and reminded him of the conditions under which permission had been granted for this *oratoire*. It was to be wholly and exclusively private, but the Grand Ducal Government had been informed that all those who desired to take part in the service were freely admitted. The custom of praying and catechizing in the Italian language had been introduced, with the result that many Catholic Tuscan subjects 'imbibe these principles and sentiments contrary to the dominant religion, and publicly propagate the same'. This would not be tolerated, and the Government were resolved, if action was not taken, to take all necessary measures to prevent Tuscans from participating in the Anglican services. Casigliano was careful at this stage not to threaten the actual existence of the church. Scarlett submitted the accusations to the scrutiny of the church, and his reply to Casigliano on 16 January was largely based on Webb Smith's to him 2 days previously.

Smith's letter was detailed, since he said it was the wish of the Vestry to provide sufficiently full information to disabuse the Tuscan Government of their groundless apprehensions. There had been no endeavour, either in the public services of the church or by private means, 'to interfere with the State Religion of Tuscany, or to lead Tuscan subjects to embrace Protestant principles'. No custom had been introduced of saying prayers or reading catechisms in the Italian language and no language had been used in the church save English. Tuscans could not have been seduced by 'services wholly unintelligible to them' (a moot point, perhaps). The next argument appeared to be more telling: no one was admitted to the body of the church who did not pay for his seat and to the best of the Vestry's knowledge there were no Roman Catholics on the books. A gallery was set apart for servants and poor people who could not pay for their seats. Smith skated lightly over the issue of their nationality – who ensured that they were all British? So rarely did Italians enter the church that, when it happened, the Select Vestry assumed that they were police officers checking whether any objection could be made to the service – a neat but hardly decisive answer. Smith concluded that the allegations had been wholly disproved and that there had been no abuse. Scarlett smugly replied to Casigliano, enclosing Smith's letter. He said he had not been mistaken in believing that the accusations advanced would be found on due investigation to be groundless and erroneous.

He then added a striking statement which did not appear in Smith's letter: 'I am further authorised to state, that no Protestant books have ever been translated, printed or circulated among Tuscan subjects with the sanction of the church in question.' Smith had in fact studiously avoided any mention of the translation and circulation of Protestant books. He must have known that the gap between the activities of the church as an institution and those of prominent members of it was very small. Leaving Pakenham aside, there would have been some very queasy consciences at the Special Select Vestry Meeting which met on 14 January to consider their reply, notably that of the chairman himself, John Maquay. John would have found it hard to disprove that he had played no role whatsoever in seducing his wife from her Catholicism or that he had not been and was not going to be involved in Bible running. His diary is typically gnomic: 'Home after a Select Vestry Meeting Communication from the Government as to the Church.' That evening, Webb Smith, Count Guicciardini and the Free Church Minister Hanna came to dine with him.[44]

When he sent the correspondence to the Foreign Office Scarlett was able to report that the explanations appeared to be satisfactory to both Landucci and Casigliano, who conceded that they might have been misinformed.[45] This rather strengthens the impression that (whatever information the government had received) the complaint had been in the nature of a shot across the bows. The new reality was that Tuscan police now attended the church service on a regular basis. The Foreign Office response to Scarlett's despatch was in the circumstances gratuitous. It claimed that the correspondence showed the weakness of relying on information presented by secret informers. Her Majesty's Government were confident that the British residents at Florence had complied with the conditions on which permission was given for the establishment of a Protestant chapel. A painful impression of intolerance was manifested in Casigliano's communication, 'which affords so remarkable a contrast with the liberal and enlightened system which prevails in the United Kingdom in regard to the exercise of religious belief'. One hopes that the Irish Roman Catholic Sheil, to whom the despatch was directed, appreciated the irony of the situation.[46]

Scarlett had also passed on the news that the Prussians, sponsors and protectors of the Swiss Church, had bowed to Tuscan complaints about their Italian-language services which (perfectly legitimately) had been held since 1850 for the benefit of Italian-speaking Swiss Protestants. There was no question but that certain zealous Swiss ministers had been involved in proselytism, although the more moderate Colombe was allowed to continue the services of the Swiss Church. The arrest of Italian Protestants, particularly after the edict of 25 April 1851 which allowed summary police process without resort to the courts, followed by bans and internal exile, turned the screw. A number of prominent converts were hit, of whom Count Guicciardini was the most prominent in Tuscany and the Madiai would be the most famous internationally.[47]

In the midst of these disturbances the English Church suffered another blow, when the Rev. George Robbins submitted his resignation to the Vestry meeting of 19 February 1851. He had been appointed rector of Courteenhall in Northamptonshire, but his departure was very far from being the last Florence saw of him. He had two sisters who had married Tuscan noblemen (one had been very soon widowed, many years before) and as the years went by he continued to spend much of his time in Florence. The Bishop of Gibraltar replaced him, not altogether satisfactorily, by the Rev. Henry O'Neill.[48]

Meanwhile, what may be termed the Pakenham papers had generated a somewhat farcical situation. Very early in the New Year Scarlett expressed his regret that Sir George Hamilton had not made more use of them; he himself had seen them only briefly, receiving the impression that they made a case against Pakenham. Now the Tuscans were resisting pressure to make them available once more, but during his brief tenure of office Sheil showed considerable diplomatic skill in obtaining a sight of them (albeit unofficially and confidentially), so that he could show them (unofficially and confidentially) to the Foreign Office. The Tuscans also agreed to allow Pakenham back for at least a month and perhaps longer to settle his affairs, on condition of his good behaviour in not undertaking anything other than observance of his own personal religion. Sheil was on the point of going to see Pakenham at Genoa when he died on 25 May 1851.[49]

Before he did, he had intervened helpfully in another high-profile case. On 7 May 1851 John Maquay's dinner guest Count Guicciardini, a nobleman of ancient Florentine lineage, was caught reading St John's Gospel privately with six companions and sentenced (without trial) to internal exile at Volterra for 6 months. The story was instantly widely publicized in England. Sheil on his own initiative saw Guicciardini in prison and obtained access to him for some of his friends. In return he received information about Pakenham, with whom Guicciardini was 'very intimate'. Guicciardini was soon allowed to leave the country, settling for a time in England.[50]

Scarlett, once again *chargé d'affaires*, reaped the reward of Sheil's diplomacy. On 11 June he was able to report that he was in possession of the Pakenham documents which, after frantic copying (there were some 150 pages of evidence), he sent to Palmerston on 14 July. Scarlett's own opinion was clear.

> Without pretending to defend the usual intolerance and illiberality of Roman Catholic Governments in Matters of religion, there can be very little doubt that in a Roman Catholic point of view Captain Pakenham has rendered himself wilfully culpable.[51]

The Tuscan decision to release the papers on condition that the British Government would agree to Pakenham's being admitted for a limited time only to settle his affairs seemed entirely justified. Even if Palmerston had had time to read the papers, the British Government was by no means on the front foot, either in this affair or that of the Stratfords which had just broken, not to mention the recent accusations against the English Church.

After Palmerston's dismissal at the end of 1851 and just before his own downfall, Granville took the precaution of referring all the papers to the Law Officers. They poured cold water indeed: as he told Pakenham on 20 February 1852, the Government was not entitled to interfere any further. Now that this was clear, Pakenham was asked whether he would accept the offer Landucci had made in the previous September of a limited permission for him to come to settle his Tuscan affairs. Under protest and with much circumlocution, he did.[52] On 12 April he at last returned with his family to Florence. Scarlett thought that Landucci would permit him to remain for as long as he needed. On 29 May Bulwer wrote that Pakenham had gone to Lucca, having stayed longer than a month, but Casigliano had reported that he was proselytizing again and begged Bulwer to encourage him to leave the country in accordance with the agreement. In the event it was not necessary; Pakenham was soon on his way to Massa, getting into more trouble there. The man was incorrigible, but at least he was now out of Tuscany.[53]

By this time yet another case of 'persecution' was headline news. Less fortunate than Guicciardini, Francesco and Rosa Madiai were arrested in August 1851 and languished in prison till June 1852 before being brought to trial for proselytism, whereupon Francesco was sentenced to 56 months' imprisonment with hard labour and Rosina to 46 months in prison. Both were released and banished from the country in March 1853. It is questionable how much influence the international campaign on their behalf – waged not just by the British but by the Prussians and the Americans – had in facilitating their release.[54]

Pakenham's expulsion from Tuscany and his subsequent attempts to return therefore coincided, unfortunately for him, with a heightened sense of irritation on the part of the Tuscans at what they saw as British interference in their internal affairs. They could accept that the British Government had a right to ask questions about Pakenham, a British subject, but Guicciardini and the Madiai were all Tuscan subjects. It seemed that the Foreign Office was being driven both by the newspapers, which, as the Tuscans saw it, the British failed to control, and by a variety of Protestant organizations in England which they both despised as heretics and execrated as cover for political subversives and revolutionaries.

There was some justification for this analysis on both counts. The row over the re-establishment of the Catholic hierarchy in England, together with the revelations of non-attendance at church produced by the census of 1851, temporarily bade fair to dominate government policy and made the noise generated by the various Protestant pressure groups seem for a time to be more momentous than in fact it was. Certainly there were many in these organizations who saw no distinction between the overthrow of Roman Catholicism in Tuscany and the overthrow of the Grand Duke. Ironically, their campaigns in favour of Guicciardini and the Madiai distracted attention from Pakenham, an increasingly forgotten man. Pakenham's fate impinged directly on the British residents, but they are almost totally silent about the Tuscan converts.

There were reasons for British interest in the Madiai. Rosa had been 17 years in the service of General Sir Henry Cumming and subsequently in that of Lady Caroline Townley; she had spent many years in England and spoke English well. Cumming called her 'a person of strong principles and unvarying propriety of conduct'. When his son-in-law, Mr Tod, went to Florence as *attaché* and fell mortally ill, 'Rosina Madiai was unremitting in her attention and services to Mr Tod and my daughter.'[55] Francesco had spent some of his early years in America before he met Rosa and their late marriage in 1842 was clearly one of affection as well as religious belief, although their conversion took place after their marriage. They were well known to English people to whom they let lodgings at their address on Piazza Santa Maria Novella. From the time of their arrest they were separated. Here was the stuff of which martyrs were made.

Somewhat unwisely, the Tuscans also arrested Captain Arthur de Noë Walker, who was visiting the Madiai house when the police raided it. Whether or not he was expounding the scriptures at this moment, it was agreed that that there was an Italian Bible on the table 'and other books were afterwards removed by the officers from the table where the party had been sitting, and a similar Bible taken also from the pocket of Mr Walker', which he always carried with him. He was arrested on the evening of 17 August and spent 21 hours in prison before Landucci ordered his release, warning however that if subsequent investigation proved there was a case to answer he would be rearrested. On 5 September Scarlett reported that there would be no proceedings against him, as there was no Tuscan law forbidding one Protestant to preach to another. It was more to the point that Walker was English; neither Guicciardini nor the Madiai were allowed to get away with the claim that they were merely Protestants exhorting one another. Scarlett vouchsafed the helpful opinion that 'Mr Walker is reported to be one of the Sect called by the name of "Plymouth Brethren", whose religious opinions incline to Communism'.[56]

Walker was unquestionably an English gentleman, articulate and outraged. Born in Florence in 1820, he had a wide range of family links and friends there, including his sisters Gertrude (wife of Count Antonio Baldelli) and Harriet, whose husband Captain Fleetwood Wilson intervened during his brief imprisonment. He had been in the Indian Army, was or had been a student at the University of Pisa, and later served in the Crimea; afterwards he was a homeopathic physician in England, strongly opposed (like his sister Gertrude) to vivisection. He was an art-lover who bequeathed paintings to the Uffizi Gallery, and a close friend of Walter Savage Landor. Unfortunately, from the Tuscan Government's viewpoint, he was also a friend of Guicciardini, and had a number of contacts in England who would not be backward in publicizing his cause.[57]

One of these was Samuel Prideaux Tregelles (another self-proclaimed friend of Guicciardini), who in November 1851 corresponded with Palmerston.

Like many others, Tregelles referred pointedly to 'the unhindered liberty with which Roman Catholics may profess and propagate their doctrines in England'. He acknowledged that (as Palmerston pointed out) 'there is no Tuscan law which forbids one Protestant preaching to another the doctrines of his religious belief', but averred (with explicit reference to Guicciardini) that 'not merely preaching but even reading the Word of God in Italian or possessing it, is now in several instances severely punished'. The circle was completed when on 28 August Guicciardini wrote to Palmerston from Upper George Street, Portman Square, about both Walker and the Madiai.[58] In the eyes of the British Protestant faithful, these cases constituted one indivisible whole, and Walker's arrest helped to unleash the hounds in support of the Madiai in England.

It was with the Madiai squarely on his agenda that Scarlett, late in September 1852, set on foot an enquiry into 'the facilities, or otherwise, for the exercise of Protestant worship in Tuscany, by Natives & Foreigners'. It is not clear whether he was acting under instruction from London. The episode is best documented in a Letter Book rather sporadically compiled by Christopher Webb Smith, who was given the task of collecting the information.[59] On 1 October he started to write letters to the ministers of the other Protestant churches in Tuscany, asking for answers to a set of questions, and concluding with a caution against giving publicity to them, 'as, although there is nothing to demand secrecy in them, yet prudence dictates the inexpediency of their being made the subject of remarks & surmises by others'.

It seems that when Smith wrote to Stewart at Leghorn, his first letter never arrived; Stewart suspected that his mail was tampered with and asked Smith always to write 'care of Henderson'. He was pleased that the embassy was taking an interest 'and I believe it is not one moment too soon – as the Ministers if they had their own way would speedily shut up all our Churches'.[60] On 3 November Webb Smith made a note that he had arranged a meeting with a Mr Savi, having recollected that the latter 'had been sent for and molested in spring last, touching his being a Protestant and attending our own Church'. Here was at least one Italian Protestant who was known to have been a member of the Anglican congregation. The meeting took place, but Smith made only a private memorandum of what passed, which does not survive.

It was against this background of intense activity that the newly formed Protestant Alliance decided to send a deputation to Florence to intercede with the Grand Duke in favour of the Madiai. It was to be led by Lord Roden, assisted by Lord Cowan and Captain Trotter, and went with the good wishes and pious hopes of all right-thinking people in England, including the *Times*. Bulwer was instructed on 8 October to give all possible unofficial support to the deputation and 'endeavour to procure for them the honour of an audience with the Grand Duke'. Bulwer had been in Rome since 7 September, but as soon as he heard of the imminent arrival of the deputation he returned hotfoot to Florence (not failing to stress how ill he was).

He was too late by 5 days.[61] The deputation's request to see the Grand Duke had been politely but firmly rejected, and they had to retire empty-handed. This may be attributed to their naivete (the Grand Duke would accept that they had no political motives and therefore they did not require diplomatic support), arrogance (their mere names should ensure an audience) or stupidity (it was easier to refuse to see them if the request had not come from the embassy, for no insult to Great Britain could then be construed). Given that neither the Prussian representative nor Bulwer was having much impact it is doubtful whether a private mission would have had much chance of success, but its behaviour certainly ensured its failure.[62]

Officially at least, the English Church in Florence maintained a profound silence on the Madiai. Its members must have heaved a sigh of relief when the Roden mission left Tuscany, for the visit caught them between a rock and a hard place. Aware of the furore in England, but trying to survive in a hostile environment and stung by the recent Tuscan accusations against the Church, the Select Vestry was well aware of the risk if it were to lift a finger to entertain Roden, let alone take any part in an approach to the Grand Duke over the Madiai. The special Select Vestry summoned on 20 October to consider a letter from the Rev O'Neill informing them of the mission produced a masterpiece of diplomacy. They did not 'deem it advisable to take any part officially in the deputation to which the letter alludes, though they cannot but take a deep interest in the subject'. John Maquay reported, 'I attended a Select Vestry Meeting whether we should do anything on the occasion of Lord Roden and deputation o/a Madiai determined in negative.'[63] There is no other reference to the issue in the Church Minute Books.

The Grand Duke seemed more than ever determined to outface his critics. As well as restoring the death penalty for acts of public violence against the government and against religion, for murder and other offences, the powers of the executive were increased independently of ordinary tribunals – delegates, prefects and sub-prefects were empowered to inflict confinement in a fortress for 3 years without trial. The attention of the police was called to the movements of foreigners, and although this was probably directed against refugees from other Italian states, Bulwer thought it likely to impinge also on the British.[64] As Elizabeth Browning remarked with some humour, 'The worst version of the Madiai story is the right one ... all badness is credible in this place.'[65] Not only were the Tuscans understandably irritated by foreign intervention in their dealings with their own subjects; they did not comprehend an alien approach to religion. Scarlett had a revealing exchange with Casigliano:

He asked me whether open proselytism against our church would be tolerated in England, to which of course I answered that no measures were ever adopted by Her Majesty's Government, and no laws existed to repress a system of proselytism to the doctrines of Rome.[66]

On 24 January 1853 the *Standard* printed a letter from Florence which asserted that 'There are much fewer of our countrymen now residing in Tuscany than there used to be before the revolution' and that the Grand Duke was now disinclined to encourage them. Half the lodgings in the town were said to be unlet. (It is doubtful how true much of this was.) The paper rejoiced editorially 'that our countrymen are avoiding Florence and its beggarly court; and we trust that the day is not distant when it will be held infamous for an Englishman to expend a single paolo in the accursed den of persecution, or upon its worthless productions'.

The writer became both apoplectic and preposterous at a report that Bulwer was in Rome negotiating with the Pope for the release of the prisoners: 'This is strange language for Englishmen to hear. Why, the whisper of a wish on the part of England ought to have been potential to unbar the dungeons of the persecuting tyrant.'

The sudden release of the Madiai on 15 March 1853 caught everybody by surprise. Erskine telegraphed the news on 17 March, Scarlett following with more detail in a despatch dated the 28th.[67] Francesco and Rosa had embarked at Leghorn for Marseille on the 16th, quickly and secretly, with French passports. Macbean got to hear about it by accident and saw them on board the steamer, supplied with warm clothes. The Pope and the French government appeared to have been active in recommending clemency. The French had maintained a distance from the British agitation, but were now seeking British support against Russia, and they had worked on the Pope – one of the few to whom the Grand Duke would listen. Elizabeth Browning, an uncritical admirer of Louis Napoleon, eagerly accepted that it was all his doing, as did the Reverend Hanna, her informant.[68]

True to form, the country had the news almost as quickly as the British Government did. The *Post* and the *Chronicle* carried the story on 19 March, and full accounts followed in most newspapers over the next fortnight. There was much portentousness and complacency and a general agreement that the Grand Duke had hardly enhanced his standing in the world at large. There was also a contribution from the Reverend George Robbins, who on 10 May delivered a sermon, subsequently printed, in which he declared that

> It has been my lot (during a residence of fourteen years as British Chaplain in Tuscany) to see and lament so much of the workings of Roman Catholicism on the minds of her deluded victims, that I cannot but shudder at the idea of the bare possibility of England being again enslaved in her soul-destroying chains.[69]

On 11 May 1853 John Maquay attended the baptism of a Jewish physician called Marco Guastalla, and on the following day his marriage to a widow whom both John and the Trollopes had known for some years, Harriet Burdett.[70] Already she had entered into one engagement which came to nothing, and her appearances in the diary tend to be accompanied by John's trademark multiple exclamation marks. This marriage resulted in a soap opera which can be followed through the diary.

First Harriet left Guastalla because of quarrels with his mother and brother, John and Trollope attempting mediation, and then she unexpectedly went back to him. He himself, some months later, ejected his mother and brother from the house.

Guastalla's baptism took place in interesting times. That he went through it in order to marry seems clear enough, but there is no evidence that this was a marriage of convenience. Even though (in obedience to the Pope) the Grand Duke was currently abrogating Jewish civil liberties, baptism should not have been necessary to enable him to continue practising as a physician (if he did).[71] The Catholic church would have welcomed him with open arms, but it was one of the theoretical conditions on which the Protestant churches were tolerated in Tuscany that they dealt only with what might be termed cradle Protestants.[72] Technically Guastalla could be regarded as a proselyte; but his conversion seems to have created no stir. There was plenty of other combustible material at hand.

Pakenham was but one of several who sought to place the Bible in the hands of the Italians, and the enterprise neither began nor ended with him. There were plenty of channels through which Bibles arrived in Italy, although few were quite so brazen as Alexander Keith and Andrew Bonar, who on their way to the Holy Land in 1839 had stopped off at Leghorn and unloaded a crate of Bibles which they distributed on the quayside. They were arrested but released without charge.[73] The British and Foreign Bible Society, which produced a Bible in 1841 which sold at 3 pauls a copy in Florence, was also active, as were the Evangelical and Protestant Alliances. Before 1848 it was all rather *ad hoc*. The revolution, which inaugurated a brief free-for-all, and the Grand Ducal reaction gave the impetus to organization. An Italian Evangelical Publication Society was established in Scotland which raised funds with which it produced Bibles and a number of other religious publications. Favourite titles were McCrie's *Reformation in Italy, Sermons* by Chalmers, and the *Westminster Confession of Faith* in a translation by Misses Rae and Pate, stalwarts of the Church in Leghorn. The Co-ordinating Committee at the Tuscan end, which was functioning by October 1850, consisted of Stewart, Hanna, and Colombe and Malan of the Swiss Church.

If Stewart and Hanna were major protagonists and the English Church in Florence kept its distance, this did not mean that all members of that church were innocents. Pakenham made himself conspicuous, but there was also John Maquay, whose Presbyterian origins gave him a sympathy with the Scots even while he took an active role within the Anglican Church. While both Stewart and Hanna had to avoid being ordered out of Tuscany, John Maquay as banker, underwriter of Grand Ducal loans and presenter of Americans at court, had a public position to maintain. The diaries contain only the barest hints of what he was up to.

The most explicit occurs just before the end of the revolutionary epoch. On 12 January 1849 John 'dined with Pakenham who had a meeting of Vaudois about printing the bible in Italian'. On 7 January 1850, not long before the trial which led to Pakenham's expulsion, he remained in town 'dining with Pakenham to meet some Italians', an enigmatic remark to make in the middle of Tuscany. On the very day that the Select Vestry considered the Tuscan Government's accusations against the English Church, Webb Smith, Hanna and Guicciardini dined with him, and Hanna was a frequent guest at his parties thereafter.[74] John must have known that Pakenham had borrowed from the bank to print his bibles in Tuscany during 1848–1849. He contrived to remain friends with him; he was the only person perceived to have any influence with him when he made his ill-advised return to Pisa, and he visited him subsequently in the south of France.

While all this might be regarded as circumstantial, the correspondence between Stewart and Hanna cannot be easily explained away. The coded references in Stewart's letter of 12 February 1851 are fairly transparent:

> Have you heard of an immense number of 'incorruptible seeds,' 'sweeter than honey from the comb' – having been landed in the Maremma; which they want to sell for a perennial crop? Ask G about them or Bet, as the information came from him. G was offered a thousand at three p. each. Of course he could not take such a supply; it is too costly for his purse: but it seems impossible to allow them to be taken away again for a soil so well adapted for the growth of them as Tuscany is, and when there has been so much demand for them. I hear the offer is only a tenth part of the stock. Now I think our friends in Ed – gh would like to have some of these, and as you have money of theirs in your hands that you could not better lay it out than in buying a considerable stock of these 'incorruptible seeds' on their account.

Stewart goes on to suggest that Hanna 'should write to P at Genoa and get him to give the £30 he was to get, as it is the best speculation he could possibly make and a famous revenge besides'. He was going to consult with the Swiss doctor about investing. Hanna replies on 21 February:

> I had heard of the Grossetto seeds, and was quite disposed to invest. In short we have no difficulty in taking a thousand, if they are sent. Mr Maquay, G., Miss Senhouse, Miss Grant, Miss Taylor, and I, form a joint stock company in re, so that there cannot be much difficulty.

The notion that these two are talking about gardening can be dismissed. P is clearly Pakenham; G is no less obviously Guicciardini, for we are told later that 'G has been at length called up before our friends the Delegates, whom he posed, puzzled and perplexed. One of our friends in whose house the reunions were held had been warned, and it is not prudent to meet any longer chez lui'. There is much more in like vein, hinting at substantial organization as well as finance.[75] Executive action was undertaken by a consortium of Leghorn merchants, of which Messrs Henderson were the most prominent. They imported Bibles under various disguises ('stationery' was a favourite), and these were stored in warehouses until they could be safely broken down into small parcels and taken by trusted couriers to

Florence by railway or private coach. Such a courier was Catherine de Swetschine, a formidable lady, daughter of a Russian nobleman and the wife of the architect Henry Roberts. She used her voluminous skirts, we are told, to profitable effect.[76]

Another key figure was Thomas Humble Bruce. Born in Newcastle in 1813, he received a deeply religious upbringing. He combined academic and religious enthusiasms, and it was hardly surprising that when he gravitated to Leghorn in 1846, at much the same time as Stewart, they should rapidly discover affinities. He became involved in running a school for the English at Leghorn and collaborated with Stewart, often secretly carrying Bibles from Leghorn to Florence and sheltering converts in his house. At the same time he began to collaborate with the Waldensian church and especially with Giovanni Ribetti, who at the time was pastor of the Leghorn community.[77] The trial of Pakenham's printers in January 1850 does not seem to have been a deterrent. By December 1850 a secret press was set up in Florence, the funds furnished by a rich American, Mr Lenox of New York, 'the committee being aware of a propaganda coup of imprint made in Florence.'[78]

Another person involved in the Bible trade was Frederick Thompson, British Vice Consul at Leghorn from 1839 to 1852. It is doubtful whether Macbean knew of this, but it is not doubtful what the Foreign Office would have said if they had known that one of their servants was breaking Tuscan law. His daughter Mary remembered:

Sometime in the 40's my father had a room in our house which was always locked up. It was full of Bibles in all the well known languages of the time and many publications of the Religious Tract Society and my father distributed Italian Bibles secretly through friends. Having so much to do with sailors of various nations he distributed Bibles and other literature among them. In what we called the Bible room, I was his chief help, though my mother came sometimes when we were extra busy. My father always said that the Jews were great helpers in distributing Bibles among the Italians. Once 500 Bibles were sent to us secretly in a large wooden case, in sheets, just as they came from the printers in England. We, in Leghorn, in that locked room cut and folded them accordingly to their pages, sorted them and arranged all the books of each Bible according to their proper order, and in chapters etc. Then some way, I cannot remember how, they were sent to be bound. An Italian lawyer Avvocato Chieso [sic] often came to help us over them, he was a secret Protestant. Mama sometimes helped us, and occasionally Helen did so, but at that time she was only 11 years old and very delicate, so she was seldom asked to come. I was, I suppose nearly 13. Some time after that papa gave it all up. He must have had the Bible room two or three years then.

Thompson's use of the Jews, who would not obviously have attracted attention, is a fascinating detail. Despite his diplomatic position, he was taking a considerable risk in the conditions of the Austrian occupation. He is believed to have given up in 1851 and emigrated to New Zealand in the course of 1852.[79]

Many years later, with the Grand Duke impotently fuming in Rome, Francesco Madiai addressed an admiring meeting at Harrison's Rooms in Clifton, Bristol. His words, delivered in Italian and translated by 'a gentleman', were reported on 14 June 1862 in the *Bristol Mercury*. He gave a pathetic account of his sufferings in prison, but also revealed facts which might have a little discomfited some of his defenders in 1852–1853. At the time of his imprisonment

> it was very difficult to get Bibles into Florence. He arranged with a grocer to bring them in casks to Leghorn, pitched at the top and bottom, so that the custom-house officers, when they examined the casks, thought they only contained pitch, whereas they were full of Bibles. That grocer sent them by another grocer to a third person, from whose house Madiai brought them in lots of forty and fifty at a time to his own residence. That plan, however, was found out, and his house was watched in consequence. He then took them to the shop of a tobacconist, and also to the residence of a merchant. A Miss Johnson, who visited his house, presented him with a beautiful quarto Bible. The officers came to his house to search for it but he put it into a footpan, and they marched past it several times without discovering it. From that Bible he was in the habit of reading to about fifty friends who came thither to hear the word of God.

If the imprisonment of the Madiai provoked a reaction, it was not surprising that the imprisonment of Miss Margaret Cunningham in 1853 provoked one even more dramatic if rather shorter-lived. The story was broken by the *Morning Post*, which on 20 September published, under the heading AMATEUR MISSIONARIES, the letter of 'An Englishman', written on the 13th from Bagni. It tells the full story and passes judgment on it:

> A circumstance occurred here yesterday, of which I hasten to apprise you, as it will most probably be attended with results both disagreeable to the English residents in Tuscany, and embarrassing to the relations of the English Government with this country. An English lady, Miss Cunningham, some few days back, committed the great imprudence of distributing Protestant tracts in the neighbouring village of Lugliano. Some of the inhabitants warned her of the impropriety of her proceeding, and protected her from the exasperated feelings of other of the peasants, who were preparing to pelt her with stones and seriously injure her. She regained the baths in safety, but on the following day had the egregious folly to repeat the experiment at another village, called Benabbio. The priest, on discovering what had occurred, descended into the baths, and informed the delegate of police of the behaviour of Miss Cunningham. Thereupon she was arrested, and, escorted by an office of gendarmerie, conveyed to the prison at Lucca – one friend being allowed to accompany her, but with the express injunction of speaking only in Italian, on pain of being immediately separated, and Miss Cunningham kept in solitary confinement.

Some of the English residents addressed themselves to the Chamberlain of the Grand Duke (who is at present at the baths), and promised the immediate departure of Miss Cunningham from his states if he would release her from confinement and overlook the offence. A speedy answer was returned, to the effect that the Grand Duke declined to interfere, and must allow the law to take its course. The affair remains at present in this state. The lady is in prison at Lucca, under the charge of endeavouring to convert, or, as it is viewed by the Italians, to seduce the people from their faith; and, by the new civil code, lately promulgated, the punishment for such an offence is fixed at five or ten years' imprisonment, with hard labour. By this time the services of the British Legation in Florence will have, of course, been required by the lady's family in the attempt to relieve her from her serious position. I do not hazard nor conjecture upon the result, but no one can for one moment entertain a doubt as to the gross culpability of Miss Cunningham's proceedings, or of her excessive folly in offending the religious feelings of a nation whose hospitality has been extended to her.

This letter was reprinted in the *Liverpool Mercury* on 23 September and the *Manchester Times* on the 24th. The *Spectator* took a similarly unsympathetic view of Margaret Cunningham's conduct: if the laws of Tuscany were objectionable she did not have to go there. Doubtless an outcry would be raised on her behalf, but British official intervention should be limited to securing a proper trial. England could go to war with Tuscany for the sake of liberty and Miss Cunningham, but it was doubtful whether any Minister would do so, or the public support him.

On the 27th, the *Chronicle* observed that the Grand Duke appeared not to be living in the modern world. Not content with the Madiai affair, the Tuscans had now imprisoned a lineal descendant of John Knox (much was made, humorously and otherwise, of Miss Cunningham's supposed ancestry). Having delivered a sideswipe at the *Pilgrim's Progress*, 'that most tedious allegory', which it was believed she had been distributing, the writer described 'the insulted dignity of the British lion' and the various reactions to it. Miss Cunningham was 'a very wrong-headed young lady, who would have been much better employed in verifying her "Murray," or looking to her knitting needles'. Doubtless it was wrong, and bigoted, to make the distribution of tracts a criminal offence, but if so it was, it was her duty to abstain. That she was not all that novel a phenomenon was indicated by the writer's quotation of Thomas Hood's *Ode to Rae Wilson, Esq.*, written some 8 years previously:

> Why leave a serious, moral, pious home –
> Scotland, renowned for sanctity of old –
> Far distant Tuscany to rate and scold
> For doing as the Romans do at Rome?
> ....
>
> People who hold such absolute opinions
> Should stay at home in Protestant dominions.

These early views of Miss Cunningham's behaviour seemed to promise that no great Protestant uproar would be created; but appearances were deceptive.

Yet again, the Foreign Office found itself having to respond to events which were already known of in the public domain. Worse, thanks to the speed with which the crisis unfolded, its instructions to Scarlett, who was again in charge thanks to Bulwer's unfortunate absence, were often out of date. It is not quite clear why Scarlett chose to ignore the telegraph (the newspapers were certainly using it) and did not write to the Foreign Office until 17 September.[80] Miss Cunningham had been arrested on the 12th, on the eve of her departure for England, and Scarlett knew of it by letter from Sir William Miller and a visit from Miller and the Rev. Gordon on the 13th. Still perhaps sore from the dressing-down he had received over Mather, he may have believed that by strenuous activity he could solve the problem, present the Foreign Office with a solution and thus restore his personal standing. He saw Landucci and Lami, who were disposed to agree that proceedings should be stopped and Miss Cunningham allowed to leave the country. They then discovered that the case, 'no doubt purposely as I have since been informed', had been taken before the Crown Prosecutor, whereupon they regretted they had no power to intervene. All that could be done was to hasten the trial and, if the lady was found guilty, appeal to the Grand Duke for commutation.

Scarlett determined to appeal to the Grand Duke direct, with the approval of Lami and Landucci, who were content to pass the buck. He waited on the Grand Duke at Lucca and pleaded with him, receiving a painful dose of reality. The Grand Duke

interrupted, lectured me on conduct of English, "Let the English who are not in the habit of breaking their own laws at home learn to respect our laws." He left me in no doubt that the case was to proceed though in some doubt as to ultimate consequences.

Scarlett pleaded with the Grand Duchess, but although she listened, she did not hold out much hope. He saw the Archbishop of Lucca, 'who feared his influence would avail little'. His difficulties continued with Miss Cunningham herself, 'who is well treated, allowed to see her mother every day', but refused to answer accusations and admitted nothing, 'which may prolong proceedings as witnesses will have to be brought to prove case'.

Having retained the advocate Salvagnoli and given him a letter of introduction to Mrs Cunningham, Scarlett discovered that the lady was by no means for turning, or for following Salvagnoli's advice. He sent a note to Casigliano, asking for a statement of the charges for the information of his government. He saw Baldasseroni, who 'assured me of his entire concurrence in the expediency of the course which I had ventured to recommend to the Grand Duke'. That he was now desperate for instructions is indicated by the fact that he wrote twice more on the same day. Salvagnoli had reported that Helen Cunningham, sister of the accused, had written 'thanking him for his attention but stating it to be unlikely that her sister will take Salvagnoli's advice'. Then Miss Helen Cunningham & Rev Gordon were 'advised to quit Lucca without delay in case anything might transpire to implicate them'. They duly escaped to Genoa via Leghorn. Scarlett meanwhile had been enlightened about one reason for Tuscan sensitivity on the subject of Bagni. The inhabitants were thought to be inclined to dissent, having been 'formerly encouraged by the ex duke of Lucca who for a short time avowed himself a Protestant'.

Further despatches followed on 24 and 25 September, including another fruitless appeal to the Grand Duke and the emotive statement that Miss Cunningham faced 10 years in prison. An interested observer of Scarlett's behaviour was Robert Bulwer Lytton, who was in Florence as an unpaid *attaché* assisting his uncle Sir Henry Bulwer. He was the very soul of indiscretion and irreverence when writing to Robert Browning on 19 September. Perhaps he had some justification for his tone, for it was he rather than Scarlett who was actually doing the running around, rushing to Bagni to present personal pleas from Lord Normanby (an old friend of the Grand Duke), 'a mighty secret wh. I have no business to divulge', as he not so innocently told Browning; chasing off to Leghorn in pursuit of the Rev Gordon and Helen Cunningham; then returning post haste to Florence, 'where I find my Coll: just fitting himself into his properest pantaloons to go the Normanby's, and find moreover that it was quite unnecessary for me to have gone to Leghorn, and that all the restaurants are shut up: thence supperless and dinnerless and cross to bed.' Lytton cheerily characterized Leopold as 'the Royal and Imbecile Mind'.[81]

None of Scarlett's despatches had been received when on 23 September the Foreign Secretary responded to private information in an unusually emotional letter, riven with misunderstandings and hardly therefore of any help to Scarlett. He had heard that 2 ladies had been 'distributing tracts at Lucca, and that one has, in consequence, been imprisoned at Florence and the other has been put on board a steamer at Leghorn'. It was deeply shocking that such a thing should happen; nowhere but in Tuscany (something of an exaggeration) would this 'imprudence' be regarded as a crime. Russell's informant was a Mr Stuart, who was in fact the ladies' brother in law, but as he had heard no further particulars he assumed that Stuart's letters had been stopped. He did not doubt but that Scarlett would have taken action, and rather significantly if redundantly pointed out 'that the occurrence will make a deep and general sensation in England'. He had hoped for better things after the Madiai, at a time 'when wise men are looking for friends instead of creating enemies'. It is doubtful whether such considerations weighed with Leopold.

The Foreign Office responded to Scarlett on 26 September. His of the 17th had been received 'with deepest pain and regret', but the obligation of British subjects to obey the laws of the countries they freely chose to visit was reaffirmed. Miss Cunningham, 'acting with that perfect freedom in such matters which exists alike for Roman Catholics & Protestants in England', had apparently contravened

Tuscan law. Scarlett was to ask formally for an audience of the Grand Duke and to request that he use his sovereign power so that Miss Cunningham could be permitted to leave the country. The tone reflected that of the newspapers to date, but there was a change in the air.

The *Times* on the 26th spoke editorially of 'yet another act of fanaticism, folly and cruelty on the part of the Tuscan Government'. As was the paper's wont, it laid emphasis on the weakness and littleness of Tuscany. Had Tuscany been of any consequence in the counsels of Europe the British would have responded promptly; but 'the more beggarly and miserable a State' the greater seemed to be its impunity.

> It is enough that any person should be an English subject and a Protestant, and it is competent to any of the little trumpery Potentates who are dotted about the Continent of Europe to incarcerate and torture them at their pleasure.

How long could this go on, when the despatch of a single battle-ship to Leghorn would spell the end of the Grand Duke's power? Tuscany was

> a mere twelfth-cake business at best, and has no more right to be treated as a European Power than Messrs FORTNUM and MASON, who import the Lucca oil which it is the highest privilege of the Tuscan Government to educe from a kindly soil.

The writer ended by appealing to the virtuous fanaticism of Queen Elizabeth and Cromwell, which would certainly have struck a chord with those Protestants who (rather like the Grand Duke) were still living mentally in the seventeenth century.

Justifiably or not, such language raised the stakes and conferred enhanced importance on Miss Cunningham. In a despatch written on the 27th Scarlett was informed that the idea that she might be sentenced to 5 or 10 years' hard labour was revolting public opinion and that 'the affair as you may suppose, is creating a profound sensation'. On 30 September several provincial newspapers weighed in. The always very Protestant *Essex Standard* referred to 'That excessively contemptible potentate, the Grand Duke of Tuscany', condensing its account from the *Times*. There were many more, which advocated solutions that ranged from breaking off diplomatic relations to sending the fleet to bombard Leghorn. The belief that Miss Cunningham was imprisoned 'in the very same place of confinement in which Rosa Madiai was', contained in a letter from James Gordon and printed in *The Era* on 2 October, was too enchanting to omit.

The Foreign Office became rather frantic in its search for a solution, sending no fewer than three separate despatches on 4 October: two approved Scarlett's efforts and the third reprobated the circumstances of the arrest as described by Sir William Miller. Four gendarmes had been in close and constant attendance on the one woman (no doubt to keep an eye on one another) and her maid or sister had not been allowed to accompany her from Bagni to Lucca. This was doubtless all very oppressive and bureaucratic, but hardly sensational. Scarlett himself seemed to have decided that to spray the Foreign Office with information at least gave the appearance of action. On 8 October he reported that the French had delivered a note critical of the severity shown to a lady for an imprudence that amounted to no more than an excess of zeal. This was in line with their already-noted last-minute intervention in the Madiai affair.

With what justification therefore did Scarlett, at last remembering the existence of the telegraph, report on 11 October 'I have obtained Miss Cunningham's liberation'? This was elaborated in a despatch of the same date. She was required to leave Tuscany immediately, but permitted a few days' grace until her mother, who had been ill, was well enough to travel. It was perhaps just as well that the Grand Duke acted when he did, because the Foreign Office, showing signs of buckling under pressure from home, had actually penned instructions which demanded that Miss Cunningham be released and allowed to quit Tuscany – well calculated to cause resentment and a rupture, with all the possible consequences for English residents.

If the *Times* of 20 October is to be believed, Miss Cunningham was most reluctant to leave prison. When informed that the Grand Duke had ordered her release she refused to accept it as an act of grace. She had been imprisoned for a month without trial and her lawyer had told her that no verdict could be obtained against her as she had not broken any law, so she would not go until she had seen him. When evening came she was politely 'told that if she did not go freely she would be carried out by force, upon which she replied, "Give me that in writing, and I will go". They did so, and accordingly out she went'. It was not a satisfactory martyrdom.

Once Miss Cunningham had been released, the Foreign Office appears to have had no difficulty in fighting off allegations which were either concerned with the technicalities of legal procedure or had no substance whatsoever. No violence had been offered to her and, although the ministrations of the Sisters of Charity may not have been to her Protestant liking, feminine dignities were preserved and no attempt was made to interfere with her own religious observances. The affair rumbled on in the English press until December, fomented by her brother Archibald, who objected to the notion of pardon where there was no guilt, Sir William Miller, who protested against the severity of the police, and the lady's brother in law Clarence Stuart.

Scarlett, who was criticized for seeking grace and favour instead of standing up for British interests, noted on 1 November that

> opinion in Florence among British residents was by no means united in favour of Miss Cunningham. There were many who took opposite view to the press in England, viz that they thought her interference with Roman Catholics to be an unwarrantable presumption and one deserving the penalty of a risk which she

must have been well aware she was running. Nevertheless all agree that 10 years hard labour for distributing tracts is out of place in the 19th century.

In fact, sections of the English press had agreed about Miss Cunningham's 'unwarrantable presumption'. Behaving as she did at the height of the Grand Ducal reaction, she was asking for trouble and duly got it.

How Scarlett arrived at his assessment of the state of British public opinion in Florence is unclear, but on balance it is likely to be correct. According to Guy Fleetwood Wilson, his parents were devout believers in the Word of God. They must have told him that there was an active Protestant propaganda in Tuscany during the Grand Ducal period, with much smuggling of Bibles. They should have known, for 'two of my relatives actively participated in both smuggling and distribution, but they neither approved of nor joined in this violation of the law'. One of the two is instantly identifiable as Mrs Wilson's brother, Arthur Walker. All the same, the Wilsons were indignant about persecution; Captain Wilson's diary, quoted by his son, records his visits to the imprisoned Guicciardini and reactions to the later imprisonment of Tuscan Protestants.[82]

The English Church had nothing to say about Miss Cunningham and John Maquay never mentions her. Just as significant, Stewart did not include her in a list of cases of persecution in Tuscany which was circulated in her and his homeland.[83] Aware of the presence of government spies, he regularly remonstrated with British journals for publishing the names and details of Italians involved in Protestant services.[84] The open blunderings of a Miss Cunningham were as much anathema to him and his associates as they were to the Grand Duke, if for rather different reasons.

Challenges to the peaceful activities of the established Protestant Churches did not come only from the Tuscan Government and the Roman Catholic Establishment. There was an outbreak of what Stewart called 'a plague of Plymouthism'. He seemed to identify both Arthur de Noë Walker and Guicciardini with these opinions, which Guicciardini would have denied.[85] Like the Tuscans themselves, Stewart saw a link between nationalism and religion: some at least of those Italians who were inclined to republicanism in politics 'showed a distinct leaning to Independency and even Darbyism in their ecclesiastical views'. Even more starkly he added that

Those that leave the Church of Rome must of necessity take their politics from Mazzini and their religion from Darby; since these two are at the opposite poles from the Pope in the absolute rule he pretends over things secular and sacred.[86]

Stewart's real wrath was reserved for three Englishwomen led by Miss Johnson (doubtless the lady who had presented Francesco Madiai with a handsome bible), who assembled some converts at her villa and dispensed the bread and wine of communion with her own hands. He was outraged, first as a male pastor with predictable opinions, and secondly on grounds of security. There was a flaming row between Hanna and Miss Johnson, in which she accused him and Stewart of patriarchy and seduced some of his converts with the allegation that Stewart merely sought priestly domination over them.[87]

It was something of a relief to the Scots therefore when these ladies attracted the attention of the Tuscan Government early in 1854. Landucci preferred an official complaint against Miss Browne and Miss Courtenay Johnson. They 'had on various occasions employed their time in making proselytes of Tuscan subjects' and they had offered religious instruction which included condemnations of Catholic doctrine and exhortations to embrace Protestantism. Landucci was 'anxious to avoid the scandal of a public trial' (he clearly had Miss Cunningham in mind) and proposed simply to expel the two by refusing to renew their *carte di soggiorno*. He showed remarkable diplomacy, even agreeing that the ladies might stay until the lease on their apartments expired in the following May, so that they would not incur financial loss.

The two ladies, however, far from showing contrition when taken to task by Scarlett, rejoiced that they were like the apostles scourged for spreading the Gospel of Christ. They were impervious to Scarlett's observation that he 'was not aware that any sanction was to be found in scripture for disobeying the laws of any Country'. He awaited instructions, but suggested that the Tuscan Government was in no way at fault. The Foreign Office agreed, and Stewart and Hanna no doubt heaved a sigh of relief.[88] Perhaps they were less pleased that Miss Browne obtained permission to return to Florence, as John Maquay noted when he called on her on 18 October.[89]

Stewart's list of Tuscan persecutions of Protestants (all Italians except Pakenham) ends abruptly in 1856. Seventeen of his 21 examples are dated between 1849 and 1853 and even he avers that the days of active persecution were over by 1857. The congregation in Leghorn had doubled and on 11 June 1857 he actually felt emboldened to celebrate Holy Communion with Pontedera converts in the Manse. At the same time as active persecution ceased 'Plymouthism' began to decline and 'more organised Protestantism' appeared with regular congregations now at Leghorn, Florence and Pontedera.[90]

One cannot be precise about the number of Bibles and banned religious books that were introduced into Tuscany during this period, for it was in the interests of Protestant groups in England to exaggerate the figures. On any reasonable computation of the number of Italian Protestants against the number of Bibles supposedly flooding into Tuscany in the early 1850s the market would soon have been saturated, for there must have been twenty or so for every Protestant. The semi-clandestine free church at Pontedera, which managed to keep going despite the attempts of the Tuscan Government to close it, elected three elders and two deacons and had for its pastor Dr Tito Chiesi (mentioned by Mary Thompson), a respected advocate of Pisa. Apart from this congregation and some individual converts there was not much to show for all the effort. For some British Protestants this would have seemed disappointing; but the generality of British residents had no reason to regret the greater tranquillity of the middle years of the decade.

Notes

1   CMB 1, 10–11 July 1845.

2   Robert W. Stewart, *An Italian Campaign, or the Evangelical Movement in Italy 1845–1887* (London, 1890), pp. 8–14.

3   FO79/127, Macbean to FO, 4 September 1847. Palmerston's comments are in two memos filed at the back of this volume.

4   FO79/134, FO to Stewart, 27 March 1848; FO to Macbean, 29 March. There is much in this episode which is revealing about Palmerston's own attitude to matters religious, significant when he came to deal with the Pakenham issue.

5   Stewart, *Italian Campaign*, p. 25. Stowe, unlike the other two, was not a long-term resident.

6   BC19, 3235 EBB to Henrietta, 26 July 1853; 20, 3484 EBB to Henrietta, 5/7 November 1854.

7   FO79/143, Hamilton to FO, 11 May 1850; 142, FO to Hamilton, 8 June 1850. The person at fault here was the Bishop, who under ecclesiastical law could have sanctioned the practice if it needed sanction. In one sense the FO was quite right: Hamilton 'cannot authorise the proposed innovation', for it was none of his business. Quite what the half-American Halls made of this is unknown. Tassinari is incorrect in saying that the matter was first brought before the congregation in 1860: Catherine Danyell Tassinari, *The History of the English Church in Florence* (Florence 1905), p. 108.

8   CMB 1, 26 January 1849.

9   Thomas Sleeman was elected chaplain of the Leghorn Church at a meeting held on 20 November 1840 (FO79/145). He resigned in 1853 when the Bishop of Gibraltar appointed him to a canonry in his cathedral (FO79/180, Macbean to FO, 12 April 1854 enclosing 1853 church minutes). John does not mention him by name until 14 July 1850 when he came up from Leghorn 'to do the duty' at Florence (JLM, E11 f.80).

10   CMB 1, 23 February 1849; Tassinari, *English Church*, p. 66.

11   CMB 1, 6 January 1853.

12   There was also to be 'set apart as at present a Pew with some distinguishing mark for the use of H B M's Legation to the Court of Tuscany'.

13   CMB 1, 26 January 1854.

14   CMB 1, 7 January & 4 February 1850.

15   CMB 1, 2 June 1845.

16   CMB 1, 18 March 1850. The various depots which had been used from time to time around the town included Samuel Lowe, Henry Roberts at the English Dispensary and Vieusseux – they were entitled to 10 per cent commission.

17   Scarlett forwarded a copy to the FO on 9 July (FO79/150). The document was deemed to be of sufficient importance to be embodied in a Confidential Print (FO881/236).

18   FO79/160, Bulwer to FO, 26 August 1852.

19   FO79/170, Scarlett to FO, with enclosure from Macbean, 10 December 1853.

20   CMB 1, 8 January 1849.

21 JLM, E10 ff. 226–7.

22 Frances Julia Pakenham; *Life Lines:Or God's Work in a Human Being* (London, 1862), p. 94. The human being in question is herself. The Lady O. who made the reported comment to Julia was almost certainly Lady Ormonde, Pakenham's aunt on his mother's side.

23 JLM E10, f. 243v.

24 Pakenham, *Life Lines*, p. 96.

25 JLM, E11 ff. 22, 24, 40v; Pakenham, *Life Lines*, p. 98.

26 FO79/140, Pakenham to Palmerston, 21 May 1849. Most of the correspondence which takes place over the next 2 years is also to be found in Confidential Print FO881/238. Except where stated, FO79 has been used in preference, since it contains very revealing marginal comments and asides.

27 It was perhaps ironic that Pakenham should lay stress, both now and later, on the length of his residence, when we learn that in October 1849 he applied for exemption from the *tassa di famiglia* on the grounds that he was 'a foreigner only temporarily resident in Florence' (ASCF, CA CC 1.79.105). On 5 November Captain 'Robert'[recte John] Pakenham was awarded a reduction in tax on the grounds that he no longer exercised the profession of banker.

28 FO70/150, Scarlett to FO, 14 July 1851, enclosing the dossier, which is also printed in FO881/238.

29 FO881/238, Hamilton to Palmerston. Hamilton says that Pakenham had been warned the previous year by the prefect of Lucca; the prefect refers only to previous general warnings from the local authorities.

30 FO79/139, Hamilton to FO, 17 October 1849.

31 FO79/136, FO to Hamilton, 31 October 1849; 79/139, Hamilton to FO, 25 November; 79/140. Pakenham to Palmerston, 30 November. In a statement which Hamilton enclosed, Baldasseroni justifies Pakenham's expulsion 'pour avoir fait un prosélytisme opiniâtre et incorrigible, contre la religion de l'Etat, et pour avoir à cet effet débité des livres dont l'expansion est défendue par les lois'.

32 JLM, E11 f. 52v.

33 FO79/143, Hamilton to FO, 27 January 1850, enclosing correspondence with Casigliano; also, 11 February.

34 FO79/146, Pakenham to Palmerston, 30 January 1850.

35 FO79/143, Hamilton to FO, 11 February 1850, enclosing note from Casigliano.

36 JLM, E11 f. 53v.; FO79/146, Pakenham to Palmerston, 2 February 1850. On the 13th young Montague came to stay for a week with the Maquays.

37 FO79/146, Pakenham to FO, 28 March 1850; FO881/238, 29 April.

38 Michael R.D. Foot & Henry C.G. Matthew (eds), *The Gladstone Diaries* (Oxford, 1974), Vol. 4, pp. 225, 227.

39 FO79/146 FO to Pakenham, 24 July 1850; Pakenham to FO, 1 August 1850; FO to Pakenham, 3 August 1850.

40 JLM, E11 f. 61v.

41 FO79/144 contains the relevant correspondence, concentrated in the last week in August when Pakenham was writing daily to Hamilton. Pakenham to Palmerston, 26 August 1850, is in 79/146.

42 FO79/142, FO to Scarlett, 20 September 1850: 'it is quite plain that Captain Pakenham is a person who takes up conclusions hastily drawn, and adheres to them without very dispassionately weighing the evidence on which they rest'.

43 FO 79/142, FO to Scarlett, 28 October & 16 December 1850; 79/144, Scarlett to FO, 9 October & 30 November (with seven enclosures); 79/142, FO to Scarlett, 16 December 1850.

44 CMB 1, 14 January 1851; JLM, E11 f. 68v.

45 FO79/149, Scarlett to FO, 20 January 1851. The correspondence is embodied in a single Parliamentary Paper, vol. 57 for 1851. Tassinari, *English Church*, pp. 80–4, draws on some of these documents.

46 FO79/147, FO to Shiel, 3 February 1851.

47 Tassinari, *English Church*, pp. 84–6. According to Tassinari the exiled Geymonat was welcomed by Pakenham at Genoa. Eventually Colombe sought a personal interview with Landucci and obtained a tacit and conditional approval for the resumption of the services for Italian-speakers.

48 Robbins and his sister Henrietta, Marchesa Inghirami, died within a few months of each other in Florence in 1873.

49 Shiel's efforts are documented in FO79/149.

50 FO79/149, Sheil to FO, 20 May 1851. Guicciardini 'came to thank me before leaving Florence for the favour which I had rendered him'. A few years later Guicciardini took out naturalization papers: TNA, HO1/85/2681 Memorial and naturalisation papers connected with Count Piero Guicciardini. Certificate issued 24 June 1858.

51 FO79/150; the Confidential Print (FO881/238) ends in September 1851 with Pakenham enquiring what has happened since Sheil's death.

52 FO79/163, Granville to Pakenham, 20 February 1852, Pakenham to FO, 3 March.

53 FO79/158, Scarlett to FO, 13 April 1852; 79/159 Bulwer to FO, 29 May.

54 See for example *The Story of the Madai; With Notices of Efforts Made, in Europe and American, in their Behalf, Comp. and Ed. by the Secretaries of the American and Foreign Christian Union* (New York, 1853). A considerable pamphlet literature was generated in England alone. There was even a confidential print produced for parliament FO881/264. Astonishingly the British Government paid the cost of their defence at their trial – some £150. With some reluctance, since he was of opinion that the British Government should not have interfered in the first place, Malmesbury authorized the cost of appeal.

55 FO79/154, Cumming to Palmerston, 12 November 1851. Thomas Tod died in Florence on 26 April 1851, just 1 month before Sheil.

56 FO 79/150, Scarlett to FO, 20 August 1851 (enclosing copy of a long complaint from Walker at Villa Strozzino); 79/151, Scarlett to FO, 5 September. On 22 August Scarlett forwarded the official reply of the Tuscan Government about Walker's imprisonment.

57 Information on his life can be gleaned from obituaries in the *Times* and the *Standard* on 3 October 1900. Although he died in Chelsea he is buried in the Allori Cemetery.

58 FO79/154 for this correspondence. Tregelles produced a pamphlet, *Prisoners of Hope: Being Letters from Florence Relative to the Persecution of Francesco and Rosa Madiai*, of which a second edition, 'with an appendix of recent information' appeared in 1852. All profits went to the Madiai.

59 This Letter Book is in the custody of St Mark's Church, Florence. The references here can be found on pp. 15–21, 24–5.

60 Stewart's letter, among the recently discovered *Church Letters*, has been mistakenly attributed to the 1830s and numbered 32 in that decade.

61 FO79/156, FO to Bulwer; 79/160, Bulwer to FO, 26 October. Ostensibly Bulwer was in Rome in order to obtain the release of a British subject, Edward Murray, imprisoned at Ancona. Malmesbury makes no reference to any other purpose in the despatch instructing him to return. It is, however, possible that he had other business

with Cardinal Antonelli, as the *Times* had speculated on 29 September, 'to negotiate a Concordat for Ireland with the Pontifical Court'.

62 Frederick William IV regarded it his duty as head of the Protestant Church in Germany to press the issue, but his *chargé d'affaires* in Florence, M de Reumont, got a predictable response from the Grand Duke: 'Protestants were all imbued with socialist and revolutionary schemes, and that he could not act otherwise'. Reumont's protest was reported in *Daily News* 3 September 1852. See also FO881/301, *Prussia and Tuscany: Depositions over Madiai*. Two foreign citizens thus managed to generate not one, but two, Confidential Prints!

63 CMB 1, 20 October 1852; JLM, E11 f. 97.

64 FO79/161, Bulwer to FO, 20 November.

65 BC18, 3146 EBB to Arabella, 13/15 November 1852.

66 FO79/152, Scarlett to FO, 27 November 1851.

67 FO79/165, Erskine to FO, 17 March 1853, Scarlett to FO, 28 March.

68 BC19, 3190 EBB to Arabella, 12 April 1853.

69 George Robbins, *The Privileges and Responsibilities of the Christian Ministry. A Sermon Preached in the Parish Church of All Saints, Northampton, on the 10th of May 1853* (private, 1853), p. 14.

70 JLM, E11 f. 109. Mrs Burdett's first husband, who was also well known to the Maquays, died in Naples in 1849. Guastalla remained a great friend of the Trollopes, and was instrumental in organizing an exhibition of Tuscan art and antiquities in Florence in 1861–1862.

71 The abrogation of Jewish civil rights caused a great deal of dissension between the Grand Duke and his Ministers in 1852, to which both Scarlett and Bulwer make reference in their correspondence.

72 Years earlier, the quarrelsome consul Falconar at Leghorn had attacked the chaplain Neat for receiving a salary from the London Society for Promoting Christianity among the Jews, claiming that this threatened to breach the conditions on which the Leghorn church was tolerated. See for example FO79/52, Falconar to FO, 10 October 1828.

73 Stewart, *Italian Campaign*, p. 27.

74 JLM, E11 ff. 34v, 52, 68v.

75 Stewart, *Italian Campaign*, pp. 254–7.

76 J. Stevens Curl, *The Life and Work of Henry Roberts 1803–1876* (Chichester, 1983), p. 38.

77 Bruce died in Rome 24 May 1881. There are a number of Italian accounts of his activities and career in Italy as agent for the British and Foreign Bible Society, particularly Giovanni Ribetti, 'Il signor Tommaso Bruce', *L'Italia Evangelica*, no. 22, 28 maggio 1881. M. Cignoni, *Thomas Humble Bruce: la Società Biblica Britannica e Forestiera ai tempi dell'Unità d'Italia 1861–1870* (Roma, 2011). See also Giorgio Spini, *Risorgimento e Protestanti* (3rd edition, Torino, 1998), pp. 218, 257, 324. Spini for some reason calls him Robert.

78 Stewart, *Italian Campaign*, p. 34.

79 Piero Posarelli, 'Reminiscences of Mary Thompson, daughter of the British Vice-Consul in Livorno' ed. Matteo Giunti, at *leghornmerchants.wordpress. com/2012/02/29/mary-thompson/*.

80 FO79/168, Scarlett to FO, 17 September 1853 with enclosures. FO79/164 contains the relevant despatches to Scarlett; 79/169, those from Scarlett during the remainder of the year. 79/171 contains letters from Archibald Cunningham and others, 79/174 the various petitions which flowed in from Protestant organizations.

81 BC19, 3268 Robert Bulwer Lytton to RB.

82 Guy Fleetwood Wilson, *Letters to Somebody* (London, 1922), pp. 36–8.

83 Stewart, *Italian Campaign*, pp. 257–63. He does include Pakenham.

84 Ibid., p. 44.

85 According to himself Guicciardini was 'neither Calvinist nor Lutheran' but 'a Catholic in the sense that Catholicism embraced all those who believed in the Gospel of the Lord Jesus': Anonymous, *Religious Liberty in Tuscany: or, Documents Relative to the Trial and Incarceration of Count Piero Guicciardini & others exiled from Tuscany by decree of 17 May 1851* (London, 1851), p. 20.

86 Stewart, *Italian Campaign*, p.103. John Nelson Darby (1800–1882) was a leading light among the Plymouth Brethren and founder of the Exclusive Brethren.

87 Ibid., pp. 81–4.

88 FO79/176, Scarlett to FO, 18 February 1854; 79/175 FO to Scarlett, 28 February. The name is variously spelt Johnston, Johnson, Johnstone.

89 JLM, E11 f. 137. John makes several references to people called Brown or Browne at this time, but the identities are not clear.

90 Stewart, *Italian Campaign*, pp. 90–2.

11 INDIAN SUMMER, 1854–1858

The year 1854 opened with the Austrians still occupying Tuscany, but their days were numbered. The underlying problems remained: the Grand Duke was weak and obstinate and would soon be left on his own in the midst of an Italian situation which he was powerless to influence, let alone control. For the British in Tuscany there were ongoing annoyances to contend with, but the reverberations of the Mather and Stratford affairs and of the Grand Duke's attempts to suppress heresy and Protestant evangelization had largely subsided. Social life continued.

With two sons in the British armed services, Elena Maquay was spending more time away from Florence, taking the youngest, William, with her. Her absence had a limiting effect on John's entertaining, but he was not averse to accepting invitations. Through his eyes we obtain glimpses of the continued hospitality of friends both old and new, including the now widowed Mrs Fombelle, who on 11 January 1854 gave a party at which there was music, but no dancing. On the following evening, Mrs Trotman gave a 'large and good' party with both, whence John proceeded to a large ball at Demidoff's where he met the second Duke of Wellington. On 8 February he went to a Court ball where he introduced fourteen Americans; he did the same on the 15th and 22nd. On the 14th he refused the offer of a ticket to a 'great Ball' given by the Jockey Club, perhaps because he was committed to another Court ball on the following night. On the 19th he went to see 'Stentorello', the theatrical personification of the Florentine common man: 'I have not laughed so much these 10 years.' On the 23rd he was truly burning the candle: 'in evening to Trotman for whist & at 11 went to Bank & dressed in Court Dress getting my head curled & powdered and went to a Fancy Ball at Demidoff's where I remained 1 ½ hours & was in bed at Bank before 2.'[1] His annual lamentations about his increasing decrepitude and need to take thought for his immortal soul must be read in the light of such entries. On 28 February he described how he had put on 'a cold supper' for his whist players but, perhaps because it was the last evening of Carnival, only six people came: 'Lever however kept us amused & laughing till 2 ½ in the morning.'[2] Lever was sharing the burden of hosting whist parties while Mrs Trollope was indisposed.

There were residents old and new who formed no part of John's circle. He mentions Frederick Tennyson only to record that Elena went to two musical parties or concerts he gave in May 1855.[3] William Blundell Spence he never mentions. The two editions of Spence's guidebook, *The Lions of Florence*, appeared in 1849 and 1852, and his career as an art-dealer seems to have taken off in the 1850s, together and often in competition with the American Jarves. The idea seemed to be to empty Tuscany of works of art, keeping one step ahead of the authorities and the Grand Duke in beating any export ban. In 1851 Spence bought a Caracci which was being hawked round Doney's tea-rooms for 9 dollars and was subsequently valued at £40. In 1853 we find him addressing the trustees of the National Gallery, not only on the merits of buying the Lombardi-Baldi collection for £12,000, but also on picture preservation and the methods in use in Florence. According to the director of the Florentine Galleries, 'no better person could be selected than Mr Spence to report on Tuscan galleries and museums' and he would 'furnish him with all particulars.' By January 1854 he had accumulated in his 'gallery' in Palazzo Corsi (later the Museo Horne) some £800 worth of paintings and bronzes and was reckoned to have one of the finest collections in Florence. By this time he had virtually given up painting.[4]

Newcomers continued to arrive. One who fled England not entirely voluntarily was the architect Henry Roberts, who with his Russian wife Catharine de Swetschine arrived in November 1853. Henry was being pursued not by the courts, but by the social obloquy that followed a mid-Victorian gentleman who got caught, in his case in an adulterous relationship with a young servant girl. His enforced resignation as honorary architect and founder member of the Society for Improving the Condition of the Labouring Classes (SICLC-President: Prince Albert, Vice President: Lord Ashley, later Earl of Shaftesbury) naturally followed and he made his way to Florence, along with his forgiving wife and family. The Russian community appears soon to have swung behind Catherine and the pair were invited to a Grand Ducal reception; within a few months he was on close enough terms with Leopold to be discussing plans for the architectural improvement of Florence and the elimination of the slums. That these came to very little was hardly Roberts's fault. Leopold was ever dreaming beyond his means about transforming Florence but effectively he was broke, finding it difficult enough to keep the government going from day to day.

Roberts remained a corresponding member of the SICLC and this bore some fruit in Florence. He persuaded the Grand Duke to institute a system of inspection of 'unseemly' properties in 1854, which included the provision of means to cleanse dwellings deemed dangerous to life. Among his close collaborators was the Marchese Torrigiani. Together they promoted a Building Society which erected a number of apartments in the suburbs, four storeys high and available for cheap rent. Another fruit was the translation into Italian of SICLC pamphlets advising the poor how to live more economically and safely. For these Roberts was elected an honorary member of the *Accademia*.[5]

John Temple Leader was another arrival in the early 1850s who was destined to be a long-term resident. He was the son of a rich London merchant who became even richer with the deaths of both his father and his elder brother. After a promising career as an MP, in 1844 Leader left (entirely voluntarily) for the continent, thereafter rarely returning to Britain. This one-time radical MP and friend of Chartists chose to purchase the Villa Pazzi, in the village of Maiano near Florence, in February 1850, as the Austrians consolidated their hold on the country and the Grand Duke teetered towards reaction. In March 1855 he bought the ruined mediaeval castle of Vincigliata, with which his name is forever associated, and in 1857 a town house in Piazza Pitti. Both were substantially altered, rebuilt, restored and stuffed full of art and antiques. His country villas were all supplied with swimming pools, for a sport which he practised well into his nineties.[6]

John Maquay first mentions Isa Blagden on 10 July 1854, but he would hardly have called on her then had there not been some prior acquaintance. On 4 August he took tea with her, making his sole reference to the Brownings, who were there with the American Kinneys.[7] Thereafter Isa was a regular in the journals and figures on his party lists. She is referred to as a friend of Hooker, the American manager of the Roman branch of Maquay & Pakenham, which suggests that the acquaintance originated when she was a customer of the bank. Isa had probably met the Brownings around March 1850, soon after she arrived in Florence from Rome. She had pretensions to write poetry and for years lived up at Bellosguardo in a villa with an incomparable view of Florence, an additional attraction for the many people whom she befriended and entertained.[8]

John was now living out the last years of his Florentine residence. It is uncertain exactly when he resolved to leave, but there is evidence that he was laying plans in 1853, if not before. On a visit to Ireland in July of that year he viewed some land at Kilteale in Queen's County (now County Laois) and got as far as authorizing John Adair to purchase it for him, showing it to Elena in May 1854.[9] He then returned to Florence, finding himself alone there when George joined his mother in July. It is illustrative of the realities of day-to-day life under Austrian occupation that when he was summoned by the police on 21 July he discovered that it was about his dog barking in the night.[10] On 21 November he and Elena (now back in Florence) had 'a long conversation about building in Ireland'.[11] The Kilteale project did not bear fruit.

By this time Elena had taken an important personal step, perhaps by way of preparation for their move. In Florence at Easter 1854 John as usual received the sacrament on Easter Day, noting in his diary 'hope Elena was doing so at the same time for the first time in Church of England'. On 12 November, only a few days after her return to Tuscany, 'I had the great pleasure of having Elena sitting by me at Church for the first time in Florence.' She attended the English Church not infrequently thereafter, but it was not until 2 March 1856 that John recorded that 'tho not Elena's first, it was first time we had communicated together'. She communicated again at Easter.[12] When the time came, she would not take up residence in Ireland as the Catholic wife of a Protestant landowner, or as a wife who did not go to church.

Meanwhile they had reason to notice international events, which John recorded in his usual abbreviated style. On 22 May 1853 he remarked, 'Russia has entered

Turkey and that the French and English fleets have been ordered immediately to the Dardanelles.' On 6 February 1854 the Grand Duke was said to have heard that Russia had 'at length declared war against England and France'. John's interest was not merely patriotic. His second son (John Popham) had attained the rank of lieutenant in the Royal Engineers and saw service in the Crimea, while his third, Tommy, who had been an idle schoolboy, had (it was hoped) found his metier in the navy. Tommy was on board the *Hannibal* which, his father learned on 20 September 1854, had reached Sheerness, 'very sickly 30 deaths coming home from Baltic with Russian prisoners'. In October the British residents were following the progress of the Sebastopol campaign, and it is in this connection that John first mentions news coming by telegraph. The physician Dr Harding had a son in the army, who was wounded at Inkerman, and on 20 December the Hardings conducted 'raffles for the wounded at Scutari hospital'. On Christmas Day John reflected that Tommy was celebrating his 16th birthday and might be fighting at Sebastopol. Some social relationships were negatively affected. On 29 December the Maquays were 'asked to a large party at Countess Botrinski but being Russians we did not go'.[13]

If the *Times* of 16 January 1854 could be believed, official Tuscan sympathies were not in doubt. The most trivial display of pro-Turkish sentiment was persecuted, while 'The word "Turkish" has been erased from the signboard of the Turkish Coffee house, and the word "Coffeehouse" remains'. The attitude of Austria was key. In May Scarlett reported Casigliano's opinion that, while Austria would remain neutral as long as possible, it had as much interest as Britain or France in limiting the spread of Russian influence; but, presumably speaking from personal information, Scarlett thought that the Austrian officers in Florence expressed much greater sympathy for Russia than for the Turks.[14] On 15 May he told the Foreign Office of reports that 'several Russian and some Greek vessels' had 'taken on board nominal Tuscan captains and sailed from the Port of Leghorn under the Tuscan Flag'. This was a cause of repeated complaint from both the British and the French, rather to the embarrassment of the ostensibly neutral Tuscans, who had to be mindful of the large Greek population at Leghorn and had no wish to reopen the debate over their sovereignty at such a moment. In time of war neutrals are at best tolerated by belligerents, but not loved, as the Austrians were finding out.

On 11 January 1855 John received a letter from Tommy, written 'in high spirits' from Sebastopol, and he was back there again on the *London* in May. The flow of news related to the war then dries up somewhat, although the death of the Russian Emperor Nicholas II in March merited exclamation marks. John makes no mention of the subscription which was got up among the British in Florence and Leghorn in aid of sufferers by the war, although his bank remitted the money to London. The lists of subscribers, published by the *Times* on 3 February and 5 April, may include the names of some mere visitors, but they also offer a remarkably inclusive list of the residents at this moment. Apart from John himself and the Marquis of Normanby, we find William Reynolds, Charles Lever, Frederick Tennyson, the Hall brothers,

Mrs Fombelle, Joseph Garrow and Thomas Trollope, Mme and Major Galeazzi, Major Gregorie, the Hardings, William Somerville (husband of the distinguished scientist), Joseph Gamgee, William Blundell Spence, Christopher Webb Smith, Isa Blagden, Thomas Kerrich, the stationer Edward Goodban, Count Cottrell, the shopkeeper Samuel Lowe and physician Dr Bankhead, the Rev. Hanna, the Rev. O'Neill, Lady Don and Sir Henry Bulwer. There were many others in a list of over 120 individuals (some subscriptions were collective and some anonymous). Francis Sloane, who might have been supposed to have Russian sympathies, was there, and among other British Catholics the Messrs Shinkwin and Miss Shinkwin and the bankers Plowden & French. The collection raised the equivalent of just over £400 sterling. The Leghorn list included all the predictable names, including both the Anglican and Presbyterian chaplains, the crew of several ships which happened to be in harbour and 'officers and men employed on the Leopolda Railway'.

A report in the *Daily News* on 1 November 1855 revealed the scrutiny to which the Briton in Tuscany might be subjected. The English wife of the Austrian ambassador, von Hügel, 'influenced by her husband' had sent lint and other necessaries to the Russians during the war. Given her well-known friendship with Demidoff (who was subject to intermittent newspaper sniping during the war), there could have been small objection had her gift remained private, but it had been much publicized, as had the special thanks she received from the Czar. 'Can there be anything more offensive to the feelings of the Florentine residents among whom she lives than such an act of servility, and want of proper self-respect, in the contest between civilization and barbarism?'

By this time the Austrians had left Tuscany. The state of siege which had existed in Leghorn since they entered on 11 May 1849 was formally lifted on 2 January 1855. On the previous day they had been superseded by a strong garrison of new-minted Tuscan soldiers, some 3,000 in all, but there was no unrest to suppress, no huzzas, no demonstrations of any kind. The same was true at Florence, where the last troops departed on 5 May. Their quiet, almost unnoticed, departure contrasted markedly with the drama of their arrival. They lost no time in quitting Leghorn, even taking with them their sick under treatment in the town hospitals. All was peaceful and there was little overt revolutionary activity, but the Grand Duke was now on his own if it were to revive.[15]

That was not, perhaps, immediately apparent. The Powers may have been distracted by the Crimean War, but Mazzini was also in recession and Garibaldi (anyway at odds with Mazzini) appeared less interested in promoting revolution than in retiring to the island of Caprera. The continued presence of a large Austrian army in Lombardy-Venetia under its veteran commander Radetsky seemed to guarantee stability in the Italian situation. The likely impact of Piedmont and the policies of its Prime Minister Cavour on the position of Tuscany was not to emerge before 1856 at the earliest. The Papal States and points south were still being atrociously governed, but there was no indication that the authorities were not in effective control. The French garrison at Rome appeared to provide reassurance that, whatever else Napoleon III stood for, he was a friend of the Catholic church and certain conservative norms would be preserved.

So the Tuscan Government to an extent relaxed. Although the Grand Duke retained some enthusiasm for the elimination of Protestant sects from Tuscany, his ministers' activity in this respect steadily declined except when they were prodded from on high. There seemed almost a reversion, as far as the English were concerned, to the good old days of the 1820s. Encouraging the Tuscan Government in this was Lord Normanby, who succeeded Bulwer as ambassador early in 1855 and represented the good old days in his own ageing person. There is no reason to doubt his account of his reception by the Grand Duke, who said that nothing could be more grateful to his feelings than for the Queen to have named 'a person whom he had known well all his life, who was thoroughly acquainted with this country'.[16] Normanby had retained a *pied-à-terre* in Florence and visited frequently. Now in the autumn of his life and in increasingly poor health, he had achieved a post he craved.

Normanby's secretary, Frederic St John, born in Florence and thoroughly familiar with the social scene, gives a pleasant picture of his domestic arrangements.[17] St John 'lived in', spending 3 months of each winter in the Palazzo San Clemente. Here a succession of travellers and residents were entertained, for Normanby was a generous host. The large ball which John Maquay attended on 6 January 1854 must have attended by more than a narrow elite, and a dinner party of 15 on 8 January 1855 included the Maquays and Levers, the *attachés* Fenton and Macdonell (son of the late Hugh), Webb Smith and the Rev. O'Neill.[18] There were many musical and theatrical parties to which Elena and George went, though sometimes John did not. Normanby's passion for the theatre conferred a measure of patronage on St John, for his Lordship daily allowed him the keys of two of the three boxes he rented in the principal theatres, which the secretary proceeded to bestow 'on the fairest and most attractive of my acquaintances, whose grateful smiles were my undeserved reward'.

During the early summer, St John accompanied his chief on pleasant excursions to the Courts of Modena and Parma. The rest of the time was spent in Normanby's out of town villa. Often there would be members of his Lordship's extended family present: Sir Hedworth and Lady Williamson (as in the 1820s), Mrs Edward Villiers (another sister-in-law) and her three daughters, Normanby's younger brother the Hon. Edmund Phipps and his son. Political friends paid prolonged visits: Lady Stanley and family, her daughter Lady Airlie with her husband, and her brother Lord Dillon and his family. The Normanbys descended from the hills to the town house around Christmastime.

During one winter the presence of Lord Minto and his son-in-law Lord John Russell, with his wife and extensive brood, at the Villa Capponi half a mile up the road produced a great deal of amateur dramatics. St John had himself lived at Villa Capponi during his childhood.[19] Perhaps this was the visit of which the *Times* reported, on 23 October 1856, that the Tuscan government would be much alarmed by the presence of Minto and Russell, who were regarded by the Grand Duke 'as a couple of itinerant demagogues' whom he would willingly imprison but for 'Lord Normanby's protecting shield'. The *Times* had noted on 14 February 1854 that a Sicilian gentleman had been summarily expelled from Tuscany for no other reason than that he had been observed regularly visiting Lord Minto. This was taken as a warning to the British to be cautious in all their dealings with 'the inhabitants of these despotic countries', to whom they might do more harm than good.

Many commented on Normanby's kindness, which was often able to touch a similar vein in the Grand Duke, and his persistence in pursuing the interests of individuals rather than standing on issues of principle. Gone however was the radical Whig of 1830, the supporter of the Reform Bill, to be replaced by a tired aristocrat supporting the powers that were, which meant Austria and the Grand Duke, unlikely to do much more than advise a little gentle reform and utterly disdaining those who urged that something more fundamental was necessary if the Grand Duchy was to reinvent itself. Normanby was not the person to prompt an equally tired and elderly Grand Duke to take the initiative. By the time he relinquished office in the autumn of 1858 a somnolent Tuscan Government was in a dangerous state of drift. Normanby therefore got little credit for what he achieved in restoring something of the good temper to Anglo-Tuscan relations. He found himself under constant attack at home, in the newspapers and in parliament, as he became increasingly out of step with a public opinion which, after Victor Emmanuel's successful visit to Britain in late 1855, adopted Piedmont as its favourite Italian son and saw advantages to England in augmenting that state and diminishing the influence of both Austria and France in the peninsula, an opinion aggravated by Austrian neutrality during the Crimean War.

Normanby did little to counter impressions as to where his sympathies lay, expressing his views with a pomposity which was not endearing. Like many of his generation of politicians, he continued to see Austria as the old ally against Napoleon, and Austria in Italy as part of the world with which he was familiar. In November 1856 he addressed a portentous homily to the Foreign Office on the Italian dislike of the Austrians. His observations concerned Lombardy-Venetia, but prefigured his reactions to the events of 1859–1860 in Tuscany. In brief, he thought that, with the exception of Venice, the urban populations were hostile; the majority on whose goodwill the government could depend consisted almost entirely of the peasantry. In all other classes the 'well-disposed' were in a small minority, which Normanby thought and hoped was growing, but the 'great body of the Upper Classes' manifested 'marked discourtesy in society to Austrians of every rank'. The Austrians deserved respect for the quality of their administration. The legitimacy of their rule in Italy was not an issue; implicitly, it rested on the Vienna settlement, which justified it in perpetuity.

Normanby's sermons to his English opponents conveyed the constant message that he alone had the correct information. The Foreign Office was warned in October 1856 against 'an endless fabrication of groundless intelligence from

Tuscany' which found its way into the newspapers. He had been reluctant to take up the Foreign Secretary's valuable time with repeated contradictions, 'believing that you would know that if any of these wonderful stories were true, they would at once be reported by myself'.[20] It is only fair to acknowledge that his experience of the country often took him in sensible directions, and he was right to challenge the notion which emanated from Shaftesbury, the Protestant Alliance and others that there were many Protestants in Tuscany.

In 1856 he sought and quoted the views on this subject of two unnamed English gentlemen, whose identities are nonetheless transparent.[21] The first was obviously Horace Hall,

> who has resided all his life in Tuscany, who is an attached member of our Church, who takes the lead in all charitable acts amongst British Residents, who is the active partner in one of the First Banking Houses in Tuscany.

In Hall's view there were isolated conversions but no Tuscan trend in that direction and no Protestant community. A suggested figure of 10,000 Tuscan Protestants was absurd. There was probably 'a diminution of Religious feeling in the body of the people', for which a number of reasons might be assigned, but no real awareness of differences between Catholic and Protestant doctrines.[22] Normanby's second informant was equally obviously Francis Sloane, an 'English Gentleman, who employs great bodies of the people as the proprietor of very extensive and valuable mines'. Himself a Catholic he (like Hall) detected a 'lukewarmness' among the people for which he was inclined to blame the priesthood; like Hall again he did not believe 'in anything approaching to a general tendency towards Protestantism, does not think that generally speaking the Tuscan population knows what Protestantism means'. There seems little reason to dissent, as Normanby saw no reason to dissent, from these opinions.

Normanby was successful in his handling of the remnants of religious persecution largely because he accepted the sensitivity of the Tuscans about foreign interference and made it clear that he did. The snag was that every Tuscan Protestant in trouble saw the British minister as the man to touch, and not all were deserving. On 30 December 1854 the *Standard* reported the prosecution and imprisonment of Eusebio Massei, a baker of Pontedera; on 11 January Captain Trotter, veteran of the abortive Roden mission on behalf of the Madiai, wrote to the same paper about the fears of Tuscans who simply read their Bibles. To British observers this case became bound up with that of Domenico Cecchetti, who was arrested in Florence in March 1855 and condemned to a year's imprisonment, according to the Reverend Stewart, 'for having failed to instruct his children in the Roman Catholic religion and also for holding Protestant opinions, and reading the Bible with his family'. The story reached the English newspapers by way of Hanna and the *Christian* Times, and on 23 April Shaftesbury and the Protestant Alliance addressed a memorial to the Foreign Secretary urging his intervention.[23]

Required to report, Normanby saw little in common between Massei and Cecchetti. Massei, he believed, had been imprisoned for blasphemy (an offence in England also), for abusing the priests and the Roman Catholic religion in a public place, although this was not how his British well-wishers represented the case. With regard to the other affected members of the congregation at Pontedera, although they had been investigated by the police, none had been imprisoned. As for Cecchetti, the willingness of the Tuscan ministers to talk to Normanby and the relative speed with which legal processes were disposed of speaks volumes. If Cecchetti would petition the ministers to commute imprisonment to exile he would be released. With a touch of Miss Cunningham, Cecchetti refused, since 'it had pleased God to place him there, and when it pleased God, He would take him out'. However, he would accept Normanby's intercession – a most improper interference in Tuscan internal affairs on the part of the English Minister. A letter sent by Cecchetti through Normanby, thanking him for his interest and signed by Anthony French the (Catholic) banker, did the trick. Cecchetti was released on 9 July and headed off with his family to Piedmont, armed with a letter of introduction to the British consul at Genoa to help him find employment. He is next heard of settled there and working in a tobacco factory. There was to be no Madiai here – instead apparently a complete triumph for Normanby.[24]

Early in 1856 Normanby repeated his cautions about the negative effects of outside interference and ended with a political assessment. Very soon the Holy See would seek a renewal of the Tuscan Concordat, with a view to obtaining 'some of the stringent provisions' to which the Austrian Emperor had recently consented. The Ministers, he did not doubt, would oppose the measure. It would be short-sighted on the part of the British to do anything to awaken priestly resentment of foreign interference in 'a flagrant case of overt contempt of the Christian religion itself'. There might therefore be quiet remonstrance on behalf of the Pontedera congregation, but no dramatic gestures.[25] Both Bulwer and Normanby were constrained to warn Hanna that he was suspected of encouraging converts to come to his house and that this must cease. Landucci once complained to Normanby that Hanna was bribing Italians to become Protestants, perhaps a deliberate misunderstanding of the fact that he had occasionally given money to relieve the distress of the families of breadwinners imprisoned for proselytism.[26] He was arguably more vulnerable at Florence, the Grand Duke's capital, where the Swiss Church had felt the wrath of the Tuscan Government, than Stewart was at Leghorn, the free port.

As for the Anglicans in Florence, early in 1858 Normanby reported regretfully, on the basis of a conversation with O'Neill, that some of the British did not 'adhere very strictly' to the prohibition of proselytism. Indeed, they encouraged meetings of converts, to which certain female English residents liked to invite 'newcomers'. O'Neill did not want his opinion of this 'imprudent conduct' to be publicly quoted, but he had promised Normanby that he would caution the guilty 'against the mischief they may unconsciously be doing to those whom they wish to protect'. Normanby for his own part would

> convey to the apparent head of this very small body of Tuscan Protestants that, if they hold mixed meetings for religious exercises without any regard to the warnings of the Government, I shall not be able, in that case, to interfere in their behalf.

No names are named, and Normanby was not acting on any complaint from the Tuscans. Bible-running was still going on and conflicting noises were still being made by the Protestant Alliance in London, the Dublin Catholic hierarchy and the Tuscan Government, but the heat had gone off.

Normanby had no doubt that he himself was the major reason for a shift in the Tuscan stance, and there is something to be said for this. With his regular attendance at the English Church the observing police were quietly withdrawn. There was to be no repeat of 1851 or even a hint of it. St John remembered acting as an informal intermediary between the Embassy and Protestant groups under threat of persecution, receiving weekly visits from them and passing information on to his chief, who would then call upon the relevant Tuscan Minister, urging him 'for the sake of Tuscany's good name to order the liberation of the prisoners before the foreign press could get wind of the occurrence and publish it to the world'.[27] St John may have exaggerated in not recalling a single case of failure, but this approach was more successful than that of the bull at the gate. It did not, however, tackle the root cause of persecution, which tended to fuel criticism at home.

Normanby's softly-softly approach was not the only cause of the Tuscan Government's apparent change of temper. He himself hinted that the Grand Duke's hesitations on the proposed new Concordat not only manifested his own inability to make up his mind but reflected genuine differences of opinion between his ministers. Leopold personally wanted a Concordat, but was aware how unpopular any increase in the power of the papacy would be in his own territory. He was burdened by the legacy of Peter Leopold and did not know what policy to pursue, given that Austria clearly no longer saw its position in Italy quite as it had done in 1815 or 1849. The message that Leopold was on his own if he provoked revolution was an uncomfortable one. His only refuge was that of the weak: to do nothing, bury his head in the sand and hope that the problems would disappear. They were far from doing so.

In August 1857 Pius 1X made an extended visit to Tuscany, with the clear purpose of putting pressure on a vacillating Grand Duke to accept a Concordat which would be entirely to the Pope's satisfaction. He departed without his Concordat and without arousing much excitement either at home or abroad. Leopold remained unable to make up his mind and the passive resistance of his ministers did the rest. The only casualties were affronted diplomats, including Normanby, who were not placed at the top table at the state reception given for His Holiness.[28]

It was in the nature of Normanby's official employment that the bulk of his reports to London concerned problems and complaints, and he had to deal with a number of inherited or recurrent issues. One who was despatched without much ceremony was the hapless John Udny, who illustrates how the Napoleonic wars could continue to reverberate half a century on. This man's grandfather, also John Udny, had been consul in Leghorn at the time of the French invasion in 1799 and accordingly suffered the complete trashing of his property and loss of his business. He escaped with his life but died in 1800. His illegitimate son, another John, the father of the later plaintiff, served for a short time as consul during the brief and uneasy peace of 1802. The renewal of the war in 1803 meant that the Udny premises in Leghorn were again sacked, but the family's claims for compensation met with no better reception than those of other merchants who suffered from the French invasions.

Repeated rebuffs did not deter the third John Udny, whose correspondence makes increasingly pathetic reading. Born in Leghorn in 1794, he settled back in Tuscany after the war and contracted two Italian marriages. With every new foreign secretary an Udny letter would appear, requesting either that he or a son be appointed to a consulship or that he receive what he thought was owing to his ancestors. In 1855 he claimed British protection against the Tuscan Government over the disposal of his property between his children. He had complicated matters by assaulting the lawyer leading the case for the *Consiglione di Famiglia*, and Normanby's response to the Foreign Office's enquiries was swift and conclusive: 'Mr Udny has long been known at Leghorn as a person of unsound mind, of which, it seems to me, obvious traces appear in his letter to Viscount Palmerston, which your Lordship has enclosed to me.' Matters must take their course in the courts; Mr Udny had not suffered excessive severity.[29]

Udny was eccentric; Normanby was required to write the final chapter in the story of the disreputable James Dennis and Mrs Mitton. All three principals turned up in Parma in 1855, with Mitton still pursuing his wife and pressing his claims from Florence in a somewhat incoherent letter in which he alleged, among other things, that it was due to Austrian influence that he could not get justice, two of his daughters having married Austrian officers. Predictably, he got no joy. Normanby regretted that his Lordship's 'valuable time should have been taken up by so utterly worthless a case', and apologized for having had to bother him with it again.[30] Dennis died at Parma later in the year (his body was brought to Florence for burial) and the Mittons disappear from history.

Should we need a further reminder that those who claimed British diplomatic protection did not always deserve it, there was Mrs Lewis, who in 1855 complained to the Foreign Office about what she called the indifference and careless conduct of the Embassy. She had arrived at the Hotel New York with a so-called daughter and friend and without any luggage, representing herself as an English princess. After 6 days she attempted a midnight flit without paying the bill. The landlord, unimpressed, restrained her from leaving and St John from the embassy was assigned to sort things out. When he saw 'the soidisant Princess' she summoned her 'private secretary', a Mr Forbes who was 'formerly known to the Police here as of a very equivocal character'. They appeared unable to agree what they were complaining about and were in fact permitted to leave 'that most respectable Hotel' without paying the bill. This had happened twice elsewhere. Mr Forbes meanwhile had been arrested 'having been involved in broils, threatening to fight in defence of the credit of his companions'. Erskine had subsequently been visited by the Minister of the Interior, 'who stated that, although they were evidently swindlers', he had no wish for litigation but proposed simply to expel them from the country, if Erskine had no objection. Erskine was confident that his Lordship would entirely approve and 'would not desire to hear any more of Mrs Lewis or Mr Forbes'. Here indeed was old-fashioned diplomacy and no pettifogging concern for due legal process.[31]

During 1856–1857, after a period of calm, Normanby confronted a sudden flurry of cases of apparent injustice against British subjects. This prompted him to move from a concentration on individual instances to a general consideration of underlying problems and to propose systemic improvements to existing practice. His despatch of 27 June 1857 enclosed a note he had addressed to the Minister Lenzoni, which would 'bring before Your Lordship the working of the system of which Foreigners become in too many instances the helpless victims'. The despatch illuminates one side of the lives lived by Britons, including humble Britons, in Grand Ducal Tuscany.[32]

Hitherto Normanby had preferred to confine himself to personal remonstrances, knowing that the government, faced with an official complaint, would take refuge behind its professed inability to interfere with 'the regular administrations of the Laws'. He had become convinced that this administration was anything but regular and that to claim that judges were not amenable to 'Ministerial supervision is to establish an impunity in wrong doing'. Within the last 20 years, petty local courts had multiplied. The judges who presided there, poorly paid and poorly qualified, were empowered to decide on issues between 'their neighbours, friends and companions on one side, instigated by low attorneys who are also often their connexions' and on the other foreigners, 'ignorant of the language, laws and customs of the Country' who often submitted to the first adverse decision, reluctant to suffer further losses at the hands of another venal lawyer.

Why did the Government tolerate or even 'tacitly encourage such a state of things'? Normanby's answer shows him at his best. It was

necessary to remember that the system here, as understood by the present advisers of the Sovereign, is that of despotism with strong democratic tendencies, that its disposition is always to seek popularity with the many, at the expence of the few, to sacrifice the weak to the strong, and that nothing can be more weak and helpless than a Foreigner in his contests with that class of the population, who seem to victimise him according to Law, unless he is in some shape or other supported by the powerful intervention of his own Country.

It was generally felt that 'an Englishman has no chance of even-handed justice' from one of these lower courts. The superior Courts were 'presided over by a very different class of men', but most of the cases in which poorer English residents were interested involved amounts of about £20 or less and did not permit the right of appeal. Thus, the system 'shuts the door of Justice against those who have been condemned behind their backs'.

The case of Mrs Jenner illustrated these points. Normanby had first raised it with the Justice Minister, Lami, whose unsatisfactory reply was also enclosed to the Foreign Office. Arriving at Pisa in January 1855, she mistakenly trusted the good faith of a landlord, Policarpo Rotondo, who persuaded her to stay one night in his apartment, even though she preferred to go to a hotel, assuring her she was making no commitment in so doing. She remained a mere two nights in the apartment, but had to pay for that imprudence to the tune of 1 month's rent with expenses, before she could regain her possessions, which had been seized by the gendarmerie on an affidavit from Rotondo. She then left Pisa and did not return until the spring of 1857, when to her shock she found that in her absence judgement for a further three months' rent had been given against her. Her carriage was seized at Leghorn, and when it proved to be of insufficient value she was threatened with personal arrest if she did not pay. She had known nothing of the case, in which she was apparently represented by the attorney Chiesi (the pastor of the Protestant congregation at Pontedera), who had sent her a bill for costs which included charges for consultations in 1856, when she had not been in Tuscany.

Normanby did not mince his words to Lenzoni: 'I have no hesitation in saying that for such an act an attorney in England would be struck off the Rolls.' Quizzed by Normanby, the landlord Rotondo admitted that during the 3 months for which he was claiming from Mrs Jenner he had in fact let the property to someone else. Mrs Jenner could not appeal against the judgement because the sum in dispute was insufficient and the time limit for an appeal to the Court of Cassation had passed. Lami's lengthy reply to Normanby's initial complaint struck all the wrong notes. Mrs Jenner had not been prosecuted under any law specifically directed at foreigners; Normanby's grievance was rather that such prosecutions were vexatiously brought against foreigners on the calculation that they would be found guilty, pay up and be unable to appeal because of the small amounts involved. As for the facts of the case, Lami simply preferred Rotondo's claim that Mrs Jenner had agreed with him for 3 months to the lady's statement that she had not. Tito Chiesi was reputed an honest lawyer, and had been recommended to Mrs Jenner by the Rev. Henry Greene. Lami then shifted his ground, admitting that there might be instances of vexatious litigation, but suggesting that Mrs Jenner was a difficult woman to deal with and given to complaining. That may have been true, but was of course irrelevant.[33]

Unquestionably difficult was Caroline Norton, another of Normanby's case-histories. Guy Fleetwood Wilson wrote of her 'ungovernable temper' and addiction to lawsuits.[34] She came to Tuscany breathing fire over her son Brinsley's unsuitable marriage, and found herself on the wrong end 'of a suit got up by a low attorney on the part of a discharged Servant, which suit was ultimately declared by the courts to be frivolous and vexatious'. This 'distinguished Lady of European literary reputation' was delayed in Tuscany for 6 weeks by the sequestration of her passport. She was in a hurry and had had no compunction in bypassing Normanby and making a personal appeal to the President of Council, asking him 'as a gentleman to relieve a lady in a strange land from unjust detention'.

In now addressing himself to Lenzoni Normanby verged on the undiplomatic, making no attempt to conceal his outrage with both the legal system and the Minister of Justice. So far from having obtained what he called 'the most exact information' (*le più scrupolose informazioni*), Lami had simply repeated *ex parte* statements full of inaccuracies. Normanby felt it necessary to remind him that his task was to respond to an ambassadorial complaint about an alleged injustice, not to deliver an *ex cathedra* judgement. The complaint required specific 'examination and rejoinder', and Normanby would have had more confidence in Lami's knowledge of his own laws if the latter had been aware that the seizure of Mrs Norton's passport was illegal, as subsequently declared by the courts.

Lami had asked rhetorically whether Normanby presumed to question the competence of the Tuscan inferior courts or whether it was credible that any court in any country would have decided differently. Normanby responded, 'I feel here the Minister meets me upon ground where my experience is at least equal to his.' Here he was able with some justification to appeal to his own long experience of the country, which extended over 30 years or more. Before changes introduced in 1838–1839 it had been the practice to hear 'all incidental disputes between natives and Foreigners' before the Commissary of Police. These proceedings might be arbitrary, but they were open to the direct intervention of the Government on the one hand and the foreigner's diplomatic representative on the other. There had rarely been any complaint, and the summary judgements that were delivered saved the foreigner both time and money.

It was now Normanby who shifted his ground, but to some effect. Was Lenzoni aware of the value of British residents to the population of the Grand Duchy?

I have made enquiries of Bankers and others most likely to be well informed, and I think I am within the mark when I state as the average of the sum spent by my countrymen, Residents and Travellers within the year as 7,000,000 of Tuscan lire. This advantageous resource, as a receipt, is worth consideration in a small state, and can be estimated by comparison with its expenditure as more than double the whole Budget of the Ministry of Justice, including salaries of Judges magistrates and maintenance of all the Prisons &c &c.

This explosive and somewhat uncharacteristic outburst seems to have caught the Tuscan government by surprise and may well have surprised the Foreign Office, which was, however, quick to give its envoy full support, threatening to lay the whole correspondence before Parliament

> in order that British subjects may have public warning of the risks to which they expose themselves by residing in the Dominions of the Grand Duke, where the hospitality and liberal treatment of foreigners for which Tuscany was once renowned, are no longer to be met with.[35]

Given Normanby's relationship with the Grand Duke, the revelation of Lami's incompetence was something that Lenzoni could well do without. Conciliation was the name of the game, and after a private exchange of letters Normanby was invited to lay his reform proposals before the Tuscan Government. In the case of Mrs Jenner he advised an appeal to the *Corte Regia*. With respect to changes in legal process he urged, first that appeal should always be open to foreigners without any arbitrary limits; second, that all judicial proceedings and legal processes affecting British subjects should be notified to the Legation; third, that in all civil suits 'a Guarantee from a Resident Banker to the amount of the sum in question' should suffice to avoid 'any other preventive process'. Once such a guarantee was obtained, the Gendarmerie were not to be employed 'unless when obviously necessary to secure due respect to the Law'.

By Tuscan standards action followed remarkably quickly. Normanby's suggestions were for the most part backed up by a Grand Ducal decree which in two respects went further: no legal process in which foreigners were concerned would in future be executed by the Gendarmerie (quite who would do so was not clear) and no passports were to be sequestrated on account of civil process. The one area where there was no immediate satisfaction was over the question of appeals, with its implications for the equality of Tuscan subjects before the law. Here the Tuscans pleaded for more time, while giving it favourable consideration.[36] It was arguably Normanby's biggest triumph. Few other British ministers could claim such an impact on Tuscan administrative process, and it was a vindication of his own personal relationship with the Grand Duke, who might not have been so gratified had he known the ambassador's opinion of the Tuscan police: 'lamentably deficient for any purpose which requires intelligence and perseverance'.[37]

In order to bring additional pressure to bear during his discussions with Lenzoni, Normanby raised the case of Mr James O'Hara, a wealthy resident of long standing, who was proposing to sell up his villa and substantial property and leave the country, driven away by his resentment of an injustice perpetrated by the Tuscan courts.[38] When he had first come to Tuscany is unclear, but it was before 1839, when he is named among several 'English' who were considered for the award of nobility by the commune of Fiesole. John Maquay mentions him two or three times, remarking in October 1840 that he was making his villa 'very nice'.[39] O'Hara was unmarried, and the cause of his troubles was his brother Barry. Barry takes up quite a lot of space in the Foreign Office correspondence, primarily because the British vice-consul on Elba, Fossi, an elderly ex-officer in the British Army who was a friend of his, had been so indiscreet as to give damaging character testimony against a Mrs Ellen Bambrick and became the subject of a complaint from her supporters. The story, which went back to 1846, was as squalid as the Dennis affair. To make any sense of it, it is necessary to explain some relationships.

It appears that James O'Hara's two brothers, Barry and William, had been cohabiting with two sisters, Isabella and Ellen Norman, whose mother (another Ellen) was said (by O'Hara) to have dumped her first husband and eloped with a Rowland Blacker. Barry was married to Isabella in London in September 1839 and they had a daughter; allegedly he promptly deserted both of them. Her sister Ellen meanwhile was married to a Mr Bambrick in London in December 1842. In 1846 she came to Tuscany to hunt down Barry O'Hara on behalf of Isabella and her child. Barry was living on Elba at the time, hence Fossi's involvement.[40]

The story unfolded in stages, driven by the financial needs of the Blackers. In May 1849 Rowland Blacker told Palmerston that his daughter (as he called Isabella) was separated from her husband and had obtained a verdict against him in a Florentine court for 'Thirteen hundred pounds past alimony and an order to sequestrate his property until the Money was paid'. His brother James had attempted to defeat this stratagem by claiming that Barry had no property in Tuscany; but Blacker asserted that according to Tuscan law 'as head of the Family [he] would be compelled to support his brother's wife or pay her alimony'. He wanted to know whether James could successfully evade this obligation by pleading that he was a British subject. The guarded reply was that he would certainly not be liable under English law; it all depended on the law of Tuscany.[41]

The next chapter opened in early 1853.[42] The exchanges between Blacker and the Foreign Office were lengthy and complicated, but it appeared that James O'Hara had been compelled by the courts to pay £30 per annum to his deserted sister-in-law and her child, and had done so for a few months, until his brother, bouncing back from a period of exile for immorality, counter-sued for custody of his daughter, whom he wished to have educated more cheaply in a convent. The relevance of Fossi's alleged libels was that Barry O'Hara had used them to blacken Mrs Bambrick's character before the courts. Furthermore, Mr O'Hara (possibly meaning James) had printed a memorial containing these slurs and circulated it round all the reading rooms and cafes in Florence with the same purpose. Mrs Bambrick hit back with an extraordinary parade of Florentine witnesses to her doubtful respectability, and Blacker made a number of subsidiary accusations, for example that Fossi had abstracted a vital document from Consul Macbean's records at Leghorn. The Foreign Office concluded that while Fossi would have done better to stay out of it, he did not have a disciplinary charge to answer (which would be strange if Macbean had substantiated the alleged tampering with his papers). Blacker described this verdict as a 'death blow'.

The later renewal of the campaign was undoubtedly due to Blacker's own predicament. Legal reports in the *Times* on 9 April 1857 and 19 February 1858 reveal a notable history of discounted bills which had not been honoured. He had been declared bankrupt on 21 December 1855 and only a few days later it was reported to the directors of the Royal British Bank (to whom he owed money) that he 'had gone abroad, and that his wife held out hopes of his getting some money through a court at Florence'. It is not entirely clear what happened next, for Normanby's summary sounds as if it refers to the original court ruling in 1849:

At the instance of a certain learned Doctor, the disreputable nature of whose relations with a member of the Family, is notorious at Florence, an order was, I am informed, obtained charging Mr James O'Hara's property with a fixed allowance for a niece, who was living in the Doctor's House with her mother and her aunt, Mr Barry O'Hara, the Father, not being domiciliated in Tuscany, but only a guest in his brother's house. By the universal principle of international Law, the Tuscan Courts had no more right, as far as right is concerned, for such a purpose to seize upon Mr James O'Hara's property in Tuscany, than they would have had upon his property in the west of Ireland.

It looks as if O'Hara had been put under renewed pressure, even if he had ceased to pay, as Blacker had alleged in 1853. The reforms that the Tuscan Government introduced may have come too late to prevent his return to his native Ireland, despite Normanby's attempts to dissuade him.[43]

Humorous echoes of Normanby's outrage sometimes found their way into the English press. In an address to a jury reported in the *Morning Post* on 18 January 1855, Mr Sergeant Byles recalled how

A gentleman in Florence was sued for some cigars which he had never had, and the case came on for trial. He was astonished to hear half-a-dozen witnesses swear that he had had the cigars, and that they had seen him smoke them; but he was utterly astounded when he heard his own advocate produce six witnesses who all swore that they had seen him pay for them.

Charles Lever in his guise as Cornelius O'Dowd told the story of an American who had his passport impounded because a fellow on the next floor down claimed he was indebted to him. The rogue produced a Count to testify that he had seen this loan made, but the American's lawyer resolved the difficulty by producing two witnesses who saw him pay the non-existent debt.[44]

Whatever the merits of his handling of these cases, Normanby suffered from an increasing image problem, which resulted largely from the fact that the English reading public, both at home and in Florence, was probably more knowledgeable about Italian affairs in the 1850s than at any previous time. Italy was rarely out of the news between 1848 and 1859. The volume of newspaper coverage was to reach a peak in 1859–1861 as unification was achieved, before falling back during the 1860s. Although the English public was informed, it was not always accurately informed; but time and again it got news as fast as the Foreign Office did.[45] The fact that much of the press became more anti-Austrian during the 1850s meant that Normanby was increasingly fair game; criticism of him was frequent and strident and coverage of Tuscan affairs ever more unsympathetic to the Grand Duke and his government.

The Thunderer led the campaign, at first more in sorrow than in anger. On 4 September 1856 it sighed

> Of Florence we fear it would be idle to speak. Old party ties, old political associations, old private friendships will continue to avail more than the public good. A pleasant retreat has been provided for a statesman oppressed with age, and, we sincerely regret to add, with bodily infirmities. England is not represented in Central Italy at the present time, and to this conclusion we must resign ourselves.

On 18 November a long report from the paper's Florentine correspondent offered an analysis of the influence of Piedmont and its impact on Tuscan policy. It listed four recent changes: the growth of what it calls *italianisme* in Tuscany, the detachment of the country from the Royal family, the impoverishment particularly of the *contadini* (two-thirds of the population) and the collapse of the power of the government, which had lost its base in the people's attachment to the royal family, largely dissipated by the Grand Duke's attachment to Austria. Baldasseroni had not succeeded in reducing the expense of an inflated bureaucracy which (in a chance echo of Normanby's own assessment in a different context) 'is the socialism of the government'. The government was mistaken in placing its reliance on 'this greedy host', for it was 'an army that puts itself up for auction, and with a promise of slight augmentation in the salaries it would be at the service of the revolutionists to-morrow'. The correspondent's full wrath was reserved for Landucci, 'a blind Reactionist' who ensured that the efforts of the police were 'always directed against liberal ideas rather than against thieves and robbers'.

The significance of all this for Normanby was now revealed. He was not alone in his incompetence, for the writer had no great opinion of the *corps diplomatique* as represented at Florence; they all had their enthusiasms, Normanby's being gastronomy. All the same, if the British Government really wanted to understand what was going on in Italy,

> it should send a real representative here, and not continue to be misrepresented by a nobleman who, though justly popular for his many amiable qualities in private life, makes no secret of his opinion that Austrian influence and Austrian occupation are necessary for Italy.

The writer claimed that unnamed people at Florence 'express great astonishment at the want of accord between the language of our Ministers in Parliament and in congress and that commonly held by their representative in Central Italy'.

Here was a message which, if repeated often enough, was bound to make an impact. Not only did the name Landucci come to stand for negative reaction, but the gap between the wishes of the British government at home and the policy of its representative on the spot was highlighted. The report conveyed another message which many British (though not all) wanted to hear, that the Tuscan peasantry were not an inert loyal mass, but increasingly alienated from the Grand Duke and his Austrian dynasty. Their economic position had deteriorated, and they had learned to see this as a consequence of 'an anti-nationalistic system'. In this writer's view, the peasantry were everywhere talking politics and all were impassioned for the 'national cause'. Normanby would continue to deny this; there would be no agreement on the point down to unification and beyond.

The campaign, sustained throughout 1857, reached a crescendo early in 1858 and could not but ultimately undermine the noble Lord's position. The sheer range of issues covered by papers which were available in Florence ensured that English residents were kept informed. In addition, the time-lag by the late 1850s was getting ever shorter. Reports from Florence were being published in a little over a week and the papers were returning to Florence at about the same speed; thus residents were certainly in the know at least as quickly as the embassy might be receiving instructions from the Foreign Office. Those who were familiar with either French or Italian were thus enabled to weigh what they received from a censored Florentine newspaper or from Paris against what they received from England. Normanby's tendency to suppose that his knowledge of Tuscany was unequalled could therefore be hazardous. He had been around a long time, but there were others in Florence who could compete with him.

As he travelled back in early July 1855 from another visit to England, John Maquay heard that the cholera was raging in Florence. Its stirrings had been felt by the Brownings already during the spring, when both Pen and Robert were unwell. The imminence of the cholera meant that Elizabeth was more reconciled to leaving Florence during the summer: 'there was a case in our street this morning. You know how little brave I am about such things.'[46] The disease blighted the summer and autumn of 1855 and is a recurrent presence in the Maquay diary. Both Elena and their youngest son William were unwell at this time, for other reasons. John was indirectly affected in his capacity as banker, when Arthur Boyd died on 28 July. In the absence of any relatives, John organized the funeral, and 'looked over some of his things & found his will & 172 dollars which I took possession of The Legation would not seal his effects hunted about for Wilson to give a certificate that he did not die of cholera'. On 19 August John experienced one bizarre side effect: the robbing of his garden of every lemon, 'some 25 or 30 dollars worth at least they are in great demand on account of the Cholera'.

On the following day he heard from both his son John and from Tommy, whose prolonged silence had been worrying him. Tommy had been ill in the Crimea but was recovering. The reality of the disease was further brought home on 24 August when Iandelli, *custode* of the English Church, died of it in 6 hours. John's belief that the epidemic was abating proved illusory with the renewal of the heat in early September. He himself was temporarily unwell with his 'bowels much out of order' and, perhaps paradoxically, for once recorded his birthday (his 64th) without any pious reflections on the need to prepare to meet his Maker.[47] Between July and September there were 3023 deaths from the disease in Florence, out of the 4663 who contracted it. Normanby had nothing but praise for the *Misericordia*, which seemed at times overwhelmed, but he had doubts about the government.[48] At least, as far as the cholera was concerned, the onset of winter promised relief.

In October, unnoticed or at least unmentioned by John Maquay, a sensational and unusual crime was committed against an English resident. One of the attractions of Florence to the British was that violence against the persons of foreigners was very rare, and if Thomas Trollope, among others, was to be believed the crime-rate in general was exceedingly low. Trollope's chronology, as so often, is vague, but he thought that there was a 'very remarkable absence of all crimes of violence in the earlier time of my residence there', in which he seems to have included the 1850s. This was not due to police vigilance, there being no police worthy of the name, but both burglary and pocket-picking were unheard of and the streets were safe by day and night even for unaccompanied women. This was perhaps an idyllic view: John Maquay was robbed in Florence for the first time in 1823 and for the last in 1852 (apart from losing his lemons to the cholera).[49] Nonetheless it was disquieting when on the morning of 17 October 1855 John Corry was found murdered in his apartments.

Aged about 65, Corry (or Corrie – the spelling varies) had been resident in Florence for about 4 years but was something of a recluse. He had recently made the acquaintance of a young man at the tavern where he usually dined, and on two or three evenings before the murder had brought him back to his apartment 'and remained playing at Dominoes with him till half past nine or ten o'clock, when the young man had always taken his departure'. On the night of the 16th no one heard or saw the young man go. On the morning of the 17th the door was found locked on the inside with the key removed, and when it was broken down by the police Corry's body was discovered, his throat slit from ear to ear; 46 ½ Napoleons in gold, 3600 Tuscan *lire*, some railroad shares and his silver watch were found to be missing.

The police investigation appeared to have been exemplary. The prime suspect was discovered to be Ernesto Fambrini, who had recently come to Florence from Montepulciano where he was in bad odour with the police. He was duly arrested and charged on 21 October. Evidence of bloody clothes found in his possession seemed conclusive, but the trial was delayed as the police began to find evidence to link him with other unsolved crimes, and it was not until 2 June 1856 that he stood trial for three other murders to which he confessed as well as that of Corry. He died in prison shortly after the trial, whether or not from suicide, which he had already attempted, is not clear.[50]

With the promptitude that was now normal, the *Times* and other papers reported the murder on 26 October, without much detail.[51] To the *Times* correspondent the incident was symptomatic of a wider malaise. Tuscany represented 'a fearful state of increasing distress, caused partly by bad harvests, partly by cholera, and partly by misgovernment'. The writer assumed that Corry had been killed for the sake of plunder. No one of the causes mentioned could be held solely responsible for this state of affairs, but 'the Government has destroyed confidence, and consequently crippled trade during the last seven years'. A hard winter was in prospect.

For John Maquay, it began badly. More letters came from Tommy in late September, after Sebastopol was taken, but at the end of October his father received the unexpected news that he had arrived in Malta with the *London*. Nothing more was said until, another month later, John learned that his son was in hospital at Valletta with a fever. December was largely occupied by a journey to Malta to find Tommy and (when it became possible to move him) to bring him back to Florence to convalesce. It was a traumatic experience, but they got home on Christmas Day, Tommy's birthday.

After these alarums, 1856 began with the appearance of normality. On New Year's Day John went to court to introduce visiting Americans and did so again at a court Ball on the 16th, which was attended also by his eldest son George. George was of an age now to accept invitations (for example to Lady Normanby's) independently. Tommy made progress, but John was clearly feeling his age; on 4 February he intended 'to go to the last Ball at Court but when the time came preferred the Chimney corner'. Despite being afflicted with rheumatism he planned and gave four big weekly parties, of which the first suffered because two other parties took place on the same evening: 206 were invited but only 85 came. Nonetheless there was dancing until 3 am, although John himself went to bed at half past one; today one would regard this as strange behaviour for a host.

His guest-lists provide another snapshot of a sizeable social circle, largely but by no means entirely Anglophone. John noted how many had attended which party and asterisked the Americans. The lists altogether comprehend an impressive range of friends old (such as Madame Galeazzi and Mrs Fombelle) and new (such as the young men from the embassy). During this period, the relationship between the Maquays and Charles Lever became closer, thanks to Lever's growing friendship with John's young cousin and frequent guest in Florence John Adair, whom Lever appointed an executor of his will. On 10 May 1856 Maquay records that 'Lever came up to witness a deed as he intends accompanying John Adair to England tomorrow'.

Lever's first biographer, William Fitzpatrick, later acknowledged the help he had received from John Adair when gathering information for his work. Among the informants whom he quoted on the subject of Lever's life in Florence was a Mrs M--, who left a lively picture of Lever at the Tuscan Court:

In one part of the palace card-playing would be going on, while the intoxicating whirl of the dance held sway in another. When deep in his game of whist and with me as his partner, he often, on hearing some favourite air struck up by the band, flung down his cards, saying 'I must give my little wife a turn;' which having done, he rapidly resumed his place at the game. The polka was at all times the dance of which he was most fond. Mrs Lever was so small and he so fat that in heeling and toeing it I must admit he cut a rather comical figure; but all admitted his abiding love for her; and he certainly looked supremely happy in her companionship.[52]

It is tempting to think that Mrs M—- was Elena Maquay, who at the time Fitzpatrick was at work was a widow, living not far from Adair's seat at Bellegrove, but it is impossible to prove.

On 27 May 1857 John had a 'Long chat with Lever at his house about his trip to England & negociations with the Derby party &c'.[53] Lever was importuning the Conservatives for a diplomatic post, which bore fruit, when Derby came to power in 1858, in the grant of the vice-consulship at La Spezia on £250 a year – a useful little addition to his income given that, although his earnings from books and journalism sometimes exceeded £2,000 per annum, he tended to spend up to the hilt. Lever would have preferred Naples, but contrived to spend most of his time at Florence, there apparently being nothing to do at Spezia, and to hang on to the post for 9 years before it was abolished.[54]

In general John's diary gives the impression of an established social routine unfolding without much disturbance other than bouts of indifferent health. He abstained from involvement in one craze which obsessed many of his compatriots. On 2 January 1856 he 'went up in evening to Colombaia to see Table turning. Many rotations &c, but was told they were not good that night'.[55] It is his sole reference to Florentine spiritualism.

It was not new. From late 1852 onwards Elizabeth Browning's letters show not only that she was fascinated by it but that it had become a major talking-point among the expatriates. It was a web woven between Florence, Rome, England and the United States, with intelligence conveyed by both personal contact and correspondence. On 8 January 1853 Elizabeth asked Miss Mitford whether her American friends had told her anything about 'the rapping spirits': 'Most curious these phenomena'. In the same letter she referred to Frederick Tennyson as a fellow-explorer, and also to her discussions with young Robert Bulwer Lytton, in whom she found the spiritualist soulmate that her sceptical spouse was not. Tennyson she thought was 'a loveable upright truthful person, interesting in many ways – an earnest Christian too, which is a pleasant thing to meet with … but rather heavy in conversation, it must be allowed'. His Christianity was of a distinctive kind, if we are to believe that 'He said the other night quite seriously that the sea would be abolished to make more room, & that Christ would reign at Jerusalem & carry on the government of the world by means of the electric telegraph'.[56]

Lytton brought to the spiritualist party the influence of his father Sir Edward, also a believer. In another letter to Henrietta, written from Bagni in the summer of 1853, Elizabeth reported at length on Sir Edward's views on the 'character of the agency' which produced the phenomena. He would not come to any definite conclusion as to whether this was or was not the spirits of the departed, but excluded 'all notion of imposture', which Elizabeth proclaimed to be anyway 'perfectly impossible'. Elizabeth also told Henrietta about the American William Wetmore Story, who claimed from Rome that he could move both tables and men. Even Elizabeth found his display unconvincing, but conceded that he might be 'a good mesmerist'.[57]

There were, of course, sceptics, with Robert Browning nearest to hand. One might expect the Scottish Free Church Minister, Mr Hanna, to be sceptical, but he expressed it rather oddly: he thought of the Roman manifestations that 'First, they are not poetical, & then they are contradictory to Revelation'.[58] Lady Normanby was also hard to convince. Early in 1854 Robert Lytton told the Brownings that she 'tells me that she has seen a table follow a person about a room, *without any imposition of hands*, but as having a will of its own, yet seeing she did not believe'.[59]

In marked contrast to the sceptical Lady Normanby was Seymour Kirkup, the most enduring of all English residents and a friend of both the Brownings and the Trollopes. Reference has already been made to his role in the discovery of Giotto's supposed portrait of Dante in the Bargello. When his housekeeper's attractive 17-year-old daughter Regina conjured up the spirit of Dante for him, he was conquered. Early in 1855 he came to see the Brownings and announced his conversion from atheism to belief in the spiritual world, thanks to Regina's rappings. Robert thought Regina was a humbug. While not going so far, Elizabeth wished to apply stricter standards of proof: 'Mr Kirkup is deaf, & though a man of great intelligence, he is not philosophical in his modes of carrying on experiments.'[60] Regina bore a daughter in 1854 and, when she lay dying at the age of 19 in 1856, managed to convince Kirkup that the child was his.

Frederick Tennyson had his own take on the phenomena, saying that 'it's a device of Satan, to persuade man that his will is omnipotent, and so give him over, body & soul, to a legion of devils'. Meanwhile, 'in the midst of all this visionariness, my poor Robert is in a glorious minority, trying hard to keep his ground as a denier' 'I cant understand, says Mr Tennyson in his grave slow way, on what possible principle you can resist the evidence'. Robert maintained that he had an open mind and was 'ready to believe what he shall see & hear himself'. He was 'prepared to try some experiments' but his standards were perhaps too exacting.

> We tried the table-experiment the other day ... Mr Tennyson, Mr Lytton, Robert & I, & *failed*. We tried only for twenty minutes though – & Robert was laughing all the time ... which was wrong because there ought to be concentration of thought.[61]

It was from America or Americans that Elizabeth and others received a lot of their information about the manifestations. From the summer of 1854 onwards much came from the art-dealer Jarves. It was also from America that a celebrity came to ride, for a short time, on the crest of this wave of faith. Born in 1833 at Currie near Edinburgh, David Dunglas Home moved with his family to Connecticut when he was 9. In 1850 his mother died and this seems to have prompted the 'studious, dreamy, and sensitive boy often ill' to have visions. Spirit rapping and ostensible communications from the dead followed, but his aunt, a strict Presbyterian, would have none of it and threw him out of the house. His career sprouted in the fertile soil of New York.[62]

In January 1855 he was diagnosed with pulmonary consumption, and a voyage to Europe was recommended. In April 1855 he arrived in London. Armed with introductions from American spiritualists, Home was admitted to English houses throughout the spring and summer. One of the most important was that of Mr J. S. Rymer, an Ealing solicitor, with whom he stayed for some weeks. Many of the big names of Victorian England attended the Ealing *séances*: Sir Edward Bulwer Lytton, Lord Brougham, Robert Owen, Buckle, Thackeray, Dickens, Anthony Trollope and more significantly the Brownings and Thomas Trollope and his mother. Home announced his intention of coming to Italy for his health; Thomas Trollope had accommodation and every reason to encourage.

Home had no intention to defraud in the sense of relieving the gullible of large sums of money. He moved around as a sort of professional guest, taking up the invitations which increasingly flooded in to come to stay and perform, to make the tables move and the spirits rap, to commune with the dead. He received hospitality and benefits in kind, but never performed directly for payment. The vicious lampoon, *Mr Sludge the Medium*, perpetrated by the unbeliever Robert Browning in 1864, was a gross exaggeration. Whether Browning would have written it had Elizabeth still been alive is questionable. As it happened, the Brownings were to be absent from Florence during Home's visit, but in a letter written just before they left Elizabeth specifically referred to his refusal of the money that had been pressed upon him by some of the '200 infidels' whom he had converted to a better way of thinking. A potential recruit to their ranks was Mrs Trollope, who, Elizabeth knew, had set off with her son to London 'EXPRESSLY to investigate'. She thought this 'quite rational in Mrs Trollope, inasmuch as she is in a state of profound scepticism as to a future prospect for man of any kind, & is willing to catch at a means which had led many to happy conclusions'.[63] Clearly her own belief in the spirits, although like others she intellectualized it, answered an emotional need which may be sensed in her yearnings for her absent family and for the acceptance from her father which never came. Her references to spiritualism and to Swedenborgianism, with which she had early become acquainted, are often interwoven.

Home arrived in October, accompanied by Mr Ryder, the son of the gentleman with whom he had stayed in Ealing. The visit began well. Many *séances* were held, the manifestations were reported strong and many prominent Anglo-Florentines made visits, sometimes multiple visits, to Villino Trollope. However, John Maquay's regular visits to the house for whist suddenly vanish from the journal, only to resume after Home's departure. Clearly the new craze had replaced the regular whist parties and was not, one imagines, to John's taste.

Two accounts give some detail of Home's visit. The first was written by Frances Eleanor Trollope, Thomas's second wife who, writing the life of Frances Trollope some forty years after the event, used a detailed journal kept by Thomas but since lost. The second is Home's own autobiography, published in 1864. They deal with different aspects of the experience. Trollope was determined to understand the phenomena, Home, taking them for granted, wished to explain his own role in producing them.[64] Thomas noted plenty of physical phenomena, such as 'moving of heavy tables, the twirling round of heavy lamps in the sight of all the company' and the rest, all agreed to have happened by everyone present, but he was less convinced by the metaphysics: 'generally vague and even when distinct, absolutely worthless as purporting to come from – I will not say higher intelligences, but – intelligences equal to those of the beings who were stated to be present'. Moreover the spirits appeared to be uneasy under Trollope's cross-examination, seldom enduring it for more than a few minutes at a time. This increasingly persuaded him that there was no truth in 'the communion of disembodied minds, with minds still acting through the medium of material bodies'.

It was ominous for Home's continued residence in the Trollope household that Thomas, if not others, was reaching 'the decided opinion' that 'Mr Hume is not in the ordinary affairs of life an honourable or true man'. He also suspected that to some degree he habitually embellished or assisted the manifestations. Suspicion once admitted made it 'extremely difficult to draw any line, even approximately satisfactory, between the true and the false'. Mrs Trollope for her part was not 'peculiarly agitated' by the spirits, even though Home apparently managed to conjure up her father, mother and some children. Nevertheless in her old age she remained more of a believer in him than her son was. Her last novel, *Paris and London*, published in 1856, contains an account of a *séance*, the medium Mr Wilson an unmistakable portrait of Home.

In Home's own account there is (perhaps significantly) no mention at all of the Trollopes or of the month he spent as their guest.

Early in the autumn of 1855 I went to Florence accompanied by the son of a gentleman with whom I had been residing at Ealing. I remained in Florence till the month of February 1856, and although some persons there did all they could to injure me by false statements, I was only the more cherished by those who best knew me ... The manifestations while I was at Florence were very strong.

He proceeds to narrate a *séance* at the Countess O's, before giving a lengthy description of a number of *séances* at the house of an English resident in Florence which harboured an unhappy ghost. This was the Villa Colombaia, home of John Maquay's close friends, the Crossmans. (It may well be relevant that the Reverend George had died in February 1854.) Along with Home, Mrs Baker (née Crossman) left a detailed account of her experiences with the ghost of a monk called Giannana, who had been a murderer and now sought rest for his soul. There was a cold atmosphere wherever he appeared, but he promised to refrain from disturbing Mrs Baker 'if she prayed that he might find some repose. After the departure of this ghost, other *séances* were held in her bedchamber, at which good and holy spirits manifested themselves, and behaved in a very comfortable and encouraging way'. The ghost returned after the Crossmans left the villa, according to a letter from Mrs Baker to Home in April 1860.[65]

Home was living alone when on the night of 5 December 1855 he was attacked by a man with a knife when on the way back to his lodgings through deserted streets. His life was providentially saved by the door key over his heart and the thickness of his clothing. 'I never discovered the perpetrator, nor the cause of my life being attacked. Many reasons were assigned, amongst them robbery, mistaken identity, and religious intolerance.' From this moment it appears to have been downhill all the way. Landucci allegedly sent him a quite extraordinary message, requesting

that I would not walk about the house at night between the lights and the window, or go out in the streets in the daytime, giving as a reason that some of my enemies had been playing upon the superstitions of the peasantry, and telling them that it was my practice to administer the seven sacraments of the Catholic church to toads, in order by spells and incantations to raise the dead. This had so enraged and excited them that they were fully bent on taking my life, and for that purpose were concealed about the neighbourhood with fire arms.

Who were these 'enemies' who were telling peasants this extraordinary story? Home had hardly been in Florence long enough to make Italian enemies. That Landucci was prepared to tolerate armed men skulking in the streets of Florence, in preference to providing this somewhat down at heel and unwelcome visitor with the fastest possible exit visa, seems unlikely. British subjects had been expelled for less than Home had been up to. On Home's own admission, he was now abandoned by friends who had given him lodging a few weeks before. 'I was left in Florence without money, and my friends in England having their incredulity imposed upon by some scandalmongers, and thinking me to be leading a most dissolute life, refused to send me even money of my own entrusted to their care.' Thus ended the Home episode as far as Florence was concerned. His powers apparently deserted him. For a year he attached himself to a Polish Count B and trundled off to Naples in February 1856. On the way he decided to become a Roman Catholic and met the Pope.

On 1 April 1856 Mrs Browning wrote to Arabella from Paris with the latest bulletin about the seer's tribulations, transmitted to her from Florence. The word was that he had been forced to leave Florence 'through a notification from the government – the spiritual movement extending further than could be tolerated, papistically'. Apparently the Government had in January informed Lord Normanby that no Tuscan subjects could be permitted to attend *séances*, and this had been followed by an outright prohibition from the Archbishop of Florence on the holding of *séances* at all, which Normanby conveyed to Major Gregorie. Landucci's supposed warning to Home must have preceded these moves; it would otherwise have been unnecessarily oblique. Home himself says nothing about the Archbishop's prohibition, and Normanby evidently did not think it proper or necessary to inform the British Government about these goings-on. If Elizabeth was correctly informed (by Jarves), British Catholics were among those drawn into the craze. The banker French had asked his father's spirit to prove its credentials by playing on the accordion an air which he had composed for the banker's wedding, 'which had never existed out of manuscript, or been known to any person in Florence except himself. The air was played *instantly, & most beautifully*'.[66]

The end of Home was not the end of Florentine spiritualism. Some 9 months after he left Mrs Browning wrote to Henrietta:

I have heard quantities on the Home question and everything confirmatory. It is curious how persons who agree in nothing else except in disliking Hume (for the foolish young man has succeeded in making himself universally disagreeable) all agree in considering the phenomena above nature.

Count Cottrell, who had turned his back on Home at Lady Normanby's as a 'worthless fellow', in the next breath affirmed a communion with his dead baby. Sceptical friends of Robert's had been totally convinced by Home's performance in their own home. The American Mrs Kinney 'thanked Robert vehemently for his violence to Home', before talking of a lifting table. Everyone hated him and wanted not to believe in him, but could not, for the 'facts' spoke for themselves.[67]

To the end of her days Elizabeth retained her belief, as Robert retained his unbelief. It may be that Major Gregorie also remained an unlikely seeming believer: Elizabeth told Arabella in November 1857 that he had invited Home (last seen in Paris) to Florence, but she doubted whether he would come, and if he did she would avoid him for Robert's sake. In March 1858 she reported what sound like conflicting rumours about Home's movements; he had been in Florence briefly; he had been at Pisa; he was coming to Florence next month to stay with the Crossmans, with whom he had stayed before; now he had gone to Rome, having allegedly confessed at Pisa that his powers were failing him. Elizabeth and Robert had agreed that Robert was not to kick him if he met him in the street.[68]

The Brownings at this period were spending a smaller proportion of their time at Casa Guidi, even when they were in Italy, than they had done in earlier years.[69] One reason was the never-ending quest for a permanent improvement in Elizabeth's health. From the middle of 1855 to October 1856 they were in France and England. Nine months at Casa Guidi were followed by two and a half at Bagni and then another nine at Casa Guidi. They spent the latter half of 1858 in France and were then in Rome for the winter, briefly touching base at Casa Guidi en route. They did not return to Florence until 30 May 1859 and therefore missed the departure of the Grand Duke. In sum, they were in Florence for well under half the period between the end of the Austrian occupation and the end of the Grand Duchy. Until 1859 political comment in Elizabeth's letters seems to be rarer by comparison with the early 1850s, as the times themselves were so much quieter. The Austrians remained hated, Piedmont was a good thing and Mazzini was unscrupulous, working his spells on the easily persuaded with 'his mesmeric eyes', but Garibaldi doesn't figure. Apart from Elizabeth's growing disagreement with Thomas Trollope about Louis Napoleon, there is very little of relevance to the theme of this book.

A major upheaval in the Brownings' domestic arrangements was caused by the marriage of their maid Elizabeth Wilson, 4 months pregnant, to Ferdinando Romagnuoli, just before they were to leave Florence for a prolonged period. The ceremony was performed on 12 June 1855 at the British Embassy, with Normanby and the Brownings as witnesses. It was, as Elizabeth admitted, 'a shake to the security of my comfort'. She told herself not be selfish; Ferdinando was 'excellent & will be an admirable husband'. She was much preoccupied with his religion and its short-term effects. Although 'he is no more a catholic than I am' and would never go to confession again once he was 'safely married', there was concern about the wedding ceremony itself, which was clearly not performed according to the rules. 'The catholic form', she writes, 'will be gone through in Paris', but the Anglican ceremony had already taken place, performed by an unnamed 'English clergyman' (revealed by the church records to have been the Reverend Huntington from Leghorn). With a touch of over-dramatization, she continues: 'It's to be considered no marriage, you understand, till after the Catholic ceremony – & we keep it secret for fear of the priests, who might get Ferdinando stopped from leaving Tuscany, & so produce a tragedy.' Ferdinando had obtained from the Archbishop of Florence a certificate which declared him free from 'matrimonial bonds' and exempted from the need for banns.[70] No mention was ever made of a papal dispensation.

The Catholic ceremony did indeed take place in Paris, evidently after some negotiations which resulted in a concession: Wilson had to swear only that she would put no obstacle in the way of the children being brought up as Catholics.[71] This was done, according to Elizabeth, to make everything right for Ferdinando 'in his own country'. Presumably obtaining permission in Tuscany would have involved stricter undertakings than the couple wished; but it remains slightly puzzling why both ceremonies could not have been performed in Paris, thus obviating any possible problem with the Tuscan clergy, and why the Florentine embassy consented to this apparent infringement of customs it had previously upheld. The child when it came was a complication and had to be parked with Elizabeth Wilson's mother in England. Only one child of the marriage was born in Tuscany, Pylades Francis on 11 November 1857, who was baptized by O'Neill on the following 3 January.

The long absences of the Brownings involved them in the problems of subletting, like other English residents who needed to make long visits back to the home country. The alternative was to give up the tenancy, sell everything including the furniture and make a fresh start when one returned, which could be expensive, particularly when return was fairly certain, perhaps within the year. As Elizabeth told John Kenyon, she could not live as far north as Paris, and if they had given up 'these delightful rooms' and packed up or sold their furniture, they would have suffered both repentance and expence. Their landlord, Centofanti, – 'in a spasm of terror at losing us', she thought – had lowered the rent by £10: 'Now, for seven excellent rooms, most of them very large, & a kitchen etc with terraces, we pay only twenty pounds a year.' The businessman Kenyon doubtless quickly perceived that the landlord, assured of £20, would more than recoup the £10 rebate by a series of short lets, as well as making something for the Brownings. Elizabeth's view was less glowing on her return. Centofanti had disappeared to Milan leaving his accounts and was 'trying to cheat us'. The accounts mentioned only two tenants, but the porter and others testified that there had been three; the house had been let for 11 of the first 12 months of their absence. She reckoned that he owed them about £22 over and above the £12 he had left them; there would be a 'vexatious' row when he returned.[72] Their experience will have been shared by others, and they were almost certain losers if as foreigners they attempted to seek redress through the Tuscan Courts.

On their return at the end of October 1856 Elizabeth immured herself for 3 months in the warm at Casa Guidi, but with the improvement in the weather and her health she gave a lively picture of the carnival, which had not been the same for some years with the prohibition on masks. This was lifted in 1857, which had a dramatic impact. 'All Florence being turned out into the streets in one gigantic pantomime, one couldn't expect people to be wiser in-doors than out.' Elizabeth got into the mood and went

> (in domino and masked) to the great opera ball … Robert, who had been invited two or three times to other people's boxes, had proposed to return this kindness by taking a box himself at the opera this night and entertaining two or three friends with gallantina and champagne.

Elizabeth very daringly left the box 'and Robert and I elbowed our way through the crowd to the remotest corner of the ball below. Somebody smote me on the shoulder and cried "Bella mascherina!" and I answered as imprudently as one feels under a mask'. She stuck it out till 2 o'clock in the morning though Robert went on till half past four with his friends:

Think of the refinement and gentleness – yes I must call it *superiority* – of this people, when no excess, no quarrelling, no rudeness nor coarseness can be observed in the course of such wild masked liberty. Not a touch of license anywhere. And perfect social equality! Ferdinando side by side in the same ballroom with the Grand Duke and no class's delicacy offended against! For the Grand Duke went down into the ballroom for a short time. The boxes were however dear. We were on a third tier, yet paid £2. 5s English besides entrance money.[73]

Truly it was an Indian summer – for both the Grand Duke and Elizabeth.

It was further warmed by a number of friendships between the Brownings and other residents which blossomed and matured during the late 1850s. The relationship between Thomas Trollope and Robert in particular developed even as Mrs Trollope declined. Isa Blagden was a firm friend and frequent visitor, not just in Florence but also in Rome, particularly when Elizabeth was unwell. Some friendships were lubricated by the presence of children. Hal, the Cottrells' son, born in 1851, was Pen's frequent playmate, and so remained after Elizabeth's death (he was present when Pen's long hair was cut). Count Cottrell was used by Robert to oversee Leighton's design of Elizabeth's tomb in Florence.[74] With the Storys too relations grew closer through the agency of young children. William Wetmore Story records that during the last 3 years before Elizabeth's death he and Robert had been scarcely apart and with Robert's departure from Florence (and his own) 'I have lost my best friend and daily companion in Italy'.[75] Their correspondence continued thereafter but, although warm, inevitably lost something of its intimacy in separation.

Another friend in whom spiritualism lived on was Robert Bulwer Lytton. 1857 saw him back in his favourite haunts with his favourite people. He had wandered off in 1854, following his uncle to Paris and The Hague, but now he was on leave and supposedly preparing for his exams to enter the civil service. Thanks to the recent Northcote-Trevelyan reforms, he needed to pass an examination in a second language other than French if he was to get paid employment in the diplomatic service. Unfortunately he fell ill with gastric fever as soon as he returned to Tuscany. He was nursed by the Brownings and Isa Blagden under the assiduous eye of Dr Trotman at Bagni di Lucca in August, and then by Isa when he returned to Florence in September. Robert Browning provided regular updates for Sir Edward, with regrets about 'a sad length' of medical bills that would have to be met. Young Lytton's grateful pay-off to his friends was to make 'Story tell me all about the spirits in America', which he is sure they have heard, but he includes an account of his last few *séances* which they may not have done.[76]

As the Brownings came and went, always intending to come back, John Maquay planned for his ultimate departure. George's coming of age in March 1856 may have further refined his father's plans. John initially does not seem to have been able to think of any career for his sons other than the armed forces, but George had managed to evade this fate. He was clearly a pleasure-loving young man and John's hopes of at least making a banker out of him met with a number of checks. On 23 June he 'had a serious conversation before dinner with George whose conduct much distresses me on acct [sic] of his general idleness & inattention to business'. Deaths and old age also had their impact on his social circle. On 12 August Maurice Baruch came and played piquet (by no means for the first time) after they had learned that 'old Mrs Trollope could not receive us'. Her whist parties had resumed for a time after the Home episode, but she was now withdrawing from the stage, and John began his own weekly whist parties in December. Another hint of the future came on 27 September when he referred to a hired carriage; he had sold his horse '& don't mean to buy another'.[77]

As usual his comments on public events are intermittent and shed no light on his reasons for leaving Florence, which may anyway have been entirely personal. On 15 December he described rather sourly the public entrance of the Hereditary Prince into Florence with his bride (a daughter of the King of Saxony): 'a poor thing it was, no applause or welcome of any kind beyond the crowd usual on all occasions when anything is going on whether they like it or not'. The old days appeared to have gone for ever, along with St Patrick's Day; 17 March 1857, he noted, passed without mark. A conversation on 21 March with Webb Smith, who was trustee for Montague Pakenham, clearly prompted a conversation with George, not entirely to the liking of father or son. We don't know what passed, for John writes only 'conversation with George!!'. The double exclamation marks speak volumes to those familiar with the code used in the journals.[78]

If John had ever intended to abandon Florence in 1857 he changed his mind, but it had clearly been decided that Elena would leave in the course of the year with William, who was to be put to school in Ireland. In February, Tommy told them that with the end of the war his ship Driver was going to be paid off, and he wanted to come home; John commented 'I am sorry I cannot let him come here'. The navy had other plans for Tommy anyway, and on 29 March John recorded a 'letter yesterday from John [Popham] says Tommy sailed for China in the Shannon which ship I see started on 17th from Portsmouth'. The Daily News on the 18th was but one of the London papers to report the departure of the Shannon. At the end of March there was disquieting news that Greene's bank in Paris had suspended payment, but even before he received confirmation of this John was making arrangements to rent a house for a year from May with the option of keeping it on for another 2 years. Charles Smyth, son of Currell, had started at the bank, staying with John in Florence, but he was seriously ill for most of the time and died of consumption back at Leghorn on 2 April.[79]

John gave his last big party on 7 May. Apart from the usual mix of Italians, Americans and British residents, Normanby, Fenton, St John and Robert Lytton were there from the embassy, as well as Prince Poniatowski and others from the Tuscan Government; some 236 in all were invited.[80] John was in Ireland from 9 July to 31 August, consolidating his finances, realizing assets in Waterford, Dublin and

London, and preparing for a definitive return in 1858. He had eventually decided on Ashfield, a house very near the Adair seat, Bellegrove, and in August they were already unpacking furniture there. John returned to Florence early in September, a mass of aches and pains, and alone.

With the end of Mrs Trollope's whist parties the name Trollope disappears from the diary. The old lady had retired from the social scene but, aged 78, remained alert enough to enjoy the visit of her younger son Anthony and his wife during the course of 1857. Anthony records in his autobiography that this was the first year his mother had not written a novel, 'and she expressed to me her delight that her labours should be at an end, and that mine should be beginning in the same field'.[81] By contrast, her other son and her daughter-in-law were writing a great deal. Thomas was increasingly occupied in researching and writing history. The year 1856 had seen the appearance of *The Girlhood of Catherine de Medici*. Sometime around 1854 he had begun his monumental *History of the Commonwealth of Florence*, a task he was to pick up and put down over the next 10 years as other themes and journalistic calls demanded his attention.[82] It was to be put down in 1859 while he rushed out his political statement, *Tuscany in 1849 and 1859*, pointing out the differences between the two revolutions. *A Decade of Italian Women* also appeared in 1859. Theodosia meanwhile was translating and writing for the *Athenaeum*. Her volume *Social Aspects of the Italian Revolution*, which gathered her related *Athenaeum* pieces together, was to provide a rare account of the events of 1859–1861 from the perspective of an English resident.

Even before those events focussed attention on Italy, the British newspapers continued to give ample space to Tuscany. The year 1857 provides a good sample of the range of their coverage. The comings and goings of Tuscan ministers were reported and their characters assessed. The Grand Duke's difficulties in finding a ministry favourable to the Pope were covered (with some relish) and even a provincial paper like the *Ipswich Journal* could on 2 May publish a letter from Florence which described 'the difficulty of finding competent persons to fill public offices in Tuscany'. Any hint of the unpopularity of the Emperor or of the Grand Ducal family was seized upon. More neutrally, the *Daily News* reported on 27 January that 'The emperor and empress of Austria are on their way to Florence, and Lord John Russell has left it'. The reader might be forgiven for concluding that the two events were connected. The *Belfast Newsletter* on 10 January assured its readers, perhaps somewhat optimistically, that Russell 'during his stay in Florence, became thoroughly acquainted with the past history and present position, with all the sufferings and wrongs of the Tuscan Protestants'. The *Aberdeen Journal* on the 11th was differently focussed: in Florence, 'judging from his appearance, Lord John has found maccaroni a sustaining and invigorating edible.'

Bad news also got wide coverage, most notably a disastrous fire at a theatre in Leghorn in June. According to the Tuscan *Monitore*, a copy of which Normanby sent to the Foreign Office on 12 June, forty-three were killed and thirty-four injured, largely from panic in the audience caused by both the fire and a guard captain who lost his head and, thinking it was a popular disturbance, charged with bayonets and prevented egress from the theatre.[83] The *Morning Post* of 18 June quoted a correspondent, who had written a mere 5 days earlier, to the effect that the *Monitore* had tried to play down the catastrophe; in fact more than 150 had died. This account was full of praise for Consul Macbean, who

> hazarded his own life in his generous attempts to succour others, for the ladder by which he had mounted to the top of the building broke under the weight of those whom he was helping to descend and he was left perched on a window exposed to the rush of those attempting to escape, and very nearly himself precipitated into the street.

The *Morning Chronicle* carried a similar report the following day with some difference of detail, but also praising Macbean, and others followed. Macbean's ears may have burned, but there is no reference to the incident in his official correspondence.

Leghorn was in the news again a few weeks later. An abortive Mazzinian rising coincided with an 8-day social visit by a British fleet under Lord Lyons and, according to some rumours, was precipitated by it. The officers visited Florence and were received by the Grand Duke; there was an open day for visitors to the ships, and a reception was held for the Tuscan Court on board the *Royal Albert*, at which the Grand Duke and Normanby were present. A number of English residents were invited, including the Brownings, but Elizabeth felt she couldn't go and therefore Robert wouldn't.[84] At the other end of town the rising, although more serious than at first thought, was soon put down. The *Daily News* on 9 July reported that efforts had been made to convince the people that Piedmont would take part in the uprising and the English ships would land troops to support it.

> Admiral Lyons, on the contrary, offered to put his forces at the disposal of the government, but they were not required. The injury done to the town of Leghorn is very considerable, as the bathing season, which usually attracts some 15,000 visitors, had only just commenced. The shops, however, are now re-opened, and everything has resumed its usual aspect.

This account was partly contradicted by the *Morning Post* of the same day, which believed that many families that had gone for the bathing had already left, unconvinced by assurances of restored tranquillity. The *Times*, also on the 9th, had the fullest report, which stressed the violence of the 'Mazzinians' and gave details of the fighting.

MPs continued to use the newspapers to address their constituents from afar; alternatively, the papers gave notice of their whereabouts. In the winter of 1856–1857 Viscount Ebrington, heir to Earl Fortescue and one of the members for

Marylebone, was driven to an Italian convalescence by a severe affliction of his eyes; anyone interested in his progress (from Florence to Naples via Rome) might have been able to follow it in the newspapers. His constituents were doubtless pleased, with a general election imminent, to read in the *Morning Chronicle* of 11 March that, although he was still in Florence, he was expected back shortly in order to be re-elected. From Pisa, Sir William Codrington, elected for the eastern division of Gloucestershire, let it be known, by way of the *Bristol Mercury* on 2 May 1857, that, although he had been in Tuscany for his health, he hoped that he would be back in a few weeks. John Bright's farewell to the electors of Manchester was written from Florence on 31 March 1857 and carried by virtually all the papers.

An interesting sidelight on what might be thought of absentee MPs was shed by Charles Hamilton who, while member for Aylesbury, had spent a great deal of time in Florence acting as right-hand man to his brother Sir George. Standing in the Buckinghamshire by-election at the end of 1857, he evidently felt that he needed to explain his previous absences from Parliament. He had been 'fulfilling a very important public duty' and rather unwisely referred his audience to the *Daily News*, which had declared (presumably after his brother's death) that Palmerston would be doing the best thing for the country if he appointed him ambassador in Florence. At this a ribald voice from the audience (as the *News* itself reported on 24 December) cried out, 'What did it cost you to get that in the *Daily News*?' Another heckler asked how much he had got for going to Florence. Hamilton lost to his liberal opponent by 140 votes.

The newspapers catered for the public's interest in Italian art, although not all of the reportage reflected credit on the Tuscans' capacity to look after their heritage. During the autumns of 1855 and 1856 Austen Layard had been hard at work with some assistants recording and making tracings of frescos in central Italy before decay and neglect accomplished their destruction. Some 700 drawings were made and placed on display at 30 Charles Street in London. On 26 June 1857 the *Times* described Layard's discovery of frescoes by Piero della Francesca at Borgo San Sepolcro, in a room used by a bank, to which five different people, all at odds with one another, had five keys. The room was full of 'corn, wool, cloth, oil-jars, and lamps' and the windows had been bricked up. When candles were brought in, 'at length was discovered, traced, and recorded in a faithful drawing, one of the most impressive representations of our Lord's resurrection'. At Arezzo, while Layard was tracing Piero's Constantine fresco,

> the workmen were breaking through the wall above it, and a brick falling struck away half the head of the page who is watching the emperor. When Mr Layard remonstrated, 'Half his face gone?' was the reply, '*Per Bacco!* then we will paint him another!' One of the finest frescoes of Fra Bartolommeo is in a cart-shed at Florence. This Mr Layard found full of water, and was obliged to extemporise a drain before he could begin his work.

Layard gave more examples, and appealed for funds and support to save remaining treasures.

On 6 May the *Morning Post* noted the exhibition in Pall Mall of a 'small but very beautiful and valuable collection, made with great care and discrimination by the proprietor during a six year residence in Italy'. This collector was Thomas du Boulay, a descendant of Huguenot immigrants into England, who had been very friendly with John Maquay during a residence in Florence which began probably in 1852. His family was grown up and variable numbers of du Boulays attended John's parties, but the diaries say nothing about his collection. The *Post* waxed especially effusive about Pampaloni's statue of the Penitent Magdalen, 'a work that would repay a pilgrimage'. Luigi Pampaloni was a pupil of the Florentine sculptor Lorenzo Bartolini, and the works of both would have been familiar to British residents and visitors.[85] One second-generation English resident received publicity in connection with the presumed discovery of a Raphael. The *Morning Post* on 7 July announced that 'the original of the "Madonna di Loreto" is now pronounced by the highest living authorities in Italy to be in the possession of a Mr Walter Kennedy Laurie, an English gentleman resident in Florence'. The verdict was mistaken. Many copies were made of this fine altarpiece (painted for Santa Maria del Popolo in Rome in 1509) and Lawrie probably had one of them; the original is thought to be now in the Musée Condé at Chantilly.[86]

The art of Tuscany attracted one visitor in the summer of 1857 whose interest may fairly be described as professional. Anna Jameson – no newcomer to Florence and its residents – spent some 7 months there collecting material for her *magna opera* on the representation of sacred subjects in art and reporting on her activities in letters to her sisters.[87] She arrived from Rome on 19 May in poor health and was entreated by Lady Herbert and Mrs Browning to get a doctor, who did not please her: 'I can manage myself better'. The Herbert daughters were kind and as useful to her as she would let them be.[88] Her lodgings in Via Maggio were close to Casa Guidi and within sight of the Pitti Palace. She had a large drawing room, bedroom, three smaller rooms, an anteroom for entrance, a kitchen all well furnished plus *servizio* (bed made, rooms cleaned, breakfast prepared), for 15 *scudi* a month (about £3.40). The lady who performed the *servizio* would cook dinner and bring in shopping for a further 3 pauls a week. Her principal expense was a carriage – there was a carriage stand opposite her door – which cost her 3 pauls an hour for hire. Food was cheap. The subscription to Vieusseux was 1 *scudo*, which she regarded as expensive, but the 'excellent' library itself delighted her: she obtained from it 'very valuable books of engravings & for reference' and was accumulating piles of notes against the day when she was fitter for work.

An unexpected diversion in her 'monotonous life' occurred when the Herbert girls were invited to the reception of Lord Lyons and the fleet at Leghorn. Since Lady Herbert could not go, Anna was persuaded to act as chaperone. She 'went reluctantly expecting to be fatigued & bored, but it turned out quite otherwise'. Capt. Blomfield of the *Osprey* was an old friend of Lady Herbert's son Douglas '&

was our constant & devoted cavalier'. In short, she had an unexpectedly good time, although she was mindful of the violence that had taken place in Leghorn a few days previously. The Florentine heat was afflicting, but Anna planned trips to Siena and Prato to view works of art. She had often driven out of an evening with Mrs Browning on the Cascine while Robert rode, but she would not accompany them to Bagni, 'too idle and expensive a place for me to stay at, tho' I may pay them a visit before they leave it'. This she did, but she returned to Florence ahead of them to continue her work.

Here she had to pay more for new lodgings, around £5 10s 0d a month. The winter was spent in Florence and it was not until February 1858 that she was able to leave for Naples because of the cold weather. She therefore witnessed the carnival, but she did not participate in any 'gaieties', not feeling up to all the invitations she had received. She did once see Stentorello, 'but it was too ridiculous – at least for sober me'. Once to the opera, once to one of Lady Normanby's parties, was the extent of her dissipation; she was clearly wedded to the work which a few years later killed her.[89]

Heat overcame everything in Florence in August, according to the *Morning Post* on 25 June 1857:

Scarcely an Englishman is left in Florence – even the temptation of seeing a migratory Pontiff has yielded to the heat. At another season of the year Pope Pius might have seen a fair proportion of the female celebrities of England. Science, as represented by Mrs Somerville, 'holds her speculative tower' in the Via del Mandorlo. It is hardly necessary to say that a house with such an Anglo-Florentine sound as 'Villino Trollope' belongs to Mrs Trollope. Elizabeth Barret [*sic*] Browning has exchanged for the baths of Lucca the first floor of that Casa Guidi which will always be associated with her verse; her friend Mrs James [Jameson?] has left the second floor (where I believe she intends permanently locating herself). And Charles Lever, who has enough to do to support the rights and dignity of the lords of creation against this band of literary Amazons, departed (and with him jokes and jollity) for Spezia the day before yesterday.

It elaborates on the theme on 27 August: Florence, normally full of English tourists, was full of clergy and peasants. Throughout August and early September readers were regaled with the papal visit.

The scientist Mary Somerville, mentioned in this report, had settled in Florence with her husband in the course of the 1850s, having visited the city several times previously. She was among the people whom William Yeames remembered from his young days as a student of art:

Though not rich, she gave delightful little receptions, at which many interesting people were to be met, and she herself was ready to talk on any subject. She was about eighty-eight when my uncle knew her, and at the age of ninety she published a book. She was a martyr to gout, and would amuse children by drawing on a slate with her chalky knuckles.

Eighty-eight was an overestimate (Mrs Somerville was born in 1780), but she was venerated for her age as well as for her intellect. It was almost certainly she who a few years later was anonymously described, in an account of Bagni, as 'that veteran blue-stocking, Mrs —-, now grown old and somewhat *passée* in comparison with her former brilliant self'.[90]

On his return to Florence in early September John Maquay 'found George well & it being my birthday 66 years old I ordered dinner from a Restaurant & he dined with me but for the future we look out each for ourselves'. His friends called, Gregorie, Baruch, Luard, Cottrell, Smith, Mrs Fombelle and the Galeazzi among them, he got letters from Elena and Tommy and decided that he did in fact need another horse. He also revived his whist evenings, but his final months in Florence almost inevitably have a certain bleakness about them. On 28 September he 'Drank a glass of Sherry to Elena's health which was all the notice I could take of the day'. When Christopher Smith told him on 18 October that he was on the point of leaving Florence for good, he reacted strongly: 'I grieve much for it on many accounts public & private.' On 21 October he had guests and 'a long evening chat about Canada most of my old friends there are dead'. There were several farewell dinners for Smith, given by Mrs Fombelle, Alfred Hall and the Dennistouns, and John himself gave one (which he had to buy in from a caterer) on behalf of the Church Committee, which George also attended. John's exclamation 'May God bless and prosper him' is eloquent testimony to the warm feelings Smith aroused. On 16 November, his successor as Secretary and Treasurer, Alfred Hall, wrote a letter of thanks to him, to be called for at the Post Office, Worthing. Ironically, Smith would soon return and John would not.[91]

Meanwhile, preparations for turning the bank over to George's management had to be made against a background which included 'sad reports of commercial distress in England'. One fortunate result of John's 3-month absence in the summer seems to have been that George had sorted himself out, for there are no complaints about his running of the bank. Probably George wanted to be left to get on with it; certainly he manifested his independent judgement in the late autumn, rather to his father's discomfiture. John was in search of a partner for him, and a good candidate seemed to be Gerard Brooks, son-in-law of John Pakenham, who would strengthen the Pakenham interest and was certainly acceptable in that quarter, while Smyth at Leghorn seemed to have no objection. Unfortunately George did, and John's careful cultivation of the Brooks during the autumn foundered on an 'Unpleasant altercation between Brooks & George!!!' on 28 November.[92] The use of three exclamation marks manifests John's exasperation. This rapidly developed into a full-scale stand-off between the two, with George refusing to go into partnership and departing for Ireland early in December.

The disappearance of familiar faces must have intensified John's sense of passing time and mortality, even when he did not cherish friendly feelings towards the deceased. On 10 November 1857 Theodosia Trollope's father Joseph Garrow died. John curtly referred to him as 'wretched man'. He seems to have attracted widespread opprobrium, although his monument in the English cemetery, with its Latin inscription, is handsome enough. Thomas said guardedly that Garrow was 'a jealously affectionate, but very exacting father'. Elizabeth Browning was censorious: 'His moral conduct had been by no means without taint – & he left everything to a wretched woman who was no more his than another's – There was an illegitimate child of uncertain parentage.'[93] This should perhaps be read in conjunction with Anthony Trollope's report, in a letter to his wife on 31 January 1858 when he was returning from his visit to Florence:

> It seems that Tom will get nearly £3000 by Garrow's death, and as this £3000 is all over & above what he expected, it ought to relieve him from all his embarrassments – he has also had a very good offer for his house – so good that were I he I should certainly take it.[94]

Perhaps Tom was pleasantly surprised to discover that all was not in fact going to the 'wretched woman'.

John was probably more saddened to attend Mrs Luard's funeral on 28 November; he was one of a tiny handful of mourners permitted to attend. He was doubtless even more saddened when her husband followed her on 26 December. John gave a little dinner party on Christmas Eve, but spent the following day in his own inimitable manner. He went to church and received the sacrament; then

> Mad Galeazzi & Mrs Brooks both asked me to dine with them but I had a fancy to dine at home alone surrounded by Elena and the boys portraits on chairs at the Table which I did and drank to all their healths individually in Champagne. I afterwards went to drink tea with Galeazzi.[95]

On 29 December 1857, under the heading 'Florentine Gossip', the *Morning Post* rounded off the year with a report sent on the 23rd by 'our own correspondent', which wove several themes, serious and less so, into a tight space. It began on a light note:

> Since the golden days of Lord Burghersh – the happy and saturnian age of Florence tradesmen, – Florence has not seen within her "third circle" such a formidable array of Anglo-Saxon visitors as in the present year. I include under this title the wandering progeny of Brother Jonathan, often more English than the English themselves in what, 40 years ago, were deemed exclusively English attributes – in the reckless expenditure and lavish prodigality that sow napoleons broadcast in every hotel from Turin to Palermo.

As for the English, the writer did not know what had caused so many of them to flock to Florence and Rome, 'but here they are; and you may hear Madame Dobbs *née* Flobbs, calling out, in delicious *lingua franca*, to her John, in the Mercato Nuovo – "Coachman, andate chez nous"!'

Carnival was now imminent, politics currently uninteresting. Baldasseroni was understood to have fended off the conspirators against him, but 'The ultramontane snake has been scotched, not killed'. It has just uttered 'a long and angry hiss' at a pamphlet written by the lawyer Salvagnoli, a familiar figure to the British and to Protestants in trouble. Supposedly about Canova's monument to Alfieri, it amounted to an appeal to Napoleon III 'to achieve the task which his uncle left unfulfilled, and to restore independence to the Italian people'. This had created an understandable sensation and had given the diplomatic body something to write home about which, apart from 'the great discovery of white truffles in the Mugello', was sadly lacking. 'No wonder that Lord Normanby takes refuge in the reminiscences of '48.' Having thus amused his readers, the writer ended 'with a melancholy theme'. The Rev. Hanna had died on 29 December at the early age of 35. The *Post* correspondent delivered a long and warm tribute to him:

> for the last eight years [he] has most zealously and faithfully done his duty as pastor of the (Free) Church of Scotland here. That loss will be felt with all the force of a personal bereavement in many a humble Italian dwelling, for the Italian Protestants had no better friend, and assuredly no safer or more prudent counsellor, than on every trying occasion he proved himself to be.

Rev. Hanna's writings in the *North British Review* and other journals

> have assisted in diffusing sound views on Italian politics, and calling forth a warm sympathy towards the moral and religious reformers of the Peninsula. Those friends of Italian Protestantism in England and elsewhere who were wont, on all occasions, to receive and act upon his counsels, will find his loss one not easily to be supplied; a man so clear-headed and so single-hearted that equal confidence was felt in the means which he employed and in the moral purity of the end for which he strove.

Hanna's funeral had taken place at the Swiss Protestant Cemetery, with his 'attached friend', Robert Browning, performing the office of chief mourner. Dr Stewart, whose wife had devotedly nursed him in his last illness, delivered, according to the custom of the Scottish Church, 'a short and impressive prayer before the body was conveyed to its resting-place.'

Hanna had probably never recovered from the death of his mother 6 months earlier. Elizabeth Browning recalled that he preached as usual on the day after he heard the news:

showing as bright and serene a face as one should do who has talked with God ... Such a bright gentle countenance perpetually smiling – in spite of his Calvinism. He is the very man for the work here – so prudent & quiet, yet persistent.

Perhaps she had adjusted to the preaching style which had previously repelled her.[96]

During 1857 the Indian Mutiny had caused more anxiety than any Tuscan event to English residents. A substantial proportion of them were either retired East Indians or had connections there. The *Morning Post* of 16 October, declared in flowery language that

> among those long residing in Florence, some have now to deplore the slaughter of sons and daughters, and nephews and nieces, and grandchildren, of all, in short, whom they best loved on earth, by the promise of whose youth, or the vigour of whose manhood, their old age was to be cheered.

Anna Jameson could cite Lady Herbert as a victim of the anxieties thus created, 'for Major Herbert is in the midst of it all'.[97] The *Post* correspondent was outraged by what he saw as not merely a lack of sympathy on the part of the Catholic press in Italy but a positive exultation in British misfortune.[98]

Early in October the Select Vestry acted on the chaplain's suggestion that a subscription be instituted for the relief of sufferers from the Indian atrocities, but it was thought best to delay a public announcement until the numbers of autumn visitors had increased to their usual levels. In February the fund was closed and the money collected remitted to England by Maquay & Pakenham.[99] Having already in October sent £50 by way of Fenzi & Co and Coutts in London, the brothers Hall subscribed again to this fund, which raised the equivalent of £161 10 11 sterling. Maquay & Pakenham contributed as well as handling the money, and Normanby, the banker Anthony French, and William Reynolds were among other names on a list that was published in the *Times* on 18 February 1858. It is hard to know how to interpret the fact that there were fewer subscribers than for the collection for sufferers by the Crimean War 3 years earlier and the amount of money raised was less.

A few wayward self-appointed missionaries apart, the English Church in the 1850s continued on its customary path. It continued to struggle with finance, although Tassinari's suggestion that receipts steadily declined between 1851 and 1862 is misleading. Figures presented to the Annual Meeting in January 1863 showed that the previous year had seen the smallest amount collected (14,520 pauls) in that period with the exception of 1860 (13,573). The other years had seen a fluctuation between just over 15,000 (in 1855 and the revolutionary year of 1859) and high points of 19,549 pauls in 1853 and just short of 20,000 in 1857.[100] 1853, we may recall, was the year in which an enthusiast for the Madiai had said that the English had deserted Florence.

One annoyance for the church was the tendency of its chaplain Henry O'Neill to absent himself for long periods. In 1855 the Select Vestry informed him 'that an uneasy feeling exists among the Congregation at large from his having no settled Residence and being so frequently absent from Florence'. The funds had never extended to the building of a house for the chaplain, but the inconvenience had not previously been felt, as the chaplains had rented and furnished apartments for themselves, which the Vestry thought should be the rule. It was agreed that O'Neill was to give notice of all absences, naming who was to act in his stead and his current residence, and the secretary was to see that all this was publicized in the vestibule. The underlying issues were not tackled, but John Maquay records the meeting as terminating 'amicably'.[101]

There were several positives. In November 1852 Lady Don deposited with Samuel Lowe 300 *francesconi* (around £69) 'for the purpose of giving pecuniary assistance to English Poor, either in cases of sickness or of requiring aid to return to their native Country'. On her death at the age of 90 in January 1855 this was bequeathed to the Select Vestry in trust. The fund was placed apart from other charitable funds which were normally controlled and disbursed by the clergyman, and its proceeds were allocated on a vote of members of the Select Vestry. By the beginning of 1856 six people had been relieved, among them servants whose stories will be told in a later chapter. Some were turned down, notably a Mr and Mrs Bell who requested the Church to facilitate their continued attendance to sing in the choir by providing them with a carriage.[102] Four more people were relieved in 1856, but there were no calls on the fund in 1857, which was just as well, for 40 per cent of it had been expended in 2 years. Late in 1858 the Reverend Gilbert, who for years had served the church in various capacities, was granted 450 pauls to help him return to England. Not all migrant clergy were affluent.[103]

In October 1855 the Select Vestry received a letter from the president of a commission which was collecting in aid of the poor sufferers by cholera in Florence. The chaplain was requested to constitute himself collector of the offerings of his countrymen to such amount as they might deem suitable to the occasion. The Vestry was quite willing to respond to such an appeal, but would it not be better to wait another month or so when more English visitors as well as residents would be in Florence? Even if it was only in order to touch the supposedly rich English for their money, the Florentines recognized that the English Church had a corporate presence.[104]

Apart from charitable work, one of the church's major achievements in the 1850s was the establishment of a library worthy of the name, as opposed to a shelf or two of books. The difference between 300 books in various states of disrepair in a single bookcase, for which no one was responsible, and well over 2,000, available for loan under a defined set of rules and under the proper governance of a librarian, was far more than a simple matter of numbers. Most of the groundwork was done in the 7 years before the downfall of the Grand Duke.[105] It was above all the achievement of Maurice Baruch, who first appears in the Church Minute

Books in January 1850 as Robbins's nominated Churchwarden, although he had been in Florence for years before that. He declined to act on this occasion, and it was not until he was elected to the Select Vestry in 1851 that he emerged into greater prominence. On 9 April, along with the Chaplain and the Rev. Gilbert, he was invited to form a sub-committee for the drawing up of rules for the library, which was now specifically put under the control of the Select Vestry.

Since Robbins was about to depart and Gilbert had other things on his mind while acting as temporary chaplain, it fell to Baruch to implement the new rules, which were agreed at a Special Meeting on 13 May. He was to retain the effective role of librarian until his death in 1875, although the rules designated the chaplain *ex officio* librarian and treasurer. He was also librarian of the Book Club from its institution by Webb Smith and Maquay in 1847 until its dissolution 10 years later, when many of its volumes were handed over to the church's library. The development of the library, its rules, contents and furnishings, can broadly be followed through the pages of the Church Minute Books; Baruch made a detailed annual report to the Select Vestry. Under his management the library was financially self-supporting, and he supplemented its income by undertaking the task of copying the registers of baptisms, marriages and burials for transmission to the Bishop of Gibraltar. In the light of the difficulties that had been experienced in the early 1850s, it is interesting to observe the resolute refusal to allow Italian subjects access to the books.

The year 1858 began with John Maquay aware that he was soon to leave the city where he had lived more or less continuously for 25 years and Lord Normanby unaware that he was about to lose his job. Neither man at this moment had any inkling of the more dramatic events to follow. The Anglican Church, meanwhile, was in remarkably good shape. The Tuscan Government seemed to have abandoned any suspicion that it was a source of subversion, political or religious. As the British went about their business in the later 1850s, few of them can have realized that they were witnessing the unfolding of an historical irony. There was more future for the British – and British Protestants – in Tuscany than there was for the house of Hapsburg-Lorraine.

Notes

1 JLM, E11 ff. 123v, 124. Stentorello was a harlequin-like character, created in the late eighteenth century and played by numerous comics who used a mixture of monologue, imaginary dialogue, music, etc., by this means smuggling satire past the censorship.
2 JLM, E11 f. 125v.
3 JLM, E11 ff. 153, 153v.
4 John Fleming, 'Art Dealing in the Risorgimento II', *Burlington Magazine* Vol. 121 1979, pp. 568–80; FO 79/167, Scarlett to FO, 3 June 1853. With some of his gains Spence purchased the Villa Medici at Fiesole in the early 1860s and it remained in his possession for more than 30 years. After the death of his first wife, Alicia, in 1851, he married her sister Enrichetta, who died in 1893. He followed in 1900.

5   James Stevens Curl, *The Life and Work of Henry Roberts* (Chichester, 1983), and article in DNB; *Monitore Toscano* 9 October 1854. The family's commitment to Italy continued long after the downfall of the Grand Duke. Henry died in 1876 and Catharine in 1905, both buried in Allori. Their daughter Theodora ran a Florentine Medical Mission for 35 years and died on 19 March 1916, joining them in Allori. This Roberts has to be distinguished from another individual of the same name, who ran a pharmacy in Via Tornabuoni.

6   See the article in DNB. Leader was married to the widow Maria Luisa di Leone on 19 August 1867 and died in 1903 aged 93. He is buried in the San Miniato cemetery, having converted to his wife's Catholicism late in life – she was buried by his side in 1906. The marriage was childless and he left £279,000 at his death, four properties in Tuscany (the fourth was the Villa Catanzaro at Maiano, bought in 1862) as well as the original family home on Putney Hill, with other property in England.

7   JLM, E11 f. 134. In the same month EBB mentioned the Kinneys (he late the American Minister at Turin) in a letter to Arabella (BC20, 3456, 22 August 1854).

8   JLM, E11 f. 135, 11 September 1854. Alfred Austin, *Poems by the late Isa Blagden, with a Memoir* (Edinburgh & London, 1873); William McAleer (ed.), *Dearest Isa: The Letters of Robert Browning to Isabella Blagden* (Austin, Texas, 1951).

9   JLM, E11 ff. 113v, 120, 130–130v.

10   JLM, E11 f. 134v.

11   JLM, E11 f. 138v.

12   JLM, E11 ff. 127v, 138, 172v. On Easter Day 1855 she and George went to church, but there is no specific mention of her taking communion (f. 151).

13   JLM, E11 ff. 106, 124v, 135v, 136v, 140v.

14   FO79/177, Scarlett to FO, 1 May 1864. This volume contains the despatches from Tuscany on the Tuscan flag issue, and 79/175 the Foreign Office end of the correspondence.

15   FO79/184, Macbean to FO, 3 January 1855; 79/183 Bulwer to FO, 3 January & Normanby to FO, 8 May.

16   FO79/183, Normanby to FO, 5 January 1855.

17   Frederic St John, *Reminiscences of a Retired Diplomat* (London, 1905), pp. 15–18.

18   JLM, E11 ff. 123, 143. John records family attendance at a Normanby function twenty times between 1853 and his own departure in 1858.

19   St John, *Reminiscences*, pp. 26–7. Villa Normanby, now the Villa Finaly, on the Via Bolognese, is the current seat of the University of Paris Sorbonne in Florence. The Villa Capponi (also once occupied by Morgan Thomas) is now the Villa La Pietra.

20   FO79/188, Normanby to FO, 24 October 1856.

21   FO79/187, Normanby to FO, 23 August 1856. Normanby added a third judgement, from 'A Tuscan nobleman of cultivated mind and liberal principles who is married to an English lady', who is less easy to identify with certainty.

22   Robert W. Stewart, *An Italian Campaign, or the Evangelical Movement in Italy 1845 to 1887* (London, 1890), p. 263, attributes this estimate of 10,000 to the Grand Duke himself when exhorting the priests of Florence to hunt out heresy at Lent in 1856.

23   Stewart, *Italian Campaign*, p. 261; FO79/185, Shaftesbury to FO, 25 April 1855.

24   FO79/183, Normanby to FO, 12 July 1855. Normanby was so eager to announce his triumph that he actually used the telegraph to tell ministers on 9 July. See also his earlier despatches of 26 May and 1 June.

25   FO79/187, Normanby to FO, 17 January 1856; 79/186 FO to Normanby approving his conduct, 31 January 1856.

26   Stewart, *Italian Campaign*, pp. 76–9; FO 79/187, Normanby to FO, 17 January 1856.

27   St John, *Reminiscences*, p. 17.

28 The snub to the diplomats is reported on 31 August in the *Morning Post, Liverpool Mercury* and many others; see also the *Times* 15 September. The Pope's majordomo, Borromeo, 'a functionary whose dignity, however great at the Court of Rome, is not recognized by ambassadors at or in other courts' was given precedence. The *Morning Post* said: 'Lord Normanby is himself one of the kindest and most courteous of men; he, above all, is entitled to the utmost courtesy from this Government and Court, for he has always treated them with, at least, due consideration.' One wonders whether the blunder in protocol, if blunder it were, was deliberate on the part of the Tuscan Government in order to sink the Concordat; certainly Hügel, the Austrian minister, treated in the same way, was none too pleased either.

29 FO79/182, FO to Normanby, 10 September 1855, enclosing letter from Udny, dated 31 August; 79/184, Normanby to FO, 24 September. In 1850 John Maquay had taken on a Mr Udny as a clerk in the Leghorn branch of the bank; probably this was Robert, born to the petitioner in 1820 (JLM, E11 f. 66).

30 FO79/166, Scarlett to FO, 14 April 1853 enclosing memo of Tuscan Minister of justice. 79/183, Normanby to FO, 12 April 1855; 79/184, Mitton to FO, 14 March. We have only been able to identify one Austrian marriage, that of Mary in 1854. Dennis received an obituary in the *Gentleman's Magazine* in January 1856.

31 FO79/182, FO to Normanby, 20 December 1855 enclosing letter from Mrs Lewis, dated 8 December; 79/183, Normanby to FO, 28 December. Could this Mr Forbes have been the son of the *garibaldino*? If so, he may still have been in Florence in June 1856 when his son was baptized by the Reverend Gilbert.

32 FO79/193, Normanby to FO, 29 June 1857, with enclosures.

33 She was the daughter of Sir John Morris Bt and wife of Albert Jenner of Wenvoe Castle, Glamorgan. John Maquay knew her and in fact met her on the boat on the way to Tuscany in 1855 JLM, E11 f. 157.

34 Guy Fleetwood Wilson, *Letters to Somebody – A Retrospect* (London, 1922), pp. 7–10. For the redoubtable Mrs Norton's career see Diane Atkinson, *The Criminal Conversation of Mrs Norton* (London, 2012).

35 FO79/191, FO to Normanby, 8 July 1857.

36 FO79/193, Normanby to Lenzoni, 16 July 1857; 194 Normanby to FO, 11 December 1857.

37 FO79/193 Normanby to FO, 22 July 1857. This view was expressed on the occasion of an abortive insurrection at Leghorn put down by troops (twelve civilians and six soldiers killed) which temporarily again led to Tuscan governmental paranoia and frantic and ill directed searches of property on the part of the police.

38 FO79/193, 23 July 1857, Normanby to FO, with enclosures.

39 JLM, E10 f. 125v, 3 October 1840; Archivio del Comune di Fiesole, IT ACF Preunitario 296 c.110v del. 341. The names of James Robert Matthews and William and John Wardle appear on the same list. O'Hara was subsequently ennobled but in 1843 renounced the title and with it the liability to pay the relevant tax.

40 According to the 1851 census Isabella was living with her mother and Rowland Blacker in Ludgate Street. There is no sign of a child, and it appears that Ellen had taken her to Italy.

41 FO79/141, Blacker to Palmerston, 31 May 1839; FO to Blacker, 12 June. Blacker claimed that O'Hara had lived in Tuscany for forty years, which seems unlikely.

42 FO79/173. The Foreign Office acknowledged receipt of Blacker's complaint (itself undated) on 7 January 1853: Fossi's statement is dated 24 December 1851. Blacker told Clarendon the story again on 22 March and acknowledged receipt of his decision on 13 April.

43 JLM, E11 f. 128 Maquay mentions O'Hara for the last time on 27 April 1854 which is not of course conclusive for his departure from Tuscany.

44 Charles Lever, *Cornelius O'Dowd upon Men and Women, and Other Things in General* (Edinburgh, 1864/5), Vol. 1, pp. 75–85.

45 The volume of newspaper coverage is paralleled by the volume of business passing through the embassy – 92 (nearly 43 per cent) of the 215 volumes in FO79, which covers the entire period from 1782, cover the 12 years 1847–1859.

46 BC21, 3533 EBB to Arabella, 11/18 March 1855; 3542 EBB to Isa Blagden, 5 April 1855; 3556 EBB to Arabella, 11 June 1855.

47 JLM, E11 ff. 157–160v.

48 FO79/183, Normanby to FO, 27 October 1855.

49 Thomas A. Trollope, *What I Remember* (2nd ed., London, 1887), Vol. 2, pp. 197–200; JLM, E8 f. 116v; E11 f. 94v.

50 FO79/183, Normanby to FO, 24 October 1855.

51 It was not until 27 May 1856 that the *Times* carried a detailed account of the murder, which other papers followed. The *Times* calls the murderer Fojani.

52 W. Fitzpatrick, *The Life of Charles Lever* (London, 1879), Vol. 2, p. 146.

53 JLM, E11 ff. 125v, 137, 174v, 194.

54 Edward Downey, *Charles Lever, His Life in Letters* (Edinburgh and London, 1906), Vol. 1, p. 336. In 1867 he was appointed to Trieste on £500 p.a., which post he was holding at his death in 1872. Lever was devotedly attached to his wife and he never recovered from her death in 1870.

55 JLM, E11 f. 168.

56 BC19, 3174 EBB to Henrietta 3 March 1853; 3190 EBB to Arabella 12 April 1853.

57 BC18, 3158 EBB to Miss Mitford, 8 January 1853; 19, 3174 & 3235 EBB to Henrietta, 4 March & 16 July 1853. The correspondence is full of references to spiritualism and only a small selection can be mentioned here; almost every correspondent gets to share Elizabeth's enthusiasm.

58 BC19, 3190 EBB to Arabella, 12 April 1853.

59 BC20, 3319 Lytton to EBB, 7 January 1854. The beautifully named Mrs Dyce Sombre also had told him 'wonderful stories of tables'.

60 BC21, 3518 EBB to Henrietta, 12 February 1855. Note 10 to this letter calls the daughter Regina. David Robertson, 'Weave a Circle; Baron Kirkup and his greatest friends' S. I. Mintz & others (eds), *From Smollett to James* (Charlottesville, Virginia, 1981). pp. 254–5 says she was Imogen, nicknamed Bibi. Bibi too proved able to summon up Dante for Kirkup. When he was honoured by Victor Emmanuel in 1865 on the 600th anniversary of Dante's birth he attributed it to the influence of Dante, which Bibi confirmed in an interview with the great man.

61 BC20, 3195 EBB to Arabella, 30 April 1853.

62 See the article by Alan Gauld in DNB and, for Home in Florence, Home's own autobiographical *Incidents in My Life* (London, 1864), pp. 86–94. His later years were covered by his wife.

63 BC21, 3556 EBB to Arabella, 11 June 1855.

64 Frances E. Trollope, *Frances Trollope, Her Life and Literary Work from George III to Victoria* (London, 1895), pp. 266–71; Home, *Incidents in my Life,* pp. 56–93.

65 H. Koel Krebs, 'Spiritisme et Piété Luthérienne en Toscane, avant le Grand Marché', *Aries* 7 (2007) pp. 185–203. Koel Krebs seems unaware of Home's stay with the Trollopes.

66 BC22, 3757 EBB to Arabella, 1 April 1856, & note 17.

67   BC23, 3923 EBB to Henrietta, 18 November 1856. Elizabeth was clearly reading the *Spiritual Magazine* in the last year of her life, since she refers in a letter to a controversy as to whether or not she herself was possessed of the devil, and also asks whether Mrs Ogilvy has read an article by Robert Bell 'Stranger than Fiction' in the *Cornhill Magazine* of August 1860: Peter N. Heydon and Philip Kelley (eds), *Elizabeth Barrett Browning's Letters to Mrs David Ogilvy* (London, 1973), p. 161.

68   Scott Lewis (ed.), *Letters of Elizabeth Barrett Browning to her sister Arabella* (Waco, Texas, 2002), Vol. 2, pp. 329, 340.

69   This was even before they achieved a greater financial independence as a result of the money left to them by their intimate friend (and Elizabeth's distant kinsman) John Kenyon, who died in December 1856. Kenyon bequeathed £6,500 to Robert and £4,500 to Elizabeth, but the will took about a year to implement. Invested for the most part in Tuscan funds, the money yielded about £550 p.a. – more than enough to live comfortably on in Florence. John Maquay had calculated his household expenses as around £700 per annum but he was supporting four children and went in for much more entertaining.

70   BC21, 3556 EBB to Arabella, 11 June 1855. The archbishop's certificate is reproduced opposite p. 176.

71   BC21, 3565 EBB to Arabella, 27 June.

72   BC17, 2913 EBB to John Kenyon, 1 May 1851: 18, 3146 EBB to Arabella, 13–15 November 1852.

73   BC24, 3971 EBB to Sarianna, 3 March 1857.

74   The relationship is well summarized by Scott Lewis, 'Sophia Cottrell's Recollections', *Browning Society*, 24, 1977.

75   Henry James, *William Wetmore Story and His Friends* (Edinburgh & London, Blackwood, 1903), Vol. 2, p. 67.

76   Aurelia B. & J. Lee Harlan jr. (eds), *Letters from Owen Meredith to Robert and Elizabeth Barrett Browning* (Waco, Texas, 1937) p. 139, RB to Sir Edward Bulwer, 27 August 1857; pp. 140–43, Robert Lytton to EBB, 3 October 1857.

77   JLM, E11 ff. 176v, 178v, 180v.

78   JLM, E11 ff. 184v, 190.

79   JLM, E11 ff. 188, 190v.

80   JLM, E11 f. 192.

81   Michael Sadleir & Frederick Page (eds), *Anthony Trollope, Autobiography* (revised edition, London, 1999), p. 112.

82   It was published in 1865, by which date he had put scholarship temporarily to one side to write bad novels which paid more.

83   FO79/193, Normanby to FO, 12 June 1857.

84   Lewis (ed.), *Letters to Arabella*, Vol. 2, p. 307; FO79/193 Normanby to FO, 6 July. The rising first surfaces in the *Morning Post* 7 July 1857; *Times* 9 July 1857.

85   Pampaloni, who had died in 1847, was responsible for a work which was endlessly reproduced, 'The Infant Samuel at Prayer'. Readers of P.G. Wodehouse may recall that Bertie Wooster's Aunt Dahlia, when under stress, found relief in smashing one such reproduction.

86   His ownership of the painting is referred to by Baron Alfred von Wolzogen, *Raphael Santi, His Life and His Works*, translated F.E. Bunnett (London, 1866). p. 105. He is here called 'Sir', which reflects the fact that he was invested as a Knight of the Order of San Stefano on 14 October 1851. Lawrie died in 1875 'in the flower of his age', which suggests that he cannot have been much more than forty. He was buried at San Miniato, as was his mother Clorinda in 1889 and his wife Giulia in 1907.

87   Beatrice Erskine (ed.), *Anna Jameson: Letters and Friendships (1812–1860)* (London, 1915), pp. 305–19.

88   Lady Herbert was the widow of the physician Sir Charles Lyon Herbert, who died in Florence in 1855.

89   She died of pneumonia 17 March 1860 in London after spending long hours in the British Museum and walking home in a snowstorm. Her book from this research *The History of Our Lord*, was finished by Lady Eastlake.

90   M.H. Stephen Smith, *Art and Anecdote; Recollections of William Frederick Yeames RA* (London, 1927), p. 80; Anonymous, 'The Baths of Lucca', *New Monthly Magazine*, 109 (1859), p. 136. Dr Somerville died in Florence in 1860 and was buried in the 'English' cemetery. Mrs Somerville moved to Naples and died there in 1872.

91   JLM, E11 ff. 200–201v. CMB 2, 4 November, records the submission of his resignation. This was not quite final, for 'he trusts if spared to be again in a position to offer his services to the Congregation of the Church at Florence'. Alfred Hall's letter to Smith is copied into the Secretary's Letter Book.

92   JLM, E11 ff. 202–202v. On 25 November John waited on Lord Normanby to take soundings about the possibility of Pakenham's visiting Florence on business.

93   JLM, E11 f.202; Trollope, *What I Remember*, Vol. 2, p. 372; Lewis (ed.), *Letters to Arabella*, Vol. 2, p. 329, 22 November 1857.

94   Bradford A. Booth (ed.), *The Letters of Anthony Trollope* (London, 1951), p. 59.

95   JLM, E11 f. 203v.

96   Lewis (ed.), *Letters to Arabella*, Vol. 2, pp. 307–8. JLM notes Hanna's death on 21 December: E11, f. 203v.

97   Erskine (ed.), *Anna Jameson*, p. 311.

98   On 23 October the *Post* gratefully acknowledged sympathy from Piedmont, reflecting a yet further rise in the British stock of that state at the expense of Tuscany.

99   CMB 2, 7 October 1857, 17 February 1858.

100 CMB 2, 30 January 1863. Tassinari, *English Church*, p. 89, bases her judgement on a comparison of the average for 1851–1853 with that of 1860–1862. 1861 in fact saw healthy receipts of 17,421 pauls.

101 CMB 2, 3 October 1855; 13 November 1855; JLM, E11 f. 162v, 13 November 1855.

102 CMB 2, 7 November 1855.

103 CMB 2, 22 October 1858.

104 CMB 2, 5 October 1855.

105 See Peter Hoare, 'A Room with a View – and a Book: Some Aspects of Library Provision for English Residents and Visitors to Florence 1815 to 1930' in Barbara Schaff (ed.), *Exiles, Emigrés & Intermediaries: Anglo Italian Cultural Transactions* (Amsterdam, 2010). The authors were privileged to see this essay in draft.

12 DOCTORS AND PATIENTS: THE QUEST FOR HEALTH

Marianna Starke's travels in the early 1790s were probably motivated by the health of her mother. One result, a continental guidebook published in 1802, proved to be the first of a series, the forerunners of the guides subsequently produced by John Murray, who became Mrs Starke's English publisher. The last was published in 1839 after her death.[1] The advice to invalid tourists which she included in her first edition reflected a preoccupation of travellers and their advisers that is almost entirely absent from modern guidebooks, which implicitly assume that the tourist will at least be fit when he or she sets out.

Mrs Starke began by advising invalids to travel by sea to Leghorn rather than overland. The winter climate of Pisa was to be preferred over that of Nice for 'pulmonary complaints'. She believed that Pisa had been much improved by the recent drainage of the surrounding land, which had resulted in an increased population that 'dispensed cheerfulness and health throughout this elegant city'. Both the cheerfulness and the healthfulness of Pisa were disputed, but there can be little doubt that many believed in its winter virtues for invalids. A few years after Mrs Starke another widely read author, Joseph Forsyth, approved of Pisa's winter ('full as mild as our Spring') but deplored its summer, with its 'damp, close, suffocating' nights: 'Pisa may reverse what physicians say of the capital – "They hardly conceive how people can live at Florence in Winter, or how they can die there in Summer".[2]

Mrs Starke thought Florence suitable for 'consumptive persons' from early May until midsummer, but they should then seek out a villa on the hills just beneath Fiesole, where there was a constant refreshing breeze which tempered the still considerable heat. Thanks to the mysterious power of the nearby Apennines to 'attract the noxious vapours', this situation avoided the rapid temperature changes which were so dangerous to 'weak lungs'. Florence in the height of summer was too hot for comfort, but Mrs Starke regarded it as still 'wholesome' then. A more 'bracing' summer climate was to be found at Bagni di Lucca or Carrara. Siena too, being on a hilltop, enjoyed refreshing breezes, but in July and August suffered from the reflected heat inseparable from large cities.[3]

The 'wholesomeness' of Florence was open to doubt. A letter published in the *Morning Post* on 15 November 1817 declared that

Its hospitals, or rather human slaughter houses, are full, and the sick throughout the city are numerous. The physicians seem to know nothing of the means of remedy, and catarrhal complaints, colds, &c, are extremely prevalent although the weather is still hot. About a week ago the thermometer was at 82 an hour after sunset; now it is at 72, but the wind sharp and cold. One circumstance to which much of this disease may be owing is, that the Arno, which divides the city, is rendered nearly stagnant by a number of mill-dams, so that clouds of noxious exhalations may be seen ascending almost every day from its muddy bottom.

Mrs Starke and Forsyth stated themes which would be endlessly elaborated by later writers. The absence of any accurate idea of the causes of disease was bound to handicap the search for cures, and left scope for beliefs and speculations which empirical observation did not suffice to confirm or refute. Great attention was paid to the likely impact of minute climatic variations on sufferers from a variety of finely distinguished afflictions, nervous, digestive and, above all, respiratory. Modern instrumentation made it possible for writers to blind their readers with science: winter and summer temperature ranges and variation, barometric pressure, humidity and the direction and force of the winds were all produced in evidence. Prevalent opinions about the climate of particular Italian cities might help to determine where health refugees, and others, pitched their tents. According to some, a residence in Florence was only for the robust, but even the claims of Pisa could be disputed, while the relative merits of Leghorn, Bagni and Siena also attracted some attention, as did those of Rome (Pisa's major winter competitor).

In 1852 Dr Thomas Burgess published a comprehensive attack on the idea that the Italian climate was beneficial to British invalids. His ghoulish eloquence is irresistibly quotable:

> The English cemetery at Leghorn is singularly touching. In spite of the excessive brilliancy of the marbles, the aspect of so many tombs of foreigners, who died on their arrival or when about to embark on their way home, is melancholy. Most of the inscriptions are remarkable for an affecting conciseness and simplicity. Many of these strangers, full of youth and hope, came to recover their health in the land that has devoured them.[4]

Burgess was to the health hazards of continental travel what the Rev. Cunningham a generation earlier had been to its moral and spiritual dangers, but he might reasonably have pointed out to his readers that they only had to read the deaths columns in the newspapers or to listen to travellers' tales to be convinced that he was right. John Maquay's only sister Betsy died aged 30 at Pisa in May 1817, probably of consumption. She was preceded to her Leghorn grave by the MP Francis Horner, who died, also at Pisa, on 8 February 1817. In a description of the cemetery which appeared in the *Leeds Mercury* on 27 January 1827 it was remembered that 'Mr Horner died of a consumption, which was too far advanced when he left England to be removed by the air of Italy'. Within a few years he and Betsy had been joined by a number of their compatriots who were explicitly declared, in memorial inscriptions or newspaper notices, to have come to Italy for the sake of their health. One was Thomas Rae, bookseller of Sunderland, who 'came to Italy for the recovery of his health and died at Pisa February 6 1819 aged 26 years'.[5]

In 1820 James Clark, the royal physician who, among other negative accomplishments, has been credited with hastening the death of John Keats in Rome early the following year, published what turned out to be the first of a series of studies of the efficacy or otherwise of 'a residence in the south of Europe', which appeared, under changing titles, down to 1846.[6] The Maquays consulted Clark in Rome between 1824 and 1826, and it is clear from John's diaries that like other fashionable physicians he was very much part of the social scene. Towards the end of 1825 John was being treated by a veritable consortium of doctors, including Clark, until he decided to put his faith in Dr Jenks. We get other glimpses of this mixture of co-operative and competitive doctoring which the moneyed Briton could indulge in at Rome or Florence as at Cheltenham or Bath. Clark seems only to have been a visitor to Florence, but in the various editions of his work he cited the opinions of British physicians who had had experience there and elsewhere in Tuscany.[7]

For Clark, the debate was about the best place to go in winter; nowhere in Italy was suitable for consumptive invalids in the summer. Pisa suffered from 'sharp spring winds', as attested by Dr Kissock, who had spent the spring of 1818 there.[8] Clark admitted that Pisa's alleged superiority over other destinations had yet to be properly investigated, and sensibly asked whether the merits of either Rome or Pisa justified the sick in undertaking such a long journey and abandoning the comforts of home. Taking refuge in southern Europe was more likely to help prevent disease than to cure it.[9] In his second edition Clark was safe in reporting that Pisa had long enjoyed a good reputation with consumptive patients and was patronized by native Italians as well as by the British. He offered advice as to when and where they could safely take their walks, and echoed Mrs Starke's view that the place was less fever-ridden than formerly.

In 1829 and more fully in 1841, Clark gave attention to other Tuscan resorts. Siena was to be recommended for people who were not sensitive to the rapid temperature changes to which it was liable because of its 'high and exposed situation'. 'Dry and healthy', it was better in the summer 'for nervous relaxed people' than Naples or Bagni, while like the latter it was free from mosquitoes. For the pulmonary patient, it was unsuitable at all times.[10] By 1846, he believed that Pisa was now less popular with invalids because of the easy steam-boat connections between Leghorn and Rome and Naples. Those who stayed there for more than one season usually spent the summer at Bagni, as indeed residents elsewhere in Tuscany also did.[11]

That was probably what Dr Plowman Young, both physician and health refugee, had done. A native of Bury St Edmunds, he was already at Pisa in the autumn of

1836, when he attended Isabella Wilmer before and after her confinement. Early in 1837 he saw one infant son die and another born within a month of each other and himself died aged 44 at Bagni in July 1840. In his brief will he described himself as of Pisa, where in November 1841 the shopkeeper Joseph Cordon advertised the sale of certain 'objects' which had belonged to him, including 'a big electrical machine', a 'galvanic battery', a 'pneumatic machine' and a case of surgical instruments.[12]

Clark's views of Florence underwent some modification between editions. From the beginning, despite all its attractions, he pronounced it unsuitable for invalids, especially the consumptive. Dr Down was quoted to the effect that the native inhabitants, thanks to their cold damp dwellings, were peculiarly liable to chest trouble (*mal di petto*). Confronted with a young man at Florence who was struggling as the heat increased in May, Down had instructed him to get north of the Alps at once.[13] Florence was particularly bad for children, but if the individual was not vulnerable to changes in temperature and could endure the heat of summer, 'it holds out many inducements as a residence during the whole year'.[14] By the time his final edition appeared in 1846, Clark had thought better of this concession, now quoting as his chief authority Dr Playfair, who had practised in the city for many years. He gave a brief description of the climate, believing that the reader would by now understand 'what diseases are likely to be benefited or aggravated by a residence at Florence' and summed up in a manner which shows that the traveller-patient had to be as certain of what health category he or she fell into as horoscope-fanciers need to know their birth sign:

> In consumption and all inflammatory diseases of the chest it is injurious; Dr Playfair never allowed a patient of this class to remain at Florence after October: indeed, acute inflammation of the lungs is one of the most prevalent and fatal diseases among the inhabitants in the winter and spring. On the other hand, the dry bracing character of the climate renders it useful in diseases accompanied with relaxation. Dr Playfair describes it as very beneficial in humid asthma, and even in the purer spasmodic form of that disease; also in atonic dyspepsia, but injurious in the inflammatory form. Gout is much relieved, and scrofulous swellings of the glands disappear during a residence at Florence. Every person who can should leave Florence during the months of July and August. With children the summer disagrees extremely, and an attempt to wean a child at this season is attended with extreme danger. The Baths of Lucca afford a convenient and cool retreat during the hot months.[15]

Clark said little actually to deter those who had imbibed the prevailing opinion in favour of Pisa, which may help to account for Thomas Burgess's energetic efforts to demolish an entrenched, though not quite unqualified, orthodoxy. The Scottish physician Andrew Combe, on the strength of a visit for the sake of his own precarious health in 1820, occasionally offered advice to prospective travellers. In 1839 he told one lady that Rome and Pisa were both very suitable for 'irritable' conditions of the chest. However, when his brother, the phrenologist George Combe, was planning a trip to Italy in 1843, Andrew told George's wife that Rome was probably the best all-round choice: 'Pisa stands in like position, but morally it is dull and depressing, although mild and cheap.' Florence was not recommended: 'Its climate is extremely variable, often severe, and always trying.'[16]

Burgess differed from Clark in concerning himself solely with consumption and with Italy. With masterful and gloomy relish he communicated the message that it was better to stay at home. Nowhere in England was there a climate less suitable for 'consumptive invalids' than at Florence,

> a town built in a deep ravine, almost surrounded by the Apennines, and intersected by a squalid river. But Florence is within a few hours' ride of Pisa, one of the chief depôts for foreign patients of this class in Italy, and the fame and artistic attractions of the city of the Medici are irresistible to the dying visitors who at all move about. In the renowned capital of Tuscany, wandering amongst its splendid, but cold and damp, churches, its palaces and picture galleries, many an English invalid annually hastens his end.

This process was materially assisted by the cramped and ill-ventilated conditions of the chief attractions. In the *Tribuna* of the Uffizi Gallery the ill-advised invalid was condemned to breathe

> a heated, confined, and impure atmosphere. An observer will not remain long before his attention is arrested by the ominous, short, dry, jerking cough, and, on looking around, he is sure to see the same stereotyped picture of the 'English disease' so painfully familiar to travellers throughout Italy, supported on the arm of an attendant, staring at the marble statue 'that enchants the world,' which often seems more alive than the gazing invalid.

Burgess gave a lengthy account of the Florentine climate, with measurements, and declared that the weather materially affected the progress of any disease. It had a 'powerful action' on the nervous system, which could be beneficial 'in cases of paralysis, melancholia, and in persons of a sluggish and lymphatic habit'; but for those afflicted by respiratory diseases it was injurious, 'and in pulmonary consumption its baneful effects are rapid and fatal'.

Of other Tuscan resorts, Leghorn was summarily dismissed: 'the point of arrival and departure of many foreign invalids, [it] has little to recommend it even as a temporary residence.' Its population was distinguished by beggars, chained galley-slaves, assassins and smugglers, and as for 'the promenade of Ardenza, the Corso of Leghorn', it 'extends along an arid beach, which is ill-suited as an exercising-ground for persons suffering from disease of the respiratory organs'.[17] Some years earlier, Sir George Seymour had taken a different view. In the early summer of 1835 he asked the Foreign Office for permission to spend a couple of months at

Leghorn on the grounds that 'The change of air is highly necessary to my Wife's health'.[18] Perhaps her lungs were not her problem. Numerous Anglo-Florentines, including the Maquays and Christopher Webb Smith, risked their well-being by taking a summer break at Leghorn, while a review of the Pisan church sources alongside the Leghorn subscription lists suggests that some Pisan residents chose the sea air of Leghorn over the mountain air of Bagni in the summer months.

Burgess devoted his entire tenth chapter to an assault on Pisa.[19] Some other places in Italy were rather dreary, but Pisa was the most dismal of the lot, 'and is calculated to inspire the mind of the stranger with anything but cheering emotions'. Burgess surpasses himself in what follows, largely an elaboration of this *leitmotiv*.

> Here and there the gaunt figure of some moribund invalid stands before the traveller, while viewing those few monumental relics of former greatness which Pisa still retains, – a dying foreigner vainly seeking, amidst these mouldering and silent walls, for some respite from a doom that is only hastened by the means taken to avert his fate. If Pisa is not the 'city of the dead', it is most assuredly the city of the dead alive; for who can walk through its streets, especially in the English quarter, without mourning over the traditionary delusion which has enticed so many natives of England to seek a renewed lease of life in a foreign country, and find only an Italian grave?

Pisa's reputation was due to 'tradition, and some vague unsupported statements, and random assertions', a process abetted by the undeniable beauty and historical associations of Tuscany. It was 'as much frequented as ever by invalids' and mortality continued to overtake the very people who had thought to find sanctuary there. So it did. On 24 January 1851 the *Glasgow Herald* lamented the death at Pisa of a distinguished clergyman, the Reverend Dr Black, who 'had retired to Italy a few months ago for the benefit of his health; but the milder climate of the south failed to remove his malady'.

Ill health was unquestionably a major reason for the British presence in Pisa. In July 1848 Sir George Hamilton told the Foreign Secretary that his physicians were anxious that he should 'pass some of the severe winter months at Pisa, where the climate is so mild in comparison with Florence'. The existence of the railway between Pisa, Leghorn and Florence would make it easy for him to remain in touch. He was hoping to receive permission at an early date, for 'I must look out for a house, as they are generally taken early in Autumn'.[20]

Only a few weeks later Consul Macbean transmitted to Hamilton a proposal from a Mr James Irving of Pisa that in these disturbed times he should take on the duties of an unpaid British Vice-Consul; he repeated the offer in April 1849.[21] In August 1848 Irving wrote that he had been there for more than 6 years and 'owing to the long and severe illness of my son, (who cannot be removed without the greatest danger), am unable to leave it at present'. Irving and his family were subscribers to the Pisan Anglican Church, where he was elected the chaplain's churchwarden in November 1846. In April 1849 he told Hamilton that 'There are probably not less than forty English families in Pisa, most of them residing here on account of the ill health of some Member of their family, which renders their departure either dangerous or impracticable'. Not all the moribund, then, were deprived of family support.

During the few months the Brownings spent in Pisa in 1846–1847 they became friendly with the Irvings. Writing to her sisters in November 1846 Elizabeth said that Mr Irving had told them that he had been 4 years in Pisa and had thereby saved 'a son in the last stages of consumption'.[22] She was, as so often, initially reluctant to cultivate the acquaintance, but by the following February she had warmed to Mr Irving: 'Really an intelligent, *very* gentlemanly [per]son – & with a benevolent countenance & smile.' He was totally convinced of the benefits of the climate, wondering how anyone who had the option of living in it could do otherwise; he could not bear the English winter. Of the two sons he had at the University of Pisa Elizabeth only mentions one (the younger James) who, she remarked when the Irvings visited them in Florence in October 1848, was in 'a sad state of health'.[23]

Elizabeth and Robert ran into the Irvings again when they visited Pisa in June 1849, and Elizabeth expressed pleasure at their son's greatly improved condition; he had lately taken honours at the university, to his father's delight.[24] Sadly, this improvement was not to last. The younger James made his will at Leghorn on 27 May 1855. Referring to his grave illness during his time in Pisa, he made a thanksgiving bequest to his friend Dr Charles Nankivell of Torquay, who had attended him there and refused all payment. The elder James Irving died at Leghorn on 10 December 1855 and his son survived him only by 2 months, dying at Pisa on 10 February 1856.[25]

The numbers of British invalids in Tuscany entailed a need for medical advice, and the guidebooks identified British physicians where they could be found. In Mrs Starke's first edition there was not a great deal to tell, but she was able to note that 'Mr Polhill, a skilful Surgeon, who lately had the care of our naval hospital at Leghorn, resides in the *Palazzo Bertolli*, near the *Port-nuova*; and Persons who employ this Gentleman may be supplied by him, with English Medicines'.[26] The early Maquay journals reveal the presence of physicians among the Britons who were unleashed on the continent by the ending of the wars, genteel participants in the social round, occupying the place in this transplanted society that they might have occupied at home. Some practised their profession only incidentally and on request, just like the equally numerous clergy. A doctor (like Plowman Young) might come to Italy for the sake of his own health and stay to practise. In 1820 Andrew Combe met Dr Peebles, 'who had come to Leghorn some six years previously in a much more hopeless condition' than Combe himself, but 'had now regained so much health & strength that he was able to practise as a physician among the English in that town and Pisa'.[27]

Peebles was recorded in Leghorn in 1821, witnessing a couple of weddings, and he is mentioned as having attended a William Owen who died there in May

1823. In his 1829 edition, Clark described him as 'of Rome', but he had also been in Florence, where he subscribed to Vieusseux at intervals between 1823 and 1831. That he maintained contact with Tuscany is indicated by the fact that in 1842 Falconar accounted to the Foreign Office for donations Peebles had collected in Edinburgh for the benefit of the church to be built at Leghorn.[28] He was described on the title-page of his ominous-sounding *Cases of Great Enlargement of the Stomach* (1840) as a Fellow of the Imperial and Royal College of Physicians of Florence; and in the census of 1851, when he was living in Cheltenham, he claimed to have a doctorate from the University of Pisa.

In Mrs Starke's 1826 edition the only British physician recorded as resident in Florence was Dr Down. Clark's reference to him suggests that he was already practising there by 1820. In 1823, he was described in a book advertisement as 'Member of the Medico-Chirurgical society of London, of the Royal Academy of Georgofili of Florence, and Physician in Ordinary to H.R. Highness the Duke of Clarence'. When the Grand Duke Ferdinand was dying in 1824, Burghersh offered the Court the services of both Peebles and Down, but the offer was not taken up.[29] Together with Kissock, these two represented the first wave of British medical men to put down roots in post-war Tuscany, although they were not the only ones. A son was born to Dr Down in Tuscany in May 1826 and may have caused the death of his mother, for Louisa Down was buried at Leghorn at the end of June. We do not know whether this contributed to Down's decision to return to Britain, or exactly when he did so, but Clark in 1829 calls him 'of Southampton'. By contrast the Scot David Kissock was to spend his life in Italy and became a long-standing friend of the Maquays; he was older than John only by a few months. We have Clark's word for it that he spent the winter of 1818 at Pisa. He first appeared as a Vieusseux subscriber in March 1823 and in the following November Elizabeth Maquay told John that Kissock had attended to his brother George.[30]

If the seasonal British colony in Siena needed medical advice it often had to be summoned from Florence. In May 1824, when the Maquays were there, George's leg was troubling him and his mother sent to Florence for advice from Kissock and Down: the latter advised a 'muriatic bath' which alleviated the discomfort. In June 1825 a Mr Bond became very ill at Siena, and John sent his servant to Florence to summon Peebles, but it was Kissock who came, Peebles being busy at Leghorn.[31] The relationship between Peebles and Kissock seems not have been of the best, to judge from a letter written by Charles Brown to Severn:

> The other night we had a duel between our Doctors, – no – not well nigh, for one of them had no stomach for it; Dr Keebles [*sic*] had spoken shockingly of Dr Hyssop [*sic*], so the latter proves his innocence, calls for an apology, and hints at an exchange of pills – bullets I mean. Well! Dr K declared he would go to the Police for protection, not liking to swallow a bitterer draught in making such an apology than ever he had administered to any of his impatients. This however [he] would not do, and he was obliged to apologise to his rival for

having spoken against his character! – an awkward affair! – and as I hate all Doctors but myself, I delight in this tattle of Florence.

It is not difficult to identify the two antagonists (although it is unclear which was which), and there is virtual confirmation in a note in John Maquay's diary that one day at Siena he and his companions 'sat a long time partly arguing about Peebles & Kissock'.[32]

Kissock was now established in Florentine society and remained there for some years after the departures of Down and Peebles. He was a stalwart of the developing English Church, alongside John Maquay and Horace Hall. His name appears in the modern literature on the history of multiple sclerosis because he was consulted in Florence by Augustus d'Este, grandson to George III and often thought to be the first to give a detailed account of the symptoms of this disease. On 17 October 1827 Augustus described his experiences in his diary. He had begun to suffer from double vision, and Kissock 'supposed bile to be the cause'. The usual horrific remedies were administered and Augustus once again 'saw all objects naturally in their single state' and was able to go out and walk. At this point 'a new disease began to show itself: every day I found gradually (by slow degrees) my strength leaving me'. If he was suffering from multiple sclerosis Kissock was no more able to help him than any physician of the time.[33]

By this time another British physician had enrolled himself in Anglo-Florentine society. Dr Charles Bankhead was already something of a celebrity. It was in his arms that the Foreign Secretary Lord Castlereagh expired in 1822 after cutting his throat, and later in the same year he was again in the news when his opinions about the dubious sanity of Lord Portsmouth attracted comment. He had the additional distinction of being mentioned in no very complimentary manner in the *Memoirs* of Harriette Wilson.[34] He was evidently a large man (Harriette calls him 'Herculean') with what might tactfully be described as an outgoing personality. She had been told that when consulting him 'maids, wives and widows were often obliged to pull their bells for protection', and she (no fragile flower) did so herself.

When Bankhead first appeared in the Vieusseux registers in October 1826 he was already in his late fifties, but he continued to practise. The *Morning Post* reported on 11 December that year that he was 'the most popular and eminent physician in Tuscany'. On 19 February 1827 the *Morning Chronicle* called Lord Burghersh his 'great patron' and said that his 'close attention and advice' had effected Lady Burghersh's recovery from a severe illness. On the following 29 May Bankhead and Kissock together witnessed a codicil to the will of John Dearman Church, as physicians often did. John Maquay registered the presence of the doctor and his daughter among his acquaintance in the winter of 1826–1827.[35] In 1840, when he was over 70, Bankhead began to take out an annual subscription to Vieusseux and did so at least until 1848. His name occurs in the registers until 1853, although by this stage he seems prudently to have decided that it was not worth subscribing for more than a few months at a time.

By the end of the 1830s Dr James George Playfair had moved into the gap left by Down and Peebles and enlarged a few years later by Kissock's departure for Rome. He signalled his arrival by taking out a year's subscription to Vieusseux on 1 September 1828 and he seems to have remained there until 1845.[36] In Mrs Starke's posthumously published 1839 edition, he and Dr James Harding were named as the two British physicians resident in Florence as of 1835 (confirming that Kissock had departed). An 1840 guidebook said that he had resided some years in Florence and was 'well acquainted with the climate, a gentleman of great talent in his profession, and much respected by English residents'.[37] In May 1839 he attended Mr Fraser, the Secretary of Legation, who had been overcome by a fatal malady and died in the doctor's arms. With Fox and others Playfair attended his Catholic funeral.[38] Playfair was supposedly Lady Holland's favourite physician, and a portrait of him by Watts used to hang at Holland House, but was irreparably damaged by fire. He was also consulted by Hiram Powers, who executed a bust of him in gratitude for his services.[39] As he was a member of the Church Committee in the 1830s John Maquay must have known of his existence, but he is never mentioned in the diaries.

Several of the physicians already mentioned had military or naval experience, and some continued both to draw their half-pay and to practise. In Mrs Starke's final edition it was stated that a Doctor McManus, 'a skilful and well-known English Physician', had for some years resided at Pisa in the winter, but the information was out of date, for he had returned to England by 1838.[40] Dr Roger David McManus, once a naval surgeon, had spent time in other Italian localities, including Siena, where in November 1827 John Maquay had wanted Elena to consult him, and Rome, where they encountered him in the following March. In 1833 McManus performed the not very difficult feat of annoying Consul Falconar at Leghorn. He complained to the Foreign Office that he had been overcharged at the consulate for the attestations of his signature that he had to obtain in order to claim his half-pay. Falconar retorted that the charges were posted up on the wall for all to see and that McManus, who had been coming into the office for some years, always referred to them and always complained about them.[41]

In the early 1840s, at least for a brief period, the small British colony at Siena enjoyed the services of one or more temporarily resident physicians. William Flewker, a native of Lincoln, was married at Florence towards the end of 1842, and may have regretted choosing to stay at Siena during the following summer, for he became involved in the affair of Charles and Lady Eleanor Law. His only child was born at Leghorn very early in 1844, probably not long before he left Italy. Also at Siena in the summer of 1843 was Dr Alexander Delisser, a Tuscan resident for somewhat longer. First recorded as a Vieusseux subscriber in February 1841, he had entered the Maquays' circle by the end of that year. For a few years he spent his summers at Siena, returning to Florence and renting a house for the winter. He seems not to have got involved in the Law affair, although his name appears next to those of Lady Eleanor and Miss Souper in the list of Siena church subscribers. When John visited Siena in August 1843 his son George socialized with 'the young Delissers'.[42] In October Delisser was expected back from Siena, but a curious rumour spread that he was dead. Was his health perhaps known to be precarious? In John's diary he appears principally as a participant in the whist-playing, party-giving social round, but pleasure was occasionally combined with business, as when one evening in November 1843 Delisser both 'dined and applied leeches to my tooth'.[43]

For John's mother too, Delisser and his wife were friends. She does not mention consulting him professionally until on 1 May 1844 she sent for him because she was feeling ill. A few days later she commented on the 'cold harsh winds which affect every one more or less'. Delisser came to her on the evening of the 4th before he had finished his dinner,

> when he lookd to me very ill but sat a long time & ordered something for me when he took Francesco in the carriage with him to the apothe[ca]ries to bring it back he went from thence to Mrs Smiths where his Wife was to join him but when he arrivd there the Porter who opend the Carriage door saw him as he thought dead & with the greatest difficulty they took him up stairs where he expird in a few minutes after had he remaind here half an hour longer he would have expird sitting beside me his death has been a very great shock to me he has been attending me several days from a very serious attack of bowels for which reason I was not told of his death until two days after.

Mournfully she reported on the 7th that he has been 'taken to his long home' with many carriages in attendance; 'he has not left his equal'.[44]

Elizabeth frequently fell victim to 'an attack of bowels'. Deprived of Dr Delisser, 6 weeks or so after his death she was sending for Sir Charles Lyon Herbert on a similar pretext. Born in London in 1784, Herbert was practising as a surgeon there before his marriage in 1813 and he was knighted by William IV in 1836, but by 1839 there were signs that his affairs were not in good order. In July 1839 it was reported that he was a candidate for outlawry, at the suit of a creditor called Henry Clark, and on 19 November the *Times* announced the sale of the furnishings of his house in Portman Square, which portended his move abroad.[45] By October 1840 he was subscribing for 3 months to Vieusseux, giving an address in Via Maggio. In 1842 the first of Murray's guidebooks to Florence named him as one of four British physicians in Florence. Playfair, Physician to the British Minister, and Harding were long-term residents; Bankhead, 'an old London practitioner', normally resided in Florence, and Herbert 'also attends as a general practitioner'.[46] The Maquays first mention him in the spring and early summer of 1844. It becomes evident that music was an important ingredient in their social relationship, in which Elena and the growing George were at least as active as John himself. Elizabeth too records seeing the Herberts from time to time for as long as she kept her diary.

Dr James Harding was another friend. On 19 March 1836 Elizabeth recorded that she had had a 'very satisfactory' first visit from a 'Mr Harden', who, a few days later 'certainly has been of service to my Rheumatism'.[47] He was not a newcomer to Florence. A native of Wiltshire, born about 1787, he had made a career as a surgeon in London and was able to call himself Surgeon Extraordinary to Prince Leopold. He served as surgeon to the Norwich Union Life Assurance Society and to the Westminster General Infirmary, and was a director (alongside Michael Faraday) of The National Drug and Chemical Company. He became the father of a large family and in about 1823 moved from Gower Street to a new house in Cavendish Square. Ominously, its opulent contents had to be sold in 1830; the *Morning Post* carried a description of them on 15 November. By December a Mr Harding was subscribing to Vieusseux. It was he who in February 1835 attempted to resuscitate the unfortunate Colonel Forbes at a Court Ball. On the following 9 May his name appeared in the *Morning Chronicle* in a list of 'debtors in high life who have left their residences, or are living in secret, or beyond the jurisdiction of Westminster'. Later in the year he attended the Wilmers amid fears of cholera. In 1840 Jousiffe carefully designated Playfair a physician and Harding a surgeon, but Harding clearly treated a wide variety of conditions.[48]

In September 1842 Harding talked to Elizabeth about himself and his settling in Tuscany; unfortunately she says no more than that.[49] That the Maquays never mention a Mrs Harding strongly suggests that he was a widower. He lost a child in Tuscany, for his 12-year-old son Berkeley was buried in the Leghorn cemetery in April 1834. At least four daughters accompanied him to Florence, of whom the youngest was no more than 5 in 1835 and the oldest (Adeline) about 20, old enough to support her father as guest and hostess.[50] The Maquays often mention father and daughters, both giving and receiving hospitality. A junior Mr Harding makes occasional appearances; this may well have been James Augustus, the artist who got into trouble with the Tuscan authorities in 1851.[51] Harding left Florence shortly before John Maquay in 1858 and by 1861 was living with his eldest daughter at Lymington in Hampshire, where he died in 1868.

The Maquays afford glimpses of the routine doctoring undertaken by such practitioners as well as the self-medication that was practised among the British residents, which was probably no more or less horrifying than would have been the case at home. Elizabeth Maquay's accounts of her physical state are occasionally enlivened by her original spelling (on one occasion she was apparently suffering from 'Diara'). On 9 November 1836 she felt unwell, went to bed and took the omnipresent 'blue pill', which made her very sick in the night. She then took castor oil and unsurprisingly felt so ill that she sent for Harding, who rather remarkably declared that 'he could not have prescribed better for me that I did myself'. In September 1841 she sent for him one evening while he was at the Pergola Theatre: he prescribed a mustard bath for her feet, so it does not sound as if her condition was life-threatening. John Maquay had to consult Harding for erysipelas, and in

April 1845 the surgeon performed 'a little operation' on young George.[52] References to purely social encounters with Harding and his daughters are numerous.

Harding's services were once required because of violence done by another physician. Jousiffe in 1840 named a recent arrival in Florence, Dr Sealy, 'a gentleman of distinguished talent in his profession and the author of *Medical Essays* and other medical works of great merit'.[53] Sealy's stay seems not to have been a long one and it may have been unusually lively. According to the *Satirist*, Sealy overheard a dubious character called Mapleson making remarks which reflected on Mrs Sealy's reputation and gave him such a beating that Harding, called in to attend the victim, declared 'that he had never seen a man so punished in his life'. It is implied that Sealy was ultimately the loser by this episode, although he was 'a gentlemanly man' and had been 'in good practice' in Bath and London.[54]

The *Satirist* rarely missed an opportunity to libel Harding. It dismissed a rumour that Mapleson had lost an eye in this affray, for had that been possible Harding would have made certain of it. He created large numbers of widows and widowers and was single-handedly responsible for the sudden and premature death of Harcourt Popham, who had allegedly been the picture of health 5 days previously. John Maquay gives a slightly different impression: Harcourt died of 'apoplexy', 'having been complaining for a few days'.[55] The *Satirist*'s correspondent may have known that Harding was a fugitive debtor, a type at which the journal liked to loose its shafts. At all events, he was sufficiently well regarded to be employed to attend on both Sir George Hamilton and Peter Campbell Scarlett.[56]

Bagni had by now become a common place of summer resort for British physicians. Their intersecting migratory movements reflected those of their clientele; the physician's trade, like the banker's, followed the flag. Dr Kissock's departure for Rome did not mean that nothing more was seen of him in Tuscany. In May or June he would pass through Florence on his way to Bagni, where he spent the summer simultaneously practising his profession and enjoying the equable climate of the spa. In the autumn he performed the return journey to Rome. Elizabeth Maquay monitored his whereabouts. Sometimes in the summer she took the waters at Montecatini. At the end of June 1837 Kissock and Harding called on her there on their way to Bagni for the summer season; a few weeks later she was sending for Kissock to come from Bagni to attend to her. In the autumn he stayed in Florence, as he often did, for a short time on his way back to Rome, and during this stay Elizabeth was

taken very ill last night with a violent Shivering was oblig'd to ring for Nannette who gave me Hartshorn & coverd me with my Duvet which soon reliev'd me sent for Kissock early in the mor'g who immediately bled me & gave me James's Powders three hours in the course of the day.

She followed this up with Castor Oil and more James's Powders 'which caused a gentle perspiration all night'.[57] In the following summer, once again at Montecatini, she was disappointed to learn that Kissock had not been seen at Bagni.

Kissock departed from this routine to be married in Edinburgh in July 1840, but this did not lead to a happy old age; his wife died in Rome less than 2 years after the wedding. Only a couple of months later, in June 1842, John Maquay noted that Kissock had not been well since. The Maquays both saw him at Bagni in the summer of 1844, but John remarked that he was 'very lame and unwell' and back in Florence in September he was 'very weak on his legs'.[58] The only further mentions of him occur when John visited him in Rome in 1847 and 1848; a silence then falls which was not broken even by his death in 1854. In his last years he became housebound and his patients had to come to him. His circle was increasingly confined to the Romans – and Catholics – who perseveringly visited him. On 22 July 1852, the *Daily News* reported that the conversion of this stalwart Protestant had been announced with some fanfare. It can hardly be supposed that John did not hear of this, or that it pleased him, at a time when such a scenario was every British Protestant's nightmare.

Kissock was not the only exponent of the annual round between Rome and Bagni. Jousiffe named alongside him a Dr Deakin, who from October to May resided at Rome and in summer attended the Baths: 'Dr Deakin is a gentleman of distinguished merit in his profession and of most agreeable manners'.[59] His connection with Bagni was not merely that of seasonal physician. In 1839 he was involved at the outset of the campaign to build an Anglican Church there, and was appointed a trustee together with George Robbins, Colonel Stisted and Consul Falconar. Subsequently he served as treasurer and collected money at Rome for the building fund. During the 1843 season he was Robbins's churchwarden at Bagni and when he was married in Sheffield in 1846 it was Robbins who performed the ceremony.

This connection continued into the 1850s. There are some glimpses of Deakin's social life at Bagni in letters exchanged in 1852 by members of the Phillips family of Mold in Flintshire. He was driving with Miss Bowyer when a disgruntled former servant of hers, lurking by the roadside,

> aimed a tremendous blow at her with a weighty stick. The Doctor saw it coming & took the force of it on his own arm between the shoulder & elbow it however struck Miss B in two places. Ye Carriage was stopped the Coachman jumped off to seize the man & Dr did the same – he made for a cottage and rushed in. The Doctor finding a key in the door on outside locked ye door and sent for the police but ye culprit got thro' a high window at ye back & ran into ye woods.

There are also humorous references to Deakin's 'train' setting off to bathe at Leghorn and later to his autumnal 'cortege back to Rome'.[60]

The Phillips correspondence also mentions a Dr Gason at Bagni. An Irishman, John Gason was a later arrival in Tuscany than Deakin, and for a few years represented another variant pattern, which combined Bagni with Pisa. His church associations were even stronger than Deakin's. On 12 May 1849 he was married in Florence to Elizabeth Greene, sister to the Reverend Henry Greene, who had replaced George Robbins in the joint chaplaincy of Bagni and Pisa and sometimes filled in at Florence during O'Neill's absences and after. The annual movements of the brothers-in-law for some years moved in parallel. In November 1848 Gason was Librarian, Secretary and Treasurer of the Pisa Book Club, and he appears as churchwarden at Pisa in the winter of 1849–1850 (where his wife played the organ) and at Bagni in the summer of 1850. In 1854 he replaced Deakin as trustee of the Bagni church on the latter's resignation. He attended on Peter Campbell Scarlett when he was taken ill at Pisa in 1852.[61] His clerical brother-in-law exemplified the extraordinary subtleties (not to say contradictions) of contemporary beliefs about climate and health. In 1858, after 12 years in the job, Greene declared that 'a lengthened residence in these relaxing climates' had injured his health. He was therefore seeking an exchange with an English incumbent whose condition by contrast required 'a southern climate'.[62]

The minutes of the Pisa Book Club, like those of the Pisan and Bagni churches, reveal the persistent presence of the physicians on their management committees alongside the predictable clerical and military gentlemen. Dr Richard Saunders was a founder member of the Club in 1844, and had already been there for some years, to judge by Jousiffe's announcement that he was about to take up residence at Pisa, probably in the winter of 1839–1840. According to Jousiffe, he had studied medicine at Bologna.[63] From 1839 he was deeply involved in the deliberations at Pisa and at Bagni which resulted in the building of the church at the Baths, and he was one of those who organized the congregation's expressions of regret when George Robbins announced in 1843 that he was leaving to take up the Florentine chaplaincy. He got to know John Maquay when the latter spent the summer of 1844 at Bagni on bank business and in 1846 they exchanged invitations at Florence, where Mrs Saunders died 4 years later. Her husband continued to purchase sittings at Pisa for the winter and at Bagni in the summer and presumably practised his profession there. He died in March 1862, aged 53, and was buried at Bagni. For most of his recorded lifetime he had exemplified the Pisa-Bagni winter-summer pattern.

Dr Charles Benjamin Nankivell, who attended the sickly James Irving junior at Pisa, displayed a variant pattern and had a distinctive history. Born around 1805 a native of the United States, he obtained his doctorate of medicine at Pisa in 1828 and then came to England, becoming surgeon to the newly established pharmacy at Coventry, where his first children were born.[64] At some time in the early 1840s the family moved to Tuscany. In December 1845 Nankivell was a member of the Pisa Book Club, and we know from later census evidence that two children were born to him in Tuscany. He also lost a daughter at Leghorn in September 1847. This, with the fact that he subscribed to the Leghorn church in 1848, hints that Nankivell may have put his services at the disposal of those British residents who chose to spend the summer there and not in Bagni. It looks as if he returned to England before 1850 and (as the younger James Irving's will suggests) settled at Torquay.

When William Snow summarized the medical facilities available at Bagni in his 1846 handbook he revealed how the various circuits intersected there in the summer. Dr Deakin had attended from Rome for nine seasons, and had a 'well-known practice'. Dr Trotman, a Florentine resident, had attended for five seasons and was highly recommended. (Trotman is often to be found, between 1844 and 1861, subscribing to the church at Bagni.) Dr Saunders had been there last season, but was not expected this (1846 was the year of his Sheffield marriage). Dr Cook was 'the resident English physician at Pisa during the Winter'; there was also a Dr Squires, who was, 'I believe, established at Florence and is considered skilful'. There was a dentist from Leghorn, Dr King.[65] If an individual remained at Bagni out of season it might be necessary to summon or send aid from Florence, as John Maquay did one day in October 1845 when he sent Harding to attend to Mr Cave.[66]

The Anglo-Florentines did not lack for physicians. If an accident occurred at the racecourse, there would be medical men on hand who were not there simply on standby. The *Satirist* of 4 July 1841 claimed that Harding cared for little except 'horses and w—-'. (It is left to the reader to choose between a number of alternative readings of the last word.) In 1852 *Murray*'s stated that

> There are four excellent English physicians resident at Florence. Dr Harding, who is the Locock of Florence; Sir Charles Herbert; and Dr Wilson, MD, late Physician to one of the London Hospitals, possessing considerable experience both of English and Continental practice. Dr Trottman, Via della Scala, 4280.

This suggests that Sir Charles Herbert was still practising, but he died on Christmas Day in 1855 at the age of 71.[67] The reference to Queen Victoria's obstetrician, Sir Charles Locock, was presumably intended to be complimentary.[68] Elizabeth Browning noted *Murray*'s description of Harding, who attended on her before and at the birth of her son in 1849 and also during her miscarriages and in other afflictions. Whatever opinion the *Satirist* may have entertained of his competence, both she and Robert came to have a high regard for him.

Doctors were key figures in Elizabeth's life. Her judgement of them was influenced by their agreement with her own view of her condition and how to manage it. The Brownings had not long arrived in Pisa, late in 1846, when Dr Cook had to treat Elizabeth's maid Elizabeth Wilson. It is not explained why it was he who was consulted and not Dr Nankivell, whom Elizabeth refers to only once, as 'the most intelligent physician in Pisa'. Wilson had suffered from sea-sickness on the journey and thought fit to swallow a large quantity of an English patent medicine. When (in her opinion) this proved not strong enough Robert was sent to 'the English dispensary' for calomel and rhubarb, and Wilson followed this with a native remedy strongly recommended by their landlords. After all this she was unsurprisingly worse than ever, and Cook was brought in to set her to rights, which he eventually did, by imposing severe dietary restrictions among other things. He assured Wilson and her mistress that the trouble was entirely due to the sea sickness and had nothing to do with the climate, which hints at the prevalent inclination to look in that quarter for explanations of sickness. That Wilson should have left well alone and let nature take its course in settling her stomach does not seem to have occurred to her or perhaps anyone else, although Cook did observe that her condition had been 'aggravated' by the English pills.

Cook was himself a firm believer in the efficacy of the Italian climate. Elizabeth said he had told her that

the advantage of being *here* is incontestable. He himself is in Italy on account of weakness of the chest, many of his family having died of consumption. He says that he could not *breathe* while he was in England a month ago.[69]

Cook and James Irving must have been in perfect agreement; but however ardent an advocate of Pisa Cook was, he too joined the migration to Bagni in the summer. 'Most Pisans', Elizabeth remarked, 'do the same. This place is untenable in the hot weather.'[70] Cook was another of the many Edinburgh graduates to ply their trade in Tuscany, and (as both Elizabeth and William Snow noted) had published a book on pulmonary tuberculosis in 1842, before coming to Pisa. Between 1845 and 1848 he is recorded in the minutes of the Pisa Book Club. When the club was wound up for the summer season on 8 April 1848 he was thanked for his services, and this hint that he was about to leave is confirmed by an obituary in the *Cheltenham Chronicle* on 22 August 1903, which stated that he had served the hospital in that town for 45 years until his retirement in 1893. Neither his weak chest nor the English climate prevented him from living to the age of 92.

Wilson flourished when the Brownings moved to Florence in the spring of 1847, although she was obviously still determined to be worried by her symptoms. In August her employers reluctantly sent her to consult Sir Charles Herbert. Elizabeth would not have done so herself, but would have simply 'kept to the old prescriptions … & walked more & eaten still less'; Wilson, however, 'gets nervous'. A little later Elizabeth said with evident approval that Wilson had thrown away Sir Charles's medicines. She may have been right that castor oil seemed more effective, but more sensibly repeated her view that diet and exercise were better remedies (assuming there was really something to remedy).[71]

Elizabeth and her maid were at one in a kind of tacit defiance of authority on the subject of the Florentine summer heat, which they were convinced was doing Wilson no harm. In the following October Elizabeth declared that 'Florence seems to me a very safe residence for me as to climate, under certain conditions. It wdnt be worth returning to Pisa, I think, on the mere ground of climate'. In the same letter she remarked that, although 'There is a Dr Trotman whom Robert has heard wonders of', there was no need at the moment to consult anyone, for despite a bad episode she had experienced in Pisa she knew (so she believed) all the right things to do.[72] There were clearly reservations about the elderly Herbert. Robert had already told his wife's sisters that in settling in Florence they had been assured 'that one of the Physicians here is an able and desirable man – (unfortunately, this "one" is *not* Mrs Jameson's old friend, Herbert – who may be getting *too* old a friend.)'.[73]

Another physician they seem to have deliberately avoided. In April 1848 Elizabeth described 'a tete à tete with Dr Alnutt' as one of the few things she was afraid of. Dr 'Alnutt' had fortunately been away from home when she had been ill recently: Trotman and Harding too had been out, but Harding came promptly in response to a note.[74] Richard Allnatt obtained his degree of MD at Glasgow in 1830 and appears to have had wide medical interests. He was author of a work on *tic douloureux* and at different times is to be found offering recommendations for the treatment of hydrophobia and cattle plague, and expressing opinions on the deleterious effects of tobacco and the positive effects of rum. In addition to all this, he was a keen archaeologist and was elected a Fellow of the Society of Antiquaries in 1842. He evidently spent a few years in Tuscany. In February 1849 Elizabeth reported that he was still in Florence and attending a few families, but did not, she thought, 'prosper gloriously'. She surely appreciated him for one thing: at Bagni during the summer of 1849 he paused to admire her baby (as did Dr Trotman). It was through him that Mrs Trollope proposed to visit the Brownings in December 1850, an initiative that Robert 'rudely' repelled.[75] At least for a brief period John Maquay saw quite a lot of him. Allnatt attended his great friend Edward Horne when he was dying in March 1851 and then helped him to make a catalogue of Horne's and then of John's own books. It is from John's diary that we know that in May he was about to leave Florence.[76]

It seems to have been the crisis in Elizabeth's health in the spring of 1848 that brought Dr Harding to the Brownings' notice. Elizabeth's choice of him, despite the advertised merits of Trotman, may have stemmed from personal recommendation, for he 'had attended an aunt of mine who besought me to have nobody else on any account'.[77] Thus began an amusing episode of what might be termed competitive doctoring in retrospect. Like much else connected with Pisa, Dr Cook, who had attended Elizabeth as well as Wilson, was suddenly 'out', whereas Harding at Florence was 'in'. Elizabeth was infinitely pleased with Harding, who was 'of the pleasant right age, with a benevolent yet acute countenance, & is very decided in his opinions and advice'. Cook had recommended the use of port wine and tried to reduce her intake of morphine. When Harding came to see her he pulled terrible faces over 'what was suffered at Pisa and hoped that he could pull her round'. 'The morphine he did not disturb in any way', Elizabeth reported, observing truly enough that 'if I diminish, so as to feel the diminution in the least degree, I shall have to double the dose as has been proved'. (Robert nevertheless contrived by 'sorceries' to reduce the quantity she took in the course of the year.) Unlike Cook, Harding 'puts away wine altogether'. It was quite wrong for her 'vivacious temperament' and 'in every way likely to do harm by quickening the circulation & producing fever'. Harding 'shook his head to and fro at the idea of my having ever taken it in any proportion'. Even milk was deemed 'over-nourishing or exciting'.

As for exercise, she was to go out every day if possible in the carriage. Elizabeth entirely approved of this in preference to walking, which old-fashioned people had declared to be better, solely (in her opinion) because in times gone by carriages had jolted like carts.[78]

Harding's influence at least during her pregnancy appears to have been positive. By assiduous visiting at the height of the revolutionary ferment and telling Elizabeth frequently that he never saw her looking so well, he clearly struck the best note possible to enable her to cope with her condition. Elizabeth records a passage of arms with Mrs Ogilvy, who, 'being accustomed to walk ten miles a day herself, thinks it heinous of me to be so still', and had lectured Robert on the subject. So Elizabeth consulted Harding, who pronounced it 'quite a mistake, besides, to fancy that exercise facilitates at the last'.[79] Mrs Ogilvy was the author of *A Book of Highland Minstrelsy*, first published in 1846. Elizabeth describes her slightly cuttingly 'as a young & pretty woman, with amiability more than sufficient to cover the heights of other pretensions'. She had her uses: with two young children, she had recent experience of motherhood. She recommended an English nurse, Madame Petrie, who had just helped her through a difficult confinement, and who began to attend Elizabeth.

Sophia Cottrell also had a young child at the time, and had recommended Madame Annina Biondi, but Elizabeth was at first intimidated by Biondi's impressive list of clients, thinking she would be 'too great a personage for us', not to mention her high charges.[80] However, she changed her mind and Biondi superseded Petrie, who was 'highly aggrieved'. Elizabeth thought that Petrie was 'a gossipping woman', and Wilson feared that she would spread stories that the Brownings had entered into a firm engagement with her. Certainly Harding was in her bad books. As for Biondi, Elizabeth said that 'she has a gentle voice and cheerful manner and Wilson thinks that she will be a pleasanter person in a house than our countrywomen'.[81] In *Murray*'s 1854 edition both Petrie and Biondi were named as excellent monthly and sick nurses; Madame Biondi was to be contacted at the English pharmacy in via Tornabuoni.[82]

Naturally enough, much of Elizabeth's correspondence in this period was associated with the health of what turned out to be her only child, Pen. Those who knew which side their bread was buttered on were fulsome in his praise. Dr Harding early endeared himself to Elizabeth with his combination of flattery ('a specimen of a beautiful baby, and I wasn't in the least surprised I can assure you') and practicality. He supplied a wet nurse whom he described as 'a regular cow woman', who 'would have enough milk we might be sure'. This treasure had 'enormous red cheeks, & a rosy mouth smiling to the ears, & broad enough in her proportions to bear "cutting up the middle" (said Dr H), "into a tall woman"'. Elizabeth seems to have been lucky too with Madame Biondi, who, although old and fat, was cheerful: 'active, quicksighted, quick-hearing and light-hearted.' It may have made her blase about the problems of others, for example Sophie Cottrell, who she claims admitted she could not achieve what she had done.[83]

The Brownings made a friend of Harding and he of them, often, as Elizabeth said, kindly continuing to call 'as a friend' after giving a course of treatment. They became well acquainted with his daughters ('accomplished women – sing & paint beautifully'). One day in 1850 Harding poured out to Robert his sorrow over his scapegrace artist son.[84] He paid due regard to a change of air, recommending the neighbourhood of Leghorn to them 'for its dryness and healthfulness, besides the cheapness' and packing them off to Siena, rather against Elizabeth's will, in the summer of 1850. His opinions were relayed to England; when Elizabeth's sister Henrietta was suffering from severe morning sickness, she was offered consolation: 'Never mind! Dr Harding says that no excess of sickness is bad – he never knew harm come of that.'[85] By this time both Brownings were pronouncing themselves more and more satisfied with his 'skill and decision'.

His practice was extensive, as they noted. Another of his clients was Lady Don, as we can infer from the fact that between 21 February 1842 and 6 December 1852 he witnessed her will and subsequently no fewer than seven of its codicils.[86] His departure from Tuscany meant that he did not attend Elizabeth in her last bouts of illness. When she was dying in June 1861 Dr Wilson came to her, but only because Dr Gryzanowski, who had become her regular physician, was away. The Brownings' American friend Kate Field regarded this as 'most unfortunate'. Writing on 29 June 1861, she declared that Wilson, who was 'most forbidding in physiognomy … hastened Mrs Browning's death'. He began by frightening her, telling her how ill she was. The absent Gryzanowski, by contrast, 'knew her constitution'.[87] The 1861 Murray's recommended both men. Wilson, in the Casa Niccolini opposite Palazzo Strozzi, was 'Licentiate of the Colleges of Physicians of London and Gottingen, and accoucheur, formerly Physician to a London Hospital and to the British Legation'. Gryzanowski was 'a German physician, familiar with English and American practice'. In 1865, when he was married in Devon to an Englishwoman, Jessie Wright, he was described as 'of Pisa'. He and his wife were both buried in the English cemetery at Bagni.[88]

On 23 November 1855 John Maquay attended a party at which three doctors were present: Harding, Trotman and Luard.[89] Unlike the other two, there is no indication that Luard was in practice, unless we can thus interpret John's rather strange observation on 8 March 1853: 'A Mr Bateson has gone outrageously deranged today apparently from loving a Miss Stiffe but it is supposed he was inclined to it before he committed great extravagances at Trotman's & with Dr Luard.'[90] Like Harding and Luard, Thomas Trotman became a friend. Born and married in Barbados, he first appears in the diary in April 1846 and is recorded thereafter as a member of the whist-playing circle which included Mrs Trollope. Like John he often hosted whist parties. He attended young Tommy Maquay when the latter was brought back sick from Malta late in 1855, and John sometimes called upon him for himself. One diary entry, on 23 April 1857, is as alarming as anything his mother could have perpetrated:

Taken very ill last night just as I lay down in bed, stomach swelling and I thought myself very bad, drank a tumbler of Salad oil & sent for Trotman who gave me clysters, Calomel Castor Oil &c and by the morning I was much better, I staid in bed all day much purged and eating nothing.[91]

John was in Florence in the spring of 1861 when his American daughter-in-law Nina gave birth to her first child; Trotman came to her both before and after the birth. There were humbler people among his clientele. When the widowed coachman John Russell called on the English Church for financial help in 1859 Dr Trotman was among the people to whom he owed money, probably for attendance on his sickly child.[92]

Russell also owed money to the apothecary Ferrai. Gaetano Ferrai or Ferrari was one of two 'highly respectable chemists' who, according to Jousiffe nearly 20 years earlier, 'divide between them nearly the whole of the English business'. Ferrai's premises were in the Piazza Santa Trinità, where the British were so often to be found; also recommended was Forini of the Piazza Gran Duca. Both prepared medicines with great care and attention, and with English weights and measures, as well as stocking English patent medicines.[93] It is evident from the Maquay diaries alone that there was a brisk demand among the Anglo-Florentines for calomel, hartshorn, castor oil, blue pills and James's Powders. Such items were among the stock-in-trade not only of Italian apothecaries but of British shopkeepers who advertised patent medicines alongside their groceries. For prescriptions, it was necessary to go to an apothecary, as Dr Delisser did on Elizabeth Maquay's behalf just before he himself died. The Brownings were able to patronize an 'English' dispensary at Pisa, and there was no difficulty in obtaining medicines during the season at Bagni. At Montecatini in August 1841, however, Elizabeth Maquay had to send to Florence for 'Opodeldoct' (opodelduc was a soap-based liniment) when she suffered a fall.[94]

Murray's in 1842 more or less echoed Jousiffe's information, but by 1847 there was a new name among apothecaries or druggists. Henry Roberts now kept 'the Farmacia del Sole, opposite the Corsi Palace, 4190 in the Via Tornabuoni'.[95] An advertisement in the *Gazzetta* of 16 January 1845 indicates that he was established in Florence by then. By 1861 *Murray*'s could state that his was the best place to go for English prescriptions, and by 1864 he had several English assistants. His pharmacy was now described as that of the British Legation and in 1867 he was said to run a flourishing wholesale trade, supplying nearly all the apothecaries in the neighbourhood of Florence.[96] Dr Wilson for a time was located opposite Roberts's premises.

It is not to be supposed that all the British in Florence consulted British doctors exclusively. There were Italian physicians, as well as Italian pharmacists, who were equipped to deal with the English-speaker. Medical men might be treated like any other tradesmen. In December 1823, John Maquay and his brother George required the attention of both apothecary and surgeon and John (very early in his experience of Italy) had what he called an 'unpleasant battle' with both men before he beat the surgeon down from 589 *francesconi* to 400 and the apothecary from 189 to 100 – the total for both himself and George.[97] As a householder he frequently employed Florentine doctors, sometimes alongside his old English friends. In February 1834 Kissock did not quite agree with Nespoli about Elena's condition, but in October 1836 he and Lazzarini were entirely of one mind as to how to treat the infant George and John accordingly 'ordered him a little calomel.'[98] Lazzarini attended the whole family and in 1836 was paid 21.6 *francesconi* for 39 visits.[99] Successive editions of *Murray's* listed the 'most celebrated' Italian physicians alongside their English counterparts and joint consultations were not uncommon. When Scarlett was ill at Pisa in 1852 the *attaché* Barron sent Harding and Bufalini to him, and they were reported to approve of the treatment already ordained by Dr Gason in conjunction with Drs Wilson and Bartolini.[100]

Mental afflictions might demand Anglo-Italian co-operation, as British doctors had no means at their disposal for treating or if necessary restraining such patients. In 1831 Seymour reported that a Captain Pattulls of the Royal Artillery had arrived in Florence in a violent frame of mind. '2 English physicians of the greatest respectability' (unfortunately unnamed) had applied to the Minister to obtain an order from the Tuscan government for hospital assistance, which was most graciously granted, but at first seemed unnecessary as Captain Pattulls had apparently benefitted from another mode of treatment. He set off for Leghorn, but by the time he arrived his malady had become more violent than the doctors had anticipated and it had been necessary to place him in confinement.[101] In 1845 John Maquay and Harding were jointly confronted by a Mrs Skinner, who thought herself dying although Harding had 'no such opinion'; they decided to call in Dr Bini of the Lunatic Asylum.[102]

Lower-class Britons were more likely than their social superiors to experience Italian hospitals. In 1853 the church committee noted that Englishmen (presumably indigent) who died in the hospital had been placed in the restricted category of those who were buried 'altogether gratuitously' in the cemetery.[103] In Leghorn, the numbers of British hospital inmates may well have been greater than in Florence, given that this was a port visited by British mariners, who were particularly liable to illness and injury. In 1824, the merchant William Macbean (the later consul's father) prepared a memorandum on the regulations of the so-called British Factory, which included the following explanatory note:

> It has been and is still usual to send the indigent sick to the Public Hospital of this Place, where they are received and attended to on payment from the Factory of three pauls a day which expense in cases of Merchant Seamen, is recovered from the Master or owner of the vessel to which they belong.[104]

The consul sometimes struggled to reclaim the expenses of hospital care in accordance with these rules.[105]

From time to time proposals were floated for the building of an English hospital at Leghorn. The Reverend Charles Neat referred to the existence of such a project at the very end of his tenure of the chaplaincy, but nothing came of it.[106] In 1849 a surgeon named Henry Green, who said he had established himself permanently at Leghorn, advised Lord Palmerston that he had offered his services gratuitously to the Consul in the event of the opening of a British hospital. Such a foundation, he believed, was urgently necessary. Sick British sailors had to be placed in 'the general Italian hospital, where they were placed in large and ill-ventilated wards filled with Italians'. They were attended by Italians who could not speak English and whom they could not understand. In many instances, men had taken private lodgings in preference. The consul had, however, refused Green's offer, for reasons which will become apparent. The doctor had therefore on his own initiative 'resolved to open an Hospital to be supported by the voluntary contributions of Merchants and Masters of Merchantmen'. This had been running successfully for a year; 115 men had been admitted in that time.

Unfortunately, there was a snag. If a patient's ship cleared the port before he could be discharged, the consul was apparently only permitted to make himself responsible for his expenses if he was in the Italian public hospital. Green therefore petitioned the Foreign Secretary, with the consul's support, to put mariners who were treated in his hospital on the same footing as those who went to the Italian hospital. Here they could have 'airy well ventilated rooms and the use of a good Library, at the same rate as is paid in the Italian Hospital'. There was also an appealing religious advantage.

> The British Clergymen residing here find that they can visit the men much more satisfactorily in an establishment where all the patients are British, than in one where they are surrounded on all sides by Italians and Roman Catholics.

Green emphasized that 'not a farthing of additional expense' would be incurred by the consul or by the government; four or five men a year would be affected. The response was curious and on the face of it obtuse, as if Green was actually requesting permission to found a hospital and (by probable implication) soliciting financial assistance. Palmerston sent a negative response, having referred the letter to the Admiralty, which blandly replied that 'there is no occasion for a Hospital at Leghorn, as every attention is paid by the Consul there to British Seamen', whatever that was supposed to mean. This was despite the fact that the consul had backed the proposal.[107]

Fresh life was given to the issue by political events. In 1853 Macbean informed the Foreign Secretary that, thanks to the Austrian occupation, there was a felt need for a hospital, specifically for British sailors.[108] Presumably because of the greater numbers now being accommodated, there was an enhanced risk of 'infection by their close contact (for want of more room,) with those who have other complaints'. The Austrians had 'gradually appropriated to themselves all the best accommodation' (which had previously, for all its shortcomings, allegedly gone to the British). Macbean gave two case histories of convalescent seamen, neither seriously ill, who had respectively contracted pleurisy and smallpox as a result of hospital conditions. There were other anxieties, entirely typical of the time:

> Our Protestant Sailors are also exposed in the Royal Hospital to the attacks of Romish Priests; I know of several cases in which they have endeavoured to pervert, and there is an Irish Priest here who is disposed to be active and troublesome in that respect. In Oct 1851 I had occasion to complain to M. Ronchivecchi against a Priest, employed in the Hospital, who had repeatedly annoyed a Scotch Ship Master (under treatment there for a mental affection) by compelling him against his will to kiss a crucifix.

Four years earlier Green had made a more oblique reference to this source of inconvenience.

At no point in their communications with the Foreign Office did the consuls mention by name any British physician resident in Leghorn. They themselves, like many of the long-term inhabitants of the merchant colony, would have been quite able to deal with Italian doctors. In 1849 Henry Green's name appears among a small cluster of known members of the Free Church of Scotland who signed the memorial protesting at the summary expulsion of Pakenham, but how long he remained in Leghorn is unclear. Also signatories were two physicians who died only a few months later. The 28-year-old William Henry Bellingham MD died at Pisa in April 1850, only some 18 months after his marriage, to be followed in the same month by Henry Harrington, who was 49.[109] We get a glimpse of a longer-term fixture in the shape of Edward King, 'surgeon and dentist', whose child Frances Jane was baptized at Leghorn on 10 January 1847. His presence can be documented, principally by way of the church subscription lists, from 1843 into the 1860s, and we have William Snow's word for it that in the 1840s he was attending at Bagni in the summer. In 1863 the consul mentioned Dr Hubert des Vignes, who had been appointed by Thomas Brassey specifically to attend to his railway employees.[110]

John Maquay and his mother make several references to undergoing dental treatment in Florence, but the dentist either remains unnamed or is Italian. When Isabella Wilmer was tormented by a tooth one day in January 1836, she had recourse to the omnicompetent Mr Harding, who pulled it out. In October 1834, a Mr Parsons, 'Surgeon Dentist and Cupper', advertised from an address in Piazza Santa Maria Novella, but his wife died the following year and his stay in Florence may have been brief.[111] On 7 November 1844 Henry Dunn, the son of a London dentist, advertised from the same piazza. He died in Florence, aged only 34, early in 1856. During the winter of 1847–1848 a Mr Kemble, surgeon-dentist, was practising at 1186 Lungarno, near the Ponte S. Trinità.[112] For years Murray's could only recommend Campana, a father and son team in the Piazza Gran Duca.

John Maquay first mentions going to Campana in 1836 and was still using father or son at the end of his time in Florence.[113] In 1863 Murray's at last recommended an Englishman, another Mr Dunn, in Piazza Santa Maria Novella, who was said to be 'highly spoken of'. Charles William Dunn, probably brother to the earlier Henry, had received adult baptism from the Reverend Robbins in 1848, when he was 18, and died in Florence in 1915.[114]

When Dr William Wilson died in 1896 at the age of 82 he was said to have been 51 years a physician in Florence; at least six children were born to him there. He attended Landor in his last years.[115] The 1863 *Murray's* elaborated on its earlier recommendations of him. He was 'long established in Florence, and is consequently well-acquainted with its climate and its effects upon disease; an important consideration in the selection of a physician in every part of Italy'. Such men were able to enjoy the amenities and social pleasures of Tuscany, while drawing fees from compatriots who believed in their expertise and accepted their reassurances that being where they were was of benefit to their health.

Notes

1   In chronological order the editions cited are: *Travels in Italy between the years 1792 and 1798* (London, 1802); *Travels on the Continent, Written for the Use and Particular Information of Travellers* (London, 1820); *Information and Directions for Travellers on the Continent. Fifth edition, thoroughly revised and with considerable additions* (Paris, 1826); *Travels in Europe between the Years 1824 and 1828 Adapted to the Use of Travellers Comprising an Historical Account of Sicily with Particular Information for Strangers in That Island* (London, 1828); *Travels in Europe, for the Use of Travellers on the Continent, and Likewise in the Island of Sicily* (London, 1833); *Travels in Europe, for the Use of Travellers on the Continent and Likewise in the Island of Sicily* (Paris, 1839).

2   Joseph Forsyth, *Remarks on Antiquities, Arts and Letters during an Excursion to Italy in the Years 1802 and 1803* (London, 1816), pp. 25–7. Based on his travels in 1802–1803, Forsyth's account was not published until 1816. He did not describe the climate of any other Tuscan city.

3   Starke, *Travels in Italy* (1802), Vol. 2, pp. 257–8.

4   Thomas Burgess, *Climate of Italy in relation to Pulmonary Consumption, with remarks on the influence of foreign climates upon invalids* (London, 1852), pp. 145–6.

5   Montgomery Carmichael (ed.), *The Inscriptions in the Old British Cemetery of Leghorn, transcribed by G. Milner-Gibson-Cullum and the late F. Campbell Macauley* (Leghorn, 1906), p. 5.

6   James Clark, *Medical Notes on Climate, Diseases, Hospitals, and Medical Schools in France, Italy, and Switzerland, Comprising an Inquiry into the Effects of a Residence in the South of Europe in Cases of Pulmonary Consumption* (London, 1820). *The Influence of Climate in the Prevention and Cure of Chronic Diseases, More Particularly of the Chest and Digestive Organs* (London, 1829) went into a second edition in 1830. This was followed by *The Sanative Influence of Climate, with an Account of the Best Places of Resort for Invalids in England, the South of Europe, &c* (London, 1841) which in turn went into a final edition in 1846.

7   Clark's not very distinctive name makes it difficult to be certain of his identity amidst the entries in the Vieusseux subscription books, but there are possible sightings in September 1821, June and October 1823, May and October 1824 and March 1830. These dates are compatible with the usual pattern of seasonal movement to and from Rome.

8   Clark, *Medical Notes* (1820), pp. 65–7.

9   Ibid, pp. 113–17.

10 Clark, *Influence of Climate* (1829), pp. 135–6; *Sanative Influence* (1st ed., 1841), pp. 252–3.

11 Clark, *Sanative Influence* (2nd ed., 1846), p. 227.

12 TNA, Prob11/1935; *Gazzetta,* 19 November 1841. The *Essex Standard* on 31 July 1840 said that Young had gone to Italy 'for the benefit of his health'.

13 Clark, *Medical Notes* (1820), pp. 87, 90.

14 Clark, *Influence of Climate* (1829), pp. 98–102.

15 Clark, *Sanative Influence* (2nd ed., 1846), p. 225.

16 George Combe (ed.), *The Life and Correspondence of Andrew Combe M.D.* (Edinburgh, 1850), pp. 365, 460.

17 Burgess, *Climate of Italy,* pp. 144–5.

18 FO79/79, Seymour to FO, 12 May 1835.

19 Burgess, *Climate of Italy,* pp. 147–62.

20 FO79/134, Hamilton to FO, 26 July 1848.

21 FO79/132, Hamilton to FO, 10 August 1848 and 79/137, 18 April 1849.

22 BC14, 2630 EBB to Henrietta and Arabella, 21/24 November 1846.

23 BC14, 2656 EBB to Arabella, 24 February 1847; 2707 to Henrietta, 20 October 1847.

24 BC15, 2797 EBB to Arabella, ? 23/25 June 1849.

25 His will is in TNA, Prob11/2240. The doubly bereaved Mrs Irving may not have left Tuscany immediately, for a person of that name continued to subscribe at Bagni in the summer and Pisa in the winter for several years to come.

26 Starke, *Travels in Italy* (1802), Vol. 2, p. 275. Polhill, a native of Maidstone in Kent, had his troubles during the French wars, but his son and grandson both made Leghorn their home.

27 Combe (ed.), *Correspondence of Andrew Combe,* p. 105. Combe's cousin Jean Newton was the wife of the Leghorn merchant John Scott.

28 FO79/40, Lord Courtown to Mr Canning, 23 December 1823; FO79/41, Burghersh to FO, 21 February 1824; FO79/108, Falconar to FO, 20 September 1842. Born in Ayrshire in 1785, John Home Peebles subsequently returned to Scotland but died at Warwick in 1867, having lived at different times in Torquay, Cheltenham and London.

29 FO79/41, Burghersh to FO, 18 June 1824. Burghersh spells his name Downe. John Sommers Down had been a naval surgeon, entering that service in 1807. He obtained his MD at Edinburgh in 1815, discoursing on 'inflammatory bilious fever'.

30 JLM, E8 f. 154v. Mrs Starke's 1826 edition says that Kissock was resident in Naples, although by this date he was certainly in Tuscany.

31 EM, C1 f. 73; JLM, E9 f. 21v. John mentions Down again in October 1824 (JLM, E8 f. 187v) but not subsequently.

32 Grant E. Scott and Sue Brown (eds), *New Letters from Charles Brown to Joseph Severn* (www.re.umd.edu/editions/brownsevern), 11, 9 August 1825; JLM, E9 f. 27v, 29 August 1825.

33 The diary entry was printed by Douglas Firth, 'The Case of Augustus d'Este (1784–1848): The First Account of Disseminated Sclerosis', *Proceedings of the Royal Society of Medicine* 34 (1941) pp. 381–4, and has been cited subsequently

in the literature on the history of the disease, although the diagnosis has recently been disputed.

34   Lesley Blanch (ed.), *Harriette Wilson's Memoirs* (London, 2003), pp. 243–4. For the Portsmouth case, see Elizabeth Foyster, *The Trials of the King of Hampshire* (London, 2016).

35   TNA, Prob11/1737; JLM, E9 f. 65v. Penelope Bankhead was married in Florence on 9 February 1828. Bankhead's Vieusseux record over a period of nearly 30 years enables us to chart with fair accuracy where he was living from year to year. In 1831 he was described as attached to the British Embassy (*The Satirist* 1 May 1831).

36   It was on the merits of Pau that Clark quoted Playfair, 'now of Florence', in 1829; and he was also mentioned in the same connection by Alexander Taylor, *The Curative Influence of the Climate of Pau and the Mineral Waters of the Pyrenees on Disease* (London, 1845), p. 48.

37   Capt. M.J. Jousiffe, *A Road Book for Travellers in Italy* (2nd ed., Brussels, Paris and London, 1840), p. 54. Born in London in 1788, Playfair belonged to a distinguished family of professional men originating from Edinburgh, where he graduated MD in 1819 and remained for some years thereafter. In 1801, he was listed as a 'hospital mate', presumably a medical assistant in the navy, becoming an army surgeon later. He remained on the half-pay list until 1831.

38   FO79/93, Fox to FO, 9 May 1839.

39   Princess Marie Liechtenstein, *Holland House* (London, 1874), p. 169; Richard P. Wunder, *Hiram Powers, Vermont Sculptor* (Cranbury, NJ, 1989–1891), Vol. 1, p. 107. Powers's original bust is now in the Smithsonian; when Playfair left Florence in 1845 Powers made a copy for him which is exhibited at the Royal College of Physicians in Edinburgh.

40   Starke, *Travels in Europe* (1839), p. 93. McManus had entered the navy as a surgeon in 1809. In 1838 he appears in a poll-book as living in the Knightsbridge area; he died at St Albans in 1859.

41   JLM, E9 ff. 88v, 89v. 98; FO79/68, Falconar to FO, 3 December 1832.

42   JLM, E10 f. 202; Siena Church Book (LMA, CLC/164/Ms39295, unpaginated).

43   JLM, E10 ff. 205v, 208.

44   EM, C7 ff. 114v, 119v/120.

45   *Morning Post* 5 July 1839. In London at this time we can find evidence of a linen-draper, a tailor and a livery-stable keeper, all called Henry Clark or Clarke.

46   Murray, *Handbook for Travellers in Northern Italy* (London, 1842), p. 474. This first edition was the work of Francis Palgrave, but his name does not appear on the title page.

47   EM, C5 f. 20v.

48   Jousiffe, *Road Book*, pp. 54–5.

49   EM, C7 f. 82v.

50   Adeline and Margaret accompanied their father back to England. Their sister Julia was married in Florence in 1856 but died back in England the following year; Augusta was married in England in 1857.

51   Another son, Francis, became a distinguished soldier in India and the Crimea, and ultimately Lieutenant-Governor of New Brunswick. In November 1854 John Maquay noted that a son of Dr Harding had been wounded at an action identifiable as Inkerman (JLM, E11 f. 139).

52   EM, C5 f. 43; C7 f. 55; JLM, 10 ff. 229v, 242v.

53   Jousiffe, *Road Book*, p. 54. The *Medical Essays* appeared in 1837, one on pulmonary phthisis (an interesting subject for an English doctor in Italy) and another on the role of the imagination in health.

54 *Satirist* 7 February 1841. Mapleson was supposed to be a friend of the Dr Crook who had already been involved in a duel at Bagni and was shortly to die in another one with Plowden.

55 JLM, E10 f. 132.

56 With Herbert and a Dr Hodgson he signed a bulletin on Sir George's health in February 1847 (FO 79/123 Scarlett to FO, 10 February); and in 1852 was sent to Pisa to give his opinion on Scarlett's treatment (FO 79/162, Barron to FO, 12 May).

57 EM, C5 f. 74.

58 JLM, 10 ff. 224v, 229.

59 Jousiffe, *Road Book*, p. 83. Deakin was a considerable botanist, who published extensively on the British flora; his *Flora of the Colosseum* was published in London in 1855. He may have had previous family connections with Tuscany, for a Samuel Deakin, a merchant originally from Sheffield, died at Leghorn in 1839 at the age of 66.

60 Flintshire Record Officer, Hawarden, Ms D/HE, nn. 607, 608, 610.

61 FO79/163, Barron to FO, 12 May 1852. By the early 1860s at the latest he moved to Rome and it was there that both he and his wife died, in 1882 and 1896 respectively; but both were brought to Bagni for burial. Henry Greene had predeceased them in 1876.

62 This letter, dated 1 September, was enclosed by the Reverend George Robbins to Bishop Tait of London on 9 October 1858 (LPL, Fulham Papers, Tait 419, ff. 112–13).

63 Jousiffe, *Road Book*, p. 160. Born in 1809, Saunders was married at the Genoese chaplaincy early in 1833 and it is quite possible that his only known child, another Richard, was born at Bologna and brought to Florence for his baptism, which took place in February 1835.

64 Here he was a friend of the free-thinker Charles Bray, another Coventry resident, who was close to Mary Ann Evans, otherwise George Eliot, and he is one of several candidates as model for the physician Lydgate in *Middlemarch*: M.C. Rintoul, *Dictionary of Real People and Places in Fiction* (London, 2014), p. 698.

65 William Snow, *Hand Book for the Baths of Lucca* (Pisa, 1846), p. 56.

66 JLM, E10 f. 252v.

67 Murray, *Handbook for Travellers in Northern Italy* (4th ed., London, 1852), p. 452. Herbert's wife and daughters remained in Florence, where Lady Herbert died in 1860. References to 'Herberts' in the Maquay diaries are frequent but are not always to this family, for the Hon. Mrs Frances Herbert, the widow of a son of the Earl of Caernavon, was also a long-term Florentine resident with other members of her family.

68 Sir Charles Locock, Bart. (1799–1875) is among other things credited with the introduction of potassium bromide as a treatment for epilepsy.

69 BC14, 2650 EBB to Henrietta, 29 January 1847.

70 BC14, 2664 EBB to Henrietta, 31 March 1847.

71 BC14, 2697 EBB to Arabella, 29/31 August 1847; 2701 EBB to Arabella and Henrietta, 13 September 1847.

72 BC14, 2707 EBB to Henrietta, 20 October 1847.

73 BC14, 2705 RB to Arabella and Henrietta, 4 October 1847.

74 BC15, 2728 EBB to Arabella, 15/17 April 1848.

75 BC15, 2773 EBB to Henrietta, 10/20 February 1849; 2809, EBB to Arabella 17 August 1849; 2896 EBB to Arabella, 16/19 December 1850.

76 JLM, E10 ff. 71, 72, 72v, 73 passim.

77 BC15, 2740 EBB/RB to Anna Jameson, 15 July 1848. This aunt has been identified as Jane Hedley, whose daughter Elizabeth Jane had been born in Florence in 1834.

78 BC15, 2729 EBB to Henrietta, 22 April 1848.

79 BC15, 2773 EBB to Henrietta, 10/20 February 1849.

80 BC15, 2751 EBB to Henrietta, 18/20 November 1848. Biondi also served Elena
    Maquay; JLM records a payment of 25 *francesconi* for nurse tender to Elena on
    30 April 1837: E10, f. 38v.
81 BC15, 2768 EBB to Arabella, 19/22 January 1849; 2773 to Henrietta, 10/20 February.
82 Murray, *Handbook for Travellers in Northern Italy, Part II* (5th ed., London, 1854),
    p. 446.
83 BC15, 2768 EBB to Arabella, 19/22 January 1849; 2783 to Arabella 8/16 April.
84 BC16, 2829 EBB to Arabella, 23 January 1850; 2875 to Eliza Ogilvy, 28 August.
85 BC16, 2864 EBB to Henrietta, 7 July 1850.
86 TNA, Prob11/2211.
87 Carolyn Moss (ed.), *Kate Field: Selected Letters* (Carbondale & Edwardsville, Ill.,
    1996), p. 27.
88 Murray, *Handbook of Florence and Its Environs* (London, 1861), p. vi. Gryzanowski
    was born in Koenigsberg in 1824. He is said to have called upon Henry Adams
    and his wife in Florence in 1872 'and drenched his hosts in Hegelian metaphysics':
    Ernest Samuels, *Henry Adams* (Cambridge Mass, 1989), p. 101. His wide cultivated
    acquaintance included William and Henry James.
89 JLM, E11 f. 163.
90 JLM, E11 f. 126.
91 JLM, E11 f. 191v.
92 For Russell's problems see chapter 14.
93 Jousiffe, *Road Book*, p. 55.
94 EM, C7 f. 52.
95 Murray, *Handbook for Travellers in Northern Italy* (3rd ed., London, 1847), p. 476.
96 By 1867 there was another British pharmacist in Florence, Groves in Borgo
    Ognissanti. Roberts has been credited with the invention of talcum powder in the
    1870s and also distilled a famous rose-water. He died before 1891, but his widow and
    daughters lived on in Florence, his daughter Sophia dying there in 1946. Of his sons,
    Henry (also described as a chemist) died in Florence in 1886 and Edmund in Boston
    in 1898.
97 JLM, E8 f. 155v.
98 JLM, E9 f. 246v; E10, f. 22.
99 JLM, E10 f. 29v.
100 FO79/163, Barron to FO, 12 May 1852.
101 FO171/2, Seymour to FO, 1 February 1831.
102 JLM, E10 ff. 74, 252v.
103 CMB 1, 4 May 1853.
104 FO79/43, Falconar to FO with enclosures, 2 July 1824.
105 See for example FO79/115, Macbean to FO, 16 May 1845, an enormous dossier
    recording Macbean's problems with Mr Robert Jackson, master of the Brig
    Industrious, who was engaged in multiple disputes with his crew.
106 FO 79/61, Falconar to FO, 1 January 1831. The outgoing Neat had written a letter to
    the Church Committee on the subject and a committee (including a Dr Harrington)
    was appointed to consider it.
107 FO79/140, Henry Green to Lord Palmerston, 26 June 1849; Palmerston to Green,
    27 July 1849.
108 FO79/171, Macbean to FO, 26 October 1853.
109 Was this the Dr Harrington who nearly 20 years earlier had been appointed to
    a committee to consider the feasibility of establishing a hospital at Leghorn? A
    Dr Harrington is to be found subscribing to the Pisan and Leghorn churches at
    different dates, but the record is discontinuous.

110 FO45/47, Macbean to FO, 1 July 1863. Macbean's reference to Des Vignes is dated 1 July.
111 *Gazzetta* 14 October 1834. Sophia Parsons was buried in Florence 14 July 1835.
112 *Tuscan Athenaeum* 11 December 1847.
113 JLM, E9 f. 250; E10 f. 22.
114 Murray, *Handbook of Florence and Its Environs* (London, 1863). It is likely that both Dunns were the children of an Irish-born dentist, John Dunn, who in 1841 was recorded in Wigmore Street. In October 1863, Charles William was married at Came Church in Dorset to Julia Eliza Barnes, the second daughter of the Rev. William Barnes, poet and friend of Thomas Hardy, by the Rev. A.C. Ponton, 'late officiating chaplain of Florence'. The couple returned to Tuscany, where at least three sons were born to them. Dunn's wife's sister, Lucy Emily Barnes, otherwise known as Leader Scott, was herself married to a chemist, Samuel Baxter, in Florence in 1868.
115 Wilson was buried in Allori with his wife Jeannette, who died in 1874.

13 MEN OF STRAW AND MEN OF IRON: HATS, MINES AND RAILWAYS

In the cloister of the church of San Francesco at Prato, 12 miles north-west of Florence, there are several inscriptions commemorating local worthies who were involved in commerce and industry. Among them is a surprise. Translated, it reads:

> James Askew, an English gentleman, of Broughton in Lancashire, having become a fervent Catholic, conscientious and loyal, managed the industries and trade of the Vyse for thirty years in Florence and in Prato, where he was overseer of the great factory from which straw in the finest plait and in hats made in various styles went as far as America. He reached his seventy-fourth year, always thinking of others more than of himself, but on the twenty-ninth day of [January] 1857 Teresa Niccoli, his devoted consort and testamentary heir, was deprived of that life, precious to her and to so many.

Teresa had tearfully buried her spouse but did not long survive him, as the Italian inscription goes on to indicate.

The name 'Vyse' probably means little more than that of James Askew to the few people who may today pause to look at this inscription; but these men were representatives of one of the most distinctive trades that brought Britons to Tuscany. On his first visit to Florence early in November 1822, John Maquay remarked, 'I observe there are few or no Leghorn hats worn here altho' it is the place for making them.'[1] He probably did not realize to what extent this was a product made for export. In the later eighteenth century this export, encouraged by the Grand Duke, had become a source of respectable profit to Tuscan producers.

There were several ways of acquiring a Leghorn hat. One might purchase the real imported item, or one that had been made in England from imported straw plait, or one made in a similar style from native-grown straw. Soon after the term came into use, war and the Napoleonic occupation of Italy began causing problems for the trade. Italian supplies never entirely dried up, but they became erratic and expensive, and efforts to find home-grown alternatives multiplied. One, using native rye straw, was devised by William Corston and presented to the Royal

Society of Arts in 1804. An Italian account of the industry written half a century later suggested that Corston's achievement (for which the Society awarded him a gold medal) was such that 'for a long time England stopped placing orders [from Tuscany] and almost forgot Tuscan hats'.[2] For many years to come, patriotism and protectionism exerted an influence on the industry.

London traders did not always claim specifically to be marketing Leghorn hats. James Askew and William Wright, who did business in partnership from a variety of addresses in the City in the first decade of the century, simply called themselves 'straw hat merchant' or 'straw bonnet manufacturers'. During these same years a young man called Thomas Vyse was also establishing himself as a hat merchant in London. Born in Birmingham in 1782, Thomas was advertising his 'Straw, Leghorn and Chip Hats' in the *Times* in July 1804. Naturally they were 'of the newest fashions, and in a style of elegance superior to those of any other house'. Now and for some years to come he had premises on Holborn Hill. With the ending of the war he scented fresh opportunities. A notice inserted in the *Morning Chronicle* and *Morning Post* on 3 April 1817 warned customers against spurious imitations and informed them that the fashionable popularity of 'these celebrated hats' had induced one of 'our principal hat manufacturers' (doubtless Vyse himself) to visit Italy to obtain the best raw materials.

The appetite for the superior Tuscan product could now be satisfied without difficulty, and the international appeal of the Leghorn hat had a considerable impact on Tuscany itself. Much later in the century, Sir Dominic Ellis Colnaghi, Consul-General in Florence, wrote:[3]

In 1810, Signor Giuseppe Carbonai of Leghorn, having established himself at Signa and improved the manufacture, was the first to open out a trade with France and Germany. In consequence, the straw industry which, till then, had been confined to the Communes of Signa & Brozzi, spread to those of Sesto, Campi, Carmignano and Prato. Between 1815 and 1818 employment was given to some 40,000 persons, almost all women and girls. Further orders from England brought the number of persons engaged in the industry between 1819 and 1822 to 60,000. America next came within the radius of the export trade, and more hands were required, so that not only the female population of the communes of Empoli, Fucecchio, Castelfranco di Sotto and many others, but even the men of Signa, Brozzi and Campi abandoned their ordinary occupations to work in straw. The number of persons engaged in the industry was at that time calculated at 80,000. During these palmy days several new villages rose in the country district, and the increase of prosperity among the peasantry was general.

A company continued to trade under the name of Carbonai until 1828.

Among the villages mentioned by Colnaghi, Signa had first become a centre for the production of straw a century earlier (and today possesses an attractive museum devoted to the subject), while Brozzi was known to produce some of the finest straw plait, if not the finest of all, and grew in population as a consequence.[4] It became commonplace for British and other travellers in Tuscany to devote space to a description of the cultivation of straw and the important part that plaiting and hat-making played in the lives of the peasantry, especially the women. One of the first was Lady Morgan, who declared that 'The most barren districts are dedicated to the growth of straw, for the manufactory of hats; and so great is the demand for this article, and such the price of the goods, that the cultivator is amply remunerated for his labour'.[5]

The 'further orders from England' to which Colnaghi referred included those placed by Thomas Vyse. In Pigot's *Directory* for 1822 Vyse appeared as one of seven London 'importers of Leghorn hats', while James Askew was among the mere retailers, but like others claimed to be marketing 'hats of the first fabric'.[6] In March 1826 a *Times* advertisement announced that 'Vyse, of Ludgate Street, is the first house in London to get the real Brozzi fabric Leghorn Hats, which for their superior make and colour surpass all others'. It is not clear from this for how long Vyse had been using the Brozzi fabric, and there is no knowing how many exploratory visits to Tuscany he or his agents may have made.

The appeal of the authentic imported item was for the time being good news for those who were exporting hats or plait from Italy. The omnipresent Emanuele Fenzi had his finger in this as in many other pies, assisted by Horace and Alfred Hall.[7] Together with their uncle Sebastian Kleiber and others they were partners in the Carbonai firm. The opening up of a transatlantic market added to the promise and the possibilities. In 1822 'extensive deposits' of straw hats were established at London and Paris and in the United States.

There was a snag. English producers of plait and hats were not as happy with the inroads made into the British market by the real Tuscan straw as were Vyse and Askew, their fashionable customers, or exporters such as Fenzi and Hall. The eloquent, not to say strident, voice of William Cobbett was among those raised in defence of a native industry that was concentrated to the north of London, in the counties of Hertfordshire and Bedfordshire, with major centres at Luton and Dunstable. In his *Cottage Economy,* published in book form in 1822, Cobbett gave detailed instructions for the cultivation, plaiting and bleaching of straw. He acknowledged that as things stood the Italian product was 'greatly superior, in beauty and durability, to those made in England', but saw no reason why this should not change.[8] In 1823 the House of Commons received several petitions from native producers against the importation of straw plait, and in 1826 the government imposed heavy import duties on both foreign plait and foreign hats. Horace Hall was sent to England to seek relief, unsuccessfully, and he then travelled across Europe seeking new outlets for Tuscan straw (and silk), at a time when he was managing the bank alone because Fenzi was unwell.[9]

When Cobbett returned to the subject in 1829, protectionist measures were therefore in place, but there had been other developments. As he discovered when he visited Tring in Hertfordshire in 1829, straw was being imported from Tuscany in its raw state, to be worked up by native plaiters and hatters.[10] Foremost among those who imported the raw material was Thomas Waller, who with his elder brother Edmund dominated the production of straw hats at Luton.[11] Edmund, it was believed, had observed the damage done to home industry by the importation of the finished article and initiated the introduction of Italian plait from which local labour could make the hats; Thomas took a further step. His attempts to grow a suitable straw locally had been foiled, despite Cobbett's optimism, by the unreliable English weather. In 1825 he 'made a journey to Florence, for the purpose of examining the economy of the Tuscan manufactories'. Convinced that 'the superiority of this article arose from the durability, delicacy, and beauty of the straw of the country', he began to import it. The higher price of labour in England compelled him 'to vary and elaborate his patterns', producing bonnets and hats which could command three or four guineas apiece.[12] He is supposed to have invented a novel eleven-ended plait which gave a very fine finish, and with it devised a confection known as 'the Tuscan grass' which, to judge by the volume of advertising in the provincial press, was launched in time for the summer of 1829. The Tuscan Grass achieved the patronage of Queen Adelaide and established itself as a rival to the Leghorn hat, but Waller's English manufactures were not the whole story.

It was perhaps no coincidence that Tuscan hat-makers from about 1825 petitioned their government to increase duty on the export of 'grey' straw, which had facilitated the opening of 'a large hat factory at Bedford' [sic]. Given the raw material, they ingenuously complained, it was not technically very difficult to produce the hats.[13] British efforts to cultivate the straw continued at least for a short time. The *Caledonian Mercury* on 22 February 1827 reported that the Highland Society of Scotland was offering prizes for specimens of native straw and intriguingly referred in this issue and also on 26 April to information about the Tuscan cultivation that been received from none other than Horace Hall, this during what many identified as a period of crisis for the Tuscan industry. It also implied that the Grand Duke had given permission for the export of the raw straw only recently, and that this had discouraged efforts to grow it in other countries.[14]

By the mid-1820s Thomas Vyse was increasingly moving out of direct involvement in the manufacture and marketing of hats and into the management of a growing commercial empire; but it was impossible for his business to be unaffected by the punitive increase in import duties. One response to the challenge was forceful advertising which played on the affluent consumer's desire for assured quality. Emphasis continued to be placed, for example in a *Times* advertisement on 10 March 1828, on the indispensable 'real Brozzi fabric'. Mr Vyse of Ludgate Street (Thomas's younger brother Charles) could supply the genuine article. Meanwhile Thomas had taken the radical step of establishing himself in Tuscany to produce hats for export.

Colnaghi described how, after about 1826, a need was felt for something new.

This was found in the eleven-end plait, one strip of which, in making up the hat, was sewn so as to overlap the other. The merit of introducing this plait was chiefly due to Messrs Vyse, first established at Florence about the year 1827. After some temporary changes the factory was finally removed to Prato, about the year 1844, where the centre of the business has ever since remained.[15]

Innovations which mitigated the negative impact of the export of 'grey' straw on Tuscan hatters were attributed jointly to Vyse and to Luigi Giunti, an aristocratic entrepreneur of Prato, whose premises Vyse eventually took over. The eleven-ended plait was Thomas Waller's invention; but there was a connection between Vyse and Waller. At much the same time as Vyse set up in Tuscany, he also established a factory at Luton, to be directed by his second son, Richard, who in March 1827 was married to Charlotte, the eldest daughter of Edmund Waller. By now, Vyse's nephew Charles Vyse Palin was also involved in the business and from the old Vyse premises on Holborn Hill could offer 'that most fashionable article the TUSCAN GRASS', originally the brainchild of Thomas Waller.

Vyse's logic may well have been that in face of the British duties it made sense to take control of the entire productive process and also to establish a presence in the North American market. In 1830 he was responsible for another innovation which proved successful after a slow start: the division of the straw into *punta* and *pedale*, the upper and lower parts of the stem, which were then used for different products. Previously the entire stem had been used, 'resulting in hats of a non-uniform colour, as the *pedale* was whiter than the *punta*'. Hats made with *pedale* straw achieved success on the foreign market by reason of their novelty, whiteness and cheapness.[16]

As long as the English interest in Tuscan straw had been limited to importing hats or plait, which were commodities just as olive oil was a commodity, little or no dedicated British presence was really required in Tuscany. With the establishment of Vyse (and, as we shall see, Waller) on Italian soil, this changed. The greater part of the employment they created was for local labour, but British managers were now deemed necessary. There is little evidence that either Thomas spent any prolonged period of residence in Italy, but they created the need for others to do so. Most were their relatives, James Askew being an exception.

If it is a correct assumption that this was the same Askew who had traded in London, Vyse was employing a factory manager who had first-hand experience of the straw-hat business. It is also possible that Askew willingly grasped the opportunity to absent himself from England, for all had not been plain sailing in his life. In September 1824 he was briefly imprisoned and then prosecuted for larceny by a young French milliner whom he had brought over from Paris late in 1823 to work for him. Having been found not guilty, rather to the surprise and disapproval of some observers, Askew caused more surprise and disapproval by himself suing the milliner for conspiracy and winning, despite the best efforts of Henry Brougham in the defence.[17] He did not emerge with much public credit from either case, and after 1827 he vanishes from the London trade directories. This would fit neatly with a hypothetical departure to work for Vyse in Tuscany and with his memorial inscription, which suggests that he had been in Tuscany since 1826 or 1827.

He was not alone for long, if at all. On 17 May 1828, Thomas Andrew Vyse, Thomas Vyse's eldest son, scrawled his signature in the Vieusseux subscription register, giving as his address 1876 Via 'Magio' and subscribing 'per un ano' – the spelling mistakes perhaps indicating a newcomer who was determined to try to use Italian. His arrival was probably recent, for his daughter Mary Jane had been baptized in Hornsey on Christmas Eve 1827. A few months later a daughter was born to him and called Florence, very likely after the city of her birth. We know of her existence only because she died, aged 15 months, in November 1829 and was buried in the English Cemetery. The family remained in Tuscany for at least 2 years; another daughter, Carlotta, was baptized at Bagni by Charles Neat on 16 August 1830. In 1831 the Vyses were back in England, where four sons and another daughter were born by 1840, all baptized in Hornsey. This substantial entourage followed Thomas Andrew from England back to Tuscany, to New York, to Tuscany again and then back to England.[18]

Before 1830 was out the manufacture of straw hats in Tuscany had claimed a spectacular English casualty. On 25 November the *chargé d'affaires* Edward Bligh sent to the Foreign Office his correspondence with the Tuscan minister Corsini on the subject of a 'respectable gentleman' called Denzil Ede who had met his death 'in suspicious circumstances' on the previous Saturday night.[19] Ede employed three hundred people in the manufacture of straw hats and was said to be much loved by his workforce. He had apparently been visiting Italian friends and drinking heavily; on his way home he got involved in a brawl with some young men whom he heard making remarks about foreigners and was fatally stabbed. Four people had been arrested. Bligh reported that some British residents suspected that Ede was the victim of local business rivals who could not compete with him for want of capital, but while Corsini did not dispute that there was some such ill feeling, he denied that this was actually the cause of the murder. He may well have been right, for the contemptuous remarks that lured Ede into trouble are as likely to have been about his intoxication as about his business activities.

Bligh sent to the Foreign Office a translation of the police report on this sad episode, which gives a vivid picture of a young Englishman who had made himself thoroughly at home in Tuscany. He had spent the greater part of the day which ended in his murder 'playing at a game called Forma with several neighbours & acquaintances'. The report continues:

> After 4 o'clock he went to a ball at the house of one Lewis Bicchierai in the Parish of San Colombano where most of his time was taken up in talking to his Straw hat polisher one Gaetano Bicchierai no relation to the Master of the house; He spoke besides to a girl of the name of Caroline Ciottoli, with whom

one Giovacchino Germi was in love & who was present; it is necessary to state that this Germi was very jealous and had previously forbidden the girl to go & work at Mr Ede's manufactory, but as the girl had not obeyed him, he no longer spoke to her – Moreover the night before when seeing Mr Ede talk to the girl he was observed to shew strong symptoms of displeasure.

This jealous suitor was one of those who later set upon Ede. The murder took place after he left the house where the party had taken place, in company with his hat polisher and the latter's father. Running into a gang of youths who had been fighting, he actively courted trouble:

In passing by Mr Ede heard some of those who were standing there together talk of Foreigners, and he said, 'I too am a foreigner', and a little while after was heard to add 'who is it that will give me blows let him come'. Bianchi [another of Ede's local acquaintances] hearing these expressions, & knowing Mr Ede's voice came out of his cousin's house & went up to him to prevent his getting into a quarrel but Mr Ede had already taken his coat off & with his sleeves tucked up offered to fight whoever came forward – he did not content himself with mere threats, for he gave one Giuseppe Martelli a blow in the mouth which broke one of his teeth and cut his lips – by this time he was surrounded by several individuals who ran up against him and immediately Mr Ede fell into the arms of Gaetano Bicchierai who had come up at that moment saying 'I am dead'.

The incident took place at San Colombano, which lies just south of the Arno to the west of Florence, and is not far from Granatieri, in the parish of Lastra, where Ede lived.

The inscription on Ede's tombstone in the English Cemetery in Florence reads as follows: IN MEMORY OF/DENZIL EDE/LATE OF LISKEARD IN CORNWALL/WHO DIED THE 21ST DAY/OF NOVEMBER 1830 AGED 23. He received his rather distinctive Christian name at his baptism at Quethiock, near Liskeard, on 15 July 1806, so at the time of his death he was at least 24. He had been in Tuscany perhaps for as much as 4 years. Was he himself, at this young age, the owner of the capital which made it hard for native producers to compete with him? If he was only a manager, for whom might he have been working? Neither the police report into his murder, nor the observations made by Bligh and Corsini, shed any further light on his business connections. An informed guess is, however, possible. Reporting his death, the *Gentleman's Magazine* described him as the son of Captain John Ede of Liskeard. The Captain's brother Francis, a London businessman, helpfully named all his siblings in the will he made in 1845. They included a Charles who many years later was himself buried in Florence, and Jane, the wife of none other than the straw-hat merchant Thomas Waller. The murdered Denzil was Waller's nephew by marriage.[20]

Waller reputedly made one of his visits to Florence in 1825; on 20 October that year Denzil subscribed for a month to Vieusseux. Perhaps he had accompanied his uncle. On 14 November 1826 he took out a year's subscription, which suggests that he had now taken up residence in Florence. All of this would be consistent with the supposition that Waller established a factory there after the 1825 visit and that he employed his young nephew as a manager. That Ede was on his own in Tuscany is suggested by the fact that the Florentine authorities placed an advertisement in the *Gazzetta* on 14 December 1830, giving anyone who could prove an interest in his estate a period of 4 months in which to come forward. A week later it was announced that the banker William Johnstone had been appointed provisional administrator.

If Thomas Waller's nephew was managing a factory for him in the Florence area and there was a hat polisher among its employees, he was doing more than merely export straw. There is no reason why he should not have produced hats for export to the American market as Vyse did. Later in the century it was recalled that his brother Edmund was a large exporter of plait, bonnets and Leghorn hats to New York, where he was represented by a John Reynolds, and we know from Thomas's will that he had property there as well as in Luton and Florence.[21] John Reynolds, just to complete the circle, was another nephew of Thomas Vyse, the son of his sister Caroline. Given that Vyse was represented in Tuscany by his own son and by James Askew, it is plausible that Ede was there on behalf of his Waller uncle.

If so, Waller now had to make other arrangements. His own sons were still children: Thomas junior was born in 1820 and Robert in 1821. It is possible that he may have called upon John Reynolds, who later certainly worked for Vyse in Florence and Prato, where he died at the age of 82 in December 1887. The inscription on his monument in the Allori Cemetery says that he was 'Born in England but in early life he came to Italy and was a faithful citizen'. It would be reasonable to suppose from this that he was there by the age of 25 or so.

While Vyse and Waller established themselves in Tuscany, the high levels of British import duties constituted a grievance which the Tuscan Government more than once attempted to raise through diplomatic channels. In 1830 the Tuscan minister Fossombroni complained to the British government about the 80 per cent duty imposed on Leghorn hats imported into the UK, pointing out that no English goods were taxed higher than 15 per cent on their entry into Tuscany.[22] A year later the Foreign Office was told of fears that the Grand Duke might be inclined to raise tariffs on British manufactures. Seymour received continued complaints and tried to supply some context for the anxieties of the natives. The Grand Duchy was overwhelmingly agricultural, but it was an under-developed agriculture, and straw hats were virtually the only manufactured article it had to export. The Tuscan Government contended on behalf of the exporters that the relative value of their product had declined catastrophically. The only response Seymour obtained from Palmerston was that 'owing to the conflicting claims of the British manufacturers of the same Article, the question is involved in some difficulty'.[23]

In 1837 John Bowring remarked of the Tuscan hat industry that it was 'somewhat reduced but still very considerable'. It employed 'a vast number of hands in Florence, Prato, and in all the districts from Florence to Pistoja on one side, and from Florence to Pisa on the other. It is estimated that between Florence and Prato alone there are 50 manufactories of straw hats.' Pointedly Bowring observed that straw hats were among the items exempted from all export duty by the Tuscan government and that 'No state profits more than England by the liberality of Tuscan legislation'.[24] In April 1842 Thomas Waller and his brothers attended a public meeting at Luton to protest against Peel's proposed reduction of the import duties on straw plait. Waller was happy to advertise his support for a protectionism which did not affect his importation of raw straw.[25]

On 29 June 1839, the *Gazzetta* announced that Thomas Waller had appointed Henry Brind, an English gentleman now living in Florence, to be his representative in 'all the dealings of his business house in Tuscany'.[26] Brind was the son of a silk merchant and ribbon-maker based in Paternoster Row in the City of London; perhaps Thomas Waller had trimmed his hats with his father's ribbons. It is not clear whether Brind was recently arrived, or whether he was in Tuscany on his father's behalf or on his own. When he died there in 1866 he was described simply as a 'merchant' and his life seems to have been unobtrusive. On 15 May 1839 he took out a year's subscription to Vieusseux, giving as his address the Villa Tempi outside the Porta San Frediano. On the very same day, Robert Waller, Thomas's younger son, now 18, also took out a subscription for an unspecified period, giving the same address. A year later, it was the turn of Thomas Waller junior, Robert's elder by just over a year, to stay at Villa Tempi and subscribe for 6 months to the reading room. Both brothers make later appearances in the subscription books, and by the mid-1840s it looks as if Thomas junior was living and working in Florence. He was certainly there to contribute to the collection in aid of victims of the flood in November 1844.[27] When Thomas senior died suddenly 'by the visitation of God' in 1845, both the younger Thomas, 'merchant of Florence', and Robert, who was in New York, renounced the duty of executing his will.[28] His splendid monument in Luton Parish Church is apparently the only known work in England by a Florentine sculptor called Pietro Costa; surely it was commissioned by Thomas the younger.

On 28 February 1840 Frederick Vyse, son of Thomas, died in Florence, aged only 23. Perhaps he had been taking his turn in the family business and it was now necessary to replace him. At all events, it was only a few months later (on 9 July) that Thomas Vyse senior, of Cripplegate Buildings in the City of London, entered into a covenant with Thomas Andrew Vyse of Hornsey which established the terms of their future relationship.[29] It is a curious document. The elder Vyse had 'for some years carried on business as a Leghorn Hat manufacturer in the city of London, Luton, Florence & elsewhere', in which he had been assisted by Thomas Andrew. He had never admitted any of his sons to partnership, but, in consideration of the assistance he had received from them and of their 'maintenance', and with their best future interests at heart, he had been in the habit of privately putting money by on their behalf. In the ledger in which he entered these amounts 'there is now standing to the credit of the said Thomas Andrew Vyse a sum of eight thousand pounds or thereabouts'. Thomas Andrew now indemnified his father for this sum on condition of the establishment of a trust fund for himself and his family. Within 4 weeks of the execution of the deed, he and his family were to remove themselves and live henceforth at least 100 miles from London, not returning there except by his father's express written permission.

What lay behind the making of this arrangement we can only speculate, but it would have ruled out Hornsey, where Thomas Andrew had been living for the past decade. He promptly complied with the stipulated residence requirements, for on 1 September 1840 he took out a year's subscription to Vieusseux. He subscribed for another year on 17 November 1843 and a year later, like the younger Waller, he contributed to the flood relief fund. The list of contributions suggests that the direction of the business in Tuscany was, in fact, at this moment chiefly in the hands of John Reynolds, who gave 1,000 *lire* on behalf of the London firm, as if he was its spokesman, as well as 600 on his own account. (Another contributor was 'Gio' Askew, almost certainly James.)

Within a year, Reynolds (probably) was overseeing the transfer of the Vyse business from Florence to Prato. In February 1846, described as *titolare* of a straw hat works in Prato, he petitioned the Florentine municipality for tax relief. Investigation confirmed that in the previous November he had relocated his straw works from Via Faenza to Prato and had ceased to live in Florence.[30] The new premises had once belonged to Luigi Giunti and stood opposite the old Hohenstaufen *fortezza*. A plaque on the Palazzo Fiorelli today records that the building originated in the thirteenth century and was enlarged in the fifteenth and reconstructed by the 'Wise' around the middle of the nineteenth.

In 1845 the Grand Duke was petitioned by local notables at Prato to elevate Thomas Vyse and his family to the nobility of the city in recognition of the benefits their business had conferred upon it. Recording this episode, Enrico Fiumi described Vyse as 'born in London but for some time resident in Tuscany'.[31] This was a correct description of Thomas Andrew rather than of his father. It is possible that the two Thomases, one the owner of the capital, the other physically present and visible in Tuscany, merged into one. 'Vyse' has been described by another Italian historian as 'one of the many foreigners who at Prato as in the rest of the Grand Duchy came to plug the local entrepreneurial gap which was characteristic of nineteenth-century Tuscany'.[32] Thomas Andrew evidently remained in Florence; in October 1845, on the eve of the factory move, he asked for six new sittings in the church.[33] In London on 15 July 1846 he made a brief will, describing himself as 'Thomas Andrew Vyse of Florence in the State of Tuscany, Gentleman'. His dear wife Mary Jane received the bequest of 'all my household furniture, plate, trinkets, linen and other effects', but everything else was to go to his father, effectively to form part of the trust for his family.[34]

Whatever role Thomas Andrew played, John Reynolds certainly came to be identified with the Vyse interests in Prato and, as his tomb inscription reveals, James Askew had also clearly moved there to manage the factory. When in February 1847, the charitable collection was made in Florence in aid of sufferers by the Irish famine, both Thomas Andrew and Reynolds contributed, and so too did Reynolds's two sisters, Jane and Amelia; were they visiting or had they already taken up residence?[35] In the following year Reynolds himself was on the move again. On 27 July 1848 Thomas Vyse senior entered into a new co-partnership with his sons Richard and Henry and with Reynolds, all of them described in the deed as 'Straw Hat manufacturers'. The firm thus constituted was to be known as 'Vyse & Sons in London, Luton, New York and Florence', and John Reynolds, 'late of Florence and now about to proceed to the City of New York', was to be in charge of the American branch. As far as Florence was concerned, the deed stated only that the business there was to be conducted 'by such persons or person as the said Thomas Vyse and after his decease as the said Richard and Henry Vyse shall appoint'. 'The factory at Florence and Prato and the store at New York shall be considered the partnership property,' regardless of the individual name in which they might be registered. Thomas Andrew was not mentioned.

Meanwhile the Waller business continued in Tuscany. Waller Son & Co subscribed to the petition of 14 April 1846, 'praying for a direct Postal communication by Steam between Gibraltar and Leghorn', as did John Reynolds and Thomas Andrew Vyse. In June 1849 Macbean informed the Foreign Office that the English firms based in Florence which had traded through Leghorn in 1848 included Vyse & Co. and Thomas Waller, both with outlets also in London, Luton and New York.[36] On 25 May 1850, the *Hertford Messenger and Intelligencer* reported that Waller's widow had run a stall at a Wesleyan Bazaar in aid of the Chapel at Luton (all their children had received Methodist baptism). The stall was 'adorned with alabaster statuettes and models of the most exquisite grace from Florence'. Was it from her own travels, her late husband or her sons that she had obtained them?

Thomas Andrew subscribed more or less continuously to Vieusseux from the autumn of 1846 until the spring of 1851. During this period he gave as his address Villa Spinelli at S. Felice a Ema, just south-east of Florence. On 4 August 1851 the entire family (he and Mary Jane, with seven children) were recorded as arriving at New York in the steamer *Atlantic*. Was he perhaps changing places with John Reynolds? Thomas Waller junior was in Philadelphia in the spring of 1852, when he was married to Amanda Mellon, and it would be interesting to know whether Thomas Andrew Vyse, who must surely have known this cousin by marriage, was a guest.[37]

By 1850 the Vyse business in Tuscany, working exclusively for export, was said to be 'superior to all others for the extent of its trade'. Its capital was estimated at 1,000,000 *lire*, whereas the other two straw-hat factories in Prato could muster only 200,000 *lire* between them. Mariotti declared in 1859 'that the house of

Vyse and sons of Prato alone annually provides work for no fewer than 15000 operatives'.[38] At the Great Exhibition of 1851 prizes were won by both Vyse & Sons of 76 Wood Street, Cheapside, and Vyse & Sons of Prato and Florence. Vyse of Prato was praised 'for a selection of very fine Leghorn hats & capotes'.[39]

Both the younger Thomas Waller and Thomas Andrew Vyse were able to lead a genteel existence in Florence in the 1850s, and it was only then that John Maquay began to notice them. On 15 November 1854 he noted that the Vyses had invited his 19-year-old son George to a party, accompanying their name with an exclamation mark. By analogy with other passages in the journal this may signify that he knew that they had been in Florence for some time, but that there had been no previous social contact with them.[40] What may have helped to bring the families together was that both now had children in their late teens or twenties. Where the Vyses were living in 1854 we are not told, but on 16 June 1855 Thomas Andrew took out a subscription to Vieusseux which was to last until the following 10 April, giving an address outside the Porta Nuova.

Thomas Waller and his American wife spent 2 years or more in Tuscany shortly after their marriage. On 19 April 1853 two Wallers attended John Maquay's last party for the season and on 4 May he and his son George went to 'a very nice party at Mrs Waller beautifully furnished rooms and recherché supper'. In the summer the Wallers betook themselves to Bagni di Lucca, subscribing for two seats in the church there on 11 July 1853. Maquay records several later encounters with them. This looks very much like one of those social relationships in which Elena and George were more active than John himself; Thomas Waller was nearly 30 years his junior. On 20 February 1855 Elena went to the opera with Mrs Waller and on 12 March there was 'beautiful music' at a concert given by the latter. Between those dates the Maquays went to see the portrait of Mrs Waller that had been painted by the American artist Thomas Buchanan Read, who also painted the Brownings and sent photographs of his works back to America with the Wallers shortly afterwards.[41]

On 28 May 1856 Thomas Andrew's eldest daughter, Mary Jane, was married in Florence to William Henry Schall of New York. Apart from Mrs Vyse, Thomas Andrew's cousin John Reynolds, and the interesting presence of Francis Sloane, the witnesses included Mary Jane's siblings Carlotta, Emily, Howard and Faulkner.[42] This helps us to identify the numerous Vyses who came to Maquay parties; in February of the same year seven had been invited and six came, and on 6 January 1857 six turned up to a New Year party which the Wallers, back again, also attended. Mr Waller came to dine and play whist on 13 March, the last mention of the name. On 29 April 1858, not long before he finally left Florence, John 'went out at 7 to the Vyses at Villa Dulci who commence being at home on Wed evenings' and on 13 May George had 'young Vyse' to dine with him. It is more than likely that George continued to socialize with the Vyses after his father's departure.[43]

Maquay never mentions John Reynolds, who was settled back in Tuscany at least by the mid-1850s. On 14 April 1855, Amelia Reynolds was married to

Charles Vyse Palin in Florence. The witnesses included her sister Jane and James Askew. Born in 1812, Amelia was about 14 years older than her bridegroom, but it is impossible to know whether or not this was purely a business arrangement. Charles Vyse Palin was Thomas Vyse's great-nephew, the son of the Charles Vyse Palin who had advertised his Tuscan Grass wares in 1830, and he was undoubtedly now in Tuscany to do his bit for the family business alongside Reynolds. Together, they are said to have shown patriotic solidarity with their workforce at the time of the plebiscites which resulted in the annexation of Tuscany to the Italian kingdom.[44]

Were we to take an imperfect census of the Britons in Tuscany in the 1850s who had some direct or indirect connection with the straw business we would be able to name Thomas Andrew Vyse and his wife and children; the younger Thomas Waller and his wife; James Askew; John Reynolds and his sisters; and Charles Vyse Palin. Back in England Thomas Vyse the elder died at Herne Hill Abbey on 5 January 1861, aged 79. He left a bequest of £500 to John Reynolds but made no specific mention of what was to become of the Prato factory.[45] It was doubtless convenient for all concerned that Reynolds should remain in charge, and by the time he himself came to make his will, in 1885, he described himself as proprietor of the site opposite the Fortezza. Both his sisters had predeceased him. Jane died in Prato on 9 April 1867 and was buried in the old English cemetery in Florence; Amelia died in Florence on 28 November 1883 and was buried in Allori. John was the last survivor. In his will he asked to be buried as near as possible to Amelia and named her husband Charles Vyse Palin as one of his executors.[46]

Nothing in the inscription on his gravestone betrays Reynolds's connection with Vyse or specifically with the straw industry, but it is eloquent on other counts:

Prato bears witness to his worthy deeds; there he promoted trade and industry, to his workpeople he was just and generous, to the poor a kind and generous almoner, to the children he gave the school in which they learned their infant lessons. All the good he did this stone cannot relate. He lies here in the land in which he lived so long and which he loved so well.

Reynolds lived and died a bachelor, and his will is evidence for the intimate friendship he contracted with a Pratese family named Falcini. Signora Enrichetta Falcini, wife of Lorenzo Falcini, was to be his principal heir. She received all the movables to be found in his villa at Talano and in his house in Piazza della Fortezza, which was partly let to Emilio Falcini (her son) and Company. Charles Vyse Palin and Henry Vyse were to have their choice of 'family souvenirs' and Reynolds also excepted all the 'books furniture maps drawings and other articles' in the school directed by Mrs Adela Falcini. This school, mentioned on Reynolds's tombstone, was at the heart of his will and he made elaborate provisions for its future maintenance and direction. Emilio Falcini, one of his executors, was evidently still engaged in the straw business, and his mother was to accord him 'the gratuitous use for three years of the machines utensils and other articles existing in the building in Piazza della Fortezza'. The will was found in a drawer of a desk in a room they had both used in that building.

Reynolds had made his life in Tuscany, but one aspect of his will may strike us as typically English. Among the burdens he imposed on Enrichetta Falcini was to ensure that his horses and asses were to be kept and taken care of for as long as they were able to work; thereafter 'they are to be kept at rest or killed as the said legatee may consider the most human(e)'. He also left money 'To the Victoria Street and International Society for the protection of animals from vivisection' and to the Royal Society for the Prevention of Cruelty to Animals in Jermyn Street. In Tuscany itself, another Briton was to be aided in her work in the same cause. Countess Gertrude Baldelli received assistance for her dogs' home in Florence or alternatively for other measures 'to protect animals from cruel treatment and remediable suffering'.

The straw business by the time of Reynolds's death was not what it had been, inevitably overtaken by technological innovations as well as by the importation of plait from the Far East. Reynolds had seen other changes. He may have first come to Tuscany not long after the last Grand Duke came to his throne; he outlived the first King of a united Italy, Victor Emmanuel II, by 9 years. During the period in which he presided over the Vyse concern a new industry had been established which brought large numbers of Britons to Tuscany – the Tuscan railway network. Men such as Fenzi, Hall and Sloane who had been interested in straw were interested both in railways and in other economic possibilities. So too was Reynolds. In November 1844, together with an entrepreneur named Gustave Méjean, he had entered into an agreement to explore an area in the Tuscan Maremma for the mineral antimony. In 1847 he and Méjean negotiated new conditions with the Tuscan Government, but the following year they abandoned the project, alleging that the quantity of ore discovered did not suffice to cover their expenses.[47] Perhaps Reynolds also knew that he would soon be returning to America on behalf of Vyse.

In a report on the Tuscan economy which was laid before Parliament in 1838 John Bowring devoted several pages to mineral resources, which included the iron of Elba, sulphur from near Grosseto and boracic acid from the region of Volterra. The various Tuscan extractive industries attracted the attention not only of British entrepreneurs but of engineers, including military men with engineering interests. One example was Bowring's 'intelligent friend' Captain Charters, who had 'examined and reported on the capabilities of the copper mines of Tuscany'. Captain (later Major) Samuel Charters was in Florence around the time of Bowring's own visit, but a few years later was serving in South Africa; later he was among the few Britons to settle at Pistoia, where his wife Emily died in 1855 and he himself in 1866.

Bowring thought it probable that there would soon be more British investment in Tuscan mines. The general impression which he had received and now transmitted to his readers was of resources which had in many instances been well known for some considerable time (even centuries) and might yet prove profitable, but had been exploited insufficiently or incompetently. At Roccatederighi the copper mines had been carried on 'without machinery, steam-engines, or any of the improvements which are usually applied to such enterprises', and the rich veins of ore around Massa awaited effective exploitation: 'There are no steam-engines, nor indeed any practised miners.' This situation created a market for both British personnel and British machinery. British investment was beginning even as Bowring wrote, and it did not necessarily require the immigration of new men.[48]

In 1837 Francis Sloane and the brothers Hall acquired the under-exploited copper mine at Camporciano near Montecatini. Thomas Trollope later wrote that while still tutor to the Russian Bouturlin family Sloane had been taken 'by reason of his geological attainments' to see the mines 'which the Grand Duke had conceded to a company under whose administration they were going utterly to the bad'.[49] In association with the Halls he obtained a new and favourable concession and under their management improved techniques resulted in a much increased production, which came to amount to 10 per cent of the Italian total. Much was exported in crude form to the UK, while the rest was processed at a plant near Prato known as the Briglia, established by Sloane and the Halls in 1845 together with an Italian partner. It was reported in 1854 that in the first 9 years the Briglia had produced 4,030,846 *libre* of copper, with some annual fluctuations but nothing below 350,000 *libre* per annum since 1847.[50]

This achievement was recognized in an advertisement that was placed in the *Times* on 31 January 1854 by the promoters of the new Copper Mining Company of Tuscany, who informed the public that they had obtained the concession of 'two extensive and valuable mineral properties' in the same area as Camporciano. No names were mentioned, but it was acknowledged that Camporciano, 'which had been rudely and unprofitably worked for several years by native proprietors, was purchased some years since by two English gentlemen; and by a moderate application of capital, it now returns a very large annual revenue to its owners'. The hopeful proponents of the new enterprise had instructed the distinguished mining engineer John Petherick to undertake a detailed survey, and he had reported favourably. The company's bankers in Florence were to be Plowden & French. What happened next is hard to discern, but one of the London bankers behind the project, Strahan, Paul & Co, and one of the nominated directors, Robert Bates, were only months later ruinously implicated in the failure of the railway contractor Gandell (as were Plowden & French). Matters were made worse by the fact that the copper mines had not represented their only Tuscan investment.[51] The repercussion of this failure were still being felt when Leopold fell in 1859.

Bowring devoted some space to the subject of marble, which interested the British from both an artistic and a commercial point of view. William Paget Jervis gave a full account in the early years of the Italian kingdom.[52] Carrara, which is now part of Tuscany, then lay in the Duchy of Modena (although it was from time to time coveted by the Grand Duke). It was a frequent stopping-place for British tourists; Elizabeth Maquay visited the quarries with her son George in March 1824 and much enjoyed what she saw. There were also quarries at Seravezza, in Tuscany proper but not very far south east of Carrara, which Bowring thought became 'daily of greater interest and importance', partly because Carrara marble was, in his view, burdened with excessive export duties. Here 'many beautiful varieties of variegated marble were to be found' and Bowring remarked that an area which had once been virtually deserted was now increasingly inhabited.

There is evidence of British interest in exploiting these new resources over a decade before Bowring wrote. The *Gazzetta* reported on 12 June 1824 that 'a superb quarry of statuary marble' had been discovered near Pietrasanta (close to Seravezza) thanks to the efforts and intelligence of one John Beresford. We may well wonder whether it was this which was referred to in a letter from Thomas Townley that Strangways forwarded to the Foreign Office in 1826. Having learned that George IV was engaged in ambitious building works, Townley wanted to draw attention to the marble that was being produced from a quarry in which he had interests: he recommended particularly a very beautiful variety called 'Mischio' (which certainly sounds as if it might be 'variegated'), of which he could produce ten, twelve or even more columns as much as 20 feet long.[53]

A few years later a British entrepreneur appeared upon the scene who would become more specifically identified with the Anglo-Italian marble trade. On 17 March 1835 William Walton placed an advertisement in the *Gazzetta* announcing that he had recently opened two *cave* on the slopes of the Pania, north-east of Seravezza, one of which produced fine white marble for statuary, the other a stone with violet veining. Walton's efforts to promote his business at Seravezza were apparently frustrated by local jealousies and litigation, and he transplanted himself to Carrara, where he remained until his death in 1872. He retained links with Tuscany, for Leghorn was the port through which his marble was exported. For many years he was a subscriber and indeed a pew-holder at the Leghorn church; he contributed to the building fund and on 9 May 1840 was paid for 16 marble slabs for the new church.[54]

Engineers who were interested in mines might well also take an interest in the railways.[55] In 1836 the British papers began to report plans to build a railway between Leghorn and Florence, which, it was believed, 300,000 passengers would use annually. In the spring of 1838 it was announced that the Tuscan Government had given its sanction and later in the year that none other than Robert Stephenson had been engaged to survey the line, which would be christened the Leopolda in homage to the Grand Duke.[56] Behind this enterprise stood the ubiquitous Emmanuele Fenzi, who in April 1838 entered into a government-approved agreement with another banker, Pietro Senn of Leghorn, to build the line. Fenzi himself was the majority shareholder. Stephenson visited Tuscany in May 1839 as part of a 3-month tour made necessary by the various invitations he had received to build European railways, but the principal work was deputed to his lieutenants

William Hoppner and Robert Townshend. Between them they determined that the line should follow the Arno valley.[57]

Not everyone was enthused by the prospect of a Tuscan railway. *Murray's* in 1842 reported one negative reaction (probably that of the author, Francis Palgrave) at a moment when the line had been completed from Leghorn to Pisa and was 'threatened' to Florence. In this view

> every wellwisher to Italy must hope that it may fail; any thing more useless in a territory of such small extent, and more destructive to comfort and pleasure than such a mode of travelling in this lovely country, cannot be conceived … At present, Tuscany enjoys an unexampled degree of prosperity and comfort. Her operatives know nothing of strikes and turn-outs, – her agriculturists suffer no distress, except when God denies the fruits of the earth; – and the attempts thus made to emulate the forced and unnatural opulence of England will, if they succeed, succeed only as a bane.[58]

John Ruskin would have agreed.

A very different perspective was offered by Consul Macbean when in the spring of 1845 he replied to a Foreign Office request for a report on the importation of British machinery into Tuscany.[59] He remarked 'that the Machinery in Tuscany is very limited in quantity – that it is chiefly of British Manufacture, and that it has been in the Country for some time'. There had been a prejudice against the adoption of machinery because of its effects on hand labour, but he had noticed a very recent change, which he attributed to the success of the new Pisa-Leghorn railway. Large quantities of presses, lathes and mills of various kinds, 'principally from Glasgow', had arrived at Leghorn. Macbean went on to list the examples of British-made machinery which he had found in Tuscany. The list included four locomotive engines made by Stephenson & Longridge, as well all the turntables and machinery used on the Pisa-Leghorn railway.

Macbean remarked further that an English engineer (unnamed) was about to establish a foundry in Leghorn with machinery and fittings imported from England; 'an establishment for smelting Copper about to be put in activity in the neighbourhood of Pescia' would similarly use British machinery, and another unnamed 'English Mechanic (who came to this country for the purpose of erecting a Marine Engine)' was constructing a 16-horsepower engine at Leghorn for the coal-mines at Monte Bamboli in the Maremma, but some parts were being imported from Glasgow to be finished in Tuscany. The mere importation of machinery did not necessitate a proportional importation of British personnel, but the railways, probably more than any other single economic enterprise, did bring Britons to work in Italy.

The section of line between Pisa and Pontedera opened amid great rejoicings on 19 October 1845. In July the following year John Maquay, back from England, paid a flying visit to his family, who were holidaying at Leghorn, and went on to

Florence by way of the train as far as Pontedera.[60] Meanwhile work had begun on a second line. From the beginning, business interests at Prato had been agitating for an alternative route to Pisa and Leghorn by way of Prato, Pistoia and Lucca. Initially no countenance was given to proposals involving Lucca, which was not yet part of the Grand Duchy, but in 1845 the go-ahead was given for a line which came to be known as the Maria Antonia – the name of the Grand Duchess. The company that was set up to carry out the work was called the *Società Italo-austriaca*, although in fact the greater part of the capital was raised in Britain. Active and prominent in this company was Raphael or Ralph Bonfil, who received the title Conte di San Giorgio from the Grand Duke and enjoyed favour at court. Its financing nonetheless proved problematic.

Despite the appearance of rivalry or even hostility between the Leopolda and the Maria Antonia, it is suspected that Fenzi, and with him the Halls and Francis Sloane, were also interested in the second line. Where Stephenson had been nominated to survey the Leopolda, Brunel was called in for the Maria Antonia, and he too delegated the substantive work to a subordinate, Herschel Babbage. Although the plans Babbage produced did not please the royal Commissary, Carlo Reishammer, the Grand Duke decided broadly in favour of them. Work began, but continued to be dogged by disagreements and financial difficulties, which were reflected in falling share prices. Babbage pressed on with the line from Florence to Prato and by May 1847 plans had been drawn up for the station at Porta al Serraglio (not far from the ancient centre of Prato and today still busy with commuters into Florence).

A humorous indicator of the interest aroused by all this activity was published in the *Tuscan Athenaeum* on 27 November 1847, under the title 'Railway-Improvement Scheme'. The author was anonymous, but one might suspect the hand of Charles Lever, recently arrived in Florence and on other evidence known to be interested in the railways. At all events, he claimed to have

> two great passions: Railway-travelling and Verdi's music. Strange combination, you will say, but to me they are but one and same thing. I find in each, the same rapidity, the same want of variety, the same puffing and blowing, the same screaming, the same rattle of brass and iron, the same jerking and bursting, and lastly the same destruction of human powers in the artists in either occupation – singing or railway driving.

The writer therefore proposed that sopranos who had ruined their voices trying to sing Verdi should be employed to remedy the present situation of 'defective communication between the head and tail of a train', which was the cause of most railway accidents. An audition should be held in the Palazzo Vecchio for the post of 'Railway-whistle' and various pieces of music selected to convey particular messages; for certain purposes, 'as the Engine men are generally English, perhaps "Old King Cole" would be best'.

This allusion to the predominance of 'English' drivers is significant. Obviously the railways created employment opportunities which were not confined to imported Britons, from simple labouring to manning ticket-offices. In September 1849 the Select Vestry was told that Charles Perrier, who a few months previously had been appointed *custode* of the English Church, had submitted his resignation with effect from 1 October, as he had obtained superior employment on the railways at Sesto, today one of the principal suburban stations to the north of Florence.[61] From building the machinery and servicing the trains to driving them, there were jobs to be done in areas in which British workers already had experience. Men who had worked for Stephenson, Brunel or Thomas Brassey in England formed part of a diaspora which ended by depositing some of them at the ends of the earth. The records of the Anglican churches afford glimpses of them, and it is also possible sometimes to discern the existence of bonds between them and their families, as if they constituted a loose kind of community within the expatriate population.

On 7 July 1844 Thomas Jeffrey, described as an engine-driver on the Pisa railway, was married at Leghorn to Sarah Parker, a native of Derby. The witnesses were Robert Jeffrey and George Summerside. Robert was Thomas's elder brother, and when his daughter Sarah was baptized at Leghorn in the following October his occupation was given as 'railway engineer' of Pisa. The brothers came from Shilbottle in Northumberland, fertile railway ground. Robert had been married to Dinah Dobson in South Shields in 1838; she died and was buried in Leghorn in 1852, which suggests that her husband worked for some years in Tuscany. George Summerside too was a railway engineer, as we learn when his infant daughter Ann was buried in September 1844.[62] In the previous March, yet another engineer on the Pisa and Leghorn railway, John Parker, had a daughter called Emma baptized at Leghorn. It is hard to resist the suspicion that he was in some way connected with the Sarah who would shortly be married to Thomas Jeffrey. In 1847–1848 children were born in Tuscany both to Herschel Babbage and to William Bray, who in 1845 succeeded Hoppner as Stephenson's representative. We hear also of George Horton, an 'engine man' on the Leopolda, who was buried at Leghorn in May 1852, and George Richardson, a 'mechanic' on the same line, who married a Swiss woman, Rose Uranie Larsche, in Florence in 1850; two sons were born to them in the next couple of years.

The first train ever to leave Florence departed for Prato from the Maria Antonia station, at 10 am on 2 February 1848. The trains made five return journeys a day, taking half an hour less than the diligence. In its first 20 days the line carried 22,414 passengers, representing 150 per journey and yielding a revenue of 20,802 *paoli*. At this moment the final link which connected Florence to Leghorn via the Leopolda had not yet been made, but on the following 13 June John Maquay noted that 'The Leghorn railway was opened last Saturday all the way from Florence'.[63] The continuation of the line beyond Prato to Pistoia and Lucca had its difficulties, in what were anyway troubled times.

Profitability seemed remote. On 14 July 1848 the *Times* summarized the annual report that was about to be presented to British shareholders in the Italo-Austrian company. With passenger traffic only and very low fares, the Maria Antonia was receiving about £200 per week. To reap maximum rewards from the investment, 'the line must be finished to Pistoia' where it would join a line to Pisa by way of Pescia and Lucca that was already being built (under the direction of Charles Pohlmeyer). Income would increase when this was achieved, and again if a projected line from Pistoia to Bologna was built. 'The realisation of these prospects, the directors consider, will produce a dividend of 10 per cent per annum on the share capital of the Maria Antonia Company.' This was the good or at least encouraging news, but it will scarcely escape observation that, aside from the progress that had actually been made on the Pisa-Lucca line, it rested on prospects as yet unfulfilled. The proposed trans-Apennine route to Bologna had for some years been the subject of yet more contention and work on it had not yet begun.

More to the immediate point was the fact that a third of the shares in the Maria Antonia were not owned by the Italo-Austrian company but had been subscribed for in Tuscany. It was the practice as work progressed for shareholders to meet a series of 'calls' on their investment, that is, demands for specified portions of what they had undertaken to subscribe. A substantial number of the Tuscan shareholders had proved unable to meet their calls, with the result that all the working expenses had been thrown on the Italo-Austrian Company. As a further consequence, payment of interest on shares had been suspended since 30 June 1847. Tuscan Government support might theoretically have been forfeited in these circumstances. Meanwhile, of course, the estimated cost of completing the line had risen. Now the directors were making a fresh call of £1 per share, payable in instalments. In the *Morning Post* of 17 July it was stated that the extra capital required 'must be chiefly found in England, but the amount is small, compared with the beneficial results to be obtained from its expenditure'. It added the intriguing detail that the principal Tuscan shareholder had first become insane and then died, while a large number of the others had defaulted.

The *Daily News* on 29 September reported one of the disconcerting results these troubles had in Tuscany. John Maquay and others like him were not merely passengers on the new Tuscan railways, but shareholders in it. They were notably aggrieved when the local directors of the Italo-Austrian company in Florence announced that on 20 September a thousand shares in the company would be auctioned to the highest bidder. These were not new shares, but had been pronounced forfeit, although it is not clear that this was because the holders had in any way failed to meet their obligations. Some of those affected, outraged, 'assembled at the Board Room of the station, to oppose what they conceived to be an arbitrary confiscation of their property'. They included John, the banker French, Arthur Vansittart, Charles Lever, Mr Barron (*attaché* at the embassy), the physician Dr Harding and the engineer Babbage himself. They were met by Ralph Bonfil with the bland assertion that 'in his official character' he could not recognize the meeting, 'however respectable'. The assembled shareholders nonetheless elected Arthur Vansittart their chairman and proceeded to make their feelings known.

Among their objections were the facts that no meeting had been called before the forfeiture was decreed and no reference made to the chief director of the company, William Jackson of Birkenhead. An Italian lawyer was now introduced who 'harangued' those present to the effect that the confiscation was perfectly legal in accordance with certain rules made by the local directors. Bonfil declared that the only legitimate business the meeting could transact was the sale of the shares, and that he would be happy to receive bids; every other question was out of order. At this the temperature rose. Dr Harding struck a humorous note, recalling a cartoon that had appeared in the early days of the French Revolution, showing the finance minister Necker as a cook, addressing a group of turkeys who represented the Estates General. When Necker asked them what sauce they would like to be cooked in, and they objected to being cooked at all, he replied that they were evading the issue. John was more choleric.

> Maquay (banker), after a violent speech, wound up by saying that the conduct of the company was dishonest and disreputable, whereupon M. Bonfils, in very indignant language, said he felt the imputation on the society he had the honour to represent in Florence as a personal insult. He had kept his temper up to this moment, but he would not tolerate the aspersions of M. Maquay, were he the highest financier in the country, much less when he was nothing but a 'jobber in lodgings, bad wine, and worse bills'. A perfect storm ensued, and M. Vansittart had to separate the belligerents, some sort of apology being ultimately tendered. The auction, however, did not take place, no bidder having had the courage to show under the strong protest of all present. An emphatic remonstrance on the whole affair will be forwarded to Mr Jackson of Birkenhead, in whose equity and business habits the fullest confidence is reposed.

The eventual outcome was not reported in the British press. John Maquay makes no mention of the incident (or of the meeting) in his diary. We do know that he had been in contact with Herschel Babbage in the summer of 1848 and had dined with him on 17 September, only a few days before the explosive meeting. We can understand why a year later he was surprised to be invited to Bonfil's funeral.[64]

On 10 August 1849, the *Times* reported on a meeting of the English shareholders, held at the London Tavern with William Jackson in the chair. It was told that 'During the whole of the disturbances in Italy it was gratifying to know that the railway and works had suffered no damage whatever'. (This meant the line to Prato, not the Leopolda, which had suffered temporary damage.) On 26 September Ralph Bonfil died, his railway shares among the assets he left to his wife.[65] The Italo-Austrian Company folded, but already on 2 October it was announced that a new Anglo-Italian company would take over from it under the presidency of William Jackson. According to one historian, 'The entry of the

English was providential.' They could muster the necessary capital and call on the services of 'the most famous contractors that the market at the time had to offer, Brassey and Mackenzie'. The new administrative council included some interesting English names. Apart from Jackson and the inevitable Hall and Sloane there were Thomas Kerrich and John Gillhuly, a long-standing merchant and resident of Leghorn, who died in 1852. Among the Italians was Filippo Corridi, professor of mathematics at the University of Pisa and tutor to the children of the Grand Duke. His daughter over a decade later would become the much younger second wife of Horace Hall.[66]

On 25 October 1849 the *Morning Chronicle* reported another shareholders' meeting. Seemly regrets were expressed for the death of Bonfil, which Jackson did not doubt had been hastened by his zealous negotiations with the Tuscan government; but it was made clear that the new directors would not recommend the policy he had been pursuing, to obtain a guarantee from the government which would only come with strings attached. This would require the company to muster a large sum by way of deposit which could, in their view, be better used for other purposes. Jackson was able to announce that receipts on the line from Florence to Prato had been much the same in the current year as in 1848, despite the unsettled state of the country, and expressed gratitude to the Tuscan government for their efforts in preventing damage to the company's property. His advice for the future was to trust to the company's own exertions and to the traffic on the line for the repayment of the debts that had been incurred and the raising of the funds that somehow or other must be obtained to make possible the completion of the line to Pistoia. On this (and also on its further extension to Pescia to meet the line already built through Lucca), future prosperity depended. It was clear that the reverberations of the Tuscan shareholders' default were continuing.

At a further meeting, reported by the *Daily News* on 12 July 1850, Jackson, who had himself visited Tuscany in the preceding April, was able to announce some progress and to make proposals for increasing revenue in the short term. Thomas Brassey's agent, Mr Woodhouse, had visited Florence at the same time to inspect the line and agree certain improvements with Jackson. The company had consented to purchase the necessary land for the extension to Pistoia and hand it over to Brassey by October 1850. This entailed a degree of financial urgency, for Brassey had insisted, as a condition of his agreement to complete the line (together with its stations), that the company should liquidate its existing debts by June 1851. Jackson felt able to offer the shareholders assurances about the future returns on their investment, and Brassey himself was seen as an asset which would boost the value of the stock. This meeting, and Brassey's involvement, were widely reported.

The financial difficulties which had dogged (and continued to dog) the Tuscan railways doubtless had some adverse effects on their employees. On 25 November 1851 Scarlett informed the Foreign Office that he had been appealed to for assistance in the case of three 'English' engineers, Clark, Grettham, and Irwin, who had been in dispute with their employers to the extent that they had had recourse to the Tuscan tribunals and required poor relief from the embassy. Irwin was employed at an iron foundry in Leghorn, Clark and Grettham on the Leopolda. Clark's case proved more intractable than the other two, which Scarlett expected to be easily settled.

According to his own statement, a copy of which was submitted to Scarlett, Joseph Clark, a native of Melrose, had been engaged in August 1846 to work as a 'fitter and turner' on the Leopolda for a period of 2 years, at a salary of 50 shillings a week. At the end of this period a new 2-year contract was agreed, by which the company agreed to bring out Clark's family, paying all their expenses to Tuscany and back, and to increase his wages to 60 shillings a week. On the expiry of this contract Hoppner (now Director of the company) requested Clark to stay on 'to assist in several services, which Mr Clark assented to; and performed his duty in such a manner as to merit a very flattering attestation from Mr Richardson, Director of the Department in which he was employed'. (This was probably the already-mentioned George Richardson, 'mechanic' on the Leopolda.)

In July 1851 Clark had decided to return home and informed Hoppner, who to his surprise informed him that 'his Contract was worth nothing'. Hoppner offered him £70 to cover the expenses of his return home with his family. Clark told Hoppner he wanted at least £12 per head, a total of £84 (he had five children). It was on Hoppner's refusal that Clark went to law. Hoppner allegedly also refused to pay the expenses of the family's coming out, which Scarlett reckoned to be 'say £15 from Melrose to Newcastle where the family embarked for Leghorn, but also £15 due the Captain of the Flora for balance of passage Money from Newcastle to Leghorn'; this despite the express inclusion in the contract of 'All his family's expences out and home'.

The Tuscan court at first found in Clark's favour and appointed an agent to determine the amount it would cost to take the family home, but on appeal this decision was reversed and Clark was informed that he must either take the £70 Hoppner had offered or abide by Robert Stephenson's arbitration. Stephenson had originally only been intended to act if issues of 'art' arose, but Clark's competence was not the issue here, and Scarlett believed he had weakened his position by appealing to the elusive Stephenson, who was possibly in Egypt. The family was now destitute. Scarlett had advised Clark to seek employment on another line in Tuscany (the Maria Antonia was now well under way), but alternatively sought authorization from the Foreign Office to pay his expenses home, where he would undoubtedly be able to find work. It would be cheaper if he was sent by ship from Leghorn to Newcastle. The Foreign Office looked favourably on this request, but in the following April Scarlett was able to report that the case had been settled and Clark enabled to pay his own way home without public assistance.[67]

The railway had an impact on everyday life, which was apparent even before the line from Florence to Leghorn was fully open. On 7 August 1847 John Maquay gives us a glimpse of the new realities of travel in Tuscany:

started for Pisa at 4 o'clock taking Mr Hooker in Biga to Empoli and thence by railway to meet Pakenham on American business Capt de Courcy and Henrietta were in the train going to Lucca and we all breakfasted together at Vittoria and having done our business Pakenham returned to the Bagni and I and Hooker started for Empoli, expecting to find Elena in the train from Leghorn but she was not there and I waited at Empoli for the next train 3 ½ hours later. Mr H went on to Florence. Elena came by next train having been too late for the right one and we did not get back to dinner till 10 o'clock.

It made for a long and tedious day, although fortunately it was fairly cool. This was not the only time Elena missed the train; like others, she had to get used to the rigours of the timetable.[68] A pious pilgrim to the imprisoned Miss Cunningham at Lucca in the autumn of 1853 was much edified by her conversation, 'which lasted upwards of an hour, and might have been longer, had I not been obliged to leave for the railway'.[69]

Once the line was fully open, new possibilities opened up of making a return journey within the day or of taking cheap excursion trains. John Maquay first records getting to Leghorn and back within an admittedly long day on 20 July 1848, only a month after the opening of the completed line. He accompanied Elena, John Adair and the family to Leghorn by the 6 am train and himself returned to Florence by the last. On 25 April 1855 he remarked that the train from Florence to Leghorn made the distance in 1 hour and 40 minutes 'without stopping'; on 7 September 1856 Currell Smyth took advantage of an excursion train to come up to Florence from Leghorn and went back that evening.[70] In 1860 Macbean could emphasize the ease of communication between Florence and Leghorn. There were seven trains daily from Leghorn, and five from Florence, taking 3 hours by ordinary and 2 hours by express trains.[71] The railway touched people in other ways. A Miss Elisa Jones who had 'resided for many years at Florence where she supported herself by teaching' died in October 1861 and left her scanty property for the relief of the poor. As the Select Vestry reported a few months later, this proved to include 'two shares in the Livornese Railway, which yield fr.25 per annum'.[72]

That the railways represented the thin end of a political wedge, appealing to rulers who were interested in technological innovation but did not perceive all its long-term implications, was already hinted by a writer in the *Dundee Courier* on 16 September 1845. Under the heading 'Railway Mania', he listed Italy among 'Countries mostly inert and unimpressible by passing changes' which had been roused to action 'by the pervading passion'. Even the Pope had yielded. The point was not lost on Thomas Trollope, who on 12 July 1851 'made one of a merry little party invited by the directors of the Maria Antonia railroad to be present at the opening of a newly completed portion of their line', that is the extension to Pistoia.

The line has been undertaken by a company almost entirely English, and the works have been executed by an English contractor. The road was therefore delivered ready for public traffic on the day on which it had been promised some 9 months since, – to the infinite astonishment of the Italians.

Trollope described with great good humour the ceremony of blessing the new line, which was undertaken by the archbishop of Pistoia. 'Whether from mismanagement of the steam by a heretic British stoker' or from the personal intervention of the devil, his words and those of the attendant priests were totally drowned, first by the noise of the locomotive and secondly by the band at the far end of the platform, who concluded from the engine noise that the ceremony was already over.

> In the midst of the absurdity of the anomalous scene, it was pregnant with suggestions of interest to a thoughtful spectator. A young Sicilian, who stood next me in the crowd, remarked: – 'He – the Archbishop – little dreams that he is giving his blessing to the instrument destined to be the means of his own destruction.'

In Trollope's view, the Pope was in fact only too well aware of the potential dangers of the railways and it was with immense reluctance that he had given his consent to the building of a line from Rome to Florence, Bologna and Mantua, there to join the one already built by the Austrians from Venice to Milan.[73]

Pius IX was to travel, if only once, on the very line that the Archbishop of Pistoia had inaudibly sanctified. In August 1857 the Pope was taken by train from Florence to visit Prato and Pistoia. On arrival at the terminus he 'conversed most affably' with Thomas Kerrich and the other directors, 'addressing to Mr Kerrich, just at starting, the request, 'Don't go too fast.'[74] The notion that the significance, and retrospectively the justification, of the building of the Italian railways were political rather than commercial may gain strength from some figures published in the Daily News on 29 August 1856. The Maria Antonia had taken £217 in the week ending 21 August, a marked improvement on the £131 it had taken in the corresponding period in 1855. (It is perhaps scarcely fair to observe that in England in the week ending 23 August 1856 the North Eastern alone had taken £38,421.)

In 1852, it was reported that Brassey and Jackson had contracted to build what was called the Central Italian line, 169 miles from 'the plain of Pistoia' to Bologna and on to Piacenza, with branches connecting to the railways of the kingdom of Sardinia and to Mantua. The names of Fell and Jopling were later added to the 'powerful company' which would undertake the work.[75] Clearly the new enterprise was of importance to Tuscany and the Maria Antonia railway which would be linked to it, but so too was the completion of the link between Pistoia and Pescia and thus of a second line from Florence to Pisa and Leghorn. As the Morning Post reported on 23 March 1853, the Anglo-Italian shareholders were told that this was now going to happen, for the Company had amassed sufficient funds. The meeting was also told that 'Mr Sloane' had been confirmed in the position of 'honorary director'. Scarlett reported that the concession for the line between Pistoia and Pescia had been granted to 'an English contractor named Gandell', who had also offered to construct a line from Leghorn into the Duchy of Modena by way of Massa and Carrara. Not everyone was happy:

> The President of the Tuscan Council Mr Baldasseroni doubts if Mr Gandell is able to undertake so large an enterprise. He has been strongly recommended here to the Government by the House of Plowden and French, but he does not appear to be much known, or to be much connected with Mercantile Houses in England of any note.[76]

Baldasseroni was right. It might have been taken as a sign that before the year was out Plowden and French had quarrelled 'about Gandell's affairs' and, as John Maquay reported on the following 28 January, dissolved their partnership.[77]

Anyone who has taken the slow train from Florence to Pisa by way of Pistoia and Lucca will have noticed the immense hill through which the line passes below the village of Serravalle. This was the major obstacle the engineers now had to overcome. On 23 May the *Morning Post* quoted an optimistic report on the progress that was being made. Messrs Gandell had 'more powerful machines quite ready against the time when the shafts should have attained such a depth as will render them necessary' and the sheer solidity of the rock created confidence 'that the tunnel will remain sound and not subject to slips'. In July it was being widely reported that Gandell had obtained the concession of the projected line towards Rome via Arezzo, which was confirmed by Scarlett: Gandell had consented to deposit 20,000 dollars as security. He was still negotiating for the line into Modena and was thought likely to obtain the concessions for both that and its continuation to La Spezia.[78] Charles Lever was pleased to be able to tell a friend, on 22 August, that Gandell had taken on his son Charley with the promise of making a civil engineer of him.[79]

The firm's prospects proved as illusory as Charley's. Early in February 1854 it became known that by failing to meet the stipulated conditions Gandell had forfeited the Arezzo concession. He had also forfeited a total of 140,000 Tuscan *lire* which he had paid as security to the Government, and according to Scarlett blamed the unsettled state of European politics for his failure.[80] Gandell, who was still nominally responsible for the Pistoia-Pescia extension, was at Leghorn in May, but his affairs in the Duchy of Parma were in trouble and there was worse to come. In the closing months of 1855 the bankruptcy of the London bankers Strahan & Paul created a sensation. On 10 October several London papers reported that Gandell Bros were indebted to the bank for upwards of £300,000 but were themselves 'bankrupt in France'. The Gandells later claimed that they had been undone by the failure of Strahan & Paul, but the consensus was clearly that it was the other way round, although the bankers had been recklessly imprudent. Plowden and French too suffered. On 18 February 1859 the *Morning Post* reported that 'the guarantees given by an English banking-house in Florence' had been among the causes 'of endless litigation before the Florentine Courts, and a source of ample profit to the Florentine lawyers'.

In May 1857 Lord Normanby wryly recalled the history of the affair when he reported on certain exchanges he had had with Edward Gandell, who was based in Paris but had apparently told 'an English gentleman' at Florence that he had been briefly imprisoned at Massa and escaped to Tuscany with his wife disguised as peasants. John Gandell had 'wound up a career of reckless personal extravagance, with hopeless insolvency, and I have frequently myself had to give charitable relief to unfortunate English subjects who had been deluded here in his employ'. He had inevitably brought a number of small fry down with him. Normanby had no great hopes (as Gandell apparently did) that he would obtain an honest livelihood in the Duchy of Modena.[81] It does not look as if he did; he was still subscribing to the church in Leghorn in 1862.

One practical consequence of this debacle was delay in completing the line between Pistoia and Pescia. On 29 February 1856 *The Times* reported that Messrs Jackson, Brassey, Jopling and Fell (with the financial backing of the Leghorn banker Pietro Bastogi) had ridden to the rescue, undertaking to complete the line within 9 months, except for the Serravalle tunnel. On 15 May 1857 the same paper reported that a special train had for the first time traversed the line between Pistoia and the 'viaduct of Serravalle'. The railway was completed 21 months later, as described in the *Morning Post* of 18 February 1859:

> On the 1st of the present month there was finally opened to public traffic the last part of the railway between Pistoja and Lucca. M. Baldasseroni and the Minister went down to Lucca to assist at the opening, and stopped and attentively examined the different points of interest on the newly-completed branch. The tunnel at Serravalle has been a work requiring great skill and labour. The Grand Duke went over the whole line about two months ago, and slept in the small iron-roofed house which the English engineers had erected for their own accommodation at Bracchia, near San Marcello. It was lucky for his imperial and royal highness that he did not sleep there two nights later, for one of the most terrific storms ever known in the country whirled the whole roof clean away like an umbrella, and then let it down unbroken at a distance of some yards from the house.

Two months later a more severe storm would break over the head of the Grand Duke. The reference to the cabin in which the contractors on the Pistoia-Pescia line had been accommodated is a salutary reminder that below the level of the financiers and the eminent engineers in whose name the railways were built there were the men who actually built and serviced them.

Naturally we know more about their social and professional superiors. John Barraclough Fell (1815–1902) is most celebrated for his contribution to the engineering of mountain railways, the Fell Centre Rail System. Like the Joplings, he worked from 1852 onwards on a variety of Brassey projects in Italy. John Maquay first registered his presence when George went to a party given by Mrs Fell on 5 January 1855 and references to the Fells continue down to May 1857. Fell turned his technical mind to the perennial problem of heating the Florentine Church. The congregation had doubtless shivered its way through another winter when 'Mr Fell of the Florentine railway' suggested in March 1855 that 'the church could be thoroughly heated by the system of heated air generated by a boiler through pipes'.[82]

The Joplings left a bigger biographical mark on the Tuscan records, but were centred in the Leghorn area. The oldest of them, Joseph, was married in London in 1849 to a widow, Elizabeth Ball née Attfield. A daughter who was given the names Elizabeth Attfield was born to them in Tuscany on 23 November 1855, but her mother died a few days later. In 1858 Joseph was married in Switzerland to her sister Louisa. He was joined in Tuscany by two brothers, the younger of whom, Samuel, died in Florence on 1 December 1858. The other, Charles, like Joseph worked on Brassey's Tuscan projects, but contracted malaria and died in Leghorn early in 1863. It was later recorded that Joseph had been employed by Brassey between 1860 and 1862 in laying out the first section of the Maremma railway, and then worked in Austria until 1868.[83] In 1861 the subscribers to the Leghorn church included Brassey himself, Charles and Joseph Jopling, Charles Jones, another of Brassey's lieutenants, who is recorded in the 1851 census as an 'assistant railway contractor' at Newcastle under Lyme, and John Attfield, the brother of Joseph Jopling's wives and himself a transport engineer.[84] Attfield was among the Leghorn merchants who signed a letter disputing Lord Normanby's picture of the state of Tuscany in 1860 (*Morning Post*, 12 March).

The extension of the Maria Antonia and the projected Central Italian Railway (or, as it came to be called, the *Porrettana*) created new employment opportunities and a new focus of activity around Pistoia.[85] In April 1859 the Reverend O'Neill asked the Select Vestry to consider the appointment of an assistant curate, which would enable him to meet such extra calls on his time as 'an additional Sunday evening Service at Pistoia to Railway officials'. It is not clear whether they had asked for the service or whether this was a missionary effort; anyway it seems to have been recognized that it was impossible for the 'officials' to get to Florence to attend regular worship.[86] Scraps of evidence identify Britons who for a time lived and worked in this locality. James Shields, a goods manager on the Pistoia & Prato railway, was married in Florence in 1852 but died only 2 years later. John Foster, whose wife gave birth to a daughter in October 1854, was a 'superintendent' on the railway at Prato. George Picture, who was living near Pistoia when his infant son died in February 1854, was employed on the railway, but we are not told in what capacity. There is a possible clue in the English 1861 census: he was then living with his wife and daughter at Chapel-en-le-Frith in Derbyshire and was described as a 'railway miner'. Had he helped to blast a path through the great mound of Serravalle?

Then there was a 'civil engineer' called David Jackson, a Londoner by birth, who on 7 April 1861, when the census was taken, was in Camberwell with several children and a servant called Giuseppa Bonacchi, a native of a place in Tuscany apparently called Pittega. This may have been an error for Piteccio, a small town just north of Pistoia, for Piteglio, a little further away to the north-west, or even for Pistoia itself.[87] It was also the birthplace of Jackson's 4-year-old daughter Maria. His wife Elizabeth was buried in the cemetery at Leghorn on 23 February 1861; he had promptly left for England with his children and his servant, after 4 years or more in Tuscany. His daughter Rosaline was buried alongside her mother at Leghorn in November 1863; perhaps he returned to work in Italy.

At some point Jackson got to know John Trewhella, a Cornish-born railway contractor who had been working in Piedmont before his daughter Beatrice was born at Petrucci (just north of Pistoia and not far from Piteccio) in February 1855 and baptized by the Rev. O'Neill a couple of months later.[88] In the autumn of 1857 Thomas Trollope took Trewhella to visit Francis Sloane's copper mines near Volterra.[89] Born in Ludgvan about 1820, he belonged to a miniature dynasty of railwaymen which stemmed from an area of England historically as much associated with mining and engineering as Northumberland. Their activity extended beyond Tuscany and into the period of the Italian kingdom. It may have been after the fall of the Grand Duke that his younger brother Robert, also a railway contractor, joined him in Italy. In 1862 Robert was married at Leghorn to Kate Thrupp, the sister of John's wife Anna Maria. The Tuscan railways took up only part of the family's working lives, but unlike many others they ended by putting down roots in Italy.

Another who did so was Thomas Downie, whose marital affairs gave the Foreign Office so much bother in 1851–1852. In 1851 he was described as a millwright, a term which covers a wide range of possibilities connected with machinery; alternatively he was simply an 'engineer', and it is not clear whether he was already employed on the railways.[90] The births of two of his children and the death of another were registered at Leghorn in 1852 and 1854 and around 1860 the Downies were living at or near Florence, where early in 1861 Thomas signed the memorial praying for the restoration of British diplomatic representation. In 1862 he was put in charge of the engineering workshop which supplied the line being built from Siena to Poggibonsi, ultimately to link Siena with Florence. He was not the first 'Englishman' to occupy this post, for an individual named Young, recommended by Stephenson, had helped to organize the workshop.[91] At least three children were born to him during this Sienese period.

Thomas was laid to rest in the Allori Cemetery just outside Florence in 1911, aged 89, and was later joined there not only by Albina in 1916, but by a host of children and grandchildren whose lives spanned the twentieth century and for whom Italy was their native land. The Italian inscription on his monument classified this Scottish Presbyterian as a 'Waldensian', 'Engineer on the Italian railways' and *Cavaliere*. The inscription was dedicated 'To the tireless worker, to the man of the highest integrity, good, pious, of adamantine character, to the exemplary husband and father', whose family now awaited their reunion with him in the celestial resting-place. The image of a locomotive adorns the monument.

Then, as now, railways were not solely concerned with passenger traffic. Among the many undertakings the over-committed Gandell had entered into was the building of a railway at Carrara to convey marble from the quarries to the port. He handed the concession over to another British consortium, consisting of William Walton and his partners Lambert and 'Beck'. Early in 1855 Walton recommended himself to Bulwer as unpaid British consul at Carrara, where he said he had lived for 20 years. The long-established marble trade with England had lately increased to upwards of 20,000 tons annually and at considerable expense to himself he had in effect created a port facility at Carrara, 'thus avoiding the heavy expense attending on the transmission to Leghorn or Genoa and the consequent enhanced price of the Article to the English Consumer'. His long residence and the 'liberal support' he had always given to the Duchy's institutions had earned him the favour of the Sovereign. The Modenese government had just conceded to 'an English Company' the right to build a railroad 'for the transport of Marble from the Quarries to Sea Side'. The £300,000 capital required 'will be almost exclusively English and the Engineers and personals principally employed of the same Nation'.[92] Walton was indeed appointed British consul, having already acted as American consul at Carrara, and although he experienced some difficult moments during the transition to the Italian kingdom he survived the disappearance of the Duke of Modena. However, problems which neither he nor his associates could surmount delayed the building of the *marmifera*, the marble-bearing railway, until after his death.

Of his partners in this abortive enterprise, Alfred Lambert had been much in Tuscany over a period of years; it is unclear when and how his interest in Carrara began, but it clearly occupied much of his later life.[93] 'Beck' was probably William George Beek, an engineer whose adventurous life had taken him to Persia and the Dead Sea before he was married in Naples in September 1838. From then until his death in Brixton in 1873 he spent much of his time in Naples and Sicily, but two of his children were born in Tuscany (at Leghorn in 1854 and Bagni in 1857), while another died at Leghorn in 1864. These dates suggest that his Tuscan years (he was variously described as of Leghorn and of Messina) broadly coincided with the period in which Walton was hoping to build the *marmifera*. Subsequently he worked in mining enterprises in Sicily and Southern Italy. Here again, an interest in mining and geology led to at least a temporary connection with railway-building.[94]

Railway building and its associated concerns were scarcely interrupted by the political upheaval which resulted in the Kingdom of Italy. Problems on the one hand with migratory British labourers, on the other with the occasionally violent Italian employees of British contractors, continued to demand Consul Macbean's attention and even to receive newspaper coverage.[95] Here, as in so many other fields of endeavour, the essential continuity of Anglo-Tuscan existence remained undisturbed for many years to come.

Notes

1 JLM, E8 f. 66. There are historical outlines of the straw trade in Filippo Mariotti, *Notizie storiche, economiche e statistiche intorno all' arte della paglia in Toscana* (1858, reprinted Florence, 2002); ed. R. Lunardi, *Condizioni della industria fiorentina delle trecce e dei cappelli di paglia nel 1896* (Florence, 2003); G. Pierotti, *La Paglia in Toscana* (Florence, 1927). There are also valuable references in *Prato, Storia di una città* (Prato, 1986–1997), Vol. 3, *Il tempo della industria (1815–1943)*.

2 *Transactions of the Royal Society of* Arts 23 (1805), pp. 223–4; Mariotti, *L'arte della paglia*, p. 41, note 88.

3 Dominic Colnaghi, 'Notes on the Florentine Straw Industry', *The Antiquary* 12 (1886), pp. 122–4.

4 Emanuele Repetti, *Dizionario geografico-fisico-storico della Toscana* (Florence, 1833), Vol. 1, pp. 363–4.

5 Lady Morgan, *Italy* (London, 1821), Vol. 2, p. 122.

6 The *Post Office Directory* for 1824 described the firm as 'Askew and Co, Leghorn hat merchants to the Royal Family'.

7 Andrea Giuntini, *Soltanto per denaro: La vita, gli affari, la ricchezza di Emanuele Fenzi negoziante banchiere fiorentino nel Granducato di Toscana (1784–1875)* (Florence, 2002), pp. 62–70. Born in 1810, Alfred's involvement during the 1820s can scarcely have been very great.

8 William Cobbett, *Cottage Economy* (London, 1823) chapter 8 contains his full thesis. This is partly reproduced in his *Weekly Political Register*, in which on 17 July 1823 he declared that English plaiters were producing from native rye-straw a product 'equal to any I can find that has come from Leghorn', while plait made from certain grasses was superior.

9 Giuntini, *Soltanto per denaro*, pp. 63–6. In 1828 Fenzi, recovered, himself undertook a long trip on the same quest, taking in London, Paris, Geneva and Milan.

10 Asa Briggs (ed.), *William Cobbett Rural Rides* (London, 1957), Vol. 2, p. 207.

11 Copious material. including printed ephemera, on the local hat industry is held by the Wardown Park Museum, Luton and also the Luton Public Library. There is an extensive bibliography on the Luton Hat trade, including Stephen Bunker, *Strawopolis: Luton Transformed 1840–76* (Bedfordshire Historical Record Society, 78, 1999).

12 *Leeds Intelligencer,* 20 November 1828. Frederick Davis, *History of Luton* (Luton, private, 1855), pp. 156–7, says that Waller went to Italy in 1825 'to make his arrangements', that is to import the raw straw. A later account by one of his nephews credited Thomas with 'extensive experiments and frequent visits to Italy' (*Luton Times and Advertiser* 27 September 1895).

13 Giuntini, *Soltanto per denaro*, p. 64.

14 The ups and downs of the Tuscan industry in the 1820s were summarized in Giuseppe Sacchi (ed.), *Annali Universali di Statistica, Economia, Pubblica Legislazione, Storia, Viaggi*, 3rd series, 29, (Milan, 1859), p. 314.

15 Colnaghi. 'Florentine Straw Industry.' pp. 122–4.

16 Pierotti, *La Paglia*, pp. 67–8, note 24.

17 See in particular the *Times* 24 September 1824 and 1 December 1855. The proceedings at the trial of Askew himself can be found at www.oldbaileyonline.org.

18 We have no record of Florence's baptism. Carlotta was married in Spain to a civil engineer called William Lewis and in 1860 bore a son who was given the names William Waller, commemorating the link between the Vyse and Waller families.

This child became a famous actor in Edwardian England, taking the name Lewis Waller.

19 FO79/55, Bligh to FO with enclosures, 25 November 1830.

20 TNA, Prob11/2104. Charles Ede was buried in the English Cemetery in August 1863, aged 70. He had no apparent connection with the straw business, and it is likely that he simply retired to Florence, where his daughter Fanny Catherine was married in 1857. The record of the marriage describes him as 'late of Constantinople' and we know that his son Edward Francis (also buried at Florence in 1909) was born at Smyrna in 1828.

21 TNA, Prob11/2202. Thomas named his friend (in fact his brother-in-law) Edward Ede of Manchester as one of his executors, and two of his children were given the second name Ede. The source for Edmund's New York business is some 'Memory Sketches of Luton' by Joseph Hawkes, which were published in the *Luton News* around 1895 (cuttings in the Wardown Park Museum collection).

22 FO79/60, Burghersh to FO with enclosures, 8 October 1830.

23 FO79/75, Seymour to FO, 30 March 1834; 79/74, FO to Seymour, 29 August.

24 John Bowring, *Report on the Statistics of Tuscany, Lucca, the Pontifical, and the Lombardo-Venetian states, with a Special Reference to Their Commercial Relations* (London, 1837), p. 18.

25 *Hertford Mercury & Advertiser* 30 April 1842. On 10 May Peel caused a 'considerable sensation' in the Commons when he produced a bundle of unplaited straw (liable only to a nominal duty of 1 penny per pound weight) in which had been concealed a small packet of plaited straw (theoretically liable to a duty of 17 shillings and sixpence per pound). This little exhibition was intended to demonstrate that the current level of duty on imported plait did not ensure as much protection to the livelihoods of the women and children who plaited raw straw as its advocates supposed.

26 An Edward Brind who was almost certainly his elder brother died in Siena in May 1833; it is equally unclear whether he had been in Tuscany on business, or on what business it was.

27 *Gazzetta* 3 December 1844.

28 Robert Waller of Luton was married in Philadelphia on 12 March 1846, as reported in the *Times* on the 18th.

29 LMA, CLC/B/227–181/Ms12057. This is a bundle of twenty-five items concerning the Vyse business and includes the various deeds later referred to as well as Thomas Andrew's will of 1846.

30 Archivio Storico del Comune di Firenze, Documenti dell'Archivio preunitario del Comune di Firenze 1782–1865, Pratica 61030, no.reg.1846, 16. Colnaghi was therefore nearly right in thinking that Vyse & Sons had moved to Prato around 1844.

31 Enrico Fiumi, *Demografia, movimento urbanistico e classi sociali in Prato dall' età comunale ai tempi moderni* (Florence, 1968), p. 507. The Grand Duke is supposed to have acceded to the request, but the name and arms of Vyse seem never to have been officially registered (p. 206, note 17). Fiumi also remarked that the Vyse did not possess Pratese citizenship (p. 233).

32 *Prato, Storia di una città*, Vol. 3, p. 1240.

33 CMB 1, 6 October 1845. He may have been in London on the following 16 May, when a new indenture was drawn up between Thomas Vyse of Cripplegate Buildings of the first part, Thomas Andrew Vyse, 'of Florence, Gentleman', of the second part, and the latter's brother Richard and trustee George Faulkner of the third part. The purpose was to change the method by which the trust fund was supplied. This is to be found in the bundle of Vyse business papers already referred to, above note 29.

34 By this time Thomas had lost another son, who died of 'apoplexy' in New York early in 1844, as well as all but one of his daughters.

35 *Gazzetta* 15 February 1847.

36 FO79/140 Macbean to FO, 6 June 1849. Macbean's list in fact names Leiden as one of the Waller outlets, but this is surely a mistake for Luton.

37 The Vyse family's stay in America was clouded by one sad event, the death of Ernest William in 1852, but the eldest son, Thomas Andrew junior, was married in New York on 21 October 1853; the rest of the family may already have returned to Europe. Thomas Andrew junior spent the rest of his life in the United States. He became a US citizen in 1854 and died in New Jersey in 1913.

38 *Prato, Storia di una città*, Vol. 3, p. 19; Mariotti, *Notizie storiche*, p. 41, note 88.

39 *Great Exhibition Official Illustrated Catalogue*, Vol. 1, p. 1297; Vol. 2, p. 577.

40 JLM, E11 f. 138.

41 Letter now in the Winterthur Library, written by Read on 28 March 1855. John refers to the Wallers E11, ff. 107v, 109, 126, 137, 138v, 141, 144, 145v–147.

42 When Thomas Andrew junior's daughter Emily applied for an American passport in March 1885 she was supported by her uncle by marriage, William Schall.

43 JLM, E11 ff. 170, 186, 190, 209v, 210. When Thomas Andrew himself left Florence is not known. He was living in Brixton when he died in the spring of 1865.

44 *Prato, Storia di una città*, Vol. 3, pp. 1227–8.

45 The will was made 3 August 1855 and proved (with codicils) on 15 February 1861 (National Probate Register).

46 The will was proved on 9 April 1888 by Charles Vyse Palin of Preston Park, Brighton. Reynolds left personal estate of £11,314 1s 0d. in England (National Probate Register). There is a copy of the provisions which affected Prato in Prato, Archivio di Stato, Comune 45, ff. 137–9.

47 Marco Sorelli, 'Una miniera maremmana nell' età preindustriale. Le zolfiere granducali di Pereta, dagli inizi all' abbandono della attività estrattiva (secoli XVIII–XIX)', *Bollettino della Società Storica Maremmana, Fascicolo speciale* 49 (1985).

48 Bowring, *Report*, pp. 51–3.

49 Trollope, *What I Remember*, Vol. 2, pp. 90–2.

50 *Prato, Storia di una città*, Vol. 3, p. 13. The plant employed about 60 people but was unpopular with local landlords who alleged environmental and social damage. An investigation failed to uphold their complaints, but (whether or not this was connected) in 1856 the manager of the plant, Luigi Bastogi, was shot dead in nearby woods.

51 *Times* 13 May 1863. The failure of Strahan, Paul & Co was widely reported and discussed, for example in the *Examiner* 16 December 1855.

52 William Jervis, *Mineral Resources of Central Italy* (London, 1862), pp. 1–25.

53 FO79/46, Strangways to FO, 4 July 1826. It is reasonable to suppose that this was the shopkeeper Thomas Townley who settled in Florence soon after 1815.

54 FO79/108, Falconar to FO, 20 September 1842. An appreciative Italian biography of Walton can be found at Carraraonline. com. He was born at Wakefield in 1796 and came to Italy in 1827, Leghorn in 1830.

55 Apart from the newspapers, the following account has drawn on a number of sources, including the works of Andrea Giuntini: *Soltanto per denaro*, q.v.; 'Le communicazioni stradali e ferroviarie', in *Prato, storia di una città*, Vol. 3, pp. 539–87, especially pp. 543–56; *Leopoldo e il Treno: Le ferrovie nel Granducato Toscano 1824–1861* (Naples, 1991); *I Giganti della montagna: Storia della ferrovia Direttissima Bologna-Firenze (1845–1834)* (Florence, 1984). Also to be mentioned are Pier Liuigi Landi, *La Leopolda: La ferrovia Firenze-Livorno e le sue vicende (1825–1860)* (Pisa,

1974); Adriano Betti Carboncini, *Firenze e il Treno: nascita e sviluppo delle ferrovie nella città* (Cortona, 2004); Nicola Marchi, *I treni di Pistoia* (Pistoia, 2003); Giuliano Catoni, *Un treno per Siena: la strade ferrata centrale toscana dal 1844 al 1865* (Siena, no date). The *Gazzetta* frequently published company prospectuses and legal notices respecting the railways.

56   *Caledonian Mercury* 5 December 1836; *Morning Post* 3 May 1838; *Morning Chronicle* 18 October 1838.

57   Townshend was able, during his stay in Tuscany, to undertake a study of the ancient bridges in the neighbourhood of Lucca, on which subject he delivered a paper to the Institute of Civil Engineers (*The Era,* 13 February 1842).

58   Murray, *Handbook to Northern Italy* (London, 1842), p. 481.

59   FO79/115, Macbean to FO, 11 March 1845.

60   JLM, E10 f. 270v.

61   CMB 1, 26 September 1849. Perrier's nationality is unclear, but a Mrs Charles Perrier appears as a subscriber to the Leghorn church in 1843 (FO79/112, Macbean to FO, 30 March 1844).

62   Surely there was a connection here with the Robert Summerside who worked as a mine supervisor for George Stephenson, and whose son Thomas in 1878 published reminiscences of Stephenson. George Summerside, engineer, was living in Derby at the time of the 1841 census.

63   JLM, E11 f. 23.

64   JLM, E11 f. 47.

65   TNA, Prob11/2180.

66   Giuntini, 'Le comunicazioni', p. 553.

67   FO79/152, Scarlett to FO, 25 November 1851; the correspondence continues in 155 and 158.

68   JLM, E11 f. 8; see also f. 25, 21 July 1848, where Elena also missed the train.

69   *Essex Standard* 14 October 1853.

70   JLM, E11 ff. 15, 152v, 180. In 2018 the regular hourly regional express from Firenze SMN to Livorno took 1 hour 20 minutes, admittedly stopping along the way but possessing the advantage of the new line bypassing Signa.

71   FO79/215, Macbean to FO, 23 April 1860.

72   CMB 2, 6 November 1861.

73   *Athenaeum* 16 August 1851. Trollope's comments about the Pope were more applicable to Gregory XVI than to Pius IX, during whose pontificate a number of railway miles were built in the Papal States.

74   *Liverpool Mercury* 31 August 1857.

75   *Times* 29 October 1852, 4 November 1852, 9 February 1853. The idea for this line had been in the air since 1845, but it would prove as troublesome as the others to bring to fruition.

76   FO79/166, Scarlett to FO, 12 April 1853.

77   JLM, E11 f. 124.

78   FO79/168, Scarlett to FO, 12 August 1853. In the autumn it was being reported that Gandell had undertaken to build a line in southern France and had also obtained the concession of three lines in the Duchy of Parma.

79   Edward Downey, *Charles Lever, His Life in Letters* (Edinburgh & London, 1906) Vol. 1, p. 134. The hapless Charley did not stay with the firm, but left them in 1856 to pursue a military career.

80   FO79/176, Scarlett to FO, 6 February 1854; *Morning Chronicle* 4 February 1854.

81   FO79/195, Normanby to FO, 9 April 1857. For other examples of fall-out from Gandell's failure see the reports of the bankruptcy of an employee, Charles James

Russell (*The Standard* 11 November 1855) and of a suit brought by a Captain Aaron Smith who had lent Gandell money (*Daily News* 1 August 1859).

82 CMB 2, 7 March 1855. JLM, E11 ff. 143, 144v, 145, 150, 186v, 192. Fell experimented with his centre-rail system in Derbyshire and it was later used in the temporary Mont Cenis railway, opened in 1862, which preceded the building of the tunnel under that section of the Alps.

83 Obituary in *Proceedings of the Institute of Civil Engineers* 160 (1904), p. 400. Jopling had been elected an Associate of the Institute in 1852. We are told that (with Fell) he was present at the opening of the Mt. Cenis railway. In 1873 he went to work in Canada, where he died in 1904.

84 They were the children of a London upholsterer, Richard Attfield. A few months after his marriage to Louisa (*Morning Post* 10 February 1858) Joseph Jopling was among the signatories to a petition presented to Lord Derby in favour of a change in the law which forbade marriage to a deceased wife's sister (*Daily News* 5 May).

85 The line still exists and until 1934 was the main line from Bologna into Tuscany. It takes its name from the spa town of Porretta Terme.

86 CMB 2, 18 April 1859.

87 Piteccio had a railway station, opened in 1864 and now closed. A great viaduct was built nearby to carry the line.

88 They worked together later in the Midlands: *Staffordshire Advertiser* 24 March, 14 April 1866.

89 Trollope, *What I Remember*, Vol. 2, p. 376. At least two more children were born to Trewhella at Petrucci. He and his wife Anna Maria were much taken by Italy, to judge from the fact they called these later children Fernando Roberto and Guglielmo Romolo Atto.

90 He is described as having been 'employed at the new works in the manufactory of the Jew Carmi at Massa' (FO79/155, Scarlett to FO with enclosure, 19 March 1852).

91 Catoni, *Un treno per Siena*, pp. 68–9.

92 FO79/183, Bulwer to FO with enclosure, 4 January 1855.

93 In 1885 (6 years after his wife's death in Florence) Lambert purchased a former property of the Modenese dukes, the Villa Rinchiostra, at Massa di Carrara. When he died in 1900, he left a bequest to one of his executors, Sydney Bush Cripps (*Birmingham Daily Post* 12 July 1900), who belonged to a family of marble merchants which had been in partnership with Walton and his nephew John Gooddy.

94 For Beek, www.apame.org/2013/09/research-more-on-bekes-neeks.html. The Probate Registry, s.d. 12 September 1873, described him as 'late of Fiume Di Nisi in the Island of Sicily'.

95 See for example *Morning Post* 4 September 1862, for a report of attacks on British railway employees by disgruntled Italian workers; FO45/47, Macbean to FO, 1 July 1863, on the squalid story of John Carney, a labourer on Brassey's Maremma railway, who was accused of murdering his wife.

14 THE SERVICE SECTOR

In 1842, the first edition of *Murray*'s guidebook to Tuscany offered this advice to the British:

> By the law of Tuscany, every servant engaged at *yearly* wages is entitled to six months' notice to quit or to six months' wages; the better way is to engage by the month, and to have a written agreement, stating that you are entitled to discharge at a fortnight's notice. Any foreign servant brought by a stranger into Tuscany, and discharged by him there, however bad his conduct may have been, can, upon applying to the tribunals, compel the master to pay his full coach-fare and expenses back to his own country, unless the employer have a written agreement, signed by the servant, to the contrary. Families intending to winter in Florence generally engage a cook at a stipulated price per month, to furnish every thing required for the house; but, in this case, it is necessary for the stranger to advertise in the *Gazzetta di Firenze*, giving his name and residence, and stating that his servants have orders to pay for every thing in ready money, and that he will not be accountable for any debts they may contract in his name: failing to do this, the cook will probably pocket the whole of the money paid him for housekeeping, and the master will be compelled to repay all the tradesmen's bills. It is also necessary to be extremely particular to take a written receipt for every weekly or monthly payment made to the cook, as, in default of this, he will probably, on the eve of the departure of the family, go into court, and swear that he has been supplying the house upon credit during his master's whole stay.

As the householder was not permitted to take his own oath on the facts or to produce testimony from his relatives or other servants, the odds were heavily stacked against him, and he would very likely be forced to repay the whole amount. This was 'of very common occurrence'.[1]

The pages of the *Gazzetta di Firenze* show that British householders, Lady Popham, Arthur Vansittart and John Maquay among them, had been anticipating this advice in quite large numbers from the mid-1820s onwards. The few who, like Walter Savage Landor, acquired rural properties might take the precaution of advising the public that their peasants were not authorized to buy or sell livestock on their behalf. Maquay's years in Florence must have made him well acquainted with the state of the law. His diary hints at the vulnerability of servants rather than of masters, although there is no reason to suppose that he mistreated his employees. More than once he decided against dismissing a servant when they promised amendment, although their repentance, and his, usually proved short-lived. His diaries were obviously not intended to give posterity a clear account of how the household of a Florentine resident was put together. Names appear and disappear without explanation; he gives global figures for servants' wages and often refers anonymously to 'coachman' or 'cook'. Nevertheless some hints emerge.

During his years as a tourist and in the early days of his marriage, when he spent a lot of time in Ireland, John often hired servants there and transported them to Italy, with mixed results. In Dublin in 1827 he took on a 'Groom and general servant' called Patrick Daly, who was to receive £3 a month while travelling and £3 6s 8d and his bed when 'stationary'. Patrick had his limitations, including ignorance of French (in July 1827 John bought him a phrase-book) and 'great want of punctuality'.[2] By April 1828 his deficiencies proved too great, but we do not know what happened to him when he was discharged at Florence. In Dublin again in the autumn of 1829 John hired a new coachman, Joseph Shaw, but Joseph and Elena's newly hired lady's maid 'could not agree' and he was replaced by John Jefferies, who was to receive

34 Guineas a year finding his own clothes 4/- & 4 francs travelling board wages if I part with him abroad for my own convenience I pay his expenses home or find him a place if I discharge him for misconduct he finds his own way home.[3]

In July 1831 there was a fresh round of recruitment in Dublin, including Joseph Brown as coachman and a 'boy' called William Kelly.

When the family was settled in Florence in the autumn of 1832 new names appear, including a Luigi who seems to have been in overall control of the household. It was natural that John should have Italian servants – the cook was invariably a native – but for some months he experienced a rather rapid turnover in the position he sometimes designates 'butler'. On 31 July 1833 there was terrible quarrelling among the servants which was patched up, whether by themselves or by his intervention is not clear. Joseph continued in charge of the carriage and horses, and in August John had to pay a fine when his dog bit a man. In October, having gone through two apparent successors to Luigi, he hired Emidio Ruggieri who, at '9 crowns a month including wine', proved more adhesive. In the summer of 1834, when John and Elena as usual moved out of town, William and a maid called Louisa accompanied them while Joseph and Emidio remained in charge of the town house. One night in October, having taken Miss De Courcy home, Joseph got drunk and the horse ran away with the carriage. This presaged the end of his employment, and John gave him the equivalent of £6 to help him return home.

William had in the meantime proved capable of taking charge of the carriage and horses, at least temporarily.

It is not clear why Emidio was discharged in January 1835, while John was away in England dealing with his late brother's affairs, but he reappeared in September 1836, having been with Captain Napier, now leaving Florence after his wife's death. Emidio was now to be paid 8 dollars a month including wine. Elena had meanwhile acquired a Sienese maid called Cici, and a Luigi appeared or reappeared in John's accounts, establishing an enduring presence alongside Emidio. By now the household seems to have achieved a degree of stability. On 1 August 1837 John sketched what he intended to be its future shape, while reviewing his finances in the light of a recent diminution of income.[4] It consisted of coachman (presumably Luigi), cook, butler (presumably Emidio), nurse and maid (presumably Cici). William Kelly was still present as 'extra', but would leave when he obtained another place, which he did in September, with a departing tip of 10 *francesconi*. After 5 years in the household, this Dublin boy should now have been a finished servant.

Had John needed warning that servants must be kept on a tight rein, his mother's troubles would have reminded him. On 1 November 1836 he recorded that 'Fombelle sat some time with me horrible story!!!! how guarded we ought to be about servants'.[5] As so often, we are left wondering what exactly this was about. One day in June 1840 Elena sent a note to John at the bank to say that the cook had not returned from market and had been taken to prison; his response was to engage a man by the day. Then he had a flaming row with the coachman, which was patched up when the latter made a suitable apology. The household seems to have become more Italian as the years went by, but in May 1842 Elena engaged an English maid called Williams, and John paid the expenses of her journey to Florence (where from is unfortunately not stated). On 1 March 1844 John noted that he had parted with Luigi Delicati, his coachman, after nearly 10 years' service. He was replaced by Francesco Bandini, who was still there 4 years later. Emidio remained in post until April 1847; John reckoned he had been with him for 13 years, which suggests that he was adding the two periods of Emidio's employment together. Pietro Agostini was engaged in his stead.

By May 1841 John felt in need of instruction for his young sons, the eldest of whom, George, was now 6 years old, and a Miss Lucy Fisher was engaged as governess. (John had probably mistaken the name, for Lucy mysteriously turned into Julia.[6]) She was to receive 30 louis per annum, and naturally associated with the family in a manner that set her somewhat apart from other servants, accompanying Elena to concerts and sharing in various excursions with the children. Two of her sisters, Ellen (or Helen) and Fanny, deputized for her at different times over the next 2 years. They were the daughters of Henry Fisher, 'merchant' of Leghorn. It would not have been difficult for John to get to know of their existence and their desire and suitability for a situation.

In March 1843 Miss Fisher was succeeded by 'Miss Wilkinson now living with Mrs Bacon' as governess at 3 louis per month.[7] Her mother was the widow of an attorney, and nearly a decade later took charge of John's second son, John Popham, while he was in London preparing for the army. She obtained lodgings for John himself when he visited London in 1852 and he clearly regarded her and her daughters as acceptable company. Miss Wilkinson, who was only about 20 in 1843, remained with the Maquays for a little over 2 years, until John decided that George and his brothers required a tutor rather than a governess. Her successor, a Mr Paisley, failed to turn up at the expected time in November 1846, but once arrived he stayed the course for a couple of years until on 27 December 1848 he 'much surprized' his employer with the news that 'he was so much oppressed both in mind & body that he must leave me', which he promptly did.[8] This marked the end of home tuition for the boys, who were now sent out to a day school run by a Mr Au Capitaine.

The sometimes bleak conditions of servant life are revealed in several entries in the Maquay diaries. It was said to be very inconvenient when servants were ill, which it doubtless was, especially for the servants. In July 1838 Elena's maid, Isabella, who had not previously been mentioned by name, became dangerously ill and expired after six days' suffering. In early May 1842 the Pakenhams set off for Bagni, leaving their nurse Carlotta sick behind them, and she died on the 7th in one of the rooms at the bank. Just as poignant is the entry for 28 July: Luigi had to go to Lucca Baths, 'having heard his wife is dying there'.[9]

A change in John's mode of recording his monthly accounts in his diary makes it more difficult to trace his household personnel, and he seems in general to become more sparing of references to them. From early 1850 an Agostino had the oversight of the household in town and country and supervised the preparations for the family's moves from the one to the other, also sometimes taking charge of William, the youngest child. When John finally left Florence for Ireland in May 1858 he was accompanied by Agostino and his son. It was not only British-born servants who were uprooted from hearth and home.

Getting back to Britain, for some unfortunate servants, proved problematic. On 12 October 1836 John went with his mother to meet the clergyman, Mr Knapp, to discuss the possibility of sending Joseph Shaw home at the expense of the church fund, for he had gone blind. There is no evidence that Joseph, once briefly engaged by John in Ireland, had ever been with him in Italy; if he had been with Elizabeth she never names him. At all events, John seems to have taken responsibility for sending him home. In his October and November accounts, without further explanation, he records disbursing sums of money to Shaw.[10] As this incident reveals, British servants who had fallen on hard times were among the calls made on the charitable funds of the English Church.

As Secretary and Treasurer to the church Committee John knew this very well. In 1838 he was involved in the sad case of a Scottish servant-girl called Jane Gavin, who was detained in the 'mad house' of the hospital of San Bonifazio. It seems that she had come to Florence with the family of Mr Allen Crombie, who went on to Pisa leaving her sick in the York Hotel. In hospital her inability to speak anything but English made it hard for the staff to treat her adequately. Some charitable people tried to hire an English-speaking attendant for her, but Mr Crombie, who was paying the hospital the agreed sum for her subsistence, refused to pay for a nurse. He thought that Jane was stubborn and had brought her troubles on herself by previously refusing medical treatment in London and Boulogne. He had wanted to send her back to Scotland from Boulogne and warned her that if she became ill 'on the road' he would have to leave her behind to shift for herself. It is a sad picture. Crombie was willing to pay for Jane to return home when she was cured, but this seemed a remote prospect, and the Committee feared that if she remained in the hospital when her employer left Tuscany, she might remain a permanent call on their charitable funds.[11]

Some years later another female servant suffered rather similarly. Alfred Hall brought the case of Sarah Latford to the attention of the Select Vestry in April 1855. She had been left in Florence when the family she was serving abruptly left the city. Her mind was 'so deeply affected' that she had to be admitted to the Insane Hospital. She became more composed after the arrival of her sister, who wished to take her home, and Hall reported that the hospital would allow her to travel if a guard accompanied her. A grant of £18 was accordingly made from Lady Don's charitable fund.

Lady Don also posthumously helped to rescue a working family in difficulties. In June 1851 John Russell, a coachman, was married in Florence to Elizabeth Field. Two sons were born to them and baptized at the English Church, James in May 1856 and John in October 1858. Elizabeth died of a 'decline' early in 1859 and by the autumn the bereaved husband and father was unemployed and had debts of 440 Tuscan dollars. We do not know how this had come about or with whom he had previously been in service, but he now applied to the church, hoping to take the children back to England and seek employment there.[12]

Fortunately he had friends in need. His wife had once been a servant with the Nicholl family of Bridgend, and Christopher Webb Smith, as Secretary, read to the Select Vestry two letters he had received from Miss Lucy Nicholl, expressing the family's willingness to contribute to the expenses and upkeep of the young Russells. Called before the Vestry, John Russell estimated that he owed the nurse of his younger child 12 dollars and that 18 dollars would cover his other debts, except those to the clergyman Mr O'Neill and to Dr Trotman. He was required to produce a schedule of these owings, which included sums for charcoal and ass's milk, rent, and payments to a 'woodman' and a chemist.

Smith now entered into direct correspondence with Mrs Nicholl. The maximum payment the Vestry was prepared to make was 45 dollars, half of what was left of Lady Don's fund, and Mrs Nicholl was asked whether she was prepared to meet the rest of what was needed to send the children home. On 15 January 1860 Smith thanked her warmly for her 'ready and liberal donation of £25'. Up to now it had seemed likely that Russell would accompany his children to England, but he had found service with a Polish nobleman near Florence, and was no longer in need of lodgings in the city. As long as he remained in employment, it would be better that he should not accompany the children to England, but how were they to get there?

At this point help appeared, in the shape of Sarah Blackburn, a friend of Russell's late wife and apparently 'a respectable and intelligent person', who in April volunteered to escort the children home, on payment of her expenses. She would set out in early May and was not asking for her fare back to Florence. Sarah was probably another servant, who wished or needed to go home herself. Smith did the sums and concluded that 15 Napoleons would cover the children's expenses, including food and clothing. He respectfully asked Mrs Nicholl for another modest amount to cover the anticipated shortfall and also asked her to send him instructions as to how the children were to be conveyed to her.

The issue now was timing. It was thought wise to send Sarah and the children off in the first week of May, the time of the great seasonal migration back northwards, when they would have the company of another family en route. Not having heard from Mrs Nicholl, Smith instructed Sarah (who was paid only as far as London) to take the children to his brother, Henry Smith, principal of Morden College at Blackheath. By early June Sarah had faithfully performed her charge, Mrs Nicholl's servant had taken delivery of James and John, and Mrs Nicholl had sent another £6. Given the tragedy of their mother's death, the Russell children were luckier than they might have been. James, at least, survived and can be traced in the English censuses later in the century. The woodman was paid off and Russell was enabled to meet another debt of 40 pauls to General Sewell's servant 'at the Baths'.

Here we glimpse relationships between servants. Russell seems to have regarded what he owed General Sewell's servant as a kind of debt of honour, which he wanted to pay himself out of savings. Was it a small gambling debt or the repayment of a loan? We may know a little more about the man to whom it was owed. James Bansfield died on 11 January 1862 at the age of 49 and was buried in the Sewell family plot in the English cemetery, with an inscription which hailed him, in the words of the *Epistle to Philemon,* 'not now as a servant, above a servant, a brother beloved'. He had been 'for 20 years the faithful and devoted servant of General Sir W. H. Sewell K.C.B, by whose widow this tomb was raised'. Lady Sewell had been overtaken by events, for her husband had died only 2 months after Bansfield.

Lord Burghersh had much earlier erected a monument over a servant's grave, when his groom Samuel Chappell died aged 37 in July 1824 and was buried in the old cemetery at Leghorn. He was commemorated as 'an honest man and faithful servant' who since 1808 had traipsed over the continent in his Lordship's service, from the Peninsula to Germany, France and Naples. In May 1829 Chappell was joined in the same cemetery by Andrew Jordan, who died at Lucca having spent 60 of his 72 years serving 'faithfully and confidentially as coachman in the family of Sir Robert Gore Booth Bart' (presumably he was not a coachman at the age of 12).[13]

Female servants sometimes achieved a special degree of intimacy with their employers. On 8 October 1852 John Maquay recorded that 'Mrs Burdett was to have spent today in the country with us but the death of her friend Mrs Tom Trollope's favourite maid obliges her to remain with her'. This is complemented by an inscription in the English cemetery which describes Elisabeth Shinner as 'for more than twenty years the faithful servant and attached friend of those who laid her body here'. Trollope echoes these sentiments in his memoirs: they all felt Elisabeth's death as that of a member of the family.[14] A sum of 572 *paoli* was spent to give her a first-rate funeral. As these examples show, not all master–servant relationships were problematic, and it was common for Anglo-Florentine testators to leave bequests to their Italian servants. John's friend Edward Horne named an Italian cook and another Italian servant in his will, but all his 'furniture, plate & linen & carriages and harness' went to his principal servant Heinrich Köppe, who was evidently neither Italian nor English. In early 1843 Köppe had been in service in Florence with a 'signor Berwitz', so it is likely that Horne had recruited him locally. John, administering Horne's estate, had a 'scene' with 'Enrico' shortly after his death.[15]

Sometimes it is not a monumental inscription but a mere note in the burial register that informs us of the status or origin of the deceased. Thus we learn about Edward Pearson, who died of consumption at the age of 37 in December 1833. He was servant to Thomas Tenison, who to judge from the Vieusseux subscription books had spent most of his time in Florence since late 1829. Charles or Caleb Hopkins of Lambeth succumbed to 'apoplexy' in March 1834 only a few months before the death of his employer, Miss Harriet Disbrowe. Elizabeth Martin from Stithians in Cornwall, a servant to Lady Don, died suddenly in 1836, without any previous illness; she was only in her thirties. The commonplace experience of going into service, for these individuals and many others, resulted in their transplantation to a foreign clime and a foreign graveyard.

There were happier outcomes. Perhaps it was in succession to the unfortunate Elizabeth Martin that Lady Don engaged another servant called Mary Deards. When her ladyship made her will in February 1842 Mary merited a legacy of £40, to be paid annually in two equal instalments; so too did her butler James Haynes.[16] In the following July Mary and James were married. It is quite possible that they had met in Lady Don's household, for he was a native of Leicestershire while Mary came from Ware in Hertfordshire. By the end of 1850 Mary had given birth to five daughters (one of whom had died) and a son. Lady Don was rather given to adding codicils to her will and between 1849 and 1852 James Haynes was called upon to witness five of them. It is not always easy to discover what became of British servants after their years in Tuscany, but it appears that at some time after Lady Don's death in 1855 Haynes set himself up as a farmer near Exeter and gave his children an education which enabled his daughters to work as governesses and a son to become a clerk and then an accountant. We cannot know what recollections he and his children preserved of their years in Florence, but for as long as they lived the latter would tell the census-takers that they were British subjects born in Tuscany.

John Maquay gives some insights into the process of obtaining servants, but one method, for servants and employers alike, was to use the newspapers. A couple who advertised in the *Times* on 2 November 1847 wanted employment 'as travelling servants'. The husband was Swiss, the wife a Florentine; they spoke French, German, English and Italian; could offer excellent references and had no objection to separate engagements. On the 27th of the same month, in Florence, a young man advertised in the *Tuscan Athenaeum* indicating that he was desirous of travelling with a family as a secretary; he taught French, German and Italian and claimed to speak English, Spanish, Latin, Russian and Polish. Salary, he said, was of little importance. In the same issue an Italian lady's maid who was willing to make herself useful in a family thought fit to state (in English) that she spoke French. Perhaps she was successful, but the young man had to go on advertising.

Fate clearly sometimes deposited Italian servants in the English watering-places which were so much frequented by continental travellers. In the *Times* of 18 May 1850 a 'Butler or Butler and Valet' advertised from an address in Bath, claiming to be 'a steady trustworthy servant from Florence, with five years' good character'. He was 35 and spoke English, French and Italian well. From Leamington Spa, on the following 17 July, 'A native of Florence who speaks the purest Italian, seeks a SITUATION as LADY'S MAID. Perfectly understands her business, speaks French and English sufficiently, is middle-aged, remarkably active, and can have the best recommendations'. Advertisements reveal also that returned travellers sometimes wished to get rid of their Italian servants as humanely as possible. On 23 August 1846 a lady was 'desirous of sending back her MAID (a native of Tuscany) to Italy, can RECOMMEND her highly to wait upon a lady, or take charge of children, going to that country, and will pay her travelling expenses as far as Florence'. Was the maid homesick, had the family on returning to England discovered that she was less help there than in Tuscany or had it been agreed in advance that she would be sent back? On 14 January 1858 a lady announced in the *Times* that she wanted 'an ITALIAN WET-NURSE wishing to return to Florence or Rome immediately'. Presumably she thought it likely that such a person would have come to England with another family.

In a distinct category was the courier, who was mobile by definition. On 14 January 1831 the *Times* reported a lawsuit brought by Joseph Callo, who in August 1827 had been engaged for 12 months at £10 a month as courier to a Mrs Brouncher of Manchester Square. He complained that he had been 'causelessly' turned off at Florence and was now suing for damages, the wages he should have received and £25 to cover the expenses of his journey from Florence to England to bring his case. The hearing was enlivened by the testimony of Mary Ann Sleep, 'an interesting-looking female' who had accompanied the family as lady's maid. She stated that, having settled in at Florence for the winter, Mrs Brouncher had dismissed Callo in December on the grounds that she could get someone else cheaper. Under cross-examination (by none other than Mr Scarlett, the father of the future Secretary of Legation at Florence) Miss Sleep admitted that she had herself left the family a week later and taken service with Mrs Hope Johnstone, who later also engaged Callo as courier; she denied that there was any improper relationship between them. The Brounchers contended that Callo had been insolent and disobedient and fully deserved his dismissal, but were nonetheless willing to pay him something in compensation. The judge pointed out that Callo had obtained another situation immediately, but the jury appear to have thought that there was something in his claim, for they awarded him a substantial £145, subject to the deduction of anything he had already received. Francesco and Rosa Madiai became celebrated examples of the courier and the maid who had seen service with English families.

Not all British servants went home, even when they ceased to be servants. In April 1850 the English Church in Florence needed a new *custode*.[17] Three Englishmen were among the applicants, but one was disqualified by his inability to write. George Walton, who had applied for the post when it was vacant 5 years previously, had served Rowland Standish for 17 years and was also able to produce certificates from three prominent Leghorn residents: Mr Sandiford, Dr Foster and Mr Gower. Robert Cox, who supplied seven testimonials, had been a servant and groom, and was now a lodging-house keeper. He had served for 10 months in 1847 with Mr C. Desloges; Mrs Hoare provided a testimonial to his service, not further particularized, and a Mrs Sarah Edwards, housekeeper (whose is not stated), gave him a character reference, as did Dr Trotman. He had at one time been groom to Mr Scarlett, who said that he was honest, and Randall Plunkett testified that he had lived with him for 3 months as a groom and was active, sober and intelligent.

The successful applicant, Elisa Iandelli, was also English, despite her married name. Born Elisa Mackrill, she had been in service with Lady Popham and was also able to produce references from John Maquay, Captain Pakenham and Samuel Lowe. It is possible that her husband was the saddler whom John Maquay patronized from time to time. Elisa's had probably been a Catholic marriage, but she remained a Protestant, for when she died in 1877 aged 71 she was buried in the English cemetery, where an inscription erected by her children paid tribute to 'her sterling worth unassuming christian piety and noble deeds of charity'.[18] Her career, like those of Cox and Walton, shows how servants were passed from hand to hand between British expatriate households. Later in her Florentine life, also like Cox, she provided board and lodging near the Ponte Carraia.[19]

Robert Cox had left England around 1845 and in March 1848 was married at the embassy to Margaret Jackson Ward. They had seven recorded children in Florence, and a rough chronology of Cox's employment after 1850 can be constructed from their baptismal records. In June 1853 he was still called a lodging-house keeper; in May 1856 he was 'employed on the railway', and in October 1858 'lately employed on the railway'. In October 1861, he was still, or again, employed on the railway; but in January 1865 he was once more described as a lodging-house keeper. The couple may have had the lodging house throughout, for Margaret could have run it in Robert's absence. She died in 1882 aged 58, Robert in 1883 aged 63. This ordinary working man had spent at least 35 years earning his living in Italy, to all appearances entirely respectable and no trouble to anyone.

The Coxes were typical in several respects. We have already seen evidence of other Britons who worked on the Tuscan railways. Many of the grooms and coachmen employed by British families were British, often brought out with them (as Cox may have been). From time to time some of them played a subsidiary role as jockeys in the races on the Cascine. An exceptional case was Thomas Ward, a Yorkshireman, who became a favourite of Duke Charles of Lucca and rose from directing his stables to become his chief finance minister, ennobled as Baron Ward.[20] Another Yorkshireman, Duncan Nevin, married a widow called Mary Judge in Florence in 1845 and was identified as groom to the former Duke of Lucca when their daughter was baptized in 1852. He probably served more than one master during his time in Italy, for he won Arthur Vansittart's praise when he rode for Prince Poniatowksi in 1841.[21] Richard Perry Harvey, a native of Devon, who was married to Mary Dunn in Florence in 1842, was also employed by the Duke of Lucca. His son Charles, baptized at Bagni in July 1843, may well have been named after the Duke; one of his other children was a banker in Florence in the 1880s.

Also not untypical was the transition the Coxes made from domestic service to running a lodging house. Francesco and Rose Madiai had done likewise. Ferdinando Rindi, who by 1863 was running a modest hotel, the Corona d'Italia, in Via Palestro, had an English wife called Jane. When they had a son baptized in 1851, Rindi was a servant and Jane may well have been too.[22] The most illustrious of servants turned hoteliers, Madame Hombert, was neither Italian nor English, but was exceedingly well known to the British in Florence and extensively patronized by them. Fanny Margerie came to Florence as a chambermaid with her French employer in 1808; was married there to a *valet de chambre*, Robert Hombert; and stayed with him when the French left.[23] Stendhal (who always calls her 'Imbert') thought she provided an excellent *table d'hôte*, but the traveller would have to share it with thirty Englishmen. Stendhal had apparently done so himself, for he says he has based his conclusions about the Florentine character partly 'upon impressions gathered *à l'anglaise,* that is around the *table d'hôte* provided by signora Imbert'.[24] John Maquay stayed with her when he arrived in Florence shortly after New Year 1823 and later that same year Leigh Hunt was doing likewise when he subscribed to Vieusseux. Her premises were then in the Palazzo Acciaiuoli, near the Ponte Vecchio.[25]

Sinclair had some reservations about the hotel, although it was 'delightfully situated' and 'much frequented by the English'. At much the same date James Cobbett regarded it as a very good bargain 'the best house, take it altogether, that we have found anywhere'. The prospective traveller could compare several accounts of Mme Hombert's hospitality, with prices. Dr William Boyd thought her hotel the best place for a single man newly arrived in Florence and like James

Cobbett spelled out her charges, but by the time his guidebook was published she was on the move.[26] On 23 February 1830 she announced in the *Gazzetta* that she was transferring her hotel to the Palazzo Torrigiani in Via Porta Rossa, near Santa Trinità and the Gabinetto Letterario (i.e. Vieusseux). A humorous piece in Daniel MacCarthy's *Tablet* imagined the trials of an English bachelor who wanted to find both a wife and the 'best society' in Florence. He went 'to a hotel in one of the back slums called Madame Hombert Porta Rossa where I understood I should meet the very best society, and pay 11 pauls a day'. His quest was unsuccessful.[27] In 1834 Madame purchased Palazzo Feroni in Piazza S. Trinità, where she opened the Hotel de l'Europe, and she also ran a *Hotel garni* (loosely, 'bed and breakfast') in Piazza Pitti, which seems to have been exceedingly popular with English visitors. Her many guests were usually content to say that they were staying with Madame Hombert, or at her hotel, *locanda* or *casa*, without specifying the address. She died in 1843 and by 1846 all references to her name cease.

The first edition of *Murray's Handbook* (1842) reviewed the current state of the Florentine hotels.[28] The famous Schneiderff's had 'greatly fallen off'. This hotel, on the south bank of the river close to the Ponte Carraia, was a Florentine landmark for a lengthy period, as well as a standing challenge to the spelling of its English clients, to judge by the Vieusseux subscription books. Lord William Russell thought in 1822 that 'tho good [it] does not merit its great reputation'. His view that it was 'immensely dear' was confirmed by James Cobbett later in the decade. Dinner cost at least '10 pauls (4s 6d); but then it is always a better dinner than any body should *wish to have*'.[29] *Murray's* analysis concluded that Madame Hombert's Hotel d'Europe was probably one of the best for 'moderate persons'. The Nord, also in Piazza Santa Trinità, was small and quiet with an excellent *table d'hote*. The York was good and principally frequented by commercial travellers; the Grande Bretagne also was good but more expensive than the Europe; the Albergo dell'Arno was only tolerable. The Porta Rossa was 'an economical house, and much resorted to by French and Germans'. The Hotel d'Italie, alternatively Hotel Balbi (recte Baldi), faced the Arno and was to be avoided during the summer because of the heat and the mosquitoes.

This particular hazard had received humorous treatment from George Irby, the future Lord Boston, in a piece entitled 'The Autobiography of a Gnat' which he contributed to Daniel MacCarthy's *Tablet* in 1835. The gnat in question was born under the Hotel de la Grande Bretagne, on the sunny (that is the north) side of the Arno. Irby himself stayed there in 1833.

> The national sign, and its warm situation, luckily for my first taste of our favourite food, tempted many strangers from Britannia's cloudy isles to sojourn there, and a long train of equipages, containing a colony, usually called in the phraseology of that people 'a small family' (the children being ten in number) had that morning arrived, anxiously expecting a quiet and sound repose after a long journey.

The gnat describes the nocturnal depredations carried out on these unfortunates, but as dawn approaches his mother withdraws high up in the bed-curtains before returning to the Arno. Aware that a 'strict search' will be made for them at the Grande Bretagne they cross the river to the Quatre Nations, where the young gnat takes up his position in 'a manifold mass of drapery, tastefully arranged by our friend Bonajuti expressly for our use' and awaits his prey, a 17-year-old English girl of such beauty that out of compassion he confines his attentions to her finger. Rejoining his mother, he learns that his father has rashly returned to the Grande Bretagne and been squashed by a fat chambermaid. At this moment a swallow dives and carries off his mother; the gnat is an orphan.

When George and Elizabeth Maquay arrived in Florence in 1815 their daughter Betsy intriguingly recorded in her journal that the York Hotel was kept by an Englishwoman who had lived there for 20 years. Unfortunately she does not give this woman a name, but there is a faint clue in the diary of her uncle John, who had already been some days in the same hotel and gives an uninviting picture of their ground-floor rooms, where he found 'Bug, Fleas, Lizard, Mouse & Scorpion' in his wife's bed. A little later he seems to refer to the landlady as 'Mrs S'.[30] In 1820 a Domenico Sambalino was running the 'Hotel de Yorck' in Via Forca.[31] Is it possible that the Englishwoman who had been able to live in Florence through the years of French occupation was Signora Sambalino?

Ferdinando and Jane Rindi much later sound like an Anglo-Italian couple, as of course were Ferdinando and Elizabeth Romagnuoli. The Signor Baldi who in 1847 was running both the Hotel d'Italie and the Iles Britanniques had an English wife.[32] We know more about the helpmeet of Pietro Pagnini, whose three hotels at Bagni received endless praise from the guidebooks. Jousiffe declared that Pagnini 'is an obliging and agreeable man; he not only speaks English fluently, but he understands and attends himself to the comforts of English travellers; his kitchen department is excellent'.[33] If Pagnini, 'clever and enterprising' according to *Murray's*, spoke English fluently, there was a reason for it apart from the needs of business. His wife ('most active and helpful') was born Margaret Harrison of Hebburn Colliery near Newcastle, so there seems to have been little reason for the *Satirist* on 8 November 1840 to present her as a cockney. She died in 1867 and was laid to rest in the little Protestant cemetery at Bagni; hers had presumably been a mixed marriage.

It was with Pagnini that Colonel and Mrs Stisted stayed on their first visit to Bagni in 1834. Some years later it was reported that his hotel scored a point over the nearby Albergo de la Grande Bretagne and Albergo di Londra by having its name written in English in 'gigantic characters' on its front. Pagnini established a kind of club in the hotel, called the *Circolo di Riunione,* which incorporated a library, reading-room, billiard-room and card-room, all overlooking 'a picturesque garden and shrubbery.' The purpose was to offer a 'place of general rendezvous' as an alternative to the Casino. An entry in the minute-book of the Pisa Book Club in 1846 reveals that Pagnini had made an arrangement by which he borrowed books from the Club until the end of September, paying 30 *francesconi* for the use of them; members of his 'Circle' were governed by the same rules and had the same privileges as the 'original members' of the Book Club at Pisa, another reminder that much of Anglo-Pisan society resorted to Bagni during the summer.[34]

There were a few native Britons (other than the wives of Italians) in the hotel business in Tuscany. One was a rather difficult character, to judge by an extraordinary exchange in the Foreign Office correspondence for 1826. John Featherstonehaugh's hotel in Piazza San Gaetano in Florence was in business by September 1822. On 4 January 1823 the proprietor announced in the *Gazzetta* that it was modelled on English hotels (*Locande d'Inghilterra*) and would provide quarters to satisfy any person or family. Vieusseux subscribers sometimes call it the 'English hotel'. John Maquay mentioned it already in February 1823 and it had the privilege of accommodating Lady Blessington in 1826. In that year's edition of her guidebook, Mrs Starke called it 'excellent'. However there were storm-clouds on the horizon.

Early in June 1826 Strangways warned the Foreign Office that Featherstonehaugh, 'master of an English hotel in Florence', had been writing defamatory letters to certain people in Leghorn about a Mr Robert Wemyss.[35] Strangways had now heard that Featherstonehaugh had been arrested, in consequence of a libellous letter written to Mr Dunn of Leghorn, and was claiming the protection of the legation, not apparently reflecting (as Strangways remarked) that Wemyss might be equally entitled to it. On 20 June, the hotelier wrote a letter of complaint to the Foreign Secretary, George Canning, accompanied by a lengthy memorial setting forth his grievances. To him, the affair constituted a 'hitherto unheard of and most unmerited Outrage' for which Strangways as much as Wemyss was responsible.

Strangways described Wemyss as 'an English gentleman who has resided above a year in this country, lately at Leghorn'; Featherstonehaugh called him a habitual drunkard.[36] He had taken apartments at Featherstonehaugh's hotel in April 1825 and for a couple of days his dinner was regularly provided. On the third day, he sent his servant to say that he had engaged private lodgings and would settle his account with Featherstonehaugh before he left Florence. All of this was quite usual. However, according to the aggrieved hotelier, repeated efforts to secure payment were ignored. He began a lengthy campaign of letters which met with no response. On 23 March 1826 he wrote warning Wemyss that he would expose his improper conduct in the English newspapers, but the letter was returned to him

having the name of Wemyss erased and directed to me at Florence. Aware that Mr Wemyss is seldom capable (from constant intoxication) to direct a letter, I endeavoured to ascertain and very soon proved the handwriting to be of Mr Dunn (a Man Miliner [*sic*] and dealer in English Goods at Leghorn) another of Mr W's intimate associates, and to whose Shop he was in the habit of going almost every day to drink. Exasperated at such impertinence from a Man I had never seen, I wrote to Mr Dunn to know upon what Authority he had dared to return my letter addressed to Mr Wemyss, and observed that it had been more to his credit to attend to his own affairs, than to aspire to the Service of so despicable a drunkard as Mr Wemyss. In a few days I was summoned before the Commissaire de Police to know if I was the author of the letter.

In another outburst, Featherstonehaugh said he had once thought Mr Dunn 'a respectable counter-jumper' but that he should have restricted his attention to his 'threads, tapes and other useful articles for Chambermaids'.

Featherstonehaugh was arrested and imprisoned, and unsuccessfully tried to secure Strangways's intervention. To the cast-list of his enemies, which Strangways had now joined, we have to add the Commissary of Police, who had long been determined 'to decide every case against me right or wrong' (Featherstonehaugh could supply a long list of examples). On 5 June he wrote to Strangways, who had in the meantime learned the cause of his confinement (which was to last 5 days) from Prince Corsini's secretary.

> The indifference with which you have treated my imprisonment convinces me that so far from being ignorant of the Affaire, you were informed, approved, and advised this hitherto unheard of Outrage – In a few Hours the time will be expired, but Tomorrow's Post will convey to the British Parliament a full statement of the Case, and I doubt not that a Generous British Nation will soon redress my wrongs, to obtain which I will with pleasure expend my last Shilling, and shed the last drop of blood that now boils with indignation. I fear my God, but fear no human Being, however high his Rank. I have the Honor to subscribe myself A poor oppressed Englishman.

Featherstonehaugh took his stand, as the British were naturally inclined to do, on the impropriety of imprisonment without trial, and told Strangways that Lord Burghersh would have dealt very differently with the matter.

Strangways may have seemed evasive about the legality of the imprisonment, but he reminded Featherstonehaugh that it was (and always had been) open to him to pursue his debt through the Tuscan courts. The latter became increasingly convinced that Strangways had not merely connived at his imprisonment but actively encouraged it. On 6 June Strangways told the Foreign Secretary that Wemyss had asked him in April to lay his complaint against Featherstonehaugh before the Tuscan Government, which he had initially been unwilling to do; but Wemyss had insisted on his right to be protected from insult, claiming he owed Featherstonehaugh nothing. Then the embattled Secretary was asked by Mrs Featherstonehaugh to intervene when her husband was imprisoned. The Foreign Office response was that Strangways should simply not have got involved. British subjects abroad had no right to demand protection against local laws which, it seemed, had operated unexceptionably in this case. Informed of this verdict, Featherstonehaugh announced his intention of becoming a naturalized Tuscan subject, 'to avoid in future the Tyranny and unjust persecution of British

Ambassadors or Chargés d'Affaires'; he hoped 'to forget that it has been my misfortune to be born a Briton'.[37]

References to the hotel in the Vieusseux registers continue down to 1830, although, perhaps significantly, subscribers often said that they were staying with 'Mad. Featherstonehaugh'. On 6 August 1835 the *Gazzetta* announced that there was to be a sale of furniture and fittings at 'the former Locanda called the Europa, Piazza San Gaetano No. 4193', when such items as fire-screens, writing-desks, carpets and beds would be obtainable at 40 per cent below current prices.

Another English purveyor of accommodation arguably suffered worse. According to Mrs Starke, Madame Merveilleux du Plantis was 'an English lady of high respectability, married to a Captain in the Royal Navy of France'. She let lodgings in Piazza Santa Maria Novella where 'travellers may be comfortably accommodated with board and lodging, for a moderate price'.[38] This lady, whose daughters Zoide and Louisa lived with her, entertained some noteworthy guests, including the future Mrs Charles Darwin in 1825. Earlier, her premises had been located in the Palazzo Marini in Via Valfonda, where Mary Shelley gave birth to her son Percy Florence. Today a plaque on a building across the road from the railway station commemorates the fact that Shelley wrote the *Ode to the West Wind* on this site. Unfortunately the Shelleys' stay ended unhappily, for it seems that they carried off not only some of the landlady's spoons but 'her "Chiroplast", a device designed to teach piano students the correct hand positions'.[39]

Losing spoons and even the Chiroplast was as nothing to the troubles that awaited the unfortunate lady, if we can believe her will, which bears very little resemblance to the normal will, largely because, as she said, she had virtually nothing to leave. She and her family had fallen victim in Florence to a German confidence trickster who bore many names including that of the Baron de Falkenstein, although he was known to them as Mr Piper. Under this name he taught the German language and Madame's daughters were among his many pupils. Alas, he 'contrived to rob me of my daughter Zoide Adelaide my house my furniture and all that I possessed and having left a name covered with opprobrium in France Spain and England he is no[w?] residing in Frankfurt on the Main'. Madame retired to England with her other daughter Louise and what little they had left. Louise died in Southampton in 1838 and her mother followed her in 1841 in London, leaving her blessing and a few trinkets to the unfortunate Zoide if she could be found.[40]

Much of what we know about Madame Merveilleux du Plantis and John Featherstonehaugh we know because in their very different ways they got into trouble. A quite different and more tranquil career unfolded alongside and outlasted theirs, providing England's modest answer to Madame Hombert. In 1838 *The Catholic Directory, Ecclesiastical Register, and Almanac* carried the following advertisement, under the heading 'Boarding Houses. Italy – Florence':

A Catholic Lady, of well-known respectability, having established, more than ten years since, a select Boarding-House in the above delightful City, is advised by her

Friends to make her Establishment better known to the Catholic World, through the medium of this Directory. Ladies, Gentlemen, or Families, travelling on the Continent, resting at Florence, and being unwilling to form an establishment of their own there, will find every domestic comfort they can desire in a quiet and respectable home. The charge (including every expense, except extra fires in the winter) is, for two months certain, One Dollar, or Four Shillings and Sixpence per Day, each person. Address, Mrs F. Clark, Lungo l'Arno, Florence.

Mrs Clark died in her seventieth year on 24 April 1842 and was buried at Santa Maria Novella. The inscription erected by her grieving children gave her maiden name as Brent, and she can probably be identified as the Frances Brent who married a calico printer called William Clark in Manchester on 13 January 1794; she herself was a native of Liverpool. When and why she came to Italy we do not know, but the evidence of the Vieusseux subscription lists is that she was already running a boarding-house in Florence in July 1822. As time went by she gained in reputation and attracted the attention of the guidebooks.

It seems that like Madame Hombert, albeit on a smaller scale, Mrs Clark had more than one set of premises. When the Maquays arrived in Florence in the autumn of 1830 John 'drove to Mrs Clark 1491 Piazza Gaetaneo [sic] where rooms were taken for us in Pension, no one in the house but an old Scotch maid'.[41] When Mrs Starke first mentioned Mrs Clark, a few years later, she too located the hotel in this piazza, but already in 1823 a Dr Chisholm, subscribing to Vieusseux, said that he was staying at 'Mrs F Clarke, Lung'Arno'. In later years, certainly, it was her house on the southern side of the Arno that was well known. It was celebrated at length by Captain Jousiffe in 1840, and his description of its amenities and charges is worth quoting *in extenso* as an example of what the modestly affluent British tourist might expect to pay.[42] It was 'very agreeably situated':

It has long had the reputation of being a highly respectable and very comfortable house. The apartments are numerous and very neatly and conveniently furnished; most of them command pleasing views of the Arno and the principal promenade on the opposite side of the river.

| For breakfast, dinner, tea and bed-room | 10 pauls a day |
| " " " " for servant | 6 " |

In winter half a paul is charged extra for each person, for drawing-room, fire and lights.

	Extras	
For	a friend to find	6 pauls per day
	a basket of wood	4 "
	four bundles brush-wood	1 "
	a pair of wax-lights	3 "
	a warm bath	4 "

a cold bath	2 "	
stand for a carriage	5 pauls a week	
stall for a horse	5 "	

Mrs Clark and her daughter conduct their house in a highly creditable manner, and much to the satisfaction of the numerous very respectable families who resort to their clean and comfortable establishment; they are very agreeable, and always anxiously alive to the wants of their guests. In 1838 they were so full that many families were obliged to wait at their hotels until they could be received. Parties desiring apartments at their house would do well to write a few days previous to their arrival.

Murray's believed that the establishment was particularly suitable for ladies and for families unacquainted with Florence and the language. The business was still functioning in the 1860s. Henry Cole, in Italy to buy works of art for the South Kensington Museum, stayed there and described its proprietor, Mrs Clark Molini, as 'a little fat quaint old lady with a great deal of native English sense if not polish'. This was surely Mrs Clark's daughter.[43] Here Cole met Dr Giuseppe Molini, 'a bookseller and an intelligent man' who had succeeded to the celebrated business established by his father. The marital linkage between the English Catholic Clarks who for years ran a hotel in Florence and the Molini who for years ran a business with a branch in London seems appropriate.

One very young Englishman owned a Florentine hotel but may never have had anything to do with running it. On 11 May 1839 the guardians of the infant Walter Kennedy Lawrie (*i tutori Laurier*) announced in the *Gazzetta* the dissolution of their partnership with Vincenzo Taffetani, with whom they had jointly run the Albergo Reale dell'Arno. On 11 June, the guardians, Luigi and Pietro Aretini, further announced the reopening of the hotel under the direction of the obviously related Alessandro Aretini. It was clearly the young Lawrie's property; what is not clear is whether his father, who had died on 29 November 1837, had bequeathed the hotel to him or whether it was a subsequent investment by the Aretini in his name. Their partnership with Taffetani had existed at least since March 1838 (a few months after the elder Lawrie's death) but Taffetani had been running the hotel, on the sunny northern side of the Arno near the Ponte Vecchio, since the previous May. Now that the partnership was ended he proposed to reopen the Quattro Nazioni on the opposite bank of the Arno.

At Leghorn a Scottish ex-sailor, David Thomson, was running the Hotel San Marco in time to receive Mrs Starke's recommendation in her 1826 edition.[44] To judge by the recorded baptisms of his children, he had been established in the city ever since the end of the Napoleonic wars. He enjoyed some distinguished patronage, as when the king of Naples (preserving the strictest incognito, according to the *Times*) stayed in his hotel during a brief visit to Leghorn in June 1836. In 1842 *Murray's* still judged his to be much the best hotel in the town, but it was now in recently built premises in the Piazza de' Cappucini on the quayside. *Murray's* eulogium evoked what British travellers were looking for:

> for comfort, cleanliness, and attention, [it] cannot be exceeded. It is furnished in the best style of an English gentleman's house, and Mrs Thomson is an excellent manager in every respect; and families remaining for the bathing season may be comfortably and economically lodged. The charges are very moderate.

Thomson's reputation with the natives had its uses for his fellow-countrymen. The new arrival at Leghorn was advised to tell the boatmen that Mr Thomson (near whose door he would be landed) would settle with them; otherwise they would infallibly cheat him. *Murray's* also suggested that 'families about to reside for a time in Florence, would do well to get their supplies of tea from Leghorn, which they can effect more economically through Mr Thompson [*sic*], the hotel-keeper there'. Premises previously occupied by Thomson had by now become Fisher's Hotel, 'also a good house, though not in so convenient a situation'.[45]

Henry Fisher was another early post-war arrival at Leghorn, where he was married to Eliza Sewell in 1817. The young women who tended to John Maquay's children were among the 9 daughters that (along with one son) had been born to the couple by 1831. If the *Satirist* was to be believed (24 January 1841), Fisher's hospitality was abused by Mr Wentworth Beaumont ('nasty beast Beaumont', as the paper liked to call him) who 'thought to seduce a Miss Fisher at Leghorn, at whose father's hotel he stopped'. If it was the San Marco hotel that Fisher had taken over, it may soon have changed hands again. On 24 February 1842 the Florence shopkeeper Samuel Lowe announced in the *Gazzetta* that the Grande Albergo di S. Marco in Leghorn was still in being, 'equipped with everything that can make a stay more comfortable and more agreeable'. It was being managed by a Mr John Smith who would go to any amount of trouble to oblige. Late in 1844 this Mr Smith took it upon himself to organize and collect subscriptions in Leghorn to the fund in aid of sufferers by the Florentine flood.[46]

Of all Florentine hoteliers, perhaps the most interesting was Silvestro Gasperini, who well illustrates the proposition that one man in his time plays many parts. Gasperini was hotelier, coach-builder and more besides. In the 1820s Mrs Starke declared that his inn was 'excellent' and the dinners there 'better cooked and more comfortably served than at any of the other hotels'. (Cobbett however called it 'a second-rate house' and 'decidedly' preferred Mme Hombert.) It was in the Piazza S. Trinità and was known alternatively as the Pellicano or the Hotel des Armes d'Angleterre.[47] Vieusseux subscribers sometimes simply called it 'Gasperini's'. Mrs Starke went on to add that 'Gasperini repairs English travelling coaches particularly well' and John Maquay employed him in this capacity on at least one occasion. Vansittart called him 'a professor of many sciences, and a dabbler in many professions', and endorsed Mrs Starke's high opinion of his hotel and cuisine.[48]

For Vansittart, Gasperini was 'a tip-top coach-maker'. He confessed to having been surprised, when he arrived in Florence, to see so many carriages of the best make (Baxter, Hobson, Adams) in the streets, until he realized that they were all made by Gasperini and 'stamped to order'. Florentines wanted to look like the owners of English carriages, and Englishmen homeward-bound wanted to avoid paying duty 'by passing off Tuscan-built drags as of British manufacture'. Vansittart went on to relate how the coachbuilder Adams, when staying in Gasperini's hotel, confronted his landlord when he discovered that he was the perpetrator of forgeries he had detected with his own eyes. Gasperini disarmed him by admitting that he had 'borrowed' his name and gave him permission to use his freely in return. In the *Tuscan Athenaeum* on 13 November 1847 Gasperini advertised a Britzka built by Hobson of London, for which he wanted £50 sterling; one may entertain one's suspicions.

In 1841 the *European Indicator* joined the chorus of praise, but made a further claim: 'M. Gasperini is I believe an Englishman [*sic*], at any rate he speaks excellent english.'[49] One might think that his excellent English had created a misleading impression, but there was more to it than that. In October 1813 Maria Gasperini, née Billington, was buried in the British cemetery at Leghorn. The inscription over her grave stated that she was aged 44, a native of Manchester and the wife of Silvestro Gasperini. She looks like the Maria Billington who was married to a man of that name at St James's Piccadilly on 8 April 1797. Clearly this was not the later carriage-builder and hotelier, but very probably his father. A Silvestro Gasperini ran a cafe in Via Legnaioli from at least 1817 to 1828, and this establishment was sometimes called the Pellicano.[50] Every year in the spring he applied to the Comune for permission to put tables and chairs outside his premises and to erect an awning during the summer season. Occasionally, like other cafe owners, he was rapped over the knuckles for abusing the conditions on which this permission was granted. The cafe surely became the hotel.

The first reference to a Vieusseux subscriber staying at 'Gasperini's' occurs in the first year of the reading-room's existence, 1820, when 'Gas' would have been a very young man; but, whenever he took over the management of the hotel and initiated his coach-building business, he was soon making other use of his linguistic skills and English connections. The clue to this, and to his approximate age, comes from a statement made on his behalf by the last Secretary of Legation, Edwin Corbett, in 1860:

Mr Silvester Gasperini has been in the employment of successive Ministers at the Court of Florence as Chancery Messenger and Extra Courier since the year 1821. He has received from all of them the highest testimonials. He is in the receipt of a regular salary of £80 a year from Her Majesty's Government. He is above 60 years of age and if deprived of his present salary, will be left without resources, at his time of life he can scarcely hope to find any other employment which would procure him the means of existence. I can bear willing testimony to the great value of his services to this Mission and to his zeal and intelligence during the year and a half I have been at Florence.[51]

Apparently Gasperini was now no longer a prospering hotelier (or carriage-builder). It is not easy to say when the hotel business ended. References to 'Gasperini's' in the Vieusseux registers seem to cease in 1846, but the Pelicano was still his address in 1847–1848, according to the *Tuscan Athenaeum*. On 25 January 1849 John Maquay referred to a 'fire at Gasperini' which entailed a lot of 'mailing' from the Bank.[52] Then, as already mentioned, in 1852 the letter from 'Britannicus' to Lord Derby criticized Scarlett for using the 'Pelecani' as a kind of agency and Gasperini as his 'factotum'.

This criticism was clearly more of Scarlett than of Gasperini, who retained the good opinion of the Legation. In 1853 he was being employed to convey despatches to and from Marseilles and sometimes Paris, and he had other uses besides. In May 1854 Scarlett told the Foreign Secretary that Gasperini

> was not only useful as a messenger but as a most efficient assistant at this legation in all disputes between British Subjects and the Tuscan authorities of an inferior class when the former get into scrapes & require to have things explained and interpreted for them, and by his intervention frequently much disagreeable correspondence has been averted.

The only pay he received at this date was for going twice a month as a courier to Marseilles. If (in consequence of British government cost-cutting) he was henceforth only to be sent 'on very special occasions' he would have to seek some other source of livelihood, 'and in my opinion a good & efficient servant will be lost to this mission'. Was this special pleading, or was Gasperini not still running his hotel? In the following year, Lord Normanby echoed Scarlett's judgement and, more strikingly, described Gasperini as a British subject.[53]

On 30 March 1860 the British Legation at Florence received a humorous obituary in the *Morning Post*:

> Strange to say, in the minds of all Tuscans the English Embassy was incarnated, not in the person of the Minister, but of a burly old Italian greatly resembling in appearance the old Duke of York. We believe, but are not quite sure, that some years ago he obtained from the English Government a pension for his long and faithful services. He certainly deserved it; and if this be not already the case, the Embassy, in its last moments, imitating the thoughtfulness of the Merry Monarch as he gasped out, 'Remember Nell!' has, we hope, given the parting charge – '*Don't forget* Gasperini!'

Neither Edwin Corbett, in charge of the expiring Mission, nor Sir James Hudson at Turin, forgot Gasperini. Hudson was only too willing to continue to use him in view of the increased volume of business that the Turin Mission now had to handle, but in July 1860 Gasperini died, his only surviving relative a nephew.[54]

Among Gasperini's associates in his capacity as coach-builder and racehorse-owner were two unquestionable Englishmen, James Huband and Joseph Gamgee. Writing as the 'Turfite', Arthur Vansittart advised 'the would-be driving youth', when in Florence, to apply to James Huband,

> for not another man in Florence can turn out, in the superior style he does, such neat equipages, such clever cattle, and such steady drivers. Choose, of the ninety tits in his stable, the spiciest clippers; down with the dibs; he will serve you right well. With him you will be satisfied, and to me grateful for the recommendation.[55]

Vansittart's description of Huband evokes a reality of the lives of sporting men: people who would never figure on their party guest lists could be bosom companions in the paddock. Huband is delineated in quasi-Dickensian terms (he had 'a somewhat sinister obliquity of vision') and comfortably placed in the social hierarchy:

> an out-and-outer, a thorough trump, and nothing but a good' un! Ushered into the world with but a wooden spoon in his chaff-box, he chopped it away, long since for silver one ... He deserves his success, if industry and indefatigable perseverance ever merited aught in this world.

Huband had inherited his business, for in 1836 he married Elizabeth, the widow of a Benjamin Mills who had died in 1834, having run a stable on the Lungarno near Schneiderff's hotel. Newly arrived back in Florence in the autumn of 1832, John Maquay noted that 'My horses are all at Mills'. The Wilmers hired 'a very neat little pony carriage' from Huband in the summer of 1836. According to Jousiffe,

> Here horses are taken great care of and attended to by English grooms. Mr Huband has also dry and secure standing for carriages of all descriptions, which are received and kept in order at a reasonable charge per day, week, or month. He has a number of ladies or gentlemen's saddle-horses, which may be hired for any period. He also buys or sells horses and carriages upon commission. Mr Huband conducts his business in a respectable way and deserves the patronage of his countrymen.[56]

Huband followed the example of other Florence traders by transplanting himself to Bagni during the summer months. Snow said that he had two locations there, one at the *Ponte*, the other near the English Church. Here too the horses were cared for by English grooms, and 'an English coachman of known worth is in attendance during the season'.[57] Huband died in 1851, leaving his property to the twice-widowed Elizabeth; it seems that the business continued to be represented at Bagni during the summer season.

Vansittart declared that for 'English saddlery, and whips, and clothing' Joseph Gamgee was 'superlative', and he had also just imported twenty-six 'clever nags' from England. Jousiffe knew that Gamgee was 'a member of the London Royal Veterinary College, has been several years established at Florence as veterinary surgeon, and livery-stable keeper'. His dependably superior saddlery, harness and so forth were manufactured by 'Whippy of London'; he could hire 'horses of a very superior description' to ladies or gentlemen. His business was 'upon an extensive scale; it is conducted on a most respectable system, and much to the satisfaction of all who patronise his establishment'.[58]

Gamgee had been settled in Florence since at least 1830, having already led a remarkable life.[59] A native of Essex who started work at the age of 9, he displayed a precocious talent for dealing with horses, which led to employment with a prince in Naples. Returning to England (on foot), he enrolled in the London Veterinary College and earned his diploma in 1823. He married in 1825 and with his wife went back to Italy, where their children were born. He made several moves during his years in Florence. In 1830 he was advertising from the Via della Vigna Vecchia, promising not only to cure horses of their ailments but to deliver farrier's work of unexampled precision. He assured the public that no item of his manufacture left the premises without his stamp upon it; they should accept no imitations. In November 1831 he made it known that he had moved across the Arno to the Via Pizzicotti, near the church of Santo Spirito and behind the Albergo di Quattro Nazioni. By the time of the Turfite and Jousiffe (1839–1840) his business was located in Piazza San Gaetano, where he had only recently moved, obtaining 'a spacious house stabling for the horses and a covered ride in which to exercise them'.[60] He never converted tenancy to ownership and was forced to move from Piazza San Gaetano when the property was bought over his head; his last address in Florence was in the Via Tornabuoni.

Gamgee became prosperous but never abandoned early frugal habits. An early riser, his one indulgence was a visit to the local cafe for breakfast and to read Galignani's *Messenger*. Any further leisure was spent in studying early Italian texts on the anatomy and diseases of the horse. All his children spoke Italian and French and the boys were required to learn German. Science and mathematics were at the centre of the boys' activity, which they turned to good account in their later careers. All the children were engaged in the keeping of silkworms, whose products they went to the market to sell. Music and dancing also figured on the curriculum, and Gamgee's daughter Clementina was later able to offer the teaching of Italian and music in Edinburgh. Gamgee himself funded a school in the 1830s, as well as campaigning for an English circulating library. His sons returned to Britain to initiate distinguished careers and Gamgee followed them in 1855; he died in Edinburgh in 1895 at the age of 94. In 1859 his daughter Emma was married in Paris to a Florentine physician, Lorenzo Capei, the son of an eminent lawyer.[61]

The British influx after 1814, and specifically the re-establishment of the Embassy, had created special opportunities for the bilingual Gasperini, but he was not the only one to seize the moment. In the spring of 1815 James Douglas, 'a native of England recently arrived in Florence', took space in the *Gazzetta* to advertise his intention of teaching English according to the most approved method. A little later he announced that together with Francesco Cheloni of Leghorn he had opened a school for the teaching of English, French and Italian, handwriting and arithmetic, but he later reverted to one-man operation and seems to have succeeded in making a living. In 1831 he was advertising a course for beginners in English, identifying himself as one of the teachers at the *Privato Istituto Letterario e Scientifico* in Via della Stufa, where he was already teaching more advanced students. Like others, he would either offer lessons at his own lodgings in Borgo San Jacopo, or attend his pupils at their private addresses.[62]

He was by no means alone. For a few years from late 1824 a Mr Johnson of London promised his students access to the 'beautiful verses' of Milton, Pope, Dryden, Thomson and others. Like his competitors, he would use either French or Italian as the medium of instruction.[63] In 1827 Mr Brown, another native of London, had devised a very simple method based on 'an ingenious choice of phrases' by means of which grammatical rules would be progressively inculcated, and his pupils exercised in hearing, speaking and writing. In October 1830 he announced that he had just returned to Florence after some months of absence, and again offered his services; he would also attend English families as a tutor.[64] It seems likely that young men on their travels sometimes hoped to earn a little pocket-money by offering tuition. That might account for the otherwise unknown Mr Wyatt, *nativo di Londra*, who hoped to get pupils in 1825, while Mr Patterson of the University of Oxford, who was fluent in French and German and offered English lessons early in 1834, undoubtedly fell into the gentlemanly category. By 1841 he was a member of the Inner Temple; married to a daughter of Sir Joseph Huddart, he spent enough time in Florence in 1842–1843 for Mrs Patterson to give birth to two children there.[65]

Some teachers advertised a variety of subjects. On 9 July 1831 Ferdinand Green offered to teach the young of both sexes not only singing and piano, but 'numerical-practical geometry, universal geography, and the principles of astronomy', using either English or French as his medium. The following month, a Mr McCarthy gave notice that he was continuing his school for young boys (*signorini*) both English and Italian in Borg'Ognissanti. As well as English he offered Latin, Greek, history, geography, chronology, arithmetic and calligraphy. The inclusion of Latin and Greek would have been bait for expatriates who wanted a classical education for their sons. In May 1834 the former secretary of the recently deceased Lord Wenlock, claiming to be among the most knowledgeable exponents of his own language and its pronunciation, would give lessons at the lodgings of his clients, who were to apply to Mr McCarthy in Via de' Servi.[66] In December of the same year, those interested in acquiring a pure accent, conversational facility, business English (*stile commerciale*) and a knowledge of the best English authors, were advised to contact Mr W. Keegan, who by his own account had a varied and interesting pedigree. He was a pupil of the English School at Rome, graduate of an (unnamed) continental university and well known (he said) for his works in French and English; on top of all this he had for some years run a hotel in London.[67]

Many, if not most, of these advertisers seem to have envisaged teaching on a one-to-one basis by private agreement, and only occasionally do we get a glimpse of an institutional framework. Mr Douglas implied that he taught classes at an 'institute' and Mr McCarthy spoke of his 'school' for boys. For 4 years between 1824 and Christmas 1828 Charles Armitage Brown sent his young son Carlino to an elementary school run by a Miss or Mrs Smith. He may have noticed her advertisement in the *Gazzetta* on 24 July 1824. She had moved from Borgo'Ognissanti to Via del Giglio, where she would impart English, the beginnings of French, arithmetic, history and geography, and for 'young ladies' the feminine accomplishments. Walter Savage Landor described the school as comprising about a dozen small children, with Italian, dancing, drawing and 'accounts' in its curriculum. At the end of 1828 Brown took his son's education over himself.[68] Some 20 years later, a Mlle Dupre, apparently English, opened a 'well recommended' school for girls; she charged £50 per annum 'for all branches of general female education'. The English chaplain attended to impart religious instruction.[69]

Other female teachers expected to work within a domestic framework. Early in 1822 an English governess (*istitutrice*), who could offer the grammatical teaching of English and French, arithmetic, geography, pianoforte and other genteel pursuits, referred those interested to James Douglas in Via Ghibellina.[70] It was at just this time that Claire Clairmont, Mary Shelley's half-sister and the mother of Lord Byron's daughter Allegra, was serving a Russian family in Florence as governess. Female advertisers did not usually publicize their names and addresses. In the early 1850s Maquay and Pakenham could provide particulars of a Miss Henning who was said to be a 'good daily governess for children in French, music and general education'.[71] There were doubtless others, male and female. In 1856 Lady Don's bequest was used to rescue a Mr Box, who had come to Florence in the expectation of finding employment as a teacher, but was disappointed.[72]

Earlier, a teacher had used his linguistic skills to develop a second line of business. We know that John Thompson had already been teaching in private families when he announced in the *Gazzetta* of 17 January 1822 his intention of opening a school of English for Italians at Leghorn. In 1824 he was married there to the widow of a naval surgeon who was entitled to a pension by virtue of her late husband's service. In order to obtain payment she had to attend periodically at the consular office, accompanied by her present husband, to make affidavit. One day in 1828 Thompson ('formerly a schoolmaster') failed to doff his hat as he entered the door. This was regarded as a grave breach of the respect due to the representative of the British Crown, which Thompson allegedly compounded by declaring that the Consul meant less to him than his little dog. Falconar, who could be enraged by much less, laid a complaint with the Leghorn police against

Thompson, who found himself briefly in prison. He objected strenuously to this and gave his version of events in a petition to the Foreign Secretary.

Both Falconar and his vice-consul asserted that this was not Thompson's first offence and that whenever business had brought him to the office he had behaved in the same contemptuous and insolent manner. In a second petition, Thompson denied virtually everything that had been alleged against him and showed a nice gift for hyperbole when he asked Lord Burghersh for 'redress for an act of prepotency, perhaps unequalled in his Country's annals'. Neither Burghersh nor the Foreign Office was much interested.[73] Falconar was probably pleased when Thompson removed himself to Florence; in 1840 Jousiffe stated that he not only taught English, French and Latin there but was 'interpreter to the courts of law'. It was in this capacity that late in 1851 he called Scarlett's attention to the case of the engineers Clark, Grettham and Irwin.[74]

Obtaining English books was not a problem in Florence. The guidebooks regularly recommended British visitors to Florence to patronize Molini's (where English was spoken).[75] In 1825 Charles Brown was settling with the firm on behalf of the departed Leigh Hunt, and John Maquay records several payments to Molini (he purchased *Nicholas Nickleby* from him in 1839).[76] By the time Giuseppe Molini, 'the Nestor of booksellers', died at the age of 84 in 1856, there was an Englishman selling books and prints in Florence. The 1854 edition of *Murray's* reported that Edward Goodban had 'opened a shop for prints, drawings, stationery, &c, opposite the Cafe Doney'. Goodban had previously been an assistant to a native dealer, Bardi, whose premises were in the Piazza San Gaetano.[77]

Goodban was born the son of a musician in Canterbury in 1824. Music and dealing in prints and artists' materials were family activities, and *Murray's* noted that Goodban could provide enquirers with a list of music-masters in Florence. Early in 1853 the Secretary to the Select Vestry reported that he had undertaken to produce 50 copies of a hymn-book at 2s 5d. apiece, and he continued to work for the church from time to time.[78] On 18 June 1859 the following advertisement appeared in the *Times*:

TO PARENTS AND GUARDIANS. WANTED, by an English and foreign book and printseller and stationer at Florence, Italy, an APPRENTICE to the above trade. A well-educated youth, with a knowledge of French, is required.

Applications were to be addressed 'to E.G., care of Messrs Williams and Norgate, 14, Henrietta-street, Covent-Garden, W.C.' The initials suggest that the advertiser was Goodban, who clearly expected to recruit despite political upheavals. In 1851 his brother Frederick had been assistant to a print-seller in Covent Garden; he subsequently came out to Florence to help in the business and died there in December 1865. Edward himself returned to England in 1861 to get married, but most of his children were born in Florence, where his wife died in 1880. He himself survived until 1893, to be followed a few weeks later by another brother, Thomas, a music-teacher like their father.

His business, while clearly specialized to a degree, nonetheless covered a range of products and activities, as *Murray's* reported in 1863.[79] Goodban was 'agent for these handbooks' and

> is well provided with English, French, and German books, works on art, and maps and books useful for travellers in Italy, photographic views, &c; and will procure all modern Italian and other books. He also sells English and foreign stationery, drawing materials, Newman's water colours, &c. He is a very obliging person, and will give every information to English and Americans as to masters, &c. He packs and forwards parcels to England. An address-book of English and American visitors to Florence is kept in his shop. He is agent for Alinari's photographs, and Giusti's (of Siena) elegant wood sculptures and picture-frames.

The appearance of photographs among Goodban's stock in trade was a sign of the times, and it is hard to imagine that he was not acquainted with another Kentish native in Florence. John Brampton Philpot, born in Maidstone in 1812, is said to have established himself in Tuscany around 1850. Few particulars of his biography seem to be discoverable, apart from the fact that in 1854 he published a bad novel, *Sabina*. He was probably wise to exchange this trade for that of photographer, in which he achieved some distinction. He exhibited views of Florence in Edinburgh in 1856 and specialized also in stereoscopic images and photographs of works of art.[80] It is more than likely that Goodban handled his photographs. He died in Florence in November 1878.

Goodban and Philpott, like Huband and Gamgee, may be described as specialists, but it was commonplace for tradesmen to fulfil a variety of roles. Those who sold provisions typically not only dealt in an enormous range of goods but dabbled in other services. Shopkeepers gave advice to those in search of lodgings and might themselves have apartments to let; bankers acted as estate agents. David Thomson ran a hotel and sold tea as well. It naturally took time for British shopkeepers to establish themselves in Tuscany after the end of the wars. In the first edition of her guidebook Mrs Starke had very few English names to play with, although a Captain Williams was the best wine-merchant in Leghorn and Mr Polhill sold his English medicines there. Leghorn had something of a reputation as a shopping Mecca. Mrs Starke informed her readers that

> Tea, coffee, sugar, English mustard, foreign wines, brandy, rum, arrack, porter, Bristol beer, and Gorgona anchovies, may all be purchased cheaper at Leghorn than in any other City of Italy; so likewise may soap, starch and hair powder.[81]

She would continue to repeat these observations into the 1820s, as hair powder, at least, became a thing of the past. *Murray's* in 1842 stated more simply: 'In no part of the Continent are travellers able to obtain at so cheap a rate, English articles, or so varied an assortment, as at Leghorn.'[82]

Already in 1802, however, Mrs Starke could assure English visitors to Florence that they did not have to go to Leghorn for everything. They could patronize Molini for English books, artists' materials including Reeves's colours, and other English goods, while

> Meggit in the small Palazzo Medici, on the Lung'Arno, sells foreign wines, and spirits, porter, Bristol-beer, tea, English bark, James's powder, &c he likewise has English camomile flowers, which can be purchased no where else in Italy, but of Mr Polhill, at Leghorn.

Mrs Starke also noted that an apartment in the *palazzo* where he kept his shop was available for rent and that he kept some of the best carriages to be had, but he 'charges very high'.[83] When Megit died in 1814 he was rather grandly commemorated on his tombstone in the Leghorn cemetery as 'merchant and banker of Florence'. A more accurate description might have been 'shopkeeper and moneychanger'. He was remembered for the oddest reasons. A letter published in *Trewman's Exeter Flying Post* on 15 December 1836 recalled

> what occurred to me about half-a-century or more ago at Florence, at the Hotel de Londres, kept by an Englishman, called Jack Megget, a poodle Dog, with a lantern in his mouth, lighted myself and some other Gentlemen to the Theatre, returning again to the Hotel, what is more singular, he walked on both his hind legs, and kept himself perfectly upright the whole way both to and from.

In Florence in 1815 the elder John Maquay visited the shop, now run by Gabriel Megit, 'son of John', where he bought a quire of paper.[84] In January 1818 Gabriel inserted an advertisement in the *Gazzetta* informing the public that he was continuing the business his father had established, although the premises were now in the Piazza del Duomo, opposite the Baptistery. He sold wines, different types of sugar and a variety of English goods, and had just received fresh stock from England.

Megit now faced competition from newcomers such as Thomas Townley, who was already in Florence in 1817. Townley had brought a wife and at least one small child with him from England and established himself in the Palazzo Feroni in Piazza Santa Trinità.[85] A few months later Falconar, who was having trouble obtaining the English newspapers at Leghorn, learned that Townley was successfully receiving the *Observer* by post, using (with permission) Lord Burghersh's address.[86] On 19 May 1818 he took an advertisement in the *Gazzetta* to announce that he was opening a shop in the Via Grande in Leghorn, and Mrs Starke a few years later referred to it as selling flannel (of which the British appear to have been in dire and permanent need) among other English goods. He also opened a branch in Rome and, some years before he died in 1839, a second shop in Florence.

On 4 February 1834 Townley's son James informed readers of the *Gazzetta* that he was about to leave for England by way of Paris and would gladly fulfil any commissions that were entrusted to him. Those interested were invited to apply to either of the two family businesses, one of which was in the Piazza San Gaetano, 'under the Pasquali palace'.[87] It was here that the Townley shop was located when in 1840 Jousiffe gave it a generous amount of publicity. Mrs Townley and her sons sold a wide variety of articles, 'the whole of them of a very superior description, most of them received direct from England'. Apart from the expected teas, coffees, sugars and wines, these included 'pickles and sauces of every description' and 'English patent and other medicines'. In addition there were to be had 'saddlery, harness, articles for the stable', 'Irish and other linens', beaver hats and a great deal more besides. 'Mrs Townley keeps ready-made and makes to order a variety of articles of utility and fashion', including children's dresses. It was 'an extensive and very long established house' and

> travellers will do well to apply to Mrs Townly [*sic*] for lodgings, and any other information they may require, which is afforded gratis; luggage, parcels, or letters addressed to the house will be carefully attended to; lodgings are also procured for parties who write previously, stating the description of apartments they require. Travellers or sojourners in Florence, should patronise Mrs Townly's [*sic*] establishment; they will find every article they may require, either for travelling or a residence. I can with confidence recommend it.[88]

One could not say fairer than that, but Isabella Wilmer, shopping for baby linen in May 1836, had been unimpressed: 'Was not successful, everything being so bad, and dear.'

The business continued for some years; George and Robert Townley, and also 'widow Townley and son', were among the English firms who in 1846 desired a postal communication with Gibraltar, and in 1849 Consul Macbean listed G. and R. Townley among merchant houses doing business through the consulate.[89] The Townleys still had the premises in Piazza Gaetano and by 1847 had acquired another base, south of the Arno near the Ponte Carraia, where Spence located 'Mr Townley's shop of English goods'.[90] Mary Townley died in 1852, Robert in March 1870 and George in December 1871. George had made an Italian marriage, some time before 1857; Robert, the only one of the Townley children to be born in Florence, spent his entire life there.

At Leghorn the re-establishment of the British merchant community was accompanied by an influx of tradespeople which included the already-mentioned Henry Fisher. Fisher was described by Jousiffe as a

> wine and spirit-merchant and dealer in teas and groceries, patent medicines, fine Havannah segars, Rowland's Macassar oil, and a great variety of articles for the toilet, etc. Mr Fisher has also an extensive stock of fine London porter, ale and brown stout.

Another early post-war arrival was Henry Dunn, who attracted John Featherstonehaugh's ire in 1826. Dunn's first wife died at Leghorn in 1830; he remarried a few years later and died in 1867 at the age of 91. Jousiffe was enthusiastic about his 'old-established English warehouse', where 'an immense variety of goods of a superior description are constantly on sale, consisting of wines, spirits, teas, groceries, manufactured goods, fancy articles, etc'. Dunn 'has also for sale a large collection of pictures by celebrated artists; some of them highly valuable' and seems to have kept in his warehouse a kind of museum of 'articles of curiosity' which could be seen on application. All this notwithstanding, when David Wilmer went on a shopping expedition from Pisa to Leghorn in October 1836, he found that Dunn 'has nothing'. It was clearly not unknown for shopkeepers to dabble in art, for another prominent Leghorn merchant, Thomas Dickie, whose warehouse in Via Borra concentrated on fabrics and articles of dress, including hosiery, shawls, gloves and 'best London hats', also sold teas, port and sherry, spirits, stationery and 'a few old pictures'.[91]

Dunn's activities were typically varied. *Gazzetta* advertisements over many years show him acting as agent for everything from a seaside villa, conveniently close to the baths, which was to be let by the English family who occupied it, to an elegantly decorated English pianoforte, carriages and sailing boats. A 30-year-old Englishwoman, bred in high society, who wanted a situation in a family with children, invited those interested to apply to Mr Dunn. A tradesman who put down roots in the locality became the indispensable source not only of goods but of help and information, and the newcomer to Italy could benefit from the links that existed between tradesmen at the different stops along his route, as Robert Heywood discovered in 1826.

Mr Heywood preserved a quantity of ephemera connected with his visit to Italy, including the letter of introduction that Dunn wrote on his behalf to Samuel Lowe at Florence. Addressing himself cheerily to 'Dear Sam', Dunn wrote

> The bearer of this, Mr Heywood, a gentleman from Manchester, visits your city on his way to Rome and Naples. As he is a perfect stranger in this country you would oblige me much by giving him every information and assistance in your power during his stay in Florence, and also in procuring him a good conveyance to Rome.

Lowe engaged a *cicerone* for Heywood and got him a place with the courier to Rome, more expensive but faster than the *vettura*. He also supplied him with a letter of introduction to 'Dear Clarke' at Rome; would he in his turn provide 'every assistance' and secure a conveyance onward to Naples?[92]

Samuel Lowe was a little later to arrive in Tuscany than Townley, Thomson, Dunn or Fisher, but this letter shows that he was well established in Florence by 1826. He was accompanied throughout his Italian career by his younger brother William, who represented the family in Rome (but was away at the time of Mr Heywood's travels).[93] In an advertisement in the *Gazzetta* on 27 December 1828 Samuel made it plain that he was 'the sole and absolute proprietor' of the business in both Florence and Rome. William's children were born in Rome and he died there in 1876, but he was brought to Leghorn, where there were other Lowe tombs, for burial. Samuel survived him for only a few months, dying in Florence in April 1877 at the age of 81. He seems to have disappeared from the pages of *Murray's* by 1867.

The business run by the Lowes in both Florence and Rome was of the kind already familiar. Mrs Starke said that Samuel's Marsala was excellent, but it was of equal importance to his clientele that, like other British shopkeepers, he was in constant communication with British suppliers. One guidebook remarked that the traveller in Florence should know

> that many articles, the possession of which he may consider comforts, can be had there of Mr Love [*sic*] such as, genuine English medicines, drugs, and soda powders, from Savory and Moore; stationary [*sic*], papers, colours, pencils, sketch-books, etc. from Waller of Fleet Street, and other goods from the first houses.

Savory & Moore (a brand which still exists) had named Lowe in Florence and Rome as their agents some years earlier.[94] In the autumn of 1834 advertisements began to appear in the *Gazzetta* which identified the Lowes as sole agent in Florence and Rome for the products of Rowland and Son of Hatton Garden in London, notably their famous Macassar Oil (Fisher stocked it at Leghorn).

Given that Bagni's Anglophone society was so highly seasonal, it is not surprising to find that shopkeepers, as well as bankers and physicians, transplanted themselves there for the summer. According to Mrs Starke, Lowe did so at some point in the 1820s, but by about 1830 he had passed the baton to an Italian, Joseph (Giuseppe) Cordon, who was Genoese by birth. In 1833 Mrs Starke said that he ran his shop at Pisa in the winter and Bagni (where he professed to charge 'Leghorn prices') in the summer. Jousiffe's account of him confirms that he stocked the usual range of goods and

> is happy to furnish strangers with a list of lodging-houses, and to give any other information in his power. Mr Cordon has an establishment at the Baths of Lucca, at which place the whole of the articles enumerated and a great variety of others are to be had. *Galignani's Messenger* may be had of Mr Cordon, who keeps a list of arrivals at Pisa and the Baths of Lucca, which may be seen by applying to him.

Snow adds that Cordon would act as an 'agent'; in effect he would do anything anyone wanted done, and was 'most attentive in his manners'.[95] The Pisa church books show that subscribers took apartments in 'Casa Cordon' and he stocked (and even printed) publications other than Galignani. Here was another Italian whose interest in the 'English' seems to have transcended commercial opportunism. In 1831 he was briefly brought to the notice of the Foreign Office because he had, allegedly, tried to contract a marriage with an unnamed Englishwoman at Leghorn, and although Catholic-born was prepared to make affidavit that he was a Protestant.[96] In 1836 the Wilmers patronized Cordon's shops at both Bagni and Pisa, and on 18 October Isabella consulted Mrs Cordon about finding a servant. Was this Mrs Cordon an Englishwoman?

It was with Lowe in Florence as it was with Dunn in Leghorn or Cordon in Pisa or Bagni. If a British dog or other item of property was lost, or if a carriage or a pleasure-boat was for sale, application should be made to Mr Lowe. When somebody wished to hire an 'English harp', those interested in responding were referred to Mr Lowe. At one time tickets for sittings in the English Church could be had from him; indeed, in November 1849 he was elected a member of the Select Vestry.[97] Jousiffe said that he would receive 'works of art, baggage, etc. to be forwarded to the care of Mr J.F. Chinnery, Custom-House and shipping agent, Thames Street' in London. In later years he was one of several Florentine firms who dealt with J. & R. McCracken of Old Jewry in the City.[98] When Consul Macbean in 1849 drew up his list of the British firms in Florence doing business through the Consulate, Lowe (described as a Commission Agent) was among them.[99] Lowe enjoyed the rare distinction of being exempted from the habitual sneers of the *Satirist*'s Florentine correspondent, who described him ('banker and general dealer') as 'one of the fairest shopkeepers here'.[100] *Murray's* in 1847 observed that Lowe was 'banker to many English families', and when in November 1852 Lady Don deposited with him the 300 *francesconi* that she wanted to leave for the benefit of the English poor, she called him 'banker of Florence'.

Tourist and resident alike needed clothes. Snow noted next door to Cordon's shop at Bagni a John Pay who was 'a good workman and fashionable tailor'. At Florence John Maquay patronized an Italian tailor called Raffaele, but he also gave custom to Timothy Haskard. Jousiffe called Haskard 'a tailor and habit-maker from London' who could furnish 'Every article of dress got up in the latest fashion of London and Paris, of the very best materials and at moderate prices'. Haskard 'appears anxious to merit the patronage of his countrymen; he will wait upon them at their hotel' or lodgings at any time they desire'.[101] Perhaps, when in October 1845 he and Samuel Lowe witnessed one of the many codicils to Lady Don's will, he was making just such a professional call. When he died in 1874 he was said to be 66 years old and to have been 30 years a resident of Florence, but this must have been an understatement, unless he was not yet a resident when he was married to Elizabeth Martin there in July 1839. Elizabeth helped in the business, to judge by *Murray's* comment in 1863 that 'Mrs Haskard is well supplied with English hosiery, outfitting articles, &c'. They established a Florentine dynasty which lasted deep into the twentieth century.

Haskard was neither the only nor the earliest English tailor in Florence. Already in her first edition Mrs Starke noted the presence of a Mr Robinson whose prices were 'tolerable' and who also had a small apartment for rent.[102] A Robinson, presumably not the same individual, and Haskard both appear in John Maquay's accounts from time to time. Elizabeth Maquay went shopping for fabrics, gowns and bonnets, most often mentioning in this connection a Madame Besançon.[103] She also said one day in November 1833 that she had gone 'to the Jews about Linnen [sic] but came away the shop was so full'. Mrs Starke had already written that 'The best linen-drapers' shops are kept by Jews, near the Mercato-nuovo'. No name is mentioned, but one such business belonged to a family called Philipson. They were already located in the Via del Proconsolo in 1829 and the 'brothers Philipson' were still there in 1842. John Maquay bought a variety of items from them, including horsehair and things for the children, and in 1848 the English Church was buying grey cloth from Philipson for covering chairs.[104] The Philipsons had another string to their bow. In April 1840 a Mr Philipson played a modest part in the Bourbel-Bogle affair when he raised doubts about a forged letter of credit. Most likely this shrewd observer was either Marco, a draper or mercer, or one of his sons. The Brownings later employed them; already in 1848 Elizabeth Browning mentioned 'our obliging Jew banker', and in 1853 Robert reported that Marco was on the point of retirement. The business seems then to have been divided between his sons Benjamin and Abraham, the latter concentrating on the banking end.[105]

The combination of banking with another line of business was so far from uncommon that *Murray*'s could advise its readers that most British tradespeople would discount bills for their compatriots. Samuel Lowe was one example, James Tough another. Tough was born in 1793 in Palermo, where his father was for some years consul.[106] *Murray*'s designated him 'both banker and wine merchant', and declared that he was 'better supplied with foreign wines than any other in Florence'. He was also 'extremely obliging' and 'will obtain lodgings, and attend to all the wants of his customers, giving advice, &c'.[107] Tough may have been obliging to visitors, but not only did the church committee have reason to rue getting embroiled with him in 1839 over the purchase of a house for the accommodation of divine worship, they later had their doubts about his wines and his prices. In January 1856 they were debating the quality of the communion wine. Believing that the local product was not good enough, they were paying Tough 12 pauls a bottle for wine from the Trentino. After a great deal of discussion and sampling, it was resolved to purchase a quantity of Malaga at 6 pauls a bottle – a considerable saving.[108]

On 11 December 1847 and subsequently the 'The London and Florence Wine and Tea Company' advertised in the *Tuscan Athenaeum* good black tea at 4 ½ pauls a pound and a variety of other increasingly expensive blends. It also had the best wines and Barclay's Stout and Bass's Ale at the most moderate prices as well as the highest exchange for bank notes, sovereigns and foreign coins. This company was located close to the Piazza Santa Trinità, always a hub of British activity. In 1852, a Mr Brown kept 'a large grocery and wine warehouse' in the Via

Rondinelli and claimed 'to take bills on England without commission, by which a saving of 1 per cent is effected'. He had adopted 'the useful plan of posting the rate of exchange daily at the door of his bank'.[109] A few years later this individual had moved to the Via Legnaioli (very close indeed to Piazza S. Trinità if not actually in it) and was calling his premises 'The English Bank and Exchange'. From this address, giving his name as J.A. Brown, he wrote a letter to the *Daily News*, published on 19 June 1856, in which he entered into a current controversy about the authenticity of a supposed Botticelli. He admitted that 'the purchase of pictures' was 'foreign to my regular business', but had obviously been dabbling in that dangerous trade and thus drew upon himself the fire of the cantankerous Morris Moore, scourge of Sir Charles Eastlake, Director of the National Gallery. Moore referred contemptuously to him as 'tea and picture dealer'.[110] The following year he was in the papers again as having lent money at Florence to an insolvent debtor who went by several names in the course of his duplicitous international career.[111]

That selling wine could be a gentlemanly business was shown by the example of Mr W.H. Wood, the brother-in-law of Colonel Stisted of Bagni and one of the sons of John Brock Wood, of Huntington Hall, Cheshire.[112] On 13 November 1847 he advertised in the *Tuscan Athenaeum* wine and tea, 'these important articles of consumption', which were to be had, 'genuine, in great variety, and at most moderate prices' at his premises in Via Larga. In the next issue he offered wines 'just arrived from Bordeaux' by the case of 3 dozen. There was prime claret, Sauterne and Barsac 'of the vintage of 1811' for prices ranging from 180 to 387 pauls a case, as well as black tea at 6 pauls a pound. During at least part of his Italian life, Wood was in business with William Wardle, son of the late exiled MP Colonel Wardle. In 1849 Macbean recorded 'Wardle & Wood' among the handful of English-owned Florentine firms which did business through the Consulate, but he did not specify what their business was.[113]

It is not much before 1840 that the guidebooks begin to mention English bankers in Florence. Mrs Starke commends the firm of Donato Orsi, in the Piazza Granduca, as 'very obliging to foreigners', and it was undoubtedly widely used, by John Maquay among others. Also obliging was 'Sig. Sebastian Kleiber, in Via Larga'. Mrs Starke does not name his associate Emanuele Fenzi, for whom Horace Hall (Kleiber's nephew) had already been working for some years; in 1820 the poet Shelley was corresponding with Hall about his monetary affairs.[114] That there was some competition for British business between these firms is suggested by two advertisements which appeared in rapid succession in the *Gazzetta* early in September 1831, just at the season when the tourists began to arrive in large numbers. On 8 September the public was informed that Fenzi, in the Piazza del Gran Duca,

are authorised to pay the circular notes of Mess. Coutts, Morlands, and Hammersleys, and in case of any difficulties arising on other credits from the

Said Bankers, any persons bearers of these Letters of Credit will be supplied with the needfull at the aforesaid Bank in Piazza del Gran Duca.

Two days later, Orsi & Co assured the same public that they 'never ceased to pay and will continue to pay' the same notes.

In 1840 Jousiffe named Fenzi and commented that Hall, albeit 'not very gracious', was 'extremely honourable in his dealings'. He also recommended two English firms, both located in the Piazza Santa Trinità. Plowden and French he called 'old established highly respectable and very obliging', while Bogle, Kerrick [sic] & Co differed from them only in being 'recently established (about two years)'.[115] This firm, it will be remembered, had been somewhat in the wars in 1839–1840. As a result of the acrimonious upheavals in the English Church the church's funds were withdrawn from their keeping; then Allen Bogle was involved in the Bourbel conspiracy to defraud the banks of Europe.[116] The firm (without Bogle) nonetheless remained in being for a few more years. The first edition of *Murray*'s in 1842, like Jousiffe, had difficulty with Kerrich's name, calling the firm 'Kerridge and Macarthy', but it was able now to name 'Macuay and Pakenham' in addition to Fenzi and Plowden.

There had in fact been at least one earlier British banker in Florence (Hall apart). A 'Johnston' or 'Johnstone' is well attested in John Maquay's diary and elsewhere. William Gracie Johnstone was born in 1793, the son of a Bolton fustian manufacturer. In 1817 he was married in London to Anne Halliday, the daughter of a partner in the bank of Herries, Farquhar & Co. Herries was credited with the invention of the circular letter of credit, on which British travellers often relied in order to obtain cash in foreign parts. It is not clear whether as a result of his marriage William Johnstone was sent to Florence to set up a bank, but he was in Tuscany at the latest by early 1825, to judge from the fact that his wife died in Florence and was buried at Leghorn on 24 February.[117]

John Maquay mentions him for the first time at the very end of 1830, and early the following year records that he was going to 'Johnston's' to read the papers, as his had not arrived for several days. We get glimpses elsewhere of this service that bankers offered to their customers; banks were meeting places as well as sources of ready cash. Johnston's premises were in the Palazzo Bartolini Salimbeni in Piazza Santa Trinità. They were used for other purposes, for example to host the discussions of a leaving present for Mr Seymour, and Johnston gave dinners both to say farewell to Seymour and to welcome Abercrombie.[118] John Maquay succeeded him as Secretary and Treasurer of the English Church in December 1837.[119] There are indications that Johnston was in some way associated with Walter Kennedy Lawrie, whom Lord Malmesbury later remembered as a banker. The younger Walter Kennedy is occasionally referred to in the records of the Commune as 'Walter Johnston Kennedy', which may hint that his father was in some way associated with Johnston and his bank.[120]

There was a connection too between Johnston and the ill-starred Allen Bogle. It emerged from the *Times* report of the libel hearing that on his arrival in Florence Bogle had taken employment as chief clerk with Johnston, and it was on the latter's 'failure' in 1837 that he very briefly set up for himself, before entering into partnership with Kerrich and MacCarthy.[121] John Maquay sheds no light on this 'failure', but Johnston had lost his eldest son in Florence in February 1837 (John attended the funeral). He did not leave Florence, but died there in 1844.

Jousiffe called the firm run by Charles Plowden and the Irishman Anthony French 'long established' by 1840. Plowden had been involved in an earlier business, for he and Walter Tempest took space in the *Gazzetta* on 22 January 1835 to announce the dissolution of their banking partnership, which had been located in Via Legnaioli. Tempest, a member of a Yorkshire gentry family, was Catholic, like Plowden and French. John Maquay certainly knew of 'Tempest's bank' for it was there on 10 March 1835 (several weeks after the dissolution of the partnership) that the meeting was held to discuss the arrangements for St Patrick's day, the celebration of which was improved by French's singing.[122] Plowden's new partnership may well have been already in view and the business remained located in Via Legnaioli (alternatively, Piazza S. Trinità).

The fact that French and Plowden were Catholics may have sweetened their relations with the Tuscan authorities, at the same time as it fuelled the scurrilous hostility that the *Satirist* consistently exhibited towards them, but the guidebooks were unanimous in recommending them to the traveller. They may have been the first Anglo-Florentine bankers to open a summer branch at Bagni which, the *European Indicator* informed its readers, was open from 1 June to 15 October. In addition, Plowden & French

> transact every description of banking-business and have connexions in all the principal towns of the continent, upon whom they accommodate their friends with credits in the usual way ... [their] correspondents in London are Messrs Herries Farquhar et Co., Messrs Glynn and Co., and many other eminent banking establishments; they are also agents for Mr WAGHORN of Alexandria, for the transmission of letters to India.

This last may have been a recommendation for British residents who had friends, sons or other relatives in India. The reference to Herries may suggest that Plowden & French had taken over this connection from Johnston's defunct bank. They continued in being until 1854, when the partners fell out over their dealings with the railway contractor Gandell and agreed to divide the Roman part of the business from the Tuscan.[123]

For some time before Captain Pakenham came to John Maquay with the proposal that they should jointly found their own bank, the diary affords its customary oblique evidence of John's increasing interest in the subject. He records frequent visits to the 'Bank', not specifying which it was, its whereabouts, or his precise purpose. That it was not just to read the papers is made clear by his entry for 12 May 1840: 'went to bank answer to my proposition yesterday of joining them'. On the previous day, Bogle had resigned from his partnership with Kerrich and MacCarthy. It seems likely that John was proposing to take his place, and that the 'bank' to which he had earlier referred was theirs. It was clearly being rumoured that the scandal would enforce the firm's closure, for on 14 May John made a bet with Mr Wardle 'that Kerrich and McCarthy would not close their bank before the end of the year'.[124] Then, on 22 May, came Pakenham's proposal.

To begin with, the business was conducted from Pakenham's lodgings. The *European Indicator* located it at the corner of Piazza Santa Maria Novella, remarking that it had been

> formed in June 1840 principally for the cashing of British credits of all descriptions, but embracing all other banking business, they are already in correspondence with the first houses in London, Dublin, Paris, and other continental cities.

A branch had been opened at Siena, and it was thought likely that the business would be expanded to other 'Italian cities, the resorts of British subjects'.[125]

From now on, John ceaselessly entered 'Bank all morning' or 'all day' into his diary and he not infrequently slept there. In early August 1840 the new partners decided to turn down a proposal from Le Mesurier (a banker at Rome who had suffered from the Bourbel conspiracy) that he should join them, and towards the end of that month they moved 'into our new rooms down stairs, which we have made very comfortable offices'.[126] The Bourbel trauma did not put an immediate end to Kerrich and MacCarthy, and John Maquay must have won his bet with Wardle. In 1842 *Murray's* gave the firm priority among bankers:

> These gentlemen, who are correspondents of Messrs Barclay and Co., are worthy of all confidence; Mr Kerridge [sic], who is domiciled in Tuscany, can give much useful information to British subjects desirous of making any stay in the country.[127]

On 23 June 1845 Maquay recorded that 'It was finally arranged today that Kerrich & McCarthy will retire from business in our favor'. He and Pakenham were to give them '£800 for their good will or in case Barings decline to support us £300'. It had clearly not been irrelevant that Kerrich was married to a Baring. The new bank acquired the premises previously occupied by Kerrich and MacCarthy in Piazza Santa Trinità (and perhaps before them by Johnston).[128] It seems that Kerrich turned to other interests, including the Tuscan railways, while MacCarthy at some point returned to England, where his wife died of smallpox in 1847.[129]

In 1842 Maquay & Pakenham opened a seasonal branch at Bagni di Lucca. It was usually Pakenham's job to run this, which had consequences for his future in

Tuscany. Snow described the bank as 'highly respectable', adding that 'the partner attending the Baths is a honourable and courteous gentleman'.[130] It was during the early summer of 1842, as Pakenham prepared for the opening of the branch, that John began once more to mention the name Johnston. This individual was something of a dogsbody, helping John to balance his books and in July being sent off to Pakenham at Lucca with a supply of money. Mentions of him recur, and on 22 April 1843 Walter George Farquhar Johnston witnessed Elizabeth Maquay's will, together with Pakenham.[131] He was William Gracie's second son, born in France around 1822 and since the death of his elder brother in 1837 destined to succeed to his family's landed interests in Galloway. For the moment, he was pursuing a banking career, and on 2 June 1843 John Maquay recorded that 'Johnston left the Bank today to go to England on Monday and on his return sets up for himself'.[132] It is not clear for how long he did so. He became closely acquainted with the family of the Dubliner Currell Burston Smyth, who managed the Leghorn branch of Maquay & Pakenham, and on 21 October 1846 he was married to one of Smyth's daughters, Catherine Wilhelmina, known as Minna. John Maquay had urged the bride's father to effect the marriage 'immediately' and on the wedding day mysteriously observed that she 'looked & behaved very well'. Perhaps she was pregnant.[133]

As John's thoughts turned back towards Ireland, he embarked on a lengthy process of disengagement, and we are reminded that he too had been engaged in another kind of dealing. In the course of the year 1855 he wound up the wine side of his business, recording in his accounts at the end of the year an amount representing the share due to him 'on closing the Wine Depot'.[134]

More could be said about those who serviced the English residents and tourists of Florence. Many have slipped below the radar because their activities either went unrecorded or came to an early end. Selectivity anyway is unavoidable. Those who can be observed make up a diverse bunch, of very different degrees of prosperity and pretension, who wove a web of relationships with one another and with the British residents in general. They illuminate the realities of expatriate life, the daily need for lodgings, foodstuffs, medicines and commodities of all kinds. Together they and their customers represented 'the Englishmen of every kind, mentality, profession, and social class' who, as Giorgio Spini observed, swarmed over nineteenth-century Italy.

Notes

1   Murray, *Handbook for Travellers in Northern Italy* (London, 1842), p. 427.
2   JLM, E9 ff. 75v, 79, 94v passim.
3   JLM, E9 f. 150v.
4   JLM, E10 f. 45.
5   JLM, E10 f. 24v.
6   JLM, E10 f. 143.
7   JLM, E10 f. 191v.

8   JLM, E11 f. 32.

9   JLM, E10 ff. 168v, 174.

10   JLM, E10 ff. 22v, 25, 27 passim.

11   *Church Letters,* 1830s, 46, 47. John as secretary of the church committee wrote to Aubin, temporarily in charge of the Legation, about the problem.

12   CMB 2, 2 November 1859; the case is last referred to on 18 January 1861.

13   Montgomery Carmichael (ed.), *The Inscriptions in the Old British Cemetery at Leghorn, transcribed by Gery Milner-Gibson-Cullum & Francis Campbell Macauley* (Leghorn, 1906), pp. 4, 44–5.

14   JLM, E11 f. 96v; Thomas A. Trollope, *What I Remember* (second edition, London, 1887), Vol. 2, p. 375.

15   TNA, Prob11/2132; JLM, E11 f. 72. In the *Gazzetta* of 25 April 1843 Köppe announced that he was about to leave Florence, obviously temporarily, and asked his creditors to present themselves at the Palazzo Capponi.

16   TNA, Prob11/2211.

17   CMB 1, 20 April 1850.

18   Her husband Agostino succumbed to the cholera in 1855, and presumably received Catholic burial, perhaps at Santa Maria Novella, where their son William, who died in 1845 aged only 14 months, was buried in the Chiostro de' Morti. However, another son, Alessandro, who died at the age of 32 in 1871, was buried in the English cemetery.

19   Murray, *Handbook of Florence and Its Environs* (London, 1861), p. iii.

20   See the article in DNB, which cites the study by Jesse Myers, *Baron Ward and the Dukes of Parma* (London, Longman, 1938) and also Lord Lamington, *In the Days of the Dandies* (Edinburgh & London, Blackwood, 1890). Contemporary sources include *Burke's Peerage* (1852), s.v. 'Foreign Noblemen'; 'An English Adventurer' (*Times,* 20 August 1852). A long article on Ward, reprinted from the *Family Friend,* appeared in the *Bradford Observer* on 28 April 1870. He is several times mentioned in FO79 and in Florentine memoirs, including Trollope, *What I Remember*, Vol. 2, pp. 44–5. Ward followed the Duke when he exchanged Lucca for the Duchy of Parma in 1847 and died near Vienna in 1858.

21   Arthur Vansittart, 'Florentine Races 1841', *New Sporting Review* Vol. 2, 1841, p. 20. A rider called Nevin took part in the Florentine races in 1829, as reported in the *Times* on 5 December; this could have been his father.

22   Murray, *Handbook of Florence and Its Environs* (London, 1863), p. ii. It is perhaps unlikely that a hotel under this name would have been opened before Italian unification, and there is no sign of it in *Murray*'s for 1861. Rindi disposed of the business in 1869: *Gazzetta Ufficiale del Regno d'Italia* no. 219, 12 August 1869.

23   E. Buonincontri, 'Madame Hombert: da femme de chambre ad albergatrice nella Firenze granducale', *Antologia Vieusseux* 17 (2011), pp. 135–43.

24   Stendhal, *Rome, Naples and Florence* (trans. R. Coe, London, 1959), p. 311; Y. du Parc, *Quand Stendhal relisait les Promenades dans Rome: marginalia inédits* (Lausanne, 1959), pp. 56–9.

25   In 1825 Robert Hombert made over to his wife his half-share in the business which was located there and known as the Hotel of Madame Hombert; henceforth she would be the sole proprietor. *Gazzetta* 29 October 1825. Already in 1820 Mrs Starke named the *palazzo* as one of many where apartments could be had, although she does not call it a hotel as such: *Travels on the Continent, written for the use and particular information of travellers* (London, 1820), p. 99. The palazzo and surrounding area were badly damaged in 1944.

26   J.D. Sinclair, *An Autumn in Italy, being a Personal Narrative of a Tour in the Austrian, Tuscan, Roman and Sardinian States, in 1827* (Edinburgh, 1829), p. 122; James Cobbett, *Journal of a Tour in Italy, and also in part of France and Switzerland* (London, 1830), p. 321; William Cathcart Boyd, MD., *A Guide & Pocket Companion through Italy* (London, 1830), p. 113.

27   *The Tablet*, p. 15.

28   Murray, *Handbook* (1842), p. 485.

29   Georgina Blakiston, *Lord William Russell and His Wife, 1815–1846* (London 1972) p. 60; James Cobbett, *Journal* p. 321. If Schneiderff's was still functioning in 1842 it cannot yet have been taken over by Mrs Clarke.

30   Elizabeth Maquay jr., D1 ff. 57, 102, 104; John Maquay sr., A4 ff. 102, 104. He met 'Mrs S' on the stairs at 11 at night, to beg a carriage.

31   *Gazzetta* 26 March 1818. Via Forca is now the Via Ferdinando Zannetti. Sambalino was still the proprietor in 1839.

32   Murray, *Handbook for Travellers in Northern Italy* (London, 1847), p. 474.

33   Capt M.J. Jousiffe, *A Road Book for Travellers in Italy* (2nd ed. Brussels, Paris and London, 1840) p. 164; Murray, *Handbook* (London, 1847), p. 417.

34   Mabel Sharman Crawford, *Life in Tuscany* (London, 1859), p. 55; Murray *Handbook* (1847), p. 417; LMA, CLC/387/Ms22926, f. 10a.

35   FO79/46, Strangways to FO, 6 June 1826. This initiates a lengthy dossier. Featherstonehaugh's complaint to Canning is in FO79/48, 20 June.

36   The *Gazzetta* on 21 June 1823 mentioned a 'Roberto Weimyss' as the master of a merchant vessel called the *James Coleyn* which had docked at Leghorn in June 1823 with a cargo of Indian goods.

37   FO79/48, FO to Featherstonehaugh, 28 July 1826; Featherstonehaugh to Canning, 13 August 1826.

38   Marianna Starke, *Information and Directions for Travellers on the Continent. Fifth edition, thoroughly revised and with considerable additions* (Paris, 1826), pp. 81, 374.

39   Edna Healey, *Emma Darwin* (London, 2001), p. 84. For the Shelleys' stay see several references in Richard Holmes, *Shelley, the Pursuit* (London, 1974); for the spoons and the Chiroplast, D. Reiman (ed.), *Shelley and His Circle* (Cambridge, Mass. & London, 1986), Vol. 8, p. 922.

40   TNA, Prob11/1951. 'Mr Piper' advertised his services as a teacher of German in the *Gazzetta* 1 January 1824.

41   JLM, E9 f. 165v.

42   Jousiffe, *Road Book*, pp. 47–8. Murray, *Handbook* (1847), p. 474 located Mrs Clarke in the house formerly inhabited by the poet Vittorio Alfieri at Lungarno (now Lungarno Corsini) 2041, but by the time of the fourth edition in 1852 she was occupying the premises of the former Hotel Schneiderff on the south side of the Arno p. 455.

43   C. Wainwright, 'Shopping for South Kensington: Fortnum and Henry Cole in Florence 1858–1859' in Ben Thomas and Timothy Wilson (eds), *C.D.E. Fortnum and the Collecting and Study of Applied Arts and Sculpture in Victorian England* (London, 1999), p. 172. Murray, *Handbook for Travellers in Northern Italy, Part II* (London, 1854) made it clear that the house was now being run by Mrs Clark's daughter, but in some later editions it was said to be by her sister.

44   Starke, *Information* (1826), p. 112 note. Mrs Starke had not mentioned the hotel in her 1820 edition.

45   Murray, *Handbook* (1842), pp. 480–1, 487.

46   *Gazzetta* 10 & 17 December.

47   Starke, *Information* (1826), p. 81; James Cobbett, *Journal*, p. 321.

48   Arthur Vansittart, 'Florence Races', *Sporting Review* Vol. 1 (1839), p. 33.
49   Anonymous, *The European Indicator or Road-Book for Travellers on the Continent* (Florence, 1841), p. 110.
50   Via Legnaioli no longer exists; it was the more southerly part of the present Via Tornabuoni, which ends in Piazza S. Trinità. The Pellicano is almost certainly now the Hotel Beacci-Tornabuoni in Via Tornabuoni and would not be given the Piazza address today.
51   FO79/214, Corbett to FO, 2 April 1860.
52   JLM, E11 f. 35.
53   FO79/177, Scarlett to FO, 1 May 1854; FO79/183, Normanby to FO, 7 January 1855.
54   FO45/257, Hudson to FO with enclosure from Fenton, 7 July 1860.
55   Arthur Vansittart 'Autumn on the Arno', *Sporting Review* Vol. 2 1840, p. 355.
56   JLM, E9 f216v; Jousiffe, *Road Book*, pp. 59–60.
57   William Snow, *Hand Book for the Baths of Lucca* (Pisa, 1846), p. 59.
58   Jousiffe, *Road Book*, p. 60.
59   Gamgee's life is summarized by Jean Robin, *Elmdon: Continuity and Change in a North-West Essex Village 1861–1984* (Cambridge, 1980), p. 168. See also Ruth D'Arcy Thompson, *The Remarkable Gamgees: A Story of Achievement* (Edinburgh, 1974), whose early pages are useful for Gamgee's life in Florence, although the chronology is sometimes vague.
60   *Gazzetta* 26 January, 20 February 1830, 22 November 1831.
61   All three sons merit an entry in the DNB: Joseph as a vet and pathologist; John as a vet and inventor in the field of thermodynamics; and Arthur, the youngest, as a physiologist. In 1846 Joseph was at the public school in Florence, where he excelled in geometry, and he also began a course on botany at the City Hospital. The following year he left Florence to attend the Royal Veterinary College in London and in 1849 his brother John joined him.
62   *Gazzetta* 29 April, 13 June, 19 August 1815, 18 February 1826, 24 May 1831.
63   *Gazzetta* 22 February 1824, 5 August 1826.
64   *Gazzetta* 10 July 1827, 26 October 1830.
65   *Gazzetta* 22 May 1825, 2 February 1834.
66   *Gazzetta* 27 August 1831, 17 May 1834. Even if he possessed superior qualifications, it would seem rash to identify this gentleman with the Daniel MacCarthy who married the daughter of Lady Popham.
67   *Gazzetta* 18 December 1834.
68   Robert H. Super, *Walter Savage Landor* (London 1957), p. 172; Jack Stillinger (ed.), *The Letters of Charles Armitage Brown* (Cambridge Mass., 1966), pp. 202, 283.
69   Murray, *Handbook* (1847), p. 477.
70   *Gazzetta* 26 January 1822.
71   Murray, *Handbook for Travellers in Northern Italy* (London, 1852), p. 447. A 'Lidia Laura Henning' died in Florence aged 87 in January 1874.
72   CMB 2, 6 August 1856.
73   FO79/51, Burghersh to FO, 2 February 1828, enclosing Thompson's first petition and annexed correspondence. Thompson's second petition is in FO79/52, with another copy of the first and some other related items. As so often, the name appears both with and without the 'p'; 'Thompson' has a small majority.
74   Jousiffe, *Road Book*, p. 55.
75   John Maquay sr., A5 f. 45v. English sources reveal that there were several Molini in London in the late eighteenth century.
76   Stillinger (ed.), *Letters of Brown*, p. 223; JLM, E10 f. 104v.

77 Murray, *Handbook Part II* (1854), pp. 454–5. Goodban's name appears alongside that of Molini as publisher of the 1853 edition (effectively a reprint of 1852), suggesting that it may have been in that year that he went into business on his own account.

78 CMB 1, 26 January 1853.

79 Murray, *Handbook* (1863), p. viii.

80 Marilena Tamassia, *Firenze ottocentesca nelle fotografie di J. B. Philpot* (Livorno, Sillabe, 2002). His premises at one time were at 17 Borg'Ognissanti. Tamassia and others mention a 'Jackson' as a collaborator of Philpot's. He can be identified as James Burrough Jackson, the son of a bookseller, printer and stationer of Bury St Edmunds, who died in Florence at the age of 50 in 1894. He was married at Leghorn in 1872, and his collaboration with Philpot presumably belonged to the later years of the latter's career.

81 Marianna Stark, *Travels in Italy between the years 1792 and 1798* (London, 1802), pp. 274–5.

82 Murray, *Handbook* (1842), p. 481.

83 Starke, *Travels* (1802), pp. 294–5, 300.

84 John Maquay sr., A4 f. 106.

85 If the George Townley, child of Thomas Townley, merchant, and his wife Mary, who was baptized at St Leonard's Shoreditch on 28 August 1814, can be identified as the individual who died in Florence in 1871 aged 58, it gives us a good idea of the speed with which such a tradesman might transplant himself to Italy to explore the possibilities opened up by peace and tourism.

86 ASCFI, CA 29.c.119 or., 10 November 1817; FO79/32, Falconar to Harry Rolleston, 7 March 1818.

87 The Piazza San Gaetano, already several times referred to, no longer figures on the street map, but can be identified as the present Piazza Antinori, which is scarcely more than a widening of the road: the church of San Gaetano is obliquely opposite Palazzo Antinori and the Pasquali palace is at Via Rondinelli 2, which runs through the 'piazza' and into Via de'Tornabuoni.

88 Jousiffe, *Road Book*, pp. 58–9.

89 FO79/140, Macbean to FO, 6 June 1849.

90 William Spence, *Lions of Florence* (1st ed., Florence, 1847), p. 26

91 For these Leghorn shopkeepers, see Jousiffe, *Road Book*, p. 156.

92 R. Heywood, *A Journey to Italy in 1826* (privately printed, 1919), pp. 38–42, 92–3.

93 They were the sons of Peter and Eleanor Lowe of Bristol, where they were baptized at the church of St Augustine's the Less, Sam on 13 November 1796 and William on 6 July 1800.

94 William Brockedon, *Traveller's Guide to Italy* (Paris, 1835), p. 133; *Gazzetta* 3 November 1827.

95 Jousiffe, *Road Book*, p. 161; Snow, *Hand Book Baths*, pp. 54, 58.

96 FO79/61, Falconar to Bidwell, 11 March 1831 enclosing Maddock's affidavit.

97 CMB 1, 23 February 1849.

98 Jousiffe, *Road Book*, pp. 57–8. McCracken were wine merchants and also 'agents generally for the reception of works of art, baggage, &c'. They dealt with the bankers Fenzi, French, and Maquay & Pakenham, and with Edward Goodban and James Tough as well as with Lowe.

99 FO79/140, Macbean to FO, 6 June 1849.

100 *Satirist* 8 July 1841.

101 JLM, E9 f. 222v (31 January 1833); E10 ff. 9v, (4 February 1836), 247 (30 June 1845); Jousiffe, *Road Book*, p. 59. Murray, *Handbook* (1863), p. ix. An account of the Haskards in Florence was given from memory by a kinswoman, Catherine

Carswell, *Lying Awake: An Unfinished Autobiography and Other Posthumous Papers*, first published in London in 1950. The second edition (Edinburgh, Canongate, 1997) contains an introduction which acknowledges corrections from Catharine's childhood playmate, Sir Cosmo Haskard, a direct descendant of Timothy. Even so, the picture is rather confused. Timothy is said to have run away to sea as a boy and to have lost a leg. Carswell believed that he arrived in Florence in 1823 (when he would have been only 15 or so); this was then altered to 'not long before' the fall of the Grand Duke in 1859! In this version Timothy was accompanied by his wife and 20-year-old son William, who was in fact born in Florence in the autumn of 1843. William established a bank and became a prominent member of Anglo-Florentine society.

102   Starke, *Travels in Italy* (1802), p. 301. There may have been a dynasty of Robinsons, for there was still a tailor of that name on the Lungarno in 1863, and it is hard to believe that this was the man who had been at work in the early 1790s: Murray, *Handbook* (1863), p. ix.

103   Successive editions of Murray, *Handbooks*, locate this business next to the Cafe Doney and describe it as 'fashionable and good but by no means cheap'.

104   Starke, *Travels* (1820), p. 101; EM, C4, ff. 24v-25; CMB 1, 7 May 1849.

105   BC19, 3229 RB to Reuben Browning, 18 July 1853; 15, 2751 EBB to Henrietta, 18/20 November 1848. Abraham's daughter Virginia was married in 1868 to the immensely wealthy landowner, baronet and MP Sir Julian Goldschmidt.

106   The elder Tough died in Florence in 1834, at the age of 85, and received an elaborate tomb with a lengthy Latin inscription in the English Cemetery.

107   Murray, *Handbook* (1842), p. 486.

108   CMB 2, 16 January 1856.

109   Murray, *Handbook* (1852), pp. 455–6.

110   David Robertson, *Sir Charles Eastlake and the Victorian Art World* (Princeton, 1978), pp. 145, 298. The tondo in question, now classified as 'School of Botticelli', is in the reserve collection of the National Gallery. Murray, *Handbook for Travellers in Northern Italy, part II* (London, 1858), p. 521 noted that Brown was a picture-dealer.

111   *Morning Post* 13 November 1857; *Liverpool Mercury* 8 November.

112   He had been married to Eliza, Colonel Stisted's rather younger sister, at Naples in 1831, and they had numerous children, of whom several found burial in Tuscany or elsewhere in Italy. Eliza herself died at Florence in 1855.

113   *Morning Chronicle* 30 October 1850. In 1837 John Maquay referred to Wardle as 'of Leghorn', JLM, E10 f53v; and it was here that his activities apparently centred and where a daughter was born to his wife Eugenia in 1850. Was this a mixed marriage? A Donato Wardle was buried at an unspecified age in the English cemetery in 1857, which suggests that he was known or believed to be Protestant. Wardle subscribed at Leghorn to the fund for victims of the Crimean War.

114   Starke, *Information* (1826), p. 375; Reiman (ed.), *Shelley and His Circle*, Vol. 8, pp. 890–1, 915–18, 1058–59.

115   Jousiffe, *Road Book*, pp. 53–4.

116   CMB 1, 10 February 1840. In November the funds were still with Guerber & Gonin, but the Secretary was instructed to seek more favourable terms, which were refused. Nonetheless the Church continued to use the Swiss firm for about 4 years. By the summer of 1844 money was being deposited in the Banco di Risparmio (Savings Bank) and then with Maquay & Pakenham.

117 There is no indication that he remarried, but he must have contrived to bring up at least three sons and perhaps a daughter during his years in Florence. Simon Halliday Johnstone died in Florence in 1837, at the age of 18, and another son died a few years later in Rome.

118 On at least one occasion, in July 1833, John bought wine from Johnston (JLM, E9 f. 231). We learn his business address from the advertisement in the *Gazzetta*, 18 December 1830, in which as 'provisional administrator' of the estate of the murdered Denzil Ede he invited applications from claimants.

119 JLM, E10 f. 54

120 See for example an 1840 report on a planning application in Borgo SS. Apostoli (ASCFI, CA 164, c. 760. m.). On his monument in the English Cemetery, Johnstone is designated 'of Garroch' in Galloway, not far from the Lawrie family property of Woodhall. The younger Johnstone dined with Mrs Lawrie more than once in December 1851 (JLM, E11 f. 83v).

121 His premises were on the Lungarno near the Carraia bridge, according to the *Gazzetta* of 30 September.

122 JLM, E9 ff. 268–268v.

123 Anon, *European Indicator*, pp. 107–8.; JLM, E11 f. 124.

124 JLM, E10 ff.116v/117. John's uncle, John Leland Maquay senior, had been a director of the Bank of Ireland.

125 Anon, *European Indicator*, p. 107.

126 JLM, E10 ff. 122–3.

127 Murray, *Handbook* (1842), p. 486.

128 JLM, E10 ff.245v, 248. One of the Baring sisters often stayed with the Kerriches and was included in John's invitations.

129 John heard the news on 17 July 1847 JLM, E11 f. 7.

130 Snow, *Hand Book Baths*, p. 56.

131 TNA, Prob11/2037.

132 JLM, E10 f. 197.

133 JLM, E10 ff. 273v-274. Minna unhappily died on the Isle of Bute only 4 years later, having given birth to two sons. After a brief return to Tuscany in 1851–1852, Johnston seems increasingly to have divided his time between Galloway (he became a Major in the Scottish Borderers Militia) and Cheltenham, where he remarried in 1866 and died in 1878. On his death the Probate Registry Index described him as 'formerly banker in Florence'.

134 JLM, E11 f. 166v.

15 DEPARTURES AND SURVIVORS, 1858–1860: THE END OF THE GRAND DUCHY

Early in 1858 the Tuscans provided Lord Normanby an opportunity to deal with an issue which must have been meat and drink to him. On 6 February he forwarded a despatch with nine enclosures, describing an attempt on the part of the authorities

> to establish the novel and arbitrary doctrine that the public within the walls of a Theatre, have no right to express in the usual manner disapprobation of the demerits of the performance. This pretension was on the first night enforced by the arrest of many individuals, on quitting the Theatre, who were alleged by the Gendarmes to have hissed the performance.

Among those arrested was the *attaché* Frederic St John, and reparation was instant. The gendarmes had erred in apprehending a member of the *corps diplomatique* when they could not even be certain that he was one of those expressing 'disapprobation', and the offenders were disciplined. Lenzoni, the Minister of the Interior, seemed, however, to defend proceedings against anyone not so privileged.

The next day Mr Lester Garland, 'an English Gentleman, settled here and married to a Milanese lady', was ordered not to attend the theatres for 2 months on pain of imprisonment for a similar period. His fate was shared by some half a dozen or so Florentine gentlemen who had also hired boxes for the season and were now denied the use of them. Garland was told that if he signed a paper declaring 'that he had not shared in the general expression of disapprobation', supported by two witnesses on oath, the prohibition would be withdrawn. He wisely consulted Normanby, who told him not to do so. It would amount to an admission that the authorities were justified in punishing those who had expressed audience dissatisfaction in what his Lordship regarded as the normal way. Did the Interior Minister really mean that a foreigner should, without notice, be forbidden to use a box for which he had paid, on such grounds?

That a despotic regime should display nervousness about displays of disapproval in theatres or other public places was not unprecedented, but the entirely arbitrary nature of these proceedings suggests a worrying sense of insecurity. The Tuscans wriggled, but they finally conceded and both Garland and the Florentines were permitted to attend the theatres. If the Government wished to enact laws altering social customs that was its right; but it had to be done openly by decree, with notices in all the theatres. Normanby also took the opportunity to complain on behalf of all the British who, having subscribed for the season, saw it coming to an end without the operatic productions they had expected to see when they paid their money. This had aroused 'universal and deserved discontent'.[1] Perhaps it showed that nothing much had changed in the way Florence was governed, or misgoverned, which was doubtless exactly the way the Grand Duke wanted it.

Robert Lytton tells a story about the mentality and poor quality of petty Tuscan officialdom at just this time:

> On moving from the villa to the town I sent my servant forward with two boxes, the one containing clothes, the other private letters, books and a little portrait of Dante. Dante of course being in the costume of the Cinque Cento, appears in the picture with a red cap on his head. Will you believe that the employes at the gate on opening the box took the picture of Dante for the portrait of a revolutionary chief (in consequence of the red cap) and arrested the books and papers as seditious! I had to reclaim the intervention of Normanby, and I believe the employes are to be reprimanded. So you see that Dante is still in exile here![2]

It is not surprising that intelligent Englishmen bridled at this sort of stupidity, for it was with petty officialdom that they mostly had to deal.

Normanby continued to monitor the once-vexed issue of Protestant proselytism, and on 11 March 1858 submitted a long despatch with an analysis of the Tuscan budget that clearly took somebody some time to prepare. His health was less troublesome than it had been and, blissfully unaware of the blow about to fall on him, he could not be accused of failing to do his job. The immediate cause of his downfall was less the hostile campaign which had been waged against him in the press than the unexpected ending of Palmerston's government. Palmerston resigned on 20 February 1858 and Derby formed a minority administration. The less than competent Malmesbury returned as Foreign Secretary, which he remained until June 1859, by which time the political situation in Italy had altered out of all recognition and he was totally out of his depth.

Unlike the newspapers, Malmesbury did not seem to comprehend that Normanby was now scarcely distinguishable from himself in his support for the Austrian position in Italy. Frederic St John commented that the symptoms of the coming change were clear for all to see who did not wilfully shut their eyes:

> But my excellent chief and benefactor, so liberal on other subjects, continued to the last, both in and out of Parliament, to advocate the cause of reaction in

Italy and the maintenance there of a system which, but for the support given it by Austrian bayonets, would have crumbled away long before.[3]

Nevertheless, Normanby had to go, to be replaced by some worthy Tory placeman. Perhaps aware of the capacity of the press to get hold of information as quickly as the Foreign Office did, Malmesbury decided to make use of that new toy the telegraph, and indulged in the crassest form of man management. On 26 March he telegraphed Normanby, telling him without forewarning that he had been sacked and 4 days later that he had recommended to the Queen the appointment of the Hon. Henry Howard as his replacement. He said he was writing by special messenger but was meanwhile telling Normanby all this in case he should hear it from other quarters first![4] If we recall that at this time a Foreign Office messenger had to take a telegraph down to the Post Office, so that confidentiality could be achieved only if code was employed – and in this instance it was not – our sympathy for Normanby may be increased.

He can hardly be blamed for the curtness of his reply using the same instrument: 'I should willingly and at once have placed my resignation in Your Lordship's hands had the slightest previous intimation of the wishes of the Govt left me such an option.' His bewilderment and outrage at the abrupt manner of his dismissal, with its apparent implications of incompetence and inattention to business, now consumed him. On 6 May, awaiting his successor's arrival, he composed a long despatch in which he delivered, with icy politeness, a long justification of his conduct in office. Malmesbury cannot have been best pleased by his references to Mather and the Madiai, a reminder of the embarrassments that occurred 'during the few months of your Lordship's former tenure of the same office'. Normanby's thrust was clear: he was the victim of a purely party decision, a charge which Malmesbury did not deny when he at last replied in July.[5]

As the instructions Howard received on 27 April made clear, no change of policy was contemplated. The new ambassador was told at some length that he could expect to have to deal with the ill-judged enthusiasm of Protestant missionaries, who had no right to set the laws of the host state at defiance; he was to attempt to deal with any such problem 'by amicable representation to the Tuscan Minister rather than by formal and official interference'. Normanby had done just this with some success. Nor would he have had any difficulty in continuing to work and hope for reform in the papal government, and (rightly or wrongly) he would not have dissented from the Foreign Office view that, although Austria was unpopular in Lombardy-Venetia, the inhabitants of those regions were unlikely to join willingly in an Italian kingdom.[6]

What followed was pure undignified farce. Howard seems to have been one of that tiny minority of unfortunates who, on making the acquaintance of Florence, conceive hatred at first sight. Within 3 days of his arrival in late May he was on his way home again, citing ill health as the reason for his abrupt resignation. In this short time, he had stuck his foot in the diplomatic mire by making an appointment with Lenzoni to present his credentials, which he then failed to keep. Normanby reported this bizarre turn of events to the Foreign Office by telegraph on 27 May and proposed that he should delay presenting his Letters of Recall until he received further orders. It took Malmesbury until 11 June to reply with his approval. On the 12th Normanby was informed, again by telegraph, that the Queen proposed to appoint Mr Lyons (the son of the Lord Lyons who had been received at Leghorn some months previously). The Foreign Secretary hoped that this would be agreeable to the Grand Duke and also that Normanby had apologized for Howard's conduct.

Whether Normanby did so through gritted teeth or with some degree of satisfaction is hard to tell. He would have been within his rights to withdraw from the arena, but his old friendship with the Grand Duke cannot have been a disadvantage in this embarrassing situation. In his usual ponderous manner he expressed the opinion that Howard would have acted differently had he known the country to which he had (apparently involuntarily) been appointed. He warmly approved of the choice of Lyons and it was indeed a good one. Lyons had earlier been attached to the mission and since 1854 had shown considerable skill as Britain's quasi-official representative at Rome. His appointment was acceptable to the Grand Duke and on 13 July Normanby notified the Foreign Office by telegraph that he had arrived.[7] Lyons was not in office 3 months, however, before he learned of the serious illness of his father and returned to England. His father's death and his succession to the title meant that as Lord Lyons he was cut out for higher things, and he did not return to Italy.[8]

The fact that Normanby had been 'recalled' did not, of course, mean that he was compelled physically to abandon Florence; he continued to reside there until an even greater calamity overtook him and his friend Leopold in April 1859. Another old Florence hand had left the city, entirely of his own free will, a few days before the ignominious flight of Henry Howard. John Maquay was preoccupied till the last with the future management of the bank, which involved repeated discussions with Currell Smyth, Mr Brooks and others. On 11 January he was 'perplexed' by a letter from George, and he was in frequent correspondence with Pakenham, who arrived in Florence on 8 March for a short visit. This gave rise to yet more discussions, which took place in George's absence, for he did not return to Florence until the 28th. It was agreed that Montague Pakenham was to continue in the bank under certain conditions (he was still a minor), but George was to make his own decision as to partnership and Brooks was to be compensated if he 'goes out'. Smyth had been of opinion all along that even if the present dispute had not occurred George and Brooks would have been unable to co-operate.[9] On 18 April John registered a disagreement between George and Smyth, which may have been prophetic of more to come; John had had his own problems with Currell in the past.

Bank business apart, these months were naturally much occupied with social calls and farewells. John must have reflected on times past on 25 January when he attended 'a great ball at Poniatowski first time of opening his house formerly Casa Standish & completely transmogrified it was & very handsome'. He had known this house and its theatre when Rowland Standish owned it and Charles Lever rented it; he had acted as agent for it for many years. A few days later, he spent exactly 1 hour at 'Lord Normanby's last reception'. He saw a great deal of his old friends the Galeazzi and Mrs Fombelle, whose will he helped to draft on 20 March: 'She made Elena a present of a very handsome India gold bracelet & me of a very pretty silver egg stand for four eggs.' On 6 May he handed over responsibility for the house expenses to George and on the 10th he was occupied all evening with the lawyer Caprili drawing up deeds. Then there was a fortnight of entertaining, but more importantly being entertained, before his departure from Florence on the 24th May. He was returning to his native Ireland, where he had not lived for any prolonged period since 1810.

Within a year of his departure there were further losses of people who would never know Tuscany without the Grand Duke. David Thomson, hotelier of Leghorn, supporter of Stewart and thorn in the side of Consul Macbean, died at the age of 82 on 27 April 1858. He was followed on 25 May by James Tait of Edinburgh, who had been in Florence since at least 1845, copying pictures in the galleries, subscribing to Vieusseux and banking with Maquay & Pakenham; he expired a victim of *delirium tremens*.[10] Major Charles Gregorie died on 16 October. John had said after George Crossman's death in 1854 that the Major planned to sell Villa Colombaia, but he had not done so. Guy Fleetwood Wilson leaves an endearing picture of the Waterloo dragoon 'who honestly believed that frogs formed the staple food in France, and never opened his mouth without damning all Frenchmen'. Gregorie bred bull terriers and was at war with Charles Lever, who bred cats. The Reverend O'Neill expressed surprise when Lever attended his funeral, to which Lever supposedly replied, 'Why the devil shouldn't I have been here? He would have been precious glad to have come to mine.'[11]

Cumberland Reid, shipbuilder at Leghorn, and Henry Gousse Bonnin, Deputy Purveyor General in the Army, both residents who dated back to the immediate post-Napoleonic years, died within 2 days of each other in November 1858, leaving large extended families. On the 30th the *Morning Post* and *Morning Chronicle* mentioned Bonnin's death and his 50 years of service in the armed forces.[12] January 1859 saw the end of Jane, the wife of Joseph Robiglio. The most unobtrusive of residents, the couple had lived continuously in Florence since their marriage there in 1833, when the Scottish-born Jane Martin had been a widow in her forties, her Piedmontese bridegroom rather younger. It does not look like a mixed marriage, and Robiglio was friendly enough with Christopher Smith to be a guest at his Christmas dinner parties in 1853 and 1854.[13] In February Anna Walker, the widow of Captain Charles Montagu Walker RN, died at the age of 67. They had been in Florence in 1819 when their daughter Florence was born, and, although some of their other children were born in England, it was in Florence that Captain Walker had died in 1833. At the time of her death Mrs Walker had more than one hundred relatives in Tuscany.[14]

Other established families continued to add to their numbers. Some had such frequent events that they could scarcely stay out of the newspapers. William Miller's marriage to Marianne Rae on 11 August 1858 was performed by the Reverend Stewart at the Leghorn consulate, with announcements in many London papers. Miller contracted three legal marriages (at least) within a relatively short space of time (in 1856, 1858 and 1869) with births and deaths of children (and, of course, deaths of wives) in between. This second marriage into the Rae family, prominent Presbyterian merchants at Leghorn and closely linked to the Hendersons, ensured an enormous family circle. Between 1832 and 1873 nearly forty children belonging to these families were welcomed into the Tuscan world, and not a few family members ushered out of it, with notices in the newspapers.

The year 1858 also saw the return of previous residents. Christopher Webb Smith was welcomed back at the Select Vestry's meeting on 22 October, when he was unanimously re-elected to their number. Alfred Hall expressed the hope that Smith might 'long remain a resident among us', and so he did.[15] The body he now rejoined would have been largely familiar to him; he had known George Maquay, who had promptly taken his father's seat, since his childhood. Smith flung himself back with a will into the church's affairs, including the vexed question of the heating; on 28 January 1859 it was even noted that he had been able to lend the church 'one Stove on the American Principle'. Before the year was out he was once again discharging the duties of Secretary and Treasurer in Alfred Hall's absence in England. Perhaps a deterioration in his wife's health had brought about their return to Tuscany. In May 1861, on a return visit to Florence, John Maquay reported that she was 'pretty well' albeit she was suffering from 'cancer internal'.[16] She died later that year and it may well be that this removed the last prospect that Smith would return to England.

A very different character, who had not resided in Florence for 23 years, also returned in 1858. Walter Savage Landor's departure from England was not entirely voluntary, but resulted from an adverse legal judgement and award of damages against him. The absence of any extradition treaty between Britain and Tuscany ensured his safety. Messrs Slack and Simmons got the predictable cold shoulder when they approached the Foreign Office asking for advice on enforcing the judgement.[17] John Maquay never mentions either Landor or Julia, the wife he had left behind him, which should not surprise us, as she appears to have been generally ostracized. Augustus Hare, one of the few who made contact with her, clearly found her monotonous complaints tedious, referring to 'the foolish wife of our dear old Landor, who never ceased to describe with fury his passionate altercations with her, chiefly caused apparently by jealousy'.[18] Julia had the added problem of the illegitimate child borne by her daughter Julia in 1850, which encouraged a low profile in a community as talkative as the English.[19]

Landor could hardly have been under any illusion that he would find a warm welcome at Fiesole. The 9 months he now spent there saw a mixture of studied unkindness from Julia and Arnold, his oldest son, who refused to make an allowance for him from the property, with more dutiful treatment from the two younger children. He finally left in July 1859 and by good fortune ran into Robert Browning (the Brownings had been away for much of the time since his return to Tuscany). Thereafter his living conditions improved. It was Browning who negotiated an allowance of £200 per annum for him from his brothers and retrieved his personal possessions from Fiesole, while his old friend William Wetmore Story looked after him physically at Siena. The allowance gave Landor some independence in his last years.[20]

That he had not lost his feistiness despite his age was shown by a much-quoted exchange with Normanby who, he believed, had snubbed him when they encountered each other in the Cascine in the presence of his family:

> We are both of us old men, my lord and are verging on decrepitude and imbecility, else my note might be more energetic. Do not imagine I am unobservant of distinctions. You by the favour of a minister are Marquis of Normanby, I by the grace of God am Walter Savage Landor.

Given that Normanby was some 25 years younger than Landor this was hardly flattering, but his Lordship kept his temper, replying that he intended no personal slight but was not in the habit of acknowledging members of Landor's family. Landor records in a letter on 8 September 1858 that 'I have received a very kind note from my old friend Lord Normanby who is paralytic. Lady Normanby wrote it'.[21] The old man was incorrigible but not without friends.

While in Florence in 1858, Browning was able to help Ferdinando and Elizabeth Romagnuoli to set up a lodging house, which provided a home for their children and also, from late 1859, a refuge for Landor. Ferdinando remained in their service, but Wilson's place with Elizabeth had been taken by Annunziata. Wilson hankered after old times, proposing in the autumn of 1858, as Elizabeth wrote, that 'she should return to me, send for her sister to take care of her house and children, and go on with us to Rome'. Elizabeth was tempted, and recognized Mrs Romagnuoli's desire to be with her husband, but good sense prevailed. How could she possibly part with Annunziata, who had given such excellent service during their recent trip to France? Furthermore,

> it did seem to me very unwise of Wilson (for her own sake) to give up her children, & the management of a lodging house in Florence, to an inexperienced English woman who does not know an Italian word, just as the house was beginning to answer and pay.[22]

Mrs Romagnuoli, as it turned out, would witness the departure of the Grand Duke, which her late employers and her husband would not.

Before their autumn departure for Rome, the Brownings received some interesting visitors, notably Frances Power Cobbe and Nathaniel Hawthorne.

The first-named was making a European tour, having been relieved of the burden of her dominating father, who had died the previous year. Before arriving in Florence she had been in Venice and before that Constantinople, where she had encountered a party of discourteous Americans who refused to allow her to join them in viewing Hagia Sophia. In an amusing illustration of how the latter-day Grand Tour worked, she arrived in Florence a month before them and told her story, with the result that they were comprehensively snubbed when they in turn arrived. They particularly wanted to meet the Brownings, but 'Mrs Browning frankly expressed her astonishment at their behaviour', while Mrs Somerville, who had also befriended her, had nothing to say to them. Miss Cobbe also met the Trollopes, Isa Blagden and Walter Savage Landor. Elizabeth Browning she admired, but she reserved her warmest admiration for Mary Somerville, who reciprocated it, calling her 'the cleverest and most agreeable woman I ever met with, and one of the best'.[23]

Hawthorne visited Casa Guidi with his wife and Miss Shephard, his children's governess, on 8 June 1858, arriving at 8 o'clock in the evening, to be greeted by Robert and Pen. The latter rather alarmed him. He thought he resembled his mother and had inherited her weakly constitution: 'He is nine years old, and seems at once less childlike and less manly than would befit that age. I should not quite like to be the father of such a boy.' Elizabeth herself was

a pale little woman scarcely embodied at all; at any rate only substantial enough to put forward her slender fingers to be grasped and to speak with a shrill yet sweet, tenuity of voice. Really I do not see how Mr Browning can suppose that he has an earthly wife, any more than an earthly child; both are of the elfin-breed, and will flit away from him some day, when he least thinks of it.

What most struck him about Browning himself was that he

was very efficient in keeping up conversation with everybody, and seemed to be in all parts of the room and in every group at the same moment, a most vivid and quick thoughted person, logical and common sensible.

His conversation was surprisingly clear and to the purpose considering the obscurity of his verse. It was a 'pleasant evening' which broke up after 2 hours at 10 o'clock because of the state of Elizabeth's health, but 'there was no very noteworthy conversation'. Spiritualism was the most interesting topic, but Hawthorne thought it 'now wearisome', noting that Elizabeth was a believer and Robert 'an infidel'.[24]

Some 2 months later Hawthorne visited Seymour Kirkup with Isa Blagden. 'He lives in an old house, formerly a residence of the Knights Templars, hanging over the Arno, just as you come upon the Ponte Vecchio.' Isa had warned him that Kirkup's personal hygiene left something to be desired, but the old man had spruced himself up for the visit. Hawthorne thought that he had a perpetually surprised look, deriving from this the impression that he was 'somewhat crackbrained', but he conceded that 'his appearance and manners [were] those of a gentleman, with rather more embroidery of courtesy than belongs to an Englishman'. Here again Hawthorne could not get away from the spirits. Shown the portrait of the now-dead Regina, he commented humorously that Kirkup 'did not quite know that he had done anything' to bring about the birth of her daughter.[25]

On 28 August he met Browning again at Isa's villa, with its 'especially fine' view of Florence and the hills beyond. Elizabeth was not there and two or three other gentlemen were present whom he did not know, but there were also Hiram Powers and Thomas Trollope. He found Robert in a much more relaxed and playful mood, commenting that 'He must be an amiable man. I should like him much (and make him like me) if opportunities were favourable'. Still the spirits were not to be avoided, and the conversation turned to Miss Shephard's 'faculties as a spiritual writing medium'. Then 'Mr Powers related some things he had witnessed through the agency of Mr Hume who had held a session or two at his house'. The medium's visit was still a topic of conversation more than 2 years afterwards. Hawthorne gave it as his decided opinion that he was a knave but 'a particularly good medium for spiritual communications'. On this evening he conversed principally with Trollope, whom he may have half-mistaken for his brother. He was 'a very sensible and cultivated man, and I suspect an author; at least there is a literary man of repute, of this name, though I have never read his works'. Hawthorne disapproved of Trollope's long absence from his native land, which he felt deprived life of its 'reality'.[26]

At the moment the Brownings left Florence to winter in Rome, Britain was again without an ambassador in Florence. The departure of Lyons to attend his father's deathbed meant that before he left on 6 October the newly arrived Secretary of Legation, Edwin Corbett, was hastily presented to Lenzoni as *chargé d'affaires*. In the event Corbett proved more than efficient during the last days of the Grand Duke and beyond, assisted by the scarcely less able Fenton. Normanby had told the Foreign Secretary on 16 July that Fenton had capably discharged almost all the duties normally undertaken by the Secretary of Legation. He had won his spurs under Bulwer and 'I can state as a fact that few Englishmen have taken such successful pains to inform themselves of the past history and present state of Italy, as Mr Fenton has done during his constant residence of above six years'. Coming from Normanby, who had such a high opinion of his own knowledgeability, that was praise indeed.[27]

For the third time in less than a year Malmesbury was called upon to advise the Queen on who was to preside at the Florence embassy. His choice was less than inspired: Peter Campbell Scarlett, who had been in Brazil since his previous Florentine posting. Nominally at least he had now reached the top of the pile, but in reality this was scarcely a promotion and was not to last long. His appointment prompted an extraordinary (and distorted) outburst in the *Birmingham Daily*

Post of 15 December. At Florence he had previously 'connived at the shameful treatment of a British subject'; his Brazilian posting had been a cover-up for this disgrace,

> and now he is brought back again to Florence, the very scene from which he was removed under circumstances that should have for ever prevented him appearing where his presence can only bring a blush to the cheek of any Englishman conscious of the transaction we refer to.

Mather was not forgotten, by this writer at least. Scarlett did not leave England till 2 February 1859, arriving in Florence on the 25th after a delay in Paris which he had to explain to Malmesbury.[28] Some 9 weeks of dilatory exchanges took place between the two of them, while rather serious events were taking place in Europe which would have a profound impact on Tuscany. From their Florentine vantage point Corbett and Scarlett monitored and reported on the gathering storm.

This was heralded by clear signs of a Franco-Piedmontese accord, to be cemented by the marriage of the Emperor's nephew Prince Napoleon to Princess Clotilde of Sardinia, which was aimed squarely at Austria's Italian hegemony. Florentine demonstrations of approval for Piedmontese policy stimulated a police crackdown. Still Tuscany was quiet, but 'some movement in Lombardy' could alter that.[29] Corbett was assured that Tuscany desired to remain neutral, could rely on its own army to maintain order and had no intention of allowing Austrian troops to enter the Grand Duchy. If the experience of 1848–1849 was anything to go by, these were mere pious hopes. The Tuscans believed there was nothing to be gained by exchanging the dominance of Austria in Italy for that of France, and looked to the Powers to uphold the Vienna settlement.[30]

The Tuscan Government at the end of March 1859 committed the supreme blunder of attempting the seizure of the *Biblioteca Civile Dell'Italiano*, a journal which analysed the political grievances of Tuscany following the abolition of the constitution under Austrian occupation. The police failed to secure the work itself before it was in general circulation, and were able only to destroy the type that had been used to print it. The seizure was illegal under the present press law and the government's next move was to issue a *motu proprio* rescinding the law. Scarlett wagged a finger at all concerned. The government's violation of the law was all very deplorable, but it was regrettable

> that at this moment when efforts are making by a union of the Great Powers to ameliorate the condition of Italy, the Constitutional Liberals of Tuscany are only widening the breach between the Grand Duke and his subjects by publications calculated to lower him still more in their estimation.

As a statement of Conservative policy this could hardly be faulted, but it did not reveal a very firm grasp of political realities.[31]

Ricasoli, Ridolfi and Peruzzi, with others, had founded the *Biblioteca Civile* in 1857. Capponi apart, they were the most prominent members of the liberal constitutionalist establishment. Ricasoli, who was to be very much the leader in Tuscany during the 2 years after the exit of the Grand Duke in April and would be Prime Minister of Italy after the death of Cavour, was no red revolutionary. The antiquity of his aristocratic pedigree exceeded the Grand Duke's. Much the same might be said of Ridolfi and Peruzzi, and it should never be forgotten that the names of these and other moderate constitutionalists (who had sometimes been snubbed by the house of Hapsburg-Lorraine) were deeply embedded in centuries of Florentine history. After the failure of the 1848–1849 revolution Ricasoli had supported the return of the Grand Duke, but refused to serve as a minister, becoming a model proprietor on his Chianti estates, whose wine would become world renowned. Periodic efforts had been made to tempt him out of retirement, but he had steadfastly refused. He had never concealed his view that Tuscany needed a liberal constitution, but he was hostile to foreign interference. He did not, as Scarlett suggests, set out in 1859 to drive a wedge between the Grand Duke and his subjects. Leopold had already lost the respect and affection, if not the allegiance, of many of the latter and his survival was now largely dependent on what happened elsewhere.

Despite grandiose statements from the Government that Tuscany was tranquil and its troops sufficient to maintain order, it rapidly became obvious, after the Austrian ultimatum to Piedmont on 23 April requiring her to disarm, that it had no control whatever. The speed with which the Grand Duke's neutral posture was revealed to be untenable precluded any effective intervention on his behalf, even if it had been contemplated. On 26 April Scarlett was already telegraphing to Malmesbury:

Revolution in Tuscany considered probable unless the GD joins in war against Austria. Loyalty of the troops very questionable. What should GD do? British interests require that ships of war be sent to Leghorn immediately.[32]

Before the Foreign Office had any chance to respond, the following was sent from Florence on the 27th at 3.15 pm, arriving at 2.20 am on the 28th:

Last night all Tuscan troops fraternised with the people. The Tuscan cabinet resigned as a body. Grand Duke attempted to place Marquis Lajatico at the head of a new cabinet. This failed altogether. This morning Grand Duke assembled the diplomatic body at the palace and informed them that his abdication was demanded but that he had refused that he threw himself on the protection of all the powers of Europe. He intends to leave Tuscany immediately and will, I suspect, go to Bologna. I request immediate instructions. There is no ministry at present. Italian tricolore is flying from most public buildings.

Later the same day Scarlett sent the following:

> Revolution accomplished. Florence tranquil. Piedmontese General Ulloa commands troops junta of three persons (Cav. Ubaldino Peruzzi, Magg. Vincenzo Malenchini, Magg. Alessandro Danzini) in Piedmontese interest has established provisional government. Tuscan arms removed everywhere. Macbean reports similarly from Leghorn, same date. All calm – Piedmontese effectively in charge.[33]

In little more than 2 days it was all over. There was next to no bloodshed. It was indeed all calm, at least in Tuscany, which is more than could be said for Italy further north.

Details of the unfolding of the final crisis emerged only after a lapse of some days. At midnight on 27 April Scarlett wrote a despatch giving a full account and making clear his own opposition to the Grand Duke's departure. It largely amounted to an expansion of the narrative already embodied in his telegrams. Leopold had resolved to leave the country at once with his family and to 'throw himself for his justification and protection upon all the Powers of Europe'. Scarlett understood that he would make for Vienna, as von Hügel informed him. He disapproved 'of this very sudden retreat', convinced (rightly enough) that 'in placing himself thus at once in Austrian hands the Grand Duke compromises the principle of neutrality, and endangers the future interests of the dynasty he represents'. Scarlett therefore refrained from being present when 'The Imperial party took their departure by the Bologna route soon after 7 o'clock, escorted out of the town by a few cavalry'.

Without comment, which he probably thought superfluous, Scarlett enclosed a copy of a printed handbill addressed to the English in Florence. It called upon them to take note of the Italian spirit of nationality, and was not complimentary to the present British government: 'the fall of the Derby ministry and the naming of a truly English and national government, are the liveliest desires and warmest hopes of the Tuscan people.' Scarlett did not doubt that similar events would by now have unfolded at Leghorn 'and in other Tuscan cities where the efforts have been unceasing of late to determine people's minds in favour of the war of independence'. Von Hügel had removed the arms of Austria from his embassy and left Tuscany. Looking on the bright side, Scarlett concluded, 'I am happy to add that these most unprecedented events have not given rise as yet to any violence done to either persons or property.'[34] A few days later he expressed his satisfaction on hearing that the Grand Duke had made for Munich rather than Vienna, but this was premature if he took it to mean that he was not going to enter body and soul into the Austrian camp.

Leopold's flight was not altogether dignified. Guy Fleetwood Wilson, who was then 8 years old, recalled seeing the Grand Duke pass 'through our carriage drive, and I was struck by the fact he wore blue carpet slippers'. He further mused: 'It was not his fault he was born an Austrian and a noodle.' Thomas Trollope recalls the departure as entirely peaceful:

> I saw him pass from the Porta San Gallo on his way to Bologna among a crowd of his late subjects, who all lifted their hats, though not without some satirical cries. He had the misfortune to fall on his bottom saying farewell to the few friends who accompanied him to the frontier. But no one impeded the departure of the man who had abandoned his throne without any sort of resistance – thus undermining those who wished to resist on his behalf.[35]

On this very day Theodosia fired off a report for the *Athenaeum*, which appeared on 7 May and began with the memorable announcement, 'We have made a revolution with rosewater.'

Mary Somerville's account is just as revealing. The family was taking its usual drive on the Cascine at the time that the whole Imperial family departed 'unmolested amid a silent crowd'. She noted that 'The obnoxious ministers were also permitted to retire unnoticed to their country houses', a detail which sufficiently differentiates this revolution from many others. So quiet was it that 'my daughters walked about the streets, as most ladies did', to see what was going on. Captain Fleetwood Wilson had a slightly more exciting time. Hearing firing and shouting, he walked down into the city, only to be seized by a cheering crowd who noted that 'he happened to have put a red rose in his buttonhole, which with its green leaves and a bit of white handkerchief showing out of his pocket created the beloved tricolour'. Young Guy professed to believe that this was accidental, and that his father had 'punctiliously' observed the official British advice to the Anglo-Florentines to maintain strict neutrality.

The Somervilles went to the theatre in the evening, and the following day passed normally, with everyone at work as usual. In the evening they went to a reception at the embassy (Mary miscalls Scarlett 'Sir James') 'where we heard many predictions of evil which were never fulfilled. The least of these was the occupation of Florence by a victorious Austrian army'. If this shows that some people were nervous, she herself was not. On 5 May she wrote to her son Woronzow Greig, who had clearly written to her in some alarm as soon as he heard the news in England. His letter 'would have made me laugh heartily, were we not annoyed that you should have suffered such uneasiness on our account; the panic in England is ridiculous and most unfounded'. Having reassured him on this point she concluded, 'Not a word of republicanism, it has never been named. All they want is a constitutional government, and this they are quietly settling.' This faith was important to many British observers, and Mrs Somerville reinforced the message in a succession of letters to her son over the next few weeks.[36]

No shot was fired on Florence from the Belvedere, despite the rumoured existence of instructions that in the event of an uprising the garrison was to do just that. Trollope saw the hand of the Grand Duke's second son, the Archduke

Charles, if not of the Grand Duke himself, in these supposed orders. In later life he was less certain about Leopold's involvement, which Fleetwood Wilson also doubted on the rather general grounds of Leopold's amiable character and love of Florence. Scarlett described the allegation, which was repeated in a Memorandum sent to the diplomatic representatives by the Provisional Government, as 'a gross exaggeration of facts, if not altogether untrue'. A written plan was in existence by which Florence would be divided into military districts in case of unrest, 'but it is absolutely denied by less interested parties than the Conspirators themselves against the Grand Dukes authority' that the measures contemplated included bombardment. Scarlett damned the Memorandum with faint praise that was as eloquent as the capital letter of 'Conspirators': it was on the whole 'a well written and able production'.[37]

Clearly such a bombardment might have had devastating effects in terms of loss of life and damage both to the Florentine artistic heritage and to foreign property as well as that of Florentine residents. Whether it would have prevented or provoked revolution is another matter. From Leghorn Macbean wrote that despite great excitement 'order was not disturbed to the slightest degree'. The Italian *tricolore* had been raised in place of the Tuscan flag among general rejoicing, which was somewhat dampened by the subsequent announcement 'that the Grand Duke had refused to accede to the wishes of his People and had taken his departure with all the Royal Family'. Sardinian involvement was confirmed with the arrival of General Ulloa to assume the command of the Tuscan army, and political prisoners had been liberated. In a report to Scarlett written on the same day Macbean added that it 'was very evident that, if the Grand Duke had no friends, his Dynasty had still a large number of partisans in Leghorn'.[38]

The *Times* carried the news as early as 29 April, printing a telegraph from Turin (one suspects the hand of Cavour, ensuring that the English newspapers were able to react as soon as the Government). On 3 May, it printed a full account from a correspondent in Florence dated 27 April. This (like Theodosia's of the same date) emphasized the peaceful nature of the revolution and included the proclamation issued by the Provisional Government, which began 'The Grand Duke and his Government, rather than satisfy the just demands of the country, manifested in so many ways and for so long a time, have abandoned it to itself.' The *Times* distanced itself from the policy of the Conservative government and others were even quicker off the mark. The *Morning Post* received a telegraph by way of Paris on the 28th, recording the flight of the Grand Duke, 'whom no one respects', along with 'the jesuitical members of his cabinet'. Others followed over the next few days, almost uniformly hostile to Leopold, Austria and English policy. The hostile press campaign during May suggested that the British government might soon be going the way of the Grand Duke, to the distress of Queen Victoria and the pro-Austrians at court.

With Leopold's departure doubt was immediately thrown on Scarlett's status. Any unfinished business which required dealings with the Tuscan Government was now formally suspended, awaiting the clarification of the situation. In legal terms Scarlett was now inferior to Macbean. On 1 May he asked urgently (by telegraph) whether a marriage celebrated in his house in Florence would now be legal. The answer was negative, but thanks to an interruption of the telegraph it took almost a week to reach him.[39] On 4 May, therefore, Arthur Matthews, whose late father had for some years inhabited a villa in the hills just to the north of Florence, was married at the Legation to Augusta, the sister of the future Lord Leighton, who was a witness; she and her brother had spent part of their childhood in Florence.

Communications were now reaching Scarlett via Turin, bringing with them a *de facto*, if not *de jure*, subordination to Sir James Hudson. It was through Hudson that Scarlett received the instruction to remain for the moment at his post, although his official functions were in abeyance.[40] During May Malmesbury seemed unable to make up his mind what Scarlett should do; his future was as uncertain as the Grand Duke's. It was left to Russell, now Foreign Secretary a week into a new government, to put him out of his misery by calling him home, leaving Corbett in charge. The tone was slightly dismissive: Scarlett was told 'not to inconvenience yourself as there is no hurry'.[41] The centre of the Italian world was now Turin, and within a week two of those most unsympathetic to what had happened in Tuscany, Malmesbury and Scarlett, had disappeared from office.

There were varied reactions to Leopold's flight, which at the time few perhaps recognized as the end of the Grand Duchy. The Brownings were not in Florence until the end of May, and John Maquay, however laconic he might well have been, had gone. Another notable English resident fled, at considerable speed. On 11 May the *Daily News* reported that 'The Marquis and Marchioness of Normanby have left Florence, where they have been resident for several years past, for Munich, owing to the unsettled state of political affairs in central Italy'. Several other papers carried this news; the *Leeds Mercury* on the following day was somewhat behind the times, reporting it as the departure of the British Ambassador, which was doubly misleading. Obviously, Normanby intended to consult with Leopold. By 23 May the Normanbys had arrived in London. As the event would sadly show, the Grand Duke's old friend would consume much of the time that remained to him in trying to reverse the decisions that had been taken in April 1859. This aroused some irritation on the part of the new regime, not to say of those who had to listen to him in the House of Lords.

Another reaction was both very unobtrusive and arguably very significant. Archibald Campbell Dennistoun was a frequent subscriber to the Vieusseux reading rooms and on 4 May he took out a fresh subscription for a whole year. Evidently he did not anticipate that rapine and pillage would disturb his reading. On 7 May he attended a meeting of the Select Vestry, whose members signally failed to record any reaction to what was going on around them. Instead, they considered O'Neill's request for the appointment of a curate, and a week later approved a small rise in the seat tariff in order to pay for it. In July Ridolfi, the Minister for Foreign Affairs in the Provisional Government, told Corbett that the government was contemplating a new law granting total liberty of conscience. It wished to have the views of the Anglican clergymen at Leghorn and Florence and Corbett was asked to request the British government to instruct those worthies to enter into communication with the Minister for Ecclesiastical Affairs on the subject. This seemingly roundabout approach may indicate an awareness, or belief, that the clergy could not be expected to communicate with the Provisional Government without the direct authorization of the Foreign Secretary, which was promptly provided.[42]

This resolutely 'business as usual' attitude was well illustrated in the autumn. O'Neill's long summer absences had already caused annoyance. On 14 September, from the comfort of Vevey in Switzerland, he wrote that Mrs O'Neill's health made it necessary to spend the winter in Rome and that he had already applied to the Bishop of Gibraltar for permission to do so. As if aware that this would arouse criticism, not least because of his discourtesy in applying to the Bishop before informing the congregation, he attempted a pre-emptive strike. He would be sorry if, when the circumstances were known, his flock 'should express any thing but sympathy with their Minister', for this would mean that 'his Ministry among them had been productive of little benefit', which he was reluctant to believe. Mrs O'Neill was nervous of Florence's 'present unsettled state', although he had 'no apprehensions' himself.

Webb Smith replied testily. Residents and visitors were now returning to Florence, and O'Neill was reminded that, on his own recommendation, the Select Vestry had agreed in April to raise the tariffs in order to appoint a curate. They still had no curate, while the chaplain was absent and apparently had taken no steps to arrange a substitute. O'Neill's arrival in Florence on 29 October prevented a final breach, and he stayed for the winter. His attempt to appoint a curate, he claimed, had foundered on the outbreak of the revolution, when his candidate refused to come out. It was agreed that since he was now present he would fulfil his duties, a curate would not be appointed, and the tariff was reduced to that in force in April, with appropriate refunds to those who had paid extra.[43]

Several noteworthy Tuscan residents departed the scene in the course of 1859, but not because they fled. Colonel Henry Stisted died in Rome on 19 May and was brought back to Bagni for burial. A link with the Florentine past that John Maquay had known was broken when Major Galeazzi died in November; what was his reaction, as an old Austrian officer, to the recent transformation? He was closely followed by Dr Charles Bankhead, aged 91; he had been in Florence for almost as long as Leopold had reigned. If the living did not rush to leave Tuscany, it was partly because the peaceful change of government coincided with a greater threat to travel in Northern Italy because of the war. Many believed at this date that the Grand Duke would be back at the behest of the Powers, although more were sceptical than in 1849. There were some considerable differences between the present situation and that of a decade earlier. Most obviously, the war against Austria was successful, and the direct involvement of France seemed to ensure that, whatever else emerged, the Hapsburg monopoly on power in the peninsula was now at an end. From the outset, also, the Provisional Government seems to have won the confidence of the English residents.

This was a much more competent administration not only than that which had briefly held office in 1849 but than the outgoing Tuscan Ministers in any conceivable combination. Foremost among its personnel was Ricasoli, whose belief in Italy made him more sympathetic to the ambitions of Garibaldi and Mazzini than to those of Cavour and Piedmontese aggrandisement. The early manifestations of the Government's determination to maintain law and order, even to the extent of using Sardinian troops with Tuscans away at the war, clearly supported a 'wait and see' policy, with those in trade or business going on as usual. Ridolfi early established a working relationship with Corbett, which helped to reassure the English. While Ricasoli was aware of official niceties about recognition, he wanted the British embassy to remain as a counterweight to the pressures being exerted by the Sardinian and French representatives. Thus Corbett found himself being consulted on all sorts of matters outside his remit. For example, at Ridolfi's request he asked the Foreign Secretary's advice on putting the electoral law of 1848 into force and convoking a National Assembly 'to deliberate on the future destiny of the Country'. With the change of British Government in June 1859 advice was not backward in arriving. Now Ridolfi, while thanking Russell for his recommendations (which he had adopted), was anxious to know whether Her Majesty's Government thought it desirable to hasten the meeting of the Assembly, which might be delayed if all the prescribed formalities were observed.[44]

In mid-1859 the future shape of things was by no means certain, which gave hope to those who, like Normanby, deplored the threatened changes. Thomas Trollope familiarized his readers with the term *codini* ('pigtails'), which denoted reactionaries both Italian and non-Italian, and his wife also made use of it. That British specimens of the breed were making their feelings known was indicated by the circulation of a reproachful handbill in Florence, reported by the *Times* on 25 May. The authors thought it 'positively incomprehensible how certain English subjects in Florence abuse the toleration of the Tuscan people, and while beneath the protection of the laws conspire for the ruin of the country'. These people were known to be promoting 'manifestations of sympathy for the fallen house of Lorraine'.

The handbill continued: 'The Tuscans do not wish to include all the English in the complicity of a few. They well know those against whom their indignation is excited.' These were reminded that 'as guests of a civilized land', it was

> manifestly unworthy of free citizens of Great Britain, to conspire against a people who have received them generously and hospitably, at a moment when, in the cause of common independence, they were able in a few hours to destroy a dynasty that existed upwards of a century, because it had proved itself palpably opposed to the interests and wants of their country – Italy.

The Florence correspondent of the *Morning Chronicle* remarked sardonically that 'some of these very easily alarmed admirers of a "paternal" government' were now complaining that they were 'threatened', and that 'the English were to have their throats cut'. The *Caledonian Mercury*, on 30 May, went so far as to report that 'the only adherents who venture to regret publicly the twice-fugitive Leopold are, strange to say, a few English residents, whom the great landholders and influential native nobility, now in charge of public order, have found it necessary to "caution"'.

The bloody war between France and Austria ended as suddenly as it had begun with the truce of Villafranca in July, but it was not short enough to avoid giving a massive stimulus to Italian national aspirations. Even in peaceful Florence, Corbett had to report that the publication of the terms of the truce, which seemed to portend a restoration of the previous regime, might well cause unrest.[45] However, Austria was in no position to renew a war she had just lost in pursuit of the restoration of a weak ruler who, at the first sign of trouble, had abandoned his post. After a half-hearted attempt to make Prince Jerome the ruler of Tuscany during the war was rebuffed, the French were certainly not going to war to enforce their own agreement with the Austrians. The resignation of Cavour after Villafranca, far from weakening the revolutionary stimulus in central Italy, strengthened it, for until he returned to office 6 months later he could deny any responsibility for outcomes he was helping to promote. When he did return, the outbreak of revolt in Sicily finally ensured that there was to be no partial solution which would leave Tuscany or any other area of central Italy outside the framework of a new Italy.

With the epic events of 1860 we are not directly concerned; but Garibaldi's subversion of Sicily and then mainland Naples, and the enforced Piedmontese invasion of the Papal States while the Powers froze, rendered the return of any Hapsburg ruler a dead issue. Leopold might have entertained hopes until October 1860, but they were extinguished when the erstwhile Holy Alliance met at Warsaw in a vain attempt to recover its dignity and resolved on inaction in the face of British intransigence. After all, if Italy could do it herself, who were the British to complain? There was nothing more for Leopold but to retire to his spiritual home, Rome, where he died on 29 January 1870.

Meanwhile neither Normanby in England nor the *codini* in Tuscany were silent. In a piece dated from Pistoia on 15 January 1860 Theodosia Trollope imagined a dialogue between a 'liberal English traveller' and an 'English resident'. The former has got the idea that 'the feeling of Italian nationality has of late been making great progress among the agricultural population'; the 'resident' dismisses it as 'all falsehoods got up by those red Republicans who infest the towns'. They 'will get their deserts by the end of Carnival at latest', for he is privy to secret knowledge about the imminent counter-revolution. Theodosia's aim was precisely to confirm the popularity of the recent changes among ordinary rural or small-town Italians, which continued to be denied (rightly or wrongly) by opponents of the changed order.

One day in late December 1859 two young English ladies named Sperling chalked on a Florentine wall the slogan 'Viva Ferdinando IV', thus causing a minor tumult. The Ferdinando in question was the eldest son of the late Grand Duke, who had now belatedly abdicated in his favour. Unfortunately Ferdinando had blotted his copybook by appearing on the Austrian side at the battle of Solferino. Yet again, this minor episode was promptly reported in the English press. In a report filed on 23 December and published on 4 January, the *Times* correspondent Antonio Gallenga quoted the brief report that had appeared in *La Nazione*, which did not name the guilty parties. Corbett did, but he was writing, as it were, behind closed doors. According to his account, the young ladies were 'living with their brother in the house of a Florentine gentleman, formerly an officer in the Grand Ducal Body Guard, well known as entertaining opinions favourable to the late reigning Family'. As a result of their indiscretion the police searched the house, but nothing incriminating was found. The miscreants' brother, the Reverend F.H. Sperling, had called upon Corbett to ask him to prevent their expulsion, which Corbett had achieved on application to Ricasoli, 'upon the understanding that their brother would become responsible for their proper behaviour during the remainder of their stay in Tuscany'.[46]

Corbett regarded this as the end of the affair, but the voracious British press had more contributions to make. In the *Times* of 10 January Gallenga offered a curious reinterpretation of the incident based, he believed, on better information. The ladies had been motivated by zeal not for the fallen dynasty, but for evangelical truth. Persuaded somehow that the new government was as intolerant as its predecessor, they had been 'tempted by a well-known *Codino*, or reactionary partisan' to commit an offence which was no more than 'an act of unpardonable silliness and imprudence'. Gallenga wished to clear their names of the accusations that had been laid against them and (truly enough) to dismiss the rumour that they had been expelled from Tuscany. Theodosia Trollope, writing in the *Athenaeum* on 14 January, named the young ladies and reproduced the original story. The girls had been living 'for the last month with an Italian family marked among those who are eagerly dabbling in petty plots for the restoration of the fallen dynasty'.

The Reverend Sperling, who was rector of Papworth in Cambridgeshire, indignantly demanded the right of reply, and the *Athenaeum* on 4 February published his alternative account, rather spoiling the effect by the editorial observation 'That his explanations appear to make the case weaker and worse is not our fault.' Of their Italian host, who had been called a conspirator, Sperling stiffly remarked that 'His only crime – and to honourable minds it must ever be considered a virtue – is that of loyalty to the Sovereign whom he has so long and so faithfully served'. In other words, he said little to support Gallenga's alternative version. The *Lancaster Gazette* on 11 February was one of several newspapers to quote Theodosia's piece and Mr Sperling's reply, adding its own sideswipe:

By the way would it not be more seemly if the rector of Papworth were at home amongst his parishioners, instead of gadding about and getting into mischief among the Florentines. Surely he must have some use in his parish; if not the sooner a successor is appointed the better.

All references to the Sperlings were omitted from the version of Theodosia's article reprinted in *Social Aspects of the Italian Revolution*.

What, apart from legitimist conservatism, might have motivated these British dissenters from the general enthusiasm for Italian 'freedom'? Many politicians, and others, remained wedded to the notion of Austria as 'our old ally' (against Napoleon) and were correspondingly suspicious of the designs, in Italy and elsewhere, of a France now headed by Napoleon III. Some observers looked to another kind of explanation. A lengthy account of the Florentine situation published in the *Daily News* on 3 January 1860 acknowledged that

> among the numerous host of our countrymen who have planted their tents on the banks of the Arno, there are many who openly advocate the interests of the Lorraine dynasty. Some of these belong to a class of her Majesty's subjects who would never be met in good society at home, but whom everybody is astonished to find moving in the highest circles abroad. Some others, though respectable both in character and education, have been induced to espouse the cause of the dethroned princes only because they were much thought of by the court and always invited to the balls and dinners of the Pitti Palace. The prototype of the last-named class was the Marquis of Normanby, whose directions they constantly followed, for it was through his lordship that the invitations were asked and obtained … They had settled in this fair country for amusement's sake, and they could not endure the thought of seeing the next carnival spoiled because it had pleased the Tuscans to assert their political rights.

The new Tuscan government was, in fact, conscious that it needed to offer some social gatherings and entertainments to compensate for what had been lost. As the *Daily News* correspondent cynically remarked,

> The Florentines are very fond of amusements, especially when they get them for nothing. When they see that balls and dinners are not wanting, the few remaining adherents of the dethroned Dukes will desist from their harmless opposition.

Gallenga in his *Times* reports had a great deal to say, in sardonic vein, about the various lavish entertainments that were given by certain parties to gratify this perceived appetite. The Piedmontese representative in Florence, Buoncompagni, gave a ball to mark the New Year of 1860, which Edwin Corbett attended. Explosive devices were detonated outside the palace and more bombs went off later in the month outside the residences of prominent members of the Provisional Government.

It might be argued that for some the point of living in Tuscany rather than in England was not only to enjoy a more agreeable climate and lower prices, but to escape both the ugly aspects of industrialization and commercialization and the associated social and political changes. Not all British exiles shared the religious enthusiasms that caused some to applaud a revolution which promised religious toleration and to dream of the advance of Protestantism in Italy. As Theodosia Trollope regretfully wrote, displays of patriotism by the Italian priesthood displeased some:

> Not many days since, a *Codina* of triple-piled retrogradism (a countrywoman, alas! of my own) was heard pathetically lamenting over the growing apostasy in the Church and saying, though herself a *Protestant*, 'Italy has no hope but in her priests, and now they too are beginning to fall off.'[47]

The Catholicism of the Italians was important because it formed part of the picture of a country still rooted in its past. It fed British condescension and authorized a view of ordinary Italians as scarcely less benighted than the Irish, if more picturesque, and comparably unfit for political self-determination. Normally there to play walk-on parts as servants and peasants against the backdrop of the Tuscan landscape, they could also be invoked, in the present crisis, as the salt-of-the-earth silent majority who were being forced to acquiesce in changes that they did not desire. This line of argument was espoused by Normanby and others.

Early in 1860 Normanby was complaining that his post was being stopped by the Tuscan Post Office. He was almost certainly right that it was being examined, but the Tuscan Government totally denied that it was being stopped.[48] He now had another grievance to espouse. Maria Amelia Tassinari, daughter of Sir Edward Thornton, complained to him that her husband, the *cavaliere* Giovanni Tassinari, had been seized and imprisoned for 5 weeks without trial. She complained of Corbett's unhelpful attitude and failure to obtain permission for Tassinari to remain confined to his own home, despite his failing health and eyesight. If Corbett himself is to be believed, he had obtained this permission on the very day (15 February) that Madame Tassinari directed her complaint to Normanby. He in his turn complained that she had not acknowledged his assistance. On 21 March Tassinari himself wrote to Lord Wodehouse at the Foreign Office, courteously complaining that the charges made against him had been misrepresented, and asserting that his wife had indeed thanked Corbett for his efforts.[49] A few days later, with the finalization of the annexation to Piedmont, Corbett's mission was at an end.

On 10 March the *Morning Chronicle* carried an article from the new Florentine political daily, significantly entitled *La Nazione*, 'in which Lord Normanby's pretensions to speak with authority in the House of Lords on the subject of Central Italy are reduced to their proper value'. The author excoriates

Normanby's claims to knowledge of the country, as opposed to 'what was told him by the Austrian Minister, by the Tuscan courtiers, and by his own parasites'. His lack of real knowledge had prevented him from seeing the rising of the tide of national opinion which swept away the Tuscan Court. He had believed those reactionaries who

> told him that the 'few factious individuals', by letting loose the mob, would cause the houses of the wealthy to be sacked, and the noble lord fairly took to his heels. In his flight he showered down curses on the 'few factious individuals' who had disturbed his digestion. He showered down curses on Tuscany, and, whilst running away, he wrote circulars to all the English ladies of his acquaintance, imploring them to do the same, because they could no longer remain in safety in Florence. It gives us unfeigned satisfaction to assure Lord Normanby that both his villa and his gardens are in a state of the most perfect preservation. We, who have actually witnessed the life which the noble lord led when he was in Florence, who know the polluted sources from which he receives his private information – we should be lowering too far our own dignity if we condescended to relate in detail the various heads of the accusation which he brings against us. We can make but one reply to him, one of the most temperate character, to the effect that in his words there is not a syllable of truth.

One feels a certain sympathy for Normanby, an increasingly sick and isolated man, whose voice was the voice of minorities, of Malmesbury, of Albert and Victoria, and some disappointed individuals back in Tuscany.

A little later in 1860 the Foreign Secretary received a slightly incoherent *cri de coeur* from one of the more colourful British *codini*. Mary Margaret, Lady Sussex Lennox, was the estranged wife of Lord Sussex Lennox, who lived and died a pillar of the Conservative party in Brighton (although the scandal sheets gave him a rather racier character than that might imply). She is to be found in Paris in the 1840s, frequenting the company of exiled Italian radicals, two of whom she took as lovers. It seems that she left Paris for Tuscany at the end of 1845, and when she converted to Catholicism in 1850 any radical sympathies she may have had were at an end. By her own account she had lived since then not in Florence but some 30 miles to the south, in the valley of the Casentino.

It is evident from her complaint to the Foreign Secretary that she had made her opposition to the late political changes, or what she termed 'the paid and fixed revolution', all too obvious locally. 'I must, as an eye and ear witness, declare that such corruption, and such terrorism as was exerted to procure & maintain the said revolution, I suppose never was practised.' She had chosen in 1859 not to subscribe to the war effort, when asked to do so by her parish priest, who told her in confidence that he was obliged to make the request. The prefect of Arezzo had thought that, as the only British person in the area, she could exert an influence on the people 'in favour of what they were, in the great majority, against.' When she refused to co-operate, he mounted a campaign against her, and she detailed the various annoyances to which she had been subjected and the expedients locally employed to rig the elections in favour of annexation to Piedmont. As she supposed the Provisional Government was 'not aware of the petty tyranny exercised by the Provincial Delegates', she asked the Foreign Secretary to intervene with Ricasoli to obtain protection for her and her household from the Prefect of Arezzo. She hoped she would be permitted

> to express the sentiments of the largest portion of the Tuscan Aristocracy and that portion of the people who form a body very considerable in numbers, & of most quick & true perception & right judgement which are Contadini or Agricultural part of the Community.[50]

This view of the unpopularity of the rosewater revolution and the oppressiveness of the new regime could scarcely differ more from the one espoused by Theodosia Trollope. There was simply no agreement to be had about the extent of arbitrary arrest and imprisonment perpetrated in defence of the new order, any more than there was about whether or not the Grand Duke had intended the bombardment of Florence. Edwin Corbett's reports to the Foreign Office from time to time expressed concern about repressive measures undertaken against supporters of the former regime, but he seems gradually to have become more and more persuaded that the old days were gone. He also pointed out that the repression was directed as much against republicans as against 'reactionaries'. In March 1860 he reported that there were 14 persons imprisoned in Tuscany for republican conspiracy, 15 for intrigues on behalf of the Grand Duke.[51]

The Annual General Meeting of the Florentine Church in January 1860 opened 'with prayer for the Divine Blessing on the Government – the spread of true religion throughout the land and for increasing unity and good fellowship among all classes'. The Select Vestry

> in adverting to the political events of the past year, find abundant reason to ascribe praise and thanksgiving to the Great Head of the Church for His gracious protection under which the holy Services of the Church have been continued without interruption.

At this same meeting one outward-looking gesture was made, a little belatedly: it was agreed that the church should include a prayer for the President of the United States. This was already done at Genoa and at Bagni, and its omission had apparently deterred a number of American gentlemen from subscribing to the church. A few graceful words of thanks were spoken by George Maquay's father-in-law, James Cooley, who a year later was elected to serve on the Select Vestry.[52]

On 6 June 1860 a number of distinguished ladies, including the Marchesa Guadagni, brought to the notice of the Select Vestry the predicament of a

'Madame Achilli', British despite her name. She had three children with her, one of them delicate and another sick, but her husband, who was in America, had failed to send her any money and she had been making ends meet by needlework and instructing English families as a *parlatore* (teacher of Italian conversation). It was now the close season for English society in Florence and she had no more than 20 *paoli* a month to live on. Things might pick up in the autumn, but in the meantime any prospects of help from England were quite uncertain. The Minute Book discreetly manages not to identify the neglectful husband, but it must have been the most open of secrets.

In 1852 John Henry Newman had encountered the full force of British anti-Catholic prejudice when he was found guilty (probably wrongly) of libelling Giacinto Achilli, a former Dominican friar who had turned Protestant propagandist (and whom Captain Pakenham had invited to speak at Bagni). In 1849 Achilli had punctuated a long history of sexual misdemeanours by taking as his wife a young Englishwoman, Josephine Hely. It has been said that he had become acquainted with her family when in England earlier in the decade; he himself describes her as having been carefully brought up in Protestant principles by her dear friend Mrs Tennant, the wife of the Florentine chaplain.[53] Josephine gave birth to her fourth child in Florence in 1856, but if Achilli had not already deserted her he soon did. The libel case was well remembered for years, but no one seems to have taken much interest in the abandoned wife. Now that her predicament was known, Webb Smith proposed paying her 10 *scudi* per month for the next 3 months, as long as no help came to her from England. Lady Don's fund was approaching extinction, but Smith added that 'a friend' had agreed to meet any shortfall. A note in his Letter Book discloses that the friend was Smith himself. He gave Maquay & Pakenham instructions to draw on his private account unless they were informed that Madame Achilli had received something from home.

The new Italian regime gave the British Government a golden opportunity to do what some had wanted to do for forty years. The Florence embassy was, so to speak, abolished by force of circumstance and from the government's perspective there was no reason to replace it with any lowlier form of diplomatic representation. As long as the invaluable Fenton remained semi-officially at Florence he served at least as a channel to Hudson at Turin, but he did not have full consular powers, and when in September 1860 it became known that he had received his orders to depart, the residents got together to submit a petition to Lord John Russell.[54] The preamble eloquently stated their case.

We, as British Subjects, beg leave respectfully to submit, for your Lordship's consideration, the following brief statement of the great inconvenience to which a very considerable number of Her Majesty's subjects will be exposed should there no longer be any Official British Representative at Florence.

We would submit to your Lordship that there are permanently residing at Florence, Bankers, Professional Persons, Half Pay Military & Naval Officers, a large number of Private families and various traders many of whom have been induced to invest their Capital in this Country under the impression that they would continue to enjoy the protection of Her Majesty's Mission at this place. That, in addition to such permanent British Residents, Florence is visited in the course of the Year, for longer or shorter periods, by many hundreds of our Countrymen – surpassing perhaps, in this respect, every other Capital City on the Continent of Europe, Paris only excepted.

Among so considerable a number are very many, as your Lordship may believe, who, under various circumstances, require official advice or assistance – it may be protection – not to mention Attestations to Half Pay Certificates, or other Documents which our Countrymen frequently have occasion to transmit to England. To persons requiring aid of this description (in many cases urgent) it is needless to point out how hopeless it would be were no other resource at their command than application to Her Majesty's Representative at Turin or even the British Consul at Leghorn.

We therefore venture to express the hope, if your Lordship should not deem it incompatible with your well-known sense of public duty, that your Lordship will take a favorable view of our present representation, and be pleased to appoint some Gentleman to reside at Florence who may officially watch over the interests of our Countrymen to which we have alluded.

The appended list of signatures included the names of many Anglo-Florentine businessmen as well as those of Seymour Kirkup, the physicians Wilson and Trotman, and the sculptor C.F. Fuller, but it was shorter than the one which would accompany a later memorial on the same subject a few months later. It had no effect, and the residents were obliged to make their way to Leghorn to obtain signatures on official documents from the ever obliging Macbean – that is, if he did not come to them.

On 20 September Macbean told the Foreign Office that he had been three times to Florence since May and the Vice Consul once. With obvious reference to the memorial just mentioned, he spoke of the need for an office at Florence, which he was willing to set up. Hudson gave qualified support to this proposal on 5 October, observing that he thought consular representation was more necessary at Florence than at Milan. Almost simultaneously Macbean was pointing out to the Foreign Office the inadequacy of his salary in view of the expenses he had to meet. In November he received permission to establish a Florentine office on a strictly temporary basis, and he submitted, as requested, an estimate of its costs. It would be open every day between 11.30 am and 3 pm under the supervision of an Italian messenger and office-keeper who already knew the majority of the residents. He himself would attend as often as he thought necessary. No sooner had the Treasury got a glimpse of the estimates than it refused to sanction the arrangement until clearer evidence of practical inconvenience to British residents should emerge.[55]

The consequence was a second memorial from the latter, dated 12 February 1861 and intended to provide the evidence the Treasury claimed to require. It recapitulated and elaborated what had already been said in September. Leghorn was 60 miles away, and experience had shown that the local authorities in Florence took little notice of any representation that did not have the backing of 'a resident British official'. A list of the occasions on which consular action might be required was appended. They included the issuing of passports, signatures on a wide variety of documents, the administration of the property of the intestate and a great deal else. It was pointed out that the Prussians and Americans had already opened consular offices at Florence. In face of this remonstrance, the Government subtly and predictably shifted its ground. In an echo of several previous responses, for example to the requests of the English Church for government support, the reverse of the document is endorsed: 'The Treasury will not consent; and it is to be observed that the residents are probably there for their own convenience or pleasure not promoting any public interest.'[56]

The most interesting features of this abortive petition are the list of signatories and the evidence that it was a more highly organized enterprise than its predecessor. The Rev. Henry O'Neill is named 'Chairman' and Alfred Hall 'Secretary to the Committee'. The commercial community was again well represented: Francis Sloane, George Maquay and Currell Smyth all signed, as did Horace Hall on behalf of the Fenzi business empire, and there were several lesser businessmen such as Sam Lowe. The sculptor Fuller and the physicians Trotman and Wilson were there again, and from the church establishment Christopher Webb Smith, William Reynolds and Archibald Dennistoun. Frederic Leighton, a frequent visitor rather than a resident, also signed, as did his brother-in-law Arthur Matthews, who was also brother-in-law to Alfred Hall. Henry Yeames and William Blundell Spence were there and 'H. Roberts' may have been either the exiled architect or the pharmacist. Mary Somerville was one of several female signatories, accompanied by her son Woronzow Greig (her husband William had died in Florence in 1860). Others were Harriet, Countess Inghirami (sister to the Rev. George Robbins), Harriet Dennistoun, Anne Crossman, Harriet Guastalla (widow Burdett, as she called herself) and the recently widowed Grace Galeazzi.

The efforts of the petitioners, for the time being at least, were in vain; but despite this and other travails Anglo-Florentine life continued. The church's Annual Meeting was told in January 1861 that 'The same cause that occasioned the decrease in the receipts of 1859, the unsettled political aspect of the Country, has operated with even more deteriorating effects in the present year'. Fortunately extraordinary expenses had been in 1860 only one-seventh of what they had been in 1859. The same meeting acknowledged that Lady Don's Fund was exhausted. Despite a gift of 50 *francesconi* from Horace Hall at the end of 1858 in memory of his late wife Costanza Lamberti, it now amounted to a trifling 18 pauls, and with many expressions of regret it was wound up. Twelve people or families in total had received assistance from it.[57]

In April 1861 the railing which had kept Lord Normanby secluded was at last removed from around his pew. The Secretary had 'received no reply to his letter of last year and last year's subscription has not been received'. Clearly the noble lord was too far advanced towards heaven to observe the courtesies; by contrast, John Maquay in 1865 subscribed 125 francs for 5 years from his retirement base in rural Ireland.[58] Normanby's pew was no more, but Maquay & Pakenham remained as a memento of the palmy days of the Grand Duchy of Tuscany.

Notes

1 FO79/198, Normanby to FO, 6 February 1858; 79/197, FO to Normanby, 11 February, expresses total approbation.
2 Betty Balfour (ed.), *Letters of Robert Bulwer* (London, 1906), Vol. 1, p. 86.
3 Frederic St John, *Reminiscences of a Retired Diplomat* (London, 1905), p. 29.
4 FO79/197, FO to Normanby, 26 & 30 March 1858.
5 FO 79/198 Normanby to FO, 6 May 1858; 79/197 FO to Normanby, 19 July 1858. The FO response was obviously tricky to draft. There are corrections even within the passages which have subsequently been deleted altogether, and, to compound the researcher's difficulties, the document is so bound in that parts of the amendments are on tightly curved inner margins.
6 FO79/197, FO to Howard, 27 April 1858.
7 FO79/197 FO to Normanby, 12 June 1858 tel; 79/199, Normanby to Lenzoni, 14 June; 79/198 Normanby to FO, 16 June tel.
8 He became ambassador to the United States. His replacement at Rome was Odo Russell.
9 JLM, E11 ff. 206, 208.
10 Alyson Price, *Florence in the Nineteenth Century* (Florence, 2011), pp. 10–11.
11 Guy Fleetwood Wilson, *Letters to Somebody – A Retrospect* (London, 1922), p. 5.
12 Bonnin had familial links to Fisher, Ede, Pillans, Sewell, Dal Pino, Broughton, Shields and Polhill, all long established in Tuscany – in the case of Polhill going back well into the eighteenth century.
13 JLM, E11 ff. 121v, 141. Robiglio signed the petition protesting at Captain Pakenham's expulsion in 1850 and subscribed to the Crimean appeal in 1853. As a widower he made a second Scottish marriage (in Edinburgh) to a much younger woman who bore him twins in Florence in 1864. He died in Nice in 1878, described as a noble of Tuscany, and was posthumously described as 'of Florence' when his son got married at Nice in 1883.
14 Her children included Arthur de Noë, who was involved with the Madiai, and Gertrude Baldelli, and the family's links included the Fleetwood Wilson, Macdouall, Whyte, Moyser, Chichester, Reader, D'Arcy Irvine, Hill Trevor, Bossi Pucci and Incontri families.
15 CMB 2, 22 October 1858.
16 JLM, E11 f. 271.
17 FO79/210, Slack & Simmons to FO, 7 February 1859; 79/210, FO to Slack and Simmons 9 February 1859. 'I cannot assist you in the matter to which it relates, being unacquainted with the law in Tuscany & having no knowledge of any of the Lawyers practising in Florence. I can only recommend you to send some person to Florence to obtain such information as you require.' See Malcolm Elwin, *Landor: A Replevin*

(London, 1958), pp. 417ff; also the less sympathetic Robert Super, *Walter Savage Landor* (London, 1957), pp. 438ff for details of the case.

18 Quoted by Elwin, *Landor,* p. 435. JLM makes a few references to a Landor who may be Arnold.

19 Julia Ada Bishop Landor, born 31 January 1850, mother Julia Savage Landor, was baptized by Rev Robbins 18 February 1850. The father was 'not known' (LMA, CLC/369 Ms 23774/179).

20 Elwin, *Landor.* pp. 439–40.

21 Stephen Wheeler (ed.), *Letters of Walter Savage Landor* (London, Duckworth, 1899), pp. 220–1.

22 Scott Lewis (ed.), *Letters of Elizabeth Barrett Browning to Her Sister Arabella* (Waco, Texas, 2002), Vol. 2, p. 375. Ferdinand was to travel by sea to Rome overseeing the heavy luggage, while the Brownings took advantage of the kindness of some rich friends in putting a closed carriage at their disposal.

23 Frances Power Cobbe, *Life of Frances Power Cobbe* by herself, (London, 1894), Vol. 1, p. 263; Dorothy McMillan (ed.), *Queen of Science; Personal Recollections of Mary Somerville* (Edinburgh 2001), p. 247. Miss Cobbe made a substantial contribution to the editing of Mary Somerville's recollections.

24 T. Woodson (ed.), *Nathaniel Hawthorne: The French and Italian Notebook*s (Columbus, Ohio, 1980), pp. 303–5.

25 Ibid., pp. 390–96.

26 Ibid., pp. 396–401.

27 FO79/199, Normanby to FO, 16 July 1858.

28 FO79/202, FO to Scarlett, 5 March 1859; 79/203, Scarlett to FO, 5 March.

29 FO79/203 Corbett to FO, 20 January 1859; 79/209 Corbett to FO, 18 January (tel.). 79/209 is the first volume in which telegraphs have been separated out and bound separately. While the FO may have known of an event by telegraph before it received the details by despatch, it was considerably hampered in its responses not only by the unrest when war actually broke out at the end of April, but the fact there was only one telegraph line at this date from Malta up through Italy, which only went as far as Genoa.

30 FO79/203, Corbett to FO, 29 January & 5 February 1859.

31 FO79/203, Scarlett to FO, 30 March 1859.

32 FO79/204, Scarlett to FO, 26 April 1859 (tel.).

33 There are three different copies of this message filed in three different places (FO79/204, 205, 209) with slightly different times, revealing Scarlett's desperation to get meaningful instructions. The Austrian ultimatum was delivered on Saturday 23 April, Easter Saturday. It was not until well into the 28th, i.e., the following Thursday, and more than 24 hours after the Grand Duke had left Florence, that the FO first responded, telling Scarlett to offer the Grand Duke passage on board a British ship and to remain at his post FO79/202, FO to Scarlett, 28 April 1859, (tel.).

34 FO79/205, Scarlett to FO, 21 April 1859; 27 April 1859.

35 Fleetwood Wilson, *Letters to Somebody,* pp. 16–17; Thomas A. Trollope, *What I Remember* (2nd ed., London, 1887), Vol. 2, pp. 109, 220–1.

36 McMillan (ed.), *Queen of Science*, pp. 251–63.

37 FO79/205, Scarlett to FO, 7 May 1859. For Trollope's opinions see Thomas A Trollope, *Tuscany in 1849 and in 1859,* (London, 1859), especially Chapter XIX and appendices, and *What I Remember,* Vol. 2, p. 220, where he doubts whether the alleged orders were given by the Grand Duke, who he is sure 'would have given or even done much to prevent any such catastrophe'.

38 FO79/211, Macbean to FO, 28 April 1859; FO79/205 Scarlett to FO, 7 May, with enclosure, Macbean to Scarlett, 28 April.
39 FO79/204, Scarlett to FO 1 May 1859, FO to Scarlett 7 May.
40 FO67/241, FO to Hudson, instructing him to inform Scarlett, 6 May 1859; 67/244, Hudson to Scarlett, 6 May.
41 FO79/202 FO to Scarlett, 20 June 1859.
42 FO79/206, Corbett to FO, 29 July 1859; 79/202. FO to Corbett, 4 August.
43 CMB 2, 21 October, 2 November 1859.
44 FO79/206, Corbett to FO, 20 July 1859.
45 FO79/206, Corbett to FO, 14 July 1859.
46 FO79/213, Corbett to FO, 4 January 1860.
47 Theodosia Trollope, *Social Aspects of the Italian Revolution* (London, 1862), p. 36, originally *Athenaeum*, 13 June 1860.
48 FO79/214, Corbett to FO, 5 March 1860.
49 Madame Tassinari's letter to Lord Normanby, dated 15 February 1860, is bound in FO79/215. Corbett's reply (FO79/214, 1 March) is contained in a private letter to Lord Wodehouse and is followed by telegrams containing more details. Russell clearly wanted to be in a position to refute Normanby in the Lords on a number of issues connected with Tuscany.
50 FO79/215 Lady Susan Lennox to FO, 15 April 1860. This is almost the last letter in the final volume of FO79. Fenton was ordered to make enquiries (FO 79/212, 21 April 1860), but there is no trace of a report, which is hardly surprising since the embassy was formally closed on 26th April and Fenton himself put under the jurisdiction of Turin (see correspondence in FO67/256). Fenton records a cordial reception on 2nd May after he received Hudson's instructions; Ricasoli wished to ensure the continued protection of British subjects (FO67/257 Fenton to Hudson, 2 May 1860).
51 FO79/214, Corbett to FO, 4 March 1860.
52 CMB 2, 27 January 1860.
53 Giacinto Achilli, *Dealings with the Inquisition, or Papal Rome, Her Priests and Her Jesuits* (London, 1851), p. 319. Achilli's imprisonment in Rome and the expulsion from the city of his brother-in-law, Henry Hely, a sculptor, made British headlines and helped to ensure the hostility with which Newman's supposed libels were greeted. One son was born to Achilli and Josephine in London and two more in New York, where they went in 1852 with a group of Swedenborgians. Achilli applied for naturalization in the United States in 1858, was accused of adultery with a woman with whom he had been living in New York and vanished from human ken in 1860. At least 3 of the sons can later be traced as US citizens. What became of Madame Achilli is obscure.
54 FO67/262, Memorial to FO, September 1860.
55 FO79/215, Macbean to FO, 20 & 24 September & 21 November 1860, FO to Macbean, 20 October, Treasury to FO, 22 December; 67/258, Hudson to FO, 5 October, 67/254, FO to Hudson, 6 November.
56 FO45/4, Memorial to FO, 12 February 1861.
57 CMB 2, 25 January 1861. After a hiatus the British Relief Fund was established under the auspices of the church in 1865: Catherine Danyell Tassinari, *History of the English Church in Florence* (Florence, 1905), pp. 111–13.
58 CMB 2, 3 April 1861; 27 January 1865.

EPILOGUE

John Maquay visited Florence in the spring of 1861 and again in the autumn. The first visit lasted 46 days and saw business (the dissolution of the partnership between the Maquays and Currell Smyth) combined with pleasure (the birth of John's first grandchild, a daughter for his son George and his American wife Nina). As of old, banking business meant consultations with Reynolds and Smith, and Pakenham too was there, no longer a problem for the Italian authorities. There were old friends such as Mrs Fombelle and Madame Galeazzi to be seen and on 19 April Nina's father James Cooley gave a dinner party which was attended by such familiar faces as the Reverend O'Neill, A.C. Dennistoun, Drs Trotman and Wilson, Hiram Powers and Alfred Hall.[1]

The second visit was much shorter at 26 days, during which John celebrated his 70th birthday. He was accompanied by Elena, who stayed on until December. The business with Currell Smyth which he had thought concluded in May needed further attention: 'at last Dissolution of Partnership & Hooker Liquidation concluded & also the new firm of MP & H concluded.' With typical casualness in the midst of all this he registered on 14 September a profound change in the Italy he had known: 'King of Italy passed under the windows great crowds.'[2]

Did John reflect on his travelling times in October 1861? Starting from Florence early on the morning of the 6th he was in London, by way of Basle and Paris, by 8 pm on the 11th. In 1824 he had left Florence on the evening of 3 February, and arrived in London at 9.30 on the 26th. Expectations had, of course, been transformed along with the technology of travel; one could now anticipate and plan for a much faster journey, even though the railways did not yet run through the Alps. John left behind him a son firmly in charge; retirement was now a reality. He kept his diary until the end of 1862, making no reference to Florence while he was in Ireland, where he settled into the role of the Protestant landed gentleman and magistrate.[3]

John died in 1868 at the age of 77. The surprise is less that Elena died at the ripe age of 88 in 1894, than that she did not return to live in her native Tuscany. Despite all the problems and possible disadvantages for her of Ireland over Tuscany – from climate to being a former Catholic – as a widow she chose a changing Ireland over a changed Tuscany. Certainly, she visited Florence, where she had two sons and several grandchildren; but the careers of her two unmarried sons, John Popham in the Royal Engineers and Tommy in the navy, were centred elsewhere. None of the sons made very old bones. Tommy died in Brighton in 1881, aged only 41, and George in Florence on 2 January 1893, aged 57. John Popham died with the rank of Major-General at the end of 1894, having lived with his mother in Ireland to the end. William, who after a brief career in the army joined his eldest brother in the management of the Florence bank and married in Florence, was the last to go, in 1912. It was his daughter Marjorie through whom the Maquay diaries were transmitted to posterity.

In June 1861 Elizabeth Barrett Browning's soul migrated from her beloved Florence. Secure to the last in her belief in spiritualism and Napoleon III, was her death hastened by the demise of her new hero, Cavour, little more than a month previously? Robert then departed physically and never came back – a perfectly understandable reaction. Florence was nothing to him now. The English cemetery in 1861 saw some twenty other burials in addition to Elizabeth's. Two of these were prominent individuals who had arrived only to die: Arthur Henry Clough the poet, and Thomas Southwood Smith the physician. In July 1862 John's old friend Dr Trotman died: how many patients and how many whist parties had he attended?

Early in the same year another physician met a violent end. In January 1862 the British newspapers recorded an outrage which led to questions in Parliament, a murder by one of the predatory porters who notoriously infested both Pisa and Leghorn, battening on to travellers and insisting on excessive payment for minimal or even non-existent baggage-carrying services. Dr George McCarthy had been in Tuscany for some years when he was stabbed by a disgruntled specimen of this breed, and the wound proved mortal. On 30 January Consul Macbean reported that Dr Wilson had sat with the dying man (who was sufficiently conscious to advise on his own condition) for three nights.[4] An old problem (we may remember Captain Napier's experience in 1816) had been exacerbated by the coming of the railways.

In 1863, the Foreign Office consented to the appointment of a Vice Consul at Florence, a Mr Proby, on the usual conditions: he was unpaid, cost them nothing and had no call on the government if he was sacked. He was refused a licence to perform marriages in case Macbean's fees suffered excessively. Macbean was now a little half-hearted about the appointment, suggesting that the residents exaggerated the difficulty of getting down Leghorn, given the train service. He did not want to lose his marriage fees, but on the other hand he did concede that there was work at Florence which needed doing and he was perhaps not looking for more.[5] In 1865 Florence became for a few years the capital of Italy; the embassy returned and Proby was made redundant. With Rome established as the national capital after 1870, it was not until after Macbean's death (in 1883) that a full consulate was established at Florence. Leghorn, now much less important as a port, was downgraded to a vice-consulate. A notable incumbent of the new Florentine post was Sir Dominic Ellis Colnaghi, whose daughter Catherine became the historian of the English Church.[6]

While the church no longer had to close its doors to Italian converts, it was slow to modify the siege mentality which had served it well during the 1850s. There was no wholesale overhaul of the library rules before 1865, and no hurry to change the rule which barred Italians from borrowing books. There was no sense of mission, a luxury the church had had to eschew, officially at least, in previous decades. The Florentine Anglicans had got out of the habit, and they were now surrounded by rapidly multiplying Protestant churches of different hues. It seems both predictable and intensely parochial that the disputes over ritual which rent the mid-Victorian church should now, with outside pressure removed, transfer themselves to Florence and lead to a split. From 1877, with the foundation of St Mark's, two churches competed for the small English congregation. Christopher Webb Smith did not live to see the schism. He continued as secretary to the Select Vestry until in late 1870 his doctors ordered him 'to give up any mental occupation'. He died on 18 January 1871, as genuinely lamented by all who knew him as a man well could be.

The year 1863 saw the death of Lord Normanby back in England, not as regretted as he should have been thanks to the controversies of his last years; he had contributed mightily over many decades to Florentine social life. In the same year Mrs Trollope died. For Thomas Trollope this blow was followed in 1865 by the devastating loss of his wife Theodosia. Though he was to marry again and live some years more in Florence, the bonds which bound him to the city had been loosened and his subsequent move to Rome was no surprise. Walter Savage Landor finally laid his ancient bones to rest in September 1864. Early in January 1865 Mrs Fombelle followed, and a few days later William Reynolds, who was accorded a rare obituary in the church minute books in recognition of his continuous service since 1849.

One development might or might not have surprised John Maquay: in 1864, a few years after the death of his wife Dorothea, the Duc de Talleyrand became the second husband of Ida Macdonell. Since Hugh's death in 1847 she had made Casa Annalena a lively centre of pro-Austrian and pro-papal sentiment; it was known to the Florentines as 'La Casa Austriaca'. Prince Windischgratz had lodged on the upper floor during the period when he commanded the imperial forces in Florence. The family even attempted to convert Mr Gladstone to Catholicism. Anne Macdonell described Ida in later life as very fair and very stout, 'kindness itself to me', living in this enormous house with numerous secret passages and staircases, which was still in the family's possession in 1872.[7]

Other people the Maquays had known lived on and died in Florence: Horace Hall in 1867, Francis Sloane in 1871, Isa Blagden, Hiram Powers and George Robbins in 1873, Maurice Baruch in 1875, the Reverend Henry Greene in 1876 and Alfred Hall in 1877. Each snapped another link with our story of the past. *Firenze capitale* saw the beginnings of a major transformation of the urban environment that these individuals had known as the walls were torn down. There would be many British (and Americans) in the new Florence, but the world of Ouida, Henry James and Berenson was not the world of Burghersh, Normanby and John Maquay.

Notes

1   JLM, E11 ff. 268–271v.
2   JLM, E11 ff. 281–281v.
3   He was appointed magistrate for Queen's County in 1860, as reported in the *Belfast Telegraph* on 7 May.
4   This letter and the other official correspondence generated by the murder were included in a Confidential Print for the use of the Foreign Office, printed on 26 June 1862. 1862 [3019] 4/65.
5   FO45/47, Macbean to FO, 14 October 1863.
6   Born in 1863, she was married to Herbert Daniell de' Tassinari, a grandson of the *cavaliere* whose imprisonment in 1860 had annoyed Normanby. She died in Florence on 21 September 1950 and received an obituary notice in the *Times* on the 26th.
7   Anne Macdonnell, *Reminiscences of a Diplomatic Life* (London, 1913), pp. 73–5. Ida died aged 80 in 1880.

SELECT BIBLIOGRAPHY

This does not set out to be a comprehensive bibliography of the British in Tuscany, but lists the works of which particular use has been made in writing this book. Other works and primary sources referred to will be found in the notes. A descriptive account of the primary sources used is incorporated in the Introduction.

Aglietti, Marcella (ed.), *Nobildonne, monache, e cavaliere dell'Ordine di Santo Stefano: modelli e strategie femminili nella vita pubblica della Toscana granducale* (Pisa, 2010).

Anon., 'The Baths of Lucca', *New Monthly Magazine* 109 (1859).

Anon., 'The Baths of Lucca in the Summer of 1840', *Metropolitan Magazine* 30 (1841).

Anon., *The European Indicator or Road-Book for Travellers on the Continent* (Florence, 1841).

Anon., *Religious Liberty in Tuscany: Or, Documents Relative to the Trial and Incarceration of Count Piero Guicciardini & Others Exiled from Tuscany by Decree of 17 May 1851* (London, 1851).

Anon., *The Story of the Madai; With Notices of Efforts Made, in Europe and American, in Their Behalf, Comp. and Ed. by the Secretaries of the American and Foreign Christian Union* (New York, 1853).

Balfour, Betty (ed.), *Letters of Robert Bulwer* (London, 1906).

Barnes, Malcolm (ed.), *Augustus Hare, The Years with Mother* (London, 1952).

Barrington, Mrs Russell, *The Life, Letters and Works of Frederic Leighton* (2 vols, London, 1906).

Bennett, Betty (ed.), *Letters of Mary Wollstonecraft Shelley* (Baltimore, 1989).

Berbeglia, Simona, 'Count Cottrell at the Court of Lucca', *Browning Society Notes* 33 (April 2008).

Berbeglia, Simona, 'James Montgomery Stuart: A Scotsman in Florence', in Barbara Schaff (ed.), *Exiles, Emigrés and Intermediaries: Anglo Italian Cultural Transactions* (Amsterdam & New York, 2010).

Blakiston, Georgina, *Lord William Russell and His Wife 1815-1846* (London, 1972).

Bowring, John, *Report on the Statistics of Tuscany, Lucca, the Pontifical, and the Lombardo-Venetian States, with a Special Reference to Their Commercial Relations* (London, 1837).

Boyle, Sir Charles (ed.), *Mary Boyle Her Book* (London, 1901).

Burgess, Thomas, *Climate of Italy in Relation to Pulmonary* Consumption, *with Remarks on the Influence of Foreign Climates upon Invalids* (London, 1852).

Carmichael, Montgomery (ed.), *The Inscriptions in the Old British Cemetery of Leghorn, Transcribed by G. Milner-Gibson-Cullum and the Late F. Campbell Macauley* (Leghorn, 1906).

Carter, Grayson, *Anglican Evangelicals: Protestant Secession from the Via Media, c. 1800–1850* (Oxford, 2000).

Cherubini, Bruno, *Bagni di Lucca fra Cronaca e Storia* (Lucca, 1978).

Clark, James, *Medical Notes on Climate, Diseases, Hospitals, and Medical Schools in France, Italy, and Switzerland, Comprising an Inquiry into the Effects of a Residence in the South of Europe in Cases of Pulmonary Consumption* (London, 1820).

Clark, James, *The Influence of Climate in the Prevention and Cure of Chronic Diseases, More Particularly of the Chest and Digestive Organs* (London, 1829; 2nd ed., 1830).

Clark, James, *The Sanative Influence of Climate, with an Account of the Best Places of Resort for Invalids in England, the South of Europe, &c* (London, 1841; revised ed., 1846).

Clearkin, Christina and Simona di Marco, 'A Tale of Three Cities: Calcutta, Southampton and Florence: The Stibbert Family and Museum', *British Art Journal* 9 (2009).

Cobbett, James P. *Journal of a Tour in Italy, and Also in Part of France and Switzerland* (London, 1830)

Colnaghi, Dominic, 'Notes on the Florentine Straw Industry', *The Antiquary* 12 (1886).

Cunningham, Reverend John W., *Caution to Continental Travellers* (London, 1818).

Curl, J. Stevens, *The Life and Work of Henry Roberts 1803–1876* (Chichester, 1983).

Dickens, Charles (ed.), *The Life of Charles James Mathews, Chiefly Autobiographical, with Selections from His Correspondence and Speeches* (2 vols, London, 1879).

Downey, Edward, *Charles Lever, His Life in Letters* (Edinburgh and London, 1906).

Elwin, Malcolm, *Landor: A Replevin* (London, 1958).

Fantozzi, Federigo, *Nuova Guida ovvero Descrizione Storico-Artistico-Critica della Città & Contorni di Firenze* (Florence, 1842).

Fitzpatrick, William, *The Life of Charles Lever* (London, 1879).

Fleming, John, 'Art Dealing in the Risorgimento II', *Burlington Magazine* Vol. 121 (1979).

Foreman, Harry Buxton (ed.), *Letters of Edward John Trelawney* (London, 1910).

Foulkes, Nick, *Last of the Dandies: The Scandalous Life and Escapades of Count d'Orsay* (London, 2003).

Gallenga, Antonio, *Episodes of My Second Life* (London, 1884).

Garrett, Martin, *A Browning Chronology* (Basingstoke, 2000).

Giuntini, Andrea, *I Giganti della montagna: Storia della ferrovia Direttissima Bologna-Firenze (1845–1834)* (Florence, 1984).

Giuntini, Andrea, 'Le communicazioni stradali e ferroviarie', *Prato, storia di una città*, 3.

Giuntini, Andrea, *Leopoldo e il Treno: Le ferrovie nel Granducato Toscano 1824–1861* (Naples, 1991).

Giuntini, Andrea, *Soltanto per denaro: La vita, gli affari, la ricchezza di Emanuele Fenzi negoziante banchiere fiorentino nel Granducato di Toscana (1784–1875)* (Florence, 2002).

Guaita, Ovidio, *Le Ville di Firenze* (Rome, 2005).

Harlan, Aurelia B. and J. Lee jr. (eds), *Letters from Owen Meredith to Robert and Elizabeth Barrett Browning* (Waco, Texas, 1937).

Hoare, Peter, 'A Room with a View – and a Book: Some Aspects of Library Provision for English Residents and Visitors to Florence 1815 to 1930' in Barbara Schaff (ed.), *Exiles, Emigrés & Intermediaries: Anglo Italian Cultural Transactions* (Amsterdam, 2010).

Home, David Dunglas, *Incidents in My Life* (London, 1864).

Hunt, Leigh, *Lord Byron and Some of His Contemporaries, with Recollections of the Author's Life, and of His Visit to Italy* (Paris, 1828).

Ilchester, the Earl of (ed.), *The Journal of the Hon. Henry Edward Fox (Afterwards Fourth and Last Lord Holland) 1818–1830* (London, 1923).

Ingamells, John, *A Dictionary of British and Irish Travellers in Italy 1701–1800* (London, 1997).

Jousiffe, Captain M. J., *A Road Book for Travellers in Italy* (2nd ed., Brussels, Paris and London, 1840).

Layard, Austin, *Autobiography* (London, 1903).

Lever, Charles, *Cornelius O'Dowd upon Men and Women, and Other Things in General* (Edinburgh, 1864/5).

Lewis, Scott (ed.), *Letters of Elizabeth Barrett Browning to Her Sister Arabella* (Waco, Texas, 2002).

Lewis, Scott, 'Sophie Cottrell's Recollections', *Browning Society Notes* 24 (1997).

Linaker, Arturo, *La Vita e i Tempi di Enrico Mayer con documenti inediti della storia della educazione e del Risorgimento Italiano (1802–1877)* (Firenze, 1898).

Lohrenz, O., 'The Life, Career and Political Loyalties of the Reverend Thomas Hall of Revolutionary Virginia and Leghorn, Italy', *Fides et Historia* 31 (1999).

Lucarelli, G., *Lo Sconcertante Duca di Lucca: Carlo Ludovico di Borbone Parma* (Lucca, 1988).

Macdonnell, Anne, *Reminiscences of a Diplomatic Life* (London, 1913).

Malmesbury, Earl of, *Memoirs of an Ex-Minister: An Autobiography* (London, 1885).

Marco, Simona di, *Frederick Stibbert 1836–1906: Vita di un collezionista* (Turin, 2005).

Mariotti, Filippo, *Notizie storiche, economiche e statistiche intorno all' arte della paglia in Toscana* (Florence, 1858, reprinted Florence, 2002).

McCullagh, William Torrens, *Memoirs of the Right Honourable Richard Lalor Sheil* (London, 1855).

McMillan, Dorothy (ed.), *Queen of Science: Personal Recollections of Mary Somerville* (Edinburgh, 2001).

Murray's Handbook for Travellers in Northern Italy (1st ed., London, 1842) [by Francis Palgrave]; (3rd ed., London, 1847; 4th ed., London, 1852; reprinted, 1853).

Murray's Handbook for Travellers in Northern Italy, Part II: Florence, Pisa, Lucca, and Tuscany as Far as the Val d'Arno (5th ed., London, 1854; 7th ed., 1858).

Murray's Handbook of Florence and Its Environs (London, 1861, 1863, 1867).

Pakenham, Frances Julia, *Life Lines: Or God's Work in a Human Being* (London, 1862).

Pierotti, G., *La Paglia in Toscana* (Florence, 1927).

Posarelli, Piero, 'Reminiscences of Mary Thompson, Daughter of the British Vice-Consul in Livorno' ed. Matteo Giunti, at *leghornmerchants.wordpress.com/2012/02/29/mary-thompson/*.

Prato, Storia di una città particularly Vol. 3, *Il tempo della industria (1815–1943)* (4 vols in 6 parts, Prato, 1986–1997).

Price, Alyson, *Florence in the Nineteenth Century: A Guide to Original Sources in Florentine Archives and Libraries for Researchers into the English-Speaking Community* (Florence, 2011).

Reeve, Henry (ed.), *The Greville Memoirs* (new edition, London, 1904).

Repetti, Emanuele, *Dizionario geografico-fisico-storico della Toscana* (Florence, 1833).

Robertson, David, 'Weave a Circle; Baron Kirkup and His Greatest Friends' in S. I. Mintz & others (eds), *From Smollett to James* (Charlottesville, Virginia, 1981).

Rudman, Harry, *Italian Nationalism and English Letters* (New York, 1940).

Rumbold, Horace, *Recollections of a Diplomatist* (London, 1902).

Sadleir, Michael, *Blessington-d'Orsay: a Masquerade* (London, 1933).

Sanacore, M., 'Il Reverendo Thomas Hall, cultura e affari in una città commerciale', *Studi Livornesi* 7 (1992).

Schonfield, Hugh (ed.), *Letters to Frederick Tennyson* (London, 1930).

Scott, Grant E. and Sue Brown (eds), *New Letters from Charles Brown to Joseph Severn* (www.re.umd.edu/editions/brownsevern).

Sinclair, J. D., *An Autumn in Italy, Being a Personal Narrative of a Tour in the Austrian, Tuscan, Roman and Sardinian States, in 1827* (Edinburgh, 1829).

Smith, M. H. Stephen, *Art and Anecdote: Recollections of William Frederick Yeames RA, His Life and His Friends* (London, 1927).

Snow, William, *Hand Book for the Baths of Lucca* (Pisa, 1846).

Spence, William Blundell, *Lions of Florence* (Florence, 1847; 2nd ed., 1852).

Spini, Giorgio, *Risorgimento e Protestanti* (3rd ed., Turin, 1998).

St John, Frederic, *Reminiscences of a Retired Diplomat* (London, 1905).

Starke, Marianna, *Information and Direction for Travellers on the Continent, Fifth Edition, thoroughly revised, and with considerable additions* (Paris, 1826).

Starke, Marianna, *Travels in Europe, for the Use of Travellers on the Continent, and Likewise in the Island of Sicily* (London, 1833).

Starke, Marianna, *Travels in Europe, for the Use of Travellers on the Continent, and Likewise in the Island of Sicily, … ninth edition, considerably enlarged and embellished with a map* (Paris, 1839).

Starke, Marianna, *Travels in Italy between the Years 1792 and 1798* (London, 1802).

Starke, Marianna, *Travels on the Continent, Written for the Use and Particular Information of Travellers* (London, 1820).

Stewart, Robert W., *An Italian Campaign, or the Evangelical Movement in Italy 1845–1887* (London, 1890).

Stillinger, Jack (ed.), *The Letters of Charles Armitage Brown* (Cambridge Mass., 1966).

Stisted, Mrs Henry, *Letters from the Bye-Ways of Italy* (London, 1845).

Stuart, James Montgomery, *Reminiscences and Essays* (London, 1884).

Super, Robert, *Walter Savage Landor* (London, 1957).

Tamassia, Marilena, *Firenze ottocentesca nelle fotografie di J. B. Philpot* (Livorno, 2002).

Tassinari, Catherine Danyell, *The History of the English Church in Florence* (Florence, 1905).

Taylor, Miles (ed.), *The European Diaries of Richard Cobden 1846–1849* (Aldershot, 1994).

Tennant, Robert J., *Sermons Preached to the British Congregation at Florence* (London, 1846).

Thompson, Ruth D'Arcy, *The Remarkable Gamgees: A Story of Achievement* (Edinburgh, 1974).

Trollope, Frances E., *Frances Trollope, Her Life and Literary Work from George III to Victoria* (London, 1895).

Trollope, Theodosia, *Social Aspects of the Italian Revolution* (London, 1861).

Trollope, Thomas Adolphus, *Tuscany in 1849 and in 1859* (London, 1859). *What I Remember* (2nd ed., 2 vols, London, 1887).

Vansittart, Arthur, 'Autumn on the Arno', *The Sporting Review* 2 (1840).

Vansittart, Arthur, 'The Festival of St John the Baptist at Florence', *New Sporting Magazine* 3 (1842).

Vansittart, Arthur, 'Florence and Florentine Sporting: The Carnival of 1839', *The Sporting Review* 1 (1839).

Vansittart, Arthur, 'Florence Autumn Meeting 1840', *The Sporting Review* 4 (1840).

Vansittart, Arthur, 'Florence Races', *The Sporting Review* 1 (1839).

Vansittart, Arthur, 'Florence Races, April 1839', *The Sporting Review* 1 (1839).

Vansittart, Arthur, 'Florentine Races, 1841', *New Sporting Magazine* 2 (1841).

Vansittart, Arthur, 'The Forest of Pisa and the Grand Duke's Stud Farm', *New Sporting Magazine* 1 (1841).

Vansittart, Arthur, 'Leghorn and Her Sports', *The Sporting Review* 3 (1840).

Vansittart, Arthur, 'Sketches of Horse Racing in Italy', *The Sporting Review* 4 (1840).

Wardle, Gwillym, *Colonel Wardle to His Countrymen* (London, 1828).

Wilson, Guy Fleetwood, *Letters to Somebody – A Retrospect* (London, 1922).

Wolff, Henry Drummond, *Rambling Recollections* (London, 1908).

Woodson, T. (ed.), *Nathaniel Hawthorne: The French and Italian Notebooks* (Columbus, Ohio, 1980).

Wunder, Richard P., *Hiram Powers, Vermont Sculptor* (2 vols, Cranbury, NJ, 1989–1991).

Zangheri, Luigi, *La Villa Medicea di Careggi e il suo Giardino* (Florence, 2006).

INDEX

No attempt has been made here to index every mention of individuals who appear repeatedly throughout the book, such as the Maquays, the Grand Duke Leopold II or Lord Palmerston. Other British ministers, officials or legation staff, when simply performing their duties (e.g. as authors or recipients of despatches), are not normally noticed. Individuals who were known by different names during their lifetime, for example because they succeeded to a peerage, are indexed under the name by which they usually appear in the sources for their time in Tuscany. Most of the numerous references to the Brownings as a couple are indexed under Elizabeth's name. Recurring place-names such as Florence, Leghorn, Pisa and Bagni di Lucca are omitted.

Blacker, Rowland 348–9
Blagden, Isa 335, 337, 362, 498–9, 523
Blessington, Earl and Countess of 43,
    60–1, 62–3, 65, 127, 459
Bligh, Edward 131, 416
Blomfield, James, bishop of London 17,
    164–5, 171–2, 183 n.29
Bogle, Allen 87, 98–102, 159, 163, 165,
    480–2
Bonfil, Ralph 236, 428, 430–2
Bonnin, Henry Gousse 294, 495
Borghese, Camillo 46–7, 74
Boston, Lord. *See* Irby, George
Bourbel, Marquis de 87, 98–9, 136
Bouturlin, Russian family 34
Bowring, (Sir) John 419, 424–5
Boyd, Arthur 351
Boyle, Mary 73, 95, 133–4, 146, 222
Brassey, Thomas 404, 432, 435, 438
Bray, William, engineer 429
Bright, John 366
Brind, Henry 419
'Britannicus' 263–4, 466
Brock Wood, John 80, 479
Brooks, Gerard Lake 299, 369, 494
Brown, Charles Armitage 41, 43, 44, 45–6,
    49–50, 65, 78, 125, 155, 470, 471
Brown, J. A., wine merchant 478–9
Browning, Elizabeth Barrett 204–5, 208,
    210, 212–14, 216, 217, 220, 221,
    222, 225–6, 238, 270, 278–9, 280,
    291, 315, 351, 359–62, 365, 367–8,
    370, 371–2, 387, 478, 497–8; death
    522; and physicians 396–400; and
    spiritualism 354–6, 359, 498
Browning, Robert 204–5, 221, 222, 235,
    272, 303–4, 322, 362, 371, 478,
    497–9; leaves Florence 522
Bruce, James Stewart 65–6, 127
Bruce, Thomas Humble 318
Brunel, Isambard Kingdom 428
Buchanan, Andrew 176
Bull, Øle, violinist 134
Bulwer, (Sir) Henry 90 n.2, 117, 254–5,
    261–2, 264, 279–80, 313, 337
Bulwer, (Lady) Rosina 117–18
Bulwer Lytton, (Sir) Edward 117, 355, 362
Bulwer Lytton, Robert 280, 281, 322,
    354–5, 362, 363
Burdett, Harriet (Guastalla) 22, 281, 315,
    452, 516

Burgess, (Dr) Thomas 384–6
Burghersh, Baron 39, 40, 44, 46–7, 55,
    61–3, 71, 126, 127, 130–1, 137,
    153–4, 388, 389, 452; criticism of
    47, 51; as Earl of Westmorland
    253–4, 256; as musician 43, 128,
    130–1, 132
Burghersh, (Lady) Priscilla 39, 44–5, 47,
    126, 127, 128, 130
burial grounds 2, 9, 11, 155, 160, 180–1,
    185 n.78, 290–1, 382
Byron, Lord 44, 53–4

Capponi, Gino 96, 219, 300, 501
Carbonel, (Captain) George 239–40
carta di soggiorno (residence permit) 240,
    265, 266–7, 271
Catalani, Angelica 73–4, 135, 136, 190
Cave, William 140, 396
'Cavendish, Henry', confidence trickster
    277–8
Cecchetti, Domenico 340–1
cemeteries. *See* burial grounds
Charters, (Captain) Samuel 424
Chiesi, Tito 318, 326, 345
cholera 82, 86, 351–2, 392
Church, John Dearman 389
civic guard 211–12; in Florence 210–11;
    at Leghorn 212, 218, 220
Clairmont, Claire 44, 69 n.56, 83, 470
Clark, (Mrs) Frances, hotelier 194,
    461–3
Clark, (Sir) James 383–5
Clark, Joseph, railway engineer 433
Clough, Arthur Henry 522
Cobbe, Frances Power 497–8
Cobbett, James 50, 54, 456, 457, 464
Cobbett, William 50, 413–14
Cobden, Richard 203
Codrington, (Captain) Henry RN 92 n.44,
    218, 220, 229
Codrington, (Sir) William 366
Coesvelt, William Gordon 21
Cole, Henry 463
Coleridge, Samuel Taylor 162
Colnaghi, (Sir) Dominic Ellis 412, 414,
    523
Combe, (Dr) Andrew 384–5, 387
Combe, George 135, 385
Cook, (Dr) Francis 396–7, 398
Cookes, Denham 66, 140–1

Fox, Henry (Lord Holland) 46, 59, 60, 86, 89–90, 95, 97, 100, 103–4, 114–15, 116, 119–20, 144, 202, 222; and the English Church 164–70, 174, 175, 177

Fox-Strangways, William 18, 58, 61–2, 89, 168, 459–60

Fremantle (Admiral Sir) Thomas 43, 126

French, Anthony, banker 102–3, 105, 107, 142, 341, 372, 430

Fuller, Charles, sculptor 515, 516

Gage, (Sir) Thomas 134

Galeazzi, (Madame) Grace 22, 41, 111, 188, 281, 337, 353, 369, 370, 495, 516, 521

Galeazzi, (Major) Michelangelo 22, 41, 73, 111, 337, 369, 495, 506

Gallenga, Antonio 12, 96–7, 287 n.90, 509, 510

Gambier, (Rev) Samuel 109

Gamgee, Joseph 137, 206, 273, 337, 468

Gandell brothers, contractors 425, 436–7, 440, 481

Garland, Augustus Lester 122 n.24

Garland, Lester 491

Garrow family 204

Garrow, Joseph 206, 337, 370

Gason, (Dr) John 303, 394–5

Gasperini, Silvestro 105, 106, 137, 142, 263, 464–6

Gibraltar, Bishop of 176, 177, 178–80, 290, 292, 296, 506

Gilbert, (Rev) William 295, 373–4

Gilhully, John 432

Giuliani, Michele 106, 135–6, 138–9

Gladstone, William 160, 184 n.45, 306, 523

Glossop, Joseph 152

Goggi, Emilia, singer 135, 146, 281

Goodban, Edward, bookseller 337, 471–2

Gordon, (Captain) John 56

Gordon, (Rev) James 321, 322, 323

Gosse, Edmund 5

Gower, George 212

Grabau, Charles 61–2

Grahame, William Cunninghame 87, 98, 101, 159, 163, 165

Grant, Isaac 56

Green, (Dr) Henry 303, 403–4

Greene, (Rev) Henry 345, 394–5, 523

Greenough, Horatio 57, 278

Gregorie, (Major) Charles 117, 281, 304, 337, 359, 369, 495

Gregory XVI, Pope 72, 120, 201

Greig, Woronzow 503, 516

Greville, George 43, 45

Gryzanowski, (Dr) Ernst 400

Guadagni, (Marchesa) Louisa (née Lee) 65, 87, 188, 513

Guardabassi, Francesco 77–8, 96, 271

Guastalla, Harrriet. See Burdett, Harriet

Guastalla, Marco 22, 315–16

Guicciardini, (Count) Pietro 309, 312–13, 317, 325

Hall, Alfred 21, 28, 30, 35, 241–2, 337, 369, 413, 425, 428, 451, 496, 516, 521, 523

Hall, Horace 21, 23–6, 36 n.11, 57, 86, 287 n.91, 337, 340, 523; business interests 35, 203, 413, 425, 428, 432, 479, 480, 516; and English church 157, 159, 163, 165–7, 176, 179, 389

Hall, (Rev) Thomas 11, 17, 21, 40, 151–2

Hallam, Arthur 162

Hamilton, Charles Baillie 118–19, 366

Hamilton, (Sir) George Baillie 144, 146, 202, 208, 210–11, 218–20, 224, 228, 235–6, 241, 263, 267, 366, 386, 393; and Pakenham affair 301–7

Hanna, (Rev) James Maxwell 272, 291, 303, 309, 315, 316–17, 326, 337, 340, 341, 355, 371–2

Harding, (Dr) James 87, 208, 214, 226, 281, 336, 337, 390, 430–1; and the Brownings 398–400; as medical practitioner 80, 139, 140, 391, 392–3, 396, 402, 404

Harding, James junior 245–6, 392

Hare, Augustus 67 n.18, 496

Hare, Francis 43; sons 246–8

Hare, (Rev) Julius 43, 192

Hare, (Rev) William 159

Harrington, (Dr) Henry 404

Harvey, Richard Perry 456

Harvey, (Rev) Thomas 80, 159–60

Haskard, Timothy, tailor 477

Hawley, (Sir) Joseph 104–5

Hawthorne, Nathaniel 498–9

Hayes, Catherine, singer 146

Haynes, James 453

Wiseman, (Cardinal) Nicholas 35
Wolff, Henry Drummond 280, 281
Wolley, (Rev) Thomas 293, 294, 303
Wolley, William 207
Wood, John Brock 479
Wrey, (Sir) Bourchier Palk 83, 88–9
Wyatt, (Mrs) Mary 84–5, 89

Yeames, Henry 35–6, 516
Yelverton, (Rev) Frederick 158, 159
Young, (Dr) Plowman 383–4